IN DEFENSE OF TRADITION

RICHARD M. WEAVER

In Defense of Tradition

Collected Shorter
Writings of
Richard M. Weaver,
1929–1963

EDITED AND WITH
AN INTRODUCTION BY
TED J. SMITH III

Liberty Fund
INDIANAPOLIS

This book is published by Liberty Fund, Inc., a foundation established to encourage study of the ideal of a society of free and responsible individuals.

⫞⊠ ⯗⟍⫸

The cuneiform inscription that serves as our logo and as the design motif for our endpapers is the earliest-known written appearance of the word "freedom" (*amagi*), or "liberty." It is taken from a clay document written about 2300 B.C. in the Sumerian city-state of Lagash.

Frontispiece photo: from the collection of the editor.

04 03 02 01 00   C   5 4 3 2 1
04 03 02 01 00   P   5 4 3 2 1

Library of Congress Cataloging-in-Publication Data

Weaver, Richard M., 1910–1963.
In defense of tradition: collected shorter writings of Richard M. Weaver, 1929–1963/edited by Ted J. Smith III.
p.   cm.
Includes bibliographical references and index.
ISBN 0-86597-282-6 (hc: alk. paper)
ISBN 0-86597-283-4 (pbk.: alk. paper)
1. Civilization, Modern—Philosophy.
2. Weaver, Richard M., 1910–1963—Political and social views.
3. Intellectual life.   4. Rhetoric.
5. United States—Civilization.   6. Southern States—Civilization.
7. Weaver, Richard M., 1910–1963.   8. Weaver family.
I. Smith, Ted J.   II. Title.

CB358.W43   2000
814'.54—dc21   99-046335

Liberty Fund, Inc.
8335 Allison Pointe Trail, Suite 300
Indianapolis, Indiana 46250-1684

Contents

SECTION 3: *Education*

SECTION 4: *Rhetoric and Sophistic*

SECTION 5: *The Humanities, Literature, and Language*

SECTION 6: *Politics*

Section 7: *History*

Introduction

TED J. SMITH III

On Wednesday, April 3, 1963, the quiet routine of the College of the University of Chicago was disrupted by reports that Professor Weaver had failed for a second day to meet his classes. Those who knew him well received the news with surprise and concern. A fixture on the campus for almost two decades, Weaver had acquired a reputation for a devotion to teaching that was remarkable even where those duties were still taken seriously. He was also well known, even notorious, for the regularity of his daily activities. On a typical day, he would arrive at his office in the early morning, teach two classes, and depart at exactly 11:30 for lunch at the Commons. After lunch he would walk to his apartment to write a few pages and take a nap before returning to campus to teach his afternoon class and attend to other academic chores. At 5:30 he went back to the Commons for dinner, walked home, and worked until 9:30. Though it was a source of merriment among some members of the university community, Weaver was proud of this strict regimen and often noted with approval the story of the citizens of Königsberg setting their watches by Immanuel Kant's perambulations in the town square.[1] For a man such as this, only the gravest necessity would compel him to miss classes without notice, and when a telephone call to his apartment went unanswered, the concern of his friends changed to alarm. Their worst fears were confirmed that afternoon, when word came that Richard Malcolm Weaver was dead at the age of 53, the victim of a heart attack, alone at night in his bed.[2]

1. Wilma R. Ebbitt, "Richard M. Weaver, Friend and Colleague," paper presented at the Conference on College Composition and Communication, St. Louis, March 19, 1988, pp. 1–2.

2. There is some confusion about the exact date of Weaver's death. A news release distributed by the University of Chicago (number 63-178, dated April 4, 1963) states that he died on Wednesday, April 3, the day his body was discovered, and that date appears in nearly all contemporary obituaries, official documents (including his death certificate), family

There followed the usual and proper rituals of a civilized community. The flag in front of the university's Administration Building was lowered to half-staff, and on the afternoon of April 10 a memorial service was conducted in Bond Chapel by the Rev. John Pyle of the campus Episcopal Center. By then, Weaver's body had been returned to Weaverville, North Carolina, where funeral services were held at the United Methodist church on April 7. He was buried near his father in the Old Weaverville Cemetery, just a few blocks down Main Street from the house he had shared with his mother, Carrie Lee Embry Weaver, his brother Embry, his sister Betty, and her son Larry, then twelve years of age.

More lasting tributes to his memory took the form of a small number of published eulogies. The first, written by Mark Ashin, a colleague of Weaver's on the English staff, appeared in the campus newspaper on April 5. It was followed some months later by two pieces in the *Georgia Review*, one by Wilma Ebbitt, a close friend and colleague at Chicago, the other by Ralph Eubanks, a professor of rhetoric and public address at the University of Arkansas who had brought Weaver there in 1961 to speak in the university's Distinguished Lecturers series. Weaver's passing was also noted in several conservative publications with which he had been associated during the last decade of his life. Foremost among them are the memorials by Russell Kirk in *National Review*, by Eugene Davidson in *Modern Age*, and by the editors of the *New Individualist Review*.[3]

---

correspondence, and subsequent accounts of his life. It also appears on his headstone. However, the obituary in his hometown newspaper, the *Asheville Citizen*, states that Weaver failed to meet his classes on April 1 and 2, and that when police found his body on April 3 they estimated he had been dead for two days. This account is corroborated by a power of attorney executed in North Carolina on April 6, 1963, which lists his date of death as April 2, and by the recollections of several of his colleagues at the University. It is also partly confirmed by a memorandum written on April 4, 1963, by Weaver's brother-in-law, Kendall Beaton, which notes a conversation with Alan Simpson, then Dean of the College of the University of Chicago, in which Simpson said Weaver had last been seen alive in class on April 1. When all of the evidence is considered, it seems almost certain that Weaver died sometime during the night of Monday, April 1, most likely in the early morning hours of April 2. Accounts also differ on whether Weaver's body was discovered by police alerted by concerned colleagues or by a maid who entered the apartment to clean his rooms. The official cause of death was listed as coronary thrombosis; no autopsy was performed.

3. Mark Ashin, "A Tribute to Richard Weaver," *Chicago Maroon*, 71/87, April 5, 1963, p. 1; Wilma R. Ebbitt, "Richard M. Weaver, Teacher of Rhetoric," the *Georgia Review*, 17/4,

These tributes are of interest because they mark the first of many attempts to assess the significance of Richard Weaver's work. As would be
expected, all are suffused with admiration, respect, and a sense of great loss.
But viewed from the vantage of time, their assessments of Weaver's achievements seem narrow and restrained. For example, the memorials written by
Weaver's colleagues cite few of his accomplishments as a scholar and focus
instead on his qualities as a teacher of composition and rhetoric at the undergraduate level. Only Ralph Eubanks characterizes him as "one of the
ablest cultural critics of our times, and a brilliant rhetorical theorist," and
only he calls attention to Weaver's considerable body of scholarship on
Southern history and culture. Similarly, while Russell Kirk does note mildly
that *Ideas Have Consequences* "was one of the first works in the revival of
conservatism in America—and surely the first to find a wide and devoted
audience," Eugene Davidson's quiet appreciation offers no general evaluation of Weaver's impact, and it is left to the editors of the *New Individualist Review*—a student publication produced by the University of Chicago
chapter of the Intercollegiate Society of Individualists—to conclude that
"Few men have been as important in the intellectual renaissance of American conservatism as Richard M. Weaver."

The tributes are also valuable because they provide the first detailed view
of Weaver's life and character from the perspective of those who knew him.
That view is neither very flattering nor, in some important respects, very
accurate, but it has become widely known and accepted through long repetition. On some points, all of the eulogists quite rightly agree: Weaver was
a kind, courteous, and principled gentleman of the old school, thoughtful
and deliberate in his speech, powerful and incisive in his writing, and deeply
committed to the restoration of truth and order in contemporary society.
In pursuit of that goal, he adopted a strict regimen in his daily activities,
kept largely to himself and his work, and lived a life of high seriousness and
austerity. Beyond these points, however, the accounts diverge, and inaccuracies of fact and emphasis begin to appear.

One set of problems concerns the precise nature of Weaver's connection

---

Winter 1963, pp. 415–18; Ralph T. Eubanks, "Richard M. Weaver: In Memoriam," the *Georgia Review*, 17/4, Winter 1963, pp. 412–15; Russell Kirk, "Richard Weaver, RIP," *National
Review*, 14/16, April 23, 1963, p. 308; Eugene Davidson, "Richard Malcolm Weaver—Conservative," *Modern Age*, 7/3, Summer 1963, pp. 226–30; and "In Memoriam Richard M.
Weaver," *New Individualist Review*, 2/4, Spring 1963, p. 2.

with Weaverville, North Carolina, a town settled by and named for his ancestors. According to Eubanks, Weaver "was born and brought up at Weaverville"; Kirk also places Weaver's birth there and adds touchingly that for "most of his life he saved money to buy a little house there, for a day when college teaching should end." In fact, however, Weaver was born in Asheville, North Carolina, and brought up in Lexington, Kentucky. Except for some summer vacations, he did not live in Weaverville until 1953, when, after only a few years of saving (thanks to the generous help of his old friend William Maury Mitchell), he purchased the house at 100 South Main Street that became his home for the rest of his life.

Eugene Davidson in his eulogy also emphasizes the Weaverville connection but uses the point to transform Weaver into a full-fledged agrarian traditionalist distrustful of modern technology and indissolubly linked to the land. In one widely known passage, Davidson reports that Weaver "plowed his land in Weaverville, North Carolina, with a horse-drawn plow; he never used a tractor." He then notes that had Weaver lived but a little longer, "he would have been again in Weaverville for the plowing and harrowing and weeding of the land," and concludes that "despite his years in Chicago, Dick remained a countryman."[4] In fact, however, Weaver lived all his life in towns and cities—Asheville, Lexington, Nashville, Auburn, College Station, Baton Rouge, Raleigh, Chicago, and Weaverville—and never, aside from visits to relatives, on a farm. In Weaverville, "his land" consisted solely of the house on two acres a block from the town center he had purchased in 1953, and his farming was limited to growing a large backyard vegetable garden and tending a few peach, quince, and crabapple trees. There is no evidence Weaver ever plowed the garden himself, preferring to hire someone else to do the job, and it is very doubtful that he ever had it plowed by a horse (or mule, in other versions of the story); certainly it was not a regular occurrence. He did sometimes speak to friends about plowing fields with a horse, apparently on some visit to a farm, and it may well be that he said or implied that he still used such methods. But none of the surviving members of his family, including a brother and a nephew who

4. Eubanks, p. 413; Kirk, p. 308; Davidson, pp. 227 and 230. Davidson also notes (p. 227) that Weaver "flew only once in his life" and enjoyed it, but "never flew again." In fact, there is proof that Weaver flew on several occasions in the last few years of his life and was doing so with greater frequency as demands on his time increased and train service deteriorated.

lived in the Weaverville house at the time, can remember seeing a horse or mule at work on the property, and the nephew recalls that the garden was plowed "many times" by a hired man with a tractor.[5]

More serious problems arise in the depiction of Weaver's lifestyle and personal relationships. There is no question that he lived a quiet and retiring bachelor's existence in rented rooms near the Chicago campus and that he impressed most people as reticent and self-contained. But there has been a persistent tendency to emphasize and embellish these facts almost to the point of caricature. Thus Mark Ashin's tribute, although not unkind in tone, makes Weaver's reserve a principal focus of discussion. In the space of nine short paragraphs, Ashin twice claims that few on campus knew Weaver well, speculates that "perhaps he was seldom able to tell [his students] how much he liked them," and asserts that even those who admired and respected him "were kept at a distance by his reticence, his sense of decorum, his rather formal courtesy, and by a calm stability which seemed to invite neither offers of aid nor the exchange of confidences." In Russell Kirk's memorial—by far the most widely distributed and influential of the early eulogies—the portrait is darkened to suggest a kind of stunted reclusiveness.[6] "Solitary by nature," Kirk wrote, Weaver "inhabited a single room

5. Among those who recall discussions with Weaver about plowing with horses are P. Albert Duhamel, Henry Regnery, and William R. Smith. Family members who deny that the garden was plowed with a horse or mule include his cousin Josephine Osborne, his brother Embry Weaver, and his nephew Larry Ludlam. From personal interviews conducted by the editor with P. Albert Duhamel, Boston, Massachusetts, May 17 and November 11, 1994; Henry Regnery, Chicago, Illinois, November 1, 1992; William R. Smith, New Paris, Pennsylvania, July 13, 1994; Josephine Osborne, Weaverville, North Carolina, August 11, 1995; Embry Lee Weaver, Weaverville, North Carolina, August 11, 1995; Larry Embry Ludlam, Asheville, North Carolina, August 13, 1995. It should also be noted that Weaver wanted to buy a house in Asheville, not Weaverville, but purchased the one he did primarily to please his mother.

6. In addition to appearing in *National Review*, Kirk's eulogy was reprinted under the title "Richard Weaver" in his *Confessions of a Bohemian Tory*, New York: Fleet, 1963, pp. 193–96, and in abridged form under the title "Richard M. Weaver, RIP" in *The Individualist*, 2/2, September 1963, p. 2. This somewhat negative view was strongly reinforced in Kirk's "Foreword" to Weaver's posthumous *Visions of Order*, Baton Rouge: Louisiana State University Press, 1964, p. viii, in which he quoted Canon Bernard Iddings Bell, a mutual friend, as follows: "'Richard Weaver distresses me,' Canon Bell said to me one day, only half in jest, 'he grows more like a little gnome every day.'"

in an obscure hotel near the University of Chicago," "dined frugally in the cafeteria of International House or in some little hash house," and "lived chaste and withdrawn." We are also told that "[s]ome of his closest Chicago friends did not see him for a year at a time" and that he "never traveled." The image is then extended to the realm of religion:

> Weaver attended church only once a year, I believe—and then a high Epis-copalian service. Somehow the solemnity and mystery and ritual, strongly though he was attracted by them, overwhelmed his soul; such a feast would last him for another twelve months. Frugality even in religious observance was woven into his character.

While these observations may faithfully reflect the impressions of their authors, they do not provide a very accurate picture of the reality of Richard Weaver's life and character. The fact is that Weaver had a fairly wide circle of friends and socialized frequently. This is acknowledged, for example, by Eubanks and Davidson, who both note his conviviality,[7] and even by Ashin, who mentions that Weaver's correspondence was "staggering" and that he was "always writing letters to friends and strangers" on the ancient portable typewriter in his office. It also happens that Weaver was an avid and rather frequent traveler. In the late 1930s, for example, he twice drove groups of friends from Texas A&M to Monterrey, Mexico, and he spent much of the summer of 1938 in Paris; in the few years preceding his death, he took a driving tour of the Rockies with his mother and brother, and he gave speeches or lectures in venues ranging from New York, New Jersey, and Washington, D.C., to Oklahoma, Arkansas, Utah, and Washington state. Regarding his religious observances, it may be that occasionally Weaver attended Episcopal services in Chicago—the University Hotel, where he lived during most of the 1950s, was located less than a block from the high Anglican Church of the Redeemer, where his friend Canon Bernard Id-dings Bell, the Episcopal chaplain at the University of Chicago, sometimes officiated—but there is clear evidence that he also attended Methodist and Presbyterian services with some regularity when he was at home in Weaverville.[8]

7. Eubanks, p. 415; Davidson, p. 230.
8. The best evidence comes from several small notepads from the early to mid-1950s which were found among Weaver's papers. Among other things, he sometimes used them to record his expenditures, and a number of entries show small amounts spent for "church."

Nor is there anything very remarkable about Weaver's living arrangements in Chicago. It is hardly surprising that, as a bachelor who spent each summer away from campus, he rented furnished rooms and took his meals in restaurants. Precisely where he slept and ate was determined partly by convenience and availability, but largely by his financial circumstances and family obligations. When he arrived at the University of Chicago in September 1944, Weaver had spent more than a decade in graduate studies and a succession of low-paying temporary teaching positions. His new job did offer a comparatively generous annual salary of $2,800,[9] but the appointment was only at the rank of instructor and only for one year; not until 1948 did he receive a promotion to assistant professor and his first multiyear contract, and not until 1951 did he enjoy the security of tenure. Further, by 1944 Weaver had accepted primary responsibility for the support of his mother, a widow of 70 with few means and not in the best of health. Until 1953 he helped to maintain her in various apartments, usually in North Carolina; he then installed her (along with two of his siblings and a nephew) in his Weaverville house, where in addition to lodging he provided her with a car, domestic help, and, as her health declined, paid companions and nurses. Given these obligations, Weaver had little choice but to lead a modest and frugal existence in Chicago during the academic year: he was, after all, trying to maintain two separate households on a single academic salary. Although he accepted his situation with good grace—there is, for example, no hint of bitterness or complaint in his correspondence with family and friends—it would be wrong to think that he was fully satisfied with it. To the contrary, as his financial position improved during the last decade of his life, he modified his lifestyle accordingly. Beginning in the early 1950s he adopted the habit of eating at least one meal a week (usually on Friday) in a better-quality restaurant. In 1957, long troubled because his living arrangements did not allow him to repay the hospitality of his friends and colleagues, he joined the private 1020 Club on Lake Shore Drive not far from the Loop so that he could entertain his guests at dinner.[10]

9. The benefit of the higher salary was undercut by the fact that Weaver, like all newly appointed Chicago faculty at the time, was given a so-called "4E" contract which stipulated that any outside income he earned had to be surrendered to the university. See William H. McNeill, *Hutchins' University,* Chicago: University of Chicago Press, 1991, pp. 127 and 163.

10. See, for example, the letter from Weaver to William C. Mullendore dated January 8, 1957, in which Weaver asks Mullendore to dine with him at the club, which he describes as "a

And by the end of his life Weaver had replaced the "single room in an obscure hotel" with a bright and modern efficiency unit (composed of a living room, bedroom, kitchen, and bath) in the Sylvan Arms Apartments near campus.

The fact that the early eulogies are sometimes inaccurate or misleading in their depictions of Weaver's life and often rather restrained in their evaluations of his work does not detract from their value as candid, thoughtful, and sympathetic accounts of the impressions he made on several of his friends and colleagues. But it is worthwhile to ask why such defects are so common in these (and many subsequent) accounts. At least three major factors would seem to be involved, the first of which is Weaver's celebrated reticence. Although not averse to conversation, he seldom spoke of either his personal life or his work in progress, and almost never in any detail. This meant that even those closest to him during his years at Chicago knew little beyond what they could observe, and there has been a consequent tendency to attribute undue significance to the few personal comments he made.

The second factor is the pronounced compartmentalization of Weaver's activities. The most basic and rigid division was between his professional life in Chicago and the wider world and his private life among family and friends in North Carolina, to which he returned at every opportunity. There is no evidence that any person knew him well in both settings; regardless, it is clear that all of his early eulogists knew him only in a professional context. But his professional life was itself highly compartmentalized. Although Weaver's writings are bound together by an underlying philosophical perspective, they divide easily on the basis of subject matter into four fairly distinct and self-contained groups: Southern literature, history, and culture; political conservatism and the critique of modernity; rhetorical theory; and pedagogical materials in English composition and rhetoric. From the earliest stages of Weaver's career, his different groups of writings have tended to attract separate audiences, each only dimly aware of the existence of the others and the larger body of his work. The result has been

---

club for artists and writers established by the former Mrs. Adlai Stevenson." The letter is located in Box 3 of the William C. Mullendore Papers at the Knight Library of the University of Oregon and is quoted by permission.

a tendency, clearly evident in the early eulogies, to marked parochialism in discussions of his life and work.[11]

The third factor, closely intertwined with the other two, involves several of Weaver's publishing practices. Russell Kirk was only expressing a common view when he noted near the beginning of his memorial: "Dr. Weaver wrote slowly, though with power; so he will live only through two books—*Ideas Have Consequences* (1948) and *The Ethics of Rhetoric* (1953)—[a] textbook in composition, and some pamphlets and periodical pieces." It is true that Weaver was not a prolific writer, but his output was actually much greater than his contemporaries could have known. One reason was that his shorter writings—of which at least 125 were published during his lifetime—appeared in an unusually broad range of outlets, including newspapers and newsletters, popular magazines such as the *Commonweal* and *National Review*, encyclopedia yearbooks, educational pamphlets, and scholarly books and journals in a diversity of academic fields. But the more important reason was that a great deal of Weaver's work remained unpublished at the time of his death. Included in this body were final drafts of two book manuscripts plus several chapters from a third, an advanced revision of his composition text, and almost a score of completed essays, verbatim texts of significant speeches, and near-final drafts of various works in progress.

Because of these factors, it is doubtful that anyone at the time of Weaver's death—not even his family or his closest friends and colleagues—had a full understanding of who he had been or what he had accomplished. Since then, the gradual accumulation of knowledge about his life and work has been matched by an extraordinary and continuing expansion of his reputation and influence. In marked contrast to the limited claims of some of the early eulogists, Weaver is now widely recognized as one of the most original and perceptive interpreters of Southern culture and letters, one of the century's leading rhetorical theorists (along with I. A. Richards, Kenneth Burke, Richard McKeon, Chaim Perelman, Stephen Toulmin, and

11. As one indication of the degree to which Weaver's professional life was compartmentalized, several of his closest colleagues at the University of Chicago have said they were completely unaware until well after his death of his extensive network of friends in Chicago associated with *Modern Age* and the conservative movement. See, for example, the interview of Wilma and David Ebbitt conducted by the editor in Newport, RI, on August 16, 1997.

Jürgen Habermas), and a founder of modern conservatism, among whose adherents he shares with Russell Kirk the role of principal defender and advocate of moral and philosophical traditionalism. Only in the field of pedagogy has his influence waned, but that is less a function of the merit of his ideas than of the wholesale abandonment of the ideal of educating students in the knowledge and service of truth.

One impetus for the heightened appreciation of Weaver's work has been the publication of a number of the writings he left in manuscript form. *Visions of Order*, a set of essays on politics, culture, and rhetoric completed in 1958 and submitted to the Louisiana State University Press in 1961, was finally issued in 1964. It was followed three years later by the second edition of his writing textbook, *Rhetoric and Composition*, which he was completing at the time of his death. In 1968 Arlington House published *The Southern Tradition at Bay*, a defense of Southern culture based on a highly original analysis of Southern letters in the postbellum period. Having initially written it as his doctoral dissertation at LSU, Weaver revised the manuscript for publication in 1945, but abandoned the project after it was rejected by the University of North Carolina Press the following year. Finally, eight unpublished essays and speeches edited by various hands have appeared in print since 1963.[12]

Weaver's reputation has also benefitted from the continuing dissemination of his published works. Three of his five books—*Ideas Have Consequences* (1948), *The Ethics of Rhetoric* (1953), and *The Southern Tradition at Bay* (1968)—have remained in print more or less continuously since their initial release, and *Visions of Order* (1964), which went out of print in 1978, was reissued by the Intercollegiate Studies Institute in 1995. In addition, three collections of his shorter writings have been published posthumously: *Life Without Prejudice* (1965), a set of eight essays and speeches on politics and culture; *Language Is Sermonic* (1970), a group of eight book chapters, essays, and speeches on rhetoric; and the fourteen essays (one of them actually the transcript of a lecture) comprising *The Southern Essays of Richard M. Weaver* (1987). Finally, at least twenty-four of his book chapters and essays have been reprinted in a total of thirty-six different publications since 1963.

---

12. See the Bibliography for a comprehensive list of Weaver's writings ordered chronologically by date of first publication.

As the body of Weaver's published writings has grown, so, too, has the discussion of his ideas and methods. Beginning with a handful of essays in the 1960s (most of them appearing in scholarly journals in the field of speech and rhetoric), the secondary literature on his work now includes well over 100 articles, chapters, and sections; at least 170 reviews of his books; two dozen doctoral dissertations; and scores of academic conference papers. He has also been the subject of four books, all published since 1993. They include a detailed analysis of his rhetorical writings by Bernard Duffy and Martin Jacobi, a collection of previously published writings on his life and work edited by Joseph Scotchie, and two slim "intellectual biographies," one by Scotchie and the other by Fred Douglas Young.[13]

There has also been a small but steady trickle of work on Weaver's life and character. It includes, in addition to the early eulogies, a number of later tributes and reminiscences published either in article form (such as the essays by Victor Milione, Willmoore Kendall, Clifford Amyx, and Henry Regnery) or as prefatory materials in his posthumous books (especially those by Russell Kirk, Eliseo Vivas, and Donald Davidson). Other valuable insights may be found in two unpublished but widely circulated memorials by Wilma Ebbit and Weaver's brother in-law, Kendall Beaton, and in various biographical sketches.[14] Finally, both of Scotchie's books begin with a

13. Bernard K. Duffy and Martin Jacobi, *The Politics of Rhetoric*, Westport: Greenwood, 1993; Joseph Scotchie (ed.), *The Vision of Richard Weaver*, New Brunswick: Transaction, 1995; Joseph Scotchie, *Barbarians in the Saddle*, New Brunswick: Transaction, 1997; Fred Douglas Young, *Richard M. Weaver 1910–1963: A Life of the Mind*, Columbia: University of Missouri Press, 1995.

14. E. Victor Milione, "The Uniqueness of Richard M. Weaver," *The Intercollegiate Review*, 2/1, September 1965, p. 67; Willmoore Kendall, "How to Read Richard Weaver: Philosopher of 'We the (Virtuous) People,'" *The Intercollegiate Review*, 2/1, September 1965, pp. 77–86; Clifford Amyx, "Weaver the Liberal," *Modern Age*, 31/2, Spring 1987, pp. 101–6; Henry Regnery, "Richard Weaver: A Southern Agrarian at the University of Chicago," *Modern Age*, 32/2, Spring 1988, pp. 102–12; Russell Kirk, "Foreword," in Richard M. Weaver, *Visions of Order*, Baton Rouge: Louisiana State University Press, 1964, pp. vii–ix; Eliseo Vivas, "Introduction," in Richard M. Weaver, *Life Without Prejudice and Other Essays* (ed. Harvey Plotnick), Chicago: Henry Regnery, 1965, pp. vii–xvii; Donald Davidson, "The Vision of Richard Weaver: A Foreword," in Richard M. Weaver, *The Southern Tradition at Bay* (ed. George Core and M. E. Bradford), New Rochelle: Arlington House, 1968, pp. 13–25; Wilma R. Ebbitt, "Richard M. Weaver: Friend and Colleague," paper presented at a panel of the Conference on College Composition and Communication, St. Louis, March 19, 1988; Kendall Beaton, "Richard M. Weaver: A Clear Voice in an Addled World," tribute presented at

brief biographical essay and Young's intellectual biography devotes several full chapters to Weaver's life.

This great outpouring of material by and about Richard Weaver has added immeasurably to our understanding of his life and work. But the process is far from complete. Concerning his work, the most obvious deficiencies are the lack of any comprehensive bibliography of his writings[15] and the fact that a number of significant essays and speeches remain unpublished. More generally, there has been a marked and persistent tendency for discussions of Weaver's work to focus on his four major books and the three posthumous collections of his shorter writings. In the recent intellectual biographies, for example, that focus is explicit. The body of Scotchie's book consists solely of a biographical essay followed by chapters on each of the seven books (except for *The Ethics of Rhetoric* and *Language Is Sermonic,* which are treated in a single chapter), whereas Young alternates between chapters of biography and chapters devoted to *The Southern Tradition at Bay, Ideas Have Consequences,* and *The Ethics of Rhetoric.*[16] The difficulty with this emphasis is that the posthumous collections include only a fraction of Weaver's shorter writings, and thus a large body of his work has remained largely unexamined. This is especially problematic in the case of the numerous book reviews and review essays that constituted the bulk of Weaver's writing in the last eight years of his life but were systematically excluded from the collections.

The deficiencies of knowledge are even more pronounced in the case of

---

an annual reunion of the Weaver family in Weaverville, North Carolina, on August 5, 1963. The most accurate and informative of the biographical sketches are by Melvin E. Bradford, "Weaver, Richard M.," in Charles Reagan Wilson and William Ferris (eds.), *Encyclopedia of Southern Culture,* Chapel Hill: University of North Carolina Press, 1989, p. 309, and by Sonja K. Foss, Karen Foss, and Robert Trapp, *Contemporary Perspectives on Rhetoric,* Prospect Heights: Waveland, 1985, pp. 45–50.

15. The first edition of *The Southern Tradition at Bay* included an extensive bibliography of Weaver's writings compiled by Paul Varnell but based largely on the list developed by Louis and Carla Dehmlow shortly after Weaver's death. Although incomplete and marred by numerous errors, it provided a useful research tool, but it was deleted from subsequent editions of the book. A slightly expanded version, still incomplete and retaining most of the errors of the original plus a number of new ones, is included in Scotchie's *Barbarians,* pp. 151–55.

16. It is difficult to understand why Young excluded *Visions of Order* from his analysis. For whatever reason, it is mentioned only in a few passing references.

Weaver's life and character. Like the early eulogies, the more recent tributes and reminiscences provide a wealth of valuable information. However, by their very nature these writings can offer only fragmentary views of their subject and, again like the early eulogies, they are prone to errors of fact, interpretation, and emphasis. What is needed is a more detailed and comprehensive treatment which would correct the record where necessary and weave the scattered fragments into a more accurate and coherent whole. In this respect, the recent books on Weaver have been somewhat disappointing. Duffy and Jacobi make no attempt to provide a comprehensive view, offering only a brief (and sometimes inaccurate) sketch of Weaver's life based almost exclusively on his autobiographical essay "Up from Liberalism" and several of the posthumous tributes and reminiscences.[17] The intellectual biographies do make the attempt, but because they are based on little (Young) or almost no (Scotchie) primary research, they add little to our store of knowledge and often repeat or extend the inaccuracies of the secondary sources on which they largely rely.[18]

This book is intended to address these deficiencies, at least in a modest and preliminary way. Its primary purpose is to complete the long process of assembling and disseminating Weaver's writings in the hope of facilitating a more comprehensive understanding and appreciation of his ideas. To this

17. See Duffy and Jacobi, pp. 2–8, and Richard M. Weaver, "Up from Liberalism," *Modern Age*, 3/1, Winter 1958–59, pp. 21–32. Among their more obvious errors are the claims that "very little of [Weaver's correspondence] has survived" (p. 2); that he "spent most of his youth" in Weaverville (p. 2) and "attended a public high school in Lexington, Kentucky" for a time (p. 4); and that he "had at an early age devoted himself to a humanistic life of scholarship, inquiry, and reflection, preferring solitude and meditation to the enticements and temporal satisfactions of social intercourse" (pp. 4–5).

18. For example, on a single page (p. 4) in his "Introduction," Young claims that "it would be a serious error to pigeonhole [Weaver] either as a conservative sage or as an Agrarian born a generation too late" because "Weaver did not see himself as a partisan of either cause" and "had no close ties to either group"; that "Weaver did not attend conferences frequented by conservatives"; that he "had no close friends, exchanging letters regularly over the years with only two people—his mother and Donald Davidson"; and that "he was a virtual, if not an actual, hermit," all of which are demonstrably false. Scotchie avoids such generalizations, but salts his biographical sketches with dozens of factual errors, ranging from Weaver's age (*Barbarians*, p. 10) and place of residence (p. ix) at the time of his father's death, to the reason he was hired at Chicago (p. 13) and the date of his death, which is listed as April 9 in both *Barbarians* (p. x) and *Vision* (p. 37).

end, the book reproduces all of Weaver's published shorter writings, including those which have appeared posthumously. The only exceptions are the fourteen essays anthologized in *The Southern Essays of Richard M. Weaver,* which is available from Liberty Fund, and a brief essay entitled "Southern Agrarianism" or "Our Southern Agrarians," which was published in the July 1935 issue of a short-lived Kentucky periodical called *The Commonwealth* and now appears to be lost. Also included here are eleven previously unpublished essays and speeches which were left in near-final form at the time of Weaver's death. Their publication exhausts the body of significant completed manuscripts contained in the three known collections of his papers.[19] Given the recent reissue of *Visions of Order,* this means that all of Weaver's published and significant unpublished writings except his composition texts are now available in book form. The present volume also provides a comprehensive bibliography of his published works.

The problem of understanding Weaver the man is more difficult to address. A full and accurate account of his life is needed, but that project must await another occasion. The most that can be offered here is a biographical sketch that may serve to dispel several common misconceptions and provide some little context for the reading of his works.[20]

19. The three collections are the Richard M. Weaver papers at Vanderbilt University, the uncatalogued Weaver library and papers at Hilldale College, and a large collection of books, manuscripts, papers, photographs, and documents acquired by the current editor from the estate of Mrs. Polly Weaver Beaton and scheduled for eventual donation to Vanderbilt. Of the eleven unpublished essays and speeches included in the current volume, seven are from the Vanderbilt collection and four from the Polly Weaver Beaton collection. A substantial body of unpublished material remains in the three collections, including Weaver's M.A. thesis; ten student essays; about fifteen early, incomplete, or undecipherable drafts of essays and speeches; typescripts of several brief presentations to the College English faculty; and numerous notes and fragments. Although useful for scholars, none of the remaining material merits publication in its present form. Most of the longer typescript drafts from the Vanderbilt collection have been reproduced (albeit with numerous transcription errors) in Gerald T. Goodnight's "Rhetoric and Culture: A Critical Edition of Richard M. Weaver's Unpublished Works," unpublished doctoral dissertation, University of Kansas, 1978.

20. This sketch reflects the fruits of five years of research for a large-scale biography of Weaver currently in preparation for the University of Missouri Press. Thanks in large part to a 1992–93 appointment as a Bradley Resident Scholar at the Heritage Foundation and a 1996 fellowship research grant from the Earhart Foundation, it has been possible to assemble from more than fifty public and private sources over 1,100 letters to or from Weaver and to locate and interview at length more than sixty individuals who knew him well. Almost 100 other

Richard Malcolm Weaver was the eldest of the four children of Carrye Lee (later "Carrie") Embry and Richard Malcolm ("Dick") Weaver. Carrye was born on January 13, 1874, near the town of Athens in Fayette County, Kentucky, but spent much of her life in nearby Lexington. Small in stature, stylish in dress, and an accomplished horsewoman, she was strong-willed and fiercely independent, with a personality often described as "fiery" or "pungent."[21] In 1902, as a single woman of 28, she founded Embry & Company, a millinery shop on East Main Street in Lexington. Two years later her brother William joined the venture, added women's garments to the stock, and initiated a series of expansions which soon made Embry's one of the leading stores in the city. Well before that transformation was complete, however, Carrye had embarked on a different course. While traveling by train on a buying trip to New York City in February of 1907, she fell into conversation with a man from North Carolina who shared her interest in horses. Born near Weaverville on March 8, 1870, Dick Weaver was the junior partner in Chambers and Weaver, a successful livery stable in the resort town of Asheville. Handsome, outgoing, and worldly, he was a popular local figure, a talented violinist, and an acknowledged expert on thoroughbred horses. He also was married, but was living separately from his wife. After a relatively brief courtship, and just two months after his divorce became final, Dick and Carrye became engaged on June 4, 1908. They were married in Lexington five months later, bought a house in Asheville, and settled down to raise a family. Richard M. Weaver was born on March 3, 1910, followed by Polly on July 29, 1911, Betty on March 12, 1913, and a second son, Embry Lee, on May 17, 1916. But Embry never knew his father. On December 16, 1915, Dick Weaver retired to bed early, complaining of dizziness; by 1 A.M. he was dead, felled by a stroke at the age of 45.

Although precise dates are unavailable, it is known that Carrye stayed in Asheville for some time after her husband's death, but then moved the family to Lexington, most likely in the summer of 1918, and took a house at 370 Aylsford Place. In about 1920 Carrye opened the Palais Royal, a shop

---

persons who were more casually acquainted with him have provided information by letter or telephone. All claims about Weaver in the following discussion are supported by documentary evidence, but for the sake of clarity and simplicity only direct quotations from these sources will be referenced.

21. Polly Weaver Beaton in an interview conducted August 11, 1995, in Weaverville, North Carolina.

specializing in hats and ladies' furnishings located on the same block as—
and in direct competition with—her brother's store. But that venture soon
failed, and she eventually returned to Embry & Company, where she
worked as buyer and manager of the millinery department until her retirement in the late 1930s.

Even though his family was not wealthy, there is no evidence that Richard Weaver experienced poverty as a child. To the contrary, the house on
Aylsford Place where the family lived until about 1932 was a fairly large and
modern frame structure located in a middle-class neighborhood a few
blocks from the University of Kentucky campus. More importantly, Carrye
(quite likely with the assistance of her family) was able to provide at least
her older children with superior educational opportunities. Richard began
his education in North Carolina at a tiny private school conducted in one
room of the teacher's home.[22] In Lexington he enrolled as a new student in
the third grade of the public school near his home, but did not return for
the fourth grade and presumably attended some private school for the remainder of his elementary education. In 1924 he was sent as a freshman to
the Academy of Lincoln Memorial University in Harrogate, Tennessee.
Following graduation in 1927, he enrolled at the University of Kentucky,
where he was awarded an A.B. degree in 1932. Although he did work in the
kitchens at Lincoln Memorial to help pay his tuition and board, there is no
evidence that Weaver held a job during his undergraduate years at Kentucky. Both of his sisters completed high school at Cardome Academy, a
Catholic boarding school in nearby Georgetown; Polly then studied at the
University of Kentucky for three years. Only Embry, the youngest child,
received his education solely in the public schools of Lexington. All of this
suggests that if there were a deficiency in Weaver's childhood it was less one
of money than of parental contact. Because Carrye's job required long hours
at the store and frequent buying trips to New York, the children were often
left in the care of a sitter. When they were young, all spent their summers

22. See the brief description of his experiences in Richard M. Weaver, *The Role of Education in Shaping Our Society*, Bryn Mawr: Intercollegiate Studies Institute, undated pamphlet, p. 10. The reference there to "our little village" suggests the possibility that Weaver's
family lived in Weaverville for some period after his father's death, but there is no other
evidence of this, and it is difficult to understand why they would give up their house in
Asheville to move to Weaverville.

with relatives in Weaverville; as adolescents, all but Embry were sent to boarding schools. This may help to explain both the marked respect and admiration Weaver showed for his mother and his firm conviction, expressed repeatedly in his early writings, that a woman's place is with her home and family.

Nevertheless, what evidence we have suggests that Weaver enjoyed his years at Lincoln Memorial Academy and made the most of the social and educational opportunities it afforded. Already a serious student, he benefitted from the example of William Maury Mitchell, a freshman in the university when they met in 1924 who became his lifelong friend. Weaver, Mitchell, and a third student, Vadus Carmack, joined together to form a philosophical society which met each week to discuss ideas. Weaver was also an officer (most likely the president) of the campus chapter of the Christian Endeavor Society, a key member of the debating team, and a star competitor on the track team. He graduated as valedictorian of his class, having completed his program of study in only three years.

Weaver extended this record of achievement during his years as an undergraduate student at the University of Kentucky (1927–32). He joined the freshman track team and performed well enough to be awarded a numeral (the freshman equivalent of a letter) at the end of the season. But he soon dropped track in order to concentrate on other activities, especially debate. After winning a place on the varsity debate team in his freshman year, he competed with great success in more than fifty intercollegiate contests over the course of his undergraduate career. Another focus was the campus Liberal Club, which he helped to organize near the end of his sophomore year; he also served as its vice president and president. Although neither large nor particularly active, the club gained substantial notoriety on campus and throughout the state for its perceived links to the League for Industrial Democracy and its opposition to compulsory military training, as well as for some minor agitation during the Kentucky coalfield strikes of 1932.[23] As this association suggests, Weaver's period at Kentucky was marked by a growing commitment to socialism and pacifism. Included in the change

23. The memoir by Clifford Amyx, a close friend of Weaver's at the University of Kentucky and for many years thereafter, provides detailed accounts of the activities of the debating team and the Liberal Club and Weaver's political views at the time. See also Weaver's "Up from Liberalism."

was a wholehearted embrace of progressive morality which led him to pursue a kind of studied debauchery during the decade of the 1930s. These experiments in dissipation had no discernible effect on his academic performance. Despite having to withdraw from school for the 1930 spring semester, apparently because of an eye injury which made it impossible for him to read, Weaver maintained the equivalent of a 3.83 grade point average over 142.3 semester hours of work. In January 1932 he was inducted into Phi Beta Kappa, and five months later he was awarded an A.B. degree in English "With High Distinction," the highest level of honors conferred by the university.[24]

His accomplishments notwithstanding, Weaver's prospects in June of 1932 were far from bright. With the Depression near its lowest ebb, few good jobs were available, and his mother was finding it increasingly difficult to support the family. Within a year of Weaver's graduation, both Polly and Embry dropped out of school to find work, and the family gave up the house on Aylsford Place for smaller rented lodgings a few blocks away on Stone Avenue. It was in these circumstances that Weaver joined the American Socialist Party and served as secretary of the Lexington "local" until about 1934. But the experience was far from fulfilling, and he later noted, "My disillusionment with the Left began with this first practical step."[25] Meanwhile, he sought to continue his education by applying for graduate fellowships at Duke and other Southern universities. But his only offer was a $200 scholarship from the University of Kentucky and so, in September 1932, he enrolled there to begin work on a master's degree in English. In the spring of 1933, Weaver again applied to other schools for aid, and this time his efforts were rewarded with an offer of a $300 scholarship from Vander-

24. This contradicts the common suggestion (see, e.g., Amyx, p. 105) that Weaver's deliberately low grades in military science prevented him from attaining the highest level of academic honors. Although it is true that his only grades of "C" were received in Military Science 1a and 1b, these courses carried only 1.3 semester hours of credit each and therefore lowered his overall GPA by only three one-hundredths of a point. Further damage was avoided when Weaver was excused from the second-year military science requirement, presumably because of poor eyesight or some other health problem. Of much greater importance to his GPA were the eight grades of "B" he received in geology (3 courses), hygiene (2 courses), anatomy and physiology (1 course), Spanish (1 course), and the second semester of freshman English, which he took by examination.

25. Weaver, "Up from Liberalism," p. 22.

bilt. Although he had completed a full year of courses at Kentucky and was already working on a thesis entitled "The Revolt Against Humanism: A Study of the New Critical Temper," he accepted the offer and enrolled as a master's student in English at Vanderbilt in the fall of 1933.

The move to Vanderbilt required Weaver to repeat the coursework for his master's degree. However, he was able to salvage the research he had done on his thesis, which was completed under the direction of John Crowe Ransom at the end of his first year of study. He received his M.A. degree in June of 1934 and enrolled in the doctoral program in English in the fall, now supported by a $500 teaching fellowship. The next two years were devoted to completing the coursework and other preliminary requirements for the doctorate. In June of 1936, he left Nashville to begin searching for a full-time teaching position to support him while he wrote his dissertation, a study of Milton, once again under Ransom's direction.

It would be difficult to overestimate the importance of Weaver's period of study with the Southern Agrarians at Vanderbilt. As related in his auto-biographical essay "Up from Liberalism" (included here in the first group of his writings), most of the seeds of his later work were planted at that time. But the period at Vanderbilt was important for other reasons as well. For one thing, Weaver made a number of long-term friends among the graduate students and explored with them poetry, art, and music. The most notable of these students were John and Esther Randolph, with whom Weaver shared an apartment during the 1935–36 academic year.[26] Weaver also maintained close contact with his friends in Lexington, many of whom had continued to work for the socialist cause. Their most ambitious project was a monthly "journal of opinion" devoted to political and economic reform in Kentucky. Launched in May 1935 with Lexington attorney Byron Pumphrey as the editor, James Porter as associate editor, and Weaver and Prof. Thomas D. Clark as contributing editors, the *Commonwealth* was a commercial failure and folded after only three issues. But the experience led Weaver to form an abiding interest in book and magazine editing which eventually found expression in his work for the *Commonweal, National Review*, and, most notably, *Modern Age*.

26. Weaver's correspondence with the Randolphs from 1934 to 1945 has been preserved and provides the only detailed account of his activities during that period.

As the summer of 1936 progressed, Weaver became increasingly anxious about his inability to find a teaching post; at one point he even considered volunteering to fight for the Republicans in Spain. Finally, he was offered a one-year appointment as an instructor in English at Alabama Polytechnic Institute (now Auburn University), which he eagerly accepted. Little of note seems to have happened during his brief tenure there except his purchase of a used car, the first of a series of Ford sedans he would own and drive over the course of his life. The purchase was tied to his acceptance of a better job, an appointment as acting assistant professor and director of forensics in the Department of English at Texas A&M.

Weaver taught at Texas A&M for three years beginning in the fall of 1937. Although he enjoyed coaching debate and was held in high esteem by his colleagues, he was deeply disturbed by the mood of militant philistinism he encountered there. He later told friends that, in order to escape the oppressive atmosphere in College Station, he spent most weekends carousing in a nearby city (probably Houston). He also traveled rather widely. Over the Thanksgiving breaks of 1937 and 1938 he drove groups of friends to Monterrey, Mexico. In July of 1938 he sailed to Europe on the *S.S. Volendam* to spend a month in Paris, ostensibly to audit lectures at the Sorbonne. Although he duly registered for a course, he spent the early part of the visit seeing the sights with a Miss Darling of Boston, whom he had met on the crossing; after her departure, he seems to have devoted himself to buying prints at the Louvre, arguing politics over schooners of Alsatian beer at sidewalk cafes, and sampling the pleasures of such establishments as "Les Belles Poules" at 38 Rue Blondel, which he characterized in a letter to John Randolph as "an amazing place," staffed with "a prostitute of every nationality," and "better described by word than in writing."[27] In 1939 Weaver reported spending "the pleasantest summer of my life" at Harvard, where, interspersed with trips to New Hampshire, the Maine coast, and "an art colony out on Cape Ann," he audited courses by Robert Hillyer, Theodore Spencer, and John Mason Brown and luxuriated in the resources of the Poetry Room of Widener Library.[28]

27. Letter from Richard Weaver to John Randolph dated August 30, 1938. Quoted by permission of Mrs. Esther Randolph.

28. Letter from Richard Weaver to Esther Randolph dated August 12, 1939. Quoted by permission of Mrs. Esther Randolph.

On the drive back to Texas after his summer at Harvard, Weaver experienced an epiphanic moment that radically altered the course of his life and career. As he noted in "Up from Liberalism," "it came to me like a revelation that I did not *have* to go back to this job, which had become distasteful, and that I did not *have* to go on professing the cliches of liberalism, which were becoming meaningless to me."[29] This revelation was the product of several factors. Work on the Vanderbilt dissertation was not going well, and what little enthusiasm Weaver had for the project evaporated in 1938 when John Crowe Ransom moved to Kenyon College and Claude Finney replaced him as thesis director. Not long after, Weaver also lost faith in the Left. In a January 1939 letter, he announced, "I am junking Marxism as not founded in experience," and immediately he began what he later described as "a kind of religious conversion" to the "Church of Agrarianism." At the core of that conversion was a commitment to restoring "the kind of poetic-religious vision of life which dominated the Middle Ages," as well as a conviction that the grounds for such a restoration could be discovered through a more profound appreciation of his cultural heritage.[30] Accordingly, in January 1940 Weaver began the process of applying for admission to the doctoral program in English at Louisiana State University. His intentions were made clear in an application for a graduate fellowship in which he concluded his biographical sketch with the statement: "My travels have made me a Southern nationalist rather than an internationalist, and I now want to do an important piece of research in the history of my section."[31]

The period at LSU (1940–43) was a time of real financial hardship for Weaver. His sole income during the first year of study was a $450 fellowship, a drastic reduction from his $2,000 salary at Texas A&M. Even as a third-year teaching assistant he received only $1,200 for the equivalent of a full-time teaching load. To make matters worse, his mother had retired and

29. Weaver, "Up from Liberalism," p. 24.

30. Letters from Richard Weaver to John Randolph dated January 26, 1939, and January 20, 1942. Quoted by permission of Mrs. Esther Randolph.

31. Richard M. Weaver, Application for Fellowship to the Graduate School of The Louisiana State University, undated, p. 3. Located in the Richard M. Weaver file in the Department of English Records, RG# A0607, Louisiana State University Archives, LSU Libraries, Baton Rouge, Louisiana, and quoted by permission.

taken up residence in a New York City hotel where she could be close to her daughters, leaving him no home. He therefore spent the summers of 1941 and 1942 in residence, respectively, at the Universities of Virginia and North Carolina. Another impediment to his plans was the unexpected closing of the *Southern Review* at the end of 1941. Weaver had come to LSU undecided whether to pursue a career in teaching or editing, and he had hoped to work himself into a position at the journal. Just when that goal seemed within his grasp, the journal's funding was eliminated, and even a nationwide campaign directed at the LSU administration failed to produce a restoration. Finally, like others of his age and sex, Weaver had to deal with the constant threat of military induction. He registered with the Baton Rouge draft board in October 1940, passed a physical examination the following May, received a I-A classification a year later, and was ordered to report for induction on June 3, 1942. Poor vision led to his rejection, but his classification was changed only to I-B, and by February 1943 he was again listed as I-A. Only in May 1943 did he receive a IV-F classification and final exemption from military service.

Weaver responded to these circumstances by devoting his energies completely to his work. Before the end of his first year of study he began writing a dissertation under the direction of H. Arlin Turner. Entitled "The Confederate South, 1865–1910; A Study in the Survival of a Mind and a Culture," the first draft was completed in December 1942 under the direction of Cleanth Brooks. Although the connection with Brooks was to prove quite valuable, Brooks had little impact on the dissertation, having replaced Turner (who was called into military service) only in October 1942 when the project was almost finished. Weaver also used the time at LSU to begin submitting for publication a steady stream of essays on Southern history and culture. The first of these, "The Older Religiousness in the South," appeared in the *Sewanee Review* in April 1943, just a month before his graduation.

As in 1936, Weaver had great difficulty finding a job during the summer of 1943. In the end, the best he could manage was a temporary position as an instructor in the Army Specialist Training Program at North Carolina State University. In September, therefore, he moved to Raleigh, where he was joined by his mother, now partly dependent on him for support. But the job lasted only eight months, and in April 1944 the two moved to Asheville, where he began the search anew. Armed with three recent publications and the active support of Cleanth Brooks, Weaver's quest this time was more favorable. Although it seemed at first that he might have to settle for a four-month contract teaching a Navy composition course at Yale, a telegram arrived on September 6, 1944, from Dean Clarence Faust of the University of Chicago offering a one-year appointment as an instructor in English in the College. Weaver accepted the offer with delighted relief—and carried the telegram in his wallet for more than a decade.

Despite the great prestige enjoyed by the University of Chicago, Weaver's position during the nineteen years he taught there was far from glamorous. Under the administration of Robert Maynard Hutchins, who served as president from 1929 to 1951, the university was organized into an undergraduate College (formerly the Junior College), four primarily graduate Divisions (Humanities, Social Sciences, Biological Sciences, and Physical Sciences), and six Professional Schools (e.g., Law, Divinity). The College differed in at least three important respects from a typical undergraduate institution. First, and most importantly, students could be admitted at any time after completing their sophomore year of high school and were expected to fulfill the requirements for a bachelor's degree in four years of work (or less, for those entering with more than two years of high school). Second, all undergraduates were required to complete an integrated program of study designed to provide a broad general education in the liberal arts and sciences. In 1944 a student entering the College after two years of high school would receive a Bachelor of Arts degree after successfully completing thirteen year-long courses, including a three-course sequence in English reading and writing. Finally, students could receive credit for a course only by passing a comprehensive examination covering the entire year of work.

The seminal fact of Weaver's academic career at Chicago is that he was appointed to the College English staff rather than to the more prestigious Department of English Language and Literature in the Division of the Humanities. Although many of the distinctive features of the College program were eventually modified or eliminated, and although the College and Division English staffs were combined a few years before his death, Weaver worked almost exclusively within the College. He spent his first two years toiling largely in English 1 and 2—both in essence high school courses—and thereafter taught mostly the equivalent of freshman composition, plus occasional sections of Humanities 3 and its successors (an interdisciplinary course in criticism), the History of Western Civilization, and a one-quarter graduate (later upper-level undergraduate) class called Advanced Composition: Exposition. Significantly, he taught no other graduate courses—and none at any level in literature—and had little opportunity to work either with graduate students or even advanced undergraduates. More importantly, because College faculty were hired and evaluated primarily as teachers, Weaver's instructional load was unusually heavy for a professor at a major research university. Typically his responsibilities included teaching three courses per quarter, attending weekly staff meetings to plan content for each of the courses, assisting in the preparation of a "syllabus" of readings and exercises for each course, and grading the final comprehensive examinations. In these circumstances, there was no expectation that College faculty would engage in extensive programs of research and publication, and few in fact did.

By all accounts Richard Weaver was a dedicated, effective, and conscientious teacher. But he was also determined to follow a higher calling, as indicated in an August 1945 letter to John Randolph in which he expressed his reactions to the end of the Second World War:

> And is anything saved? We cannot be sure. True, there are a few buildings left standing around, but what kind of animal is going to inhabit them? I have become convinced in the past few years that the essence of civilization is ethical (with perhaps some helping out from aesthetics). And never has the power of ethical discrimination been as low as it is today. The atomic bomb was a final blow to the code of humanity. I cannot help thinking that we will suffer retribution for this. For a long time to come I believe my chief interest is going to be the restoration of civilization, of the distinctions that make life intelligible.[32]

Weaver never thereafter strayed from this course. His considerable body of writings—made possible only by enormous self-discipline and self-sacrifice and accomplished with little of the academic support and intellectual stimulation most scholars take for granted—serves as a monument to his determination.

32. Letter from Richard Weaver to John Randolph dated August 24, 1945. Quoted by permission of Mrs. Esther Randolph.

His first priority after arriving at Chicago was to publish his dissertation, now retitled "The Southern Tradition at Bay." After making minor revisions and adding an epilogue, he traveled to Chapel Hill in July 1945 to spend a week discussing the manuscript with William Terry Couch, then director of the University of North Carolina Press, and with Couch's assistant, George Scheer. Couch gave an oral commitment to publish the work, but recommended the addition of an introduction and conclusion to clarify its focus. These were completed by the end of the summer, but by then Couch had left North Carolina to accept the position of director of the University of Chicago Press. T. J. Wilson, Couch's successor, asked to review the manuscript, and it was sent to him in March 1946, but he rejected it later that year; Weaver made no further efforts to have it published.

"The Southern Tradition at Bay" was ultimately abandoned as the result of a meeting at Couch's home in Chicago early in the fall quarter of 1945 among Couch, Weaver, and Cleanth Brooks, who had accepted a visiting professorship at the university for the 1945–46 academic year. Couch had refused to consider the dissertation for the Chicago press because of its Southern focus. However, he did suggest that if Weaver would "take the conclusions . . . and apply them in a general way to the modern world," the press might be interested in the result, and the three men spent the evening exploring the idea.[33] Weaver immediately began work on the new project, but much of the writing was done the following summer, which he spent in residence at the University of Wisconsin. The product was a manuscript entitled "Steps Toward the Restoration of Our World," which he submitted to the University of Chicago Press on October 26, 1946. Couch responded enthusiastically, but several outside reviews were highly critical and the first half of 1947 was devoted to extensive revisions. On July 18, 1947, a contract was issued, and the manuscript, now entitled "The Adverse Descent," was scheduled for publication.

33. Letter from Richard Weaver to H. Arlin Turner dated July 3, 1946. Located in the Richard Weaver file in the Arlin Turner Papers (2nd 84:A) in the Special Collections Library at Duke University and quoted by permission. This account of the inception of *Ideas Have Consequences* differs from the one offered by Weaver in "Up from Liberalism" (p. 30) but is supported by other contemporary materials, especially his letter to Cleanth Brooks dated May 31, 1948, located in Box 15, Folder 320, of the Cleanth Brooks Papers in the Beinecke Rare Book and Manuscript Library at Yale University. It should be stressed, however, that the two accounts are not necessarily incompatible.

Clearly hoping to repeat the phenomenal success of the press's American edition of Friedrich Hayek's *The Road to Serfdom* in 1944, and contemplating sales of as many as 30,000 copies, Couch put the full resources of his organization behind the book. He ordered an unusually large initial press run of 7,500 copies, with provisions for a second printing of equal size, and authorized a promotional budget of $7,500, an extraordinary sum for a book with a retail price of $2.75. He also worked tirelessly to secure endorsements from such notables as Reinhold Niebuhr, Paul Tillich, and Norman Foerster, in addition to Brooks, Allen Tate, Donald Davidson, and John Crowe Ransom. But perhaps his most important contribution was the book's title, *Ideas Have Consequences*, which he first proposed in early October of 1947. The difficulty was that Weaver loathed the formulation and, following a heated argument with Couch at a party on October 25, seriously considered withdrawing the manuscript from the press. In the end, however, Weaver apologized and acquiesced, with the result that a phrase which he later described as "hopelessly banal" has now become indissolubly linked with his name.[34]

Ideas Have Consequences was released on February 16, 1948, supported by a major (albeit poorly conceived) promotional campaign which featured multiple news releases, full-page advertisements in all of the leading literary publications of the day, and even a special spotlighted display table at the main entrance to the book department at Marshall Field and Company. As hoped, the effort generated extensive discussion, including over 100 published reviews. As anticipated, however, the reviews were decidedly mixed in tone: those in regional newspapers and religious publications were generally quite favorable, whereas those in organs of the liberal establishment tended to sneering vituperation. The most damaging were a review by Howard Mumford Jones in the February 22 issue of the *New York Times Book Review* and an essay by Dixon Wecter in the April 10 issue of the *Saturday Review of Literature*, which began with an attack on Robert Maynard Hutchins and his efforts at Chicago and ended by holding up *Ideas Have Consequences* as an emblem of the university's deficiencies. Although Wecter suffered the humiliation of seeing his views repudiated three weeks later in a rejoinder by *Saturday Review* editor Norman Cousins, these and similar sentiments aroused so much animosity toward Weaver on campus

---

34. Letter from Richard Weaver to Robert Heilman dated July 2, 1948. Located in the Robert Heilman Papers in the University Archives of the University of Washington Library and quoted by permission.

that he had serious concerns for his job.[35] It seems likely that the negative reviews also contributed to the book's lackluster sales, which at midyear stood at fewer than 8,000 copies.

It is clear from his correspondence that Weaver was somewhat disappointed by the book's performance and regretted not taking more care in the formulation of some of its arguments. Nevertheless, it did serve to bring his name to prominence and created an enthusiastic audience for his work. On a more practical level, the university responded on May 7, 1948, by offering him a three-year contract and promotion to assistant professor. His career at Chicago was assured the following year when he received the coveted Quantrell Prize for excellence in undergraduate teaching. In 1951 he was duly promoted to associate professor with tenure, and six years later he attained the rank of professor.

In many respects, the publication of *Ideas Have Consequences* marked the high point of Weaver's career, and the years from 1948 through 1953 may well have been the most satisfying of his life. Certainly they were among his most productive. Even before the book was published, he had resumed his work on Southern literature and culture, which led to a steady stream of essays and reviews in the *Sewanee Review*, the *Georgia Review, Shenandoah,* and the *Hopkins Review.* In 1949 he was appointed chairman of an interdisciplinary committee charged with producing a treatise on grammar for use in the undergraduate program at Chicago. More than two years of concentrated effort was required to complete the work, a slim 33-page pamphlet entitled *Elements of English Grammar,* which was published for campus use by the University of Chicago Press in September 1951.[36] In combination

35. See Howard Mumford Jones, "Listing Mankind's 'Wrong Turnings,'" *New York Times Book Review,* February 22, 1948, pp. 4 and 25; Weaver's response to Jones, "Editor's Mail," *New York Times Book Review,* March 21, 1948, p. 29; Dixon Wecter, "Can Metaphysics Save the World?" *Saturday Review of Literature,* 31/15, April 10, 1948, pp. 7–8 and 30–32; and Norman Cousins, "The Case of Robert Maynard Hutchins," *Saturday Review of Literature,* 31/18, May 1, 1948, pp. 18–19. For an expression of Weaver's concerns see his letter to Cleanth Brooks dated May 31, 1948, located in Box 15, Folder 320, of the Cleanth Brooks Papers in the Beinecke Rare Book and Manuscript Library at Yale University.

36. George J. Metcalf, W. H. L. Meyer, Jr., John P. Netherton, James Sledd, and Richard M. Weaver, *Elements of English Grammar,* Chicago: University of Chicago Press, September 1951, pamphlet. James C. Babcock, Ernest M. Halliday, and Louise A. Roberts are also credited with assisting the committee in its work. Weaver felt this work was so important that he listed it for a time under the heading of "Publications—Books" on his official "Biographical Information for University Records" form.

with his experience in teaching composition and preparing sets of readings for his courses at Chicago, this project encouraged him to try his hand at writing a textbook on composition and rhetoric. Accordingly, in October 1952 he signed a contract with Henry Holt and Company to produce by July 15, 1954, a "Complete Textbook for Freshman English." At about the same time he was actively seeking a publisher for what was to become his second book, *The Ethics of Rhetoric*. Begun in early 1949 and strongly influenced by the tutelage of his close friend and former Chicago officemate Pierre Albert Duhamel, the collection of nine essays expanded his views on language in *Ideas Have Consequences* to form the basis of a highly original neo-Platonic theory of rhetoric.

When *The Ethics of Rhetoric* was published on September 21, 1953, Richard Weaver must have felt a certain amount of pride in his accomplishments. As a tenured associate professor and a respected member of the College English staff, his academic career was secure. He had two books and a brace of shorter publications to his credit and a potentially lucrative contract for a college text in hand. Perhaps most important, he had just purchased the house in Weaverville as a permanent residence for his mother and siblings and a place where he could spend term breaks and summers. However, he was about to encounter a series of disappointments that would shadow his efforts for the rest of his life.

The first disappointment concerned *The Ethics of Rhetoric*. Weaver noted in a letter to Cleanth Brooks that "I have put into this work the best that I have" and stressed that it was "a more carefully and solidly written book" than *Ideas Have Consequences*.[37] The problem was to find a publisher. The University of Chicago Press asked to review the manuscript in the fall of 1952, but Weaver refused as a gesture of support for William Terry Couch, who had been summarily dismissed from his position as director two years before. The manuscript was then sent to the Oxford University Press, but it was rejected, and overtures to several large commercial publishers proved fruitless. He therefore decided to accept an offer from the Henry Regnery Company—a small Chicago publishing house that had entered the book market only five years before—and a contract was signed on March 16, 1953. Regnery had established a reputation as a publisher of serious (albeit often

37. Letter from Richard Weaver to Cleanth Brooks dated November 16, 1952. Located in Box 15, Folder 320, of the Cleanth Brooks Papers in the Beinecke Rare Book and Manuscript Library at Yale University.

political) nonfiction and would soon issue Russell Kirk's *The Conservative Mind,* one of the seminal works of modern conservatism, but the firm had few resources for promotion and was at best a questionable vehicle for a narrowly focused work of scholarship intended primarily for an academic audience. As a consequence, although the book did receive a handful of mostly favorable reviews, only three were in academic journals, and the author lamented to his sister that *"The Ethics of Rhetoric* continues to be one of the most unread books of the year."[38] Indeed, fewer than 700 copies were sold in the first year of publication, and by the end of the decade the total had risen only to 1,500.

The composition text was another source of frustration. Although Weaver had toyed with the material since at least 1951, it was only after *The Ethics of Rhetoric* was published that he began to work in earnest on the project. He then discovered that the writing was excruciatingly slow and difficult for him, and by the end of 1954—more than four months after the completed manuscript was supposed to have been delivered to the publisher—he had produced only a revised draft of the first chapter; two more years of effort were required to bring the task to completion. He later remarked to Donald Davidson: "The labor was enormous, and several times I was on the point of throwing it up in despair."[39]

A third blow involved Weaver's friend and patron William Terry Couch. Following his dismissal from Chicago, Couch eventually became editor of *Collier's Encyclopedia,* in which position he commissioned Weaver to write entries entitled "Reflections on Education," "Colleges and Universities," and "Propaganda" for the 1954 and 1955 *Year Book*s. The last entry was so insightful that an expanded version was requested for the 1956 edition of the main *Encyclopedia.* Despite the pressure of other commitments, Weaver took special pains with the work, producing what he felt was "one of the most careful pieces of analysis I have ever done."[40] But Couch's superior,

38. Letter from Richard Weaver to Polly Weaver Beaton dated December 16, 1953. Located in file C21 of the Polly Weaver Beaton collection and quoted by permission.

39. Letter from Richard Weaver to Donald Davidson dated April 23, 1957. Located in the Donald Davidson Papers in the Special Collections of the Jean and Alexander Heard Library at Vanderbilt University and quoted by permission.

40. Letter from Richard Weaver to William Terry Couch dated September 12, 1955. Located in File 517 of the William T. Couch Papers in the Southern Historical Collection of the Manuscripts Department, University of North Carolina, Chapel Hill, and quoted by permission.

Director of Publications Everette O. Fontaine, blocked publication of both "Propaganda" and an entry on "Regionalism" by Donald and Theresa Davidson, citing transparently political grounds. An extended dispute ensued, in which Couch apparently went so far as to submit his resignation. To Couch's evident relief, the offer was rejected, and he turned his efforts to an increasingly desperate search for a compromise, even repeatedly rewriting the propaganda essay in the vain hope of finding a version that both author and critic would accept. In the end, Weaver felt compelled to sever all ties with *Collier's* (which included abandoning a partially completed entry on "Politics and Rhetoric" for the 1956 *Year Book*) and had little to do with Couch thereafter.[41]

Faced with these disappointments, Weaver reacted with characteristic determination. In November 1954, on the advice of Russell Kirk, he applied to the Volker Fund for a grant to support a sabbatical leave to work on "a third book which might, in a sense, complete the other two" by bringing together "the problems of order, community, tradition, and expression in some more comprehensive view."[42] The grant was approved the following February, with the result that Weaver was able to devote almost sixteen full months—from June 1955 through September 1956—exclusively to scholarship. Much of that period was spent working in Weaverville on the composition text and the initial draft of the "third book," which would be published eventually as *Visions of Order*. But he also traveled widely, including repeated trips to New York, New Haven, and Nashville. In addition, the connection with the Volker Fund produced the first of a series of invitations to foundation-sponsored conferences, most of which included publication of the papers presented.[43]

41. Despite extensive searches, no copy of either the revised "Propaganda" entry or the partial draft of "Politics and Rhetoric" has ever been found, and both must be presumed lost. In contrast, the Davidsons' essay on "Regionalism" was preserved and eventually published in *Modern Age*, 37/2, Winter 1995, pp. 102–15.

42. Letter from Richard Weaver to Richard Cornuelle dated Thanksgiving Day, 1954. Located in file C6 of the Polly Weaver Beaton collection and quoted by permission.

43. The first invitation was to attend a "Conference on Democratic Theory" held at Buck Hill Falls, Pennsylvania, in June 1956. Weaver subsequently presented papers at Volker-sponsored conferences on "Individuality and Personality," held at Princeton, New Jersey, in September 1956, "Scientism and Values," held at Sea Island, Georgia, in September 1958, "Relativism and the Study of Man," held at Sea Island (or possibly Emory University) in September 1959, and "The Necessary Conditions for a Free Society," held at Princeton, New

A further benefit of the sabbatical was that it gave Weaver an opportunity to indulge his interest in journals of opinion. The importance of such publications had been apparent to him at least since the time of his association with the *Commonwealth* in 1935, and not long after his conversion to conservatism he wrote to Cleanth Brooks: "One of the great needs of the postwar period will be a publication which will do for some of the absurdities floating about today what the *Mercury* in its prime did for some of the extravagances of the twenties."[44] In the years immediately following the war he lent his support to the *Commonweal*, contributing seventeen book reviews to its pages between 1947 and 1953. In 1954 he was approached by Willmoore Kendall and William F. Buckley, Jr., concerning their plans for *National Review*, and by Russell Kirk, who was developing a proposal for a conservative monthly that eventually saw light as the quarterly *Modern Age*. Weaver pledged his enthusiastic support to both endeavors, and when the second issue of *National Review* appeared in November 1955, it included his review of Theodore Lentz's *Towards a Science of Peace*, the first of twenty-six essays and reviews he contributed to the magazine in the next two years.

The year 1957 marked the beginning of another brief period of accomplishment and satisfaction for Weaver. The early spring brought publication at last of *Composition: A Course in Writing and Rhetoric*. In May he was promoted to full professor, and the following month he had the honor of seeing his "Life Without Prejudice" featured as the lead essay in the premier issue of *Modern Age*. A note of sadness was struck in mid-December when he received word of the sudden and tragic death of his closest personal friend, Virginia attorney William Maury Mitchell, who left behind his wife of less than a year and a son only a few weeks old. But just a few days later a letter arrived from Randall Stewart, chairman of the Department of English at Vanderbilt, asking Weaver to join Andrew Lytle, Cleanth Brooks, and Warren Beck as featured speakers at a Vanderbilt Literary Symposium to be held the following April. Undoubtedly the invitation was a product of Weaver's increasingly close friendships with Stewart and Donald Davidson,

---

Jersey, in June 1961. All of these papers were eventually published in volumes of conference proceedings.

44. Letter from Richard Weaver to Cleanth Brooks dated March 30, 1944. Located in Box 15, Folder 320, of the Cleanth Brooks Papers in the Beinecke Rare Book and Manuscript Library at Yale University and quoted by permission.

one of the Twelve Southerners who contributed to the 1930 Agrarian manifesto *I'll Take My Stand* and a senior member of the Vanderbilt English
faculty. But it also reflected a more general respect for his work on Southern
literature, and his lecture at the symposium ("The Image of Man in Contemporary Southern Literature," delivered on May 1, 1958) was greeted with
widespread approval. Further evidence of his status in the field came three
months later when he was the youngest of seven alumni asked to participate
in the First Annual Alumni Seminar at the University of Kentucky, where
he chaired a discussion on "The American Political Tradition in American
Literature." Shortly thereafter, most likely in September 1958, he completed
work on "Visions of Order" and immediately submitted the manuscript to
the Regnery publishing house for review.

In December 1958 Weaver's autobiographical essay "Up from Liberalism"
was published in *Modern Age*. Ironically, it appeared in the same month that
Ideas Have Consequences went out of print.[45] Demand for the book remained
so great, however, that the editors of the University of Chicago Press re-
luctantly decided to reissue it in paperback under their Phoenix imprint.
Weaver was notified of their intentions in May 1959 and signed a contract
the following month. But by then whatever pleasure he might have taken
in the project was subsumed by a series of major reversals. The first of these
involved his composition text. That book had been written in the specific
expectation that it would provide him with a measure of financial independence. Yet it generated very few sales, and by June of 1959 he was forced to
concede that it had been "a dismal flop."[46] At about the same time, Regnery
returned "Visions of Order" with the suggestion that "additional work"
would be needed before the manuscript could be considered for publication.[47] Finally, at *Modern Age*, editorial disagreements and a steep decline

45. Although the book was technically out of print, the Press still had a small number of
slightly damaged copies in stock in June of 1959 and presumably until the paperback edition
was published.

46. Letter from Richard Weaver to Donald Davidson dated June 9, 1959. Located in Box
3, Richard M. Weaver Correspondence folder, Donald Davidson Papers (Addition) in the
Special Collections of the Jean and Alexander Heard Library at Vanderbilt University and
quoted by permission.

47. Letter from Henry Regnery to K. F. Beaton dated April 12, 1963. Located in file C33
of the Polly Weaver Beaton collection and quoted by permission. See also Weaver's description of the incident in his letter to Kenneth S. Templeton dated August 30, 1960, located in
file C32 of the same collection.

in subscription renewals resulted in Russell Kirk's resignation as editor in July 1959, and the demise of the journal seemed imminent.

Faced with the very real prospect that much of his work in the preceding five years had been wasted, Weaver responded once again with a kind of dogged determination. He spent the month of July 1959 touring the Rocky Mountains by car with his mother and brother. He then turned his attention to the plight of *Modern Age*. Although his only formal connection with the journal was an appointment as one of twenty-three "editorial advisors," apparently he played a major role in the complete (and ultimately very successful) reorganization of the enterprise in the fall of 1959. As a result, he was asked in November to serve as one of two (later three) associate editors and given the specific responsibility of editing the extensive book review section. His acceptance of the position not only committed him to a heavy and continuous burden of work but also led to an estrangement in his relations with Russell Kirk. But it had the merit of finally allowing him to try his hand at editing a journal, and there is every indication that he took great pleasure in discharging his duties. He also clearly enjoyed the conviviality of the frequent meetings of the editorial board which took place on Friday afternoons in the offices of *Modern Age* in downtown Chicago and were usually followed by dinner and drinks at a nearby restaurant.

The problems with "Visions of Order" were not so readily resolved, and Weaver spent a full year revising the text. In August 1960 he decided the manuscript "is now in about as final form as I can put it," and resumed his search for a publisher.[48] Although Henry Regnery had asked repeatedly that his firm be given another chance to review the work—and had virtually guaranteed its acceptance—the earlier rejection had convinced Weaver that he should look elsewhere. Inquiries were sent to a number of commercial and university presses, beginning with Farrar, Straus, and Cudahy and the University of Michigan, but all to no avail. At last, in January 1961, Donald Ellegood of the Louisiana State University Press responded with a warm invitation to submit the manuscript for review. Weaver decided immediately to accept the offer, but then spent more than two months soliciting comments from friends on problematic chapters and making a number of minor revisions. Not until April 4, 1961, was the manuscript finally dispatched to Baton Rouge.

48. Letter from Richard Weaver to Kenneth S. Templeton dated August 30, 1960. Located in file C32 of the Polly Weaver Beaton collection and quoted by permission.

Despite these private disappointments, the growth of Weaver's public reputation continued unabated throughout this period. In July 1959 the Intercollegiate Society of Individualists (ISI) released *Education and the Individual,* the first of four of his essays and speeches to be published in pamphlet form by that organization. Three months later an abridged version was reprinted in the *Wall Street Journal* under the title "The Purpose of Education" and promptly brought its author an Honor Certificate from the Freedoms Foundation at Valley Forge for "outstanding achievement in bringing about a better understanding of the American way of life during 1959."[49] The immediate result was to give Weaver a measure of national prominence as a critic of contemporary education. At about the same time, the University of Chicago Press released the paperback reprint of *Ideas Have Consequences,* and within six months of publication more than 3,000 copies were sold.[50] A final indication of his status was the increasing demand for his services as a speaker. Weaver had given occasional public lectures on a variety of topics since at least 1948. Beginning in the mid-1950s, these occasions became much more frequent. At first, most of the speeches were presented at conferences and programs organized by ISI and its campus affiliates and addressed topics concerning the nature and prospects of political conservatism. In 1960, however, he began to receive a steady stream of invitations to deliver more scholarly lectures at schools with which he had no prior affiliation. These led to presentations at Brigham Young University (May 1961), the University of Arkansas (November 1961), Whitworth College in Spokane, Washington (April 1962), and the University of Oklahoma (July 1962), all of which were eventually published. Significantly, the Arkansas and Oklahoma invitations asked him to speak on rhetorical theory and therefore mark the growing recognition of his work in that field.

With *Modern Age* secure and "Visions of Order" in the hands of an apparently sympathetic publisher, Weaver was able to devote much of the summer of 1961 to work on a new book. Conceived in 1957 and begun in the summer of 1960, this was intended to be his *magnum opus,* a monumental study of the profoundly opposed cultures of the American North and South

---

49. From the original Honor Certificate dated February 22, 1960. Located in file B7 of the Polly Weaver Beaton collection and quoted by permission.

50. It is not clear exactly when the reprint of *Ideas Have Consequences* was republished. Although it is dated 1959, several items of correspondence suggest that it was not actually released until February 1960.

as revealed through an analysis of the works of pairs of exemplary figures from the two regions. As such, it marked the confluence of two major streams of his work: his dissertation and subsequent essays on Southern history, culture, and literature, and the critique of modern (i.e., Northern) culture in *Ideas Have Consequences,* "Visions of Order," and many shorter works. In the end, however, he was able to complete only three chapters—"Two Diarists," "Two Orators," and "Two Types of American Individualism"—before other priorities forced him to set the work aside.

Within a week of returning from his lecture on "The Cultural Role of Rhetoric" at the University of Arkansas on November 8, 1961, Weaver received two letters that would strongly influence the course and tone of the remainder of his life. The first was from Kenney Withers, the editor in charge of English textbooks in the College Department at Holt, Rinehart and Winston, which had been formed through a merger with Henry Holt and Company twenty months before. Although "appalled" by the sales of *Composition,* he noted that the book "is rightfully admired by many—by everyone who knows anything about rhetoric" and suggested the possibility of producing a revised edition. Weaver agreed to the revision "if the outlook for success is fairly good and if it would not require *too* much labor" and began immediately to explore the project with Withers and Richard Beal, a professor at Boston University who was the publisher's principal consultant in composition.[51] The second letter was from Donald Ellegood of the LSU Press, who reported that "a couple of readings" of the "Visions of Order" manuscript "have been very favorable" and that "I am soliciting one more appraisal, after which your ms [sic] will be 'presented' to our Press Committee."[52] In conjunction with the proposal from Withers and the continuing growth of *Modern Age* under the capable leadership of its new editor, Eugene Davidson, the letter gave reason to hope that all of the reversals from the summer of 1959 might soon be recouped.

The spring of 1962 marked the final turning point in Weaver's all too brief career. It began with perhaps his greatest honor, an award from the Young Americans for Freedom (YAF) "for dedication to the preservation of the

51. Letters from Kenney Withers to Richard Weaver dated November 7, 1961, and from Richard Weaver to Kenney Withers dated November 13, 1961. Both are located in file C30 of the Polly Weaver Beaton collection and are quoted by permission.

52. Letter from Donald R. Ellegood to Richard M. Weaver dated November 13, 1961. Located in file C32 of the Polly Weaver Beaton collection and quoted by permission.

heritage of our Nation through consistent support of the principles of free-dom and individual human dignity." The presentation was made at a rally of 18,000 conservatives held in Madison Square Garden on March 7, 1962, which featured a keynote address by Senator Barry Goldwater and brief acceptance speeches by Weaver and other award recipients.[53] Six weeks later a formal agreement was reached concerning the production of a revised edition of *Composition*. As part of the arrangement, Weaver contracted with Richard Beal to assist him in the selection of readings for the book and accepted a deadline of June 1, 1963, for delivery of the final manuscript. But the most important event came in the middle of May, when a letter arrived from Randall Stewart in which he asked: "Would you be willing to come to Vanderbilt either for one year or permanently?" Although Stewart cau-tioned that his was "not an official letter," it was nevertheless clear that the position was within his control and had already been offered to John Crowe Ransom, who had just spent a semester at Vanderbilt but declined for per-sonal reasons to stay. Weaver's reaction is best indicated by the opening sentence of his reply: "Your letter came like something I have been dream-ing about for years." He then suggested a one-year appointment for 1963–64 to see "whether I have the kind of stuff that Vanderbilt can use," to which Stewart readily agreed.[54]

Although a formal offer did not come until December, Weaver began at once to organize his affairs in anticipation of the move to Nashville. His first and most pressing priority was the work on *Composition*. He had rec-ognized from the outset that "even with the most fortunate falling out of circumstances, it will be a hard push to complete the revision by next May."[55] Now it had become imperative to finish by the deadline so that he

53. The text is taken from the original award certificate located in file B7 of the Polly Weaver Beaton collection. For details of the rally see the (blatantly biased) articles by Peter Kihss, "18,000 Rightists Rally at Garden," *New York Times,* March 8, 1962, pp. 1 and 18, and Foster Hailey, "Liberals Decry All 'Extremists,'" *New York Times,* March 8, 1962, p. 20. Other award recipients included John Dos Passos, Charles Edison, M. Stanton Evans, Herbert Hoover, Roger Milliken, Marvin Liebman, Ludwig von Mises, Strom Thurmond, Moise Tshombe, and John Wayne.

54. Letters from Randall Stewart to Richard Weaver dated May 15, 1962, and from Richard Weaver to Randall Stewart dated May 19, 1962. Both are located in file C14 of the Polly Weaver Beaton collection and are quoted by permission.

55. Letter from Richard M. Weaver to Richard S. Beal dated April 9, 1962. Located in file C30 of the Polly Weaver Beaton collection and quoted by permission.

could have the summer to prepare for the new position at Vanderbilt. The difficulty was that he was already overburdened with a growing load of teaching and administrative duties at Chicago,[56] his editorial obligations at *Modern Age,* numerous writing and speaking commitments, and his continuing work with conservative organizations such as ISI (where he served as a trustee of the national organization, faculty adviser to the campus chapter, and an editorial adviser for the chapter's journal, the *New Individualist Review*) and the Volker Fund (where he was deeply involved in discussions about the future of the organization).

Through enormous effort and the simple expedient of refusing or postponing most new writing and speaking engagements, Weaver kept the revision on schedule through the end of January 1963. But then he contracted the flu, and much of February was lost to illness and worry. In addition to concerns about completing the revision, he had heard nothing from LSU Press for well over a year and was beginning to fear that "Visions of Order" had again been rejected. By the end of the month, however, he had regained a measure of his characteristic drive and optimism. On March 3 he wrote to his mother: "The first thing I thought of when I woke up this morning was that I am now 53 years old. The next thing I thought of is that I am feeling fine."[57] Despite the pressure of work, he spent spring break as usual with his family in Weaverville, returning to Chicago on March 25. Nine days later he was dead.

It was the opinion of his family that Weaver literally worked himself to death, and there is little reason to question their view. Conscientious to the point of perfectionism, he was able to accommodate the increasing demands on his time and talents only by driving himself harder, and it may well be that the textbook revision was simply one burden too many. To this perhaps should be added the continuous frustration of seeing his last three books perform so poorly. It was therefore the cruelest of fates that he should falter just when he did. Had he lived but a few weeks longer he would have learned that "Visions of Order," delayed by one negative review and a

56. Since 1958, Weaver had served most years as chairman of the College composition course and was scheduled to do so again in the 1962–63 academic year. He had also just been appointed (in April 1962, along with Milton Friedman, Friedrich Hayek, Leo Strauss, and seven others) to the new interdisciplinary Committee on a Free Society at Chicago.

57. Letter from Richard Weaver to Carrie Weaver, undated but posted on March 3, 1963. Located in file C23 of the Polly Weaver Beaton collection and quoted by permission.

change in editors, had at last been accepted for publication. Nor had his work on *Composition* been wasted. Although the full revised textbook—completed by Richard Beal and published in 1967 as *Rhetoric and Composition: A Course in Writing and Reading*—was only a modest success, two shorter paperbacks derived from the main work—*A Rhetoric and Handbook* (1967, reprinted as *A Rhetoric and Composition Handbook* by Morrow in 1974 and Quill in 1981) and *A Concise Handbook* (1968)—produced combined sales approaching 100,000 copies. But more important than these successes is the likely effect of the move to Vanderbilt. Freed there of much of the burden of teaching and administration he carried at Chicago, ensconced in the culture he loved, and enjoying the stimulation and support of colleagues who fully understood and appreciated his ideas, he might have produced works of which we can only imagine.

Although the loss occasioned by Richard Weaver's early death is irrecoverable, it is at least possible to preserve and disseminate the full body of writings he was given time to complete. It is altogether fitting that such a project should be sponsored by Liberty Fund, a private educational foundation established in 1960 to encourage study of the ideal of a society of free and responsible individuals. At the very center of Weaver's philosophy is the belief that the decline of the West has been the product not of inexorable forces beyond the scope of human control but of unwise and irresponsible choices freely made. In such a situation, the solution lies not in eliminating freedom but in restoring the ideals and circumstances required for its responsible use. As he noted in accepting the Young Americans for Freedom award in the year before his death:

> We are living at a time when the very idea of liberty, upon which our nation was founded, is threatened by open forces abroad and by insidious forces at home. There has never been a moment in our history when the sincere friends of liberty more needed to consult together and to publish to the world the real nature of that which most makes life worth living.

February 2000

IN DEFENSE OF TRADITION

SECTION ONE
Life and Family

This section brings together all of the writings that deal primarily with Richard Weaver's life and personal views, including his few public statements about his family and community. They are presented in three groups.

The first group consists of three presentations made at various meetings of the "Tribe of Jacob," the collective name of the descendants of Jacob Weaver, one of eleven children of John and Elizabeth Biffle Weaver, the first white settlers in the Weaverville area. "The Weaver Family of North Carolina: The Prospectus of a History" was written for distribution at the 100th reunion of the Tribe of Jacob on August 8, 1959, and reflects Weaver's research as a member of the family's History Committee. It was intended as the beginning of a much larger historical account, but the pressure of other commitments forced him to set that project aside. The "Address of Dr. Richard M. Weaver, Chicago University" is the text of a speech presented at the 1950 reunion. It is noteworthy not only for its defense of place, community, provincialism, and the South, but also for its harsh characterizations of Chicago, "a place where all the vices of urban and industrial society break forth in a kind of evil flower." Whether such sentiments reflected his true convictions at the time, an adaptation to his audience, or some combination of the two, it must be said that Weaver often expressed more favorable views of the city in his later years. "The Pattern of a Life" is the text of a eulogy of Ethan Douglas Weaver presented at the 1954 reunion and published "by popular demand" in the Asheville Citizen newspaper shortly thereafter. Weaver was pleased and flattered by its reception, but noted to his sister Polly the difficulty of *writing about an individual whose only "real claim to distinction was that he lived a very long time."*[1]

The second group comprises six short items written while Weaver was an undergraduate at the University of Kentucky. They are of interest mainly for what they reveal of his attitudes and interests at the time. His contribution to the symposium "A Panorama of Peace" from the December 1929 issue of The Intercollegian *(a magazine produced by and for the student YMCA/YWCA movement) is his earliest published work and reflects his growing commitment to socialism and pacifism. The remaining items were written with Clifford Amyx in the summer of 1931 for "Looking Over the Magazines," a regular feature of the* Kentucky Kernel, *the University of Kentucky student newspaper. Although in most cases it is no longer possible to determine who wrote which entries, Professor Amyx has stated that the ones on* I'll Take My Stand *and* Theodore Dreiser *were wholly Weaver's work.*[2]

The section concludes with a pair of autobiographical essays. The first of these, "Up from Liberalism," was published in the Winter 1958–59 issue of Modern Age *and is now one of Weaver's best known shorter works. It was written in the summer of 1953 at the request of Erik von Kuehnelt-Leddhin for use in a planned book of autobiographical essays by contemporary conservatives. That project fell through, but Russell Kirk "somehow fell heir to the ones that had been written" and used several in* Modern Age.[3] *The second essay, "William Maury Mitchell," is published here for the first time. Written in 1958 to mark the passing of his oldest and closest friend, it provides the only detailed account of Weaver's days at Lincoln Memorial Academy and a rare glimpse of his personal life in the 1950s.*

1. Letter from Richard M. Weaver to Polly Weaver Beaton dated September 2, 1954. Located in file C21 of the Polly Weaver Beaton collection and quoted by permission.

2. Clifford Amyx, "Weaver the Liberal: A Memoir," *Modern Age*, 31/2, Spring 1987, p. 104.

3. This account is based on Weaver's letter to Edmund Opitz dated March 18, 1959, which is now in the editor's possession and is quoted by permission of the Rev. Dr. Optiz.

The Weaver Family of North Carolina: The Prospectus of a History[1]

1. European Origins of the Family

The European origins of the Weaver family are lost in the mists of the past. One or two legends, handed down orally, tell all that the family knows of its history on the other side of the water. One of them relates, without any specific detail, that the original ancestor was "a Dutch gentleman." Another, which seems more likely on grounds of general probability, says that the Weavers were originally Swiss Germans. At some period in their history they inhabited that section of Europe known as "the Palatinate." This was a borderland region lying along the upper Rhine, which was much fought over during the Seventeenth and Eighteenth centuries. It was ravaged during the Thirty Years War, and it was twice invaded by Louis XIV while that monarch was ambitiously trying to expand his dominions, so that the inhabitants were reduced to a state of oppression and economic misery. Many thousands of these, seeing no relief from their troubles at home, began to turn their eyes toward America. The result was that during the latter part of the Seventeenth century and the early part of the Eighteenth, large numbers of Germans began to pour into Pennsylvania. The colonists already in America wanted more settlers for obvious reasons, and German immigrants were looked upon as especially desirable. Not only were they hardworking,

1. The opening sections of a projected larger work, distributed at the 100th reunion of the "Tribe of Jacob" on August 8, 1959. Portions of the text were included without attribution in a privately published history of the descendants of Jacob Weaver: Pearl M. Weaver, *The Tribe of Jacob,* Asheville: Miller Printing, 1962. Edited by Ted J. Smith III from a copy of a mimeographed typescript acquired from Weaver's sister, Polly Weaver Beaton, and currently in the possession of the editor.

sober and thrifty, but they also brought with them much needed skills, such as ironworking, weaving and cabinet work. So great was the influx that a single volume, Israel Daniel Rupp's *A Collection of Upwards of Thirty Thousand Names of German, Swiss, Dutch, French and Other Immigrants in Pennsylvania,* lists more than thirty thousand Germans and other settlers in Pennsylvania who landed at Philadelphia between the years 1727–1776.

It is very likely that the original Weaver (whose name was then spelled "Weber") came with this extensive migration, though we do not know exactly when he first set foot on American soil. The best conjecture is that sometime in the first half of the Eighteenth century, though possibly earlier, a Jacob or Johann Weber, somewhat the worse for fortune and a hard ocean crossing, came ashore to begin a new life in the New World.

2. Settlement in Pennsylvania

Nor do we, unfortunately, know anything about the career of the Weavers in Pennsylvania. It may be assumed that when the movement for independence swept the colonies in the 1770s, the Pennsylvania Weavers were among the patriots. Two entries in the *Historical Register of Officers of the Continental Army During the War of the Revolution* give the first clues toward definite identification for this period. There we find reference to a Jacob Weaver.

> Weaver, Jacob (Pennsylvania)
> Ensign, 3rd Penna. Battalion, 22 April 1776; taken prisoner at Ft. Washington, 16 November 1776; exchanged 12 December 1780; retained as captain of independent company, to rank from 13 January 1777; company annexed to 10th Penna., 7 November 1777; retired 17 January 1781. (d. 1812)

There we find also the brief listing of a John Weaver.

> Weaver, John (Pennsylvania)
> Surgeon's mate, invalid regiment, 9 October 1780 to 31 October 1781.

It is certainly within the realm of possibility that this John Weaver was the son of Jacob Weaver. The nature and length of his service suggests that he was then a young man, perhaps in his late teens. The war with Britain was over in 1781. Armies were disbanding and the ex-soldiers were looking about, thinking of new lands, and Pennsylvania was the seedfield of American migration.

3. Migration to North Carolina

We cannot say for certain, but this may have been the very John Weaver who, within the next few years, married Elizabeth Biffle, and in 1787 entered, with his wife and infant son, the beautiful French Broad Valley of Western North Carolina.

The route by which they came to this mountain paradise is known. According to research done by Dr. Bascombe Weaver, four Weaver brothers started westward from Pennsylvania. They went down the Green Briar River of what is now West Virginia to its confluence with the North New River. Here the three other brothers decided to continue north to the Ohio. But John went south up the North New River to its headwaters in the hills, picked up the trail down the Watauga River and followed this down to the Sevier settlement of "Happy Valley," near where the present town of Elizabethton, Tennessee, stands. From there he turned eastward into North Carolina.

The time of John's coming across the old Indian trail was early spring. Late in the afternoon on one of the high mountains a sudden snow storm came up, causing them to lose their way. John began scouting for a place of shelter and for wood to build a fire. In the course of his efforts he routed out a wild mother pig and her little ones and tucked his freezing wife and baby into their warm bed.

Having survived this and other rigors of the journey, John Weaver not long thereafter looked upon the scene which was to become his future homestead. Whatever else this ex-soldier and trailblazer of the wilderness may have had, he must have possessed an eye for scenic beauty. For the spot he chose lay in a spacious valley about four miles eastward from where Reems Creek empties into the French Broad River. Then the chief features of the landscape were unnamed; but today a visitor standing on the southern edge of Weaverville can see the Elk Mountain range to the south, Chestnut Knob with its foothills to the north, and to the east the great

Craggy Range, where less than thirty miles away the Appalachian Mountain system reaches its highest peak in Mt. Mitchell. It is a fertile and well-watered valley, where every prospect pleases, and we cannot wonder that this seeker of a new home was satisfied to end his search here.

4. John Weaver and His Family

Not much is known of the early days of John and Elizabeth Biffle Weaver in North Carolina. But that they were there we have indubitable proof in the first official (1790) United States Census. Asheville did not then exist as a town, and what is now Buncombe County was then a part of Burke. In the listings for Burke County we find:

Jno. Weaver   Free white males of 16 and upwards, including heads of families:

I

Free white males under 16:

I

Free white females, including heads of families:

3

Slaves:

I

Indians were all around, but tradition says that the Weavers had little friction with these original Americans. One day while her baby Jacob was sleeping and John was at work in the field, Elizabeth went to their nearest neighbor to borrow a churn. When she returned, she found the bed empty. Going to see whether the father was playing a joke, she soon spied an Indian lurking in the edge of the wood. The Indian waved toward her new homespun petticoat which had recently been dyed a rich red and left in the sun to dry. He signified his willingness to accept the red cloth as ransom, and the exchange was made. But a few days later, about dusk, Elizabeth heard a noise by the door and saw the Indian scampering off into the woods. He had left a well-dressed deer on a stone by the cabin.

Here John Weaver led a fairly typical settler's existence until his death in 1830. He grew corn and raised hogs; he was a member of surveying parties; and he served on juries with his near neighbor David Vance, the grandfather of North Carolina's most celebrated governor, Zebulon Vance. He helped to organize the community's first church. His family was blessed with eleven children. They were, in the order of their birth: Jacob, Susannah, the first white girl born west of the Blue Ridge, Christiana, Mary, Elizabeth, Matilda, Catherine, James, John, Christopher and Michael Montraville. Jacob, the eldest, was born September 13, 1786; The youngest, Michael Montraville, for whom Weaverville was named, was born on August 10, 1808.

When his time came to pass on, John Weaver held title to 672 acres of land in and near Reems Creek Valley, together with various other possessions, which he carefully disposed of in the following will.[2]

WILL OF JOHN WEAVER

In the name of God, Amen, I, John Weaver, of the County of Buncombe, and State of North Carolina, being of sound and disposing mind and memory, praised be God, do this 10th day of May, in the year of our Lord, One Thousand Eight Hundred and Thirty, 1830, make and publish this my last Will and Testament, in the manner following: that is to say,

First I give and bequeath my Soul to Almighty God, who gave it first.

Secondly, my body to the earth, to be decently buried at the direction of my executors.

Thirdly, my will and pleasure is, that should I decease first, that my property personal and real, be kept together as it is now, under the care and control of my son, Montraville Weaver, for the comfortable maintenance of my wife, Elizabeth, during her life. At her decease—

Fourthly, I give and bequeath unto my son, Montraville Weaver, the tract or parcel of land whereon I now live, containing six hundred and seventy two (672) acres, be the same more or less, with all the buildings, ways, woods, and waters thereunto belonging, or in any wise appertaining, to him and his heirs forever.

Fifthly, I give and bequeath to my six daughters, Susannah, Christiana, Mary, Elizabeth, Matilda, and Catherine, all my household furniture, to be equally divided at their mother's discretion.

2. The will was fully proved in open court by oath of all the attested Witnesses, and ordered to be registered. It is on file in the Buncombe County Courthouse.

Sixthly,   I give and bequeath the balance of my personal property, consisting in negroes, stock and farming utensils, still and such like, to
my sons and daughters, Jacob, James, John, and Christopher G.
Weaver, Susannah McCarson, Christiana Vance, Mary Adding-
ton, Catherine Pickens, Elizabeth Wells, and Matilda Garrison,
to be equally divided at the death of their Mother, and this to the
entire exclusion of Montraville Weaver, considering his landed estate to be his equal share, and I hereby make and ordain my two
sons, Jacob and James Weaver, executors of this my last Will and
Testament.

In witness whereof, I, the said John Weaver, have to this my last Will and
Testament, set my hand and seal, this the day and year above mentioned,
signed, sealed, published, and declared by the said John Weaver the testator,
as his last Will and Testament, in the presence of us, who are present at the
time of the signing and sealing thereof.

John (X) Weaver
(his mark)

Attest:
J. M. Alexander
John Chambers
G. McDaniel

Address of Dr. Richard M. Weaver, Chicago University[1]

Everybody admits, I believe, that the most difficult people of all for a man to convince are the members of his own family. And since I am here before a very complete gathering of my family, I look upon my case as a trifle hard, and shan't be surprised if I don't convince anyone of anything.

In thinking over subjects on which I might be qualified to speak, it occurred to me to look at Weaverville and the Weaver community through a perspective of Chicago. I have been condemned for the past six years to earn my living in that most brutal of cities, a place where all the vices of urban and industrial society break forth in a kind of evil flower. I sometimes think of the University to which I am attached as a missionary outpost in darkest Chicago. There we labor as we can to convert the heathen, without much reward of success. But of course we learn many things about what is happening to this country.

Anyone who removes to such a place from an old-fashioned society like ours, with its roots in the past and with its well-understood relationships, becomes conscious first of all of the absence of community. He is made aware that people existing together in one geographical spot do not necessarily comprise a community. There in Chicago we have a politically defined area, we have local laws and institutions, but that which makes true community, namely association on some non-material level and common attachment to some non-material ends, is lacking. One encounters the curious fact that the more closely people are crowded together, the less they know about one another, and the less they care about one another. And I think the man transplanted to such a place can sum up his perception of the people around him under two heads.

1. In Pearl M. Weaver, *The Tribe of Jacob*. Asheville: Miller Printing Company, 1962, 113–16.

(1) *Theirs is a condition in which nobody knows who he is.* Oh, of course one knows that he bears a name, which he got from his parents, but he does not know what went into the making of it. It does not stand for any particular thing. A name there is an index rather than a characterization. Names are spelled out rather than weighed. I am not here speaking of names that rest on empty genealogical pretense—the silliness of a coat of arms. Names can gather weight in even the humblest communities; they can become names for industry, for loyalty, for kinds of expertness, or for simple truthfulness. But in the overgrown and falsely glamorized city of which I speak, all the forces are against the establishment of names in this way. Instead, the very conditions of existence combine to make one anonymous. It has been said that the masses of a great city are people without faces. But they do have faces, and often you can see the marks of frustration on them. It would be more revealing to say that they are people without names. They come to be like mass-produced parts, polished, machined, and what is worst of all to say—interchangeable.

(2) *Nobody knows where he is from.* Oh, in a sort of objective way he knows that he had a birthplace and that he went to a certain school. But as for the more important feeling of being formed and sustained by a traditional background—this he does not have. Sometimes he tries to make this a point of pride, because the big city is on the whole the professed enemy of the local and the provincial. Usually the feud between city slicker and country fellow is presented on the level of comedy. It would be more appropriate to present it on the level of tragedy, because it conceals a deep opposition of philosophies of life. What the big city fails to see, or willfully ignores, is that provincialism is one of the chief supports of character. To be of a place, to reflect it in your speech and action and general bearing, to offer it as a kind of warranty that you will remain true to yourself—this is what it means to have character and personality. And without these things there is no individuality.

It is often observed by students of art that all the great arts of the world have been provincial. There is no such thing as an international art. It is highly doubtful that there can be such a thing as a national art. It is the province which gives to an art its particular vision of the world, or imparts to its interpretation a meaningful character. Therefore, the slickness, the anonymity, the impersonality of the great cities, which are so much sought after today, especially it would seem by the young people, are a fool's gold. These are reasons for saying that it is a good thing to have roots in a province or a locality and to express something of it in one's being. It is good to have a local habitation and a name.

I would not ascribe the fault entirely to the inhabitants of metropolis. Many of them are victims, who have never had a chance to understand what it means to be a member of a community. Often they exhibit hunger for the sort of thing community can give and make pathetic gestures in its direction. But there is no denying the tendency toward atomization of our society as long as the purely urban ideal is allowed to dominate. That is a fact which keeps the sociologists worried and keeps the philosophers pessimistic.

Now, for the first time in generations, the future of the great cities is somber. There are responsible thinkers who fear that either they are going to blow themselves up or be blown up. And I must say that I sometimes get the feeling that the big city is itself an explosive. It is only waiting the right combination to set it off. Like explosives, their leading characteristic is a high degree of instability. And that is why we hear of their more lucky citizens fleeing to cabins in the Ozarks, to New England farms, and to quiet places in our own South.

The South, as we all well know, has been made up from the beginning of what I am describing as communities. Our pattern has been that of the local neighborhood, the village or perhaps county, in which men have relationships other than that of cash exchange. For this we have been subjected to a lot of ignorant ridicule. We are the country cousins of the American family. We are behind the times; we are not sufficiently sold on progress; we are even suspected of disloyalty to the American way—as that way is pictured by advertisers and exploiters. Our capacity to resist the things that emanate from New York and Chicago has been enormous. Sometimes I think the South is best described by paraphrasing a witty French phrase: "The more it changes, the more it remains the same."

Many years ago a few men were found to prophesy that the South was destined to be the great fly wheel of American society. In the science of machinery, this is defined as a heavy wheel, rotating at a uniform speed, whose function it is to stabilize the motion of the whole machine. If the machine speeds up too much, the fly wheel holds it back; if it slows down too much, the fly wheel speeds it up. The South, with its massive weight of tradition, with its pace regularized by a steady contact with nature, seems to perform that essential function. Our role has been, and I think will continue to be, that of the indispensable conservative counterpoise. We have nothing of the hysteria of the great cities. We have long memories, and it is against our instinct to build for a day. Of course this is vexing to a lot of people. There is a school of opinion in this country which considers the South a problem child. But this problem child may yet prove to be the savior of the household.

This, from such vantage point as Chicago gives, is where I see our place in the American scene. We are provincials. We have our name on the land. These are great assets. But in the midst of self-congratulation it is well to recall responsibility too; it seems to me there are two vices which we cannot in the least afford. We cannot afford presumption and we cannot afford complacency. After all, the battle we are in—I mean in general the battle against the dehumanization of life—has been a losing one for more than a hundred years. Thus far we see only signs of change. But as society begins to look back, to ascertain the real sources of its strength, it is not presumptuous to say that we shall have to be recognized.

The Pattern of a Life[1]

On March 9 of this year there passed away Ethan Douglas Weaver, the oldest member of this family and its chairman for the last twenty-two years.

We were all touched by a sense of personal loss, from our long knowledge of him, from our appreciation of his character, and from our pride in him as a symbol of the family's unity and durability. But in addition to this, I think that most of us were made to realize that one of our links with the past had been removed.

When Uncle Doug's life came to an end, he had reached the age of ninety-seven years, and eleven months, the greatest age ever attained by a member of this family as far as our records go. It might be good for us to think for a little while about how far into the past that life extended. You will recall that it is only a year since we listened to a message from him penned in his own hand. It is only two years since he stood before us, at that meeting held at George Ward's, and made an inspiring address. But Uncle Doug came into this world in the last year of the presidency of Franklin Pierce. Our calamitous Civil War was still several years in the future. Politically the air was resounding with talk about the slavery issue, about the Know Nothings, and about the newly formed Republican Party. Kansas and Oregon had not yet been admitted to the Union. It would be another two years before an obscure lawyer in Illinois named Lincoln would run unsuccessfully for the U.S. Senate against Stephen A. Douglas. It would be another three years before the John Brown raid at Harper's Ferry.

The two sides of this continent were not even linked by the Pony Express, that coming in 1860, and it would be another thirteen years before a railroad crossed the continent. The telegraph was a novelty only twelve years old, and Uncle Doug would be a young man of twenty-three when Edison invented the electric light.

1. *Asheville Citizen-Times,* August 22, 1954, B4.

Washington Irving was still alive; Darwin had not yet published his *Origin of Species* and Karl Marx would not publish his *Capital* for another eleven years. Nobody had ever heard of, and perhaps nobody had even thought of a world war.

I cite these facts in order to remind us of what a span of time this life embraced. But here, on this memorial occasion, we are chiefly concerned to ask, what is the meaning of this great longevity? What kind of thought and feeling does it fill us with?

I cannot help feeling that a life of this length reflects great mental and spiritual health. Today, when so many people are killing themselves with worry and with emotional indulgence, we often have occasions to remark that the health of the mind is the health of the body, and that the most certain hygiene is a positive outlook on the world and honest work in the service of ideals. And when we turn to survey the life we are now commemorating, we find that it was eminent for just these things.

We see Uncle Doug as a boy, growing up in these beautiful mountains, learning, on the one hand, what nature had to teach, and on the other, imbibing from his parents the "faith of his fathers" which has been so strong a binding element with this family. We see him looking with admiring eyes upon his uncle, Captain, later Colonel James Thomas Weaver, home on furlough in his gray uniform with its gold facings. We see him approaching manhood and realizing that he must make his own way in this world, it being perhaps the good fortune of the Weavers that none of them have ever been children of fortune. Times are hard on them and opportunities look few. With a young man's natural desire to see new things, he travels over into East Tennessee. By good luck, I can give you this part of his life in his own words. "Once upon a time there was a boy raised in Western North Carolina, who, when grown to manhood, found times hard and money scarce. So he wandered over into East Tennessee and became acquainted with a fine country girl. The inevitable happened—they were married. Neither one was rich, neither one was poor, but endowed with a fine fund of practical common sense. So they began immediately planning to build them a home as soon as possible." Thus he wrote of himself many years later.

This union was blessed with children to the number of ten, and at length the little home in which they had settled down began to be crowded. By hard work and economy Uncle Doug saved enough to buy a larger farm, and there, in 1895, he built the home on Monticello Road in which he lived for almost six decades. Character and good judgment always assert themselves and before long he had become farm agent for Buncombe County, by some reports the first county agent west of the Blue Ridge, and by all reports the best agent that Buncombe County ever had. In 1918, during the First World War, we are told that eleven of his proteges grew more than 100 bushels of corn to the acre, setting some kind of record for this section; and there are many who will attest to the excellent product of his vineyard.

In the whole course and tenor of his life, Uncle Doug suggests strongly the ideal citizen as he was contemplated, near the founding of this republic, by Thomas Jefferson. He was an agrarian, living on the soil; a primary producer creating things, not trafficking in the things that other men made. He did not believe in being beholden. In that spirit of independence which we associate with the builders of this country, he believed that the individual should support the state and not the state the individual. Again like a good Jeffersonian, he viewed politics with the watchful eye of the self-sustaining citizen; and many of us will recall the pithy and shrewd letters which he wrote to the local paper after he was well in his tenth decade. His mind never lost its clarity, and I can testify from personal experience that one had to be very sure of his ground before venturing into political argument with him. There was much in this life to inspire those who cherish the early American ideals and much to rebuke those who have succumbed to easy ways and short-cut solutions.

There was also much in this life to vindicate the agrarian type of society, with its wholesomeness, its rhythms in unison with nature, and its rooted strength. What an extraordinary thing it is in this age, and what a fine thing in any age for a man to sit on his own porch and watch the shade trees he planted with his own hands grow for sixty years! This it was Uncle Doug's privilege to do, and we feel right in saying that it was an earned privilege. In a world where so much is superficial, aimless, and even hysterical, he kept a grasp upon those values which are neither old-fashioned nor new-fashioned, but are central, permanent, and certain in their reward. That is why we think of him as an outstanding example of the sturdy yeomanry which, though modest and self-effacing, has contributed so much to the fiber of this state.

Uncle Doug has gone from us now, but one of our chief purposes in setting aside this day in the year is to remind ourselves, by acts of commemoration, that the deceased are not non-existent. Apart from specific religious teachings on this subject, I think the members of this family would agree with Edmund Burke that society is a mysterious incorporation, which includes the past, the present, and the future generations in one whole. Recollections of the example of those who have departed this life influence our daily action just as certainly as do our present concerns and our speculations about the future. Only a fool tells himself that the past is dead. Therefore I take this opportunity to say that this practice of annually recalling, in a family meeting, those who can no longer be present, is neither sentimentality nor luxury. It is part of that habit of seeing life steadily and seeing it whole, of keeping fresh the memory of things, without which civil society does not exist.

The words that we speak here about the departed are tribute in return for what they have given. We are sorry to have to say that in the physical sense Uncle Doug is no longer one of us. But we keep our bond, and we show the right feeling of Veneration, if we say that we think about him earnestly.

Kentucky[1]
in "A Panorama of Peace: A Symposium"

With so many garish and superficial things on the campus and off of it to preempt the average student's attention, there is usually little of it left when a matter as relatively remote as the problem of world peace happens around. This is doubly unfortunate in these days when things of rare significance are being accomplished almost daily in the field of pacific relations between national groups. Apparently the world is just now crawling out of the slough of a post-war reaction, repeating thereby its essentially identical feat of a century ago. A Labor Government is in office in England and a Socialist one is in process of being formed in France. The position alone of these groups, so avowedly opposed to war, is bound to have a powerful bearing on the progress of the cause of peace. The splendid gesture furnished by Premier MacDonald's visit to American shores, too, has left the jingo journals sorely pressed to keep their fires of hatred glowing. It is rather unlikely that the majority of American students have kept abreast of these swift changes.

Such revolts against compulsory drill as we have witnessed lately have been of a sporadic and generally fruitless nature. Few of these uprisings have been inspired by a holy idealism or even by a conscientious objection to the performance of the duties required in soldiering in war-time. Too often they are a direct result of the drafted cadet's resentment toward a hot and unbecoming uniform or of the remarks of the sergeant on the appearance of the cadet's shoes or the angle of his gun—or because a small minority, supplied with niftier uniforms and shiny sabers, cornered the glory on parade day! Even the introduction of frills in the form of sponsors and prize competitions has not removed these sources of periodic rebellion. A student

1. *The Intercollegian*, 47/3, December 1929, 72.

anti-war movement arising out of a knowledge of present conditions and speculation on dreadful possibilities—rather than out of trivial discontent—would doubtless be better organized than those we are familiar with and possibly be longer sustained.

But as for the outlawry of war as an international issue, there appears to be little change in the average student's indifference to anything far enough away to be international. The unhealthy notion that the nation's business is none of the individual's business is widespread through the land, and college students are among the most frequent holders of it. The problem is how to break up the general lassitude in this particular quarter. Again, mere opinion is not all. Following it must come conviction and determination, for in the pandemonium preceding the outbreak of every war, many fine words and high resolves are likely to be forgotten. Student thought on world peace seems to be all right intrinsically; the crying need is for more of it.

Looking Over the Magazines[1]

[July 24, 1931]

CLIFFORD AMYX AND RICHARD WEAVER

Those of us who have been lamenting the fact that respectability is almost respectable again may take heart from an article which Bertrand Russell has in the July number of *Harper's*. The disrepute into which middle-class conventionality has fallen has been blamed, like numberless other things, on the World War. In "Nice People" Mr. Russell points out other influences which are working to undermine it and which may accomplish its final demise. For years now "nice people" have been revelling in the sadistic pleasures of prosecution, making propriety into a kind of bed of Procrustes whereon the moron was stretched and the genius suffered the loss of head or feet. Even now, he says, "they have sufficient influence to ensure that young men who write for the newspapers shall express the opinions of nice old ladies rather than their own," but, he adds thoughtfully, "to be a nice person it is necessary to be protected from crude contact with reality." Now two champions are appearing on the scene who bid fair to put an end to Victorian hypocrisy for good and all. They are (1) a belief that there is no harm in being happy and (2) a dislike of humbug. This article, like all of Mr. Russell's writings, is distinguished for acumen and candor.

* * *

Students of political science especially should be interested in an article which Dr. Amry Vandenbosch, of our own political science department, has in the April number of *Pacific Affairs*. Under the general title "Colonial Labor Problems" Dr. Vandenbosch discusses the indentured labor situation

---

1. *The Kentucky Kernel,* July 24, 1931, 3.

in the Dutch East Indies. His study convinced him that the penal labor contract, horrid as it may sound to us who are accustomed to having the praises of free labor dinned into our ears, is not entirely a thing of the devil. If the laborer is not at liberty to terminate his period of toil whenever he feels like it, neither is the company free to kick him out in the streets to shift for himself whenever business gets bad. However it appears that recruiting and management give rise to many abuses, and the Netherlands India government is working resolutely to abolish the system.

*　*　*

The reader of periodical literature is met with such a vast amount of ill-founded speculation about the duration of the present business depression that it is refreshing to encounter something in the nature of a careful comparative study of the subject. Wilford J. Eiteman, writing in the *New Republic* on "Two Decades of Depression," points out similarities between our economic condition today and that which began with the stock panic of '73. Then too there had been a tremendous expansion of industry and much wild talk about "a new era." Mr. Eiteman's conclusions will not bring much comfort to the prosperity boys. He finds that in spite of the confident pronunciamentoes of politicians and the whooping of the press, it took prices four long years to reach the bottom. We are reminded with a shiver that only one and three-quarters have elapsed since the debacle of '29.

*　*　*

Mr. G. K. Chesterton busied himself on his recent teaching expedition into this country by writing a series of articles for the *New York Times Magazine*. The last of this series appears in the issue of July 12. Mr. Chesterton, journalist above all, is at considerable pains to defend some of his previous statements concerning our well known Main Street, which has been at the mercy of our "heathens" for some time. Such peculiarly American phenomena as a God-advertising electric sign and an "unnatural individualism" are designated with an unerring finger, but are finally submerged under blanket paradoxes.

The recent issue of *The Hibbert Journal* carries an article on Chesterton's philosophy. It is a valiant attempt to wrest something coherent enough to be called a philosophy out of the great mass of material written by one of the most productive of modern writers.

* * *

That "contrary critic," George Jean Nathan, writing for the July issue of the *Forum*, takes pen in hand to charge the modern windmill, the Talkie. Nathan, long a critic of the drama, finds that the movies are beginning to make unnecessary demands on the imagination of the audience: enumerates seven as the minimum. With some of the movie producers crying pathetically to find what the dear public wants in the theatre, it would at least seem that Nathan has chosen an opportune time to cry up the return of his first love, the legitimate drama.

* * *

For quite a while now critics of higher education have had things their own way: broadside after broadside has been fired against students, teachers and administration without eliciting so much as an answering shot. Howard Mumford Jones in an article "The Forgotten Professor," appearing in the summer number of the *Yale Review*, makes out a very good defense for the university teacher. First of all, he says, it is worthy of note that a great deal of the criticism of our colleges and universities has come from professors themselves. What other group would afford such a dazzling display of disinterest? Moreover the professor is an expert in some field and the expert must command respect in any highly organized society. Mr. Jones attributes our confusion largely to sentimentalization about the young. The professor, as a general rule, is required to bend too much to the student. To quote directly: "the spectacle of men 40 and 50 years old trying to adjust themselves to the adolescent yearnings of 18 must, in all conscience, be a curious one." It is noticeable that the author does not attempt to defend the professor against the most damning of all the charges leveled at him, namely that of timidity and intellectual quietism. Probably it has cost him more prestige than all the others together.

Looking Over the Magazines [1]

[July 31, 1931]

CLIFFORD AMYX AND RICHARD WEAVER

Modern painting is the subject of an article appearing in the *Virginia Quarterly Review* for July; the title is "Picasso and Others." Through a rather tortured course, from which the reader will find many deviations, Picasso is presented as the leader of modern art. No analysis of the artist's work is attempted, the reason being that Picasso is subject to change as often as a weather-vane. Nevertheless, Picasso, urchin of the cafes of Madrid, inconstant disciple of Goya, El Greco, Puvis de Chavannes, important in cubism, is presented as the most significant figure in modern painting. In him we find the combination of technical skill and "constant definition of states of mind." In contrast the general group is portrayed as "playing the hurdy-gurdy of technique." Through two very directly conflicting statements we are left in doubt as to the real role of the "subject" in present day art. In the opinion of the author, Samuel M. Kootz, "significant form" has proved a tartar. Those interested in Picasso especially will find a short and intimate sketch of his life and works in *Living Age* for January 15, 1930.

* * *

The New Republic for July 22 carries an excellent editorial on the supposed decease of Greenwich Village. The fact that the one-time citadel of Bohemian America is no longer what it used to be is hailed in some corners as a great victory for righteousness. The august *Saturday Evening Post* has officially recognized its passing and that sniveling penitent, Floyd Dell, has spewed a tearful page or two over its sins. The writer in *The New Republic*

---

1. *The Kentucky Kernel*, July 31, 1931, 2.

draws an entirely different lesson from the story. The truth seems to be that Greenwich Village was a victim of its own popularity. The advertising it got started such a rush in its direction that rents bounded upward and the less prosperous of the villagers were forced to find cheaper locations. Most important of all, the reforms for which Greenwich Village strove have gained such general acceptance that it can very well be regarded as having fulfilled its mission. Bobbed hair and cigarettes for women, the gin cocktail party—all of the things with which the Village once scandalized the country have now penetrated even to the fastnesses of Middletown and Gopher Prairie and have spread over the Puritanical steppes of Kansas. Indeed the life of the Village was not lived in vain; we may yet see a monument raised to its cherished memory.

* * *

The Nation is running a series of ten articles on the Hoover Administration. Contributors to the group include Amos Pinchot, John B. Whitton, Paul Y. Anderson, Senator Robert La Follette and others of equal note. The present article is by Charles A. Beard who writes of the President's appointments. He emphasizes the fact that the shackles of party allegiance lie heavily on every chief executive. Too often their position is one of "servitude mocked by the pomp of power." Mr. Beard lauds Secretary Stimson as probably the best fitted member of the Republican Party for the post he holds.

* * *

The *Virginia Quarterly Review* also contains an article on George Gissing by Morley Roberts. The author's main interest is to impress us with the fact that Gissing was not the melancholy creature "remote from Rabelais" he is taken to be by the desultory reader of his works. Gissing was a hedonist, a man who had great interest in a flask of Chianti, Italian cookery, or reading *Don Quixote* in Spanish. These impressions of Gissing are based upon a personal acquaintance and a long period of correspondence; however, we are not led to believe that his smile did not have a trace of melancholy. Those men who are hedonists are also sensitive to other flows of life forces outside their own, and also sensitive to the pain of Grub Street.

* * *

H. L. Mencken yields once to unstinted praise. In his review of *Men of Art* in the July issue of the *American Mercury,* he is all praise for the most popular of the recent works on art. Of the author, Thomas Craven: "His book is the best of its kind so far done in English," and there have been many volumes published on Western art. Those who have read *Men of Art* will recall that the treatment of Velasquez was one of the impressive features of the book. The entire school of Spanish realism before El Greco is subject to a severe criticism. More than one critic has it that Craven displays for art the same talent that Will Durant has for the wholesaling of philosophy. Mencken has nothing but admiration for Craven for introducing painting as a fashionable subject for conversation after dinner; a subject in which Americans do not interest themselves readily. What magazine publishes photographs of significant paintings hung each year in the National Academy, as the *London Illustrated News* does for the Royal Academy? Small wonder that Mr. Mencken feels that Craven's book is deserving of approbation.

*   *   *

The May issue of the quarterly, *American Literature,* features an article on Swinburne and Whitman by W. B. Cairns of the University of Wisconsin. The article traces the course of Swinburne's vacillations in his opinions of Whitman from unqualified praise in his book on Blake, to a somewhat dampened ardor in later years. The author regards the change in attitude as due to the failure of Whitman to maintain the standard which first aroused Swinburne when he read *Leaves of Grass.* Vehement Swinburnisms are quoted, both favorable and unfavorable.

The same issue contains "The Anatomy of Melville's Fame," a short enquiry into the recent Melville boom. The documentation seems to be adequate enough to insure students of Melville plenty of source material.

Looking Over the Magazines[1]

[August 7, 1931]

CLIFFORD AMYX AND RICHARD WEAVER

The unenviable reputation for intellectual barrenness which the South has won for itself since the Civil War was disturbed last year when a small group centering about Nashville, Tennessee, published *I'll Take My Stand*. In essence the book was a defense of the agrarian form of industry and the kind of society it supported. Now Edmund Wilson, who certainly stands in the front rank of American critics today, has gone down to inspect for himself the source of this striking if ineffectual rally against the onward sweep of industrialism. He records his impressions in "Tennessee Agrarians," an article appearing in *The New Republic* for July 29. As sometimes happens in the case of Northerners of the reformist turn of mind, Mr. Wilson's hostility to the yet distinctly feudal nature of Southern society was somewhat softened by actual contact with it. He frankly admits that the wage-slavery system of the North offers few improvements over the former bond-slavery system of the South. He finds that agrarian life leaves people an opportunity to remain human beings which is more than can be said of the stern regimentation imposed upon the worker hordes of our great cities. He concludes his article with a rather wistful echo of the closing sentence of *Candide*.

* * *

"Old Fitz," otherwise Edward FitzGerald, is the subject of an article by Horace G. Hutchinson in the *Quarterly Review* for May. Carlyle speaks of FitzGerald as the "peaceable, affectionate, and ultra-modest man; and in

1. *The Kentucky Kernel*, August 7, 1931, 3.

innocent *far niente* life." Although he is remembered as the translator of the *Rubaiyat,* FitzGerald was an extremely productive writer and translator. His first interest was in the translation of the works of Calderon, the Spanish dramatist; later, he was engaged with the Greek dramatists. His translations were never cramped by being literal; it was his practice to omit or insert at will. Although he never was in need of money he is represented as eternally at work. He conducted a voluminous correspondence with his contemporaries; letters which ran on and on, concerned with the most trivial incidents, the weather, his garden, parties, picnics, and such. In spite of the author's attempt to show us FitzGerald as a tireless worker, we are left with the impression that "Old Fitz" turned every task into a joyous game. This "ceaseless worker" found time to render interest in opinions on his contemporaries, and become more than a dabbler in the arts.

* * *

S. Parkes Cadman usually confines himself to the verbose and airy generalities in his syndicated daily column, but in the *Forum* for August he launches his power of invective at full speed. In the article "Strafing the Church," Dr. Cadman replies to R. G. M. Neville, who wrote "Prima Donnas of the Pulpit" in the June issue of the *Forum.* Mr. Neville's article is devoted to unearthing various obnoxious practices of publicity-seeking ministers; Cadman replies in a similar tone concerning the methods of those interested in "strafing the church." Phrases such as "buttoned-up precisians and petty-fogging creedalists," "the apostolic itch for publicity," "our voluble intellectuals" are used as counters in catch as catch-can ballyhoo.

* * *

The New Republic for June 29 carries also an excerpt from Kenneth Burke's new work on esthetics, soon to be published in book form under the title, *Counter-Statement.* Mr. Burke attempts to reduce the time-honored classical-romanticist feud to broader terms by distinguishing between the absolutist and relativistic methods in art. He finds that the relativistic, historical attitude in criticism preponderates today. The old notion that romanticism finally runs into an unbridled monism he believes false: the romanticist is always confronted with a dualism, compounded of himself, or the individual in rebellion, and society. He is inclined to think the ro-

manticist has a better grasp of historical situations, his representation tending to be more typical than the so-called "normal" ones of the classicist.
Some years ago Mr. Burke translated for the *Dial* a part of the monumental
Decline of the West. The reader is left to wonder whether acquaintance with
this great work has had an influence on his philosophy of esthetics.

* * *

The *New York Times Magazine* for July 26 presents a sketch of the career of
America's veteran philanthropist, George F. Peabody, who is now in his
80th year. In many ways, George Peabody is unique among philanthropists.
Not content merely to dispense liberally the wealth which a system piled
into his lap, he came out boldly for modifications in that system itself. Although he spent many years in the most conservative of all forms of business, that of banking, he remains today a confirmed free trader and an
advocate of public ownership of the railroads. Extraordinary as it may seem,
he aligned himself with Henry George in the Single Tax movement. Mr.
Peabody is Southern-born and his services to education in the South have
been very great. He will be remembered not only for his generosity, which
success made easy for him, but also for his courage.

* * *

Julian Huxley has cooked a new witches-brew to ease the wounds of the
bleeding world. In a clear-cut article in the *Contemporary Review* for July,
this brew takes the name of "scientific humanism." He illustrates, of course,
the newer advantages man has gained over Dame Nature, but we are ad-
monished not to set these newer advantages up as God, with the new name
Science. To prevent such deification Mr. Huxley advocates that science be
linked with value. The prime task is to be that "scientific humanism clarify
her own ideas as to the limitations of the human mind." Men have been
busy at such a task for a few hundred years. Definitions are scattered rather
freely throughout the article. One example should be adequate: "Art is a
way of expressing some felt experience in communicable form; and in a way
which involves that most difficult of things to define, the aesthetic emotion.
In short, scientific humanism is to give direction to life. We are to 'have life
and have it more abundantly.'"

Looking Over the Magazines[1]

[August 14, 1931]

CLIFFORD AMYX AND RICHARD WEAVER

An article in the *American Mercury* for August, titled "The Exquisite American," deals mostly with the American as a man of literary pursuits. The author, Theodore Maynard, makes several interesting contrasts and comparisons intended to demonstrate that the American manner is not "kosmic" as Whitman terms it, but rather that it is characterized by a special aptitude for fineness and delicacy of expression. He cites as a master example Cabell, the stylist, and finds traces of delicacy even in blundering Sherwood Anderson and Theodore Dreiser; though Maynard writes: "I should describe him [Dreiser] as being, rather than an American tragedy, a teutonic muddle." Though Maynard can scarcely be considered as representing a non-American point of view (he writes as an Englishman), the article is excellent and lacks the voluble sweeping statements that are usually found in the characterizations of one country by the representative of another.

* * *

The newspapers have done an incredible amount of banal moralizing over Bernard Shaw's recent trip to Russia. Some have criticized him for going, others for returning, and still others for what he did while there. In the issue of August 5 *The Nation* takes time out to emit a few chuckles over the incident. Shaw, "the bad boy of the articulate world," is pictured as visiting Russia, the bad boy among nations. They get along famously because they

---

1. *The Kentucky Kernel,* August 14, 1931, 4.

are audacious in about equal degrees and because they both have a sublime contempt for the world's opinion.

* * *

Lewis Mumford has written an appreciation of the life and works of Thorstein Veblen for *The New Republic* of August 5. Thorstein Veblen is unquestionably one of the few men of genius America has produced, and yet it is doubtful if 10 per cent of the students of economics in the average college could even identify him if asked to do so on their final examination. Reasons for his failure to win recognition are easy to find. It was his misfortune to spend his life in a field where the laurels went not to the candid seeker after truth but to the glib apologist. He had no patience with the abracadabra of the traditional political economy, and his exposure of its fake problems was ofttimes brilliant. It was his great contribution to distinguish between the pecuniary and the technological aspects of industry. Mencken was the first to recognize in him an unusual gift for satire, and anyone who has read *The Engineer and the Price System* will testify to the wonderful lucidity of his prose. Mr. Mumford believes that the present period of deflation demands a fresh consideration of his theories.

* * *

Lewis Mumford, in *Books* for August 6, chats briefly on the last decade; the decade that saw the appearance and decline of two small, though significant magazines. The principal one was the *Dial*, which ran the course: books, social reconstruction, pure aesthetics, and a final lapse in "the timid, spindly review of its final years, proof that one of the wittiest and most audacious of poets could also be the worst of editors." Another periodical, the *Freeman*, under the editorship of Albert Jay Nock, and the symposium *The American Caravan*, are discussed by Mr. Mumford.

For the life and death of another literary magazine, *Transition*, see the *American Mercury* for June. *Transition* was published in France and barred from the United States by the Smootians. It was a magazine with a purpose and the writer of the article, Eugene Jolas, claims that purpose partially established: "The principle of liberty for the fabulist and the poet has been definitely established."

* * *

The August issue of the *Golden Book* appears in a reduced format. In consequence, the number of illustrations is less than the usual number. This magazine has been significant, not only for its policy of printing short stories by famous authors, past and present, but for the excellence of its illustrations. Their passing is to be regretted. The *Golden Book* contains stories this month by Wilde, Galsworthy, O. Henry, Chekhov, Gautier, Dumas, and Mark Twain's ludicrous "Punch, Brothers, Punch," listed as "foolishness of a high order."

*   *   *

With the exception of Russia and our own economic depression no subject arouses so much discussion today as the status of religion in the modern world and the problem of its contribution to modern life. Charles W. Ferguson writing on "The Predicament of the Clergy" in the August number of *Harper's* pictures the dilemma in which the minister is finding himself. Either he may adhere to the old dogmatic religion and go down before the onslaught of scepticism and naturalism, or he may attempt to construct a new religion based on the findings of science and motivated by an ethical humanitarianism. The clergy made its original mistake in suffering the men of science too gladly. Under solemn promises to respect all sacred things they were admitted into the temple, but they have been followed by less pious successors, so that now the temple is not only profaned but is in imminent danger of wreckage. The public that once shouted and rolled at the evangelists' camp meeting is interesting itself today in "the anatomy of faith and the psychology of religious behavior." Mr. Ferguson goes on to compare the modern clergyman to the shorn Samson.

Looking Over the Magazines[1]

[August 21, 1931]

CLIFFORD AMYX AND RICHARD WEAVER

The *New York Herald Tribune*'s literary supplement, *Books,* is running a series of feature articles by E. M. Forster. Each one presents some noted
literary figure in an unusual situation. Thus the number for August 16 por-
trays Edward Gibbon as a young captain of militia in his 24th year. This
was just after Gibbon, following a brief period of vacillation, had lapsed
into the imperturbable scepticism which he carried to his grave. He credited
his experience in the militia with having increased his knowledge of mankind. Those who have felt the spell of this extraordinary historian seize this
opportunity to get a more intimate glimpse of him. It is revealing to find
the author of *The Decline and Fall* entering in his journal after a night of
intemperance, "I could do nothing this morning but spew."

* * *

Reports of political upheaval in Spain have caused some of us to overlook
that country's reputation as a land of sunshine, color, and romance. The
August *National Geographic* carried an article by Harriet Chalmers Adams
describing how life is lived in gay Madrid. The author declares that Spain
is a place of wide personal liberty, where the enjoyment of leisure has been
made a consummate art, and where the amenities of social intercourse are
universally observed. One feature of Madrid's park system which should
interest American readers is the presence of small open air libraries whose

---

1. *The Kentucky Kernel*, August 21, 1931, 2.

books are entrusted entirely to the custody of the chance users. There is a striking photograph of the Escorial, the huge palace erected by Philip II.

* * *

One suspects that if the United States be far behind Germany and France in the publication of books, such cannot be true in the case of periodical literature. August marks the appearance of another magazine in a large group which caters to the soulful and financial longings of the young author. It blooms forth under the name *Creative World,* official publication for the International Society of Creative Minds. Its avowed purpose is stated: "A world famous scientist recently said that less than five per cent of the people living ever contribute anything to the material progress of humanity. These are Creative Minds who will find in this magazine a champion, and it cares nothing for the other 95 per cent. Devoted to Authorship, Art, Invention, primarily, it shall attempt to cover the entire field of creative thought, including scientific research in every direction." The least that can be said is that the program outlined is slightly ambitious.

The first issue contains the column "What's the Racket," a description of the "copyright racket" as practiced by certain persons who have very small regard for the accepted moral standards. In the next number we are promised "The Song-Writing Racket." Featured are: a column on Esperanto, the coming international language; the method to pursue in changing your name, your present one will undoubtedly "jinx" your whole literary future; the prices paid by the best magazines for copy (detective, western, adventure, love); "How They Got Their Start," with S. S. Van Dine as the featured author.

When such magazines as this one spring out of nothing and, in company with their literary cousins, prosper and glut the market, such magazines as the *Dial* struggle and falter and finally pass out of existence for one cause or another; one would be extremely thankful to find in America such a periodical as *Blanco y Negro,* a review without any literary pretensions which accomplished the stated purpose of *The Creative World* without using MacFadden methods and three-ring circus brand of brass and ballyhoo.

Up from Liberalism [1]

There is a saying by William Butler Yeats that a man begins to understand the world by studying the cobwebs in his own corner. My experience has brought home to me the wisdom in this; and since the contemporary ideal seems to run the other way, confronting the youth first with the abstractions of universalism, collectivism, and internationalism, I propose to say something on behalf of the historic and the concrete as elements of an education.

The discovery did not come to me as a free gift, for practically every conviction I now hold I have had to win against the propositional sense and general impetus of most of my formal education. This was owing partly to special circumstances, but mainly, I now believe, to the fact that the United States tends to institutionalize the chaotic and superficial type of education and to impose it with an air of business efficiency. This is not to imply that I was wiser than my generation, for I was filled with the formless aspirations which make such an education look like a good thing, and I fell into most of the pitfalls that were left open. But I hope that a retrospect of twenty-five years, involving much change of opinion, gives some right to pass judgment; and furthermore I wish, in this testament, to discuss education as one of the proven means of doing something about the condition of man.

I was born in the Southern section of the United States, and at the age of seventeen I entered the University of Kentucky. I have more than once recalled how well Charles Peguy's description of himself at the beginning of his career at the *Ecole Normale* fitted me at this time: "gloomy, ardent, stupid." The University of Kentucky was what would be called in Europe a "provincial university," but I have since come to believe that if it had been more provincial in the right way and less sedulously imitative of the dominant American model, it would have offered better fare. Like most of our

1. *Modern Age*, 3/1, Winter 1958–59, 21–32.

state-supported universities during the period, it was growing in enrollment and physical plant and losing in character; moreover, it was given to the "elective" system, whereby seventeen-year-old students, often of poor previous training and narrow background, tell the faculty (in effect) what they ought to be taught. After many wayward choices I managed to emerge, at the end of my undergraduate course, with a fair introduction to the history—but not the substance—of literature and philosophy.

The professors who staffed this institution were mostly earnest souls from the Middle Western universities, and many of them—especially those in economics, political science, and philosophy—were, with or without knowing it, social democrats. They read and circulated *The Nation,* the foremost liberal journal of the time; they made sporadic efforts toward organizing liberal or progressive clubs; and of course they reflected their position in their teaching very largely. I had no defenses whatever against their doctrine, and by the time I was in my third year I had been persuaded entirely that the future was with science, liberalism, and equalitarianism, and that all opposed to these trends were people of ignorance or malevolence.

That persuasion was not weakened, I must add, by the fact that my class graduated in May, 1932, at almost precisely the time that the Great Depression reached its lowest point on the economic charts. College graduates were taking any sort of job they could get, however menial or unrelated to their preparation, and many, of course, were not getting jobs at all. It seemed then that some sort of political reconstruction was inevitable, and in that year I joined the American Socialist Party. My disillusionment with the Left began with this first practical step.

The composition of our small unit of the Socialist Party was fairly typical, I have since learned, of socialist organizations throughout the world. There was on the one side a group of academic people—teachers and students—who were intellectually trained and fairly clear in their objectives, but politically inexperienced and temperamentally not adapted to politics. On the other side was about an equal number of town people who cannot be described for the good reason that they were nondescripts. They were eccentrics, novelty-seekers, victims of restlessness; and most of them were hopelessly confused about the nature and purpose of socialism. I remember how shocked I was when a member of this group suggested that we provide at our public rallies one of the "hillbilly bands" which are often used to draw crowds and provide entertainment in Southern political campaigns. This seemed to me entirely out of tone with what we were trying to do. I have since had to realize that the member was far more astute practically than I; the hillbilly music would undoubtedly have fetched more auditors and made more votes than the austere exposition of the country's ills which I thought it the duty of a socialist to make. But I am sure that the net result would not have been socialism. The two groups did not understand one another, and it is a wonder to me that they worked together as long as they did.

In the course of a membership of about two years, during which I served as secretary of the "local," as it was called, I discovered that although the socialist program had a certain intellectual appeal for me, I could not like the members of the movement as *persons*. They seemed dry, insistent people, of shallow objectives; seeing them often and sharing a common endeavor, moreover, did nothing to remove the disliking. I am afraid that I performed my duties with decreasing enthusiasm, and at the end of the period I had intimations, which I did not then face, that this was not the kind of thing in which I could find permanent satisfaction.

Meanwhile another experience had occurred which was to turn my thoughts in the same direction. I had gone as a graduate student to Vanderbilt University to pursue an advanced degree in literature. Vanderbilt was another provincial university, but it had developed in the hands of men intelligent enough to see the possibilities that exist in a reflective provincialism. It was at that time the chief seat of the Southern Agrarian school of philosophy and criticism. This was one of the most brilliant groups in the United States, but its members held a position antithetical in almost every point to socialism and other purely economic remedies. By some their program was regarded as mere antiquarianism; by others it was attacked as fascist, since it rejected science and rationalism as the supreme sanctions, accepted large parts of the regional tradition, and even found some justification for social classes. But here, to my great surprise and growing confusion, I found that although I disagreed with these men on matters of social and political doctrine, I liked them all as persons. They seemed to me more humane, more generous, and considerably less dogmatic than those with whom I had been associated under the opposing banner. It began to dawn upon me uneasily that perhaps the right way to judge a movement was by the persons who made it up rather than by its rationalistic perfection and by the promises it held out. Perhaps, after all, the proof of social schemes was meant to be *a posteriori* rather than *a priori*. It would be a poor trade to give up a non-rational world in which you liked everybody for a rational one in which you liked nobody. I did not then see it as quite so sharp an issue; but the intellectual maturity and personal charm of the Agrarians were very unsettling to my then-professed allegiance.

Moreover, during my residence at Vanderbilt University I had the great good fortune to study under John Crowe Ransom, a rare teacher of literature and, apart from this and in his own right, a profound psychologist. Of the large number of students who have felt his influence, I doubt whether any could tell how he worked his effects. If one judged solely by outward motions and immediate results, he seemed neither to work very hard at teaching nor to achieve much success. But he had the gift of dropping living seeds into minds. Long after the date of a lecture—a week, a month, a year—you would find some remark of his troubling you with its pregnancy, and you would set about your own reflections upon it, often wishing that you had the master at hand to give another piece of insight. The idea of Ransom's which chiefly took possession of me at this time was that of the "unorthodox defense of orthodoxy," which he had developed in his brilliant book *God without Thunder*. I began to perceive that many traditional positions in our world had suffered not so much because of inherent defect as because of the stupidity, ineptness, and intellectual sloth of those who for one reason or another were presumed to have their defense in charge.

This was a troubling perception, because the 1930s were a time when nearly all of the traditional American ideologies were in retreat, and I had never suspected that this retreat might be owing to a kind of default. If there was something to be said for them, if their eclipse was due to the failure of their proponents to speak a modern idiom or even to acquire essential knowledge, this constituted at least a challenge to intellectual curiosity. I had tried some of the Leftist solution and had found it not to my taste; it was possible that I had been turned away from the older, more traditional solutions because they wore an antiquarian aspect and insisted upon positions which seemed irrelevancies in the modern context. Actually the passage was not an easy one for me, and I left Vanderbilt University poised between the two alternatives. I had seen virtually nothing of socialism and centralism in practice, and the mass man I had never met; there was also reluctance over giving up a position once publicly espoused, made somewhat greater by a young man's vanity. Nevertheless, I had felt a powerful pull in the direction of the Agrarian ideal of the individual in contact with the rhythms of nature, of the small-property holding, and of the society of pluralistic organization.

I had left the University to take a teaching post in a large technical college in Texas. It has been remarked that in the United States California is the embodiment of materialism and Texas of naturalism. I found the observation true with regard to my part of Texas, where I encountered a rampant philistinism, abetted by technology, large-scale organization, and a complacent acceptance of success as the goal of life. Moreover, I was here forced to see that the lion of applied science and the lamb of the humanities were not going to lie down together in peace, but that the lion was going to devour the lamb unless there was a very stern keeper of order. I feel that my conversion to the poetic and ethical vision of life dates from this contact with its sterile opposite.

I recall very sharply how, in the Autumn of 1939, as I was driving one afternoon across the monotonous prairies of Texas to begin my third year in this post, it came to me like a revelation that I did not *have* to go back to this job, which had become distasteful, and that I did not *have* to go on professing the clichés of liberalism, which were becoming meaningless to me. I saw that my opinions had been formed out of a timorous regard for what was supposed to be intellectually respectable, and that I had always been looking over my shoulder to find out what certain others, whose concern with truth I was beginning to believe to be not very intense, were doing or thinking. It is a great experience to wake up at a critical juncture to the fact that one does have a free will, and that giving up the worship of false idols is a quite practicable proceeding.

Anyhow, at the end of that year I chucked the uncongenial job and went off to start my education over, being now arrived at the age of thirty.

In the meantime I had started to study the cobwebs in my own corner, and I began to realize that the type of education which enables one to see into the life of things had been almost entirely omitted from my program. More specifically, I had been reading extensively in the history of the American Civil War, preferring first-hand accounts by those who had actually borne the brunt of it as soldiers and civilians; and I had become especially interested in those who had reached some level of reflectiveness and had tried to offer explanations of what they did or the manner in which they did it. Allen Tate has in one of his poems the line "There is more in killing than commentary." The wisdom of this will be seen also by those who study the killings in which whole nations are the killers and the killed, namely, wars. To put this in a prose statement: the mere commentary of an historian will never get you inside the feeling of a war or any great revolutionary process. For that, one has to read the testimonials of those who participated in it on both sides and in all connections; and often the best insight will appear in the casual remark of an obscure warrior or field nurse or in the effort of some ill-educated person to articulate a feeling.

I once heard of a man who made it a lifetime hobby to study the reasons that people in various circumstances gave as to why they felt it necessary to tell a lie. I believe that it is equally worthwhile and perhaps more interesting to study the reasons that people have given for passing from the use of reason to the use of force. At what point does reason tell us that reason is of no more avail? The American Civil War, because it was a civil struggle, with an elaborate ideology on both sides, left a rich store of material on this subject.

From the viewpoint of my general purpose, I had come to believe that one way to achieve the education which leads to understanding and compassion is to take some period of the past and to immerse oneself in it so thoroughly that one could think its thoughts and speak its language. The object would be to take this chapter of vanished experience and learn to know it in three if not four dimensions. That would mean coming to understand why certain actions which in the light of retrospect appear madly irrational appeared at that time the indisputable mandate of reason; why things which had been created with pain and care were cast quickly on the gaming table of war; why men who had sat in the senate chamber and debated with syllogism and enthymeme stepped out of it to buckle on the sword against one another. Almost any book of history will give you the form of such a time, but what will give you the *pressure* of it? That is what I particularly wished to discover.

I am now further convinced that there is something to be said in general for studying the history of a lost cause. Perhaps our education would be more humane in result if everyone were required to gain an intimate acquaintance with some coherent ideal that failed in the effort to maintain itself. It need not be a cause which was settled by war; there are causes in the social, political, and ecclesiastical worlds which would serve very well. But it is good for everyone to ally himself at one time with the defeated and to look at the "progress" of history through the eyes of those who were left behind. I cannot think of a better way to counteract the stultifying "Whig" theory of history, with its bland assumption that every cause which has won has deserved to win, a kind of pragmatic debasement of the older providential theory. The study and appreciation of a lost cause have some effect of turning history into philosophy. In sufficient number of cases to make us humble, we discover good points in the cause which time has erased, just as one often learns more from the slain hero of a tragedy than from some brassy Fortinbras who comes in at the end to announce the victory and proclaim the future disposition of affairs. It would be perverse to say that this is so of every historical defeat, but there is enough analogy to make it a sober consideration. Not only Oxford, therefore, but every university ought to be to some extent "the home of lost causes and impossible loyalties." It ought to preserve the memory of these with a certain discriminating measure of honor, trying to keep alive what was good in them and opposing the pragmatic verdict of the world.

For my part, I spent three years reading the history and literature of the Civil War, with special attention to that of the losing side. The people who emerged were human, all-too-human, but there was still the mystery of the encompassing passion which held them together, and this I have not yet penetrated. But in a dozen various ways I came to recognize myself in the past, which is at least an important piece of self-knowledge.

Toward the end of this inquiry, I published my first article, "The Older Religiousness in the South." It was an attempt to explain why the South, although it was engaged in defending institutions which much of the world was condemning on moral grounds, seemed to exhibit a more intense religiosity than its opponents. It was a first effort toward an unorthodox explanation of an orthodoxy, and it showed me how much more was to be done in historical revision of the kind before the shallow liberal interpretation could be exposed in its inadequacy.

Looking back over this discipline, I feel confident enough of its principle. The aim is to strip aside the clichés of generalization, the slogans which are preserved only because they render service to contemporary institutions, and of course to avoid the drug of economic interpretation. Henry Adams felt an impulse to do something like this amid the hullabaloo of his America, and his inquiry led him—this bloodless, self-questioning descendant of New England Puritans—to ponder the mystery of the Virgin. It seems to me that in some corresponding way the process will compel any honest seeker to see that the lines of social and political force are far more secret than the modern world has any mind to recognize, and that if it does not lead him to some kind of faith, it will lead him safely away from the easy constructions of those who do not wish to understand, beyond grasping what can be turned to serve a practical purpose. Whereas conventional schoolbook history leaves men cocksure and ignorant, this multidimensional kind ought to leave them filled with wonder. Long before, I had been impressed by Schopenhauer's statement that no one can be a philosopher who is not capable at times of looking upon the world as if it were a pageant. This kind of detachment, produced by a suppression of the instinct to be arbitrary, seems to me a requirement for understanding the human condition.

The attempt to contemplate history in all its dimensions and in the fullness of its detail led directly to the conviction that this world of substantial things and substantial events is the very world which the Leftist of our time wishes to see abolished; and such policy now began to appear egotistical and presumptuous. I am disinclined to the view that whatever exists necessarily has a commission to go on existing. On the contrary, I have a strong tendency to side with the bottom dog, or to champion the potential against the actual if the former seems to have some reason behind it; and I am mindful of the saying that God takes delight in bringing great things out of small ones. To this extent I am a reformer or even a subverter. But I feel that situations almost never present themselves in terms so simple. They usually appear in terms like these: we have before us a tremendous creation which is largely inscrutable. Some of the intermediate relationships of cause and effect we can grasp and manipulate, though with these our audacity often outruns good sense and we discover that in trying to achieve one balance we have upset two others. There are, accordingly, two propositions which are hard to deny: we live in a universe which was given to us, in the sense that we did not create it; and we don't understand very much of it.

In the figure once used by a philosopher, we are inhabitants of a fruitful and well-ordered island surrounded by an ocean of ontological mystery. It does not behoove us to presume very far in this situation. It is not a matter of affirming that whatever is, is right; it is a recognition that whatever is there is there with considerable force (inertia even being a respectable form of force) and in a network of relationships which we have only partly deciphered. Therefore, make haste slowly. It is very easy to rush into conceit in thinking about man's relationship to the created universe. Science paved the way for presumption, whether wittingly or not; and those political movements which appeal to science to vindicate their break with the past have often made the presumptuous attitude one of their tenets. I found myself in decreasing sympathy with those social and political doctrines erected upon the concept of a man-dominated universe and more and more inclined to believe with Walt Whitman that "a mouse is miracle enough to stagger sextillions of infidels."

As a further consequence of reflecting upon this problem, I began to see it in theological terms. As I have suggested, "the authority of fact" is a phrase that I am a little uncomfortable with, because it is readily turned, unless one is vigilant, into an idolatry of circumstance, and this is the most unspiritual of all conditions. Nevertheless, there is a way in which "the authority of fact" carries a meaning that we can accept. It merely requires that we see "fact" as signifying what the theological philosophers mean by the word "substance." Now the denial of substance is one of the greatest heresies, and this is where much contemporary radicalism appears in an essentially sinful aspect. The constant warfare which it wages against anything that has *status* in the world, or against all the individual, particular, unique existences of the world which do not fit into a rationalistic pattern, is but a mask for the denial of substance. If one benighted class of men begins by assuming that whatever is, is right, they begin by assuming that whatever is, is wrong. Had we to decide between these two—and I hope to make it clear that I do not think we have to decide thus—the latter would appear more blasphemous than the former because it makes a wholesale condemnation of a creation which is not ours and which exhibits the marks of a creative power that we do not begin to possess. The intent of the radical to defy all substance, or to press it into forms conceived in his mind alone, is thus theologically wrong; it is an aggression by the self which outrages a deep-laid order of things. And it has seeped into every department of our life. In the reports of the successful ascent of Mt. Everest, the British members of the expedition talked of "conquering" the mountain, but the Nepalese guide who was one of the two to reach the summit spoke of a desire to visit the Buddha who lives at the top. The difference between these attitudes is a terrible example of the modern western mentality, with its metaphysic of progress through aggression.

Here again was an invitation to ponder one of the oldest and deepest of human attitudes, which is generally expressed by the word "piety." The war of the radicals against substance is a direct repudiation of this quality. It is true that a great many instances of sham, in both word and deed, have been associated with this term, so that one runs a danger by bringing it into any modern discussion of ethics and religion. Nevertheless, it seems to me that it signifies an attitude toward things which are immeasurably larger and greater than oneself without which man is an insufferably brash, conceited, and frivolous animal. I do not in truth see how societies are able to hold together without some measure of this ancient but now derided feeling. The high seriousness of this life expresses itself as a kind of *pietas,* or a respect for the tragedy of existence, if nothing else. Piety is another one of those orthodoxies which have broken down because the defenders have not been able to show what is necessary in them. They have erected their defenses on positions quite easily overrun, and the places they could easily have defended they have left unmanned. As long as the term is associated exclusively with the avoidance of foibles and minor vices, there seems no hope of restoring the vital idea for which it stands. But when one shows that the habit of veneration supplies the whole force of social and political cohesion, one hits at its enemies where the blow cannot be ignored.

The realization that piety is a proper and constructive attitude toward certain things helped me to develop what Russell Kirk calls "affection for the proliferating variety and mystery of traditional life." I feel now, in looking over the course of things, that such an attitude has always been in my nature, but that it had been repressed by dogmatic, utilitarian, essentially contumacious doctrines of liberalism and scientism, so that it was for me a kind of recovery of lost power or lost capacity for wonder and enchantment. The recovery has brought a satisfaction which cannot be matched, as far as my experience goes, by anything that liberalism and scientism have to offer.

It is what I feel when I return to the South, as I do each summer. There are numberless ways in which the South disappoints me; but there is something in its sultry languor and in the stubborn humanism of its people, now battling against the encroachments of industrialism—and with so little knowledge of how to battle—which tells me that for better or worse this is my native land. It is often said today that the hope of the world lies in internationalism. That may be true, but it is also true, and true with a prior truth, that there can be no internationalism without a solid, intelligent provincialism. That is so because there is nothing else for internationalism to rest on. And if philosophical sanction for this is wanted, there is the wise and beautiful saying of Thoreau: "I think nothing is to be hoped for from you, if this bit of mould under your feet is not sweeter to you to eat than any other in the world, or in any world."

Nevertheless, it is most important, as I have tried to suggest earlier, to draw a line between respect for tradition because it is tradition and respect for it because it expresses a spreading mystery too great for our knowledge to compass. The first is merely an idolatry, or a tribute to circumstance, which has engendered some of the most primitive, narrow, and harmful attitudes which the human race has shown. There is a worship of tradition and circumstance which is all fear, distrust, and feebleness of imagination, and to this the name "reaction" is rightly applied. There can be no hope for good things from an attitude as negative as this. But the other attitude is reverential and creative at the same time; it worships the spirit rather than the graven image; and it allows man to contribute his mite toward helping Providence. Obviously free will would be meaningless if the world were to be left entirely untouched by us. Some things we have to change, but we must avoid changing out of *hubris* and senseless presumption. And always we have to keep in mind what man is supposed to be.

At the same time that the radical is engaged in denying the substance, he is engaged in denying the existence of evil, which is another great heresy. This takes the form today, as we all recognize, of assuming the perfectibility of man, the adequacy of social and political measures for the salvation of the individual person, and all the means of state engineering which are supposed to take the place of the old idea of redemption. Apart from the dilemma that the denial of evil involves us in, it brings into our moral, intellectual, and cultural life a number of destructive fallacies. It brings in,

for example, the flattery of the popular will, the idealization of the mediocre, and along with these a spirit of rebelliousness toward anything that
involves self discipline, sustained effort, and service to autonomous ideals.
There is abroad in democracies today an idea that to criticize anybody for
anything is treasonable, that the weak, the self-indulgent, and the vicious
have the same claims toward respect and reward as anybody else, and that
if a man chooses to be a beast, he has a sort of natural, inviolable right to be
one. As far as I can see, there is no possible way of opposing this idea until
we admit the existence of evil and the duty of combatting it. Here modern
radicalism has failed again to interpret the issue.

It has been said that a disillusionment with human nature most often
turns the mind toward Christianity. I know that in my period of jejune
optimism the concept of original sin seemed something archaically funny.
Now, twenty years later, and after the experience of a world war, there is no
concept that I regard as expressing a deeper insight into the enigma that is
man. Original sin is a parabolical expression of the immemorial tendency
of man to do the wrong thing when he knows the right thing. The fact of
this tendency everyone should be able to testify to, not only from his observation but also from his personal history. And it is the rock upon which
nine tenths of the socialist formula for universal happiness splits. The socialists propose to offer man peace and plenty; and they seem not to realize
that he may reject both for crime and aggrandizement. He has done so
before in both the individual and the national units. It would be more realistic for the reformers to start with the old assumption that the heart of
man is desperately wicked and that he needs external help in the form of
grace. At least, we cannot build on the quicksand that he is by nature good,
for he is not. Whether he has inherited his sin from Adam is perhaps a
question for another level of discussion; the plain situation is that he has
inherited it, and that it will sink any scheme which is founded on a complacent faith in man's desire always to do the good thing. Nothing can be done
if the will is wrong, and the correction of the will is precisely the task which
modern radicalism fails to recognize.

It is only realistic to point out that the concept of original sin, if not anti-
democratic, is at least a severe restraint upon democracy. Democracy finds
it difficult ever to say that man is wrong if he does things in large majorities.
Yet even politically this notion has to be rejected; and that is why constitu-

tions and organic laws are created in nearly all representative governments, and are indeed regarded as the prime unifiers of such governments. A constitution is a government's better self, able to rebuke and restrain the baser self when it starts off on a vagary. If the mass of every electorate were wholly right at every period, constitutions would be only curious encumbrances. This means of distinguishing what is right deeply and naturally from what is wrong needs to be carried over also into our individual lives, where it sets a limit on indulgences of the self.

For all these reasons, those who say that evil is but a bad dream or an accident of history or the creation of a few antisocial men are only preparing us for worse disillusionments and disasters. It is necessary to recognize evil as a subtle, pervasive, protean force, capable of undoing plans that promise the fairest success, but also capable of being checked by proper spiritual insight and energy. This makes the problem of improving the individual and society continuous with known human history and not different according to different phases of economic and technological development.

The persistence of the fact of evil was then being underlined for me by the dreadful events of the Second World War. A question was posed in sharp form when the claims of modern and "advanced" civilization were being refuted by the presence of this greatest creator of misery. Wars not only were becoming more frequent, they were also becoming more absolute or more undiscriminating in their ends and means.

The prosecution of the war by the Western allies was to me a progressive disillusionment. My study of the American Civil War had made me acquainted with the principle that as a war continues, the basis of the war changes, but I had not been prepared to see the extent to which the moral aim may deteriorate. My faith in the honesty of our case was shaken by an incident that occurred about the middle of the conflict. The incident is not very well remembered because it concerned chiefly a small country, and what does a small country count for in a world where everything is decided by a Big Four or a Big Three or a Big Something? This was the abandonment of Finland by Britain and the United States, who had previously bucked up her morale and to some extent her strength against the Russian foe. I felt that if Finland could be cheerfully thrown to the wolves in the haste for victory and vengeance, much worse things must be anticipated, and so it has proved. And the Yalta Conference seemed to me at the very time when the newspapers were crowded with the most fantastic tributes and eulogies a piece of political insanity.

In sum, I felt that, thanks to our wonderful press and our Office of War Information and our political leaders, almost nobody in the United States knew what the war was really about. I recall sitting in my office in Ingleside Hall at the University of Chicago one Fall morning in 1945 and wondering whether it would not be possible to deduce, from fundamental causes, the fallacies of modern life and thinking that had produced this holocaust and would insure others. In about twenty minutes I jotted down a series of chapter headings, and this was the inception of a book entitled *Ideas Have Consequences*. At first it seemed destined to have only a *succès de scandale*, since it was so out of line with most current thinking on the subject. But many letters I later received from readers convinced me that other minds were tormented by the same questions, and that I had only gone to the point of saying what numerous people were thinking. The kind of opposition it aroused too seemed a confirmation.

It may sound odd, but it is true that the thesis of this book was first suggested by the bygone ideal of chivalry. My reading of history had encouraged the belief that at one time this had been an ideal of considerable restraining power, and that it contained one conception that seems to be absent from all the contemporary remedies for curing war—the conception of something spiritual which stood above war itself and included the two sides in any conflict. I have never had any faith in the notion of ending wars by fighting one war to a victorious and sweeping conclusion. The idea of a "war to end all wars" is worthy only of a mountebank. What such an attempt does in actuality is to scatter the seeds of war more widely, and possibly plant them more deeply. It does not take into account the intransigency of human nature.

The profoundly interesting feature of chivalry was that it offered a plan whereby civilization might contain a war and go on existing as civilization. It did not premise itself upon simplifications which are soon rejected, such as the proposition that "all war is murder." On the contrary, it tried to treat war or human combat as one of the activities of civilization, a dangerous one, to be sure, but one that could be kept under control. War under the code of chivalry might be likened to what the insurance companies call "a friendly fire." It is a useful thing to man as long as it is kept in a furnace or whatever place is intended for it. But a fire which gets out of the place created for it ceases to be friendly; it is a foe and can spread quick and terrible devastation. Thus the warfare controlled, or the war of limited objectives, is the friendly fire; but a war which has unlimited objectives has broken out of control and may, with the weapons now available, be capable of consuming civilization in a holocaust. Hence the problem is: what kind of thing is capable of controlling war, or of keeping it *within* civilization? It would be absurd to claim that chivalry accomplished all that the ideal pointed toward; there were episodes in the age of chivalry which make unpleasant reading. Nevertheless, it was a moderating influence; and it did one thing which makes it appear realistic in comparison with the solutions which are being proposed today. It insisted that even in war, when maximum strain is placed upon the passions, man may not become an absolute killer. In war there are some considerations which must not be crowded out by hatred and fear. This is true because even your foe has some rights, and these rights you must respect although your present course has his destruction in view. This may seem to some too paradoxical, but let us consider it in terms of an analogy. Modern wars have tended increasingly to resemble lynching parties. A lynching party acts in the belief that the guilt of the victim is absolute and unqualified, and that the only thing that matters is to put him to death immediately. Any means will do: beating, pistol fire, a tree and a rope. Of course this idea is contrary to that of juridical procedure. The law never takes the view that a man's guilt is so absolute and so completely known that he is not allowed to say a word in his defense. On the contrary, the most atrocious murderer is given police protection and a trial according to forms of law, with a chance to state his side of the affair.

The law is in such instances upholding an idea similar to that of chivalry, inasmuch as it takes the position that no one—not even an "enemy of society"—can be denied rights entirely. In modern international warfare, however, the idea of a binding agreement such as this is being abandoned rapidly. The object now is to pulverize the enemy completely, men, women, and children being lumped into one common target; it is to reduce a country to "atomic ashes," to recall a frightful phrase which I saw recently in a newspaper. And then, if anything remains, the next step is the unethical one of demanding unconditional surrender. No further analysis should be needed to show that this moves in a direction opposite to that of the chivalric ideal, in that it pulls everything into the madness and destruction of war and leaves nothing, as far as I can see, to help pull even the victor out again.

There are those who maintain that modern technology, when applied to war, makes all such concepts as the one upheld by chivalry simply fantastic. There is no way of restraining a technology, they say, which is so developed that it cannot produce anything short of annihilation once it is turned to destructive ends. Perhaps this cannot be disputed as a fact. Yet if it is a fact, it seems one more proof that we have allowed science to reach a point at which it no longer allows us to be human beings. If we have got ourselves into a position where our only choice is to blow up or be blown up, this circumstance refutes the idea that we have increased the mastery of our lives.

There cannot be any improvement in the world's condition until the human spirit has counterbalanced and more than counterbalanced the hectic brilliance of technological invention. The deadly trap into which the pride of the modern world in technology and invention has led us is not often described in its real nature. It has produced a world condition of unheard-of instability. The only way in which this instability can be overcome even temporarily is through rigid, centralized control of the national life. And the only way that a rigid, centralized control can be maintained is to keep the people living in a mentality of war. One can do this by filling them with desire of conquest, or one can do it by keeping them fearful of a real or imaginary enemy. Then one has a trump card to play on every occasion. If there is any relaxing or any resentment of controls, one has only to invoke "the national security" to silence opposition and even render it disreputable. We in the United States are living under the second of these policies now. The choice appears to lie between chaos and perpetual preparation for war, and the trouble with preparation for war is that it always issues in war. Here again technology steps in to make the dilemma more cruel, since it causes warfare to be increasingly total and nihilistic, and increasingly beyond the power of civilizing influences to absorb. From now on, as Maurice Samuel has pointed out, humanity will be living in the shadow of its own demonic omnipotence, and this is a calamity so great that almost nobody is able to face it. The chance that the world will not use atomic bombs if it goes on making them is infinitesimal.

How this tide is flowing even into the small interstices of our lives may be shown by a small incident. A few years ago there stood on the edge of the campus of the University of Chicago a small café. It was a poor affair, without style or pretensions; but here in the afternoons members of the liberal-arts faculties were wont to go for a cup of coffee, to get out of their professional grooves for an hour, to broach ideas and opinions, to be practicing humanists, you might say. Today a monstrous gray structure given to atomic research covers the site; the little café is no more; and the amiable *Kaffeeklatsche* no longer take place.

The chief result of what I now think of as my re-education has been a complete disenchantment with the liberalism that was the first stage of my reflective life. Liberalism is the refuge favored by intellectual cowardice, because the essence of the liberal's position is that he has no position. It may be true, with due qualifications, that in certain transitional phases, where the outline of issues is none too clear, the liberal or uncommitted attitude has its expediency. But as something to construct with, never! It is that state of mind before we have made up our mind. The explanation of why liberalism has been erected into a kind of philosophy in our time is perhaps to be sought in the fact that our world is disintegrating rapidly. It is thereby creating the impression that nothing is permanent but change, and that the very concept of truth is a stumbling block to adaptation as the disintegration goes on.

But even after this concession to the state of affairs, it is easy to see how the liberal's lack of position involves him in contradictions that destroy confidence. He is a defender of individualism and local rights, but let some strong man appear, who promises salvation through "leadership," and the liberal becomes indistinguishable from the totalitarian. Hence the totalitarian liberal of our times, a contradiction in terms, but an embodiment in the flesh, and a dire menace to government based upon rights. In times of peace, the liberal is often a shouter for pacificism, but let something he dislikes appear upon the horizon and he is the first to invoke the use of armed force. In education, he believes in the natural goodness of the child and abhors the idea of corporal discipline, but he believes in spanking nations with atomic bombs until their will is broken.

It is frequently said that while our knowledge of the natural world is increasing rapidly, our knowledge of the nature and spirit of man shows no gain, and that most of our troubles arise out of this disproportion. I think that our situation is considerably worse than this figure represents it, for I am of the opinion that our knowledge of the nature and spirit of man is decreasing, and this not relatively but absolutely. No one can study Greek philosophy or mediaeval Christianity or the other great religions of the world without realizing that these saw man as a creature fearfully and wonderfully made, and that each tried to lead him with appropriate imagination and subtlety. Today, living under the shadow of this demonic technological omnipotence, we are trying to get along by supposing such crudities as economic man, "naturally good" man, and so on. Of course they do not work, and the more they are tried in our context, the nearer we are to catastrophe.

Somehow our education will have to recover the lost vision of the person as a creature of both intellect and will. It will have to bring together into one through its training the thinker and the doer, the dialectician and the rhetorician. Cognition, including the scientific, alone is powerless, and will without cognition is blind and destructive. The work of the future, then, is to overcome the shallow rationalisms and scientificisms of the past two centuries and to work toward the reunion of man into a being who will both know and desire what he knows.

William Maury Mitchell[1]

My acquaintance with Maury Mitchell began in the fall of 1924 at Lincoln Memorial University in Harrogate, Tennessee, where he was a freshman in the college. Maury was then about 20 years of age and thus about two years older than the average entering student; I was only 14, and a freshman in the Academy.

I do not know much about his life previous to this. He was the oldest of five brothers. He received some part of his preparatory education at a place called "Ferrum Training Institute," or something like that, located in the little town of Ferrum, Virginia, not far from Bassett. Here he came to know that discipline and hard work which he was to make an important part of his life ever after. During the two years or so that intervened between his graduation from high school and his matriculation at LMU he worked in Bassett. Most of the time I think he was employed as a factory workman by the Bassett Furniture Company. I am sure that it was distaste for this work that made him resolve to become a professional man one day, whatever the cost in labor and self-denial. He once told me that the highest wage he ever made while working for the Bassett Company was 27 1/2 cents per hour.

I imagine that Maury chose LMU for the same reason I did: it was a school for "poor mountain boys" (and girls). It had been established around 1900 by some idealistic Republicans who hoped to educate Southern mountain youth under the auspices and in the ideals of Lincoln. It was, all in all,

1. The text of a memorial written by Weaver in June 1958 to mark the passing of William Maury Mitchell, his oldest and closest friend. It was apparently composed in response to a request from Mitchell's widow, Hilda, to his friends for information about his activities before their marriage in December 1956. A copy was sent to Mrs. Mitchell on June 20, 1958. Edited by Ted J. Smith III from a corrected typescript acquired from Weaver's sister, Mrs. Polly Weaver Beaton, and currently in the possession of the editor.

a good place. The location was awe-inspiring (within a mile of historic Cumberland Gap); the plant was modest but adequate; and the faculty contained some dedicated spirits. Our favorites were Prof. J. H. Moore, for Latin, whom we always referred to as "Cato the Elder," and Miss Buffum, for history, who was a real New England female intellectual. But the best thing about it was the student morale. This was "democratic" in the best sense, friendly, full of zest, and it reflected all of the virtues of the Appalachian people.

I do not remember my first meeting with Maury. It probably occurred while we were standing around outside Norton Hall, waiting for the supper bell to ring. Norton Hall, the principal residence for girls, contained the dining hall which served the entire institution. Here students would gather from all quarters of the campus about six; and I have a vivid image of Maury walking down the hill from Grant-Lee Hall, where he had his room, with that peculiar pace of his and wearing an infectious smile.

In spite of the disparity of our ages, Maury and I were drawn together by certain common interests. We were both ardent students of Latin, and in this we were pretty much alone. One year, I remember, Maury comprised the entire class of an advanced course in Latin (Livy and Tacitus, it may have been), while I was comprising the entire class in Virgil. Also we were both then contemplating careers in law and politics, though I rather nebulously. We were both addicted to the study of history. We never had classes together because I was about four years behind him academically, but we often discussed and compared our work.

Sometime during the year 1925–26 a recruit showed up to make us a sort of club of three. This was Vadus Carmack, from Cookeville, Tennessee, near Nashville. Carmack was a young man of brilliant literary gifts, and I have always believed that it was a loss to American literature that he did not decide to become a writer. He had the habits of a recluse and was melancholic. We always referred to him as "The Hermit Sage" or "The Sage of Cookeville." But we found him very congenial, and he was soon adopted into our "circle." Before very long we organized a formal society, to which we gave the high-sounding name "Societas Philosophiae Scientiaeque." To govern the society we drew up an elaborate constitution, but actually our proceedings were very simple: we would meet in the room of one of the members, usually on a Sunday afternoon, for debate and discussion. Sometimes a prepared paper was read; sometimes a subject was just thrown out for discussion. The chief topics were history, literature, politics, human nature. You may be sure that people were not banging at the door to get into the "Societas," and its membership never exceeded three. The tone at LMU was friendly, but it was not intellectual. In later years Maury always recalled the "Societas" with the greatest interest and pride. When I told him only last year that I had discovered, in a trunk that had been in storage for seventeen years, the original Constitution, he was greatly delighted and said that he wanted to have it photostated to hang on his office wall. This was a short time before he passed away.

Nearly all of the students at LMU performed some labor to pay all or part of their way. I worked in the kitchens for three years, but somehow I cannot remember very clearly what Maury did. My impression is that he did pick-and-shovel work on the campus and worked on the farm which the University owned. I think the fact is that he kept this down to the minimum that he could get by with, because he regarded studies as having strictly first place. And what a worker he was! The rest of us were frivolous compared with him. His study period began immediately after supper and rarely ended before one in the morning. Often I have heard him say that he kept going until two. And this was a regimen of work which he never relaxed. I can honestly say that his diversions were *nil,* unless the meetings of the "Societas" could be called such. I don't believe he spent a nickel a week on what is now called "relaxation." Right across from the main entrance to the campus was a little place called "The Hunkstand," which purveyed Coca-Cola, ice cream, and hot dogs to the students. I think Maury would have as soon been caught in a saloon as in that place. By this kind of strenuous application he developed that habit which marked him for the rest of his life of never going into anything unless he intended to master it thoroughly.

The only extra-curricular activity that Maury took part in was intercollegiate debating. This was of course linked with his future profession of the law.

When Christmas of 1926 came around, I invited him to spend the holiday with us at our home in Lexington, Kentucky. So one snowy December morning we carried our suitcases a mile to Cumberland Gap (the train did not stop at Harrogate) and boarded the old L & N. Poor Maury, it always made him sick to ride in any vehicle he was not driving himself. He was train-sick all the way to Lexington. We spent a jolly Christmas at our house at 370 Aylesford Place, and visited "Ashland," the home of Henry Clay, and other shrines of the capital of the Blue Grass.

In June, 1927, we both left LMU. I graduated from the Academy and was planning to enter the University of Kentucky next fall. Maury had completed just three years of college, but there was an arrangement by which one could take a year of law and have that count as the fourth year toward the A.B. degree. He took that year at Virginia in 1927–28, and in the spring of '28 returned to LMU at commencement and received his A.B. As you can see, he realized that he was a little behindhand in time, and he was making all the speed possible.

It was ten years before I saw Maury again. But it was during this period (perhaps it began with the summer of '26) that he started working in the summers as a Bible salesman. There was a Bible publishing house in Philadelphia which hired a considerable number of college men each summer to go into rural districts, especially in the South, and sell Bibles from door to door. Maury evidently decided that this was the one way he could raise the cash to carry him through law school. My recollection is that he spent his first summer in Mississippi. I remember this rather distinctly because it has always seemed to me that selling Bibles to negroes (which he was doing) in Mississippi in the summer time would be about as unpleasant a kind of work as a man could imagine. But with his usual unshakable determination he stuck to it, and he always returned with enough cash to get through the next year. Letters I have retained show that he was stationed in Kentucky in the summer of 1927, Oklahoma in 1928, and Alabama in 1929. I might add as a bit of incidental color that the Bible salesman hitch-hiked to his place of business and went home the same way at the close of summer.

During Maury's period at the University of Virginia (1927–30) my contact with him was through letters only, but these were fairly frequent. Charlottesville was a very different world from LMU and he was conscious of the difference—favorably for the most part. He worked harder than ever, if that was possible, and of course he did well. I do not know what his relative standing in his class was, but I think he became a member of the Board of the *Virginia Law Review,* and he had at least one article in it, a piece which dealt with the nature and scope of police power. He drove himself very hard during this period, I am sure, and his letters sometimes complained of fatigue and nervousness. He was also frequently beset with money worries, for Virginia has never been a cheap place to go to school.

Soon after his graduation in 1930, he hung out his shingle in Bassett. I remember clearly his telling me that the first case he had involved a man who was charged with having improper license plates on his car.

I do not know much of Maury's history during the next few years. We were both busy trying to get our careers started and hence were immersed in our own affairs. Maury early gave up interest in a political career and decided to stick to law practice. It was sometime in this period that he and another lawyer won the largest award for damages ever given in Henry County. A bus had backed into a little boy and injured him severely. The award was $30,000.

The next time I saw Maury was in the summer of 1937. I had just completed my first year of full-time teaching, at the Alabama Polytechnic Institute. I had saved a little money, and I decided on a trip to the East which would permit me to visit him *en route.* I went from Kentucky by train as far as Roanoke, where he met me in his car and took me to Bassett. I remember very little of this visit except that I passed a couple of days with him. Either at this time or later in a letter he told me something which I have always cherished as a piece of wisdom. He said, "Sometimes I get vexed with people when I discover how ignorant they are of the laws they are supposed to be living under. But then I reflect that if they knew as much about the law as I do, I would be out looking for a job." I have tried to apply that to the teaching profession.

The next time I saw him was the summer of 1941. I was then completing my doctoral dissertation and was in Charlottesville. I was not taking courses in the University, but was making use of the Library, which is especially rich in the field in which I was working. One day in late July or August Maury drove up from Bassett. He showed me his old haunts at the University, and we had dinner at one of the hotels.

Another nine years elapsed before I saw him again. I had joined the faculty of the University of Chicago, but had decided to locate my mother permanently in Asheville. In the summer of 1950 we were delighted to hear from Maury that he intended making us a visit. He arrived the last week in August and we were able to put him up in the apartment we were renting at 152 Murdock Avenue. Maury had started law practice in 1930; this was 1950, and so this was the first vacation he had taken in 20 years! He remained with us a week, and we devoted most of the time to touring the Great Smokies and the Cherokee Indian Reservation. Maury took in the outdoor Indian drama "Unto These Hills" in Cherokee and seemed greatly pleased with it. In appearance he looked about as usual to me, though of course older. Mother, however, who is a very good judge of health, commented several times on his frailness.

Maury seemed so happy over his visit that he left us with the idea of making it an annual affair. Next summer, however, we were saddened to receive disturbing reports of his health. We telegraphed him to come down and spend an indefinite period with us and really recuperate, but received no reply. Eventually we learned through one of his brothers that he had had to go to the Neurological Clinic of the Duke University Hospital, where he spent some time. Maury was very reticent about matters of this kind and would never discuss it. All he ever told me was that he had reached a condition in which it was impossible for him to sleep.

In the summer of 1952 he visited us again, and we found him looking much better. Our trip was largely a "repeat" of the 1950 one. We went to the Smokies again, but this time added Fontana Village and Fontana Dam.

In '53 Maury gave us what was literally a "Grand Tour of Virginia." We met him at Boone, North Carolina, visited my old friend Cratis Williams at Appalachian State Teachers College, and thence headed north. The tour included Charlottesville and Monticello, Richmond, Colonial Williamsburg, where we saw the thrilling "The Common Glory," Yorktown, "The Northern Neck" and the birthplace of Lee, Fredericksburg, and then the Shenandoah Valley from Winchester on down. This was the summer that Maury, through volunteered financial assistance, helped me to acquire my present home in Weaverville.

In '54 we decided to "do" Tennessee and Kentucky. Leaving Weaverville one morning, we reached Harrogate, Tennessee, in the afternoon and spent several hours revisiting LMU. Maury even climbed the hill to Grant-Lee Hall and peered into the room he had occupied there. We were intrigued with the thought that this was the 30th anniversary of the matriculation of both of us at LMU. Next day we drove on to Lexington, Kentucky, where Mother visited a few relatives. Then on to the Bardstown area and finally to Mammoth Cave, which we reached about sundown of what must have been one of the hottest days Kentucky ever had. Next morning Maury and I took one of the conducted tours of the cave. We returned home via Oak Ridge and Knoxville.

In early spring or summer of 1955 I suggested to Maury that since both of us were loyal Confederates, it was absolutely incumbent upon us to see South Carolina, and especially Charleston. He assented readily, and so this was the scene of the '55 tour. On the way we toured Kings Mountain Battlefield. We were all fascinated with Charleston, where we put up at the beautiful Ft. Sumter. Maury and I took the tour to the Fort itself, drove out to Sullivan's Island, scene of Poe's famous "The Gold Bug," and saw many of the sights of Charleston. On our way back we passed through Summerville, which was very interesting to Mother, because she had come there from Kentucky to recuperate from an operation sixty years before. When we got back home I remember Maury's saying it would take "two stout niggers and a mule" to unload the car, for we had accumulated so much in the way of Spanish moss, pine cones, sea shells, curios, etc.

This was the last trip of any length that we made. The next year, 1956, he made his visit at the usual time, but he was feeling a little under par and disinclined to a long drive. Moreover, Mother was suffering from a stomach upset and decided not to go with us this time. What we did was take the "Waterfall Tour." In the region around Brevard and Highlands there are eight or ten beautiful waterfalls, and we spent a day seeing most of these. Maury remarked at the time that it rested him to look at falling water. I have since thought that this was expressive of some deep inner tiredness. He visited the doctor once or twice while here in connection with some kind of nasal allergy. The last time I ever saw him was when he turned his car east on Reems Creek Road to get onto the Blue Ridge Parkway and return to Bassett.

We tried to get Maury to rest more on these visits, but we never succeeded. I got the impression that he had really forgotten how to rest. He had been so industrious all his life that he had come to look upon inactivity as something irrational. On the tours he insisted on doing all the driving himself; he often drove long distances; and when we were in a sight-seeing area, he insisted on seeing everything, and that thoroughly. Thus his vacations were changes, but they were not rests. He drove himself too hard, and I feel that this was the principal reason for his untimely passing in 1957.

SECTION TWO

The Critique of Modernity

These writings focus on modern American culture and the reasons for its decline. Most expound or extend the views elaborated in Weaver's first published book, Ideas Have Consequences. *They are presented here in two groups.*

Included in the first group are five essays written at widely different levels of abstraction and presented here in chronological order. The principal reason for their disparity is that three were originally prepared as speeches or public lectures. The first, "Humanism in an Age of Science," was presented at a campus Newman Club meeting in Chicago in the late 1940s and published posthumously in a version edited by Robert Hamlin.[1] *It is followed by two polished essays, "Individuality and Modernity," which was first presented at a conference on "Individuality and Personality" held in Princeton, New Jersey, in September 1956, and subsequently revised for publication in* Essays on Individuality, *a volume of conference proceedings, and "Life without Prejudice," which had the honor of being selected for publication as the lead article in the first issue of* Modern Age. Relativism and the Crisis of Our Times *is the text of a speech delivered at a conference sponsored by the Intercollegiate Society of Individualists (ISI) that was probably held in Chicago in the fall of 1960. It was published in pamphlet*

---

1. Contrary to the claim in Hamlin's "Editorial Note" at the beginning of the essay, there is no evidence that this is a manuscript Weaver "was apparently readying for publication" at the time of his death.

form the following year by ISI. Finally, "Reflections of Modernity" is the text of an address delivered at Brigham Young University on May 15, 1961, and published by the university later that year. It should be noted that Weaver declined a request to submit the speech for publication in Modern Age *on the grounds that it was "prepared specifically for an undergraduate audience, and I fear it is a little too undergraduate-ish."*[2]

The second group consists of a number of shorter writings—mostly book reviews—which examine specific aspects of the decline of American culture. The first two items, a 1950 review of Commager's The American Mind *for the* Commonweal *and an "Introduction" to a 1955 edition of* Pragmatism *by William James, focus on the defects of philosophical pragmatism. They are followed by a fragment of an unfinished essay entitled "Puritanism and Determinism." Probably written near the end of Weaver's life as the beginning of a chapter on Emerson for his book on the contrasting cultures of the American North and South, it argues that there is a "necessary progression" from the views of the Puritans of the 1600s to those of the scientific determinists of the late 1800s. It is published here for the first time. The remainder of the section is made up of six reviews of books dealing with science, Weaver's letter to the* New York Times Book Review *replying to Howard Mumford Jones' review of* Ideas Have Consequences, *and six reviews of books devoted to various aspects of culture and modern life.*

2. Letter from Richard Weaver to David Collier dated July 22, 1961. Located in the correspondence files of the Intercollegiate Studies Institute and quoted by permission.

Humanism in an Age of Science[1]

EDITED BY ROBERT HAMLIN

Editorial Note: The essay presented below has been edited from an untitled, undated typescript of a lecture which Weaver delivered to a meeting of the Newman Club at the University of Chicago shortly after the end of World War II. It is one of the many manuscripts he was apparently readying for publication at the time of his sudden death in April, 1963.

As the title is meant to indicate, Weaver was deeply concerned with the difficulties of maintaining one's humaneness in an age growing steadily more brutal. This problem is no less significant today. Clearly, the lecture speaks with pungent relevance to a much wider audience than the one which heard it.

The original typescript contained numerous revisions made in Weaver's handwriting. These have been incorporated into the text, while explanatory remarks and asides which seemed to interrupt the continuity of thought have been deleted. In those instances where the spoken word transposed awkwardly or unclearly to print, ideas have been recast. Every effort has been made, however, to preserve the "pressure" of Weaver's style, for as he once said: "It has always been my habit to write out a lecture in full because it is my conviction that a lecture should not be a speaker's random thoughts; it should rather be a distillation of his considered opinion."

I wish to acknowledge Mr. and Mrs. Louis H. T. Dehmlow for first bringing this lecture to my attention. For permission to publish it, I extend grateful appreciation to the late Kendall Beaton and to his wife Polly Weaver Beaton.

—Robert Hamlin
University of Kansas

---

1. Richard M. Weaver, "Humanism in an Age of Science," ed. Robert Hamlin. *Intercollegiate Review*, 7/1–2, Fall 1970, 11–18.

When I speak of humanism, I do not mean, as some in the past have meant by this term, an alternative to religion. *Humanism,* as I intend to use it, is something authorized by religion, but acting on a lower plane, on a plane of the prudential, if you will, but still on a plane where man is regarded as a special creation with a special vocation in life. That vocation is to be his better self, to enjoy his faculties, to live in a happy society—in short, to be humane. All religion worthy of the name implies and encourages a humanism, without at all being enclosed in or exhausted by that humanism. There is a kind of art of life which takes into account man's relations to his maker, to the great phenomenal world, and to the world as constituted by his fellows. The question I want to ask at the outset is whether we have the same chance to practice that art that other periods and peoples have had.

Now, of course, when one begins to talk about the amount of happiness or good existing in any given society, he lays himself open to attack from several quarters. There are those who maintain that the amount of good existing increases steadily as time goes on. There are those who maintain that it decreases steadily. And there are those who maintain that the amount of good is always constant, and that our impressions of increases and decreases are pure illusion. About the first, I would say that they are naive or insensitive; about the second that there is probably something wrong with their ontology; and about the third that they are despairing men who leave no room for free will or deliberate improvement, but represent us as caught up in a meaningless dance.

I take the position that the amount of positive good does vary from time to time and from group to group, and that the relative amount is closely dependent upon the amount of intelligence and good will that men exercise. This is just another way of saying that we are in great measure the authors of our own fortunes and that there is no decent refuge in either complacency or self-pity.

While this is true, it is also true that our own case is relatively hard. We have one of the toughest assignments in trying to remain humane that any age has had, and I hope you will indulge me if I describe things pretty much as I see them. There are two circumstances that I believe create our difficulties. The first is a mentality; the second is a great fact of the objective world. Discussing these involves a critique of present-day science. And since science is up for canonization, I intend to play the role of the devil's advocate. I am going to say the worst and meanest things I can about science.

We are all familiar with the assertion that we live in an age of science. So many times have we heard it that probably few of us pause to give the statement reflective content. When we do attempt to say more, particularly what the "science" is that dominates our world, we find ourselves looking at a program of inquiry, and at the solid or tangible results of that program. About the inquiry itself I shall say what may seem a dreadful thing, but I propose to offer my grounds. It seems to me that this inquiry reflects a habit of mind which must disquiet us. The habit appears to rest on a supposition that if you *can* do a thing, you *must* do it. And I can characterize that only as an infantile mentality. It is like the stage of boyhood one passes through during which one feels that if he can chin himself twenty times, he must do it; that if he can throw a rock across a certain stream, he must do it. The criterion then is not whether you should do a thing, but whether you can do it. I am afraid that much of the vast scientific activity which goes on about us is predicated on nothing profounder than that. There is a real bite in Winston Churchill's description of science as "organized curiosity."

But this attitude that if you can do a thing you must do it is one that civilized societies outgrew, and I should like to develop this proposition more seriously by approaching it through another route. Those familiar with Plato's *Phaedrus* will recall an early scene in that dialogue, before the argument settles down to a single theme and while Socrates and Phaedrus are exchanging what might be called pleasantries. The two are outside the city walls looking for a shady place to rest. As they walk along, Phaedrus is reminded that this is the place where, in the myth, Boreas is said to have carried off Oreithyia. Phaedrus then asks Socrates whether he believes the tale is true. The answer which Socrates gives has always seemed to me one of the most meaningful things in this wonderful dialogue because it pits scientific rationalism against humanism, and humanism carries off things with a high hand.

He begins his answer by remarking that many tales of this kind are open to a sort of rationalization. That is to say, one may substantiate a scientific explanation by stating that a young maiden was playing on some rocks when a blast of north wind pushed her over; and that when she had died in that manner, she was said to have been carried off by Boreas. "I think such explanations are very pretty in general," says Socrates, "but are the inventions of a very clever and laborious and not altogether enviable man. . . ." This sort of explanation produces only a boorish type of wisdom—the Greek phrase might be rendered "a countrified sort of wisdom"—and Socrates regards it as beside the point. "I have no time for that kind of investigation," he says—if I may translate loosely here—"because I don't yet understand myself. Why should I occupy my time with matters like that while I still do not understand whether I am a monster more complicated and more furious than Typhon, or a gentler and simpler creature to whom a divine and quiet lot is given by nature."

This statement of Socrates contains the essence of humanism. What it asks is merely this: Can I afford to spend all my time—or even much of it—studying the rocks and the trees while I still don't know what my nature is and therefore cannot be sure what use I would make of these studies? This is the *locus classicus* of the principle that we do not find the secret of man's life in the study of things.

Modern man has obviously taken the alternative that Socrates rejected. He has made the most prodigious researches into nature and has come up with terrifying discoveries. To use an illustration which comes very close to home, he has unlocked the secret of atomic energy without waiting to make certain whether he is a creature crueller and more furious than the monster Typhon. The first use made of this great discovery was to drop it on the heads of other men. (The parallel is so close that I cannot refrain from mentioning that Typhon in the legend was chiefly notorious for having slain his brother.)

What this illustrates to me is that after all the labors of the social scientists, we now know less about human nature than did the men of Socrates' day or the men of the Middle Ages. They recognized that man needs to be protected against himself; and they were interested in setting up internal safeguards. We seem to think that only external safeguards, in the form of bastions and air fleets directed against other men, are needful. The Greeks and the men of the Middle Ages made their failures; but they seem not so egregious as the failures we have made and the failures we may be facing, because our theory of the human being has simply ceased to be candid. It is no longer candid because it will not recognize that man has a bad nature too. This is not our whole nature, but it is a part of our nature which has to be looked after sharply. Humanism studies man as expressed through his whole nature, including his motivation; and that is why it seems to some now, as it seemed to Socrates that day in Athens, to have a prior place in the course of inquiry.

While we are on the subject of the proper study for man, let me cite a corollary fact about scientific development. Is it not a perturbing consideration that scientific progress seems to get its greatest impetus from war? Why should this be so? Taken by itself, is not this congruence of mutual human slaughter and great scientific progress, as it is called, a rather frightening conjunction of events? Among the ancients this conjunction of truths would have been regarded as an omen. Everywhere today we read about products and techniques which came into being *thanks* to wartime studies in science. Does not this raise some question about the motivation of science? If its greatest efforts are always seen in times of hatred and mass hysteria, is there not some small ground for suspecting that the very essence of this undertaking is exploitative and aggressive? And what we may be justified in asking is whether things created in that kind of crucible are in the long run good for us. Their intent is so narrow, so special, so ill-inspired. One thing we can certainly say: They are not made in contemplation of human happiness. As to whether they can be turned to the ends of human happiness—well, I think the burden of proof is on the devisers.

Now being a piece of a logician, I do not contend that this concurrence proves that one is the cause of the other. But this sort of conjunction repeated is the kind of analogy that leads to the more serious kind of investigation. Moreover, there are probably other aspects to indicate that science in its nature is not contemplative, but aggressive. Bacon's statement that knowledge is power, which he meant in some such sense as this, is one of the most dubious aphorisms ever handed down. It leaves hanging in the air the whole question of power for what.

A pamphlet issued by the Office of War Information during World War II bore the subtitle "Science at War." The first time I saw it I felt "How anomalous." Science cannot be at war. And certainly if someone were to conceive the slogan "Art at War," there comes at once a great outpouring of aesthetic theory to prove that art cannot go to war, or that such part of it as does go ceases by that act to be art. But the code of science is different, and the more I reflect upon the subtitle, the more I suspect that it is one of those locutions through which the truth slips out while we are trying to say something else. For the very fact that science has declared an implacable sort of warfare upon the unknown, upon space and time, makes us again wonder whether its aims are not hostile to our peace. It tends to set up a world of such brittle relationships that if one part gets a sharp knock, the whole flies to pieces. One certain result we can see is an increasing rigidification of our world. If there is a sneeze in Siberia, it disrupts something in Patagonia. The shock absorbers have been removed. We used to look upon space and time as cushions which protected us against phenomena we did not wish to intrude. But science seems to have declared war on both, and both are being cut down, so that everything has a new proximity.

Here I would suggest that a mind to which everything is present at once is a mind gone many steps toward madness. As human beings, we can't stand that kind of thing. We can't stand to think of all our troubles at once, or even of all the things we have to do next week at once. To do so unsettles us or makes us frantic. But this is what the new structure given our world by technology tends to make us do. An uprising in Indo-China or Malaya jolts as severely in Washington as it does in Hanoi or Singapore. And this is true, we are told, because science has made the world one. Things are put upon an all or nothing basis. We must have permanent and indivisible peace, or we must have universal war. This sort of rigor, this sort of spectacular inclusiveness, appeals to some natures, but I question whether it is a healthful development. I suspect rather that true union is through a kind of grace, and not through an unbearable tension. This sort of unity that science, at least in its applied version, is giving the world, is the unity of a rigid mechanism.

I have already introduced the second division of my topic, which is the tangible products of this great program of inquiry, and what they do to us as well as for us. Here I intend to focus upon the machine as a special construct of science, and upon its reputed benefits. There is no need for me to make a canvass of these. Every speaker who dilates upon the theme of progress reminds us of how many machines we have, of how the face of the earth has been changed through the application of mechanical power, of how modern life is sustained by a great network of energies. I shall merely summarize and remind you that we do live in a mechanized world and that many circumstances of that world cannot be explained apart from the fact.

Yet there is one aspect of the machine's existence which I think has not been sufficiently noticed by social philosophers. This is what I shall call the *moral* role of the machine. Here I seem to be dealing in anomalies myself. The machine is not supposed to have a moral nature, and in the conventional way of thinking, of course, it does not have. The conventional approach is to represent the machine as an innocent, almost as an injured innocent, since man has obviously misused it under many circumstances. The argument runs that the machine is a completely impartial agent. One can use it for good or for bad. It has no preference in the matter. Or, to put this into a figure, the science of ballistics along with some other sciences will tell you how to make a gun, but it will not tell you whom to shoot with it. And the gun itself will not tell you either. Therefore, it is said, the great tragedies of our day cannot be blamed upon science and machinery, since these never fail to exhibit a perfect impartiality.

This argument seems valid up to a point, but it leaves out one consideration, and the omission of that permits too simple a conclusion. The argument says, to repeat, that the machine does not have a character and hence cannot be good or bad. It cannot be principal or accessory in the acts where it has a part.

Now it is true that the machine does not have character, but it does have *being*. And being itself may be thought of as a kind of force.

Allow me to try to make plain what I mean here by drawing on a concept from the field of military strategy. When military strategists go about planning the defense of a country, I understand that they speak of the armies, the fleets, and whatever the other countries may possess as "forces in being." And these forces in being, although they are inactive and although they are the possessions of a nation at peace, nevertheless determine policy. That is to say, measures have to be devised which will take into account these "forces in being" even though they seem to have a purely existential status.

This means that a "force in being" cannot be treated as if it had no influence on the course of affairs. Or, if our word "influence" in its common acceptation does not quite state the idea, maybe I could say "effluence"—which means an outpouring, an outgiving of something. And what I am preparing to ask at this point is whether we must not regard the mechanical creations of science as a "force in being." It is easy enough to say that they are neutral with regard to us, that they do not affect our course one way or another. But is this realistic in the sense of admitting all the factors that are at work? Does it take into account the *effluence*?

We might use the automobile for a simple illustration. Most of us who have had the experience of owning an automobile have found that the simple existence of this piece of private property makes it relatively hard for us to get enough exercise. Not that the automobile has a moral character, not that it enters into a dialectic with us and tells us that we ought to ride when we know we have only three blocks to go. But there it is, sitting by the curb, such a masterpiece of ingenuity that we are perhaps a little proud to be associated with it. Its simple being is a standing temptation to use it. The fact that it is there seems to induce us to find additional opportunities for its use.

Now what is true of the automobile in this everyday illustration may be broadly true of the great world of machinery created by technology. Certainly it does not tell us to use it for idle or wasteful or destructive purposes. But again, there it is, a force at hand, and the very least we can say is that it imposes an added strain upon human nature. I am afraid this is seen especially in the case of weapons of war, where the temptation to see how well they will work, once they have been created, is almost overwhelming. If then what I have outlined is even measurably so, then our living in this world which science has created calls for more heroism than other ages have demanded, and it is at least well to know what the requirements are.

Not only does this science-created world act as a deflector of specifically human activity, there is yet another result, one which I am not able to analyze very clearly, but which I can indicate by pointing to certain phenomena that give cause for concern.

When the proponents of science feel they are on the defensive, they recite the things which the various sciences are able to cure, either wholly or partially. Actually the list runs from cancer to psychopathology. Our retort to this must be: "Why are there so many things today that need curing? Has the world just become more cure-conscious? Or do we actually have more forms of degeneracy, mental and physical?" Generally, I believe it is a bad sign when a man feels that he needs a cure. Is it not possible that we are curing things that we are causing, or that with our cures we are only running after things that we have started and are trying to hold back? If a world which is chiefly distinguished by its precariousness produces a great number of psychopathic individuals, and scientific techniques can cure say thirty percent of these, where is the profit? My point is simply that we should be as interested in why so many cures are found needful as we are in the brilliance of the curative techniques. I have heard it plausibly argued by an ingenious man that cancer is morally caused, and that the moral cause has something to do with the guilt complex of specifically modern man. I certainly would not attempt to settle this proposition. But taking facts apart from suppositions, here is an instance in which degeneracy has kept well ahead of the most strenuous efforts of the keenest scientific brains. To put it in my way, the need for cure is outstripping the cure available. The same is probably true of psychopathology, of suicide, of divorce, and of other afflictions of the social body. Technique, however brilliant, is an employment of means. Perhaps our error is the ignoring of first and final causes, which cannot be studied without some conception of the whole man.

I have now spent a good many minutes playing the devil's advocate against science. It is not a very fashionable thing to do, and I hope I have not appeared contumacious. Science is with us as a great empirical fact. We all make use of it to some extent, and anyone who does so much as wear eyeglasses must ask himself how well he could get along without it. It certainly is not going to be banished by one short polemic like this. We shall continue to come to terms with it. Even its devotees and followers have the necessity, sometimes personally arduous, I believe, of adapting themselves to its progressive changes.

My final consideration must therefore be: What is the best means of living with science? I do not necessarily assume here a hostility, for even where the attitude is friendly, problems do persist. The city of Chicago is perhaps the foremost example in this country of a great complex situation produced by science and technology. At the same time it is true that the leading impression many people have of Chicago is an impression of brutality. Indeed, one of her poets has celebrated this as a virtue, but I do not believe that is the considered feeling of most of us. Rather, we are perplexed over how to adjust to it.

As one looks over the scene and tries to decide his policy, two alternatives are almost certain to suggest themselves. Either one can immerse himself in the element and strive to be just as brutal as it is; or he can detach himself, cutting down to the minimum his point of contact with it. That is to say, he can try to fight it by its own means, or he can run from the fight.

I think a little reflection is needed to show that both of these have unacceptable or certainly undesirable consequences. By trying to compete in brutality, you make yourself a brute, and this man is commanded not to do. Brutality is in its essence a lack of discrimination, a lack of regard for distinctions and susceptibilities and rights. It is the action that smashes or levels or obliterates while remaining contemptuous of qualifying circumstances. This is the bestial attitude and the antithesis of humanity. On the cultural level it is fatal to what we respect as the humanities. But detachment too, while it seems to preserve intellect, draws bad things in its train. It results in isolation, decrease of sympathy, eventual loss perhaps of any vital idea of brotherhood; and it is certainly likely to engender pride. The man who is self-consciously perched above the fray comes to have a sort of disdain for those who are wrestling with the world's intractability, and that too tends to be inhumane in the way that it divides us off. We are all here to be proved, and it seems that a man should not try to save himself by individual withdrawal.

If then he is to mix in the world but not be brutal, if he is to preserve his integrity but not abstract himself too far from others, he must have some kind of guide or measure, must he not? He must, in short, look for some standard of humanity. Now one way to do this is to make a survey of history and to gather up the best that has been thought and said, as Matthew Arnold exhorted us to do. By this method humanism becomes inference and generalization about human behavior in its historical composite. But humanism so conceived cannot serve as an inspiriting goal. On the contrary it collapses from the fallacy that man is the measure of all things. The explanation seems to be that if you limit attention to the best of human achievement, you introduce a *concrete* ideal. But concrete ideals are never legislative or normative. Our opponents can always attack us, if we take such a stand, by saying that one age has as much authority as another. Why, they will argue, should we not take our human objectives from the present age? We exist just as truly as did any past age. Let the Greeks be the Greeks; we will be the modern Americans. The difficulty arises because one concrete ideal cannot sit in judgment on another concrete ideal. Before we can have the idea of relative evaluation at all, we must have a *tertium quid*, a third essence, an ideal ideal, as it were. This is why a humanism which is merely historical-minded can be learned, but cannot in the true sense be critical. Such humanism is, as I once heard a clever man express it, horse-power without the horse. Now where do we look for the horse?

Unquestionably this is the point where humanism has to seek transcendental help. Such help is indeed implied by the problem we posed for ourselves: namely, how do we practice a humanism amid circumstances tending to defeat our humanity? The answer must contain an element of prescription. Nor is there anything in this approach to outrage our basic definitions if you will grant that the human being cannot be fully defined without some reference to final ends. He can be anthropologically surveyed; he can be culturally appreciated; but these accounts merely describe him on certain levels of his existence. As Cardinal Newman said explicitly of his ideal of the gentleman: It is an attractive role with many incidental benefits, but it does not exhaust the vocation of man. Indeed, it is not really comprehensible until it is validated by something higher. In the same way, humanistic activity has to be measured, pointed up, directed by some superior validating ideal. Not long ago on this campus I heard a speaker exclaim, after expressing impatience with all this transcendental moonshine, "Why can't we just be good human beings!" The reply would be that one of the attributes of the good human being is some kind of response to the whole of existence, and that this response, however you care to figure it, lays some kind of obligation upon the respondent. Since humanism, as I have tried to show, cannot carry its own measure, it has to solicit that measure from some other source. Some higher point of view seems necessary to gather up the implications of humanism.

We find ourselves up against great pressures today in our effort to maintain a humane life and to cultivate what we rejoice in as the humanities. In this effort, we need to know how far to go and in what way. We also need a little moral bucking-up. The impetus of the trend is against us. Descriptive comparisons will not suffice, because they will merely pit this age and its ideals against other ages and their ideals. In view of the very formidable size and weight of our own, it would probably win out in any such contest. What we do, then, is look to an ultimate source of value and judgment, one of whose prescriptions is that we retain the image in which we were made. It is this ideal of the human under the aegis of something higher which seems to me to provide the strongest counterpressure against the fragmentation and barbarization of our world.

Individuality and Modernity[1]

In a world which has largely accepted "modernism" as its slogan, the status of personality becomes a matter of concern to all who think reflectively and benevolently about the human being. There is an uncomfortable basis of truth in a remark I once heard made by a philosopher: as soon as something begins to disappear, we put up signs proclaiming the virtue of it. The very fact of a symposium arranged to discuss the future of individuality may be taken wryly as a sign that its prospects are poor. But sometimes men disvalue a thing only because they have forgotten how good it is comparatively. In such cases a fresh look should lead to a revival of faith and also uncover possibilities for preserving what we would be the poorer for losing.

What I understand by "individuality" is the personality vis-à-vis society and the state. Individuality is the sign of the *persona,* and it always finds its claims in the higher sanctions of the latter. Therefore, it seems necessary to say something about the true nature of personality. In what immediately follows, I shall describe a few of its aspects as they appear to an observer from the humanities. If these do not add up to a definition, at least they may help to determine in what sort of soil and climate personality, in the sense desiderated, is most likely to thrive and be respected.

It seems a threshold fact that personality is some kind of integration. The individual whom we regard as having authentic personality appears to possess a center, and everything that he does is in relation to this. When such a person performs an act, no part of his being seems uninvolved; what happens on the outer circumference is duly controlled by the integrating center. We sense, sometimes with a feeling of envy, that this individual is a unitary being and thus "in possession of himself." Of course, there are poorly inte-

1. In Felix Morley (ed.), *Essays on Individuality.* Philadelphia: University of Pennsylvania Press, 1958, 63–81.

grated or disintegrated "personalities," but these we classify as unformed or degenerate just because they fall short in this property. The true personality is a psychic unity, preserving its identity and giving a sort of thematic continuity to the acts of the individual.

I have observed in many instances that different personalities possess different powers of insight into matters. A subject which is obscure to one person may be clear and understandable to another, even when the "IQ" measurement of the second is inferior to that of the first. A type of sentience open to one individual is simply closed to another. The older I grow, the more disinclined I am to disparage mental processes which at first strike me as naïve, foolish, or even illogical. I can recall more than one instance in which an individual who impressed me as quite naïve proved to have a better grasp of a situation than I had. Certainly some of the finest creations of civilization have been produced by persons who were regarded by their associates as simple-minded in some respects. The mysterious formula of the personality may fit the individual for unique insight and achievement in one direction while leaving him below average in others. This is the real reason for insisting that every man's view should have a chance for a respectful hearing. The Creator seems to have given different individuals different ways of cogently apprehending reality.

This selective relation of the person to the totality may suggest that personality is the final ethical tie-up of the individual. It is the special form taken by the individual in expressing the values he has recognized. When we speak of "the sacredness of the personality," as we sometimes do, we mean just this reflection through the person of ideas of the true and the good. The fact that there are as many different expressions as there are personalities need not mean that the reality is miscellaneous. It may mean rather that we are faced with a religious concept, not open to the kinds of noetic formulations that serve on other levels of knowledge. Any other conception of personality leaves it a mere aggregate of peculiarities, and the cultivation of the idiosyncratic is idiocy.

An indirect proof of this religious conception is found in the ethical maxim that the greatest wrong one can do to a person is to treat him as if he were only an instrument. To treat him as an instrument is to treat him as though he had no vision of the good to express through his particular stances and actions. There are forms of regimentation, some in labor, some in military service, and today perhaps a good many elsewhere, which the general sense regards as brutalizing because they strike down and keep suppressed any motion the individual might make toward personal discrimination and evaluation.

Our reasoning will not admit that the entire worth of a man is in his instrumental servitude. If man has a right to personality, along with the other rights that are being claimed for him today, he must have an area of freedom to express, with personal emphasis, his acknowledgment of the good. The personality is a morally oriented unit which has a duty to maintain itself against many forms of social coercion and also against the sometimes greater danger of complacence. This means a state of independence which makes the battle for personality a basic phase of the battle for freedom.

I am in agreement with those who believe that personality is on the defensive today, and I would go so far as to say that in some cases it is the object of deliberate, directed assault. That is an accusation. To justify it I shall name a few of the forces that seem to me most inimical to personality and shall discuss their impact.

There is no question that technology and industrialism are making it difficult for personality. Whatever may have been the designs of the authors of the Baconian revolution, they have produced a world in which it is increasingly hard to be human in the normative sense. Man is an organism, not a mechanism; and the mechanical pacing of his life does harm to his human responses, which naturally follow a kind of free rhythm. As a small but significant illustration: I have seen an interesting conversation terminated because a member of the party remembered that the parking meter by his car had about run out.

Most of us today have to move to the sounds of bells and whistles and to changes of light; we have to keep ourselves tense so as not to miss these mechanical signals. There can be disciplinary value in a certain amount of mechanical pacing, but ours has gone too far, and servitude to the machine today involves not just those who work in factories, but the great majority. These pressures against human personality, however, are visible to all and have been much discussed, so I shall pass on to some insidious forces, which may be all the more dangerous for being subtle and sometimes concealed.

First among these is the attack upon memory. There has never been another milieu, as far as my knowledge goes, which has sought to make forgetting a virtue. "Forget it" is a password of the time. If people make a mistake or commit a sin (to use an antiquated phrase), they are told to "Forget it." People are praised in our organs of greatest circulation for discarding all baggage of the past and conforming to a "fast-changing world." Those who live with a burden of memory are smiled at amiably, when they are not frowned upon darkly, as impediments in the way of progress. Everything is supposed to be of the moment and for the moment. In our educational programs, history, which used to be a very sobering discipline, has been dropped in favor of various scientistic studies of the human record, and that passionate sense of historical reality which is at the base of much cultural achievement is actually discouraged. The mood of the individual and of the group has become ahistorical.

I cannot see this disparagement of all memory as anything but an attack upon the mind, which must have adverse effects upon the personality. According to Joseph Jastrow, "Disorders of personality involve more or less disorganization of the memory continuum and of the group of elements which enter into normal consciousness of personal identity."[2] The human being must live in a present that is enriched and sustained by a past; it is his experience stored up in the form of memory which enables him to be something more than an automaton responding to sensory impingements.

It is equally true that a man's personality is a product in large part of the memory of things he has done, decisions he has made, with their consequences, and so on. Personality cannot be the creation of a moment, for one of the things we predicate of it, with most confidence, is its uniformity. If Sam Jones is known to have a certain kind of personality, we say that in a given situation he will behave in one fashion rather than another, which might be chosen by an individual of different personality. But unless Jones carries with him a consciousness of what he has been, we can have no ground for predicting the nature of his future choices.

By the same token, without this faculty of memory there can be no such thing as conscience. Conscience is essentially a recollection or pulling together of our ideas of what we are, what the things we deal with are, and the structure of values to which we have in our inmost feelings subscribed. It is a present awareness of many things which no longer have present ex-

---

2. Joseph Jastrow, "Personality," *Baldwin's Dictionary of Philosophy and Psychology* (New York: Peter Smith, 1940), II, 284.

istence. Thus, when an individual consults his conscience, he refers to a complex of remembered facts, insights, and ideas of obligation—all of which by their very nature cannot be manufactured out of a present moment. Conscience thus requires a re-collection of the self, a thinking of who and what we are before performing an act, and this is why meditation and contemplation are enjoined by most religions.

The craze for "living in the present" is related to the fact that the present is empirical time. It is the time we experience, if by experience we mean sensation. The great wave of empiricism which has engulfed modern thinking has had, as one of its logical effects, this discrediting of memory and denigration of the past. Its influence upon our very mode of thinking can be very grave.

Consider for a moment what it means to invite the individual to "live in the present." It means asking him to give up his habit of associating things, and indeed, to give up having any but the most superficial ideas. William James points out that people who remember best are those who have concept systems. A fact is rememberable when an individual is able to make "multiple associations" with it. The concept serves as a kind of frame upon which he hangs this and that item. When a particular fact is called to mind, it may suggest the framework and the framework in turn may suggest other facts.

What I particularly fear is that this attack upon memory may be a concealed attack upon all conceptualization, more especially since intellect is now regarded by a school of educational theory as "undemocratic" in its relation with the physical body. When we advise people not to remember, we may be advising them in effect not to conceptualize. In other words, "Don't think about it." Let the present trend of sensory experience determine the attitude and the decision. Today's mass journalism, with its lively propagation, its weak reflection, and its addiction to sensational data, lends powerful encouragement to the habit.

It is hard to see how this cult of forgetting, or of living entirely in the present, can avoid weakening the integration which develops personality. There is truth in the saying that a man is part of all that he has met—and I pointedly include here the choices he has made with reference to the problems that he has met. All of these experiences, active and passive, physical and intellectual, coalesce in what I have been calling his center, but what at other times has been called his soul. When the individual destroys his memory, he destroys in part his soul.

The fact that one has this kind of center means that one has created something as a result of his effort in living. And this something, resting on "the presence of the past in the present," to recall a useful phrase of T. S. Eliot's, gives one a defined character, or a self. If a man cannot remember what he did day before yesterday, how can he know what he ought to do day after tomorrow? And if, on principle, he should remember what he did day before yesterday, he should remember whatever of significance he did a year ago and five years ago, for there is no arbitrary point at which the past becomes dead.

It is even questionable whether those who claim to "live in the present" are getting more out of the present than anyone else. I agree entirely with C. G. Jung that denial of the past is by no means the same thing as consciousness of the present, and that "the really modern man is often found among those who call themselves old-fashioned."[3] This is because those who have well stored minds are able to live more knowingly in the present. They are constantly making multiple associations, and their very erudition, which memory makes possible, becomes a means of wider sensibility. The idea of progress itself involves retrospection and accurate comparison. The pseudo-modern, who is an enemy of the past, is actually unable to understand the nature of progress.

At the same time that this pseudo-modern temper is warring against memory, it is also warring against status, with a similar harmful result to the personality. We might call it a two-pronged offensive aimed at the same goal.

I have not thoroughly tested the representation I am now going to make, but it seems to me that man is happiest (in a sense which would include spiritual happiness) when he enjoys a kind of equipoise of status and function, or of being and action. His status at any moment enables him to know what he is (or who he is) and his function keeps him in relation with the process of human activity. In other words, the man of developed personality and achieved well-being *is* somebody and can *do* something. When these

3. C. G. Jung, *Modern Man in Search of a Soul* (New York: Harcourt, Brace, 1933), p. 229.

two properties are in balance in the individual, the ensuing condition can be described by that beautiful word *euphoria*.

An excessive inclination toward either status or function is upsetting. To rely wholly upon one's status, to stay wrapped up in it and suppose that it answers every need, leads to debility and sterility. It is a condition often observed in decadent aristocracies, and in any individual who has long been over-protected by status. It is not against this, however, that the present age needs warning, for its excess lies at the other end. We have gone to the extreme of attaching importance only to function, while deriding the idea of status. The current feeling is that the measure of man is what he does, and everybody is to be judged by results, like baseball players or salesmen. At first glance this has a plausible look; it seems honest whereas the other does not, and indeed there are situations in which measurement by accomplishment only is a very good corrective. We like to see presumptuous or unfounded status rebuked, and "functional" man seems to contribute more to the production of things.

A more circumspective inquiry, however, will show that the idea of status, while certainly capable of abuse, is an important element in one's psychic well-being. It is natural and it is right for a man to wish to be seen as something more than he is at a random moment. He wishes to be known as an individual, and individuality requires historicity. If he has by effort and sacrifice won himself a position among men, that position is part of his being; when you touch him, you touch it. When you address him, you are not addressing merely the externals of indifferently preserved flesh; you are addressing the man within, who has achieved a *state* of being. At some point in each life, owing to the inevitable ravages of time, one's functioning efficiency is lowered. We do not subtract from the individual's honor in society because he can no longer run a hundred yards in ten seconds, or perform the labor that he could at thirty, or write poetry with the passion of his youth. Rather, his achievements are listed after his name, and he is, so to speak, emeritus.

But one of the main tendencies of modernism, if I mistake it not, is to discount accumulated status, and to insist that the only worth is that which is present and demonstrable. The philosophy of instrumentalism has lent theoretical support to this notion.

The harm that is done to the individual thereby is this: every person needs to have a sense of his place, or what is often called a sense of belonging. A sure knowledge of status, I think, confers this more than does anything else. Much of the subconscious anxiety and feeling of lostness from which many people suffer today results from this broadscale attempt to do away with status, which is like doing away with home. Home is the place where our status is known and duly respected. Change for its own sake, and function as the sole criterion, have brought about a condition of mobility such that many people no longer feel that they have a place, physical or spiritual. I am inclined to think that pure function or activity, without a backdrop of status, is meaningless. The small boy who puts on a cowboy suit or a fireman's helmet shows that he wants to function as something.

Just as the individual requires a balance of status and function for his real happiness, so it appears that he requires a balance of outer and inner life. Part of his life has a public orientation, but part of it does not. He has a private self that looks inward, and he should be able to feel with some distinctness the difference between public and private roles. It strikes me that those eighteenth century individuals who wrote letters to the newspapers, signed "Publius" or something like that, were giving expression to this difference. When the writer appeared before the public in the common interest, he was conscious of stepping outside his private considerations and entering into another capacity, of assuming a posture. The rest of the time he was his own man, with his thoughts and feelings reserved for himself.

Whatever barrier made this delicacy possible has long since been broken down. It is now felt that the individual's entire life is subject to public report and review. Any claim to privacy is viewed as a form of exclusiveness, to be denied in the interest of an onrushing democracy.

When a feeling becomes as pervasive as this now is, it finds many manifestations. It affects, for example, even the architecture of our houses. We have all noted the vogue of picture windows, which leave the family livingroom open to full view and appraisal of the world. Even the interiors of modern houses are so designed as to make it impossible for the individual to withdraw and find privacy. The traditional refuge of "a room of one's own," upstairs or to the rear, is no more. All must be visible and together in "the democratic way of life." Evidences like this are often more conclusive as to the real trend of mentality than what we see reflected in our newspapers and magazines.

One of the more extraordinary invasions of individual privacy is the modern income tax. I am aware that this example will appear ludicrous to some, yet I am convinced that it has a very serious side. If we take a detached view and realize the extent to which it places everybody under surveillance, we are amazed at what it assumes. I am familiar with the arguments for it on political and humanitarian grounds. What I am pointing out is that this tax makes the individual's entire economic and financial life subject to annual government audit. It is just as if we were all criminals out on parole, required once a year to file an affidavit of our doings before a public official. The fact to be pondered is that arguments against the income tax based on the right to privacy would be dismissed as trivial or irrelevant. The claim to privacy would simply not supply any leverage.

The decline of privacy is traceable, to the best of my perception, to a belief that man is or should be one-dimensional. There should be no depths, no recesses, no area of being that cannot be unfolded simply. Such a conception seems quite in line with other attempts to simplify man through various forms of scientific abstraction and to insist that he is "nothing but" a thing that these techniques of exposition can explain. If he were not that kind of thing, we might not be able to manipulate him, and this thought is anathema to the positivistic party. Since personality means depth and uniqueness, and even mystery, it does not flourish on a plane. The abolition of privacy does away with the very regions where personal configurations must form.

Possibly the worst result of this one-dimensional concept of the person is that it makes self-knowledge deceptively easy. In spite of the popularity enjoyed by psychology in recent decades, it may be questioned whether men understand themselves any better today than they did when Socrates was exhorting the Athenians to examine themselves and to learn whether man is a creature mild and gentle by nature, or a monster more terrible than Typhon. Or, one might conclude that what psychology has done to advance such understanding, political romanticism and advertising propaganda have largely undone. The pressure against the habit of contemplation and the displacement of the humanities from a central role in our education have worked against what are probably the two best means of getting to know the nature of the human being. Self-knowledge is an extremely difficult acquisition under the best circumstances, and I think no one has better expressed this truth than Eliseo Vivas:

> My experience in general inclines me to the belief that men in general live their lives through without finding out who or what they really are. We think we are courageous when we are cowards, honest when we are cheats and thieves, truthful and generous when we are liars and pigs, and self-respecting in spite of the high coefficient of pliability of our moral spines. . . . It takes a crisis to reveal to us what values we truly espouse, and even that is often not enough, for each of us has his system of jujitsu for disposing quietly of bothersome truths.[4]

If a person is satisfied with the externality of the self, and if he gathers from the tone of current thinking that personality is just so much moonshine anyhow, it is not likely that he will take pains to search out the real springs of his attitudes and actions. Actions that appear to him perfectly respectable, or even the expression of benevolence, may become the cause of suffering to others—suffering which the agent cannot apprehend because he has a false picture of much that is involved. Such failure may become collective, and what is true of the individual in this regard may be true of the group or the nation. The same want of self-knowledge and the same self-deception regarding motives can lead nations into policies that create enmity and produce suffering. A nation, too, may have a system of jujitsu for breaking the holds of self-criticism.

I shall conclude this list of forces which are bringing about a depersonalization of the individual with one or two from the field of my professional work. Few will question the proposition that language is one of the means by which man expresses himself most personally. But in this sphere, too, we can mark the same tendencies toward over-simplification, and redefinition with the apparent object of manipulating. I have in mind especially the current fondness for something called "communication." Communication is usurping the place formerly held by expression. What used to be studied as an art, with some philosophical attention to the character and resources

---

4. Eliseo Vivas, *The Moral Life and the Ethical Life* (Chicago: University of Chicago Press, 1950), p. 190.

of the user, the truth of what was being expressed, and the character of the potential audience, is now being stripped down to a technique. Many would be surprised by the extent to which this new subject is edging out the old courses in composition and rhetoric in our colleges. The significance of the change has been noted by Allen Tate in an apt sentence. "The word 'communication,'" he writes, "presupposes the victory of the secularized society of means without ends."[5]

In this paring down of expression to "communication" there are two dangerous premises. One is that communication is primarily an engineering problem, to be solved through resort to the physical sciences. The problem is conceived as getting certain sounds from one mouth to certain ears or of getting a set of graphic symbols before certain eyes. This reflects the obsession of the scientific linguists that language is nothing more than a code, whose ends and means can be scientifically analyzed and dealt with. The intermediate stage of encoding and decoding thus becomes the whole subject. Left out of account are the way in which language is expressive of value and personality, and the way in which the use of it shapes and disciplines the mind.

The second premise is that the object of the communication is merely a passive registrar—a pair of ears or eyes ready to absorb whatever is presented to them by our now marvelous means of transmission. I shall go into Allen Tate's debt once more, this time to quote an observation from his "Reflections on American Poetry: 1900–1950." In this *Sewanee Review* article (Winter, 1956), he notes that there are "strong political pressures which ask the poet to 'communicate' to passively conditioned persons what a servile society expects them to feel." If these forces are brought to bear upon the modern poet, they are surely brought to bear much more strongly upon the journalists and all who write for our organs of mass "communication." The extent to which they assume prior indoctrination and docility on the part of their audience is amazing when one goes to the point of analyzing it. Mass communication is not conversation, and the obstacles in the way of a meeting of speaker and hearer, in what might be termed a "man to man" or "no nonsense" discussion, seem actually greater than ever before.

5. Allen Tate, *The Forlorn Demon* (Chicago: Henry Regnery, 1953), p. 12.

This development will suggest that loss of belief in personality is being reflected in language itself; and indeed, how else could it be if, as I. A. Richards has said, language is "the supreme organ of the mind's self-ordering growth."[6] I have to agree with F. A. Voigt that the English language today is losing character, strength, and resonance. What I am chiefly conscious of is the loss of resonance, and I think that this loss is owing mainly to the fact that the modern style shuns anything suggestive of value. Or, if this generalization must be qualified, it admits only values of the narrow, strident kind, such as might be expected to survive after positivism has done its work. There is even a theory to justify this narrowing down, as can be seen in the curious attempts of people like Alfred Korzybski and Stuart Chase to maintain that language ought to be somehow correlated with the spatio-temporal order. Symbolism and expression of emotion are both under attack as irruptions from a non-scientific world.

If we seat a typical modern before a chapter of the King James Bible, or a passage from an eighteenth century oration, it is problematical how much of what is there he can get. The wonderful wealth of pleonasm, metonymy, synecdoche, antithesis, isocolons, anaphoras, inversions, and climactic orders—a veritable orchestration for the soul—is, I believe, puzzling to him. His reaction, I suspect, is that the writer of the passage is saying it the best way he could, and must be pardoned, being of a primitive time. The way to say it would be in the style of *Look,* or of an editorial in the New York *Daily News,* with words of flat signification, with syncopated syntax, and with none of the broadly ruminative phrases which have the power to inspire speculation. The essential sterility of such a style is one of the surest signs we have that modern man is being desiccated. For the "modern" style is at once brash and timid; brash enough to break old patterns without thinking, and timid before the tremendous evocative and constructive powers immanent in language.

There is a temptation to suppose that by doing something to language itself we can do something about this situation. Much as I would like to think that, reason tells me that the opportunity is limited. Something will have to be done first about man's representation of himself, because that

6. I. A. Richards, *Speculative Instruments* (Chicago: University of Chicago Press, 1955), p. 9.

representation broadens or narrows the vocabulary and the rhetoric which he thinks he can use. But to the extent that language exerts a counter influence upon the representation, we can say that it is a causal factor, and we can do something through force of example. It is very easy to pick up unconsciously a tone, or to fall into a vocabulary, or to make use of figures and analogies, whose implications are opposite to the views we really hold. Any style moves along on a set of hidden or half-hidden premises, and there is a great if unconscious pressure to accept the premises of a style in popular use. These premises now point in the general direction of a philosophic nihilism. We cannot re-institute the style of an age that we feel to have been more humane toward the personality, but we can, within the idiom permitted us, avoid the kind of discourse that carries just below its surface a contempt for all values.

This seems to turn the consideration toward remedial measures. One of the obvious steps, if we are to secure the future of personality, is to clarify the relation of the individual to his society.

It is quite easy to fall under the influence of our extensive literature of protest and to assume that the individual is always engaged in a righteous warfare with his society. In my view this is not an accurate picture of the relationship. I believe that there *is* a dualism of the individual and society, but that the dualism is not necessarily, nor even normally, one of conflict. The two are complementary and mutually supporting, and it seems idle to argue which is prior in order of time and therefore prior in order of natural right.

When we speak of "the individual," we are dealing with an analytic isolate, something abstracted from its context and held up for convenience of study or reference. For all Whitman's fine phrase, there is no "simple, separate person." The person is always a person within his society, and although it probably could never be proved which owes the other more, it is certain that the individual is indebted to society for many things which allow him to be an individual. He makes use of its institutions, its customs, its usages, its settled preferences, and its means of communication in order to express himself in his own way; it is silly to think of being an individual alone in the big woods or at the North Pole. Thoreau's individualism showed itself in the rather long list of rejections of what his society presented and his continuing satire of its assumptions. This was his way of using what was offered; and we rejoice that this society was healthy enough to allow him to take the posture he chose to take and still "include" him.

It would seem to me false, therefore, to picture our task as always that of fighting the battle of the individual against any society. In a normal situation, the individual and his society are mutually sustaining in a complex, and while there will always be minor and incidental frictions, these will not be a prime feature of the relationship. We may derive some prescriptive guidance here from the principle that any sound whole respects its parts. It is made a whole by its parts; it is conscious of this, and it does not attempt to override them or distort them. And the part owes a loyalty to itself as well as to the whole; it must be itself in order that other parts may be themselves.

Following this line of analysis, I am disposed to accept the doctrine of Calhoun, which, roughly speaking, visualizes society as an organism made up of organic parts. If the organ as a whole is to function properly, the parts must be allowed to perform their offices. The head must not fight against the stomach or the arms try to take the place of the legs, and so on. This provides reason for saying that the parts have an inviolate character; they must be allowed to be what they are if the whole is to carry on its unitary function. Furthermore, there are some things the whole may not do without specific concurrence of the parts, so that in some matters the part has an absolute veto.

Taking this out of the language of metaphor and looking at society as a concrete thing, we can say that it has parts comprised of individuals and of groups and combinations of individuals emerging out of some common interest or feeling. These groups are constituents of society, and the state has no right to disregard their needs and privileges, because in doing so it would be working against its real end.

This principle contains the final rebuttal of totalitarianism. The totalitarian philosophy assumes that the unit of the whole, or the totality, has all the rights and that the constituent parts either have no rights or have rights of an inferior order. On the premise of this doctrine, there is no such thing as oppression of a minority; if a minority stands in the way of something willed by the totality (as it would work out, by a numerical majority), it is condemned by that very fact, and any means whatever may be used against it.

This can be a form of government, but it is not a society in any true sense, for society is a system of groupings which has as its purpose the expression of the many needs, desires, and inclinations that are found in a multitude of people, always of course with due prevention of invasions and excesses. The modern "mass" looks with hatred upon any sign of the structuring of society, perhaps just because its own desires are formless and irrational. As Hannah Arendt notes in her exhaustive study of totalitarianism, "Masses are not held together by a consciousness of common interest, and they lack that specific class articulateness which is expressed in determined, limited, and obtainable goals."[7] The individual has the best chance in a society which permits and even encourages many different centers of authority, influence, opinion, taste and accomplishment. These things grow out of associations freely entered into by persons of common necessity, interest, or geographical habitat.

Something toward this end could be accomplished by drawing more sharply the line between government and society. The present tendency seems to be to dissolve society altogether and make everything government. But government is the *protector* of society, not something identical with it. It is only in the kind of spontaneous life that society lives that a person has a chance to be an individual and to express himself personally.

For that reason the widespread present efforts to exterminate the idea of class and independent association, and to override all forms of particularism, are to be firmly resisted. Some of them had their original impulse in idealism, real or perverted, but their effect would be to freeze our imaginative, cultural, and social life in a *rigor mortis* of bureaucratic domination.

7. Hannah Arendt, *The Origins of Totalitarianism* (New York: Harcourt, Brace, 1951), p. 305.

Life without Prejudice¹

When one sets out to discover how "prejudice" became a fighting word, some interesting political history comes to light. Everybody is aware that this term is no longer used in its innocent sense of "prejudgment." It is used, instead, as a flail to beat enemies. Today the air resounds with charges of "prejudice," and the shrill note given it by the "liberals" and radicals suggests a considerable reservoir of feeling and purpose behind its invocation. This appears all the more striking when one recalls that in the controversial literature of a hundred years ago—or even of a couple of generations ago—you do not encounter the sort of waving of the bloody shirt of prejudice that greets you on all sides now. Men did not profess such indignation that other men had differing convictions and viewpoints. They rather expected to encounter these, and to argue with them as best they could. You do not find the tricky maneuvers and the air of what might be called ultraism that we are familiar with today.

What has changed the atmosphere? I would point to the world-wide revolutionary movement which has manifested itself in almost every land. The indictment for prejudice has been one of the most potent weapons in the armory of its agents. There is need to realize what this indictment masks and how it operates, both politically and logically.

It is getting to be a bore to bring communism into every article that deals with a topic of public concern, but here the connection is so close that one finds no option. For the doctrines of Moscow are the *fons et origo* of the great pressure to eradicate "prejudice." A prime object of militant communism is to produce a general social skepticism. Not that the communists are skeptics themselves. They are the world's leading dogmatists and authoritarians. But in order to bring about their dogmatic reconstruction of the world they need to produce this skepticism among the traditional believers.

1. *Modern Age*, 1/1, Summer 1957, 4–9.

They need to make people question the supports of whatever social order they enjoy, to encourage a growing dissatisfaction and a feeling that they have inherited a bad article. The more subtle of them realize, no doubt, that people can be made to forget how well a system is working right under their noses if they can be allured and distracted with "pie in the sky." The communist version of pie in the sky shall be dealt with in a moment when the logical method is considered. Just now I emphasize this unfixing of faith as one of the steps in a large-scale and—it must be confessed—cunning plan. This world-wide revolutionary movement, openly conducted in some countries, operating from hiding in others, wants first of all to clear the ground.

To this end, what it knows that it must overcome is the binding element, or the cohesive force that holds a society together. For as long as this integrative power remains strong, the radical attack stands refuted and hopeless. This will explain the peculiar virulence with which communists attack those transcendental unifiers like religion, patriotism, familial relationship, and the like. It will also explain, if one penetrates the matter shrewdly, why they are so insistent upon their own programs of conformity, leveling, and de-individualization.

However paradoxical it may appear at first sight, we find when we examine actual cases that communities create a shared sentiment, a oneness, and a loyalty through selective differentiation of the persons who make them up. A society is a structure with many levels, offices, and roles, and the reason we feel grateful to the idea of society is that one man's filling his role makes it possible for another to fill his role, and so on. Because the policeman is doing his policeman's job, the owner of the bakery can sleep well at night. Because plumbers and electricians are performing their functions, doctors and lawyers are free to perform theirs, and the reverse. This is a truistic observation, no doubt, but too little attention is given to the fact that society exists in and through its variegation and multiplicity, and when we speak of a society's "breaking down," we mean exactly a confusing of these roles, a loss of differentiation, and a consequent waning of the feeling of loyalty. Society makes possible the idea of vocation, which is the primary source of distinctions. The ceaseless campaign of the communists to make every people a mass has as its object the erasing of those distinctions which are the expression of this idea. In the communist Utopia Comrade Jones would work in the mines, and Comrade Smith would write political articles for the party organ, or perhaps he would be assigned the task of proving the non-existence of metaphysics. Their "comradeship" would be of far greater importance than their vocations, but to what end? The answer to this lies in some Messianic idea derived from the prophecies of Marx, Lenin, and Stalin.

The point is that their hostility to distinctions of all kinds as we know them in our society conceals a desire to dissolve that society altogether. And we see that practically all traditional distinctions, whether economic, moral, social, or aesthetic, are today under assault as founded on a prejudice. This shows itself in everything from the more absurd theorems of "democratic action" to the ideal of "non-competitive education," by which teachers who ought to be on the dunce's stool themselves have been led half the distance to Moscow.

Although the aim is this general social skepticism, the communists and their helpers are sufficiently experienced in ideological warfare to know that it is often bad policy to attack everything at once. To do this may cast doubt upon your own motives and cause people to suspect that something is wrong with you. Often the best tactic is to single out some special object and concentrate your force upon this, while feigning a benevolent attitude toward the rest of the order. This enables you to appear a critic and a patriot at the same time. It is a guiltless-looking role because most of us object to and would like to reform one or more of our country's institutions, even though we have profound attachment to it as a whole.

The difference with the communist is that this is part of a plan to discredit and do away with the whole. And this is why it is important to note the political method by which he proceeds.

He knows that if you can weaken one after another of the supporting pillars, the structure must eventually collapse. He works, then, like a termite, except that he selects and directs his effort. First things first and one thing at a time. He chooses some feature of an order where there is a potential of resentment, or he may choose some feature about which people are simply soft-headed—that is to say, confused or uncertain. It may be the existence of rich men; it may be the right to acquire and use property privately; it may be the idea of discipline and reward in education; it may be some system of preferential advancement which produces envy in the less successful. His most common maneuver, as previously suggested, is to vilify this as founded upon "prejudice." The burden of his argument usually is that since these do not have perfectly rationalized bases, they have no right to exist. You will find especially that he pours his scorn—and this seems a most important clue to his mentality—upon those things for which people have a natural (and in his sense irrational) affection. The modern communist, looking upon this world with its interesting distinctions and its prolific rewards and pleasures, may be compared to Satan peering into the Garden. Milton tells us that the arch-fiend "Saw undelighted all delight." The more he sees people attached to their theoretically impossible happiness, the more determined he is to bring on the fall.

Just as the marshals of the communist movement have worked politically with more cleverness than many people give them credit for, so they have often been better logicians than those in the opposite camp. The fact will partly explain the sense of frustration felt by defenders of our traditional structural Western society. In their polemic use of the term "prejudice," however, they have been better logicians in the shyster's way: they have confused the other side with a boldly maintained fallacy.

The fallacy contained in the charge "prejudice," as it is usually employed to impeach somebody's judgment, has long been familiar to logicians, by whom it was given the name *argumentum ad ignorantiam*. This signifies an argument addressed to ignorance. The reason for the appellation will appear in an analysis of how the fallacy operates. Those who are guilty of the *argumentum ad ignorantiam* profess belief in something because its opposite cannot be proved, or they assert the existence of something because the something possibly may exist. It is possible that life exists on Mars; therefore life does exist on Mars. In the realm where "prejudice" is now most an issue, it normally takes a form like this: you cannot prove—by the method of statistics and quantitative measurement—that men are not equal. Therefore men are equal. You cannot prove that human beings are naturally wicked. Therefore they are naturally good, and the contrary opinion is a prejudice. You cannot prove—again by the methods of science— that one culture is higher than another. Therefore the culture of the Digger Indians is just as good as that of Muncie, Indiana, or thirteenth century France.

Generally speaking, this type of fallacious reasoning seeks to take advantage of an opponent by confusing what is abstractly possible with what is

really possible or what really exists. Expressed in another way, it would substitute what is possible in theory for that which we have some grounds, even
though not decisive ones, for believing. It is possible in some abstract sense
that all men are equal. But according to the Bible, Aristotle, and most considerate observers, men are not equal in natural capacity, aptitude for learning, moral education, and so on. If you can get the first belief substituted
for the second, on the claim that the second cannot be proved, you have
removed a "prejudice." And along with it, you have removed such perception as you have of reality.

The "pie in the sky" appeal of the communists consequently comes in
this guise: you cannot prove the unworkability of the communist or statist
Utopia; therefore it is workable. I say "cannot prove," although there are
multitudinous evidences that it has never worked along the lines and with
the motivations that are always suggested in its favor. One might indeed
borrow a famous apothegm and say that all theory is for it and all experience
is against it. However, since the appeal is to the dislocated, the resentful,
the restless, and the malcontented, it has won its followers. We have seen
how they charge the rest of us with being prejudiced in favor of the present
order, or whatever feature of it they have singled out for attack. Often they
manage to conceal the fallacy underlying their position by a vocabulary and
a tone which intimidate the conservative into feeling ignorant.

A critical examination of their logic therefore deserves priority. But after
we have seen the worst that can be said against the type of ideas which they
condemn as prejudices, we ought to inquire whether such ideas are capable
of positive good.

A number of years ago John Grier Hibben, a professor of logic at Princeton and later president of that university, wrote a temperate essay entitled
"A Defense of Prejudice." Professor Hibben demonstrated in some detail
why it is a mistake to classify all those notions which people denominate
prejudices as illogical. A prejudice may be an unreasoned judgment, he
pointed out, but an unreasoned judgment is not necessarily an illogical
judgment. He went on to list three types of beliefs for which we cannot
furnish immediate logical proof, but which may nevertheless be quite in line
with truth.

First, there are those judgments whose verification has simply dropped
out of memory. At one time they were reached in the same way as our

"logical" conclusions, but the details of the process have simply been forgotten. It is necessary to the "economy of thought" that we retire from consciousness many of the facts that were once used to support our judgments. The judgments themselves remain as a kind of deposit of thought. They are not without foundation, though the foundation is no longer present to the mind with any particularity; and the very fact that we employ these judgments successfully from day to day is fair evidence that proof would be available if needed. The judgments are part of the learning we have assimilated in the process of developing a mind.

The second type of unreasoned judgments we hold are the opinions we adopt from others—our betters in some field of learning or experience. There is no need to labor the truth that we all appropriate such opinions on a considerable scale, and if we could not do so, books and institutions of learning would lose their utility. No man in a civilized society proves more than a small percentage of the judgments he operates on, and the more advanced or complex civilization grows, the smaller this proportion must become. If every man found it necessary to verify each judgment he proceeds on, we would all be virtual paupers in knowledge. It is well for everyone to know something concerning the *methods* of verification, but this indeed differs from having to verify all over again the hard-won and accumulated wisdom of our society. Happily there *is* such a thing as authority.

The third class of judgments in Professor Hibben's list comprises those which have subconscious origin. The material that furnishes their support does not reach the focal point of consciousness, but psychology insists upon its existence. The intuitions, innuendoes, and shadowy suggestions which combine to form our opinion about, say, a character, could never be made public and formal in any convincing way. Yet only the most absurd doctrinaire would hold that they are therefore founded upon error. In some situations the mind uses a sort of oracular touchstone for testing what cannot be tested in any other way. My judgment that Mr. Blank, though a well-spoken and plausible gentleman, will one day betray his office is a conclusion I cannot afford to put aside, even though at the present moment I have no publicly verifiable facts from the space–time continuum which would prove it to another. It may be true that only those minds which are habituated to think logically can safely trust their intuitive conclusions, on the theory that the subconscious level will do its kind of work as faithfully as the conscious does its kind. This still leaves room for what may be termed paralogical inference.

When one thinks about these well accepted and perfectly utilitarian forms of "prejudice," the objections of the rationalists seem narrow and intolerant. There is, indeed, a good deal of empirical evidence for saying that rationalistic men are more intolerant than "prejudiced" men. The latter take the position that their judgments are reasoned conclusions, and why should one swerve or deflect from what can be proved to all reasonable men? Such are often the authors of persecutions, massacres, and liquidations. The man who frankly confesses to his prejudices is usually more human and more humane. He adjusts amicably to the idea of his limitations. A limitation once admitted is a kind of monition not to try acting like something superhuman. The person who admits his prejudices, which is to say his unreasoned judgments, has a perspective on himself.

Let me instance two cases in support of this point. When H. L. Mencken wrote his brilliant series of essays on men, life, and letters, he gave them a title as illuminating as it was honest—*Prejudices*. What he meant, if such a dull addition as a gloss may be permitted with Mencken, was that these were views based on such part of experience as had passed under his observation. There was no apology because some figures were praised and others were roundly damned, and there was no canting claim to "objectivity." Mencken knew that life and action turn largely on convictions which rest upon imperfect inductions, or samplings of evidence, and he knew that feeling is often a positive factor. The result was a tonic criticism unrivaled in its time. Did his "unfairness" leave him unread and without influence? He castigates religion in many ways, and I have known churchmen who admire him and quote him. He thought nothing sillier than the vaporizing of most of our radicals, yet numbers of these looked to him as a mentor in writing and as a leader in every libertarian crusade. In brief, they found in him a *man*, whose prejudices had more of reality than the slogans and catchwords on political banners.

The same lesson, it seems to me, can be read in the career of Dr. Samuel Johnson. Johnson lives in considerable measure through the vitality of his prejudices. When he says to an interlocutor, "Sir, I perceive you are a vile Whig," you know that he is speaking from a context of reality. It is not necessary that you "agree" with him. How many people do we ever "agree" with in any unreserved sense? That he hated Whigs, Scotsmen, and Americans we accept as a sign of character; it is a kind of signature. The heartiness of his likes and dislikes constitutes an ethical proof of all he puts forward. And so it is with any formed personality. A hundred popinjays can be found to discuss brilliantly; but you will not find on every corner a man whose opinions bear a kind of witness to the man himself.

Mencken, like Johnson, is, in his more abstract political thinking, a Tory. But both men—and this is a continuation of the story—proved kind in their personal relations, and both of them were essentially modest. Upon one occasion when Boswell confessed to Johnson that he feared some things he was entering in his journal were too small, the latter advised him that nothing is too small for so small a creature as man. This is good evidence that Johnson had achieved what I referred to as perspective, which carries with it a necessary humility. And while some may be startled to hear Mencken called a modest man, I can infer nothing but a real candor and humility from those bombastic and ironical allusions to himself which comprise much of the humor of his writings. The tone he adopted was a rhetorical instrument; he had faced his limitations.

I have given some space to these examples because I feel they show that the man of frank and strong prejudices, far from being a political and social menace and an obstacle in the path of progress, is often a benign character and a helpful citizen. The chance is far greater, furthermore, that he will be more creative than the man who can never come to more than a few gingerly held conclusions, or who thinks that all ideas should be received with equal hospitality. There is such a thing as being so broad you are flat.

Life without prejudice, were it ever to be tried, would soon reveal itself to be a life without principle. For prejudices, as we have seen earlier, are often built-in principles. They are the extract which the mind has made of experience. Try to imagine a man setting out for the day without a single prejudice. Let us suppose that he has "confessed" his prejudices in the manner of confessing sins and has decided to start next morning with a fresh mind as the sinner would start a new soul. The analogy is false. Inevitably he would be in a state of paralysis. He could not get up in the morning, or choose his necktie, or make his way to the office, or conduct his business affairs, or, to come right down to the essence of the thing, even maintain his identity. What he does in actuality is arise at his arbitrary 7:15, select the necktie which he is prejudiced in favor of, set off relatively happy with his head full of unreasoned judgments, conduct a successful day's business and return home the same man he was, with perhaps a mite or two added to his store of wisdom.

When Mark Twain wrote, "I know that I am prejudiced in this matter, but I would be ashamed of myself if I were not," he was giving a therapeutic insight into the phenomenon of prejudice. There is a kind of willful narrowness which should be called presumption and rebuked. But prejudice in the sense I have tried to outline here is often necessary to our personal rectitude, to our loyalty to our whole vision. It is time, then, for the whole matter of prejudice in relation to society and conduct to be reexamined and revalued. When this is done, it will be seen that the cry of "prejudice" which has been used to frighten so many people in recent years is often no more than caterwauling. It has a scary sound, and it has been employed by the illiberal to terrify the liberal. And since the "liberal," or the man who has not made up his mind about much of anything, is today perhaps the majority type, it has added a great deal to the world's trepidation and confusion. The conservative realizes that many orthodox positions, once abandoned in panic because they were thought to be indefensible, are quite defensible if only one gives a little thought to basic issues. Surely one of these positions is the right of an individual or a society to hold a belief which, though unreasoned, is uncontradicted. When that position is secured, we shall be in better shape to fight the battle against the forces of planned disintegration.

Relativism and the Crisis of Our Times [1]

Few observations are more commonly heard today than that we are living in a time of crisis. Some persons, evidently becoming bored with this expression, try to scout this idea by asserting that every time, every age, is an age of crisis.

To me they are among the gravest indications of the havoc that relativism has played and is playing with the modern mind.

Now, it is perfectly true that in one sense every age *is* an age of crisis. Every age has its decisions to make, every age is confronted with some dilemmas. From the point of view of the present, the future always looks uncertain and perhaps a little threatening and unnerving; but I think it is profoundly wrong to say that every period of a society or a nation's history is equally critical. There are periods of crisis and disorder, and there are periods of stability and prosperity. And to say that we cannot distinguish between the two is to give up all hope of social amelioration and political reconstruction.

I think the fatuity of the notion can be seen by asking a simple question: How many individuals could you find who would be willing to say that every part of their lives had been equally happy and rewarding? I think that is a fair analogy. Just as there are critical and difficult periods in the life of a single individual, so there are periods of stress and strain, the periods of indecision and wrong decision, in the lives of those communities that we call groups and nations. I have perhaps belabored this thought a bit, but I think it is necessary, before we can have any possible discussion of the question before us, to get out of this relativist trap.

To say that no age is more an age of crisis than another would be the relativist way of dodging the question, or pretending that the issue doesn't

---

1. *Relativism and the Crisis of Our Times.* Philadelphia: Intercollegiate Society of Individualists, n.d. (1961), pamphlet.

really exist. I am proceeding on the assumption, therefore, that our age is very much an age of crisis. It is a time when manners, and morals along with them, are in a state of change. It is a time when institutions which are the patient creations of centuries are seriously challenged. In the past fifty years we have seen the aims of education almost completely reversed by many of our public educators. And perhaps more serious than any of these, and possibly underlying them all as a cause, we have seen the attempts to change radically the traditional image of what man is, in his nature. About the only adjective which persons agree in applying to our social and economic order today is "dynamic." Now, dynamic means moving, continuously in motion. But in motion toward what? There is an aspect of bitter truth to the saying: "We don't know where we're going, but we're on our way." And, unless we are willing to turn the whole matter over to the unknown forces of biological evolution, I maintain that we are faced with a crisis of the first magnitude. Deeply, intimately involved in that crisis lies a decay of belief in standards. I use the word "standards" here because it has a double signification, expressive of the ideas I have in mind. *Standard means, first of all, something of general application and validity. A standard is something that is set up as a measure for all. It is not contingent upon this man's preference, or whim, or that man's location in space and time.* When the Bureau of Standards in Washington sets a standard, it establishes something that is the same for the man in California as for the man in Maine. *A standard is, therefore, something of uniform and universal determination. This is one of the aspects of the meaning. But in addition to this, the term standard in its more general usage has the imperative sense of an ideal. It represents that to which we are supposed to come up to, not just in weights and measures, but in our contractual obligations with others—in our more general social responsibility and even in our personal development.*

The standard may not in every case represent the highest conceivable ideal; but it is in every case the least we are willing to settle for, and, therefore, it exerts an upward pull against man's natural impulse to do things just any way. Perhaps we can say that a standard is the ideal translated into everyday life but still recognizable through its power to discipline.

Now everyone who is in the least alive to the current of ideas knows that in the past fifty years there has been a great onslaught against the belief in standards. This has been carried on through a doctrine known as relativism.

Relativism denies outright that there are any absolute truths, any fixed principles, or any standards beyond what one may consider his convenience. A theory is true only relative to the point of view of the individual, or to the time in which it is asserted, or to the circumstances which prevail at the moment. Truth is forever contingent and evolving, which means, of course, that you can never lay hands on it. Relativism is actually the abdication of truth.

I could give you examples from my experience as a teacher showing how far this notion has seized the popular mind. Things may be changing a bit now, but for years I have known that the easiest way to get a rise out of a class was to express a generalization. It hardly mattered what the generalization was about. Somebody in the class was sure to attack it *qua* generalization. Somewhere along the line the students have been given the notion that they should discard all general propositions—reject them. If they did so actually, of course, we would never be able to teach them anything. The point I am making here, however, is that the modern mind has been induced to believe through the doctrine of relativism that you can't speak truth if you speak a generalization. And a generalization is a standard idea or observation. (Indeed, the prevalent skepticism even goes beyond this, I might add. A biologist friend of mine caustically expresses the modern attitude thus: "Why face facts: they may turn out to be no facts at all.")

It is little wonder, however, that our young people have succumbed to this when it infects the highest echelons of our social and political organization. Comparable views can be heard emanating from our once respected Supreme Court. For example, the late Mr. Justice Holmes is on record as saying: "A word is not a crystal, transparent and unchanged; it is the skin of a living thought and may vary greatly in color and content according to the circumstances and time in which it is used." And the late Chief Justice Vinson observed the following: "Nothing is more certain in modern society than the principle that all concepts are relative: a name, a phrase, a standard [and may I call attention to his use of the term "standard"] has meaning only when associated with the considerations which give birth to the nomenclature." It would be fascinating to follow out the metaphysical, ontological, and epistemological implications of these doctrines and to discuss philosophically the impasses to which they lead. But the subject of this paper is not philosophy in the abstruse sense. We are dealing here with political considerations and economic considerations, and politics is a practical science and an art. What I shall do next, therefore, is deal with the impact of relativism upon two areas in the practical realm.

* * *

The greatest injury that the idea of relativism has done to political thinking—and organizations—lies in the encouragement it gives to middle-of-the-roadism. Here I find myself speaking about my particular personal aversion. Middle-of-the-roadism is the departure of intellect from political thinking. How did the notion ever arise that the safest place is the middle of the road? I believe it arose from people who resent the very idea of logical clarity, because logical clarity always leads you to a principle. And a principle is resented because it is binding in the same way that a generalization or a standard is. Middle-of-the-roaders often try to justify themselves by dragging out the old adage: the truth is always found some place in between. But in between what? If one position is right and the other wrong, is the truth found somewhere in between these? That is, does the truth consist of a combination of part of the right and part of the wrong? If one answer is demonstrably right and another is demonstrably wrong, do we find our solution by simply averaging these? The reply to my rhetorical question is, of course, that between contradictories there is no middle ground. It is a law of logic that where A and not-A exist as alternatives, you cannot have both of them nor can you squeeze in between them.

Here I can imagine its being retorted: You are overlooking a big difference. You are talking about the realm of logical distinction; we are talking about practical facts, where things are not true or false or right or wrong in this way. My reply would be that I am attacking this attempt to pretend that intellectually conceived principles and practical policy can be kept apart in this way. Just as there is no such thing as practice without a theory of that practice, so there can be no such thing as a political policy without a theory of that policy. It has been said that politics is the art of compromise. I do not deny that practically all political activity involves some compromises or accommodations at the level where concrete facts are encountered. But I do deny strenuously that compromise itself is a political philosophy. After all, one has to have something to compromise *from*. A political philosophy takes a stand in favor of certain values and the arrangements that follow from them. It ought to be clear, coherent, self-consistent. It should be able to define itself well enough to know when it is conceding something to the opposition. Now the truth about the middle-of-the-road position is that it has no such character. It takes its bearings from the other two sides, left and right, which do have intellectually clarified positions. If they move, it must move, not because of an independent explanation of some fact or situation, but precisely because it has no independence of them.

In a manner of putting it, both the left and the right have laid out their roads. The middle-of-the-roader finds it easiest and he thinks it is safer—but it isn't—to travel along the graded way between them. Middle-of-the-roadism is not perspicacious. It doesn't see with its own eyes. It tries to get along by borrowing a little from those who have done the hard work of seeing the principles through.

I am satisfied that the popularity of middle-of-the-roadism today stems from the widespread acceptance of relativism. It is not a position based on philosophical insight, because, as I have tried to explain, it is not in reality a position. Or, at the most, it is a position relative to other positions. And I believe further that this position can be traced to an unwillingness to face the possibility that truth and falsehood, or right and wrong, exist as real alternatives. If one persuades himself to believe this, the only recourse to him is the path of expediency, which does not have to submit to the discipline of logic and moral absolutes.

An acquaintance of mine recently declared his belief that the sociological jurisprudence under which we are suffering today had its origin in the setting up of juvenile courts. It was felt that some offenders against the law belonged "in the middle of the road." They were neither children, and hence guiltless, nor were they adults, and hence guilty. So a special in-between area was created for them, with the result, as all of you know, that usually nothing was done with them. Here, in my judgment, is an important source of the tremendous upsurge in juvenile criminality which we are witnessing today. But the lack of clearsightedness in middle-of-the-roadism can lead to much worse things than this, as in those crises where nations have to deal with nations or with the international order. It was middle-of-the-roadism which brought Chamberlain to Munich. There is no solution, but rather great danger in the form of this complacency in the face of contradictions.

*   *   *

There is yet another effect of relativism which introduces a great deal of confusion into current ways of thinking and living. This takes the curious form of supposing that all values are compatible. Or to put this in another way, from which the result may be better seen, of supposing that no values are incompatible. I feel sure that this traces back to an unwillingness to be bound by logical and ethical restraints, because after all "nothing is really that true—or so true that it has to exclude something else." Under the influence of this thinking, modern man is being increasingly encouraged to believe that all values can exist in simple juxtaposition. The values of civilization and the values of primitivism, the values of the right and the values of the left, the values of self-sacrifice and the values of self-indulgence, the values of freedom and the values of regimentation, lie down together like the proverbial lion and the lamb, so that no one is forced by some tyrannical principle of contradiction or some hierarchy of the good to choose between them. The upshot then is to think that we can have them all—and at the same time and at the same place.

One of the most eloquent evidences of this trend in mentality can be found in an aspect of advertising language today. There is in a lot of advertising language today a kind of "doublespeak," which embodies or expresses this very idea. One finds in such language contradictory things predicated on the same article. Somebody has made a collection of these and I wish I had it at hand. But not having it, I will make up a few examples to suggest the kind of blurring or confusion of opposed values that I am pointing to. In this advertising double-talk a tobacco will be described as "mild" but "pungent," a whiskey as "light but full bodied," a foodstuff as "satisfying but respectful of your calorie intake," a holiday resort as "dazzlingly new but full of old-fashioned charm," something else as "delicate, but rugged." I do not think this is a trifling matter. I think it shows how deeply there enters into the general consciousness of our people the notion that one is entitled to have all the goods in one package and at one moment. In short, one does not have to make a rational choice.

Now the consequences of this may not be very disastrous when one is merely buying articles for consumption. But when one is determining the order of his life or deciding upon the nature of the state he wants to live under, nothing but luck can save him from disaster if he follows this principle very far. For there are values in life which will not lie down in simple juxtaposition. I use values here in the sense of something that satisfies desire. In this sense, accordingly, there are values that satisfy bad desires. There are some values which satisfy good desires but which have to be hierarchically ordered if the individual is to have any personality and if his life is to have any direction. There are values in political organization which serve the ideal of freedom, and there are those which are fatal to it. Individualism and communism, for example, will not drive in the same team. Supposing that a person can have all of them without any discrimination—because it is wrong to deny anyone anything—is a condition of real intellectual and moral benightedness. Yet it is the condition into which relativism is pushing large numbers of our people.

It might be inferred from these remarks that I am a heartless and extreme kind of person, who insists on seeing everything as black or white. The word "absolute" indeed seems to have a power to terrify, driving many people to relativism as to a shelter against something that is tyrannical or oppressive. At this point, therefore, a most important distinction has to be made. There is a difference between knowing an absolute and knowing an absolute absolutely. It is even more certain that there is a difference between knowing an absolute and applying an absolute absolutely. To know an absolute absolutely is something that is not given to men, unless there be such a thing as special revelation. As long as we inhabit this house of mortal clay we are none of us absolutists in this sense. This is but a recognition of our human condition.

This is not the same, however, as saying that there are no absolutes. The absolute is something that we apprehend without knowing fully, that we have fleeting intimations of, that we recognize as necessary to give validity to our intellectual and moral principles. Some notion of the absolute is as essential to these things as backbone to an animal—which reminds me that I have often heard relativists referred to as "jelly-fish." I say all this while recognizing that in this concrete world the application of an absolute principle has to be tempered by the diversity of fact and circumstance. To imagine oneself able to proceed absolutely on an absolute principle is the mark of a madman. But this is only to state the limitation that common sense always recognizes. My plea comes down to this: Belief in universals and principles is inseparable from the life of reason. And to make rational choices in those areas where reason rightly applies is a moral duty. And there is a very direct connection between the belief in principle (which may be thought of as a soften-downed word for "absolutes") and the preservation of freedom. I am entirely convinced that relativism as a doctrine must eventually lead to a regime of force. The relativist has no outside authority, no constraining transcendent idea to appeal to or to be deterred by. For him "all things flow." What is relevant today may be irrelevant tomorrow. For relativism is a matter of relevance to the moment and to the situation. Then the only things one can be judged by are success and failure. With such an outlook the temptation is very strong to see what one can get away with. After all, if one is successful, one can set up a new ethic on the basis of his success. But then, somebody stronger comes along to see what he can get away with. This is the way that leads to the rule of appetite. And appetite, in that vivid line of Shakespeare, "becomes a universal wolf," a wolf which must at last "perforce eat up himself."

Reflections of Modernity[1]

Thank you, Mr. Gassman. When Mr. Clark tendered the invitation, by which I am honored, to appear on this program, he suggested that I give something inspirational, but informal and off the cuff, as it were. Well, inspirational one can only hope to be. But as to proceeding off the cuff, I decided, after some deliberation, that the risk would be too great. There was the likelihood of boring you with what often bores me, namely, the ordinary course of my thoughts. A speech, it seems to me, ought to be some kind of distillation, or at any rate something a little better than the man is able to attain in his ordinary moments. Therefore there is to be a topic— and a title. I am going to offer some "Reflections on Modernity," by one who is characterized by his acquaintances at least as a conservative. You may decide, by the time I am through, though, that it is quite wandering enough to satisfy the original requirement.

Now the first feature of modernity that strikes one who keeps his eyes and ears open is the ceaseless talk of crisis. Everywhere it is being said that "We live in an age of crisis." We hear this until we begin to weary of the term itself, and sometimes people try to put an end to the matter by turning skeptical and replying, "Every age is an age of crisis. How is our age any more critical than another? Delve into the history books and you will find that people in every epoch have been filled with anxiety. They have been torn with doubt before large questions. Some always give in to despair and say the world is going to the dogs; the Devil has everything. It has been characteristic of men at all times to feel that the future looms as a crisis."

Now this may be a comfortable line of evasion, but the skeptical pose really does not get us out of our difficulty. We may concede to the skeptic that every age is an age of transition. Every period is a link between two

---

1. *Reflections of Modernity.* Provo: Brigham Young University, 1961, *Speeches of the Year* pamphlet.

other periods, one passing away part by part and the other coming in in much the same way. Sometimes these passages are fairly smooth.

But a crisis is something far more precarious. Its nature can be underlined by thinking of the root meaning of the term. In the Greek original a crisis meant a separation, a place where a judgment had to be made, a place where you had to choose your road, right or left, up or down, as the case might be. This older sense clarifies the nature of crisis. One cannot go along in the line in which he has been traveling; decision is called for, and the decision is going to make a difference, perhaps a big one.

The characteristic of an age of crisis therefore is that the decisions are decisive. Large issues of definition and value are up for determination, and the choice cannot be deferred. Or if it is delayed, this only enables the side we do not want to win to gain ground. In this way I think it is fair to conclude that our age is an age of crisis, and that the issues cannot be met by "wise and masterly inactivity," to recall that prescription of John Randolph's, admirable as it may be for a happier situation. A friend of mine has pointed out that in the past it was usual for presidents and chiefs of state to promise something affirmative, to pledge themselves to add to the existing store of happiness and prosperity. Now, he added, about all one in such a position can do is to promise to *try* to keep things from blowing up, or collapsing completely. This is a way of pointing to the *instability* of the modern order, but it is also a way of showing how continuing crises have put us on the defensive.

So much for description. Now if we expect to inquire with any success into the causes of this situation, we must stay away from alluring subjects like nuclear fission and the international balance of power and seek out those real causes that lie in the human consciousness. For this is where our troubles start—in the ideas we have about things. And the most controversial of all ideas in this difficult time is the idea of the nature of man.

All political arguments stem ultimately from the question, "What is man?" So do all educational arguments. This may well be a platitude, but someone has defined a platitude as a truism imperfectly realized. There is sometimes need for a little commentary on what everybody more or less knows or at least senses. All political questions have to do with how to take care of man. How to feed and house him, how to organize him, how to train him, and how to make room for that part of his life which is cultural and diversionary. In line with this, all educational controversy revolves around how best to develop him.

I think it goes without demonstrating that one cannot argue these questions in any intelligible fashion unless one has a concept of man. Unless one knows what kind of creature he is providing for, or training, or organizing, one cannot envisage goals or even methods. We train horses for one thing and men presumably for something else, but what do we train men for? Goals and methodologies both will depend upon the answer to that question.

Basically our modern confusions and animosities derive from the fact that in the last century we have lost our consensus, our agreement, about the definition of man, about this creature who lives in every one of us and who in his aggregations raises our political problems. Looking into the more recent literature on this subject, one can discover two broad schools of thought on the matter, which divide in an interesting way. One of them, which I will label the "scientistic," denies in effect that there is a nature of man. Most of these people are, in my opinion, modern Darwinians or evolutionists, whose views are actually dominated by some principle of natural evolutionism. Their views can be summed up rather simply: they say, there can be no "nature of man" because man is a creature still in evolution. He was something a million years ago; he is something else today; and in the future he will be something else again. From such a point of view it is idle to speak categorically about a "nature of man," since that nature is a fluid something. Least of all, they think, do we know what man was intended to be. Who or what was the Intender? For all one can say positively on this, he was intended to be a cannibal, or to develop two heads, or to fly through the air on his own power. I indulge in caricature here, of course, but the principle remains: if man is simply a product of natural forces and if nature has no teleology—no end in view—it is as reasonable for man to develop one way as another, and you really cannot say what form of man is more or less like man. All you can do is note what you have got at the latest stage of the evolutionary trend. For the same reason you cannot expect to prescribe for him except in a very provisional way. Now this kind of thinking is by no means found only among those who study the sciences, and indeed their handling of the problem is usually more intelligent than that of some of the followers they seem to have picked up. I find it infiltrating more and more into works of political science, sociology, and even history. One encounters among some historians a surprising readiness to turn things over to "historical forces." They are not very clear about what these are, but they think that man has no choice but to go along and make the best of whatever is in store for him.

Standing in contrast with this view is a much older one which can properly be labeled the traditional theory. This theory depends not upon scientific induction and deduction, but upon what I would call an image. It is possible, say the traditionalists, to have an image of man, and an *image* as the word immediately suggests, is something arrived at through the imagination. This is not to say that it is a fiction. It is imagined, but not imaginary. It is a product of our total awareness of what man has been, is now, and—the indispensable component of the picture—what man ought to be. This last component has been regularly supplied by religion, though there are certain other ways of arriving at it. When the Psalmist asked the question with which we started, "What is man?" he suggested the answer with an interesting clause of result, "that Thou art mindful of him." If one proceeds in this fashion, one takes the oldest and most widely received view of the subject, which is that man is a creature in whom a creator takes a special interest and whom he holds to a standard of responsibility.

No one could hope in the course of a short speech to adjudicate in detail between these two positions, each of which is in its way massively supported. But I mentioned at the beginning that I am offering only reflections. Therefore, let me suggest just this about the rival cases. The naturalist says to the traditionalist: "You cannot show any acceptable source or authority for what you say is the nature or the image of man." To which the traditionalist might reply: "Maybe I cannot, but in the absence of a vision or intuition of what man is supposed to be, you cannot show any ground why he should behave in one way rather than another, and ethics and rational politics go out the window."

As we leave them here in this unresolved argument, I may add that the second position is the one generally assumed by the conservative. He maintains that there is a nature of man which can be known and which in its better part ought to be conserved. It is on this nature of man that we found commonwealths and erect institutions and chart our courses toward good but realizable goals. He is disturbed when he hears from the other side only that this is a changing world and that we ought to be prepared to change with it. Change in itself cannot be a meaningful principle of ordering. And there are very grave liabilities in the idea of an endless or infinite change. Aristotle somewhere makes the profound observation—I cannot cite chapter and verse here—that with an infinite series it is impossible to conceive an order of the goods. That is a metaphysical proposition, but metaphysical truths have an uncomfortable way of rearing their heads when we are attempting to get to the bottom of "practical" problems. The status of good or value in a world delivered over entirely to change is not something confined to classes in philosophy; it intrudes into our common councils. That is why we all need to reflect upon what the statement can mean when we are told, as we are regularly told today, that we are living in an ever-changing world.

One of the corollaries commonly drawn from that proposition is that modern man must necessarily be "living at the height of the times." How else could it be since we are living at the furthermost point of realized time? And how full of reassurance and gratification is the expression, resounding as it does with thoughts of progress and achievement and superiority, "Living at the height of the times." Our age is thereby denoted the supreme age in the sense of—well, when we undertake to answer that question, we find ourselves in metaphysical difficulties again. But here we first need to clear up the metaphorical picture. It is appalling to realize the extent to which our thinking can sometimes be derailed by a misleading metaphor or figure of speech. The figure may come so aptly and seem to illuminate so readily that we fail to see how the points of correspondence have ceased. We are off the rails or at least on another track which does not lead to the reality we are in quest of. So let us try following out the meaning of "living at the height of the times." We see in it a concept of historical progression which has two necessary features: it is linear and it is constantly ascending. The result is that at the latest time every society or people is "higher up" than the people of any preceding time. History is thus analogized as a constant and steady ascent, and those most recent in time always have the most reason to congratulate themselves. And we, living now in 1961 A.D., a year never attained before in the history of the world, are by definition on top. By the same definition our grandchildren will inevitably be higher than we.

The idea furnished by this misleading analogy has sunk very deep into the modern consciousness. We hear it in contemptuous references to "the horse and buggy age"—we are even told that it is beneath our dignity to fight a "horse and buggy war" anymore—meaning the old-fashioned war of limited objectives. We hear it in veiled aspersions against the nineteenth century for being decorous and restrained and—well, moral. We can see it in the ignoring of some of the very real achievements of Medieval civilization. And of course it reaches back to Greco-Roman civilization and depreciates the thought and culture of that period as provincial. Manifestly it is impossible to learn anything from the past if one adopts a criterion of value so simplistic and foolish. How simple things would be if development had been strictly linear and upward. But no student of the history of thought can accept anything as distorting as that. Still less can the student of art, when he looks at the memorials of Greece and the splendor of the Italian Renaissance.

The truth is the story of intellectual culture has been one of peaks and valleys. To assume, in response to that metaphor, that we cannot learn from the art and philosophy of ancient Greece or from the literature of Elizabethan England would be a form of self-imposed ignorance. Those elevations were higher than some that have followed. And once we admit, as we have to admit, that some periods of achievement in the past have something to teach us, we are on our way toward acquiring the humility necessary for wisdom, for not all wisdom is new wisdom.

I am old-fashioned enough to think that American political wisdom was at its height over a century and a half ago when the Constitution of the United States was framed. I cannot believe any group of Americans since then has had such basic insight into the necessary conditions of a free society. The founding fathers were an assembly of educated hardheads, not eggheads. You cannot find a trace of mush in their thinking. Listen, for example, to James Madison, writing in the *Federalist*:

> Men have been much more disposed to vex and oppress one another than to cooperate for their common good. So strong is this propensity of mankind to fall into mutual animosities that where no substantial occasion presents itself, the most frivolous and fanciful distinctions have been sufficient to kindle their unfriendly passions and excite their most violent conflicts.

That is written with a candor which Machiavelli himself would have applauded. But it is not cynicism—it is realism about a part of that nature of man which we have to take into account in the framing of governments. Free government, Jefferson was later to write, when attacking the Alien and Sedition Acts, is founded in *jealousy*, not in confidence. But out of these somewhat sardonic observations something great and lasting could be made. Men who could think in these terms set up, in the course of a memorable year, safeguards against tyranny on the one side and license or anarchy on the other which still deserve the admiration of the world. Anyone who thinks he cannot go to school to these men seems to me sadly lacking in the power to recognize achievement. But these are men out of our past, out of our political infancy.

This unhistorical way of supposing that only being of the present can validate a thing has been called the fallacy of presentism. It has produced an enormous amount of confusion in education, and the end is not in sight. But meanwhile there are other forces to grapple with, and here I turn to another, for which no convenient name exists, but which impresses me as equally presumptuous. It is the impulse to standardize everything in the present.

Everybody senses that in the modern world there exists a massive trend toward uniformity and regimentation. Individualism has never before been under such pressure, not even from the most repressive forms of government. This is true not only because of certain political ideologies which fill the wind, but also because the products of modern technology have created an order which makes the expression or even the retention of individuality increasingly difficult. Actual physical obstacles are there, and then there exists the tremendous pressure to conform and be like the majority when "what is like the majority" is heard on radio and television and is portrayed in nationally plugged advertisements. A picture is created, a way of doing things is stereotyped which crosses more and more boundaries and makes itself more and more insistently the model. The result, unless some way is found to check or to elude this pressure, threatens to be fatal to cultural pluralism. By cultural pluralism I mean simply the appearance, growth, and co-existence of a number of different cultures often within one political division. A plurality of cultures affords the same kind of richness in space that the cultures of the past to which I have been alluding provide in time.

Up to now cultural pluralism has been very much the rule, expressed in the fact that cultures have developed and flourished as regional creations. I will give an instance of what I am talking about from our own country. A

friend of mine who comes from the eastern section of the state of Kentucky
has written a work on the Kentucky mountaineer. Now the people who
inhabit the Kentucky mountains came into that region nearly two centuries ago, bringing with them what many students affirm to be survivals of
Elizabethan culture, and even Chaucerian speech. These they modified
somewhat, of course, in the new situation, but a considerable part of the
inheritance they preserved, and naturally they added something of their
own until they had one of the most distinctive or individually flavored cultures in the United States. The whole cultural complex—their special way
of looking at life and of doing things—was kept intact right down to the
most recent times. Their speech, their balladry, their music, their social
codes, and their religiosity—for despite the tales of violence one hears out
of those hills, there is a strong strain of religiosity in those people. Only last
summer when I was talking with this friend, he drew the moral very tersely:
then came the radio and the television, and the Kentucky mountaineer was
no more.

There is a type of thinking today which tries to say that this is a gain,
that in the extinction of the Kentucky mountaineer, or any individual type
like that, progress has chalked up a gain. Now he can be like everyone else,
and what is progress for if not to equalize us? To me this is the shallowest
kind of philosophy, for it substitutes for what is human and creative and
diversified, something that is external and hollow, something more like a
parody of the life of the spirit than a genuine expression of it.

I use this case because I happen to know the background well. But even
if I should concede it to the apostles of progress, which I have no mind to
do—even if I should say that the disappearance of this particular example
of cultural distinctiveness is no great event, still there is the principle at
work, a principle which threatens all cultural differentiation. For the serious
truth is that in moving against this, technological uniformity is moving
against the nature of culture itself.

For when we look into the matter, we discover that all of the world's
cultures have been *regional*. Culture always develops in a region, though
sometimes it can be a fairly large one. It expresses the feelings of the people
in that place and time, and it is always conscious of itself; that is to say, it
can quickly recognize what is foreign to it. A culture, to use a word which
has certain unfortunate connotations today, operates on a principle of exclu-

siveness and can operate on no other. I am not referring here to any principle of class distinction or to that snobbishness with which the more cultivated sometimes look down on the less so. Those are totally different matters. The principle of exclusiveness of a culture is simply its integrity. It is an awareness of the culture that it is a unity of feeling and outlook which makes its members different from outsiders. The culture of ancient Greece is an outstanding example of this. The Greeks applied to outsiders the term *barbaroi,* which is the source of our term *barbarian.* But they did not mean by it *barbarian* in our sense. By *barbaroi* they signified "those speaking a different language." And since language is one of the supremely important elements in a culture, it is clear that this was a cultural, not a social or political designation of the outsider. Yet there has never been a time when the existing culture has been more widely diffused among the people as a whole than in the Greece of Pericles. Everyone belonged, everyone participated in it, but everyone sensed a difference between himself and "those speaking a different language." This is what I mean by cultural unity and by the regional character of a high culture.

Today such necessary conditions are being threatened in fact and in theory. I have not yet had a chance to learn as much as I hope to about the life and culture which have been developed in these beautiful valleys of Utah. But I should be much surprised if these same pressures were not being felt here too. The questioning of apartness, the suspicion of difference, the distrust of distinction, the jealousy about allowing privacy—these are all features of a modern mentality which, often without even knowing what it is doing, may put an end to what has always been the source of culture—a particular kind of development in response to particular values. Thus the plight of the individual is reenacted on a larger scale. Not only is the single human individual being pushed toward conformity, but the individual group or culture is met with the same demand to go along, to become more like the generality, and so to give up character. Now the thought is sometimes expressed that this trend will produce a culture that is international. But an international culture is a contradiction in terms. *There are no international roots.* Cultures are sometimes national or roughly co-extensive with the nation (if the nation is not too big a one), but in most instances they are geographically regional. In proportion as one tries to stretch a culture wide, it gets thin. And now that they are trying to bring the planets into our scheme of things, I do not know what we should contemplate. Thoreau has made (for me) the final pronouncement upon those who want to go sailing off to other worlds:

> I think nothing is to be hoped for from you, if this bit of mould under your feet is not sweeter to you to eat than any other in the world, or in any world.

Loyalty begins with what is near. It does not have to be an invidious loyalty. All history shows that culture is an indigenous flowering.

Lord Acton, one of the greatest of all historians, made the point that there is a goal higher than unity. Unity means oneness. The goal is harmony. Harmony is the fruitful co-existence together of things diversified.

The drive to efface individual character and to abolish distinctions has also political accomplices in this world of warring ideologies. The most powerful and correspondingly the most destructive of these goes by the name of Jacobinism. You should recall that Jacobin is a term applied to a group of extremists during the French Revolution, who carried their fervor to the point of paranoia—I think the word is not too strong—conducted the Reign of Terror, and were finally caught up and destroyed by their own radicalism. Since then the term has been used to characterize any group which aims at an extreme renovation of things and which is ready to brush aside all considerations of humanity in the pursuit of its Utopia. It had long been supposed that Jacobinism is a spirit which finds its home only on the political left, but recent history has shown that it can appear on the political right, too. Hitler's National Socialism—and how unfortunate that in our vocabulary that term has been shortened to "Nazi." We ought to continue referring to the phenomenon as "National Socialism," with emphasis on the "Socialism." Hitler's National Socialism was a Jacobinism of the right, as was to some extent Mussolini's fascism. But left or right, this political disease is fatal to cultural endeavor. Not a single significant literary work emerged from the French Revolution, except from those who fled from it to other countries or lived to write in criticism of it after it was over. The struggle of writers to get honest expression published in Soviet Russia is part of the day's news.

The reason is that Jacobinism hates the past, and hating the past it really hates humanity. Its zeal is all for power, systemization, regimentation—a madness for the translating of abstract concepts into the life of man. It therefore cannot respect the things with which culture has most intimately to do—the natural, unforced, and humane aspirations of men in their real setting. It is observable that wherever you find the spirit of communism strong or gaining headway, there you find culture at a discount. Not officially—oh, no—the communist theorists are too shrewd for anything like that. They give it sometimes a handsome location in their theory, but meanwhile they are cutting the roots from which it springs. What culture is always trying to express is reality—not that overlay of reality which is messianic communism; that is, communism in its role as messiah. Not the least of its enemies therefore is this modern political Jacobinism which may look so benign but which actually carries, as the philosopher George Santayana so well noted, a hatred of all human affections.

Now I am going to give this talk one more meandering turn, though I do claim a certain continuity for it. I am still speaking of aspects of the cultural crisis. At this point I advert to something that concerns me professionally, but also and for the same set of reasons, concerns me as a member of Western culture who desires to see that culture endure. Most of my academic career has been devoted to the teaching of rhetoric—the art of composition and expression. People far less directly connected with that field than I am could tell you that in the past several decades rhetoric has suffered a disastrous loss of prestige. In some of the universities it is regarded as a kind of scullery maid course which can be turned over to just about anybody. I am not interested in covering up this loss of prestige. I am interested in examining into the causes of it, which I believe to be far more ominous than most people suppose.

If you explain to the man in the street what it is that a course in rhetoric endeavors to do, he is as likely as not to exclaim: "Oh, I see; it's a course in how to make propaganda." Now it seems to me that there are some very general causes behind that misunderstanding, and that they are closely related to what I have been calling the evil factors in modernity.

We could begin by examining the reaction of the man in the street: "It's only propaganda." This looks like a reaction in favor of honesty, but if one pursues it just a little, he finds that it rests upon presuppositions that are nothing less than calamitous. The equating of rhetoric with propaganda is one of the surest signs that the modern world is trying to bid goodbye to religion and morality and indeed to any idea of normative standards of conduct. For the thing that such people really hold against rhetoric is that it is trying to *persuade* men. And who in this day of skepticism and moral relativism can presume that he knows enough about anything to undertake to persuade anybody? The very fact that a man is trying to exert some imaginative and emotional force upon somebody else is taken as proof that he is up to something guilty. By the uncritical application of certain dogmas many of our people have arrived at this absurd position: that to be in favor of anything is to be prejudiced in the opposite direction. Rhetorical expression therefore deals in prejudice and in nothing else. And no man has a right to prejudices, much less the right to put his prejudices off on somebody else.

It is most amazing how people have gotten themselves into such a blind alley of thinking. For the most obvious thing of all is that when man was given the gift of speech—or when he developed it, if you prefer that account of the matter—it was for the purpose of teaching and persuading. Without the use of speech for these purposes, imagine what would become of prophecy, of leadership, of instruction on all levels, and indeed of all that daily intercourse by which we decide our private affairs.

This ignorance of the essential function of rhetoric can be traced clearly to two things: a failure to distinguish between what is rightly called prejudice and what is conviction; and an unwillingness to grant that some persons are more entitled to convictions on some subjects than other persons, through superior natural insight, through hard study, or through that seriousness which comes with responsibility. An acquaintance of mine has aptly described the nature of this modern unbelief in words like these: all opinions are equal and of infinite worth. This, of course, would hold good also for the opinions of Adolf Eichmann. A converse of the proposition would be that all opinions are prejudices and therefore equally of no account.

The retort to this mass of confusion is a simple one: Men will always live by convictions, or they will kill themselves or go crazy. Rhetoric is the means we have of making convictions compelling to others by showing them in contexts of reality and of human values. "In a context of human values." This last phrase brings into view another reason why rhetoric has been brought under attack by the forces of modern radicalism. The more I

reflect, with some effort at detachment, upon rhetoric as a branch of learning and an art, the more I am convinced that it is the most humanistic of
the humanities. It is more humanistic than literature, because literature has
its own aesthetic standards which are at least semi-autonomous and which
constitute in this respect a kind of objective study. Rhetoric is more humanistic even than the study of a language, because a language has its structure
and its way of working which have to be mastered scientifically, up to a
point anyhow. Rhetoric makes use of the resources of both language and
literature, but its focus is always upon the human being. In any given case
its concern will be with a group of men in their historical, not their general
or abstract situation, for without this concern there is no basis for appeal. It
must take into account not only their generic nature, but what they know,
what they have experienced, how they feel, and what the chances are of
changing their attitude, if that is desired. Nothing could be more intensely
humanistic than this.

Now this unabashedly humanistic interest of rhetoric is to some moderns
but another reason to suspect it. And here we may note another phase of
the campaign to dehumanize man. The fact that rhetoric is so preoccupied
with what is human was once a point in its favor, but now an attempt is
being made to turn the point against it. This could never have happened
had we not lost or seriously perverted our definition of man. Again, what
is man?

He used to be considered a little lower than the angels, though with a
definite capacity to fall much lower. Now through a progressing series of
devaluations he has been defined as an animal and at length as an animal
that does not really have free will. Why then pay any deference to his values
and emotions, which must under this definition be contingent and ephemeral things anyhow? Instead of trying to improve him by rhetoric, which is
the old-fashioned way, we will go to work on him through chemistry and
really effect a change.

Time does not permit an examination of all the fallacies that underlie
that argument. Suffice it to say that the argument is logical in only one step:
if what is human is trivial (and we might recall here that the religious consciousness is peculiarly human), then it follows that rhetoric is a study of
things trivial. But if one believes that man is a creature with a special mis-

sion, nothing that enables him to put that idea of a mission into appealing forms can be considered less than important. Rhetorical language is by nature sermonic; that means it is the speech by which we preach sermons to ourselves and to others on all sorts of subjects in our private and public capacities. It therefore supplies the bond of community, for community rests upon informed sentiment.

William Faulkner in his justly famous speech at Stockholm declared his belief that man will prevail over the dark forces of this time. I agree with that prophecy, and I would add that a chief means of his prevailing will be, as it has always been, persuasive speech in the service of truth.

Now since a moment of time remains, a short retrospect may be in order. I realize that thinking and talking in this vein is regarded by some as the height of futility. Any suggestion of the recovery of past values is likely to be met with the pronouncement: "You can't turn the clock back." But the objection itself is ill-taken and actually frivolous. Nobody thinks of denying that the flow of time is irreversible. Both common sense and philosophy have established that beyond any need to call it into question. The real question is the relation of different kinds of things to this flow of time. The idea that everything has only a temporal status and therefore must change with the passage of time is the idea to be examined. Nostalgia may be a weakness, but there is nothing nostalgic about a belief in basic verities. To believe in basic verities is to believe that some values are not grounded in time; they move neither against nor with the clock.

Other objectors, varying the theme somewhat, say that there is no staying the march of material progress. The trend of that is so massive that to talk against it is only to help it along. I have even heard the proposition put in that form. It may be, say they, that there are some values which we would prefer to preserve. But the situation just does not admit it; they are destined to be ground under by the iron march of events. "Fate leads the willing and drags the unwilling" seems to be their slogan. And this progress is our fatality.

Such people, I am certain, greatly underestimate the power of men to achieve their real choices. But the choices must be real and primary, not secondary ones. Men will often say that they want such and such a thing, and true, they do want such and such a thing, but it turns out that they want something else more. It is what they want most that they will be most active, ingenious, imaginative, and tireless in seeking. When a person decides that he really wants something, he finds he can surpass himself; he can change circumstances and attain to a goal that in his duller hours seemed unattainable. As an old teacher of mine used to say, "When you have done your utmost, something will be given to you." But first must come the honest desire.

Review of Henry Steele Commager,
The American Mind[1]

Professor Commager's *The American Mind* may fairly be described as an extension, with some shift of emphasis, of Vernon Parrington's widely known *Main Currents in American Thought*. The comparison is not invidious, since Professor Commager announces himself a disciple of Parrington in his preface and later recounts the work of this scholar in terms of encomium. Parrington's study extended into the middle twenties; Professor Commager, taking the eighties of the last century as a "watershed" period, brings his account down to the present date, in a style of presentation reminiscent of the earlier work. It is generally recognized that Parrington adopted as his point of view the economics of Jeffersonian democracy. To what extent this provides an approach to all aspects of American culture is, of course, debatable, and in fact his cursory treatment of figures like Poe has scandalized students of American literature. But the point of view is capable of precise formulation, and it had the effect of illuminating considerable areas of American thought and experience.

Professor Commager's approach, or principle of interpretation, does not match this in clearness of focus. But one may readily infer from his chapters on evolutionary philosophy, pragmatism, and the new jurisprudence, together with the picture of William James as frontispiece, that he regards pragmatism as the chief current in the period he has chosen to describe.

It is very common in expositions of this kind for the chief current to become also the touchstone of evaluation; and despite some obvious efforts to chronicle fully, one finds Professor Commager's enthusiasm reserved for topics such as the science of society, the socialization of Christian doctrine,

1. *The Commonweal,* 52/4, May 5, 1950, 101–3.

and the jurisprudence of Holmes, with its pragmatic adaptation to social ends. These, and the movements that are comprehended under them, tend to constitute what is distinctively American, and add up, by his calculation, to what is valid in American life. Anyone is free, naturally, to adopt this principle, and we can even feel grateful to the author for making the application and providing an opportunity to assess the outcome.

Perhaps the most striking feature of this work as a cultural history is the failure of the facts and the conclusions to appear in a clear relationship. In some passages the author seems unable to account for data which, with the fidelity of a chronicler, he has incorporated into his story. In other passages he seems nonplussed by results which were plainly implicit in the conditions he has rehearsed. This is tantamount to saying that his theory of causation is inadequate. The "good" causes seem by his own report, though not by his inference, to be causes of the "bad" results.

Underlying the entire exposition is a theory of progress which may be exemplified by his sentence "Nothing in all history had ever succeeded like America, and every American knew it." This success is, on the whole, attributed to the willingness of Americans to be guided by practical results, and no one can deny that they have achieved outstanding successes of this *ad hoc* variety. But this can be progress in the most degraded sense, and Professor Commager is always having to wrestle with its manifestations.

How, for example, does such theory of progress accommodate the fact that "no twentieth-century statesman accomplished so much as Jefferson, and none enjoyed so much leisure"? Why is it, if progress signifies gain and not loss, that today almost no home builder has available to him skills like those of the "nameless craftsmen who built the New England villages of the eighteenth century"? What is there to tell us why "the popular culture represented by the lyceum or the Chautauqua of earlier generations was more sophisticated than that of the radio"? What explains the gulf separating "the *North American Review* from the *Reader's Digest,* or the old *St. Nicholas* from the comic strip magazines"? Where are our terms to account for the fact that "there seemed to be, in short, a progressive atrophy of the creative instinct of the average American"?

The truth expressed in the statement that "Of all the philosophies to which Americans have subscribed, pragmatism lent itself almost inevitably to vulgarization" is not irrelevant, as Professor Commager contends, but is an important link in a chain of causation which he has largely ignored or obscured.

These citations should illustrate how the trends which he holds in most esteem will appear to some minds the causes of things he deplores. The charge here is not that he fails to cover everything, but that his principle of interpretation fails to account for what he does cover. Such is bound to be the effect of riding two horses at the same time. One of them is patriotic eulogy of the American way; the other is depiction of the modern American scene, for which there are objective requirements.

The prevailing weakness of the work is that the descriptive and the evaluative tend to get mixed up, and I should say that this very ambiguity lurks in the author's phrase "evaluation of what is characteristically American." The characterization of what is American and the evaluation of it are perfectly legitimate undertakings, but they proceed from different bases. To overlook this is to ignore the difference between the positive and the dialectical, which is never done but at the expense of confusion. As a result, although *The American Mind* presents considerable information and offers a few good insights into circumstances, the picture as a whole is blurred.

Finally, I hope it will not appear caviling to ask whether pragmatism can properly be described as a mind at all. It is a method, perhaps a mood, but it cannot be called a mind for the same reason that it cannot be called a philosophy. A mind is a system of thoughts, not all of which are immediately validated by experience. Here the standard of pragmatism leads to the same collapsing of narration and evaluation which is visible in parts of Professor Commager's book. But the Americans have more in their heads than this would give them, and may be credited with a mind. The story of its formation must be—to borrow language the author uses in another connection—also "economic, social, and moral."

Introduction to William James,
Pragmatism (Selections)[1]

William James, celebrated American psychologist and leading exponent of the pragmatist method in philosophy, was born in New York City, January 11, 1842. His father, Henry James, was a man of wealth, who inherited a strong interest in religious questions, and who wrote a series of esoteric works on the relation of man to God. One of William's brothers, Henry James, Jr., was the famous novelist, who is regarded by many as the greatest American master of fiction. These three, together with a daughter, Alice, made "the James family" unique in American history for intellectual power and creativity.

James's youth was spent at various schools and in study under various tutors in Switzerland, France, England, and Germany, where he acquired the cosmopolitan outlook and the urbane manner which distinguish his writings. In early manhood he suffered a long period of nervous depression; and a kind of instability of purpose made it doubtful for a while whether he would pursue any line of activity with lasting success. The period 1861–68 saw him trying first one thing and another, and journeying to Europe again in search of health and intellectual stimulation. At the close of this period, however, he returned to Harvard and resumed work for a medical degree, which he secured in 1869.

In 1872 James was appointed instructor in physiology in Harvard College. He was deeply influenced by the reigning theory of evolution, but his own restless intellect sought an answer to the problem of the relations between physiology and mental phenomena. This interest led naturally to an absorp-

1. In William James, *Pragmatism (selections)*. Chicago: Gateway Editions, 1955, v–xi. Copyright © 1955 by Regnery Publishing. All rights reserved. Reprinted by special permission of Regnery Publishing, Inc., Washington, D.C.

tion in the study of psychology, which was just then being recognized as a subject worthy of investigation. The career for which James is known to posterity may be said to have begun about 1880, when he was made assistant professor of philosophy, following the transfer of psychology to the department of philosophy.

Two years previously he had signed a contract with a publisher for a book on the new science. He expected to turn it out in a couple of years, but it was not until 1890, or twelve years later, that his monumental *Principles of Psychology* came from the press. Its most notable feature was a rejection of the "associationist" psychology, which had come down from Hobbes, Hartley, Berkeley, and others. James had reached the conclusion that consciousness itself has causal efficacy and that the mind both selects and *adds* in its dealing with the phenomena of existence. This conviction was a springboard for launching into philosophical speculation.

Throughout his career, as his biographer Ralph Barton Perry notes, James was "solicited on the one side by religion and on the other by science." In the twenty years that remained to him after the publication of the epoch-making work on psychology his thought took on an increasingly philosophical and religious cast, although it must be recognized that he never gave up his interest in psychology or lost respect for the positive methods of science. The trend is indicated by his Gifford Lectures at the University of Edinburgh, 1901–02, later published as *The Varieties of Religious Experience,* and *Pragmatism,* which appeared in 1907. The latter volume, comprising a series of lectures given at Columbia University and at the Lowell Institute in Boston, may be regarded as his boldest expression of pragmatism as a philosophy competent to guide men's lives.

As the reader of these pages will discover, the basic tenet of pragmatism identifies truth with utility. Ideas are treated as functional, and the final test of an idea is whether it will "work." An idea is said to work when it produces the greatest amount of satisfaction and effectiveness for the individual person, all things considered. There are no systems, metaphysical constructs, or *a priori* assumptions by which an idea can be otherwise validated. If the idea produces some significant consequence for the individual, it is in that measure true; if it does not produce this, it cannot be rescued or made good by any logical or metaphysical system, since these systems themselves could be validated, in the view of the pragmatist, only by appeal to experience or results. As James expresses the point: "There can *be* no difference anywhere that doesn't *make* a difference somewhere. . . ." There can be no true idea which does not make itself felt somewhere in a concrete result.

This is the phase of James's philosophy characterized by the expression "radical empiricism," which we may interpret as an unqualified reliance upon experience for verification. But another phase, equally important for an understanding of his doctrine as a whole, is his voluntarism, or his belief that the will itself is an active agent which, in a world malleable and unfinished, adds something to the processes of reality. In James's view, the will can make the difference between one truth and another. Resolve that you will succeed in business and your chance of success is greater than that of another man in a comparable situation who makes no such resolve. This superior likelihood of success is created by the very act of willing. Following out the theory, James held that it is right for us to will things, including beliefs, which will redound to our happiness and prosperity. This is the message of his celebrated and controversial essay "The Will to Believe."

This is a crucial point for the place of religion in James's philosophical creed. He could not, on the principles he had announced, accept the kind of religion which posits dogmas or lays claim to supernatural revelation. In *Pragmatism,* for example, he speaks caustically of "gnostic answers to a divinely instituted world enigma." Nevertheless, he found that the pragmatist attitude toward life and the world would accommodate religion to this extent: if a man discovers that religious belief makes him a happier, more confident, and more effective person, that religious belief is justified by this practical consequence. The question becomes "which type of religion is going to work best in the long run." In *The Varieties of Religious Experience* he revealed a sympathetic and even penetrating understanding of such matters as conversion, saintliness, and mysticism, and he was not averse to noting that this work "on the whole has been regarded as making for the reality of God."

Anyone reading James for the first time is in danger of being carried away by the extraordinary energy, color, and buoyancy of his style. James was undoubtedly one of the greatest rhetoricians who ever wrote philosophy, and it is easy to be swayed by the surface brilliance of his arguments. However, when his system is exposed to the kind of examination which a trained dialectician can give, flaws and shortcomings become evident. Of the criticisms which have been made of his theory in general, the following cannot be ignored.

(1) The chief tenet of pragmatism rests upon the logical fallacy of illicit conversion. From the statement "All true ideas work" the pragmatist passes to the statement "All ideas that work are true." The second proposition, however, is not implied by the first, which says only that "No idea which does not work is true." It does not affirm that all ideas that work are true. This latter proposition would involve an assumption that the universe is wholly benevolent, so that all ideas which have perceptible effects are helpful, comforting, and otherwise adapted to man. But there is nothing in the pragmatist system to justify this antecedent proposition, which has to be brought in from the outside to support pragmatism itself. If the proposition were true, pragmatism would be revealed as depending upon a kind of piety toward the world which does not simply refer to experience but transcends it.

(2) An equally serious difficulty appears in the pragmatist theory of how the mind perceives reality. Pragmatism asserts that there is no such thing as disinterested knowledge, that out of the continual flux of experience the mind selects or carves certain objects according to the interest of the perceiver. But this leaves the perception of reality an arbitrary process, dependent altogether on the will or desire of the one who is perceiving. The result is to introduce a fatal subjectivism. If I now need an apple rather than a potato, I should perceive this object before me as an apple and use it accordingly. This contradicts, of course, the idea that phenomena contain in themselves certain features and differentiations which the mind has to recognize, whether they suit the purpose of an occasion or not. To employ another illustration: our decision to have a carefree picnic may encounter the fact that there is poison ivy where we sit down, a brute empirical circumstance which exists without harmonizing with the purpose of picknickers.

By the same test, the pragmatist theory that some postulates work and hence are true and others do not work and hence are false implies that facts do not always conform with the mind's original picture of them—that there is some kind of ontological basis other than what the mind provides. If those are treated as illusory, while the facts that work or harmonize with our purpose are treated as real, we are returned to the old distinction between appearance and reality, which pragmatism has no means of coping with.

(3) Finally, James's assertion that whereas there is no Absolute there may be an Ultimate seems only a verbal distinction. For an Ultimate may be an Absolute *in potentia;* that is to say, absolutes may not exist simply but may exist as paradigms toward which the world of actuality is moving teleologically. Systems other than pragmatism have admitted this, without giving up a rationalist or transcendentalist basis. James has expelled the Absolute from the front door only to open the back door for it. Although the idea disagrees with a radical empiricism, it seems a natural admission for a thinker who was strongly impressed by the variety and multiplicity of experience but also was moved by a virtually religious feeling for some kind of unification.

Puritanism and Determinism[1]

From the intensely religious Puritans of the Seventeenth Century to the unhappy scientific determinists of the late Nineteenth Century there may at first appear little connection, yet a necessary progression from the former to the latter can be traced.

The Puritans originally attempted to establish a spirituality on grounds which are untenable; this is in essence the history of the Puritan mind. For the tendency of Puritanism was away from any effort to conceive a knowledge of God. The classical philosophers addressed themselves directly to this undertaking and speculated profoundly about the nature of the truest or most real being. Plato, through his teleological metaphysics, arrived at a Supreme Idea of the Good, and this was for him World-reason, or the deity—not a personal god, but a final end of phenomena, through which causation could be explained. Aristotle accepted the same doctrine but gave it further exposition: God is pure form or the unmoved mover; it is the source of all change but is immutable itself; it is pure thought or thought of thought. The phenomena of this world are a longing of matter for this form. Aristotle's theology is thus a spirituality of the final cause.

Saint Augustine, drawing upon classical philosophy and Christian revelation, conceived God as a personality. The individual comes to know God through a consciousness of his own personality, but he must perceive finally that all rational knowledge is knowledge of God. God transcends all human categories so that our knowledge of Him must be by analogy and can never

1. A polished fragment of an essay, most likely written between 1960 and 1962 and apparently intended as the introduction to a chapter on Emerson in a book contrasting the cultures of the American North and South on which Weaver was working at the time of his death. Edited by Ted J. Smith III from a corrected typescript located in Box 5, Folder 4, of the Richard M. Weaver papers at Vanderbilt University.

be complete; yet our reason shows us that all things must be contained in their highest union in a divine mind.

Thomas Aquinas based a theology upon his study of Aristotle. God is pure form not united with matter. This means that God is without imperfection, and that He has a complete knowledge of things. Truth is an identity of thought with its object and there is no difference between what God thinks and what is. God first revealed Himself to man through Jesus Christ; this was the beginning, from which man's attention was first directed to the nature of God. The realm of nature is to the realm of grace as matter is to pure form, and God is this pure form itself in a unity of being. Saint Thomas represents, of course, the supreme attempt to unite metaphysics with theology.

All of these are profound attempts to seek out the nature of God. But Puritanism, when it appeared during the Reformation, carried a very different impetus. It was born as a protest against the evil and corruption of this world. Its attacks were aimed against men and institutions. Its intellectual energies were absorbed not by speculations about the *ousia*—the true being—but by quarrels over the conduct of ecclesiastical affairs. The Puritan even found his spirituality in this rebellion; he withdrew from other men, and the withdrawal was regarded by him as a sign of his closeness to God. What looks like a movement of extreme pietism already has its focus upon the world. The very narrowness of conduct which the Puritan prescribed for himself must be taken as an evidence of increasing worldliness. The things of this world did matter in a more decisive way than they had for Catholic Christianity, and this despite the fact that the Puritan began with an outward rejection of the world.

Unlike the doctrines of theological philosophers that have just been mentioned, his tended to be second-hand ones. They were re-definitions of Christian teachings by Calvin or Knox, or they were literal interpretations of the Bible by a duly chosen minister of the flock. And as a result, the feature of Puritanism which stamps it as a heresy in the broad or ecumenical sense of that term is its narrowness. Losing sight of the truth that religion is an apprehension of God and the cosmos, it centers attention upon things fragmented from this whole. Puritanical narrowness is thus literal: it substitutes for the whole vision some limited perception and in regard to this acts with an energy that is disproportionate. For history, tradition, and the church, the Bible is substituted. For the whole condition of man, man's relations to the sinful seductions of the world are substituted. For the doctrine of atonement, a system of narrow suppression is substituted.

The Puritan cut himself off from the total view, and has never been able to recover it. And the greatest resulting problem for him has been what to do about the world. It has been argued that Catholic Christianity went too far in utilizing the aesthetic and sensuous resources of the world as a means of religious symbolism and sanctification. What is much more certain is that the Puritans went too far in expelling the worldly and the material from any kind of consideration. Disaffected by what he felt was mummery, he made an idol of bareness. Logically that follows when there is no central or controlling vision to insure harmony and prevent simple antagonism.

Arrogating to themselves a right to judgment, they tended to see themselves as God's protagonists. The content of religion was their unilateral interpretation of the Bible. They were intensely concerned with Providence, and they believed that the working out of the world was a kind of judgment. Consequently, contrary to their initial attitude or position, the world gained in importance. It first became the place where the design of God was spelled out; ultimately it became the only source of knowledge and valuation. If the Puritans were victorious in a clash with the Indians, God's hand was in it on their side. If they got the worst of the encounter, God's hand was chastising them. The danger in this theory of matters is that Providence may one day become secularized, and that is precisely what happened. As long as there is high speculation about the nature of God, inscrutability is accepted, and Providence can remain mysterious yet real. When, however, religion becomes more literal and the problems become more ecclesiastical, the tendency is to look more for explication in this world. The Puritan allowed himself to become the victim of a dialectic which turned him from a professed complete unworldliness to an immersion in the world. His religion was of a reduced kind which could not allow an alternative to this course. Having deliberately chosen the narrow way, he found that he was forced to follow it. This leaves his intellectual heirs today in the *cul de sac* of scientific determinism. He who does not know how to judge the world's place will one day be dominated by the world. The cause and effect in his history can be denominated thus simply.

But this is getting a little ahead of the story.

Following from the old Puritan negation of the world on sternly moralistic grounds (deriving from an incomplete theology) there is a stage of the dialectic called Transcendentalism. Transcendentalism makes inescapably clear the attempt to assert or establish a spirituality without a spiritual reference. It appeared at a time when belief in historical Christianity was breaking down, partly under the impact of the higher criticism. The abandonment of faith in the divinity of Christ had to be compensated by something, and what arose in its place was a quasi-philosophical doctrine which taught the natural goodness of man and gave assurance of his contact with high powers, whatever they were or however they could be conceived. It was a liberalism, freeing itself from hereditary conviction, and setting up in place of the old God of justice and vengeance a deified man and a pantheistic concept of nature. The new point of departure is seen most clearly in R. W. Emerson's "Divinity School Address."

Review of Charles A. Lindbergh,
Of Flight and Life[1]

This book is the story of a man's passage from faith in the unlimited power
and benefit of science to a belief in the necessity of some transcending value
which can shape the ends of that science.

From his great wealth of experience Mr. Lindbergh relates three occasions which brought home to him the futility of our everyday measure-
ments. The first was his testing of the engine of a Thunderbolt fighter at
40,000 feet over Willow Run; the second was his return from a bombing
mission over Babelthuap in the South Pacific; and the third was his revisit
to Germany in 1945, where he saw the ruined cities of a nation which had
cultivated science so brilliantly and with such tragic result. The lesson,
which he urges with an earnestness that should leave no reader unstirred, is
that science without some moral supervision is fatal, and that our nation is
proceeding in dangerous disregard of this truth. "As the fallen walls of Cov-
entry should have warned Germany of the fate of her own cities, the devastation of Hiroshima and Nagasaki should be a warning to America. Our
atomic bombs return to haunt us, and in our science we foresee our doom."

Mr. Lindbergh writes that it took him many years to discover that science, for all its dazzling results, "lights only a middle chapter of creation."
The author calls for a more balanced and humane kind of living, for a re-
discovery of the values of simplicity, of solitude, of meditation, for a dedication to what he terms, in a singularly happy phrase, "the quality of life,"
and finally for a recognition of spiritual reality.

It is highly significant that the two Americans of our day who are pre-
eminent for encompassing both action and thought, Charles Lindbergh

1. *The Commonweal*, 48/24, September 24, 1948, 573.

and Douglas MacArthur, have declared that there is no answer to our problem short of a theological orientation.

This is a wise book, for which one can confidently predict a frigid reception. Probably no public figure in our recent history has suffered more from political malevolence than Mr. Lindbergh, and the extent to which books today are prejudged according to the politics of the reviewer is a near scandal. That his message is sober, thoughtful, and well directed no one can deny; and it seems to me that a man who has worked in close relation with the terrific pressures generated by our technology has something special to say to this age. People today are little disposed to listen to preachers; they are not much more disposed to listen to politicians; will they listen to one who has been in the heart of the whirlwind? If they will not listen to anybody, they are lost.

Impact of Society on Mr. Russell[1]

Bertrand Russell may well be regarded as the dean of philosophers of science in our time. Everyone recognizes that his contributions to mathematical and logical theory, his popular expositions of difficult scientific concepts, and his willingness to enter the realm of social philosophy with this special equipment give him a unique position. Outwardly, therefore, *The Impact of Science on Society* has the promise of an important testament.

But the reader who takes up this volume expecting both clearness and confidence is due for disappointment. He will get the impression that science, to which Russell has dedicated most of his proselytizing activity, has got out of hand, and that Russell is almost as confused as the ordinary layman as to its tendencies and future potentialities. "Confused" is a word one naturally uses with hesitation here, but the following quotations will give some indication of what I mean. On page 5 we read, "The victory of humanity and commonsense in this matter [the abolition of trials for witchcraft] was almost entirely due to the spread of the scientific outlook . . ." But on page 97 we read, "The human race has survived hitherto owing to ignorance and incompetence; but, given knowledge and competence combined with folly, there is no certainty of its survival." Our query then is, why does the scientific outlook combat folly in one case, but team up with it and increase its effects in another? On page 75 Russell says, in regard to a choice between extermination through modern war and submission to an international authority, "I think it probable that mankind will choose its own extermination as the preferable alternative." But on page 93 he says that we are nearer to actually achieving the abolition of war than ever before.

It may somewhat extenuate these contradictions—and other less spectacular ones which could be cited—to point out a characteristic feature of

1. *The Commonweal*, 57/20, February 20, 1953, 504.

Russell's method, which is to take evidence from widely different levels of phenomena. Sometimes he will draw his conclusion from a generally accepted body of historical fact; but in the next paragraph or on the next page he will draw another, about equally broad, from a more or less singular instance. At the same time he makes it a common practice to pass at one jump from a cause to a remote effect or from an effect to a remote cause. These could be rhetorical devices for securing attention on the lecture platform (the book is based upon a group of lectures); in any case, they result in giving the book a declamatory rather than a logical tone.

Such practices involve serious questions of method, but we must turn now to the prescriptive part of the work and look at Russell's recommendations for a world which shall be characterized by science and sanity. Here the reader will be struck by signs of extraordinary evolution in the author's thinking. Russell begins with the one-dimensional concept of human well-being right out of positivistic socialism. If we see to it that everyone is well fed and has an abundance of leisure time, the difficulties that now lead to revolution and war will evaporate. Thus in a chapter entitled "Can a Scientific Society Be Stable?" he names as the two essential conditions of stability a wide diffusion of prosperity and long holidays with full pay.

A generation or two ago, when life could be construed much more simply, this might have closed the case, and we would have had a QED not going beyond economics and biology. But so much has happened to call into question these simplistic assumptions that two important addenda appear in Russell's prescription.

One of these is a provision for risk and adventure. No longer may it be supposed that man will sink into a kind of bovine contentedness once his physical appetites have been satisfied. Now Russell believes that the security promised by a socialist community is but the "base camp from which dangerous ascents can begin." The future will have to allow room for initiative and for competitions because "the impulse to danger and adventure is deeply ingrained in human nature, and no society which ignores it can long be stable."

In the chapter "Science and Values" Russell recognizes, with the kind of candor which has always been one of the best qualities of his writing, that the real problem of social cohesion is still to be dealt with. There is something else in man which the prescription thus far does not take into account.

He names it correctly when he says, on page 94, "This wide diffusion of malevolence is one of the most unfortunate things in human nature, and it must be lessened if a world State is to be stable."

Well, the wide diffusion of malevolence is at once the oldest problem and the newest problem of society. The scientific outlook has not conquered it; good feeding and modern hygiene have not been able to expel it. Opportunity for initiative sometimes only opens up new regions to it. Where now do we look for help?

His answer, which deserves to be widely noted, appears as follows: "The root of the matter is a very simple and old-fashioned thing, a thing so simple that I am almost ashamed to mention it, for fear of the derisive smile with which wise cynics will greet my words. The thing I mean—please forgive me for mentioning it—is love, Christian love, or compassion. If you feel this, you have a motive for existence, a guide in action, a reason for courage, an imperative necessity for intellectual honesty."

It seems a long way around to find something which might have been discovered on the threshold. But sometimes we are firmer in our convictions for having surveyed the possible alternatives. Let us hope that this is true of all who like Lord Russell in this book make the long circuit to learn that society is not saved by bread alone.

Easy Conclusion[1]

It seems almost churlish to quarrel with a book infused throughout with good will and dedicated to making peace a constant and universal condition. But simplistic reasoning is one of the dangers, too, and I feel that Theo. F. Lentz's *Towards a Science of Peace* is a fairly extraordinary example of reaching an easy conclusion from defective premises.

The argument behind his proposal may be summarized as follows:

Humanity has within its grasp a happy tomorrow because "the dynamic surge of a scientific civilization promises to relieve man of the handicaps of ignorances and poverty and disease." At the same time, this human world is threatened with extinction through technology in the service of war. As Mr. Lentz expresses it in his own jargon, "power-harmony imbalance has been brought about by science in misorder." His conclusion is that since science has got us into this mess, science ought to, and can, get us out.

The assumption underlying his argument is the usual bleak scientific materialism. The whole of phenomena is amenable to the same investigative procedures that have produced "results" in the natural sciences. Here are some of the bald propositions. "We need here to challenge the dualism which says that man's world is divided into two parts, the one characterized and the other not characterized by the principle of ascertainable and knowable cause and effect." "Human intelligence has been fabulously successful in learning how to generate electricity; why should we assume that there is no way to find out how to generate love?" "Anti-social attitudes are as natural as measles and mumps, and like measles and mumps are not likely to be abolished by undisciplined anger and moral denunciation but by the appropriate means to be ascertained by objective study." This last is the crowning exculpation of man; war is a "societal disease" as the crime of the individual

1. *National Review,* 1/2, November 26, 1955, 29. © 1955 by National Review, Inc., 215 Lexington Avenue, New York, N.Y. 10016. Reprinted by permission.

is the individual's disease. It is "pragmatically stupid" to attach moral and political blame to warring nations. (Query: Are those who might agree to seek peace along Mr. Lentz's lines to be praised? The tone of his many rhetorical appeals says yes.)

The flaw in this work that leaps to the eye is the use of "science" as a sliding term. Mr. Lentz obviously wants to use it in the same sense as the physicists, chemists and biologists, and he does so whenever he can. But when such use becomes too restrictive even for his data, he uses it in the sense of "all knowledge." Ever and anon, though, one finds him slipping back to his real operating ground in statements like this: "One often wonders why the physical scientists, for example, do not apply their scientific method to the problem of war which their discoveries have terribly aggravated."

When Mr. Lentz comes to the problem of "volitional man," he can do little more than perorate on the need for gaining more knowledge through the channels of these sciences.

There is an ancient precept of theology that nothing can be done if the will is wrong. And in the absence of a teleology arising out of knowledge not merely descriptive, nothing can be done.

On Social Science[1]

Stuart Chase wrote this book to say, above all, that where knowledge is available, it is better to attack problems with it than without it. That answers *one* question—about as sane people, everywhere, have always answered it. But the terribly perplexing questions of what kind of knowledge is appropriate to what kind of problem, and how these knowledges can be obtained, he proceeds to treat breezily—by tossing everything into a hopper called "the scientific method."

Many social scientists, as Eliseo Vivas has pointed out, seem to think that they can make theirs an exact science by expressing their thoughts in the form of grating neologisms. Chase does some incidental gibing at scientific terminology, but shows himself a ready customer for such neologisms. He seems unaware, moreover, that a good many of the "discoveries" of social science are things that have been known from hoariest antiquity, the difference being that they are now dressed up in the new jargon and promulgated by somebody holding a position in the educational or governmental bureaucracy.

He tells, for example, about a study of juvenile delinquency: "*in every case an emotional maladjustment was found.*" I should think this would have been the primary datum rather than the conclusion. Saying that boys are bad because of an emotional maladjustment is about as helpful as saying that opium produces sleep because of its soporific powers, or that birds fly south in autumn because it is their instinct to do so. Too often the discoveries of "the science of human relations" are but new phrases, murkier than the ones they are intended to supplant.

Chase grows especially eloquent over the contributions of this science to the war effort. During the bombing of "Fortress Europa," he writes, a team

1. *National Review*, 1/25, May 9, 1956, 20. © 1956 by National Review, Inc., 215 Lexington Avenue, New York, N.Y. 10016. Reprinted by permission.

of social scientists made a study of the morale of fliers in action. And what these learned investigators came up with is that men fought best when they belonged to a group in which fighting well was the only accepted mode of behavior. I could refer him to a dozen passages in our Civil War literature in which the same thing is said, only with more insight and elegance.

His inability to see where ideas are leading sometimes involves him in contradictions. In an enthusiastic passage on the value of opinion polls, he extols the wisdom of the people. The people, he says, are often ahead of their chosen leaders in sensing reality. And this causes him to endorse the adage, "Never overestimate the people's knowledge or underestimate their intelligence." Well, are the people scientists? How is it possible, on the grounds he has taken, for the people to show intelligence without possessing knowledge? And if the people can and do judge rightly without possessing the knowledge he has declared indispensable, what becomes of his case for social science? Maybe there is room after all for the common sense which he virtually booted out the door on page four.

This is only part of the way in which Chase flubs the question of the relation between a scientific elite and the populace. On p. 41 he says that new knowledge about man has been gained in recent years which can answer some problems of society "better than a convocation of elders." For me this phrase translates "congress" or "senate." Does this mean that he is ready to turn over a substantial part of the work of governing to a soviet of technicians schooled in the methodology he celebrates? His position as a whole is so confused that one cannot be certain what he has in mind. But he is a great popularizer, and many readers could draw such an inference. Therein lies the danger of a superficial book like this one.

Social Science in Excelsis [1]

Social science is a tent covering a wide variety of performances. Nor would it be right to say that they are all of the circus variety. Here in this collection of thirty-one papers and addresses (*The State of the Social Sciences*, University of Chicago Press, $6.00) one sees the new science on parade, and the differences are striking enough to be reassuring.

Contributions range all the way from the unrelieved horror of inanity and jargon of Murray Horwitz's "Psychological Needs as a Function of Social Environments" to the subtle dialectic in which Leo Strauss reduces to absurdity the relativism embraced by many of his colleagues; from the overweening pretensions of James G. Miller's "Toward a General Theory for the Behavioral Sciences," with its frank dismissal of teleology, to the hardheaded questions propounded in James L. Cate's "Humanism and the Social Sciences."

The question immediately arising is how people of such differing commitments and approaches ever got assembled under one banner. Could it be that some of them have been dragooned into this parade? For the answer, one must go to the modern "success story" of social science, which is largely a tale of invasions and usurpations.

A century ago, the various studies of man were known by a few appropriate and easily decipherable names such as "history," "political economy," and "moral philosophy." But the dazzling success of the physical sciences in altering the external world inspired, if not a black envy, at least a desire to share in the accompanying attention and prestige. As Darwinism and other theories seemed to immerse man more and more completely in nature, it was soon being asked why the methods which had explained so much of

1. *National Review*, 2/19, September 29, 1956, 18–19. © 1956 by National Review, Inc., 215 Lexington Avenue, New York, N.Y. 10016. Reprinted by permission.

the physical world might not explain him also. With this the way was wide open for the materialistic monism which today underlies virtually all "scientistic" social science. Henceforward man was to be "nothing but" what the methods of science could reveal him as being.

The oddest fit in the new scientific conglomerate has been history. Science, as everybody knows, is concerned with abstractions, general laws, and the problem of predictability. It seeks out the recurring, because recurrence makes possible predictability, and prediction makes possible manipulation. Therefore the great inductive apparatus of science was turned upon history (especially history that was recent and statistically available) in the expectation of deducing its laws with the same success that had been achieved in the physical world.

One soon discovers that a basic tenet of this branch of social science is that man is always pushed but never pulled; he has "drives" and "strains," but neither freely willed goals nor a destiny. Even that troublesome word "value," so obstructive to the scientific rationalist, will one day be reduced to scientific handling, if we are to believe Mr. Miller. "The total of the strains within the individual resulting from his genetic input and variations in the input from his environment is often referred to as his values. The relative urgency of reducing these individual strains determines his hierarchy of values." This is what is known as turning "value" into a value-free word, and there are plenty of workers in the enterprise.

Where the new scientistic social science and history come to a real parting of the ways is in their grasp of the totality. History is not primarily concerned with abstracting, but with reconstructing unique events that happened in irreversible time. It is made, as Cate observes, "of the warp of individual experience as well as the woof of abstraction." Thus it is history which is broadminded, and social science which is narrow and partial.

Social science, because it has leaped to a premise of the infinite predictability and infinite manipulatibility of man, looks forward to some millenial reconstruction of society. For this reason, a large number of the members of this school have been political radicals in some measure or other; and those Congressmen who are reported to have confused social science with socialism may not have been so dumb after all. They had the right intuitive perception, even if they got the academic distinctions a little confused. A thing is defined in part by its tendency, and the tendency of scientistic social science, from Comte down to our own day, has been toward political and economic collectivism.

The historians, in contrast, have been predominantly conservatives, and their conservatism proceeds from a pessimism about the nature of man as revealed by his story. Here one cannot do better than quote the terrible pronouncement of Acton: "Neither paganism nor Christianity has ever produced a profound political historian whose mind was not turned to gloom by the contemplation of the affairs of men." To this might be added Gibbon's description of history as "the record of the crimes, follies, and misfortunes of mankind."

History in the sense recognized by Acton and Gibbon and the other great figures admitted the contingent, and the ineluctable, and expressed the truth of tragedy. It contained lessons, but not the kind that can be drawn out of a computing machine. A study making this appraisal of the human record is a far more sobering discipline—a diet calculated to grow hard-heads rather than soft eggheads—than the "social stew" on which the modern educationist tries to nourish the young. The latter is usually a con-coction of dubious abstractions about human nature and wishful thinking about the structure of reality, with a dash of political ideology from the left.

It may be said for certain that the inscrutable element is still in our lives. The more the social scientists proclaim their imminent control of affairs, the more the world bucks, heaves and reels. That is because, the more one assures himself that he has a complete rational control of his environment, the more he diminishes his actual capacity for dealing with it.

The course which converted the study of man into social scientificism contained a number of illogical steps. It is good to know that there are some men within the general field, like Strauss, Cate and Friedrich Hayek, who are engaged in patiently pointing these out. No one wishes to rest in a complete agnosticism about human nature. But it is better to be conserva-tive about our knowledge and about the perfectibility of man than to court the disasters which would certainly follow the scientific *hubris* evidenced by most of the contributors to this volume.

Science and Sentimentalism[1]

When Milton asked, "What is man, that Thou art mindful of him?" he intended the qualifying clause to place uppermost the relationship of man to God. Now, three centuries later, the question is generally amended to read, "What is man in terms of the scientifically analyzable factors that have combined to produce him?" This is essentially the line of inquiry of *In Search of Man* (Hawthorn, $5.95), by Andre Missenard, engineer, teacher and former collaborator of the late Dr. Alexis Carrel.

The work is not, however, an essay in simple materialism. Professor Missenard is concerned primarily to attack Descartes' notion of the independence of the body and the mind, which he regards as having done vast harm. But his concept of science is very broad, and he aims at "a view of man in the ensemble which will restore to him his integrality, and which will take cognizance of the interaction of his various aspects: the moral on the physical, the physical on the moral, and nutrition on the body and soul."

A number of the scientific dicta are interesting, and some of them are unsettling to the dogmas of modernism. For example: "all experiments designed to prove that acquired characteristics may be transmitted have failed completely." And further, not only is psychic heredity a fact, but "the social consequences of psychic heredity are so considerable that all political systems must postulate its acceptance or rejection." He believes nutrition to be of extreme importance in molding both the physical and the psychological man, but even so, the well-fed world of the modern social engineer would have its own pitfalls—that is, if men are like mice. When mice were given unlimited food, they became "passive, unintelligent, and less fertile." When the amount was cut down to half of what they would eat if allowed to eat

1. *National Review*, 4/22, December 7, 1957, 524–25. © 1957 by National Review, Inc., 215 Lexington Avenue, New York, N.Y. 10016. Reprinted by permission.

to satiety, they grew smaller, but "more aggressive, alert, and very cunning." Most "civilized" diets are so poor that when primitives adopt them, they lose their teeth and fall victim to all sorts of infections. It is commonly recognized that a hot climate is hard on brain work, but the same is true of a very cold one. Men from cold climates cannot adapt themselves to tropical ones, but the opposite does not hold; those from hot climates can adapt to cold ones. These instances will illustrate the range of facts which he thinks can be used for the improvement of mankind.

It is in the section on education and character building that he begins to emerge with a philosophy of man, and the trend of remarks here will be gratifying to most conservatives. Much of this section might be compressed into an "Epistle to the Deweyites." After sketching the tenets of progressive education (which he styles "natural" education as opposed to "didactic") here are some of the things he has to say:

> Natural education . . . was recently tried out in Hamburg, where the pupils were given every liberty, including the right of not attending classes. The failure was complete and resounding. . . . The new methods are ostentatiously careful not to demand too much effort of the student by fiat. It is no doubt disagreeable to force students to do work which is repugnant to them. But should they not be trained in the hard law of work while they are still at a formative stage, and learn early that it is not man's lot to escape toil? . . . Serious culture is not acquired by amusement. School must be a serious thing, even an austere matter. It may also be dull and irksome, but should we sacrifice life for childhood, or a part of childhood for life? . . . The campaign against examinations and scholarship competitions is sheer calumny. If the essential mission of intellectual education is to form character, examinations make real sense, for they are tests of the will even more than of the intelligence.

Despite the forthrightness of these and other judgments, I cannot overcome the feeling that this is essentially a softheaded book. On the whole it impresses one as a sequence of more or less agreeable *pensées* rather than a "scientific," or better, philosophical, attack upon the problems of man. These have their incidental value. But what distracts one throughout is the absence of a determining and synthesizing point of view.

The difficulty seems to be this: if one starts with empirical data, there is never any way of getting to moral and ethical judgments unless one is willing to postulate a *tertium quid,* a transcendent third something which can bring the two together in a meaningful relationship. To illustrate: there is no way of getting from evidence that certain diets have made men "loyal, faithful, and brave" to the statement that "In his relationship with his fellows, man must prove his honesty, integrity, and love of justice" in the terms Professor Missenard is willing to use. A mere amiability toward man finally exposes its roots in sentimentalism. Unless there is a dominant image of man, such as Milton was willing to conceive, there is no unconditional reason for trying to save him from his threatened collapse.

Editor's Mail[1]

Your reviewer, Howard Mumford Jones, has attacked *Ideas Have Consequences* as an irresponsible utterance. This raises the question of what determines responsibility. The intimation of the review is that one needs to apply somewhere for a license to discuss the topics covered by my book.

The one way for any writer to show responsibility is to make perfectly clear the premises from which he starts. His statements can then be judged with reference to those principles. I proceeded at some length to make explicit the grounds of my argument, and I have no reason to feel that they are left unclear. I maintain, as Jones correctly infers, that form is prior to substance, and that ideas are determinants. I am quite willing to be identified with the not inconsiderable number of thinkers in the Platonic-Christian tradition who have taken the same stand.

Jones further declares that I am concerned with only a small portion of mankind. I begin my exposition with reference to hecatombs of slaughter, ruined cities, mass captivity. These phenomena are not, unfortunately, localized, nor are the forces which have brought them into being. Actually the book was written out of concern for the millions over the earth, in bread lines, in bombed homes, in prison camps, whose sufferings, material and spiritual, are traceable to the kind of pragmatism which Jones so egregiously flaunts.

1. *The New York Times Book Review*, March 21, 1948, 29.

Culture and Reconstruction[1]

It is a historical truth that institutions do not produce their great apologias until they are on the point of passing away. In the days of their vigor, their value and perdurance are assumed; and it is only when that value is challenged and their existence becomes a matter of question that we are stirred to prepare a logical defense of them. This unhappy recollection is prompted by the appearance of T. S. Eliot's *Notes Toward the Definition of Culture.* Mr. Eliot's view is somber, and he is not unaware that he may be defining a thing which, for our time, is moribund. "We can assert with some confidence that our period is one of decline; that the standards of culture are lower than they were fifty years ago; and that the evidences of this decline are visible in every department of human activity." It therefore seems to him not unreasonable to anticipate "a period, of some duration, of which it is possible to say that we will have *no* culture."

Perhaps the surest sign that modern culture is in a critical state is the number of things which are today mistaken for culture; and I imagine that Mr. Eliot's work will have value chiefly as a corrective of popular misconceptions. The list of these is worth noting.

First of all, culture does not consist of a set of manners and attitudes which are the property of those at the top of the social and economic structure. On the contrary, any healthy culture is to be found diffused throughout the entire structure, and the author feels that in the end we are driven to locate it "in the pattern of society as a whole." Culture requires the persistence of classes, but it is not a class possession. It is equally wrong to suppose that the modern hypostatization Education is synonymous with culture. It appears rather that in spreading that abstraction we are lowering our standards and giving up the study of those things through which real

1. *The Sewanee Review,* 57/4, Autumn 1949, 714–18. Copyright 1949, 1976 by the University of the South. Reprinted with the permission of the editor.

culture is transmitted. Education of the modern kind is a defensive response to a disintegrating society; we have no evidence that it can improve culture, though we have evidence that it can "adulterate and degrade it." We know it to be true of the older universities that "young men have profited there who have been profitless students." The university influenced them not through giving them information about culture, but through being something itself, presenting a splendid image, or subtly instilling a way of life. That explains the distinction between being an Oxonian (a Harvard man is our closest approximation) and possessing a Ph.D. It follows that culture is not to be confused with proficiency. An excellence, even in the arts, is not in itself assurance that one has culture. "The person who contributes to culture, however important his contribution may be, is not always a 'cultured' person." This interesting observation could forestall much special pleading on behalf of those who have developed a specialty, but who have not undergone the spiritual initiation which seems prerequisite for membership in a culture. Lastly we must recognize that culture is not something for the political conjuror to play with because it can never be made programmatic. The word has come to have a fascination for demagogues, politicians, and social planners, and we have grown as solicitous about the culture of our defeated enemies as about their education. But nothing is less susceptible of bureaucratic direction.

Thus far the definition proceeds through a series of eliminations, and we expect next a look at the positive nature of culture itself. Here naturally the author moves with caution. I believe that his best thought appears in what I should term the principle of counterpoise. It explains the proportion of space he has given to a defense of regionalism and of religious diversity, and allows us to see the grounds on which he embraces the unpopular principle of the class society.

The principle of counterpoise is probably best seen in relation to the latter. Mr. Eliot is careful to distinguish class society from both the caste system and the system of elites. The United States, he notes, has never had a class society. The Civil War produced a plutocratic elite, and extensive immigration later came near to producing a caste system; but neither of these is an articulated society. The upper class in such a society is not defined by "the vanities and pretensions of genealogy" but by its function in maintaining a certain level of the whole culture. Thus "neither a classless society, nor a society of strict and impenetrable social barriers is good; each class should have constant additions and defections. . . ." But a class structure is necessary, along with other patterns, because cultures need forces that offset each other. "One needs the enemy." A nation whose enthusiasms and antagonisms are counterpoised at home is less likely to go looking abroad for a fight, and culture demands periods of real peace. It is precisely when these internal differences are made to disappear in favor of an enforced solidarity that the world begins to scent an aggressor. In this sense *culture* and *Kultur* are seen to be opposed conceptions. "A nation which has gradations of class seems to me, other things being equal, likely to be more tolerant and pacific than one which is not so organized." The same principle applies to differences of religious sect and cult. The opponent, or the counterweight, helps one to define himself. A "world" culture, or a national culture, is richer for tolerating local cultures, if indeed it does not find its very existence in the relations between these.

Mr. Eliot has so many valuable things to say about the services of regionalism to a culture that one wishes he had drawn examples from the United States, where regionalists have had an uphill battle against nationalizing and centralizing tendencies, and where the right to regionalism may well be decided for the whole world, considering the prestige of the American leviathan. He points out quite properly that the champions of local traditions are often most fiercely opposed by others among their own people. Sometimes this occurs because the defenders make out an absurd case; but it occurs more often, I should say, because the compatriots have found that they can do profitable business with the national or general culture which is swallowing the region. In any event, one of Mr. Eliot's most illuminating remarks is that to have a culture a people needs not merely enough to eat, but also "a proper and particular *cuisine*." In our own country, it should have been recognized, corn bread or blueberry pie is more indicative of culture than is a multi-million-dollar art gallery which is the creation of some philanthropist.

This is virtually the extent of the definition. Some readers will find the latter half of the book baffling because Mr. Eliot's prophetic soul has not allowed him to seize upon the essence of culture and offer it to us in a formula. *The Waste Land* and "The Love Song of J. Alfred Prufrock" gave him the stature of seer, and we cannot help feeling that he above all other men of our time is able to tell us something of its secret source and power.

But he stops with calling it "that which makes life worth living" and "the unconscious background of all our planning." In the latter chapters he discusses peripheral matters and persistently speaks as a sociologist. Perhaps this is an indirect way of expressing the view that culture is ultimately not definable. He tells us that we cannot aim at it deliberately, that we cannot grow it any more than we can grow a tree, although we can reach some conclusions about the conditions that favor growth.

The book as a whole seems directed at the bureaucratic delusion that everything is an administrative problem. If culture begins to flag, there must be a revision of administrative procedure, or the invention of new administrative machinery, to "save" it. Certainly it is no small achievement to expose the dilemmas which lie in wait for those who would reform culture by applying political catchwords.

The steps toward a definition of culture then are a series of corrections to keep an age which has confused virtually everything else from confusing culture with something material or mechanical. We realize that in the realm of contemporary politics words like "peace," "justice," and "democracy" are sometimes made to do duty for their logical opposites. The same thing could happen to "culture," and, within limits, has already begun to happen. If Mr. Eliot succeeds in saving the word from such perversion, he will have performed another important work of rescue and clarification.

Proud "City of God"[1]

This is an account, historical and descriptive, of the fabulous Eastern Roman Empire, which survived the fall of Rome by a thousand years. The work of a French scholar, it is designed to make more generally known one of the most extraordinary civilizations the world has seen. The ideal of Byzantine culture has exerted a strong fascination upon many who have come to know it. Yeats especially was attracted by Byzantium, feeling that there, as never before or since, "religious, aesthetic, and practical life were one."

The reason behind this was Byzantium's representation of itself. The Byzantines believed that their state was actually the extension upon earth of Christ's Kingdom. They kept an Emperor only for form; the real Emperor was Christ, for whom a throne, empty save for a copy of the Gospel, was always maintained beside that of the acting Emperor. "The Byzantine Empire was, in effect, nothing but the great scene of a spectacular drama, a mystery or a passion play, in which the consecrated dynast as the leading character played through the centuries the part of Christ."

The Byzantines deduced not only their constitution and their forms of government from the Gospel but their art as well. There were no statues in the churches, and people were depicted only in relief, as in pictures, icons, and mosaics. The reason was that Byzantium was a City of God and that supernatural beings do not exist in three dimensions. Artistic portrayal was of the abstract and disembodied. Gold was everywhere; it gilded the domes of the churches; it shone in the mosaics; it was woven into the court dress of the Emperor. Why? There is a passage in the book of *Revelations* which says that the new Jerusalem is entirely of gold.

In its actual life, however, Byzantium was far from a heavenly city.

1. *National Review*, 3/24, June 15, 1957, 578. © 1957 by National Review, Inc., 215 Lexington Avenue, New York, N.Y. 10016. Reprinted by permission.

Monopoly and privilege were entrenched by law; free enterprise was virtually proscribed; and a fierce class struggle continued down through the centuries. Changes of government were most often by *coups d'état;* according to M. Guerdan's figures, of 109 sovereigns, 65 were assassinated. While an Emperor reigned, it was God's will that he reign; but if he was murdered, that was God's will too. There was something Byzantine even in the cruelty of the punishments meted out by law.

If Byzantium has left a lesson for the philosophic historian, that is probably to be read in its excessive institutionalization. To divinize an institution is to make it eventually an idol, and an idol always demands tribute. The Byzantines tended to worship the forms they had created, and the forms came to exact a toll that was ruinous.

Strange though the thought may at first appear, there are nations of the modern world which, in their bureaucratic and industrial organizations, seem to be falling into the Byzantine pattern.

Cold Comfort[1]

In this slim volume Professor MacIver sets down his reflections on the meaning and value of life. "Philosophers without portfolio," as Irwin Edman termed them, sometimes write very revealingly about one or two aspects of experience. This can hardly be affirmed, however, of Professor MacIver. Amid a perfect forest of banality and truism there are but a few shoots of original perception. The work as a whole reminds us that a group of random observations does not constitute a philosophy. What he practices, and what he recommends, is a sort of intellectual epicureanism. He thinks that the pursuit of happiness requires philosophizing, yet he does not believe that philosophy can ever arrive at any real truths. The image it evokes for me is that of a man trying to warm his hands before the fire of his own skepticism.

1. *National Review*, 1/16, March 7, 1956, 29. © 1956 by National Review, Inc., 215 Lexington Avenue, New York, N.Y. 10016. Reprinted by permission.

Dilemma of the Intellectual[1]

During the eighteenth century there appeared in the culture of the West a new type which today is publicly acknowledged as "the intellectual." Most likely he arose in response to another new phenomenon, to which we now refer as public opinion. His characteristic function is intellectual brokerage, and therefore some would distinguish him from the original thinker, the scholar, and the expert. It is his part to stand midway between these and the general public which is destined to receive their ideas in some form. His identifying gift is a superior articulateness, and he operates chiefly as a higher-grade publicist, who makes it his job to present in the right light the findings of more creative or profounder minds.

That his work in recent times, if measured by simple consequences, has been important cannot be denied, and this we may regard as the occasion for the publication of *The Intellectual: A Controversial Portrait* (ed. George B. de Huszar, Free Press, $7.50). The book is a compilation of statements (many of them essay-length excerpts from longer works) about the nature, role and public image of the intellectual, by authors ranging from de Tocqueville to Valery, Schopenhauer to Camus, Stalin to T. S. Eliot, and Dostoievski to H. L. Mencken. Some of the authors have been intellectuals themselves in some of their roles; a few have been intellectuals merely. The account that one casts up from the various presentations is slightly if at all in favor of the intellectual, but no doubt is left that he is a force to be reckoned with.

I regret that I cannot give even a sampling of the many fine *aperçus* to be found in the sixty-eight different portraits. Space permits only the broaching of two or three questions that insistently appear in many of them.

1. *National Review*, 9/10, September 10, 1960, 153–54. © 1960 by National Review, Inc., 215 Lexington Avenue, New York, N.Y. 10016. Reprinted by permission.

The intellectual is best described as one who sees the world under the aspect of ideas. Inevitably therefore he is a critic of ideas, and as a critic of ideas he must be a critic of morals. Criticism of morals leads him directly to criticism of institutions, and this largely explains the actual influence he has had in history. Frequently the intellectual has been some kind of revolutionary, and when not a revolutionary he has supplied the ideas with which revolutionaries of the active and irreconcilable sort have worked to subvert the existing order.

It is an historical commonplace that intellectuals furnished the ideas with which the bourgeoisie overthrew the feudal regime in Europe; and today it is a notorious fact that intellectuals have been exceedingly active in the greatest subversive movement in history, whereby a doctrinaire Communism seeks to overthrow an order which has been the very basis of Western civilization. Political points of view aside, one theme seems to be more or less continuous: an estrangement of the men who work with ideas from the society which has nurtured them. This raises a problem: is there something in the nature of the ideologue as a broker of ideas which places very strong pressure upon him to think of himself as an outsider or even as a foe of the existing system?

One consideration is that many intellectuals of the past two centuries have been classless parvenus. The phrase is paradoxical, but it may serve to point out that they are individuals who have arrived by routes of education and professional experience where they understand the nature, the resources, and the mechanisms of society without having a real place in it. Like other men, the intellectual desires to belong, but he does not belong in the traditional, instinctive sense: he is not "declassed"; he is "classed," and yet he is without a class. Self-consciousness about this may lead him to ask the question "Why?", when it would never occur to one less privileged but at the same time less self-conscious.

Not only is the intellectual often conspicuous for this sense of insecurity, he is also a person actually in a dilemma, for it is certain that he can never de-intellectualize himself. Once he has arrived at his kind of education and awareness, he is in a state of lost innocence; he can never go back to the primeval garden. What then is the solution for him? The metaphor may suggest a solution; what the intellectual today stands in need of is atonement. He needs to recover an at-oneness with historical society. One of the atonements he must make is for a rationalism which, in the absence of transcendental guiding principles, can issue only in power-seeking and the worship of the centralized state.

Though it is impossible for him to de-intellectualize himself, to go back to the unreflective life, he can find for his special gifts plenty of defensive work of a noble sort. The mission of the intellectual in our age of crisis is to use his intellect to defeat the presumptions of other intellects which are not willing to accept the discipline of total reality—to supply sound reasons for those settlements which a free and humane society makes and must continue to make in order to survive. Not everyone is called upon to see the world under the aspect of ideas. Therefore the intellectual's peculiar virtue of clarity and cogent expression can do for the generality of men something which needs doing but which they are unable to do for themselves.

Up to the present the majority of intellectuals have been concerned to argue that the consensus, whatever it happened to be, was wrong. What they now have to do, since the depth of the conflict can no longer be ignored, is to show that there is a consensus—beneath that consensus about which we may permissibly quarrel—which is essential to the preservation of culture and civilization. This is not an assignment to write apologias for all the features of the *status quo*. It is an invocation to criticize from the basis of historical actuality and transcendental truth as well as from the vantage point of speculative freedom. It would be a reversal of the real treason of the intellectuals, and an end to nihilism.

There is no reason why the intellectual should not speak as an exponent of his social order as well as a critic of it. But before he can do that, he will have to learn some things which ordinary men seem to understand out of sheer simplicity. Lenin observed that the working class, if left to itself, would never rise above "trade union psychology." That is because it would reject the illusions of "scientific socialism" and strive for improvement within the limits of reality. Many of our intellectuals have been less wise than the workingmen. But the intellectual who can weather all the sophistications and arrive at basic verities would be complete and regenerate in a way that would allow us to look upon him as a person especially trustworthy for leadership.

If Mr. de Huszar's collection of portraits will permit this moral to be drawn, we can regard it as an edifying gallery.

A Hobble for Pegasus[1]

What was to be expected sooner or later has now arrived, an admonition from the social sciences to the humanities to reform their ways. Robert E. Lane's *The Liberties of Wit: Humanism, Criticism, and the Civic Mind* punctuates with a shot the cold phase of a war long present between the two disciplines.

One may doubt, however, that it will be enough to touch off a hot conflict of major proportions. The work is so deferential, so disarming in its modesty, and so willing to concede that the humanities after all *do* have something to teach that even the confirmed humanist may find himself nodding in assent here and there. Nevertheless, there could result a tightening of the lines as it becomes clear, under Mr. Lane's analysis, what course events will take if his proposed settlement is adopted.

Basically, he indicts the performance of the humanists measured against the obligations of democratic citizenship. The democratic citizen is to be the final end of education, and the concept of the democratic citizen is the idea that polarizes everything into place. What do we want of our citizens? he asks. "We want them to have democratic values and the personality to sustain these effectively." Important among the qualities of the citizen would be mental clarity. Mr. Lane is exhaustive in his inventory of what this means: it includes an understanding of the philosophical foundations underlying any inquiry; a capacity to analyze theoretical propositions; a knowledge of the relation between language and the real world (not as yet satisfactorily worked out by anybody as far as I am aware); a capacity to differentiate between fantasy and directed thinking—and a number of other things. With this as his major premise he is prepared for his assault upon the methods of teaching the humanities.

1. *National Review,* 12/2, January 16, 1962, 30–31. © 1962 by National Review, Inc., 215 Lexington Avenue, New York, N.Y. 10016. Reprinted by permission.

Much of this teaching, Mr. Lane argues, receives its misdirection from "original error," and I attach no little significance to the fact that he has here invented a parallel to a theological dogma to explain the curse that is on literary interpretation. This original error, he maintains, traces back to a deposit of Aristotelian metaphysics in the critics' and teachers' minds. From this proceeds a false idealism, breeding notions of absolutism, universality, and the intrinsic. All of these lead away from probative empirical research because they depend upon definitions and classifications in the mind, with boundaries which resist any adjustment suggested by sensory experience. And "since one of the mental properties of the citizen that is most useful is a tendency to look for empirical evidence obtained in certain well established ways, this subjectivity may impede the exercise of a person's citizenly functions."

Like the ill-prepared citizen, the ill-trained literary student looks for "intentions" in the work first of all, and at actual results later or not at all; his process is a form of "sentence first, verdict second," following from the metaphysical principle that if certain things are present, other things must follow. Such conclusions from original error, he decides, can be prevented by the instrumentalist epistemology which he espouses throughout. The saying that to think like Aristotle is to think like a human being would not impress him; he is far closer to saying that to think like John Dewey is to think like the ideal citizen. Thus the humanities are not sufficiently conscious of the tendency of the theories they use in analyzing and evaluating literature. Such lack of clarity about method, the argument continues, can have dangerous carryover, for the difference in the methods appropriate to thinking about *The Brothers Karamazov* and about the Politburo are often exaggerated, and moreover "the influence of teachers transcends their subject matter."

The nub of the criticism is that one can borrow from research a set of habits for knowing which will "legitimize" the wrong sort of conclusions. As he puts it in a summary passage: "The subjectivist, self-referential and occasionally autistic quality encouraged in literary criticism forms a Way of Knowing. There are times when this epistemology, too well learned, may stand in the way of an orderly and flexible society." We mark here the reappearance of his polar concept of a flexible society, or one whose goals are empirically discovered as life moves along.

Against these sallies the humanist has ample ground for retort. I would stress first that Mr. Lane's proposal is actually more parochial than that which he would have it supplant. For, acting out of that peculiar modern hubris which is likely to show itself whenever the term democracy is brought in, he would make the whole of life and art attendant upon a political device. If a judgment of a work of literature tends to interfere with the flexible processes of a democratic society, then something has slipped back there in the mechanics of judgment, and the methodology has to be overhauled.

Various art styles at different times have followed ideals that seem to us curious, but none an ideal quite so irrelevant as this one. Mr. Lane will be proved parochial just because his overture has in contemplation a curbing of the liberties of wit, which has been known to flourish under almost every kind of government, and which would go on ignoring his invitation to get into line. (Since critic and artist are sometimes the same person, I fail to see how the latter can be excluded from his prescriptions.) What, one may ask before leaving the point, would be our attitude toward Elizabethan literature under his proposed regime? Well, one might conceive his replying, we have now developed a political maturity which would preclude a literature based on that kind of class structure and aristocratic outlook. We can still study it, but our properly phrased questions will elicit answers that will not stand as obstacles to the democratic way of life. But this is the aforementioned hubris, the assumption that the nature of man has been defined for us by the democratic process. It is well to show a decent respect for the political form which is proving most useful in our time; it is quite another thing to handicap the artistic intuition of realities with prior political commitments.

Pegasus is too noble a steed to be hobbled in this fashion; Mr. Lane's wish that wit, in its older sense of the creative imagination, might be brought under the same discipline as the sciences is but a new offshoot of the scientistic fallacy. We can afford to leave the critics to their congeries of systems and approaches, confident that democracy will not be too badly damaged, and knowing that one good insight is worth any number of pointless deductions from an approved schematism.

A Further Testament[1]

Those who remember the impact of Joseph Wood Krutch's *The Modern Temper* in 1929 will be delighted that this civilized mind has now resurveyed the world from a perspective of nearly seventy years. More precisely, as the title intimates, he has described three worlds, the provincial Knoxville of his boyhood, cosmopolitan New York and Europe, where he passed his professional years, and the desert of the Southwest, where he makes his home in retirement and writes as an amateur, but very knowing, naturalist. As a peripatetic philosopher, he has learned much from all three, and the reader will find a rewarding combination of anecdote and reflection.

Much of the book is keyed in one way and another to the philosophy first expressed in *The Modern Temper*. That work was written with a poise which denotes matured power—Mr. Krutch recalls that each chapter somehow "miraculously presented itself." It was not so much a profession of faith as of outlook, and it was pessimistic, or at least it was widely regarded as such in booming 1929. Yet what the author had pointed out was that modern science, along with a good many abetting philosophers, was describing an inhuman world in which it was impossible for man to feel at home. The physical world was without source of value, yet man could not live without values. There was no longer possibility of tragedy; for this man now appeared too minuscule. Meaning could not be sought in love, since all attention was now affixed to its biological role. The modern temper was thus a dilemma, in which the human being could no longer find sanction for the values that had previously sustained him nor resign himself to an existence that was without value. These were unrelenting conclusions to draw in an era which had staked its all on faith in Progress, and we are not surprised to learn that someone wrote the author and asked him why he did not hang himself.

1. *Modern Age*, 7/2, Spring 1963, 219–22.

That he did not feel like acting on that gloomy advice we have the record of three more decades of successful and relatively contented life to show. In the interval Mr. Krutch has altered his views somewhat, although not in a way to repudiate the indictment carried by *The Modern Temper*. He continues to feel that the mass of "educated" people have rejected those ideas and values on which Western civilization was founded. He continues to feel, furthermore, that our sense of impending catastrophe of civilization grows out of a correspondent loss of faith in humanity. However, he no longer believes that consciousness, free will, and morality are mere figments of the imagination. His present creed is a kind of atheistic pantheism, in which man holds a unique position because he is at the highest level in nature's mysterious impulse toward the "higher." This may seem a rather bare theology, yet some very significant principles can be drawn from it, or at least can be made compatible with it. For one thing, such a view permits him to affirm a standard nature of man, which is a basis for judgments of value.

Difficult as the inquiry into the question "what is normal for man" may be, full of pitfalls as past history shows it, we must make it. And even the most casual consideration of the question seems to me to provide at least a few very general answers.

One is that most men at most times—all happy men I believe—have assumed (as we tend to deny) that Good and Evil, Justice and Injustice, the "higher" and the "lower" are, however difficult to define, realities beyond merely prevailing custom. Human nature thus makes us inveterately and "normally" makers of value judgments. A second constant is that human nature does not incline us to be pure materialists. Men have sought God as the ancient Hebrews did, or, like the Greeks, beauty and wisdom. Below these levels they have sometimes put the highest value on glory, courage, personal prowess, or military success and have believed that comfort as well as security were well sacrificed for them. Even the belief, in some savage societies, that a large collection of human heads is the thing most to be desired testifies to the fact that to believe something more worth having than material wealth is nearly as universal as the belief that some things are good and bad. A society which, like ours, defines the Good Life as identical with the High Standard of Living is running counter to a fundamental characteristic of the nature of man.

Moreover, he had developed a sense of sympathetic kinship with nature, strikingly symbolized by his turning his back upon cities. Friends were incredulous when he announced his intention of leaving the urban East for the Arizona desert. Would he not miss the theaters and universities and all that make city life stimulating? The answer was no; he was glad to have had these; but he had had them; and at his place at Redding, Connecticut, he was already experiencing a feeling of solace from nature, a positive satisfaction in knowing that there were around him living and growing things not of his planting or instigating. Undoubtedly in the case of some persons this anticipation of happiness in a more primitive environment would have proved self-deceptive; but for him it has been realized in the form of improved health and renewed zest.

Not the least interesting story in this autobiography is of Krutch's high resistance to communism, even when this was appearing in the sheep's clothing of liberalism. Anyone knowing only the outward features of his career might well ask how a person of his individualistic and realistic turn of mind could have remained associated with the *Nation* for twenty-eight years. Part of the explanation is that during Krutch's first years with it, and while Oswald Garrison Villard was editor, there reigned a liberalism of the old-fashioned kind—a liberalism which means what it says when it speaks of tolerating difference of opinion. With the departure of Villard and the mounting political fanaticism of the Thirties, his position grew uncomfortable. He speaks of himself as feeling like an "Old Pagan," bewildered by the conversion of many friends and colleagues to a strange new faith which had nothing in common with what they had previously stood for. But he himself remained unaffected; he could never accept the dogmas of the left. "I think I always tended to resist even the first beginnings of that sympathy with the Communist philosophy which was already tinging many Liberals." There were ingrained in his nature a pessimism and an "anti-utopianism," which made him say to every scheme for a brave new world: "that won't work either."

He sums up by affirming his belief that human nature either is "truly permanent" or that it cannot be changed radically short of "many millennia." There, whether he would care to admit it or not, speaks a true conservative. Once during a discussion of such matters, Freda Kirchwey came at him with a question as to how he had ever arrived at such a low opinion of human nature. "By introspection," was the reply. A humanist does not romanticize human nature; he simply believes that we have to work with what we have. By 1937 Krutch ceased to have any editorial responsibility for the *Nation,* although he stayed on as drama critic until 1952.

Mr. Krutch realizes that much of his happiness has been owing to the pluralism of our American society. What the Communist ideologue denounces as "the glaring inner contradictions of the capitalist regime" is in effect our greatest blessing. The fact that we are neither wholly this nor wholly that, that we accept democracy in some spheres of life and reject it in others, that we put up with centralized direction on one level and resist it with all our might on others means elbow room for everybody and a chance of happiness for the individualist. The latter can nearly always find a nook or cranny where he is protected by some autonomous interest which the theoretically rationalized state would certainly wipe out of existence. The moral seems to be that our freedom is a result of our unwillingness to sacrifice everything to freedom in the abstract.

For all his civility, one can detect in Krutch a certain disdain for those who have suffered more intensely than he has under our mechanized chaos. I find a touch of aloofness toward some subjects that tempt me to rhetoric. And some may feel that he has got only a little way beyond the Humanism of the Twenties and Thirties. But what can be said in recommending him to the judicious reader is that his candor and power of criticism have kept him from being taken in by imposing theories out of psychology, sociology, and political science. "They have attempted to explain myself to me and I reject the explanation." A critic of letters should also be a critic of life, and in this respect too he has been one of the wiser spirits of his generation.

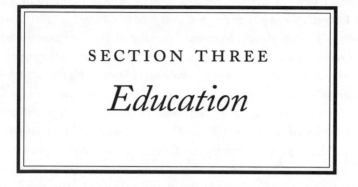

SECTION THREE

Education

Anyone who has read Richard Weaver's books will be aware of the great importance he attached to education. This section gathers together all of his shorter
writings on the subject. They are divided into three groups.

The initial group consists of five major essays, ordered chronologically. The
first two are rather prosaic analyses of the status of American education written
for the 1954 and 1955 Year Books of the Collier's Encyclopedia. The remaining
three were all published in pamphlet form by the Intercollegiate Society of Individualists (ISI). Education and the Individual was first issued in July 1959. An
abridged version entitled "The Purpose of Education" was reprinted in the Wall
Street Journal on October 9, 1959, and subsequently earned its author an Honor
Certificate from the Freedoms Foundation at Valley Forge. Academic Freedom:
The Principle and the Problems, completed in September 1962 and published
the following February, is the last essay Weaver wrote before his death. The Role
of Education in Shaping Our Society is the text of Weaver's last known speech,
an address to the Metropolitan Area Industrial Conference in Chicago on October 25, 1962. It was published some years after his death by ISI (now renamed
the Intercollegiate Studies Institute) and represents his most mature thinking on
the problems of education.

The middle group is composed of three items devoted specifically to the teaching
of composition and rhetoric. The first argues that the principal purpose of college
composition courses should be to teach students "To Write the Truth." So radical
was this thesis when the article was published in 1948 that it led to an invitation

for Weaver to debate the issue at a plenary session of a Conference on College Freshman Courses in Composition and Communication sponsored by The National Council of Teachers of English and held in Chicago in April 1949. The next item, "Looking for an Argument," provides a brief technical discussion of the Aristotelian topoi, *or topics, as sources for the generation of arguments. It is noteworthy as Weaver's only co-authored essay. Finally, "Weaver Discusses English Course" offers a description of the English composition course in the College of the University of Chicago. As chairman of the course that year (1961–62), Weaver was asked to write the article for a series on curriculum changes in the* Chicago Maroon *student newspaper. Clearly mindful that his own talents as an expository writer would be on display to the university community, he produced at least five full drafts of the article and besieged his colleagues with pleas for critical comments.*

The final group is made up of eight reviews of books on education and scholarship, all but one of them published in National Review. *Presented here in chronological order, three are of special interest because they were featured as lead reviews in the magazine's "Books in Review" section: "From Poetry to Bitter Fruit," "Mr. Hutchins as Prophet," and "History or Special Pleading?" The second of these is also noteworthy because it includes Weaver's only public evaluation of the work of Robert Maynard Hutchins, who served as chancellor of the University of Chicago from 1929 to 1951.*

Education: Reflections on[1]

Most statements today about educational policy begin with the assumption that education must prepare one for living in a democratic society. There exist, however, two sharply distinguished schools of thought on the best means to this end, and discussion of curriculums and methods has increasingly assumed the character of a debate.

On the one hand are those who maintain that an education liberal and philosophical in nature should be required for everyone, regardless of the walk of life he has in view. Their argument rests upon the principle that participation in a democratic society is an active process, that it involves the ability to reason clearly and independently, and that no potential voter should fail to receive training in the disciplines which develop the mind. Liberal education, therefore, emphasizes an acquaintance with the intellectual and cultural achievements of mankind and a capacity to use these discriminatingly and creatively. It accepts the arduous assignment of producing not merely more useful workers but better human beings, and it believes in the necessity of measuring educational attainment by ideal standards.

On the other hand are those who maintain that education is sufficient if it prepares the student to make a living and provides him with some instruction in the specific duties of citizenship. This group tends to oppose or de-emphasize liberal education on the ground that it is time consuming, that its methods are authoritarian, and that its disciplines reflect an order of society which has largely disappeared. An extreme expression of the view was given recently by the principal of a junior high school in Illinois, who declared: "We shall some day accept the thought that it is just as illogical to assume that every boy must be able to read as that each one must be able to perform on the violin, that it is no more reasonable to require that each girl

1. In William T. Couch (ed.), *Collier's 1954 Year Book*. New York: Collier & Son, 1954, 182–84. Copyright © 1954 Collier Newfield, Inc. Reprinted by permission of the publisher.

shall spell well than it is that each one shall bake a good cherry pie." The implication of this position is that there is no subject which it is necessary for every one to know. Its focus is upon practicality in the sense that it trains the hand of the individual rather than the mind of the essential man, gives greater attention to means than to ends, and assumes that an adjustment to the current (and even local) environment is all that a student need be equipped for.

Underlying these differences, at a deeper level, there appear to lie two diverse views of what a school is in its essence. One view holds that the school is simply an adjunct of the world and that the closer the two can be brought together, the better for education. Under this conception the school does not attempt to impose standards of criticism nor to point the way to higher levels of achievement: instead, it accepts the standards of the world, whatever they happen to be, and seeks only to familiarize the student with them. This attitude will explain the emphasis upon classes in civic affairs, trips to the local waterworks to see how they run, progressive abandonment of the reading of classics, and along with this a general distrust of intellectual distinction.

The other view holds that the school is not simply a part of the world, but a part set aside and reserved for progress in new areas of knowledge, for the attaining and demonstrating of higher standards, and in general for the cultivation of excellence. It welcomes rather than deplores a certain distinction between the school and the world, believing that both teachers and students are people with a mission as long as they are in that capacity, and that the world itself profits best in the long run by giving the school a certain area of freedom and asylum to carry on its work of learning, instruction, and propagation. Obviously, this view assumes a rational hierarchy of values and the authority of knowledge.

The real dilemma of modern education is that almost no one has the courage to assert that some kinds of knowledge are more valuable than other kinds. The fear stems from an awareness that once one sets the process of valuation in motion, it never stops until all kinds of knowledge have been ranked and some kind has been placed at the top. The idea of a "queen of the sciences" is one the modern mind seems unable to accept. Yet in the absence of systematic valuation, there is no basis in reason for prescribing any course of study, and the curriculum of any school or college must be regarded merely as an idiosyncratic preference.

One consequence of these opposed philosophies is a growing lack of articulation between secondary schools and institutions of higher learning. The secondary schools have increasingly subscribed to the first view, and they have accordingly instituted the student-centered or "life-centered" curriculum, with its absorption in real or supposed contemporary needs. The colleges, on the other hand, have adhered more strictly to the older, classical disciplines, which serve to train the mind and to provide knowledge. A concrete result has been that large numbers of students entering college possess too little training in basic mathematics, in rhetoric and literature, and in the foreign languages, to pursue successfully advanced studies in science and the humanities. Many colleges have been forced to alter their curriculums in ways not considered ideal to meet the problems posed by these deficiencies.

In a number of institutions, notably the large state-supported universities, a compromise has been worked out which takes the form of the "core" curriculum. This curriculum is a program of general education constituting the first two years of the student's college training. It contains courses in liberal and cultural subjects such as literature, language, history, and the arts, and basic courses in the sciences. By means of these, the student is made acquainted, during the first half of his college career, with the principles of the arts and sciences, which provide a foundation for his cultural life and to some extent for his future specialization. During the second half of his career, he begins to concentrate in the field of his future profession. Many professors of specialized subjects, it may be added, themselves believe that it is easy to over-specialize, particularly at the lower levels, and they are frequently found among those who are thus seeking to broaden the area of general education.

A few of the best known private universities, including especially Chicago, Harvard, Yale, and Columbia, have experimented with the possibility of devoting most or all of their college curriculums to general education. During the past year Yale announced a sweeping change in its college curriculum, with greater integration of studies and with a system of testing by comprehensive examinations. All of these programs represent a departure from the unlimited elective system, which allowed vocational education to begin at an early stage, toward a basic curriculum required of all students. To the extent that these institutions may be considered leaders, their new policies mark a resurgence of faith in the importance of liberal education.

Nevertheless, the struggle between the proponents of vocational and liberal education has by no means been decided, and the claims of the two groups continue to agitate, and to some extent confuse, American education at every level.

Differences over the aims of education are naturally reflected in different concepts of teaching. Various colleges and universities continue to weigh the relative merits of the lecture, the classroom discussion, and the tutorial system as means of instruction. Not all are equally free to experiment with them because the discussion and tutorial methods require larger staffs and hence are more expensive. Nonetheless, there has developed a growing interest in the discussion method. Where this method is in use, the teacher abandons the lecture altogether and appears before the class in the role of questioner and moderator. By skillfully guiding the discussion and by providing information where it is needed, he enables the students to reach by themselves answers to important questions in the subject under study. The method is defended on the ground that it encourages independent thinking, develops the critical faculty, and causes students to retain their learning longer than if they had passively absorbed it from a lecture or textbook. The tutorial system aims at much the same objective but concentrates somewhat more upon the needs and interests of the individual student.

Meanwhile the very magnitude of the American educational establishment has encouraged a tendency to think of educational progress in terms of externals. Too often it is assumed that a new school building is equivalent to a better school, that new equipment will produce greater interest in the pursuit of knowledge, and that a larger enrollment in a college or university means a more productive center of learning. When rightly used, increased physical properties may facilitate the work of education. Frequently, however, they have served as a temptation to add the superfluous, to indulge in educational frivolities, and to evade the real question of what education is for. Studies made since the Second World War have shown that some states with relatively large means have mediocre to poor educational systems, whereas states with relatively limited means have managed to create good ones. The difference is found to result from degree of interest in education, from an awareness of the true aims of the educational process, and from a more efficient employment of the resources that are available.

However, in the area of teacher recruitment it may be said that American education has suffered from obstacles of the external kind. Of these, the comparatively low salary scale is chief. Many individuals with the intelligence and energy to make excellent teachers realize that they can obtain greater remuneration in industry or in one of the professions and so are lost to the educational world. Figures show that during 1953 the average salary of all teachers in the United States was $3400, which, though a rise from the $3240 paid in the previous year, is not to be compared with what can be earned in many lines of endeavor. Good teaching requires, in addition to the proper education, the qualities of imagination and effective personality, and these are precisely the qualities which are rewarded by industry and the professions. When account is taken of the American tendency to measure social status by income, it is seen that the teacher is asked to make a double sacrifice. It would be well if there were enough dedicated spirits to make recruitment easy, but this has never been the case.

Another real deterrent is the requirement of course credits in the subject called "Education" for employment and promotion in the public school systems. Many scholars regard this as a pseudo-science, and young people who might otherwise consider teaching as a career are repelled by the triviality and barrenness of its courses. Generally, the more original and creative the mind, the less able it is to submit to this kind of teacher training.

The habit of small communities of keeping surveillance of teachers' private lives and of objecting to normal means of relaxation is a further discouragement to some who might be induced to enter elementary and high school teaching.

Academic Freedom and Communists

With the sharpening of the ideological and political conflict between the Soviet-dominated world and the West, American institutions of learning have become increasingly sensitive about the possible presence of Communists on their faculties. This is an issue which gravely involves the issue of academic freedom, and most institutions have been understandably cautious about declaring a position. The danger to the institutions, as they well recognize, is that a partial surrender of academic freedom can be a first step in a total surrender. Moreover, groups which attack schools and colleges as "communistic" are not always disinterested; they are often using the epithet to divert attention from their own selfish purposes. Yet the character of modern Communism has proved such that it cannot be ignored, even by institutions which enjoy many safeguards.

The issue took concrete form during the past year as a result of the work of the subcommittee of the Senate Committee on the Judiciary, appointed to investigate the administration of the Internal Security Act and other internal security laws. The committee was endeavoring, in the words of its chairman, Senator Jenner of Indiana, "to safeguard and protect academic freedom." It held hearings in several cities throughout the country, attempting especially to discover how many teachers owed past or present allegiance to the Communist Party. More than 100 witnesses were questioned in public sessions, and of these 82 refused to answer questions about Communist Party membership. The witnesses who so declined invoked the Fifth Amendment of the Constitution, which provides that no person can be compelled to give testimony which might incriminate him.

The status of teachers who thus refused to testify naturally excited much interest and comment. The public tended to assume that such refusal was *prima facie* evidence of Communist connection, but most of the institutions which employed the teachers took the view that they were exercising a constitutional right, and that this did not warrant suspension or dismissal from a faculty. The faculty council in one large university, however, passed a resolution to the effect that any member who refused to answer questions put by a Congressional committee should be dismissed from his post. Some educational bodies took an even more positive line of action. William Jansen, Superintendent of Schools of New York City, announced that 81 teachers had been separated from the school system since the start of an investigation.

The controversy over whether Communists should be allowed to teach really turns on the question of whether a Communist is a free agent. Those who argue that connection with the Communist Party is no disqualification for teaching maintain that all political affiliation is a private matter and that Communists can be just as objective in the classroom as professional ethics demand. They furthermore point out that asking students to read Com-

munist works and to study Soviet history is to some extent necessary because these are important influences in the modern world and must be
studied like anything else which is affecting contemporary civilization.

Those who maintain that Communists should be debarred from teaching claim that the Communist is not a seeker after objective truth, inasmuch as he has embraced a doctrine which makes him the unquestioning
agent of a political organization. They feel investigation has shown that
Communists carry on their activity in both private and professional life.
The American Association of Universities expressed its position in the following statement: "Appointment to a university position and retention after
appointment require not only professional competence but involve the affirmative obligation of being diligent and loyal in citizenship. Above all, a
scholar must have integrity and independence. This renders impossible adherence to such a regime as that of Russia and its satellites."

Both of these positions have been argued repeatedly before the public
without either winning a decisive assent, although the trend of public opinion seems to be in favor of the latter.

The entire problem is further perplexed by the fact that there has never
been a satisfactory definition of indoctrination. By one definition, all teaching whatever is indoctrination. By another definition, no teaching which is
sound teaching is indoctrination. The fairest position seems to be that indoctrination is any teaching which is done for an end that is predetermined
and in some degree selfish. An instructor who teaches a class the supposed
virtues of Communism with the object of winning adherents to the Communist Party would be practicing indoctrination. And similarly, an instructor who teaches a class "booster" material furnished by, say, the Chamber of
Commerce would be practicing indoctrination.

It appears from this that indoctrination can be recognized and checked
only by those societies which accept the objectivity of truth. If truth is regarded as dependent upon the will of the local or national government,
nothing that it wishes taught can be called indoctrination. But in a society
where truth is regarded as something having objective status, many things
can and will be taught which run counter to the views of a given political
administration. A free society will tolerate this because it regards the process of inquiry as continuous and as making its way against prejudice and

preconception. Such an attitude toward truth seems, in turn, dependent upon ethical and religious ideals.

Ethical and Religious Training

This constitutes one reason why the cry of many leaders in education is for greater emphasis upon ethical and spiritual content. Nathan M. Pusey, upon his inauguration as twenty-fourth president of Harvard University, called attention to the "gaping need" for leadership in religious knowledge and experience today. Nearly all educators realize, however, that whereas it is easy to ask for such knowledge, it is difficult to supply it, and especially difficult to implement the imparting of it. Most of the colleges and universities have been unwilling to take hold, in any tangible way, of the task of ethical and religious instruction. Part of this reluctance is traceable to the separation of church and state provided by our Constitution and reaffirmed by recent court decisions. Part of it is due to the multiplicity of religious denominations in this country and the presumptive difficulty of finding a common religious ground which would have significance. But much of the blame is undoubtedly to be placed upon the ethical confusion of the time and upon a widespread feeling that no principles of conduct, whether derived from reason or authority, should be regarded as generally compulsive. It appears that the colleges and universities will be unable to face the problem of ethical and religious training until they are willing to ask the question "What is Man?" speculatively as well as empirically.

It is universally admitted that world leadership imposes a heavy responsibility upon the United States and that the successful discharge of that responsibility will largely depend upon the education of the electorate. American education has been vigorous and adventurous in a number of respects, but it has been timid and reluctant in those fields where philosophical difficulties must be grappled with and resolved and where judgments of value must be made. Since politics on any scale is inseparably bound up with judgments of value, this is an omission which will have to be repaired. That will require more serious and thoughtful attention to the humanities, whose province it is to study the best that man has been and the best that he can be. In the past the liberal arts colleges have been the centers of such study. Today there are powerful economic and social trends whose effect has been to leave them with dwindling enrollments and with falling incomes. Either they will have to be preserved, or some means will have to be found to do the work which they have performed if the American citizen is to have an education proportionate and appropriate to his responsibilities. Once this educational duty is clearly recognized, it should be possible to organize the elementary and secondary school curriculums with foresight and relevance.

Colleges and Universities[1]

For American colleges and universities 1954 was a year of continuing crisis. Problems of financial support, of enrollment, and of basic educational philosophy mark the present as a period of transition, during which the nature of our institutions of higher learning may be determined for a long while to come.

Most of the financial problem now plaguing the colleges and universities originated in the decade 1940–1950, which was characterized by economic inflation and low interest rates. Many institutions had depended heavily upon income from endowment invested in bonds, and these two economic developments had the effect of cutting the purchasing power of such income by 50 per cent. The result was equivalent to a loss of one half of the assets which were expected to sustain them, and this at a time when enrollment was tending to increase rather than decrease. As a consequence most instinctions in this category have been driven to the unpleasant expedient of raising more money from students in the form of tuition. The new difference in tuition costs between private and public colleges and universities must be regarded as creating an unfortunate kind of differential. These facts explain why some of our celebrated universities have felt for years that they have their backs to the wall financially.

Publicly supported institutions have fared somewhat better up to the present date. Many states accumulated large surpluses during the war years because war-time restrictions cut down their normal expenditure in a number of fields. As soon as the war ended, most state institutions succeeded in getting liberal appropriations for building expansion and for salaries. However, these surpluses have been virtually exhausted by now, and state insti-

1. In William T. Couch (ed.), *Collier's 1955 Year Book.* New York: Collier & Son, 1955, 145–47. Copyright © 1955 Collier Newfield, Inc. Reprinted by permission of the publisher.

tutions are again beginning to feel the pinch, especially under the impact of newly rising enrollments.

In the economic struggle which is reflected here, the professor seems to be getting further behind all the time. Never a highly paid calling, teaching is not even holding its own in the scale of the professions. A recent study has shown that real personal per capita income throughout the country in 1951 was 164 per cent of the 1939 value. But the real per capita incomes of teachers rose only slightly more than one half of this figure. Specific figures on professional incomes will make the teacher's position clearer. A report published in the Bulletin of the American Association of University Professors showed that in 1951 the mean annual income for lawyers was $8,730, and for physicians $13,432. In the same year the mean annual salary for teachers in a selection of high-grade colleges and universities ran from $3,692 for instructors to $7,603 for full professors. The figures take on more meaning when it is realized that full professors are a small minority in every institution, consisting of men who have given most of their lives to the profession and who have achieved some degree of eminence in their field.

Most teachers who have the welfare of education at heart are sternly opposed to asking the Federal government for funds to correct the balance. While aid from this source might close the economic gap, it would certainly introduce many new problems, some of them perplexing and dangerous. Moreover, the election of a Republican administration in 1952 indicated that the people want a limit set to Federal subvention. For an indefinite period our affairs are going to be in the hands of the business community, a circumstance which presents opportunities as well as perils. If business men succeed in making our economic system run successfully, they will regain their prestige and be in position to do something for the colleges and universities. More leaders in business and industry than some people imagine are impressed with the value of liberal education, because it is this kind of training which prepares men for the "statesmanship" of business. Engineers and other technicians can be turned out by a more or less routine type of training. But skill in dealing with the public, in relating business policy to broad social trends, and in exercising the sort of imaginative insight which leads to long-term success is developed by the more philosophical, less specialized type of education. Consequently a real connection exists between our traditional liberal arts training and our traditional free enterprise system. Business men have shown some realization of this by searching for means to help our sorely pressed liberal arts colleges, though the efforts as yet are small scale and tentative. If business leadership should cope successfully with the nation's economic problems but fail to deal effectively with the problems of higher education, the plight of the colleges might become worse than it is now. Thus far, however, the auguries are fairly good.

But regardless of the source of support and control of our institutions in the near future, there seems no doubt that enrollment will continue to increase. The Second World War gave a big boost to attendance at institutions of higher learning of all kinds, and total enrollment has exceeded 2,000,000 every year since 1946. A downward trend started in 1949, but it was arrested in 1952. Fall enrollment for 1953 was 2,250,701. This figure, representing 1,432,474 men and 818,227 women, marked an increase of 4.8 per cent over the previous year. The Office of Education of the United States Department of Health, Education, and Welfare reports figures for 1953 as follows.

Universities	1,042,563
Liberal arts colleges	568,864
Teachers colleges	196,220
Technological schools	101,130
Theological schools	27,577
Other	54,080
Junior colleges	260,267

Junior colleges showed the greatest increase in students enrolling for the first time; universities the smallest. Of the total enrollment, 53.5 per cent was in publicly controlled institutions and 46.5 per cent in privately controlled. The figures represent a slight gain over the previous year for publicly controlled institutions.

The same source reports that the institutions with the largest enrollments were New York University, with 38,912; the University of California (all campuses), 33,382; the City College of New York, 28,482; the State University of New York (all campuses), 27,862; and Columbia University, 24,870.

But even these figures are due to increase sharply if the forecasts of most authorities prove correct. The Bureau of Labor Statistics has predicted that American colleges and universities will have a total enrollment of 3,800,000 by 1970. That figure might be exceeded if a larger fraction of the college-age population should go to college, or even if a larger percentage of college-age women should go. Francis H. Horn, of the Pratt Institute, Brooklyn, has published reasons for believing that the 1970 enrollment will pass 4,500,000.

In this connection it is important to recognize that modern life is more and more dominated by giant bureaucracies, governmental, business, and educational. These bureaucracies are fed almost altogether by our colleges and universities. Therefore a college-grade education, which in the past was often esteemed a luxury, is now virtually a necessity for a successful career at the professional or managerial level. A growing awareness of this fact will certainly maintain the pressure to go to college, and additional ways be sought to support financially this large college population. With the present situation in mind, the President's Commission on Higher Education recommended that by 1960 the nation be prepared to give two years of higher education to one half of the college-age population, four years to one third, and graduate education to about 15 per cent of those in the undergraduate programs.

Facts and figures like these must be cited to show the magnitude of the problems that confront those entrusted with education today. It is evident that we are entering an age of mass higher education. From one point of view this is an inevitable outcome of democratic sociapolitical philosophies. The theory that every man has equal rights leads naturally to various attempts to equalize educational advantages. And by the very nature of education, this calls for a leveling up rather than a leveling down. But the problem of how to bring an excellent education to the poor man is certainly going to prove less vexatious than how to bring it to the indifferent or the incapable man. Mass attendance at colleges and universities has made the latter problem a reality already; and this problem increases the opposition between those who favor more liberal education and those who wish to lose no time before turning the student into a competent professional man or technician.

An anomalous feature of the situation is that although liberal arts colleges have often been viewed in this country as giving an "aristocratic" type of education, the theory of liberal arts is part and parcel of the theory of democracy. The aim of liberal arts education is the "freeman"—the man educated broadly enough to make his own choices in the realms of economics, politics, and ethics. Obviously this is the ideal citizen envisaged by democracy. The mere specialist needs to have decisions made for him in fields outside his specialization. If theory and practice went hand in hand, we would behold the democratic masses surging forward to acquire a liberal education with the object of becoming fully equipped for their role as the final repositories of political power. But in actuality the situation is reversed: the great numbers besieging our institutions of higher learning are taking up special training as soon as possible and are often impatient with the meager liberal arts requirements imposed upon them. The liberal arts, meanwhile, have their steadiest following in the older and more exclusive institutions, established in the days when our country was a republic rather than a democracy and leadership was expected to come from certain classes. Educators and men in public life are sounding the warning that this is not an auspicious development for democracy. Arthur Bestor, of the University of Illinois, has observed that "the liberal arts college exemplifies, and prepares for the realization of, the motto inscribed upon our Great Seal, *E pluribus unum.*" As yet, however, the public shows little sign of appreciating the connection between what looks like a pointless general education and its own political salvation.

These pressures make themselves felt concretely by the colleges and universities especially in the area of the curriculum. Probably at no time in the past fifty years has there been more intensive thinking about the proper study requirements than goes on now. This is a consequence of the bankruptcy of the "free elective" system, which first received its impulse at Harvard under President Eliot. Under the free elective system students were allowed to choose courses according to their own estimates of their needs. The idea had a kind of specious attractiveness in its deference to real or supposed student interests and in its promise of satisfying the variegating demands of an industrialized society. But its weakness lay in the fact that it failed to face honestly one of the ultimate questions in education, which is whether a student knows what he ought to be taught. This question had been considered by Aristotle, who maintained that learners have to take some things on faith; that is to say, learners are not yet in position to judge the value and relevance of everything they are engaged in learning. As it turned out, students were not only unable to judge the value of the fundamental intellectual disciplines, they were also unable to judge the courses that would make up a good professional education. Curriculums were turned into weird collections of specialized, professional, and vocational offerings; and numberless students presented themselves for degrees with the required number of credits, but with nothing resembling a sound and coherent education.

Most curricular revisions today represent a reaction against this abuse. Harvard partially expiated its error by publishing in 1945 a report on *General Education in a Free Society*. Broadly speaking, this was a new defense of liberal education in the light of experience. It discussed the value of basic intellectual disciplines and surveyed means of introducing students to more of them. The report has stimulated interest throughout the country in "core curriculums," or curriculums in which students acquire some knowledge of the basic disciplines before launching upon their careers of special study. The expression "general education" was misinterpreted in some places, however, by those who thought it meant catch-all courses and training for that nebulous thing called "life adjustment."

A widely publicized event of the year 1953–1954 was a modification of the University of Chicago College Plan, one of the pioneering efforts in general education. The modification was the result not of educational defects but of a practical necessity to articulate the work of the college with the programs of high schools and professional schools as these are now organized.

There is another educational cleavage at the college and university level which is in some ways more serious than that between liberal and specialized training. This is the gulf that has grown between colleges and universities in general on the one hand and teacher training colleges on the other. The degree to which these are out of touch and out of sympathy with one another must prove amazing to anyone who has never investigated the situation.

Colleges and departments of education have developed in response to the need for preparing the tens of thousands of teachers required to staff our immense public school system. That they have a most important function to discharge is plain for all to see. But instead of seeing that their products are equipped with sound learning in the various arts and sciences, they have ignored this and have concentrated almost exclusively upon methods of education. They have erected a pseudo-science called "Education," most of whose courses are made up of commonplaces expressed in pretentious jargon. This kind of emphasis has led to an astonishing degree of anti-intellectualism among those in charge of public education. Their policy has been to deprecate men of learning as "subject-matter specialists" and to insist that only those trained in their peculiar methodology are prepared to instruct the nation's youth. The result is a curious situation in which the best graduates of our liberal arts colleges are unable to secure positions in the public schools until they have submitted to the requirements of a self-perpetuating body of educationists. Many of the ablest students refuse to go through this mummery, and consequently public education is largely left in the hands of the fair to poor ones. A recent study showed that of 97,800 college freshmen who took the draft deferment tests, 53 per cent made a passing grade. But of those majoring in Education only 27 per cent passed, the poorest showing made by any category of students. The rift between the world of learning and the schools of pedagogy is the greatest single scandal in education, and until something effective is done about it, our public schools will continue to deteriorate.

The problem of staffing colleges and universities has been complicated by the growing battle over communism. It is common knowledge that in the past many teachers have been receptive to the idea of political and economic change in the general direction of social democracy. A few allowed their enthusiasm to carry them to the point of joining the Communist Party, or at least of working actively in some of its fronts. Two developments especially have made the public extremely hostile to communism: the fact that the Soviet Union is a menace to the security of the United States, and the fact that many of the methods employed by communists are profoundly unethical. Where indifference or toleration once prevailed, condemnation and active prosecution are now under way. This has resulted in incidents ranging from the ludicrous to the deplorable, but so far not even the wisest heads in education have conceived a wholly satisfactory policy. On the one hand, it is of the utmost importance to preserve our tradition of academic freedom, which is the source of all that is vigorous and creative in our education. But on the other hand, we cannot leave ourselves completely vulnerable to a political force seeking to undermine all our freedoms in the name of a dogmatic philosophy. There is a conviction, now crystallizing into law, that the communists do not play the game within the rules of tolerance set by a free society. But in academic ranks there exists a difference of opinion on procedure. The liberal position is that anyone should be allowed to teach, regardless of his political affiliations, as long as he is judged by his colleagues to be working competently in his field. The conservative position is that no one should be allowed to teach who has been a member of the Communist Party, who has been active in "subversive organizations," or who has refused to testify before a Congressional committee.

Education at any level is a controversial subject. In times of special anxiety and insecurity, it is natural for people to want to scrutinize the educators to see whether they are doing the right sort of thing. Virtually all of our colleges and universities welcome this kind of review, but they desire at the same time sympathetic help with their problems. Some of these problems have now reached an acute stage, but they are not insoluble. A happy solution depends much upon public appreciation of the fact that all education is at base a discipline, and that in this realm as in others, one gets what one is willing to pay for.

Education and the Individual[1]

The greatest school that ever existed, it has been said, consisted of Socrates standing on a street corner with one or two interlocutors. If this remark strikes the average American as merely a bit of fancy, that is because education here today suffers from an unprecedented amount of aimlessness and confusion. This is not to suggest that education in the United States, as compared with other countries, fails to command attention and support. In our laws we have endorsed it without qualification, and our provision for it, despite some claims to the contrary, has been on a lavish scale. But we behold a situation in which, as the educational plants become larger and more finely appointed, what goes on in them becomes more diluted, less serious, less effective in training mind and character; and correspondingly what comes out of them becomes less equipped for the rigorous tasks of carrying forward an advanced civilization.

Recently I attended a conference addressed by a retired general who had some knowledge of this country's ballistics program. He pointed out that of the twenty-five top men concerned with our progress in this now vital branch of science, not more than two or three were Americans. The others were Europeans, who had received in their *European* educations the kind of theoretical discipline essential to the work of getting the great missiles aloft. It was a sad commentary on a nation which has prided itself on giving its best to the schools.

It is an educational breakdown which has occurred. Our failure in these matters traces back to a failure to think hard about the real province of education. Most Americans take a certain satisfaction in regarding themselves as tough-minded when it comes to successful ways of doing things

1. *Education and the Individual.* Philadelphia: Intercollegiate Society of Individualists, July 1959, pamphlet.

and positive achievements. But in deciding what is and is not pertinent to educating the individual, far too many of them have been softheads.

An alarming percentage of our citizens, it is to be feared, stop with the word "education" itself. It is for them a kind of conjuror's word, which is expected to work miracles by the very utterance. If politics become selfish and shortsighted, the cure that comes to mind is "education." If juvenile delinquency is rampant, "education" is expected to provide the remedy. If the cultural level of popular entertainment declines, "education" is thought of hopefully as the means of arresting the downward trend. People expect to be saved by a word when they cannot even give content to the word.

Somewhat better off, but far from sufficiently informed and critical, are those who recognize that education must, after all, take some kind of form, that it must be thought of as a process that does something one can recognize. Most of these people, however, see education only as the means by which a person is transported from one economic plane to a higher one, or in some cases from one cultural level to another that is more highly esteemed. They are not wholly wrong in these assumptions, for it is true that persons with a good education do receive, over the period of their lifetime, larger earnings than those without, and it is true that almost any education brings with it a certain amount of cultivation. But again, these people are looking at the outward aspects and are judging education by what it does for one in the general economic and social ordering. In both of these respects education is valued as a means of getting ahead in life, a perfectly proper and legitimate goal, of course, but hardly one which sums up the whole virtue and purpose of an undertaking, which, in a modern society, may require as much as one quarter of the life span. Education as a conjuror's word and education viewed as a means of insuring one's progress in relation to his fellows both divert attention from what needs to be done for the individual as a person.

Education is a process by which the individual is developed into something better than he would have been without it. Now when one views this idea from a certain perspective, it appears almost terrifying. How does one go about taking human beings and making them better? The very thought seems in a way the height of presumption. For one thing, it involves the premise that some human beings can be better than others, a supposition that is resisted in some quarters. Yet nothing can be plainer, when we consider it, than this fact that education is discriminative. It takes what is less good physically, mentally, and morally and transforms that by various methods and techniques into something that more nearly approaches our ideal of the good. *Every educator who presumes to speak about his profession has in mind some aim, goal, or purpose that he views as beneficial. As various as are the schemes proposed, they all share this general concept of betterment. The teacher who did not believe that his efforts contributed to some kind of improvement would certainly have lost the reason for his calling. A surface unanimity about purpose, however, is not enough to prevent confusion and chaos where there is radical disagreement about the nature of the creature who is to be educated.*

If man were merely an animal, his "education" would consist only of scientific feeding and proper exercise. If he were merely a tool or an instrument, it would consist of training him in certain response and behavior patterns. If he were a mere pawn of the political state, it would consist of indoctrinating him so completely that he could not see beyond what his masters wanted him to believe. Strange as it may seem, adherents to each of these views can be found in the modern world. But our great tradition of liberal education, supported by our intuitive feeling about the nature of man, rejects them all as partial descriptions.

The vast majority of people conscious of this tradition agree that the purpose of education is to make the human being more human. Every generation is born ignorant and unformed; it is the task of those whom society employs as educators to bring the new arrivals up to a certain level of humanity. But even with this simple statement, we find trickiness in the terms. The word "human" is one of varying implications. In estimating what constitutes a complete human being some persons today are willing to settle for a pretty low figure. To some of them, as previously noted, he is nothing more than an animal in an advanced state of evolution. His brain is only a highly developed muscle, useful to him in the same way that the prehensile tail is to the monkey; his needs are a set of skills which will enable him to get his sustenance from nature, and his purpose is to enjoy himself with the minimum amount of anxiety and the maximum amount of physical satisfaction. Others go somewhat beyond this and insist that in addition to his requirements as an animal, man has certain needs which can be described as social, intellectual, and aesthetic, and that these in turn require a kind of education which is not limited to practical self-survival. Others go beyond this and say that man is an incurably spiritual being—that he is this even when he says he is not—and that he cannot live a satisfying sort of life until certain ends which might be called psychic are met. Man has an irresistible desire to relate himself somehow to the totality, to ask what is the meaning of his presence here amid the great empirical fact of the universe. Many feel that until this question receives some sort of answer, none of the facts of life can be put in any kind of perspective.

We will not pause to weigh the opinion of those who consider man merely an animal. This view has always been both incredible and repugnant to the majority of mankind, and is accepted only by the few who have bound themselves to a theoretical materialism.

All others agree that the human being has a distinguishing attribute in *mind*. Now mind is something more than brain. Many anatomists and surgeons have seen a brain, but nobody has ever seen a mind. This is because we believe that the mind is not merely a central exchange of the body's system, where nerve impulses are brought together and relayed; it is a still mysterious entity in which man associates together the various cognitive, aesthetic, moral, and spiritual impulses which come to him from the outer and inner worlds. It is the seat of his rational faculty, but it is also the place where his inclinations are reduced to order and are directed. Most importantly for the concerns of education, mind is the place where symbols are understood and are acted upon.

Man has, in fact, been defined as the symbol-using animal. This definition makes symbol-using the distinguishing characteristic which separates him from all the other creatures with which he shares animal attributes. Even though the definition may be a partial one, it points to the faculty which has enabled man to create cultures and civilizations. The significance of the symbol is that it enables us to express knowledge and to communicate in an intellectual and not in a sensate way. Even in the matter of economy, this gain is an enormous one. If a man wishes to indicate six, he uses the symbol "6"; he does not have to lay out six pieces of wood or other objects to make his meaning clear to another. If he wishes to indicate water, he does not have to go through the motions of drinking or some other pantomime. If he wishes to express his insight into a wide complex of physical phenomena, he can do this by means of a mathematical formula, like the now famous $E = mc^2$. This is a highly symbolic form of expression, in the absence of which, it is hardly needful to point out, man's power to deal with nature would be very much smaller than it is at present. But symbolism is not used only to convey information about the physical world. Through the use of symbols man expresses those feelings and states of being which are none the less real for being subjective. His feelings of love, of delight, of aversion have been put in forms transmissible from generation to generation through the use of symbols—letters in literature, notation in music, symbolic articles in dress and in ceremonials, and so on. It is impossible to realize how poor our lives would be without the intellectual and emotional creations which depend upon this symbolic activity.

It might seem that all of this is too obvious to need a case made for it. But there exists a crisis in education today which forces all who believe in the higher nature of man to come to the defense of those subjects which discipline the mind through the language of sign and symbol.

For some while now there has been a movement among certain people styling themselves educators to disparage and even do away with the very things that were once considered the reason for and the purpose of all education. There has been a bold and open attempt to deny that man has a nature which is fulfilled only when these higher faculties are brought into play, educated, and used to make life more human in the distinctive sense. Oddly enough, the movement has arrogated to itself the name "progressive." That seems a curious term to apply to something that is retrogressive in effect, since it would drag men back toward the pre-symbolic era. In preempting the adjective "progressive" for their brand of education, these innovators were trying a rhetorical maneuver. They were trying to give the impression that their theory of education is the only forward-looking one, and that the traditional ones were inherited from times and places that sat in darkness. Now it is quite true that "progressive" education represents a departure from an ideal that has prevailed ever since the ancient Hebrews, the people of the Bible, thought about religion, and the Greeks envisioned the life of reason. This new education is not designed for man as an immortal soul, nor is it designed to help him measure up to any ideal standard. The only goal which it professes to have in view is "adjustment to life." If we examine this phrase carefully, we will see that it, like a number of others that these educational imposters have been wont to use, is rather cleverly contrived to win a rhetorical advantage. "Adjustment" has an immediate kind of appeal, because no one likes to think of himself as being "maladjusted"; that suggests failure, discomfort, and other unpleasant experiences. And furthermore, "adjustment to life" may be taken by the unwary as suggesting a kind of victory over life—success and pleasure and all that sort of thing. But as soon as we begin to examine the phrase both carefully and critically, we find that it contains booby traps. It is far from likely that the greatest men of the past, including not only famous ones but also great benefactors of humanity, have been "adjusted" in this sense. When we begin to study their actual lives, we find that these were filled with toil, strenuousness, anxiety, self-sacrifice, and sometimes a good bit of friction with their environment. In fact, it would be much nearer the truth to say that the great creative spirits of the past have been maladjusted to life in one or more important ways. Some kind of productive tension between them and their worlds was essential to their creative accomplishment. This indeed seems to be a necessity for all evolutionary progress, not merely on the organic level but on the cultural level as well. This must not be taken to mean that such persons never achieve happiness. "Happiness" as employed by today's journalism is a pretty flabby and misleading word. Certain distinctions must be made before it can be safely used. The moments of happiness of creative people, though perhaps comparatively rare, are very elevated and very intense. This is characteristic of the life of genius. And when a culture ceases to produce vital creative spirits, it must cease to endure, for these are necessary even to sustain it.

Now let us look carefully at the second term of this formula. The prophets of the new education say that they are going to teach the young to adjust to *life*. But when we begin to elicit what they have in mind, we begin to wonder what kind of thing they imagine life to be. They seem to have in mind some simulacrum of life, or some travesty, or some abstracted part. They do not contemplate adjusting students to life in its fullness and mystery, but to life lived in some kind of projected socialist commonwealth, where everybody has so conformed to a political pattern that there really are no problems any more. Adjustment to real life must take into account pain, evil, passion, tragedy, the limits of human power, heroism, the attraction of ideals, and so on. The education of the "progressives" does not do this. It educates for a world conceived as without serious conflicts. And this is the propaganda of ignorance.

Furthermore, nearly all of the great lives have involved some form of sacrifice for an ideal; nearly all great individuals have felt the call for that kind of sacrifice. But sacrifice does not exist in the vocabulary of "progressive" education, since for them everything must take the form of "adjustment" or self-realization. Were Buddha, Socrates, and Jesus "adjusted to life"? The way in which one answers that question will reveal whether he stands with those who believe that man has a higher self and a higher destiny or whether he is willing to stop with an essentially barbaric ideal of happiness. The adjustment which the progressive educators prate of is, just because of its lack of any spiritual ideal, nothing more than the adjustment of a worm to the surface it is crawling on.

When we turn to the practical influence of their theorizing, we find that it has worked to undermine the discipline which has been used through the centuries to make the human being a more aware, resourceful, and responsible person. As would be expected, the brunt of their attack has been against those studies which, because they make the greatest use of symbols, are the most intellectual—against mathematics and language study, with history and philosophy catching a large share also of their disapproval. *(There are excellent reasons for terming certain subjects "disciplines" and for insisting that the term be preserved. For "discipline" denotes something that has the power to shape and to control in accordance with objective standards. It connotes the power to repress and discourage those impulses which interfere with the proper development of the person. A disciplined body is one that is developed and trained to do what its owner needs it to do; a disciplined mind is one that is developed and trained to think in accordance with the necessary laws of thought, and which therefore can provide its owner with true causal reasoning about the world. A person with a disciplined will is trained to want the right thing and to reject the bad out of his own free volition. Discipline involves the idea of the negative, and this is another proof that man does not unfold merely naturally, like a flower. He unfolds when he is being developed by a sound educational philosophy according to known lines of truth and error, of right and wrong.)*

Mathematics lies at the basis of our thinking about number, magnitude, and position. Number is the very language of science. So pervasive is it in the work of the intellect that Plato would have allowed no one to study philosophy who had not studied mathematics. But these are the very reasons that mathematics is calculated to arouse the suspicion of the "progressives"; it works entirely through symbols and it makes real demands upon the intellect.

Language has been called "the supreme organon of the mind's self-ordering growth." It is the means by which we not only communicate our thoughts to others but interpret our thoughts to ourselves. The very fact that language has the public aspect of intelligibility imposes a discipline upon the mind; it forces us to be critical of our own thoughts so that they will be comprehensible to others. But at the same time it affords us practically infinite possibilities of expressing our particular inclinations through its variety of combinations and its nuances. Most authorities agree that we even *think* in language, that without language thought would actually be impossible. Those who attack the study of language (whether in the form of grammar, logic, and rhetoric or in the form of a foreign language) because it is "aristocratic" are attacking the basic instrumentality of the mind.

History has always been a sobering discipline because it presents the story not only of man's achievements but also of his failures. History contains many vivid lessons of what can happen to man if he lets go his grip upon reality and becomes self-indulgent; it is the record of the race, which can be laid alongside the dreams of visionaries, with many profitable lessons. Yet the modern tendency is to drop the old-fashioned history course and to substitute something called "social science" or "social studies," which one student has aptly dubbed "social stew." What this often turns out to be is a large amount of speculation based on a small amount of history, and the speculation is more or less subtly slanted to show that we should move in the direction of socialism or some other collectivism. Often this kind of study is simply frivolous; the student is invited to give his thought to the "dating patterns" of teen agers instead of to those facts which explain the rise and fall of nations. There is more to be learned about the nature of man as an individual and as a member of society from a firm grounding in ancient and modern history than from all the "social studies" ever put together by dreamy "progressive" educators.

Philosophy too is an essential part of liberal education because it alone can provide a structure for organizing our experience and a ground for the hierarchical ordering of our values. But under "progressive" education there is but one kind of philosophy, that of experimental inquiry in adapting to an environment. This has no power to yield insight and no means of indicating whether one kind of life is higher than another if both show an adjustment to the externals around them.

Thus with amazing audacity the "progressive" educators have turned their backs upon those subjects which throughout civilized history have provided the foundations of culture and of intellectual distinction.

If this has been stressed at some length, it is in order to deny the claim that "progressive" education fosters individualism. It may have the specious look of doing so because it advocates personal experience as a teacher and the release of the natural tendencies of the person. Yet it does this on a level which does not make for true individualism. *Individualism in the true sense is a matter of the mind and the spirit; it means the development of the person, not the well-adjusted automaton. What the progressivists really desire to produce is the "smooth" individual adapted to some favorite scheme of collectivized living, not the person of strong convictions, of refined sensibility, and of deep personal feeling of* direction *in life.* Any doubt of this may be removed by noting how many "progressive" educators are in favor of more state activity in education. Under the cloak of devotion to the public schools, they urge an ever greater state control, the final form of which would be, in our country, a Federal educational system directed out of Washington and used to instill the collectivist political notions which are the primary motives of this group.

No true believer in freedom can contemplate this prospect with anything but aversion. *If there is one single condition necessary to the survival of truth and of values in our civilization, it is that the educational system be left independent enough to espouse these truths and values regardless of the political winds of doctrine of the moment.* The fairest promises of a hands-off policy on the part of Federal educational authorities would come to nothing once they were assured of their power and control. If education were allowed to become a completely statist affair, there is no assurance that the content of even science courses would be kept free from the injection of political ideas. The latter might seem a fantastic impossibility, yet it has actually occurred in the Soviet Union. This is a case well worth relating as a warning to all who would put faith in centralized education under a paternalistic state.

Some years ago the leading Soviet geneticist was one T. D. Lysenko, who occupied the post of President of the All-Union Lenin Academy of Agricultural Science. Lysenko claimed that he had disposed of the genetic theories of Mendel and Morgan, his motive being that these were "reactionary" and counter to the theories of socialism. Western scientists exposed the fallacies in his work and denounced him as an ignorant quack. But Lysenko, working through a stooge named Michurin, established what he called "Michurin science" in genetics, to which Soviet geneticists still have to bow because it is in accord with the Marxist political line. How far the Communists are willing to go in perverting science to the uses of politics may be seen in the following excerpts from an article in the *USSR Information Bulletin* written by Lysenko himself.

> It was the great Lenin who discovered Michurin and the great Stalin who launched Michurin's materialistic biological theories on the highroad of creative work.
>
> Not only has the great Stalin rescued the Michurin teaching from the attempts of reactionaries in science to destroy it; he has also helped to rear large forces of Michurinist scientists and practical workers. His guiding ideas have played and are playing a decisive role in the triumph of the materialistic Michurin teaching over the reactionary, idealistic Weissmannism-Morganism in the Soviet land.
>
> The works of Joseph Stalin are an invaluable and inexhaustible fount for the development of theoretical Michurinist biology. His classic work, *Dialectical and Historical Materialism,* is an indispensable general theoretical aid to all agrobiologists, which helps them to gain a correct understanding of biological facts. Only when examined in the light of dialectical and historical materialism, the principles of which have been further developed by Stalin, does the Michurinist biological teaching gradually reveal its full depth and truth to us.

Where education is under the control of collectivist fanatics, not only is the individual's loyalty to truth despised, but the objective findings of science may be thus perverted to serve the ends of a political ideology.

Even though this may be regarded as an extreme case, we are living in a world where extreme aberrations occur suddenly, so that "It can't happen here" may be followed rather abruptly by "Now it has happened here." Dangers are always best met at the frontier, and the frontier in this instance is just where the state proposes to move in on education. Education's first loyalty is to the truth, and the educator must be left free to assert, as sometimes he needs to do, unpopular or unappreciated points of view.

Education thus has a major responsibility to what we think of as objectively true. But it also has a major responsibility to the person. We may press this even

*further and say that education must regard two things as sacred: the truth, and
the personality that is to be brought into contact with it. No education can be
civilizing and humane unless it is a respecter of persons.* It may be that up to a
certain utilitarian point, everyone's training can be more or less alike. But
in a most important area, no educational institution is doing its duty if it
treats the individual "just like everybody else." Education has to take into
account the differing aptitudes produced by nature and individual character,
and these differing aptitudes are extremely various. Physiologists are just
beginning to understand how widely men differ in their capacities to see, to
taste, to bear pain, to assimilate food, to tolerate toxic substances, and in
many other physical respects. On top of this are the multifarious ways in
which individuals differ psychologically through their nervous systems, reflexes, habits, and patterns of coordination. And above this are the various
ways in which individuals differ psychically in their ways of intuiting reality,
their awareness of ideals, their desires for this or that supersensible satisfaction, and so on. When all of these factors are brought into view, it is seen
that every individual is a unique creation, something "fearfully and wonderfully made," and that the educator who does not allow for special development within the discipline which he imposes is a represser and a violator.

*Now the educator who is aware of all the facts and values involved in his
difficult calling will recognize in the individual a certain realm of privacy. Much
of present day education and many of the pressures of modern life treat the person
as if he were a one-, or at best two-dimensional being. They tend to simplify
and indeed even to brutalize their treatment of the person by insisting that certain ways are "good for everybody." Yet it is a truth of the greatest importance
that our original ideas and our intuitions of value form in certain recesses of the
being which must be preserved if these processes are to take place. The kind of
self-mastery which is the most valuable of all possessions is not something imposed from without; it is a gestation within us, a growth in several dimensions,
an integration which brings into a whole one's private thoughts and feelings and
one's private acts and utterances. A private world alone is indeed dangerous, but
a personality whose orientation is entirely public is apt to be flat, uncreative, and
uninteresting. The individual who does not develop within himself certain psychic depths cannot, when the crises of life have to be faced, meet them with any
real staying power. His fate is to be moved along by circumstances, which in
themselves cannot bring one to an intelligent solution.*

Most people have marvelled how Abraham Lincoln was able to develop such a mastery of logic and such a sense of the meaning of words while growing up in a society which set little store by these accomplishments. Yet the answer seems easy enough; Lincoln had a very real private life, in which he reflected deeply upon these matters until he made them a kind of personal possession. He was an individual—keeping up a train of personal reflection, even while mingling in a friendly and humorous way with the people of his frontier community. Lincoln paid a price for this achievement, of course, the rule of this world being "nothing for nothing." But no one who believes in greatness will say that the price was out of proportion to what was gained. If it is true that Lincoln "belongs to the ages," it is so because he learned to think about things in a way that enabled him to transcend time and place. This is what is meant by developing a personality.

How far modern theorists have drifted from these truths may be seen in the strange remarks of the "progressive" educator John Dewey.

> . . . the idea of perfecting an "inner" personality is a sure sign of social divisions. What is called inner is simply that which does not connect with others—which is not capable of full and free communication. What is termed spiritual culture has usually been futile, with something rotten about it, just because it has been conceived as a thing which a man might have internally—and therefore exclusively.

For Dewey an inner consciousness is exclusive, aristocratic, separative. What Dewey denies, what his spurious system forces him to deny, is that by achieving a depth of personality, one does develop a power and a means of influencing the community in the best sense of the term "influence." To speak personally is to speak universally. *Humanity is not a community in the sense of a number of atoms or monads knocking together; it is a spiritual community, in which to feel deeply is to feel widely, or to make oneself accessible to more of one's fellow members. In consequence, it cannot be too forcefully argued that the education which regards only development with reference to externals is not education for a higher plane of living, for the individual and for the society of which he is a part, but for a lower—for an artificially depressed level of living which, were it to be realized, would put an end to human development.*

Although it may at first seem paradoxical to insist both upon discipline and the development of private and inner resources, the cooperative working of the two is a proved fact of education. Nothing today more needs recovering than the truth that interest develops *under pressure*. Man is not spontaneously interested in anything with an interest that lasts or that carries him beyond attention to superficial aspects. Natural interest which is left to itself nearly always proves impermanent, disconnected, and frivolous. It is only when we are made to take an interest in something that we become exposed to its real possibility of interesting us. It is only then that we see far enough into its complications and potentialities to say to ourselves, here is a real problem, or a real opportunity. We need not suppose that institutions are the only source of this kind of pressure. The situation a person finds himself in when he must earn a living or achieve some coveted goal may exert the necessary compulsion. But here we are talking about what formal education can do for the individual, and one of the invaluable things it can do is face him with the necessity of mastering something, so that he can find the real richness that lies beyond his threshold indifference to it. An interest in mathematics, in music, in poetry has often resulted from an individual's being confronted with one of these as a "discipline"; that is, as something he had to become acquainted with on pain of penalties. The subject then by its own powers begins to evoke him, and before long he is wondering how he could ever have been oblivious to such a fascinating world of knowledge and experience. From this point on his appreciation of it becomes individual, personal, and creative.

As individuality begins to assert itself in the man or woman, we realize that its movement is toward a final ethical tie-up of the personality. *Individuality should not be equated with a mere set of idiosyncrasies. Idiosyncrasy is casual, fortuitous, essentially meaningless. No enlightened believer in individualism rests his case on anything as peripheral as this. To be an individual does not mean to be "peculiar" or somehow curious in one's outlook. It does, however, mean to be distinctive.*

Individuality as a goal must be explained by men's inclinations toward the good. All of us aspire toward something higher, even though there are varying ways in which that something higher can be visualized or represented. Whether one is prone to accept an ethical humanism, a tradition of religious principles, or a creed having its authority in revelation, the truth cannot be ignored that man is looking for something better both in himself and in others. But because different persons have, through their inheritance, nurture, and education different faculties, they have different insights into the good. One man is deeply and constantly aware of certain appearances of it; another of others; and sometimes these differences are so great that they lead to actual misunderstanding. Nevertheless, the wisest have realized that such differences express finally different orientations toward values, and that the proper aim of society is not to iron them out but to provide opportunity for their expression. Variations appearing in these forms do not mean simply that one man is right and another wrong; they mean that the persons in question are responding according to their different powers to apprehend an order of reality. In this kind of perception, some persons are fast movers; others are slow but deep; some have to see things concretely; others are more successful in working out ideas and principles; some people are profoundly sensitive to place; others would do about the same kind of thinking anywhere; some do their best work while feeling a sense of security; others require the excitement and stimulus of uncertainty to draw forth their best efforts. Such a list of differences could be extended almost endlessly. But what it comes down to is this: the reason for not only permitting but encouraging individualism is that each person is individually related toward the source of ethical impulse and should be allowed to express his special capacity for that relation. This is at the same time the real validation of democracy. Democracy cannot rest upon a belief in the magic of numbers. It rests upon a belief that every individual has some special angle of vision, some particular insight into a situation which ought to be taken into account before a policy is decided on. Voting is perhaps only a rough way of effecting this, but the essential theory is clear: every person is deemed to have something worthy to contribute to decision-making, and the very diversity and variety of these responses are what make democracy not indeed a more efficient, but a fairer form of government than those in which one, or a few men at the top assume that their particular angle upon matters contains all the perception of the good that is needed.

Yet there is a very true sense in which one does not become such an individual until he becomes aware of his possession of freedom. One cannot act as a being until one is a being; one cannot *be* a being unless he feels within himself the grounds of his action. The people in this world who impress us as nonentities are, in the true analysis, people whose speech and actions are only reflections of what they see and hear about them, who have no means of evaluating themselves except through what other people think of them. These are the "other directed men," the hollow men, the men who have to be filled with stuffing from the outside, of which our civilization is increasingly productive. The real person is, in contrast, the individual who senses in himself an internal principle of control, to which his thoughts and actions are related. Ever aware of this, he makes his choices, and this choosing is the most real thing he ever does because it asserts his character in the midst of circumstances. Then the feeling of freedom comes with a great upsurging sense of triumph: to be free is to be victorious; it is to count, whereas the nonentity by his very nature does not count.

A liberal education specifically prepares for the achievement of freedom. Of this there is interesting corroboration in the word itself. "Liberal" comes from a Latin term signifying "free," and historically speaking, liberal education has been designed for the freemen of a state. Its content and method have been designed to develop the mind and the character in making choices between truth and error, between right and wrong. For liberal education introduces one to the principles of things, and it is only with reference to the principles of things that such judgments are at all possible. The mere facts about a subject, which may come marching in monotonous array, do not speak for themselves. They speak only through an interpreter, as it were, and the interpreter has to be those general ideas derived from an understanding of the nature of language, of logic, and of mathematics, and of ethics and politics. The individual who is trained in these basic disciplines is able to confront any fact with the reality of his freedom to choose. This is the way in which liberal education liberates.

Finally, therefore, we are brought to see that education for individualism is education for goodness. How could it be otherwise? The liberally educated individual is the man who is at home in the world of ideas. And because he has achieved a true selfhood by realizing that he is a creature of free choice, he can select among ideas in the light of the relations he has found to obtain among them. Just as he is not the slave of another man, with his freedom of choice of work taken from him, so he is not the slave of a political state, shielded by his "superiors" from contact with error and evil. The idea of virtue is assimilated and grows into character through exercise, which means freedom of action in a world in which not all things are good. This truth has never been put more eloquently than by the poet Milton.

> I cannot praise a fugitive and cloistered virtue unexercised and unbreathed, that never sallies out and sees her adversary, but slinks out of the race, where that immortal garland is to be run for, not without dust and heat. Assuredly we bring not innocence into the world; we bring impurity much rather; that which purifies us is trial, and trial is by what is contrary.

Freedom and goodness finally merge in this conception; the unfree man cannot be good because virtue is a state of character concerned with choice, and if this latter is taken away, there is simply no way for goodness to assert itself. The moment we judge the smallest action in terms of right and wrong, we are stepping up to a plane where the good is felt as an imperative, even though it can be disobeyed. When education is seen as culminating in this, we can cease troubling about its failure to accomplish this or that incidental objective. An awareness of the order of the goods will take care of many things which are now felt as unresolvable difficulties, and we will have advanced once more as far as Socrates when he made the young Athenians aware that the unexamined life is not worth living.

Academic Freedom:
The Principle and the Problems[1]

Some of our most inflamed controversies in recent years have involved the question of academic freedom. It is possible and even likely that such controversies will become more numerous, to the prejudice of academic freedom itself, unless there is a clearer understanding of the meaning of the concept and of the source of its validation. Anyone judging a particular issue of academic freedom needs to grasp first the essence of the principle and second its place in the general constitution of society.

The definition of academic freedom must in the nature of the case be a stipulative one; that is to say, it cannot conclude with being a mere description or generalization; it must be a statement of an ideal and a policy. All definitions that involve moral ends are of this kind. Academic freedom then is the freedom of scholars and researchers in institutions of higher learning to teach and to publish the results of their scholarship without interference from the institution itself or from outside interests.

From one point of view, academic freedom is but a new term for a very old idea. For considerably more than two thousand years there has been a tradition of free inquiry in Western civilization, which is one of its greatest glories. From the time of the Greeks there have existed in most periods "wise men," philosophers, or scholars who made it their work to seek out the structure of reality and to proclaim it by one means and another to the less initiated. The first Greeks began looking for the structure of reality in the constitution of matter: what was the prime element out of which all other things were made? Later other kinds of realities were recognized, and the scope of inquiry among them was broadened immensely to include the

1. *Academic Freedom: The Principle and the Problems.* Philadelphia: Intercollegiate Society of Individualists, February 1963, pamphlet.

nature of the gods, the nature of man, and the nature of political institutions, subjects which descend to us today as divinity, ethics, psychology, political theory, and so on.

The Middle Ages, which created the first universities in the modern sense, produced scholars of powerful intellect and accorded them a good deal more of academic freedom than the generally erroneous picture of the period would suggest. The chief subjects of study were theology and the salvation of man, and revelation furnished some propositions which they were not free to challenge. Yet the truth had to be inquired into and expounded, and within these limits there flourished a fairly extraordinary intellectual life and respect for the independence of learning. Paradoxically, the very unity of their outlook upon the world left them at liberty to argue diverse theories of reality.

With the coming of modern times, marked by the rise of science and the multiplying of conflicting political systems, the pace of inquiry has been greatly increased, and the role of men of knowledge who can bring that knowledge to others has become even more significant. At the same time tremendous political tensions and potentialities of catastrophe have developed, so that to discuss academic freedom as if these did not exist is either puerile or disingenuous.

Running through all these phases of history we find a common thread: the value set upon the fruits of free but self-disciplined inquiry. The person entitled to academic freedom has never been regarded as an irresponsible spouter of opinion. Indeed, he is not a dealer in opinion at all, but a professor of demonstrable knowledge. For the teacher entitled to voice his findings freely two things can be thought of as touchstones: a special capacity to acquire knowledge and a conscience which keeps him close to his findings, so that what he says is at the opposite pole from propaganda.

This leads us to look more carefully at the question of who is to be granted the privilege of academic freedom. There are those in America today who apparently get academic freedom mixed up with students' rights in general. While welcoming the idea that students have their rights, we should realize that after all they are probationers. It is necessary, said Aristotle, attacking an epistemological problem, for those who are learning to accept some matters on trust. That essentially defines the position of the student. He is in process of initiation, and his freedom must be apportioned in relation to that fact. It seems much safer for the integrity and the future continuation of academic freedom to limit it to those who have a commissioned responsibility. And it goes without further saying that academic freedom is not a tool for the "democratizing" of universities by turning the control of them over to students.

It is also necessary not to confuse academic freedom with ordinary civil liberty, even though they may have a common root. Academic freedom in the sense stipulated here is a privilege enjoyed by professors and other academic appointees which is a correlative of their duty—a privilege of speaking the truth. Why should this be the privilege of academic persons more than of anyone else? Everyone is privileged to speak the truth as he sees it, yet a distinction can be drawn in terms of consequences. The academic person is given the advantage of extra protection. He is not supposed to be deprived of his post or otherwise harassed if he espouses an unpopular idea or position. In the non-academic world we know that people have to take pot luck in this matter; if they have a considerate superior, they may get by with it, but in any case they run the normal hazards of deviation. To some extent they are protected by the law of civil liberty, but civil liberty and academic freedom are not synonymous, and any attempt to equate them probably weakens the cause of the professors. For in addition to civil liberty, the academicians are granted a special exemption, for several reasons easy to elucidate.

Their long training in methods of investigation is supposed to teach them how to discover the truth. The leisure for research that usually goes with their position gives them the opportunity to do so. They are not out to make money or win political office, so that what they report should be disinterested. And finally, society expects to profit by what they are able to discover.

In its ideal conception, then, academic freedom is a limited immunity accorded to those who have been considered worthy of guarding society's oracle. Their work is thought to be of such consequence that like certain other groups which make a unique contribution but are ill-equipped to defend themselves, they are protected by a covenant which says to others, "Hands off."

In the above analysis I have sought to stress two facts about academic freedom. The first is that it is the prerogative of a special group. The second is that it is an earned prerogative. The non-academic citizen has his freedom of speech. There is nothing to prevent him from taking the soap box or mimeographing pamphlets and sending them out to all and sundry. But he understands that there may be certain adverse results to this indulgence in what is essentially a personal activity. He has legal protection, but unlike the professor he has no assurance that because he has given up something, something will be conceded to him.

It is impossible not to view the professor as a kind of licensee, who thus has the right to unfettered utterance in the pursuit of his work and the opportunity to exercise this without the risk of intimidation. (At the same time the professor is in the somewhat unenviable position of having everything he says regarded by the public as coming *ex cathedra,* or from a seat of authority. This is a circumstance which must be taken into account in assessing the total situation.) Society has generally agreed that its interests are best served in the long run if academic persons, like judges, are placed beyond the range of popular retribution. Professors sometimes say dreadfully stupid things, and judges sometimes render decisions that leave us astonished. The principle cannot work perfectly, of course, but there is the long run to be considered. In the long run the public has seen the need for functionaries whose place sets them apart, so that they are free to serve but one master. The academy is thus intended to be an island of truth-seeking in a sea of self-interested contention.

The more democratic society is, the more it tends to be jealous of exemptions and exclusions of any kind, and therefore it is well to emphasize the purpose of academic freedom. Allusion has been made to the tradition of free inquiry which has been so prominent a feature of Western civilization. Generally speaking, Western man has believed that there is a truth which is knowable, that only a portion of that truth has been discovered, and that therefore the work of study and teaching should go on. Whether the age saw this acquisition and diffusion of knowledge as the spreading of philosophic wisdom, or a preparation for salvation, or as a necessary foundation for progress, the role of the scholar was regarded as a key one. Academic freedom can be viewed as a concession made to him as a key member of society.

This concession is greater than might at first appear, for society is "taking a chance." All society—any society—is made up of vested interests in the form of classes, occupations, callings, and "walks of life," which have a stake in the general social settlement. That stake may vary all the way from ownership of property to dependence upon a state-established or state-tolerated religion. For the holders of such vested interests, such things are traditionally true and practically just, and it is very human for those enjoying the benefits of the settlement to see anything threatening it as a menace. At the same time, it is generally recognized that expanding knowledge must bring some unsettlement. A balance has to be struck, and the unsettlement can be regarded as the price of renewal and increment, something society has felt it could afford within limits.

The tension between society and the academy grows almost entirely out of this relationship. The academy by the nature of its work tends to be pioneering, "adding to the total sum of knowledge"; society by the nature of social constitutions is conservatory. When this opposition of interests is enclosed or transcended by some higher, over-arching sanction, it can be productive of good. But if the two become so estranged that they can no longer see one another's position, some kind of crisis is portended.

In such times, one side may try unfairly to curb the other. Taking the side of the academy first, let us note the kinds of intervention which have been considered reprehensible by it. On occasions universities have been subjected to political interference. (Interestingly enough, this kind of interference increased markedly with the decline of feudalism and the rise of monarchs and parliaments to power, according to Walter P. Metzger in his *Academic Freedom in the Age of the University.*) At times they have been subjected to interference by ecclesiastical bodies. (Though in speaking historically we must note that most of our colleges began as "confessional" institutions, which means that those who could not accept their creed were not supposed to participate in them. This was the principle that lay behind their original supervision by the church.) In modern times, though sporadically, they have been subjected to pressure from business. These instances have been few, and attempts like Upton Sinclair's *The Goosestep* to show that American institutions of higher learning simply dance to the tune of big business are gross caricatures.

As this brief retrospect shows, there have been occurrences when the scholar and the university have been abused, if we mean by this expression restrained in their undertaking by some outside force whose main interest was not in the cultivation and dissemination of truth. These occasions, contrary to the impression given by the notoriety of some of them, have not been very numerous; and when one considers the delicacy of the relationship between the scholar, who is sometimes an innovator, and society, whose natural instinct is for self-preservation or at least continuity, it may seem surprising that there have not been more.

Much of the intemperate thinking about academic freedom derives from a supposal that whenever the academy and society fall into a disagreement, the public must be wrong. If the academy represented Truth personified, this would be so. But is it not just possible that the academy could sometimes be wrong, or that some of its influential spokesmen could be guilty of misleading? The reply may come, yes, but it has just been agreed that this is a risk which must be run. Ideas will have to meet the test of the market place even if they come from the academy, and those that are bad will remain unbought. This set of propositions has its theoretical force, which has already been recognized, but we must consider them now amid the pressures of our historical world.

First let us note that if we take the "liberal" professors as a group, we see one circumstance in particular which has called into question their commitment to the search for truth. It was noted at the beginning that "wise men" or scholars were first recognized as inquirers into the structure of reality. Most of these professors of the "liberal" persuasion have been less interested in the structure of reality before their minds and senses than in the peculiar theory of a bearded German prophet of a hundred years ago. This is to say, they have not acted as independent investigators of economic and political problems, which was their right and duty if they were to speak of them, but in a more or less herd-like fashion they have followed a doctrine. Now as this prophecy has not been borne out by history, and as the theory behind it has been exploded intellectually, they begin to look more and more silly. It would appear that they have not been professors in the sense contemplated by academic freedom. Such a professor is above all a man of independent judgment; he should not become hoodwinked about the nature of reality by some prepossessing theory. And he should not readily align himself with an Establishment. The professors who have made this mistake have, one might say, erred professionally.

As a consequence, one of the extraordinary developments of our period is a growing cleavage of opinion between the university and the general populace. This is a highly anomalous development in view of the spectacular increase in size of the universities, the amount of money they are given from various sources, and the prestige enjoyed by their graduates. But it is as true as it is unprecedented. Moreover, it is not one of those minor or local divergences which can be easily closed by explanation and concession. There has appeared a major schism which, from the point of view of the present, there seems no prospect of healing.

A striking evidence is the division of political thinking which has grown up between gown and town, if we take the former to symbolize the professoriate of our colleges and universities and the latter the great bulk of the people outside the academy. The division has been concealed to a great extent by the fact that the press and the communications media have been on the side of the academy (and moreover have been staffed through the academy) and have done much to make its opinion appear the popular one. Also, machine-run political organizations have done much to make political decisions seem to reflect that kind of thinking. But if we peer behind these machineries, we find a different state of affairs. The academicians have been "liberal," radical, collectivist in their political views, and they have furnished immeasurable amounts of ammunition to various leftist programs. Meanwhile the mass of the people, the hungry sheep who look up and are not fed their customary diet from these sources, have remained conservative and theistic, committed to faith in individualism and the American way of life, to belief in transcendental values and the dual nature of man. Consider, for example, the bitter, almost vituperative hostility of a large part of the professoriate to the House Committee on Un-American Activities, despite the almost unanimous support of this committee by the membership of the House, the people's elected representatives.

Another striking evidence of the divergence can be seen in the story of "progressive" education. The philosophy of progressive education had its birth in the universities. (Let it be said here to their credit, however, that the more strictly academic parts of the universities never succumbed to this heresy. In dealing with the realities of their own profession, most genuine academics can recognize a delusion.) Nevertheless, the doctrine of John Dewey, which one critic has aptly termed "a metaphysical rendering of communism or socialism," was propagated first from Chicago and later from Columbia, and then was taken up by the various teachers colleges. I remember once asking a distinguished professor of education, a man who had spent his life teaching teachers but who had never accepted the theories of progressivism, what American parents would do if they really understood what was being taught their children as a result of Deweyism in the schools. "They would raise hell!" was his somewhat unacademic reply.

The difference in position is so wide that I have heard another educator describe the American professoriate as a cabal. That term may be a little too strong, yet one can see what prompted it. The characterizing feature of a cabal is that it is a rather small minority engaged in trying to put something across. A case can be made showing that for roughly the last fifty years a considerable number of the professors in this country have been trying to put something over on the American people. We do not have to ascribe to them the intrigue of a cabal, for as a matter of fact their work has been quite open. To cite one instance of this frankness, a number of years ago the well-known educator George S. Counts published a work entitled *Dare the School Build a New Social Order?* By their own declaration of intentions they have been, of course, only trying to educate the people. However, education always proceeds on premises. What some of them have been offering is a theory of man and a theory of education wildly at variance with the traditional beliefs of the American people; what some others have been offering is a social and economic theory—known under its least offensive name as "social democracy"—perhaps not wildly at variance but certainly in contradiction at many points with their traditional belief in a free society. The least assumption that would justify this is that the people are so backward that their most basic values must be transvalued.

One cannot think of any society in history which has sought to educate its youth in principles contradictory to those of the society itself. To do so would produce a very unstable situation, putting it most mildly.

Here is the source of the anomaly. Seen in one way, it can be represented as a situation in which both sides are right; and my sympathy goes out to those university heads who have had to arbitrate quarrels in which these two rights were opposed. The scholar must be left free to articulate his conception of the truth. And society must be allowed to enjoy the authority and the sustaining power of its traditions. The question that now rises insistently is, how did things get so out of joint? How did the two parties ever drift so far apart that the principle of academic freedom can scarcely any longer be invoked to compose their differences? One answer would be that tradition no longer has any authority, so that everything must be created *de novo* from abstract principles, and these new ones. This is the argument of those who like to preach that we must "adapt ourselves to a fast-changing world," without inquiring as to the direction of the change.

Another answer, which will not be at all welcome in some quarters, is that the professors themselves have been guilty of a general apostasy, and as a result, it is they who have gotten academic freedom wrong. Under their conception, academic freedom, far from remaining a protective covenant whereby a professor could be assured of his job, has been converted into something much more tendentious in its effect. It has been converted into a kind of advanced barricade in an offensive campaign against the traditional foundations of our country. While it continues to serve the ordinary professor naturally and properly, it has given a kind of protection to the cabal which goes beyond its defined purpose. At least that inference can be drawn from a good many of the recent controversies over academic freedom.

Let us remember that a significant number of these cases have involved communists or the right of communists to teach in our institutions of higher learning. Now when the right of a communist to teach is challenged, one defense can readily be gotten up in this form. Suppose a political scientist or sociologist, by dint of his sober research, arrives at the conclusion that communism is the best state of society. Are you going to prevent his saying so through the normal channels of teaching and publication? If so, you will be striking at the very essence of academic freedom, even as it has been defined in this discussion. It would be the case of Socrates and his prosecutors all over again.

At this point some persons try to meet the difficulty by drawing a distinction between communists and Communist Party Members. The latter can be ruled out summarily because they are not free to teach the truth as they find it. They are bound by the dictates of the party line, which tells them *a priori* what views to hold, what ideas to propagate. They are not exercising academic freedom, and they are not entitled to its prerogative. Professor Sidney Hook, for example, accepts the principle that it is not a violation of academic freedom to refuse employment to a known member of the Communist Party, although he holds that in particular instances it may do more harm than good to discharge him.

When we turn to the communist sympathizers or "fellow travellers," however, the problem becomes far more complicated, since they cannot be defined categorically. They represent almost every degree of affiliation, from the slightest to the most serious; some are simply confused; others are "birds of passage," for whom communism is the current favorite ideology. Is there any ground for challenging their right to academic freedom?

Perhaps the most that can be said is that they are enjoying a right to which their profession of sympathy leaves them a cloudy title. It is an historical fact of life, to which I do not know any exceptions, that societies have to circumscribe public debate and expression somehow. Sometimes it is circumscribed as to subjects (i.e., we will not listen to an argument in favor of murder and arson), and sometimes it is circumscribed with reference to the people who are allowed to speak. Let us remember that John Stuart Mill, one of the most ardent defenders of liberty of expression, began his famous essay dealing with the subject by ruling out certain groups as ineligible. True, he was talking about qualities of maturity and rationality. But society has long had a custom of insisting that its speakers or mentors bring in addition to these qualifications what the ancient rhetoricians called "ethical proof"—that is, proof in the form of their character, their record for truth telling, and even their patriotism, if such a maligned word can be brought back into service today.

The next question is obviously whether the fellow traveller possesses the requisite ethical proof. If he sponsors the Soviet regime or collaborates with it on the intellectual level, he must defend some things that our traditional morality has agreed not to condone—mass killings, planned aggression, systematic double dealing, and cynical disregard for pledges, not to mention the fact that he is defending a regime which does not itself recognize academic freedom. It is clear to anyone who has known them that many of these sympathizers are *douce* people, whose personal standards of morality are high, and who personally would shrink from killing just about anything. But oddly, they have been able to swallow the blood-and-iron tactics of the communist regimes along with their disregard for the scraps of paper on which agreements are written. Their excuse seems to be that these are unfortunate incidents; they are parts of the working of history, from which we must avert our gaze, to fix that gaze upon the ultimate goal of a classless society.

Still, this does not leave them very distinctly branded. They are not the only ones who show a willingness to justify means by ends. It is a fairly common immorality.

Is it possible to brand them as people giving comfort to the enemy? That question can be answered yes or no depending on the definition of the term. Officially and in the full sense we do not have an enemy until some nation has been declared such by the Chief Executive and his action has been ratified by the Congress. Formally the communist powers are nations with which we are enjoying peaceful and friendly relations, except for our non-recognition of China.

Actually, however, almost nobody is deceived by this formalism, unless it be the most dreamy-eyed of Utopians. Long before things have reached a breaking point the rival (to avoid saying enemy) is identified thousands of times, by the general feeling in the air, by the talk of plain citizens, and by the insinuations—not always so indirect—in newspapers and journals. There seems to be a kind of psychological recognition of the rival not only before there are any overt acts but even before there is much distrustful talk. Unquestionably it is this feeling—that there is such a rival and that persons holding specially exempt posts are friendly toward his system or his purposes—which causes the public to wonder about the impulse of the professors.

It may be alleged that no one has a right to say this. But I try to deal with the problem on several levels. There is the level of psychological realism as well as that of conventional rights. Neither should be ignored. On a subject like this one the public is prone to fall into a short way of reasoning and to think quickly in terms of consequences. And if this is true in times of peace, it is true *a fortiori* in times of emergency like the cold war. When people are asked to weigh calmly the advantages of the other system of government against our own, or to appreciate it as "a Russian solution to a Russian problem" or "a Cuban solution to a Cuban problem," they show more interest in what the long-term outcome will be for their safety and survival.

It is against these facts that we have to weigh the issues in many of the controversies over academic freedom. Theory is all for it up to a point, and no academician who did not insist on it would be worth his salt. But that is the point at which the rhetoric of political and social survival becomes more persuasive than the rhetoric of academic freedom, just because in the present situation the second is a dependent of the first. A recent bulletin of the American Civil Liberties Union notes that "Restrictions on freedom have developed everywhere because our world is in trouble, and life is not as free as it should be for any of us." That expresses a true if regrettable fact, and academic freedom is part of "our world."

The Role of Education
in Shaping Our Society[1]

Viewed from one point, education is the most threadbare of all subjects. But, viewed from another point, there is ample reason why education should be the perennial theme. It concerns in a most central way two of the greatest and most vital questions that every age has to face. The first of these is the question: "What is man?" and the second is: "What should man strive to become?" It is almost too manifest to point out, but education *is* concerned with the shaping of man. From the kindergarten level, where it is decided at what and how long the children shall play to the highest level of the graduate school, where the candidate for the Ph.D. decides on the nature and form of his contribution to knowledge, the question that is faced, whether with simplicity or with knowledge and sophistication, is "What is important for man?"

Since the beginnings of reflection, there have been differences of opinion over the nature of man. Religions have declared one thing; sometimes philosophies have taught something else. In our own time, with the tremendous increase of positive science, new ways of studying man have been attempted, and the results of some of these attempts have been startling, not to say upsetting. The last one hundred and fifty years have probably seen more efforts to re-value the idea of what it means to be a human being than all previous time. I am not implying by these remarks that the results have represented progress; many of them have produced only confusion and dismay. Yet this removes all doubt as to the centrality of the question.

Once one has arrived at some kind of answer to the question "What is man?" that second question lies before him: "What should man strive to become?" And unless one answers that man is right now in his perfect and

1. *The Role of Education in Shaping Our Society*. Philadelphia: Intercollegiate Studies Institute, n.d. (after 1970), pamphlet.

fully realized state (and even philosophies which adopt that complacent position do not follow it out—they have a program for him) one must form some idea of what he should do to improve himself. Here is where education enters the debate in a crucial way, since education is the means of forming and reforming man, his mind, his character, his way of life, even his appetites. Different authorities disagree over how many of these are the proper object of education, but if education has a purpose, that certainly is not to leave man just as he was born into the world. Until that improbable time, therefore, when we shall lose interest in what is man and what kind of destiny he should try to fulfill, we shall be talking and speculating about education.

The truth of this may be appreciated even more forcefully when we realize what a peculiarly *intimate* thing education is. Education begins with our tenderest years, and according to some it never really ends, although after maturity it usually becomes less systematized and more self-administered. All the while it is doing something to our minds and conditioning our personality—its effects indeed come home to men's bosoms and their businesses. It would be a very light-minded nation, consequently, which would take education lightly. I am certainly not one of those who confuse intelligence with the ability to read, or think that only those with a college diploma have the right to succeed. Nonetheless, it is undeniable that more and more positions of leadership in all the walks of life are going to those who have been educated in institutions and often educated for a very long time.

The bearing of the nature of our education upon the nature of our society is, therefore, obvious, but here a certain amount of definition is necessary. In dealing with the term society, I give it a much broader meaning than a particular political form or a limited historical period. In a sense that is very real, our society goes back twenty-five hundred years. We are the heirs of a fairly uniform tradition of wonderful richness coming from Rome, Greece and Judea. In our antecedents are the gifts of the Hebrews and later the Christians for a spiritual life and intensity which have resulted in our belief in the reality of the inner man. There also are the gifts of the Greeks for art and philosophy and the genius of the Romans for government. We have derived much more than is usually acknowledged from the European Middle Ages; the Middle Ages created the first universities, and other institutions far from contemptible. All of these things stream down to our present time to constitute what we can proudly call Western culture. A culture is a deeper, more far-reaching, more subtly pervasive thing than a form of government or any institution. To place matters in the real order of causation it would be accurate to say that our form of government is an outgrowth of our society and our society an outgrowth of our culture. For this reason, when we talk about preserving or improving our society, we must think about preserving the culture which is its intellectual and spiritual source. A people does not enjoy a republic, at least for very long, unless the idea of a republic is somewhere forcefully expressed in its culture, and similarly ideas of justice and of law spring from the general cultural consciousness.

A Japanese of my acquaintance once observed to me that the reason the Japanese sound empty and inept when they try to talk about democracy— or some other Western concepts—is that these concepts simply have no cultural history with them. It is not so much a matter of willing or not willing; the substance is just not there to give the words the inner content and force they have with us. I do not cite this in a critical sense, but only to establish the fact that cultural heritages enter profoundly into a people's very way of thinking. No doubt the Japanese have concepts of their own nurturing which we appear extremely inept in handling. Here is all the more ground for saying that a people should not try to trade cultures, nor pretend that their own has no special significance; a person clings to his own culture as he clings to his identity, which he would not at bottom trade for anyone else's.

I do not quite agree with Plato that the state, or society, is merely the individual writ large. The comparison is a little too neat to get in all the perplexities of the case. There is a danger in hypostatizing society in this way, or treating it as something above or apart from the constituting individuals. The unique individual is the primary reality. Nevertheless, a society is going to reflect what the individuals in it have been taught, and unless they have been taught something about its integrity, it is not going to endure. I do not mean integrity here in its connotation of honesty. I mean integrity in the sense of wholeness. The more I reflect upon that problem, the more clearly I see that societies survive as integers or they do not survive at all. That is to say, they survive as distinct wholes or unitary creations, with their own constitution, their own outlook, and their own order of values. The moment they declare themselves to be open, open to every outside influence and suggestion, that is the moment they take a slow poison which will eventually undo them. A prime educational goal, therefore, must be the preservation and transmission of our cultural past as something worth preserving in its integrity. There are plenty of people about today who seem ready to ignore this, to disparage or to sell at a knockdown rate our Western culture. But I must repeat a conclusion I am very sure of: a culture, a nation, or a society which loses confidence in its right to an identity loses the will to live, and where there is no will, nothing can be done.

This raises at once the question of whether education in its fundamental orientation should be political. My answer to that would be a straightforward no, if by that term one means political in the narrow *ad hoc* sense. An education in the student's cultural tradition is not political; in fact it is the only kind of education that does not presume political ends. An education in the cultural heritage is an introduction to things enacted, realized, made historical, and become traditional, in contrast with those things which are merely proposed, wished for, or sponsored by some pressure group.

One of the great heresies of the followers of John Dewey is that they saw, and still do see, education as primarily political. The evidence for this damning proposition is that they tried to make the schools not the means of handing down the traditional knowledge and wisdom of our civilization but political instrumentalities for the constituting of a different kind of society. The schools were to be used for the implementing of social democracy or democratic socialism, whichever arrangement of the phrase you prefer. This was to be the paramount aim of education, mind you. Not the imparting of knowledge, and indeed in Dewey's system knowledge hardly exists except by his peculiar definition; since he does away with forms and fixities, a knowledge of the nature and constitution of being is for him a meaningless phrase. Neither were the schools to introduce students to the traditions of our American life, for those traditions were seen merely as an encumbrance of left-over baggage from the dark age before his brand of enlightenment.

Any so-called educator who makes a political form or condition the supreme sanction of education is not an educator but a propagandist, with special ends in view. One of the terms with which they like to dress up their activities is "education for democratic living." But even this, with the tremendous rhetorical weight it has picked up in recent years, is not a principle by which to order education. We may hope that out of a study of our common past, our hard knocks and successes, the students will come to see advantages in a republican form of government. But to narrow education down to what indoctrinates in a particular governmental form is to predetermine things in advance, and to cut students off from sources of inventiveness and wisdom. We may well speculate as to what would have happened had the Founding Fathers of this nation been brought up on an education so partial and tendentious. It is a safe inference that they could never have created our Constitution. To conceive that remarkable structure, one had to be versed in history, which they were. They knew a lot about the profits and the losses in the human story. They knew about the "mixed" form of government so successfully developed by the Romans. They had reflected upon the dangers of pure democracy—what a far cry, this, from modern hosannas to democratic living. Finally, they had studied human nature by looking it in the face, as it were, instead of indulging in phantasies of theory. Hardly anything less that this would have enabled them to produce what the profound historian Lord Acton called the most perfect form of democracy yet seen in the world because the most safeguarded against its own potential excesses.

Thus, they were prepared for great political achievement by an education which was not political in the overt sense. They had been educated in the long tradition of Western culture. It is my contention that this kind of education is nonpolitical because the tradition has presumption in its favor. It is an accomplished settlement, not perfect in any case, but again not trying to put over anything. It is those programs which are trying to put over something which have to be inspected for their political motives.

A genuine broad-based education has as its subject matter the structure of reality. I do not imply by this only physical reality; there are other realities, aesthetic, ethical, economic, and so on, which have their real structure and content, not to be explored for narrowly political reasons, which I hope by now I have discredited, but for the purpose of producing more knowledgeable and wiser human beings.

Having spoken this freely about education in the structure of reality or the nature of being, it becomes necessary for me to say something about areas of subject matter and the relationship of them.

It is not possible to introduce order and proportion into learning without making some clear commitments about value. To assume that every subject is just as valuable as every other subject is only a little less ridiculous than saying that all opinions are of equal worth. When we come to the very intimate work of shaping the human being for his life and his role in society, we are compelled to recognize that some areas of instruction are essential for him, some important but hardly essential, some worthwhile but perhaps not important, and some that should not even be considered under the head "education."

At the heart of every liberal arts curriculum lie mathematics and language—and when I name language here I include the resources and beauties of the student's own native language. Mathematics and language provide the symbolic tools with which we handle all other things. Man has been defined as the symbol-using animal; but indeed it is using symbols which *sets him off* from the animal. We do not know of any animal which can use intellectual symbols in the way that man does; and we know that without a constant use of these symbols—the formula, the written word and sentence—it would not be possible either to maintain or to pass on our civilization. Mathematics and language are basic to our lives as civilized human beings as well as the essential tools for inquiring into other areas. Significantly, these seem to be the subjects that are least well taught where "progressive" methods of education dominate.

Along with language of course goes literature, which is unique in its ability to acquaint us with modes of feeling and ways of looking at things, as well as with situations of drama and tragedy.

Next in order I should place history. After what has been said about the value of a cultural consciousness, I hardly need go much further into this. But let me point out the interesting fact that those who would overthrow, or subvert, or revolutionize our society are nearly all of them anti-historical.

Either they do not know history, or they deny the reality of history, or they satisfy themselves with some specially selected strand of it, which is about as bad as being ignorant of it. The man who is grounded in history knows something of the ever-present tension between the ideal and the prudential, so that his judgments should reflect wisdom rather than cleverness or phantasy. And while we are in this area, let me add a word for more instruction in geography—and of the old fashioned kind, despite the talk of the annihilation of space. Most of our adult citizens even are remarkably ignorant of geography, and owing to this they understand little, if anything, about the polarity of place—or the influence of one's geographical position in shaping one's outlook. It is a fact of great consequence that the American is made partly by his Western orientation. Less geographical illiteracy should lead to an appreciation of social facts like that.

It is highly important that the educated man study at least one other language, even if he should never have any practical use for it. The reason for this prescription is that one does not really understand his own language until he has studied another. Our own language we learn gradually, instinctively, and from the inside. But the foreign language we have to approach from the outside, and this forces us to learn about how a language works which otherwise we might never become aware of. Someone has said that when we take up a foreign language, all the joints show. We have to learn these joints and how they fit together, and that is an instruction in language as such. At the same time one learns how the forms of another language tend to impose ways of conceiving things, and this is a cultural lesson of high importance.

On the more advanced levels, I would certainly want to see philosophy studied, and especially its criteriological branches of logic and ethics, which of course are the branches that train us in the distinguishing of true from false and right from wrong. Nor would I shrink from the study of such philosophy as presents itself as "wisdom of life." For after all, if there is a chief end to the study of philosophy, it is just this: it provides a coherent ground for the ordering of our values and the conduct of our living. One of the truly disconcerting things about modern man is that he can hold so many incompatible values and propose so many incompatible goals. A person trained in philosophy at least tries to iron out the incompatibilities and contradictions and to lead a life more rational in the sense of more consistent.

Up to this point I have said nothing about the physical sciences. But there is little need to make a case for them. Their weight and momentum are so great today that they are already receiving a major share of attention. Subjects which have transformed the face of the earth and devised weapons capable of man's complete self-destruction of course have to be studied. But they should not be studied for what they are not—the keys to civil and moral order. The Spanish philosopher Unamuno is, I believe, the source of the saying that "Science is the enemy of wisdom." There is some rhetorical bitterness in that; what it really means is that a pre-occupation with the physical world or with stunts like going to the moon can lead us to ignore what Plato called "the great business itself"—a critical examination of the life and destiny of man.

Up to now I have also said nothing about the social sciences; but this is for another reason. I have some grave doubts about the real value of that swelling department. Possibly under the pressure of its very name—social *science*—this branch of inquiry has displayed a near fatal tendency to emulate the physical sciences; it has come forward with a sharply reduced concept of man; that is, with man cut down to something that denies his whole nature; and it is making proposals for the renovation of society which reflect these biases. I have known brilliant men in the field of social science, but the mass of them, I fear, are social tinkers and not very well educated ones at that. The character of what they have chosen to do seems to have driven them in the direction of anti-intellectualism in regard to other subjects. Not very long ago I heard a social scientist, who deplores this very tendency, speak of how shallow the training of a social scientist today can be. He does not study philosophy, so that he remains ignorant of the profounder value systems. He does not study languages, without which it is impossible to understand other cultures from within. He does not study history, which gives the concrete story of all social development. Without philosophy, without languages, and without history he calls himself a social scientist. At any rate, this is the way my acquaintance put it, and it is a travesty. Political theory and comparative government are subjects solid enough; unfortunately they are the very ones that are being dropped in favor of the new scientistic fads and behavioral analyses which have little if anything to teach.

Now, despite all that is heard about television in the classroom and various automatic devices, there remains the teacher. There is no substitute for the direct relationship of mind to mind. Minds are excited by other active, creative minds in a way that no mechanical contrivance, however ingenious, can ever match. Furthermore, teachers do not merely educate in the abstract; *they also influence.* This is incontestable. I sometimes say to classes: when a teacher walks into a room, a part of your fate walks into the room.

Because that teacher is going to determine something for you—an attitude, a conviction, or an evaluation. He does not always do this in a positive or affirmative way, for he may determine something by antagonizing a student. But his personality and what he communicates to the class are going to leave their mark or their residue.

If we desire results we can count on, we must therefore find good teachers. Experience has shown, however, that there is no single test for the good teacher. In our staff at Chicago we have once or twice tried to draw up a list of the characteristics of the good teacher with a view to future appointments, but we soon found that they made nonsense and tore them up. I have known good teachers who have had very different temperaments, very different degrees of industry, very different working habits and methods in the classroom and very different relation with students. If the good teacher can be identified by results, the standard is probably this: he succeeds somehow in getting his students to take what he is teaching seriously. But, there are many different ways of doing that. So, we need to find good teachers, and yet we can't judge what makes a good teacher except in this *ex post facto* way.

The offering of higher salaries alone will not locate them. In view of the kind of world we live in, the matter of salaries cannot be left out of account. Very low salaries might frighten away too many who are potentially good teachers. Yet there is a danger at the other extreme too; very high salaries would probably attract a type chiefly interested in salary, and this would not be good for a profession which ought to demand some denials in return for the freedom and prestige accorded the teacher.

I seem to have gotten nowhere with this inquiry, but here is a thought or two. Some recent studies have shown that teachers are actually more drawn by the prestige of a college or university than by the salary level. That might seem to indicate a sort of snobbery, yet I believe that it is to be interpreted in the favorable sense. Those institutions which have prestige possess it because they have adhered to higher standards of scholarship, because they have kept the educational ideal purer, and because they have allowed their staffs more time for thinking and research. These are quite respectable sources of incentive, and no one should blame a teacher if he swaps some differential in salary for something that will satisfy the less material but not less real urge. And here perhaps is the key to our problem; if we can give to the teaching profession the kind of sense of dedication that infuses the military profession, the medical profession, and some others that might be named, then we shall be getting what money cannot buy, a devotion and service to an ideal. If our teaching profession can escape being made into a vast national bureaucracy, I think the outlook for this is good.

We want our teachers not merely to be good teachers; we want them to play their part in leadership, again not in the narrowly political sense, but in the sense of maintaining belief in the values which our civilization has created. Here the facts become more discouraging, and the issue becomes more delicate. Why is it that more teachers have not been representative of these in their views and actions? The more one examines into the matter, the more he is impressed with the fact of an ideological estrangement between town and gown; that is, between the body of the people on the one hand and the academy on the other. This rift is more observable in the higher levels, among the professoriat, but since what exists there is certain to percolate down, it is found in the lower levels also, if to a lesser extent.

I take it as an incontrovertible fact that the body of the people still have faith in our traditions, still believe in the American way of life, in the free enterprise system, and in the high sanction to be given personal freedom. They are conservatives in the good sense of wishing to conserve the good that we have inherited and have added to.

I wish that the same could be reported of the great majority of the professoriat, but in candor it cannot be. Many of this group have been strongly imbued with leftist collectivism, so that they are quite ready to vote socialist, even if they have to vote it under a disarming name. The adjective "American" seems not to carry the weight it should with many of them; they appear ready to sacrifice our nationality to the chimera of world union or world government. When they speak of objectives, these are often not within the scope of our tradition, but reflect alien ideas and systems. The teacher who is willing to stand up and speak for the old America often finds himself an isolated figure, and he may have to pay penalties for his deviation.

Yet, I believe that there are ways of accounting historically for this situation. The minds of our older and middle generation of teachers were formed back at the time of the great boom and depression. This is a circumstance from which most of them have never recovered. The experience left them frozen in an attitude toward certain subjects which nothing since then has been able to affect very much. You know the elements of that attitude. Free enterprise cannot insure stability; the state must take over; everyone has a right to a good living—the usual cliches of welfarism. Many things have occurred in fact since that time which deny those conclusions; and the most recent economic theory gives powerful support to free enterprise as the best productive and distributive system; but they are not aware of this. They have not kept up with the times.

And the new teachers coming on the scene meanwhile have been brought up by these men, or have been much influenced by them, so that their outlook is substantially the same. So, we have a couple of generations of teachers who are really behind the times, except perhaps in the matter of their specialties. Their defect here is not lack of patriotism; the failure is a lack of hard thinking about the realities before them. It is so much easier to dispose of everything with socialist clichés.

When we speak of better prepared teachers, I should hope that preparation would include at least this: a more up-to-date economic outlook than the defeatist one of thirty years ago and a keener appreciation of the value of personal freedom than welfare bureaucrats seem able to entertain. The scholarly works which justify the former have been written and are there to be studied—a great accomplishment of von Mises, Hayek, Röpke, Voegelin and others. And the lesson of freedom can be learned through a little honest self-questioning.

With this sort of curriculum and this kind of teacher as reasonable ideals, let me touch briefly upon three great current issues in American education. These are: 1) basic education versus "progressive"; 2) private education versus public; and 3) liberal education against early specialization. In offering my view of the first issue, I must turn again for a few moments to what happened to us under the onrush of progressivism.

Increasingly over the past fifty years we have turned our lower and secondary education over to professional educators. These have not been men chiefly educated in the artistic and scientific disciplines; they have been men educated in "education." At first hearing that might sound like a good thing—like one of those intensive specializations which have had such impact upon the modern world. But inquiry and experience have proved two things to the contrary. One, there is no such thing as a science of education. Education is an art, which the great teachers and even the good teachers largely teach themselves. Of course, in the actual administration of a classroom there are better and worse ways of doing things, yet they hardly add up to a science, and even successful principles will vary according to the individualities of teachers. If you want the proof of this charge, look into the curricula of most of our teachers colleges. They are of an unbelievable thinness. What occurred was that our future teachers got trained not in what they were going to teach, but in how they should teach it, and that, I repeat, is a very limited curriculum. So far did this tendency carry that many of these teachers became indifferent to intellectual pursuits—mere acolytes of the ritual of educationalism. The result has been "educational wastelands," to borrow the phrase which Professor Arthur Bestor courageously used as the title of one of his books.

We found that our second mistake was allowing educationism, with its inherent limitations, to fall under the direction of a misleading philosophy. Here I shall have to admit again to the doctrine of John Dewey. Dewey was in some ways a powerful if perverse thinker, and that accounts partly for his influence. If not all the extravagances and aberrations of his followers can be laid on his doorsteps, we can say at least that a man who accepts a role of intellectual leadership ought to take the measure of likely consequences and insure against the bad ones. (Let me remark in passing that we ought to look more critically at the common saying that if truth and her adversary are left to fight it out in the marketplace, truth always wins. That truth will ultimately triumph is something we *have* to believe—anything else would lead to pessimism about man's existence. What we overlook is that in some cases it takes an awfully long time. I could name certain beliefs which seem to me errors, but which have been holding their ground for centuries. The moral of this is that we should not be complacent about truth's winning a speedy victory when error has gotten abroad. And by this token we must not assume that the errors of Deweyism will be soon or easily vanquished.)

At any rate, the followers of Dewey, in their entrenched positions, have been culpable in two major respects. Like Dewey, their motivation has been too political in the interest of "democratizing," as I have previously indicated; and they have offered a false, or at least a grotesquely incomplete, philosophy of life and of human nature.

Because the system of Deweyism is not interested in knowledge as that has been traditionally conceived and is not friendly toward excellence because of its deprecation of individualism, it substitutes the curious ideal of "adjustment." This term has some power to mislead just because it enjoys certain pleasing connotations—such as satisfaction and fulfillment and ease. It sounds much better to be "adjusted" than "maladjusted" or even "unadjusted." But we are not deceived when we discover its real meaning for the devotees of the theory. "Adjustment" means conformity with the needs of a necessarily emerging industrial democracy, or the communism of the future. The individual merges himself with a communal group. He even thinks and works through group impulses. There is no longer any tension between himself and others or himself and the world—those creative tensions out of which so much that is valuable in our civilization has been produced. And it is certain that Deweyism would rule out both the creative and the heroic, the one because it demands some privateness of the inner life, and the other because it presupposes an individual standing out from the crowd.

But even if we should conceive this adjustment to life as an ideal, there remains a second large and inevitable question to be asked: how is that life that is being adjusted to be defined? Men have, under certain trying conditions, adjusted themselves to an animal level of existence, but usually this was what they tried to get relieved from at the earliest opportunity. Here something equally as incomplete is being set forth as an ideal. I have just mentioned that Dewey's concept leaves out the element of the heroic; it also leaves out the element of the tragic, which has always been recognized as one of the ineluctable parts of life, so that our very greatest dramatic literature is concerned with how to meet the tragic. In the world envisaged by Dewey and the progressives, there is nothing with which to meet the tragic because there is nothing to compensate for not being "adjusted."

Basic education presents a picture of life which is steady and whole; progressive education has its gaze fixed upon this caricature of it. The latter discourages competition in the classroom, but dares not take this dogma onto the athletic field. It tells us we do harm if we say "no" to children, but, as someone has cleverly pointed out, it hardly sticks to this principle at the school traffic crossing. In a brief characterization, the return to basic education is a return to realism.

With so many of our rights to free choice being eroded away by a growing paternalism, the future of private education has to be viewed with all seriousness. Fiscal and taxation policies of the government have made it increasingly difficult for private institutions to support themselves. There are forces today covertly hostile to all private education. Measures have been introduced into Congress which would have the effect of edging private institutions out of the picture or would leave them private in name only. Centralizers of government and totalitarian liberals would like to see our educational system run from an office in Washington. We must be prepared for every kind of specious argument on behalf of such a scheme. But this would be the greatest calamity that could befall American education. I can enumerate briefly some of the consequences that might be expected. There would be a paralyzing uniformity, which always make things easier for bureaucratic administration. Under various pretexts of raising standards of achievement, it is almost certain that standards would be lowered. And with the supposedly bottomless well of the Federal treasury to draw on, it is practically inevitable that the true aims of education would be lost sight of amid preoccupation with salaries, with new buildings, cafeterias, with provisions for trips and all of the peripheral things that can eat up administrative energy. And this says nothing about the political stipulations, perhaps disguised somewhat, which would accompany the hand-out of the Federal largesse.

Whenever I think of the subject of private versus public education, memory takes me back to my childhood in North Carolina. Most of the children of our little village attended a primary school conducted by an elderly maiden lady in one room of her home. This mistress of a small private school was well along in years; she heard through an ear trumpet, and I don't know how much she actually heard. But she taught us all to read. And we read not the imbecile stuff which is given youngsters today. In the second and third grades we were reading the beautiful myths of Greece and Rome. At recess, instead of going to some elaborately equipped gymnasium or recreation hall, we had a great time chasing one another around in the side yard. I have always remembered this as one of the best and one of the pleasantest schools I have ever attended. There were no problems of discipline, no problems of motivation that I can recall. Since that time I have performed a kind of educational odyssey: I have been attached in the capacity of student or teacher to both private and public schools at various levels and in several sections of the country. And I must report that the private institutions from the one room in a home village school in North Carolina to the University of Chicago, where I am now located, have been better. And in particular, the one-room-in-a-home school has stayed with me as a permanent lesson in how much can be done with how little if the aim and means are right.

This is not a criticism of those who have gone to public schools and universities. I went to them myself in the course of that odyssey. But since almost every thing that is private is today on the defensive, it is time for someone to emphasize the merits of private schooling. There are sound reasons for not only preserving what we have of it, but for seeking to extend it. When an institution is privately supported and run, there is always a more direct relationship between what the payer wants and what he gets. He does not dictate policies, of course, but he can always change his patronage. The extra, peripheral or frivolous activities, which have grown like the upas tree in some of our public institutions, never get a start simply because the private institutions cannot afford them and at the same time do what the supporters want them to do, which normally is, to give a quality education. The economy of the school simply doesn't permit them, unless it is the kind of school set up for them, and this turns out to be a great saving for education.

In the second place, because the private school is an autonomous unit, able to decide for itself what it wants to do, it can be more independent, more creative or pioneering in the right sense. It can be free to try the promising experiment or meet the new situation.

Public education has today become such a shibboleth that to say anything against it is often to invite incomprehension or to provoke the most violent denunciation, as if one had attacked religion. But I will declare my belief on this subject, which is that our situation would be better if not only a considerable part but even a majority of our education were conducted under private auspices. Let me repeat that this comes from one who has spent about an equal amount of time in public and private schools and colleges.

Finally a few words about the college liberal arts phase of our education. Many persons are unaware that the liberal arts college is a peculiar British and American creation. Standing midway between the secondary school and the graduate or professional school, it gives the student up to four more years of general or formal education. This is not done on the Continent or in the Latin-American countries. There the student is conducted suddenly from the equivalent of our secondary school into a school of medicine or law or whatever he is going to take up as a profession. There is no intervening period for taking the philosophical approach to education and for personal maturing. I agree with Professor Bestor that the institution of the liberal arts college has contributed something highly important to the political atmosphere of Britain and America. These two nations have shown by far the most stable governments of the Western world, and that happy circumstance is owing in no small way to the liberal arts phase of education at the college level. Here young men and women who are headed for twenty different occupations meet and converse on common ground about common subjects. They are members for a while of one world of discourse. And they never thereafter wholly lose the power to communicate. This gives us an educated minority able to cooperate at the basic levels despite divergent interests and occupational points of view. That may well be the flywheel of our continuing republican–democratic form of government. At least, that seems a fair inference, and I urge it as an especially good reason for preserving our four year liberal arts college. It gives an education for politics without being political, because it gives opportunity for that consensus, that agreement of feelings and ideas, without which neither state nor society can last.

As I have endeavored to point out all along, this is the way education shapes and sustains a society. Wisdom is never taught directly; indoctrination often backfires; propaganda ends up by drawing contempt upon itself. The education that forms minds and wins converts to belief in truths is education in the arts and sciences which have brought our civilization into being, in the ideas and values which can be shown to give it unity, and in history, which is the actual story of our trials and triumphs. The deeper and more solid the individual's education is in these, the more likely he is to conclude, when years have matured him a little, that self-directed living in a free and pluralistic society is the finest fruit of man's political wisdom.

To Write the Truth [1]

The endless effort toward refurbishing college composition, with its restless shift of approach, of sequence, of emphasis, arouses suspicion that the most formidable question of all has been begged. A course so firmly intrenched in every curriculum and yet so productive of dissatisfaction must conceal a problem which needs to be set forth in its true nature and proportion.

For this reason I wish to make a certain radical, and probably impolitic, inquiry about objectives. Suppose it were possible to poll every teacher of college composition with reference to its aims; is it likely that any area of unanimous agreement could be found? I am aware of the varied philosophies, but if the question is properly phrased, my surmise is Yes; I cannot imagine anyone's denying that the aim of a course in composition is to make students more articulate. Every instructor wishes his students to write better, to talk better, and is chagrined if tests cast doubt upon the achievement. He may steal moments to introduce them to the sweetness and light of literature, but his success is measured by how his charges gain facility with their native tongue. That, at least, is the plain implication of syllabuses, course plans, and examinations. I suspect, however, that just here lies the root of our commonly felt frustration; we are not conceiving the real nature of our duty if we stop with making students articulate, even to the point of eloquence.

For at the source of our feeling of restlessness and incomplete achievement is the ignoring of a question necessarily prior: About what do we wish to make men articulate? Admittedly we who instruct in the art of speech are turning loose upon the world a power. Where do we expect the wielders of that power to learn the proper use of it? Now "proper" is, of course, a critical word, and I propose next to examine its possible meanings.

There came a moment in the fourteenth century when teachers of rheto-

1. *College English*, 10/1, October 1948, 25–30. Published by the National Council of Teachers of English.

ric and philosophy hesitated between two aims: Was it their duty to teach men *vere loqui* or *recte loqui,* in the phrases then employed? Obviously a basic question of epistemology was involved. Those who favored the former were metaphysicians; those who favored the latter had come to believe, as Bacon expressed it in the *Advancement of Learning,* that "the Essential Forms or true differences of things cannot by any human diligence be found out." Empiricism was gathering strength, and the decision was to teach *recte loqui,* as one can discover in the manuals of rhetoric of the Renaissance. Once the ontological referents were given up, however, this proved but an intermediate stage, and the course continued until today we can discern on all sides a third aim, which I shall take the liberty of phrasing in a parallel way as *utiliter loqui.* From speaking truthfully to speaking correctly to speaking usefully—is this not the rhetorician's easy descent to Avernus?

Yet these changes seem to be symptomatic of a profound trend, and it is to be feared that the course of our civilization is mirrored in the direction they indicate. The teacher of composition today, who thinks he is struggling merely with the ignorance and indifferentism of individuals, is actually trying to hold back the tide which is threatening intellectual life as such. Perhaps the picture seems melodramatic. I think it will seem less so after we have examined the implications of the trend.

Let us begin with our own time and look at *utiliter loqui,* which is usually described as a potent handmaiden of Success. It is the art of using language to better our position in the world—and heaven knows its objective comports with a great deal that has been said from high places about the aim of education. That knowledge is power has been dinned at us until it appears faintly treasonable to question the pragmatic use of speech. But, in all candor, is it the goal of our instruction in expression, both written and oral, to make men more eloquent about their passions and their interests? It would hardly do to reason from actual practice, for a large part of the teaching of composition facilitates and perhaps encourages such proficiency. From it comes the language of journalism and advertising; from it comes the language of those who study rhetoric with the object of making the worse appear the better cause. In technical and professional schools the aim may be frankly indicated in catalogue descriptions; language is a tool which will enable you to get what you want if you use it well—and well does not mean scrupulously. Says George F. Babbitt to his son Ted, who is having his evening struggle with *Comus* and Cicero, "Be a good bit better if you took

Business English, and learned how to write an ad, or a letter that would pull." Millions will agree on the point with Babbitt, and plenty have paid hard cash for training which they were told would enable them to place eloquence in the service of popularity or profit.

Those who teach English on this level are the modern sophists, as the homely realism of the world seems to recognize. They are doing what the orators were once accused of doing, making speech the harlot of the arts. More specifically, they are using the element of universality in language for purposes which actually set men against one another. They are teaching their students how to prevail with what is, finally, verbal deception.

Now *recte loqui*, because it teaches a sort of etiquette, appears more respectable; and therein lies its danger. It is the way of those who wish their speech to bear the stamp of conventional correctness. They have their eyes, therefore, upon tradition, or upon the practice of a dominant class, since they desire their style of utterance to indicate that they belong. They are more fearful of a misplaced accent than of an ambiguity, because the former arouses suspicion that they have not been with the right people. This is the language favored by the timid, who live in fear of conventions, and by the ambitious, who have learned how to use conventions as a means of self-promotion. Making allowance for those who see an ideal in purism, we can yet say that this is speech which is socially useful, and thus we are not in much better plight if we confine ourselves circumspectly to the teaching of *recte loqui*. The acceptance of such assignment still leaves the teacher indifferent to truth. He has no standard other than what was done, if he is a traditionalist, or what is being done, if he is a pragmatist. A large body of opinion, of course, believes that this is precisely the teacher's job; he is paid to be an interpreter and an upholder of established institutions; he initiates the young into the mysteries but does not question them himself. Every teacher has to make this choice between play actor and prophet, and most of them choose the play actor. The public must suspect this hopelessly servile role when it snickers at caricatures of teachers.

Certainly nothing creative and nothing revolutionary (which in the best sense is creative) can come from this dancing of attendance upon fashion in speech. It means in the nature of things a limitation to surfaces; indeed, it leaves one without a real standard of what is right, for the most massive traditions undergo change, and the teacher may at any moment find himself faced with competing old and new ways and without a criterion to judge between them. In sum, *recte loqui* requires the language of social property. Because it reflects more than anything else a worldliness or satisfaction with existing institutions, it is the speech of pragmatic acquiescence. Whoso stops here confesses that education is only instruction in mores. Is it any wonder that professors have been contemptuously grouped with dancing masters, sleight-of-hand artists, and vendors of patent medicine?

If now we are not resigned to the teaching of sophistry or of etiquette, there remains only the severe and lofty discipline of *vere loqui*. This means teaching people to speak the truth, which can be done only by giving them the right names of things. We approach here a critical point in the argument, which will determine the possibility of defining what is correct in expression; we come in fact to the relationship of sign and thing signified.

Since this involves the inherent rightness of names, let us consider for a moment the child's statement: "Pigs are called 'pigs' because they are filthy beasts." The semanticists offer this as an outstanding example of fatuity but what, I would ask, are the alternatives? They are: "Pigs are called 'pigs' because that is what they have been called for a long time," and "Pigs are called 'pigs' because this name gives one a degree of control, as when summoning them to the trough." After all, there is something to be said for the child's interpretation. It presents an attachment of thing and concept. The others, in accepting tradition and in seeking utility, offer reasoning which is merely circular. The first says that what is, is; and the second affirms in good pragmatic vein that what works, works. I would not argue that the child has the whole philosophy of the matter; but he appears to be seeking the road to understanding; he is trying to get at the nature of the thing, and such must be the endeavor of all who seek a bridge to the real.

Now every teacher is for his students an Adam. They come to him trusting in his power to bestow the right names on things. "And out of the ground the Lord God formed every beast of the field, and every fowl of the air, and brought them unto Adam to see what he would call them; and whatever Adam called every living creature, that was the name thereof." The naming of the beasts and the fowls was one of the most important steps in creation. Adam helped to order the universe when he dealt out these names, and let us not overlook what is implied in the assertion that the names stuck. There is the intimation of divine approval, which would frown upon capricious change. A name is not just an accident; neither is it a convention which can be repealed by majority vote at the next meeting; once a thing has been given a name, it appears to have a certain autonomous right to that name, so that it could not be changed without imperiling the foundations of the world.

If I begin to seem fanciful here, let us recall that Plato was deeply interested in this problem, as one can discover by reading the *Cratylus*. And he could accept the view neither that a name is an accident nor that it is a convention which a man or a state may alter at will. For him—and we should wonder why teachers have not pondered this more—a name is "a means of *teaching* and of separating reality." The word in the original is *didaskalikon*. Consequently, he goes on to add, a teacher is one who gives names well, and "well means like a teacher." Because those who give the names are in a unique position to control, the task is not to be intrusted to just anyone. "Then it is not for everyman, Hermogenes," he makes Socrates declare, "to give names, but for him who may be called the name-maker; and he, it appears, is the lawgiver, who is of all artisans among men the rarest." Plato then proceeds to a conclusion that since the name-maker is the lawgiver, he must, if he is to make proper use of this *organon didaskalikon*, have a dialectician sitting by his side. By thus arranging a philosophical supervision for name-giving, he establishes his point that name-giving is not a task for "trifling and casual persons." Certainly no one blind to the unities and pluralities of the world can be placed in charge of what things are to be called.

The task now begins to appear serious indeed, for those engaged in separating reality are in effect ordering the universe. The burden of some teachers is in fact heavier than Adam's, for teaching the names of imponderables is far more difficult and dangerous than teaching those of animals and rocks. The world has to be named for the benefit of each oncoming generation, and who teaches more names than the arbiter of the use of language? With the primer one begins to call the roll of things, and the college essay is but an extended definition.

Suppose a teacher, striving to vitalize his instruction, as the professors of education like to put it, assigns his papers on current topics. What is he to tell students, by way of preparation or correction, that "democracy" is the name of? Does it stand for something existing in the nature of things, something in accordance with "right reason," or can it be changed over-night to mean dictatorship of the proletariat? And what of "freedom"? Does it stand for an area in which the individual is sovereign, or does it signify some wide function of a centralized government? What sense of direction is carried by the term "progressive"? Consider the immeasurable harm one might do students by telling them that "history" is the name of our recol-lection of the past adjusted to suit our feelings and aspirations, as some recent historians would have us do.

I am not unaware of the questions which will come crowding in at this point. It will be asked: By what act of arrogance do we imagine that we know what things really are? The answer to this is: By what act of arrogance do we set ourselves up as teachers? There are two postulates basic to our profession: the first is that one man can know more than another, and the second is that such knowledge can be imparted. Whoever cannot accept both should retire from the profession and renounce the intention of teach-ing anyone anything.

Let those who consider such prerogative unreasonable consider what re-mains. If we cannot be sure that one person knows better than another the true nature of things, then we should follow the logic of our convictions and choose our teachers as the ancient Greek democracies chose their magis-trates, by lot. Let us imagine that on some appointed November day we here in Chicago proceed to Soldiers Field, and there from a huge kettle we draw lots, and those drawing, say, the blue slips become automatically the school staff for the ensuing year. This mode of selection would surely be mandatory under the proposition that one man knows as much truth as another about the things that are to be passed on to the next generation. I do not think the scheme would meet with popular approval. In fact, I sus-pect that it would be denounced as radical. We should have to go back then and say that whoever is willing to make the most elementary predication acknowledges thereby that he thinks he has some grasp upon reality, which is a form of saying that he thinks he possesses some measure of the truth. Such people only may be certificated to teach. For those who doubt the existence of truth, there is only what Santayana has called "the unanswer-able scepticism of silence."

There is no escape from this in the plea that, since there are today many competing ideologies, it is usurpation for the teacher to make his own the standard. Such policy throws us right into the embrace of relativism, which leaves us as helpless as the skepticism outlined above. It is very hard after a century of liberalism, with its necessity of avoiding commitment, to get people to admit the possibility of objective truth, but here again we are face to face with our dilemma: if it does not exist, there is nothing to teach; if it does exist, how can we conceive of allowing anyone to teach anything else? Those who argue that teachers should confine themselves to presenting all sides of every question—in our instance, to giving all the names previously and currently applied to a thing—are tacitly assuming that there are sources closer to the truth than are the schools and that the schools merely act as their agents. It would be interesting to hear what these sources are.

Here is the point at which teachers have to make up their minds as to whether they are the "trifling and casual" persons described by Plato. Either they are going to teach sophistry and etiquette, or they are going to teach names which are indexes to essences. I will grant that the latter course makes teachers of composition philosophers more truly than those who teach the systems of philosophy, but there is no alternative short of that disastrous abdication which says, "Write anything you please as long as you write it well." This is invocation to the asocial muse. Just anything the un-instructed mind pleases cannot be written well. Even on the most practical level there is no such separation between substance and form of utterance. Anyone who has observed the teaching of composition knows that, regard-less of how much latitude of sentiment the instructor gives himself credit for, there will be judgment of idea. When the comment is made that a paper "says something," it is being valued for recognizing a measure of reality or for being true in its assertions. Ultimately there is no evading the issue of whether any piece of writing predicates something about the world either literally or imaginatively, and this is why I am arguing that, in teaching students to be articulate, we must hold up the standard of what is true. The man who essays that task is doctor of philosophy in more than title, and he takes on stature.

Perhaps I should visualize for a moment the course I am urging. Here is our teacher, who is charged with the awful responsibility of telling a younger generation the true names of things, figuratively sitting with the dialectician at his elbow. What is the use of this counselor? I should say that his chief function is to keep the teacher out of the excluded middle. He is able to define, and he can see contradictions, and he is never going to say that B is only a mode of A. In short, he is going to stand guard against that relativism which has played havoc with so many things and which is now attacking language. He will save those points of reference which are disappearing as we fall into the trap of "infinite-valued orientation." The dialectician works through logic, which is itself an assurance that the world has order. True enough, there will not be much student-centered education here, and knowledge will take on an authority which some mistake for arrogance. The student will learn, however, that the world is not wholly contingent, but partly predictable, and that, if he will use his mind rightly, it will not lie to him about the world.

Let there be no mistake; this is an invitation to lead the dangerous life. Whoso comes to define comes bearing the sword of division. The teacher will find himself not excluded from the world but related to it in ways that may become trying. But he will regain something that has been lost in the long dilution of education, the standing of one with a mission. He will be able, as he has not been for a long while, to take his pay partly in honor.

It is often thoughtlessly said that the restoration of our broken world lies largely in the hands of the teachers. The statement is true, but the implications are not drawn. The teachers cannot contribute by teaching more disorder. When something has been broken, the repairman fixes it, with his mind not on the broken object but on the form according to which it was originally made. And so we who must repair some names that have fallen into strange distortions must not consult the distorted shapes but rather conceive the archetypes for which they stood.

A prominent educator was recently heard to declare that he hoped for a day when people would point with admiration to a member of the teaching profession and say, "Look, he is a teacher." We may be sure that day will not dawn until the remark carries the implication, "Look, he is a definer." For this reason teachers who think they have a part in the redemption of society will have to desert certain primrose paths of dalliance and begin the difficult, the dangerous, work of teaching men to speak and to write the truth.

Looking for an Argument[1]

MANUEL BILSKY, McCREA HAZLETT,
ROBERT E. STREETER, AND RICHARD M. WEAVER

I

It is widely believed that courses in composition should deal with argumentation; and few question that argumentation is related to logic. Many teachers of English stress the importance of "clear" or "straight" thinking and implement their convictions by giving their students more or less systematic training in the labyrinthine ways of the syllogism. This is clearly valuable. Because logic provides the form of good argument, it should be treated with some thoroughness.

However, most modern discussions of argumentation assume that the whole problem can be solved by means of logic. Students will be able to argue well, it is believed, if they are lectured on the principles of logic, trained in the detection of fallacies, and earnestly exhorted to think honestly. For the teaching of composition, such a point of view is not completely satisfactory, because logicians deliberately exclude subject matter. If this is not amply demonstrated by pointing to the complex sets of nonlinguistic symbols which they have concocted, it can be clearly established by a nonsense syllogism:

> If Gilbert and Sullivan wrote *Iolanthe*, then the fall of Napoleon was largely brought about by his invasion of Russia.
> Gilbert and Sullivan wrote *Iolanthe*.
> Therefore, the fall of Napoleon was largely brought about by his invasion of Russia.

1. *College English*, 14/4, 1952–53 (January 1953), 210–53. Published by the National Council of Teachers of English.

This is formally a valid hypothetical syllogism. But it must be emphasized that it is unexceptionable only in a formal sense. A single reading reveals that the argument is ridiculous. Clearly, teachers and students of composition cannot stop where the logician does.

We are primarily concerned with teaching our students to write well. While the development of skill in logical analysis is a valuable means to this end, we need other techniques and tools which will assist in the process of creation. We need to discover ways to help students to find relevant and effective arguments. Because it is formal in its nature and analytic in its use, logic, though basic to the study of argumentation, cannot entirely fulfil this need. Recognizing this problem, the English Staff of the College of the University of Chicago has recently been exploring one concrete solution. What follows is a summary account of the theory and practice of this experiment.

We may begin by recalling our implication that the student who is instructed in logic is only half-instructed in rhetoric. He has been told to write an argument, but the syllogism is only the frame of an argument. The sense of vague frustration over the syllogism not infrequently shown by students may be accounted for by the fact that the "argument" is still but a formula. In the argumentative process there is still wanting what the traditional rhetoricians called *invention,* and that means simply the discovery of content—of relevant supporting material.

All this points to the truth that, to have any power to move, an argument must say something intelligible about the actual world. Because real arguments are made up of such predications, we find most of our substance for argument by interpreting and classifying our experiences. The most fundamental of these categories of interpretation are being, cause, and similarity. To deny these is to deny all possibility of argument. But in actual practice no one denies them, for we no sooner begin to talk about the world than we find ourselves saying that such and such a thing exists as a member of such and such a class, or that it is the known cause of a certain effect (or the known effect of a certain cause), or that it has certain points of similarity with some other thing. These recognized aspects of phenomena provide examples of what the classical writers called the *topoi* or "regions," and what have come to be translated as the "topics."

They are so called because they constitute regions of experience from which the substance of an argument can be drawn. It is a matter of everyday observation that arguments are made by saying that X is a kind of thing, or that X has a known definite effect, or that X has important points of similarity with a thing better understood than itself. The "topics" represent only an analysis of these kinds of predicables that may appear in arguments. Let us suppose, for illustration, that you are accosted one night by a robber, who threatens you with a pistol and demands your money. Assuming that you could get him to listen to argument, you might find yourself ranging over the following "regions" or possibilities:

1. You could tell him that what he is attempting is a crime. This would be an argument from *genus.*
2. You could tell him that his act will result in his having to spend years in the penitentiary. This would be argument from *consequence.*
3. You could tell him that this is the sort of thing he would dislike if he were the victim of it himself. This would be argument from *similarity.*
4. You could tell him that this sort of thing is forbidden by the Bible. This would be argument from *authority.*

Although you may think that we have here overestimated the patience of our hypothetical gunman, you will have to admit that each of these arguments has a certain degree of force, which the abstract syllogism cannot have. That is why we say that we have now invented arguments. The areas from which they can be drawn here start to emerge with some distinctness, and so we have the beginning of a "topic."

In our teaching we have commonly referred to these topics as the "sources" of argument, which is another way of indicating their nature. To return to the classroom for illustration: suppose now the student is given the assignment of writing an argument about freedom of expression or democracy or world federation. With these sources outlined for him, he can begin to develop his case by consulting such recognized areas of experience and observation as genus, consequence, similarity, etc. Even the student of limited ability now finds that he has more to say about the subject than he had first supposed.

II

Naturally, introducing the topical approach into a college composition course calls for some practical decisions. One of the more important of these concerns the choice of specific topics to be presented. When we undertook to teach the topics as part of the Chicago composition course, we decided to deal with only a few topics but to choose them so that they could be related, sometimes explicitly but more often by implication, to a much longer list. This gives the teacher latitude; it enables him to emphasize one or another aspect of any one of the topics. Next we kept in mind that we wanted topics useful in the art of teaching composition. The result has been a relatively limited and pedagogically useful list, with a considerable degree of flexibility.

GENUS

The argument from genus or definition comprises all arguments made from the nature of a thing. In presenting this type of argument, we merely take whatever fact or idea is the subject of our deliberation and refer it to its class. If our audience is sufficiently impressed with the actuality of that class (i.e., with its reality as a class containing this member among others), it will grant that whatever is true of that class is true of this fact or idea in question, which is the point we are seeking to make by our argument.

For example: suppose someone is seeking to argue that a certain fiscal policy of the government is undesirable. What he may do, if he is using the argument from genus, is to take this single policy and put it in the class "inflation." Now if he is successful in doing that, he transfers the significance of (and presumably the feeling about) inflation to the fiscal policy of the government which he is attacking. We are assuming here that the speaker says no more than "This is inflation." If he goes into the consequences of inflation, he is leaving his argument from genus for a further argument from consequences. The same analysis holds for "This is treason," "This is a betrayal of the working class," "This is true Americanism," and for any other argument which seeks to find its motivation through a fixed predicable constituting a genus. It may be pointed out here, incidentally, that training in the critical and precise use of genera is the best possible safeguard against irresponsible "name-calling."

In teaching the topics, it may be necessary at some point to take into account the empirical fact that arguments employ two types of definition (and it may be possible to distinguish these as [1] *genus* and [2] *definition*). The first type employs a universally accepted convention for which the speaker does not feel that description, analysis, or "proof" is required. It is, so to speak, one of the established categories of the public mind, and one feels that nothing more is needed than to name it. Probably for a minister with a rather orthodox congregation, "sin" is such a term. Therefore, when he has categorized, either flatly or through extended exposition, such and such an action as "sin," he has made his argument. The genus is so well established that it would be superfluous for him to support it.

But there are many terms whose scope is by no means fixed, so that any successful employment of them requires a certain amount of explicit definition. One has to define them because one knows that their correct definitions are not perceived. A good example of this type of term is "liberty" in John Stuart Mill's famous essay of that name. Mill proposes to argue certain propositions about liberty and the individual, but before he can do this, he must go through a long process of defining. Only after that is completed, can he use "liberty" as a genus by which to approve or disapprove of certain actions. Anyone today predicating an argument upon "democracy" must do the same thing. "Democracy" is surrounded by so much nebulosity that one cannot, until this labor is performed, expect much similarity of conception. That is to say, it is not in the public mind now a clear genus.

The process of argument is, of course, the same in both instances, the difference being that in the first the genus is ready-made; in the second it has to be made. It is well to take notice of this because many arguments will be encountered by the students in their reading which devote most of their space to setting up the genera. Not until these are fixed is the writer prepared to make propositions with reference to special occurrences.

CONSEQUENCE

In a consequence argument, one presents the causal relationships among experiences. As with arguments from genus and definition, these arguments may employ self-evident and widely accepted causal linkings, or the writer may seek to establish linkings which are less well recognized. Such arguments most frequently move directly from cause to effect or from effect to cause. The simple cause-to-effect argument is well illustrated in Burke's *Speech on American Taxation,* where the movement of the argument is from the cause (unjust treatment of the American Colonies) to the effect (discontent, disorder, disobedience). The classic argument from effect to cause is the proof of the existence of God from the existence of order in the universe. The argument here consists of observing the effect and then postulating a cause which will explain this effect.

A more complex argument is sometimes called the "argument from sign." Many causes have a multiplicity of effects. A cold snap not only will produce ice on ponds but will cause people to dress warmly. When one observes some of the effects and argues from them to the cause and thence to another effect, he is arguing from sign. The ice and the wearing of warm clothing are effects of the cause, coldness. By observing one effect, we can reason to the cause and thence to another effect, which, in this example, is a course of action.

All these arguments are in constant use in our civilization. The politician argues that, if he is elected (cause), there will be better government (effect); he argues that the present corruption in government (effect) must have been produced by a corrupt administration (cause); and that his happy home, successful career, and firm church and civic affiliations are clear signs that he will administer the office he seeks wisely and honestly.

LIKENESS AND DIFFERENCE

Likeness and difference are really two separate topics. But their structure as arguments is sufficiently similar to warrant their being grouped together. There is no significant difference between likeness and what we are more familiar with as analogy. Similarly, difference corresponds to what some logicians call "negative analogy." An important thing to remember in both is that they rest, as arguments, on two instances; that is, in using likeness or difference, we argue from one case to another, unlike the practice in induction, where we argue from a large number of particular cases to a general rule or law.

A distinction is sometimes drawn between two uses of likeness, or analogy. The rhetorician Whately, for example, suggests that it may be used, not only "to *prove* the proposition in question, but to make it more *clearly understood.*" We must not mistake for argument, he goes on to tell us, what is used for clarification. When we reflect that "analogy" is sometimes used synonymously with "metaphor," we can see that the situation can become still further complicated. For our purposes, however, we can disregard such distinctions. Actually, it could be plausibly asserted that all comparisons are used, in varying degrees, for argument. Hence we will not go far wrong if we treat them as arguments.

TESTIMONY AND AUTHORITY

In that it seldom stands alone as the primary source of an extensive argument, testimony and authority differs from the other topics. It is an "external" source of argument, because its force is derived not from the immediate subject matter of the discourse but from consideration of the competence and integrity of the witness: if good and wise men believe this, it must be so. This topic may be directed toward the confirmation of either a general proposition or a specific circumstance. Testimony and authority involves also the writer's attempt to establish his own credibility as a witness or probity as a judge and, conversely, in some instances an effort to show that his opponent is careless with facts and unsound in judgment. Finally, style itself, through the use of terminology or even syntax associated with revered persons, ideas, or institutions, may constitute a subtle appeal to authority.

III

It may be objected that, although this approach to the teaching of argument has theoretical attractiveness, its relevance to the workaday job of writing a composition is somewhat tenuous. Some may feel, as some of us did during preliminary discussions of the idea, that, however plausible the introduction of the topics might appear when reflected upon in the teacher's study, it would only create confusion in the classroom by setting up another barrier of terminology between the student's thought and his written argument. However, on the basis of experience, we are now convinced that the topics can be intimately related to the student's problems in writing arguments, that they help the student to clarify the ideas which he wishes to set down on paper, and that, above all, they fulfil their primary purpose—the stimulation of the student's powers to discover relevant and effective arguments.

Perhaps the nature of this interplay between theory and practice may be suggested by a brief account of the way in which we familiarize our students with topical analysis. First, in order to make clear what a topic is and to exemplify the four topics chosen, we present a series of brief argumentative passages, classified according to the topic primarily employed in each. Thus, under genus, we show Tom Paine using a definition of a "true" constitution to support his argument that the British government is fundamentally lawless. As soon as the students show some ability to understand and recognize particular topics, they are asked to write a series of brief arguments in which they experiment with the appropriateness of various topical approaches. It should be noted that the students are *not* told to create an argument illustrating a particular topic but, instead, are instructed to write arguments supporting or attacking certain propositions which are chosen for their simplicity, closeness to students' interests, and capacity to stir controversy.

Obviously, in any reasonably complex argument, a skilful writer will draw upon a variety of topics, moving easily from one to another as he develops the full significance of his thought. Consequently, after introducing the topics through brief, categorized excerpts, we turn our attention to the examination of several substantial arguments—among them *The Federalist*, No. 10; Lincoln's First Inaugural Address; Thoreau's "Civil Disobedience"; Swift's "A Modest Proposal"; Bertrand Russell's "A Free Man's Worship"; Newman's "Knowledge Its Own End"—in which various topical approaches can be observed in the less artificial context of full, rich, and actual disputation. Accompanying the study of these texts is the writing of two or three fairly long arguments in which the student has an opportunity to practice not merely his ability to recognize relevant topics but also his skill in incorporating various topical arguments into a systematic and persuasive whole.

The most significant result traceable, we believe, to experimentation with the program outlined above has been a striking increase in the richness of students' arguments. With the topics providing a guideline, our writers show much less timidity about thrusting themselves into the heart of argumentative situations, instead of coyly and cautiously skirting the edges, as they have often done in the past. This fact has done much to strengthen our conviction that instruction in argumentation has a primary role in the composition course. Insofar as familiarity with the rhetorical topics improves the young writer's ability to look for and recognize rational arguments which are appropriate to the line of thought or action he is advocating, the approach we have described makes it possible to deal seriously with argumentation. Placed in the posture of argument, students who know how to employ the topics are not so likely either to freeze or to foam. They have demonstrated that, given a technique to assist them in locating and evaluating arguments, they have something to say about controversial subjects.

Weaver Discusses English Course[1]

(*Editor's Note:* With changes in UC's undergraduate curriculum imminent, the *Maroon* begins today a series discussing the present organization of College general education courses. Articles in this series will run to the end of this quarter. All articles are written by the course chairman, or members of the course teaching staff.

The first article of the series, a discussion of the College English course, appears today. It is written by course chairman Richard Weaver, a long time UC faculty member and professor of English in the College.)

English composition in the College is a course in writing and rhetoric, designed to increase the student's proficiency in the use of his language. There is no medium which he will be called upon to use more frequently than language, yet the average student begins college with only a rudimentary command of the subtle and powerful resources of English. This can be a grave handicap to his education in general and also to his personal development, for language has been rightly called "the supreme organ of the mind's self-ordering growth." In his practice of composition, the student acquires more than a simple skill; because of the close relationship between language and thought, he must constantly be exercising his power to conceptualize and as constantly testing his sense of relevance, while at the same time he is increasing the range and accuracy of his vocabulary.

Basis Explained

The course in composition is based, it could be said, upon the principle that the laws of rhetoric, like the laws of logic, were not instituted by man, but can be discovered by him and imparted. Accordingly, both English 101–2–3 and 105–6 (the two-quarter version for the better prepared students)

1. *Chicago Maroon,* February 21, 1962, 4.

follow a carefully planned sequence. Study begins with the relation between style and purpose. Examples are used to demonstrate that every competent piece of writing must be interpreted in the light of a purpose, and that this purpose may explain virtually all the elements of style, from major features of organization to the smallest matters of grouping within the sentence and choices of diction. In this phase of the program systematic attention is given to the rhetorical qualities of words and of various sentence patterns. The student learns to discriminate levels of abstraction in diction, to become aware of connotation, and to judge the usefulness of figures of speech. He learns also the importance of variety, subordination, parallelism, and position in constructing effective sentences.

Exposition Required

With this introduction to the elements of style as background, the student passes to expository writing. Here attention is focused upon the most effective types of organization for communicating facts, for informing, and for explaining. Successive papers are assigned which involve definition, classification, comparison and contrast, organization by cause and effect, and combinations of these forms. Throughout the study of exposition, stress is laid upon the logic and clarity of the controlling plan of the essay.

Exposition is followed by argumentation, which is regularly given a full quarter's time. Here the student learns something of the principles and techniques of induction, deduction, and analogy. He learns the methods of stating and supporting propositions and is shown some of the principal fallacies to be avoided in the interpretation of evidence. At the end of the period devoted to argumentation, some study is given to the rhetorical "topics"—the sources from which proofs can be drawn—as a means of finding persuasive content for argumentative papers and of adapting an argument to a given audience.

Essay Required

In English 103, and in 106 at the discretion of the instructor, the student writes at the close of the course a long essay based on an outside reading prescribed for the class. In this paper he has an opportunity to bring into play all that he has learned about exposition, argument, and persuasion.

Work in the classroom follows a pattern of discussion, writing, and criticism. The English syllabi contain a wide variety of readings, most of which are models, or at least useful examples, of exposition and argument.

Purpose Determined

After a reading has been assigned, the instructor asks the class to determine the purpose of the writing and to identify the techniques used by the author. As analysis proceeds, he invites the class to point out sources of strength or weakness in the organization, the use of evidence, and the various features of style and tone. In the writing assignment which follows, the student will be required to prepare a paper in which he demonstrates his own understanding of the expository modes or argumentative techniques he has been studying in the example. It is the conviction of the staff that all topics for writing should have serious intellectual potentiality; the trivial type of theme topic is discouraged.

Papers are not only marked for errors, but also are criticized for content, organization, and style. Papers which can serve well to illustrate special points are sometimes dittoed so that the entire class can engage in constructive criticism. The instructor always holds up positive improvement as the goal; the censure of mistakes is incidental to the larger end of achieving clear and cogent expression.

More Than Training

The writing course in the College thus offers substantially more than a training in routine rules; it is directed toward an expansion of the student's powers through analysis, criticism, and that estimate of rhetorical situations which is the inescapable duty of any articulate member of a community. And because its central concern is with the effective use of language, it provides not so much a tool for, as a key to all humanistic studies, which are traditionally the teachers of wisdom.

And for Yale[1]

The Yale man is writ fairly large in American tradition. Now, on the seventy-fifth anniversary of its founding, the *Yale Daily News* gives a portrait of him, against the background of his institution. The contributions, which are by faculty members and distinguished alumni, cover everything from his initial selection to his future in the problematical world of today.

Central to the picture is Yale College, which has maintained a certain uniqueness among American institutions of higher learning. Yale has never coveted the intellectual radicalism of Harvard, or the severe objective scholarship of Johns Hopkins; but on the other hand it has stayed far away from the curricular disorders and the confused aspirations of the public institutions. If there has been a measure of truth in the saying that a boy went to Yale not to get an A.B. degree but to get a "Yale education," the product was not entirely derogated thereby. Yale kept a firm grip on the humanities; it tended to educate the whole man; and if competitor institutions sometimes complained that it was "a trade school for success," there was some ground for suspecting envy of the formula.

In studying the contributions of faculty members, one is likely to be impressed by their humaneness. These articles contain the kind of chastened wisdom one is reassured to encounter. A teacher is engaged in many ways in sorting good from bad; yet after watching the parade of youth for two or three decades, he comes to distrust those superficial signs by which a generation is condemned as very bad, or is praised as very good and as likely to save the world. He has learned to take the long view, which is, in the words of H. Richard Niebuhr of the Divinity School, "that before God the generations are equal in goodness, sin, and prospect of deliverance from evil." The question which the teacher is professionally obligated to ask then is not "whether a present generation is more selfish than its predecessors," but "what particular form egocentrism takes in it."

That, for the liberal educator, seems to be a sensible way of keeping up with the times.

1. *The Commonweal*, 58/1, April 10, 1953, 31–32.

From Poetry to Bitter Fruit[1]

The inside story of the corruption of public school education has never been more poignantly told than in Joan Dunn's *Retreat from Learning: Why Teachers Can't Teach—A Case History* (New York: David McKay, $3.00). Miss Dunn, a young woman with ideals, decided to make teaching her career—partly because she had worked with children and liked them, and partly because she wished to bring to others her own natural delight in literature. After going through the various maneuverings necessary to get a post in the New York City school system, she showed up one Friday shortly after Labor Day at the high school to which she had been assigned.

A leap from the poetry of John Donne and Richard Crashaw, the subject of her college thesis, to an institution like that described here is about as great as any mortal could be expected to make. But she had the qualities of character and personality to make it, and for four years she observed modern public education from the firing line. Her book is an account of what she saw between that morning of hope and expectancy and the day she resigned, out of fatigue and disillusionment, to enter the happier world of journalism.

Only by a doubtful use of the term can this institution be called a school. A school may be defined, not too strictly, as a place where instruction is systematically imparted. Instruction could not be systematically imparted here—except in the case of a few honor classes and a few entering ones that had not been ruined by the school's atmosphere. Discipline and morale were practically non-existent. Classes turned into hour-long disputes between the teacher and individual students about students' "rights." The reading of comic books during recitation, insolent remarks about the teacher's appearance and personality, and muttered obscenities in the back of the room were regular features of each day.

1. *National Review*, 1/10, January 25, 1956, 26–27. © 1956 by National Review, Inc., 215 Lexington Avenue, New York, N.Y. 10016. Reprinted by permission.

It must be questioned also whether much of that which could be imparted was instruction. The pressure to use the discussion method with youngsters who had nothing to discuss except trivialities, or their own misbehavior; the willingness of school authorities to pander to the supposed interests of adolescents; the discouragement of healthful competition; and the practice of passing students merely for "being good" in the classroom naturally brought knowledge as such into disrepute. The resultant anti-intellectualism was, moreover, belligerent. "I ain't gonna read no book" was a general refrain.

These young Americans for democratic action were transforming what was supposed to be a school into a daily detention home for the lawless and the obstreperous.

Miss Dunn's analysis of the cause of this collapse will be challenged by no one who has followed the trend of "progressivism" in education. Heading the list is the "anti-formalism" of John Dewey, who applied his talents and longevity to wrecking the educational philosophy which had been built up through twenty-five centuries of classical and Christian experience. As a result of his influence, nothing is more pervasive in the doctrines of modern education than the notion that all forms and rules are evil. Yet all history and observation confirm the truth that men cannot exist together peaceably without the acceptance of certain formalizations of behavior and intercourse. If the schools are teaching that these things are wrong, they are spreading ignorance. Which is what many of us have been suspecting for a long while.

The schools began to betray their mission in society the moment they turned away from the principle that discipline lies at the heart of all education. Discipline was cast out because discipline may inspire fear, and nobody should be made afraid. (One hears the traditionalist in the rear of the teachers' meeting murmuring helplessly, "The fear of the Lord is the beginning of wisdom." But what can be done, now that "freedom from fear" has been made one of the pillars of the New Freedom?) Competition is out for the same reason. Far from helping to adjust them to their environment, these quack doctors of education are preparing their charges for something that never was on land or sea.

Compared with these fantastic doctrinaires, the founders of Utopian communities in the past were realists of a higher order. They all believed in the need of work, and most of them believed in the necessity of an overriding sanction through religion or moral commitment. Our leading public school theorists today believe in neither.

Their educational theory, to the extent that it is capable of coherent statement, sounds like a Wordsworthian version of Platonism. The child is father of the man; growing older is a process of forgetting original knowledge, so that the only thing for a teacher to do is stand by and let the students carry forward the work of education. And what is the real situation of the short-changed student? "He arrives at high school to learn only to find himself greeted by teachers who worship him simply because he is young and ignorant while they themselves are fallen from that pristine state." It is little wonder that some of these impudent charlatans have proposed abolishing the fixed curriculum, as another march on the retreat from learning.

This is the bitter fruit of that theory vaingloriously termed "progressive education." It is, as Miss Dunn rightly points out, "materialist in premise and pragmatic in application." Behind the façade of larger buildings, better equipped gymnasiums, more efficient cafeterias, and an infinitude of bookkeeping for the teacher lies the fact that the schools have abjured all rational goals. The aim is no longer learning. The students are no longer scholars, but "citizens." And though a general program of secular education is supposed to have a "unifying influence," nothing is more apparent in this case than the lack of any kind of social cement. When appeals are made for loyalty, they are either in the name of something inexpressibly vague or something that doesn't exist. As the author pointedly says, "You cannot turn a child from the ways of crime by telling him that it is uncivic to rob a store, beat up a subway guard, or murder a member of a rival gang in a street war."

Many years ago H. L. Mencken, after reviewing a kind of credo voted on by a select group of educators, declared that the most humane thing he could recommend would be to take them out in the alley and knock them in the head. Anyone surveying the depth to which the high calling of education has been brought by these fakes today may well wish that the execution could be carried out. But they are not going to be killed. They are going to be saved from that by the very traditions and formalizations of order which they have worked so sedulously to undermine. Another remedy will have to be found.

Miss Dunn believes that we must abandon immediately all the nonsensical features of progressive education and begin again to instill in the child a basic moral sense. That, certainly, is the least we should settle for. But the exposures in this book prompt one further thought, which I am going to suggest, with apology for my recklessness. Is not this sagging of all values and this dispersal of aims somehow implied in the idea of public education? I ask whether we would not have produced a more thoughtful kind of literacy if we had found a way to support a system of private subscription schools in which children could be educated according to the religious or cultural principles espoused by their parents. On these terms, education would be a privilege, and not a "right." The educationally incorrigible would simply be dropped, instead of, as now, being allowed to set the tone of the school. And the scholars who remained would feel the upward pull of definite religious and cultural ideals. If that thought seems too odious for words to the advocates of increased public education, let them show cause why it is not so.

Mr. Hutchins as Prophet[1]

For a generation Robert M. Hutchins has been calling educational sinners to repentance, and no man can fairly deny that he has been a major prophet of our time. What has raised him to this high eminence is a peculiarly clear grasp of the relationship between liberal education and the practice of democratic government. Although this relationship requires no complex demonstration, the American people have yet to see it, if we are to judge by their educational choices and expenditures. Liberal education is specifically the education of the man and the citizen. In a democratic state the common citizen is vested with the ultimate power of decision; his is the final determination of policies which affect him in the unit and the mass. And, hopefully or ominously, there is no higher court of appeal; if he votes himself trouble, he cannot, according to the theory at least, expect to be saved by a more knowing elite. This being the case, there is no excuse for not training him as a thinking man. He needs for his career as a citizen those disciplines which train the mind in the interpretation of evidence and the discrimination of alternatives. He needs some knowledge of history because being a provincial in time is at least as dangerous as being a provincial in space. In sum: he needs initiation into the habit of philosophy. That courses in history, literature, mathematics, logic and rhetoric will provide this, whereas courses in truck-driving, drum-majoring, cosmetology and even nuclear physics will not, should need preaching only to a misled or perverse generation.

In *Great Books: the Foundation of a Liberal Education* (New York: Simon and Schuster, $3.00) Mr. Hutchins returns to this theme with a few fresh applications. The Great Books conserve the intellectual and spiritual tra-

1. *National Review*, 1/12, Febrary 8, 1956, 26–27. © 1956 by National Review, Inc., 215 Lexington Avenue, New York, N.Y. 10016. Reprinted by permission.

dition of the West; they are centrally related to liberal education; their "infinite suggestiveness" makes them better suited to study by adults than by the young; and a recovery of their wisdom is the best means—perhaps indeed the only means—of finding a basis of understanding with the renascent East. Again, as one can see, he is looking at the larger perils of our cultural crisis, and he is laying it on the line.

This last reminds us that, apart from the substance of his thought, Mr. Hutchins has one qualification as prophet which cannot be overlooked. Like the prophets of old, he is prepared to damn completely. There can be no shilly-shallying in prophecy. Search the Old Testament, for example, from end to end, and you will not find a single prophet who was a "liberal" in the modern sense. To the real prophet, right is right, and wrong deserves hell-fire and damnation. There is never that middle ground into which the modern Liberal loves to crawl to avoid any meaningful commitment. By his position, furthermore, the prophet always implies that "he that gathereth not, scattereth." During his long career as an educational leader, Mr. Hutchins has mercilessly beaten over the head those relativists, pragmatists, presentists, and anti-metaphysicians who were greasing the skids for the disappearance of liberal education. In this respect, he has never been a Liberal, but a voice, and, in his own phrase, "no friendly voice."

After describing Mr. Hutchins as a qualified prophet in these terms, I must introduce one grave demurrer. A wise man has written that the word of a prophet is a *deed*. Well, when one turns from Mr. Hutchins' words to his deeds as administrator and as director, one encounters singular and unexpected failures. His words have often not issued in deeds, or they have issued in deeds that appeared to break faith with the words. I seldom think of this aspect of his career without recalling the lines that a court wit is said to have pinned to the door of the bedchamber of Charles II: "He never said a foolish thing, and never did a wise one." Of this there are so many examples that a severe critic might insist upon "Failure" as his epitaph.

Did this come about because the pressure of events worked inexorably against his high ideals? I do not believe that exculpation is so easy.

Mr. Hutchins has always been disarmingly candid about his own lack of education, and he has in fact written "The Autobiography of an Uneducated Man." I do not feel, however, that he has told us where the deficiencies of his education really lie. He has no education in common life. Despite his earnest concern with the salvation of the average man through liberal education, I see little evidence that he has understood him. Santayana once wrote that if John Stuart Mill had ever learned in what the common man, who was the object of his solicitude, found his happiness, he would have been chilled to the bone. I think Mr. Hutchins would be chilled to the marrow. As a general consequence, a figure who should have been a great public educator has progressively alienated his public.

This ignorance I refer to led Mr. Hutchins, as well as many of those he gathered about him at Chicago, into too great a dependence upon dialectic. Dialectic is altogether a logical process; it is concerned with definition of categories and the drawing out of the implications of propositions. It is most necessary, but it is not all. It has to be supplemented by rhetoric, which is an accommodation of the existing passions of men. And although Mr. Hutchins is no mean rhetorician in his own area, he seems not to have contemplated the role of rhetoric in his analysis of social tendencies and situations. In this connection it could be pointed out that the chief criticism leveled at the Hutchins plan at Chicago was that whereas it provided tremendous intellectual stimulation, it afforded little means for emotional and social maturing. Social man is to a considerable extent rhetorical man.

The obsession with dialectic has produced, among other things, a naïveté about Communism. By the dialectical process one can easily arrive at a definition of Communism; but without some understanding of the sphere of rhetoric, one fails to grasp its impulse, and its impulse is the fact we have to deal with practically today. It is one thing to say what it is in the manner of a dictionary; it is another to discern its inner motivation and predict its movement. This has led Mr. Hutchins into confusions like his ridicule of "guilt by association," which flies in the face of the ancient principle of folk wisdom that "Birds of a feather flock together." The common man absorbs that long before he begins to read the Great Books.

In this volume recommending the classics to the adult population of the Western world, Mr. Hutchins calls reading the Great Books the Great Conversation. The phrase is a good one, and let no man stand in the way of such reading. I only fear, on the basis of the record, that a great conversation presided over by Mr. Hutchins would be dialectic alone. That means that it would be carried on in a realm of great abstraction; many would be called but few would choose to enter. Dialectic by itself can be destructive, as when it erects systems that deny common perception, common feeling, and the wisdom of tradition. A humorless dialectic was midwife to Marxism.

What Mr. Hutchins says about liberal education and its relation to the great books is unquestionably the truth. But the complete educator must still ask himself whether it is the whole truth.

Flesh for a Skeleton[1]

This book is written for the layman who has received limited mathematical training but is intellectually curious about the history and major concepts of mathematics. Professor Dantzig begins with the most primitive forms of counting and proceeds down to the deep waters of today, wherein mathematical theory is hardly distinguishable from philosophy or cosmology. It is not all easy reading, but anyone willing to peruse it with a degree of concentration will be amply rewarded.

His account is filled with facts that will interest and, some of them, amaze. It is interesting to learn, for example, that the decimal system traces back to man's original habit of counting on ten fingers. Although tradition is going to preserve the decimal base indefinitely, it is not the best one, mathematically speaking. "Almost any other base, with the possible exception of *nine*, would have done as well and probably better." It will come as news to many that one of the greatest achievements of the race was the invention of zero, or a symbol standing for an empty class. It marked a virtual revolution in mathematics, and made possible many operations which before were either extremely tedious or impossible altogether. Another discovery of tremendous consequence was the idea of infinity. The Greeks, according to Professor Dantzig, had a temperamental horror of infinity and of irrational numbers, and this paralyzed their mathematics at a certain point. But when the "dilemma of infinity," which was like a "legendary dragon guarding the entrance to the enchanted garden," was finally solved, the scope of mathematical theory was immensely increased.

Again the reader may be surprised, but the author should convince him, that the history of mathematics is "a profoundly human story." Hardly less

1. *National Review*, 1/19, March 28, 1956, 26–27. © 1956 by National Review, Inc., 215 Lexington Avenue, New York, N.Y. 10016. Reprinted by permission.

than art theory, mathematical theory has had its schools and parties, its feuds, its *causes célèbres,* and its innovators who were resented. Consider what happened when Georg Cantor propounded his revolutionary "theory of aggregates."

> It was fortunate for Cantor that mature reflection had thoroughly steeled him to face the onslaught, because for many years to come he had to bear the struggle alone. And what a struggle! The history of mathematics has not recorded anything equal to it in fury. The stormy beginnings of the theory of aggregates show that even in such an abstract field as mathematics, human emotions cannot be altogether eliminated.

The book will certainly make clear how much mathematics has to contribute to liberal education. The author maintains that "our school curricula, by stripping mathematics of its cultural content and leaving a bare skeleton of technicalities, has repelled many a fine mind," and most readers are likely to agree.

Safe for a While[1]

The future of the book, along with that of many other things in a world that is cheerfully or apprehensively described as "fast changing" is now being called into question. A means of record and an instrument of education which has stood unchallenged for thousands of years finds itself competing today with films, tapes, discs, the radio, the television screen, and other products of technology. To librarians, as custodians of the book, this is a development of special concern, and last year the Library School of the University of Chicago held a conference in order to take stock of changes and assess the book's future.

There is nothing in the findings of the men represented here, who come from a number of professions and fields of learning, to inspire alarm in the breast of the book-lover. For the verdict is practically unanimous that the book has a long lease on life, perhaps not as a handsome artifact, but certainly as a means for the storage and transmission of knowledge. Its new competitors, though they may dazzle with some feature of novelty or ingenuity, prove to have limitations of their own. And the physical changes in book manufacture, which cause some to feel that the book is on the way out, are hardly greater than those in the past from papyrus scroll to vellum codex, and so on. Professor Howard W. Winger summed up the sense of the meeting when he said: "In providing for the storage of information and for its efficient retrieval, the codex book has been without a peer. It can hold more and yield it more readily than any other tool that has been devised up to now."

The real threat appears to come not so much from the new means of transcribing and reproducing as from the fact that the book is overmul-

1. *National Review*, 2/5, Jume 20, 1956, 21. © 1956 by National Review, Inc., 215 Lexington Avenue, New York, N.Y. 10016. Reprinted by permission.

tiplying itself. It is a saying among professional librarians that the modern library, like money at compound interest, doubles every sixteen years. Although certain leveling-off forces prevent the actual increase from being quite that terrifying, storage is in most places an acute problem. For the same reason, reference grows increasingly complicated. A student becoming familiar with a field needs to find his way now not among a few books, but among hundreds or thousands, so that "the sheer bulk of recorded information is today a cause of serious concern." Our methods of getting at the contents of books are lagging behind book publication. It is a fact that mathematicians are at work trying to devise more adequate means for classifying and retrieving the information piling up in libraries.

The question of the future seems to be not whether the book will be used, but how it can be coded, arranged, and recovered in libraries that will contain millions of volumes.

Informed and Urbane[1]

Whether the world should come to the college or the college should come to the world has long been an issue in the theory of education. The extensive growth of the evening college in America indicates that higher education is in fact drifting toward the market place. The Association of University Evening Colleges now has one hundred members. More than a quarter of a million students are in attendance, and if one adds to this figure the number enrolled at extension centers, the total is considerably larger. Everyone admits that the new arrival is a member of the educational family, but no one knows exactly where to place him at the table.

In this book Professor John P. Dyer, Dean of University College at Tulane, chronicles the history and discusses the main problems of the new type of institution.

The evening college student body is highly heterogeneous. Its typical member is a person who has been out of the regular channels of education anywhere from five to thirty years. The motives of those who attend are even more varied, if that is possible, than those of the hordes in residence at our state universities. Some come to get clearly defined vocational training, with job improvement in view. Others come from no other cause than a vague feeling that "more education would be good for me." The records show, however, that evening college products do about as well as those of the regular institutions when they go on for graduate work.

The author makes a special point of the fact that the evening college's clientele, despite its variety in other respects, comes very largely from the white-collar class. And since this class occupies a strategic station in the modern social organization, what their college does for these students may be important out of proportion to their numbers.

1. *National Review,* 2/6, Jume 27, 1956, 19. © 1956 by National Review, Inc., 215 Lexington Avenue, New York, N.Y. 10016. Reprinted by permission.

The question here as elsewhere comes down to whether the institution ought to give them what they want or think they want, or what they ought to have. This involves, of course, the old debate between vocational and liberal education. Professor Dyer is educational statesman enough to believe that evening colleges have responsibility for adult education of the broader kind. The white-collar worker in particular, he feels, needs to be lifted above his "stereotyped experiences." But Dyer also believes that "the evening college must devise ways and means of prying open the minds of all its students." His suggestions here are tentative, but they point in the right direction.

Professor Dyer is at his best when he writes with his own mind, and at his worst when he falls back, as he too often does, upon the authority of sociological pundits. But on balance the book is recommended as an informed and urbane study of this recent outgrowth of our mammoth educational system.

Education for What?[1]

If educators really want to know why they have fallen so low in public esteem, they need only wake up to the fact that they have abandoned concern with the very things of which educators are traditionally the custodians
and expositors. There are teachings concerning the nature of reality, the
validity of knowledge, the meaning of goodness, and the origin and final
end of man. This essentially is what Professors Redden and Ryan show in
A Catholic Philosophy of Education. The book is a systematic comparison of
Catholic belief and practice with all of the chief modern theories, and particularly with those stemming from the school of John Dewey.

Catholic education proves its seriousness by asking at the outset, "What
is man?" The answer given is that man is a body and a soul. Consequently,
education has as one of its controlling considerations man's supernatural
destiny. It cannot be exclusively for the objective of "adjustment to the environment." (Even biology now teaches that a perfectly adjusted organism
ceases to develop.) Neither should it be exclusively for "success." Failure is
just as truly a part of reality as success, and a complete education equips one
to survive that. Meantime, that prize of all modern cant phrases, "education
for democratic living," receives its due deflation. It takes no little courage
today to point out, as do the authors, that "democracy is only one form of
government that *Societas Civilis Naturalis* takes."

That modern "progressive" education is an apostasy, not only from all
faith but from all learning, is apparent to anyone who takes the trouble to
examine its premises. Man is continuous with nature, and nature is eternally
changing—toward what, nobody can say, because the universe is regarded
as self-existing. And since man is only an atom in this vast flux, free will is

1. *National Review,* 2/27, November 24, 1956, 20–21. © 1956 by National Review, Inc., 215
Lexington Avenue, New York, N.Y. 10016. Reprinted by permission.

not only intellectually untenable but also practically undesirable. The upshot is a picture in which "there are no eternal moral values or moral standards . . . no conduct intrinsically good or bad, no moral responsibility; there are no good men or bad men; no heroes, no honest men, no scoundrels; there are only 'cases' (neurotic or badly conditioned)."

Well, having dug himself into a hole that deep, how is man ever going to get out? More than thirty years ago Irving Babbitt wrote, "under certain conditions that are already partly in sight, the Catholic Church may perhaps be the only institution left in the Occident that can be counted on to uphold civilized standards." That is certainly the feeling one gets from reading this comparison of a Catholic philosophy of education with the nihilism of Dewey and his epigoni.

History or Special Pleading?[1]

Legend says that the president of a leading American university once asked the professors in the department of history to define what it was they were teaching. Apparently more astute and knowledgeable than most, they refused to come up with a definition of exactly what they were professing. Perhaps it was just as well for them; history has proved a notoriously difficult concept to define; and the "idea of history" continues to invite abstruse speculations. Nevertheless there remains on the part of the expert and the inexpert alike a solid conviction that the study of history, however the subject is defined, does have some uses. Estimates of that use range all the way from Thucydides' cautious belief that a knowledge of the past is "an aid to the interpretation of the future, which in the course of human things must resemble if it does not reflect it" to Lord Acton's forthright declaration that the use of history is to sharpen our conscience.

Harvey Wish's *The American Historian* (Oxford, $7.50) raises the problem to a new level, since now the question becomes, what is the use of a history of historians? Of course the two questions are best taken together, and out of respect to the method of historians, let us begin with a look at the data. *The American Historian* is substantial and complete: it begins with the unsophisticated and therefore delectable early writers like John Smith and William Bradford and proceeds down to Allan Nevins. All of the great names in between—Bancroft, Parkman, Fiske, McMaster, Adams, Turner, Beard, and others—receive due space if not their due meed of praise. The book moves along like a good historical narrative, notwithstanding some necessary excursions into analysis.

The reader soon becomes aware, however, that Mr. Wish has an axe to grind. Despite attention to the strict business of relation and despite

1. *National Review*, 10/1, January 14, 1961, 21–22. © 1961 by National Review, Inc., 215 Lexington Avenue, New York, N.Y. 10016. Reprinted by permission.

an ability to enter momentarily into views with which he is unsympathetic for the purposes of exposition, Mr. Wish's ideological premises are in clear view throughout. The result is that this work is not simply a history of historians; it is also a critique of them. In his conclusion the author expresses a hope for "a more meticulous and critical search for a reasonable view of the past." Evidently "reason" is his trump word, and accordingly one must look for the "reasonable" position from which his critique is presented.

This is largely and flatly that of modern dogmatic equalitarianism. In fact, I have seldom seen such an unblushing application of this Liberal dogma. For him any expression of discrimination in regard to class, or race, or economic order is traceable to "bigotry"—that term of opprobrium which is doing such yeoman service in the disvaluing of our traditions and institutions. Every historian is searched for prejudices as a suspect is searched for arms; more than this he is grilled as to whether his sympathies with the "outs" and with minority groups are sufficiently wide to pass Liberal inspection.

The warning comes early in the book, when he applauds Governor Thomas Huchinson's condemnation of "colonial bigotries" as worthy of "an enlightened twentieth century historian." Thereafter he bewails the "near monopoly of expert history-writing held by economic conservatives and Loyalists" prior to the Revolution. Most colonial historians were "conservatives at heart" who "forgot to deal with ordinary men and their everyday concerns." After the Revolution, although the Tories were heard no more, "the writing and publishing of history books proved too expensive for mere sans-culottes." Consequently "the selection as to what was important amid the endless facts of history lay in the hands of a single social class." Washington Irving, for example, belonged to an "elite of bright salon conservatives" who "shuddered at the mob unleashed by Jacksonian democracy."

Francis Parkman is condemned for his "upper-class unawareness of the personality of the common man." Although he wrote well of the "forest primeval," his history "reflected the racial errors of the day." Thus Parkman is a "hostile Anglophile," who looked without sympathy upon the "Acadian peasants." In passing Mr. Wish adds, "his social science framework is wholly untenable."

The author's bogeyman is what he thinks of as Anglo-Saxon racial exclusiveness, which he represents as distorting history from the time when the Puritan fathers could not decide what to do about the Indians down through U. B. Phillips. No matter how diligent a researcher or how gifted a narrator the historian was, Mr. Wish will ferret him out and expose him unless he embraces the modern opinion that racial characteristics must not be taken into consideration. John Bach McMaster "had unfavorable judgments about the Irish, and the newer immigrant peoples." Henry and Brooks Adams are charged with harboring racial antipathies. Woodrow Wilson "showed his ethnocentrism . . . by prejudiced comments on the Italians and other southern Europeans." The young historians who trained under William A. Dunning at Columbia could not overcome their "preconceived racist assumptions." And so it goes, to repletion. Historians are also searched for their degree of acceptance of economic determination. To cite one instance of many: Bancroft is presented as "something of a snob" whose "idealistic interpretation of history led him to minimize all economic causes." In this way Mr. Wish's own social science framework is built up.

Clearly the effect of such criticism is to implant more deeply the premises of secular Liberalism, with its strong tendency to break the social bond. Doctrinaire equalitarianism and economic determination both pave the way toward a nihilism of values. One does not have to be either Anglo-Saxon or Anglophile to be an American, but one does have to accept certain principles which are intended to exclude the political nonbeliever. It may even be expected that he will show a special affection for his country. This is not unreasonable; it is merely anti-rationalistic. When Mr. Wish comes upon McMaster's statement that "There is no land where the people are so prosperous, so happy, so intelligent, so bent on doing what is just and right as the people of the United States," he can only call it "fatuous."

This kind of approach might be regarded as trivial or as destined to be abortive did we not know that it is expressive of a widespread fanaticism infecting education today. The driving idea behind that fanaticism is to make all education an adjunct of some social thesis or other. Dewey and his adherents were quite frank to say that education should condition the young for social democracy. To Mr. Wish, the whole of historiography would appear to be in part an adjunct to race problems and in part an adjunct to some theory of economic leveling. There is a difference between relating what people in the past have said about these subjects and praising opinions that one finds agreeable as if they were the true laws of historiography. The first of these is dutiful reportage; the second is a more or less concealed form of special pleading. *The American Historian* tends dangerously toward the latter, and the pleading is for a kind of featureless social order which historically is not ours.

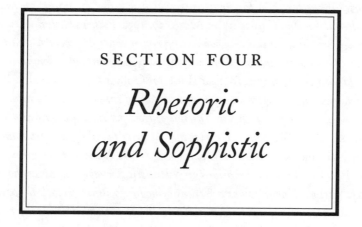

SECTION FOUR

Rhetoric and Sophistic

Richard Weaver is generally recognized as one of the five or six leading rhetorical theorists of the twentieth century. His neo-Platonic perspective was expounded in The Ethics of Rhetoric *(1953) and a small number of later essays, most of which were reprinted in a posthumous collection,* Language Is Sermonic *(1970). This section brings together all of his shorter writings—including two previously unpublished essays—on rhetoric and its negative counterpart, sophistic. They are presented here in roughly chronological order, which makes it possible to trace the significant evolution of his thinking in the last decade of his life.*

The section begins with "'Parson' Weems: A Study in Early American Rhetoric," which is published here for the first time. The essay was almost certainly intended as a chapter for The Ethics of Rhetoric, *which means that it would have been written sometime between 1949 and 1952. Weaver apparently decided to delete the chapter from the manuscript before sending it out for review.[1]*

1. The best evidence that the essay was written for *The Ethics of Rhetoric* is found in three textual references to a prior discussion of Milton. Weaver's only published work on Milton was the essay "Milton's Heroic Prose" in *The Ethics of Rhetoric.* In addition, Weaver noted in a letter to H. Arlin Turner dated February 15, 1952, that the book manuscript consisted of ten essays; in a letter to Cleanth Brooks dated November 16, 1952, that number was reduced to nine, the same as in the published version of the manuscript.

The next four items all focus on the misuse of persuasive speech. "Responsible Rhetoric" is the text of a lecture delivered at a seminar for upper level under-graduates at Purdue University on March 29, 1955. First published in 1976 and presented here in a revised and corrected form, it contrasts rhetoric and propa-ganda as forms of persuasion. The latter activity is examined at length in "Pro-paganda," an entry in the 1955 Year Book *for* Collier's Encyclopedia. *Weaver was commissioned to write an expanded version of the entry for the 1956 edition of the main encyclopedia, but it was rejected on political grounds and is now apparently lost. "The Best of Everything," a brief popular essay from an early issue of* National Review, *catalogues the defects and excesses of consumer adver-tising. Finally, "Concealed Rhetoric in Scientistic Sociology" analyzes how sup-posedly "scientific" descriptions are transformed into illicit rhetorical appeals in much of contemporary sociological writing. First presented at a conference on "Scientism and the Study of Man" in 1958, it was published without footnotes in the* Georgia Review *and later with footnotes added in* Scientism and Values, *a volume of conference proceedings. The later version has been reproduced here.*

The last three items are of particular interest because they show Weaver's gradual retreat from a Platonic emphasis on dialectic in The Ethics of Rhetoric *to a more Aristotelian view in his later writings, where he calls for a balance between dialectic and rhetoric. This change is implicit in "The Lincoln–Douglas Debates," a 1958 review for* National Review, *which acknowledges Lincoln's dialectical skill but emphasizes the limits of his vision. It is made explicit in "The Cultural Role of Rhetoric," which argues that pure dialectic in the social realm is inherently destructive of culture. Although probably written at about the same time as "The Lincoln–Douglas Debates," this essay was not published until 1964, when it appeared as Chapter 4 in* Visions of Order. *The version included here is the text of a public lecture of the same title that Weaver prepared for presentation at the University of Arkansas on November 8, 1961. It consists largely of material taken verbatim from the chapter in* Visions of Order, *but it is shorter in overall length and includes an important new section which cites court-ordered desegregation as an example of the destructiveness of pure dialec-tic.[2] The last of the trio is "Language Is Sermonic," the text of a public lecture*

---

2. In a letter to Donald Davidson dated October 5, 1961, Weaver discussed the upcom-ing speech at the University of Arkansas and noted: "I hope to get in a sideswipe indirectly at the 1954 Supreme Court decision, branding it as an irresponsible exercise of dialectic in

presented at a seminar on rhetoric at the University of Oklahoma in July 1962. First published the following year and widely reprinted thereafter, it shifts the balance even further in favor of rhetoric by arguing that language is intrinsically suasory or "sermonic." Written less than a year before his death, it is Weaver's final statement on the subject.

---

contempt of the rhetoric of history." However, Professor Ralph Eubanks, who was responsible for Weaver's invitation to Arkansas and attended the lecture, is "absolutely certain" Weaver did not include the section on desegregation in his presentation. The letter is located in the Donald Davidson Papers in the Special Collections of the Jean and Alexander Heard Library at Vanderbilt University and is quoted by permission. Professor Eubanks's comments were made in an interview with the editor conducted in Little Rock, Arkansas, on July 25, 1996.

"Parson" Weems: A Study in Early American Rhetoric[1]

It is a question worth considering whether any other writer in the range of our literature has had a greater effect of serious inspiration upon American youth than Mason Locke Weems, the first biographer of Washington. Weems has been generally forgotten except for the anecdote of the cherry tree; yet it is certain that in his time and long afterward he was a major cultural influence. Born in Maryland in 1759, ordained an Episcopal minister, engaged in the book trade after 1791, Weems looked with an active imagination upon the early years of the republic. Amid a variety of duties, he found time to write the life of Washington, of Francis Marion, of Benjamin Franklin, of William Penn, and a considerable number of moral and political tracts. From about 1800 until his death in 1825, he went up and down the Atlantic seaboard, from Pennsylvania to Georgia, preaching, writing, and selling books, including especially those of his own authorship. Sometimes it is said a sermon provided occasion for both moral inspiration and book promotion, but, as we shall presently see, the books were partly sermon too. Weems had hit upon the happy formula of presenting American heroes in a light which would gratify the rising young republic, which was hopeful, bent on success, and inclined to identify evil and pessimism with Europe.

The following which this formula drew was not only enormous; it was also distinguished. William Gilmore Simms, in a lively appreciation written in 1845, observed that Weems's qualities "have united to cast a greater spell over young America, in past days, than almost any collection of writ-

1. An essay apparently written in the period 1949–52 and intended as a chapter in *The Ethics of Rhetoric*. Edited by Ted J. Smith III from a corrected typescript (probably a final draft) located in Box 1, Folder 5, of the Richard M. Weaver Papers at Vanderbilt University.

ings within our experience."[2] We learn from Albert Beveridge, moreover, that in the very period alluded to a lad on the Western prairies named Abraham Lincoln was reading with keen attention the lives of Washington and Franklin and copying out passages for study.[3] And Woodrow Wilson, the greatest rhetorician to occupy the White House, recalled the lasting impression which the life of Washington had given him of the American Revolution.[4]

The question of why a figure of this magnitude has dropped so far from sight even in histories of American literature and culture[5] can be answered by pointing to some very general changes in taste and belief. Weems's vices as a writer were of a kind which is today peculiarly reprobated; and his virtues, which seem to me very real, have undergone a corresponding eclipse. The biographies, for example, are strangely proportioned, discursive, at times inconsistent and anything but detached in spirit. Weems regularly warmed up to his subject in a fashion which could only shock a modern biographer essaying to be critical and scientific. One might say in general that Weems has dropped from view for the same reasons that the modern American bungalow or city apartment does not resemble an eighteenth century New England home or a Southern plantation house. He was an early American, and his books are both planned and ornamented in early American style. What today impress us as disproportions, excrescences, bulkinesses and unusable spaces where we would be compact and streamlined are but parts of that style, broadly considered. That his lives of the American worthies are now period pieces is accordingly true. But in his time their vogue was very great; the *Washington* has passed through numberless editions, and the *Marion* was an early best-seller. We owe it to ourselves to look at them in the mood with which we pass through Mount Vernon or the Hermitage, not without curiosity about how much of their informing spirit we have lost.

2. William Gilmore Simms, "Weems, the Biographer and Historian," *Views and Reviews in American Literature, History and Fiction,* vol. 2, New York: Wiley and Putnam, 1845, p. 125.

3. Albert Beveridge, *Abraham Lincoln,* vol. 1, Boston and New York: Houghton Mifflin, 1928, p. 76.

4. Ray Stannard Baker, *Woodrow Wilson: Life and Letters,* vol. 1, Garden City: Doubleday, Page & Co., 1927, p. 37.

5. Van Wyck Brooks revives him briefly if skillfully in *The World of Washington Irving,* New York: E. P. Dutton, 1944, pp. 1–4.

The quality of Weems, apart from the simple pertinence of his subject matter, which made him an influence and which warrants serious literary study, is his extraordinary power of rhetoric. He was beyond doubt one of the greatest rhetoricians which this country, often accused of preferring high-flown utterance, has brought forth. There is little of classic decorum in his art, for he composed hastily, and there is a trace of the slap-dash about even his best passages; but if we define rhetoric as that which has the power to make an otherwise drab subject appealing, and to move us to take attitudes toward it, no other American of his time—not even Tom Paine—excelled him. Weems belonged to that fortunate class of persons whose way of looking at the world makes it impossible for them to be dull. He wrote upon subjects which permit the last degree of tediousness, but they began to quicken as soon as he touched them. The lives of prominent men, the saws of politics and religion, commonplace advice to the young—all were the same to his power to enliven and make immediate. To one of his imagination and sensitivity, and especially his philosophical conviction, the world was alive with implicativeness. A barked cherry tree (in the story narrated by Weems, the cherry tree was barked by the youthful Washington, not cut down) was to him not just a barked cherry tree, but the scene of a meeting between truth and its tempter; and it would scarcely exaggerate to say that for him life was a morality play. In his narratives the forces of good and evil meet in human embodiments; they engage in dialectical contests, and though evil bears itself proud for a time, it is in the end reduced to utter abjection.

The best way to introduce the subject of Weems's art is to show, by a typical illustration, that his prose is a highly *written* prose; that is to say, it is distinguished by a higher degree of the writer's artifice than is common today. Our subsequent inquiry will ask what conditions made this possible, and what the general effect was. But now, to get the problem before us concretely, I shall reproduce a brief part of Weems's account of the treason of Benedict Arnold.

> The history of Arnold's embarrassments and his quarrel with his countrymen, soon got down to New-York to the British commander, who well knowing the ticklish situation of a *proud* man, caught on the horns of *poverty,* sends him up a major Andre, with money in his pocket. The major, by means yet unknown to the public, got near enough to Arnold to *probe* him, and, alas!

found him, both in principle and purse, hollow as an exhausted receiver, and very willing to be filled up with English guineas. English guineas, to the tune of ten thousand, with the rank and pay of Brigadier General, are offered him; and Arnold agrees, Oh! shocking to humanity! Arnold agrees to sacrifice Washington.[6]

Any reader today is immediately conscious of a highly contrived style—the style of a "propagandist," it will generally be said. But a Renaissance student of rhetoric would go further to mark the presence of the following: alliteration, metaphor (two instances), ecphonesis or exclamation (two instances), anadiplosis, periphrasis, and anaphora. I think it will be fairly seen from this example that Weems is a rhetorical subject. Our next task is to look somewhat analytically at the components of his rhetoric.

The first component of his style which will impress a modern reader as peculiar to the point of being impossible today (outside of some very specialized types of discourse) is the lushness of metaphor. In the brief passage cited there were two; now I wish to illustrate this particular feature with a series of citations. In an early chapter of the life of Marion, Weems is describing the defenseless condition of South Carolina during the Revolutionary War.

The British did not, after Sir Henry Clinton's return to New York, exceed *three thousand men;* and South Carolina alone, at the lowest computation, must have contained *fifty thousand!* and yet this *host* of poor honest men were made to tremble before that handful of ruffians, as a flock of sheep before the wolf, or a household of children before a dark frowning pedagogue. The reason is immensely plain. The British were all embodied and firm as a rock of granite; the Carolinians were scattered over the country loose as a rope of sand: the British, all well armed and disciplined, moved in dreadful harmony, giving their fire like a volcano: the Carolinians, with no other than birding pieces, and strangers to the art of war, were comparatively feeble, as a forest of glow-worms: the British, though but units in number, were so artfully arranged that they told for myriads; while, for lack of unity, the Carolinians, though numerous as myriads, passed only for ciphers. In short, the British were a handful of hawks; the poor Carolinians a swarm of rice-birds, and

6. Mason Locke Weems, *The Life of George Washington: with Curious Anecdotes, Equally Honorable to Himself, and Exemplary to his Young Countrymen,* Knoxville: James Williams, 1842, p. 103.

rather than be plucked to the pin feather, or picked to the bone, they and their little ones, they were fain to flatter those furious falcons, and oft times to chirp and sing when they were much in the humor to hate and curse.[7]

Counting metaphors and similes together, we find a total of 14 in this passage of 230 words, a proportion not much under what will be found in many a passage of Shakespeare.[8]

In the life of Franklin, Weems tells the story of his hero's early association with a young man named Collins. While the future inventor and statesman was making himself a model of industry and frugality, poor Collins was beginning to succumb to drink. The scene is a conversation between the two in which Collins laments the misfortunes which have driven him to intemperance. In the relation, Weems provides Franklin with three elaborate figures for his response, and has one left for himself for the commentary.

Collins, who was exceedingly eloquent on every subject, but especially on one so nearly affecting himself, went on deploring his misfortunes in strains so tender and pathetic, that Ben, whose eyes were fountains ever ready to flow at the voice of sorrow, could not refrain from weeping, which he did most unfeignedly for a long esteemed friend now going to ruin. He could bear, he said, to see the brightest plumed bird, charmed by the rattle-snake, descending into the horrid sepulchre of the monster's jaws. He could bear to see the richest laden Indiaman, dismasted and rudderless, drifting ashore on the merciless breakers; because made of dust, these things must at any rate return to dust again. But to see an immortal mind stopped in her first soarings, entangled and limed in the filth of so brutal a vice as drunkenness—that was a sight he could not bear. And as a mother looking on her child that is filleted for the accursed Moloch, cannot otherwise than shed tears, so Ben, when he looked upon poor Collins, could not but weep when he saw him the victim of destruction.[9]

7. P. Horry and M. L. Weems, *The Life of General Francis Marion, a Celebrated Partisan Officer in the Revolutionary War Against the British and Tories in South Carolina and Georgia,* Philadelphia: J. B. Lippincott, 1857, pp. 81–82.

8. This says nothing of the figures of repetition and schemes of grammar, which are also present in Elizabethan abundance.

9. Mason Locke Weems, *The Life of Benjamin Franklin; with Many Choice Anecdotes and Admirable Sayings of this Great Man, Never Before Published by Any of his Biographers,* Philadelphia: Uriah Hunt & Son, 1854, pp. 84–85.

Not only was Weems willing to multiply metaphors, he was willing also to extend boldly the single metaphor, and there is a theory of expression to be deduced from this. Here is his picture of Washington rallying his troops before the battle of Princeton.

> The Sun had just tipt with gold the adjacent hills, when snowy Trenton, with the wide-tented fields of the foe, hove in sight. To the young in arms this was an awful scene, and nature called a short-liv'd terror to their hearts. But not unseen of Washington was their fear. He marked the sudden paleness of their cheeks, when first they beheld the enemy, and quick, with half-stifled sighs turned on him their wistful looks. As the big lion of Zara, calling his brindled sons to battle against the mighty rhinoceros, if he mark their falling manes and sees them crouching to his side, instantly puts on all his terrors—his eyes roll in blood—he shakes the forest with his deepening roar, till, kindled by their father's fire, the maddening cubs swell with answering rage, and spring undaunted on the Monster. Thus stately and terrible rode *Columbia's first and greatest son*, along the front of his halted troops.[10]

The figure used in the same work to describe the flight of the British at the battle of Cowpens is of similar design.

> As when a mammoth suddenly dashes in among a thousand buffaloes, feeding at large on the vast plains of Missouri; all at once the innumerous herd, with wildly rolling eyes, and hideous bellowings, break forth into flight, while close at their heels, the roaring monster follows—earth trembles as they fly. Such was the noise in the chase of Tarleton, when the swords of Washington's cavalry pursued his troops from Cowpens' famous fields.[11]

I now propose to cite three other features in order before taking up the special assumptions which they reflect. After noting this lavish use of metaphor, the reader is most likely to be impressed with the unflagging energy of Weems's style. Hardly a sentence that he wrote is inert. And when we come to inquire into the cause of this extraordinary aliveness, we find it to be a free and very successful use of the epithet. This practice is, indeed, related to the use of metaphor, and I believe Aristotle has observed somewhere that an epithet can be extended into a metaphor.[12] In any case,

10. Weems, *Washington,* pp. 85–86.

11. *Ibid.,* p. 112.

12. Cf. also in this connection: "Now strange words simply puzzle us; ordinary words convey only what we know already; it is from metaphor that we can best get hold of some-

Weems early discovered that if an object is to be active, the object must have its proper epithet, because it is this which evokes its contribution to the play of forces in a narration. In doing such, it rounds out the dramatic situation. When epithets are used generously, the whole environment is made to seem animate, and this circumstance seems to point up the moral character of the human actions. With these considerations in mind, I wish to take note next of the frequency of Weems's epithets. I shall begin the demonstration with another passage from the *Marion*—the liveliest of the four biographies—in which Weems describes the sociological state of South Carolina a short time after the outbreak of the war.

> The war had hardly raged above a twelvemonth and a day, before the state of society seemed turned upside down. The sacred plow was every where seen rusting in the weedy furrows—Grog shops and Nanny houses were springing up as thick as hops—at the house of God you saw nobody—but if there was a devil's house (a dram shop) hard by, you might be sure to see *that* crowded with poor Lazarites, with red noses and black eyes, and the fences all strung along with starved tackies, in grape-vine bridles and sheep-skin saddles. In short, the whole country was fast overrunning with vagabonds, like ravening locusts, seeking where they might light, and whom they should devour.[13]

Suppose now we read this passage with the object of challenging single words. Why should one go to the length of adding "sacred" to "plough" and "weedy" to "furrows"? By the parsimonious standard of denotation these make mere verbiage. Yet they are justified by their works. "Sacred" is an epithet recognizing a context of duties, which is here falling apart; and "weedy" injects the unpleasant consequence. These words have the effect of enhancing the roles of the human actors by showing their wider impingements. The plough, an ancient symbol of rational labor and peaceful productivity, is abandoned in the "sunshine and basking time of rogues," and the fields revert to nature. Succeeding epithets add to the impression of idleness and vice. Through them the setting takes on an inclination, and we have an attitude toward this decay of order.

For another useful illustration, we may take Weems's account of how the Colonial patriots responded to news of the battle of Lexington: "Even age

---

thing fresh. . . ." Aristotle, *Rhetoric* (trans. W. Rhys Roberts), bk. 3, ch. 10, 1410b, in *Aristotle: Rhetoric and Poetics*, New York: Modern Library, 1954, p. 186.

13. Horry and Weems, *Marion*, pp. 47–48.

itself forgot its wonted infirmities; and hands, long palsied with years, threw aside the cushioned crutch, and grasped the deadly firelock."[14] Again the epithets flock to the substantives. There would be a number of reasons for excising both "cushioned" and "deadly" from this sentence; but a sentence so pared would not make the same gift to the story. What they supply is the dimension that is missing from mere commentary; it is the kind of treatment which conveys the thick rotundity of the event instead of an abstraction of it. And when we read, in his account of the battle of Kings Mountain, that the ball which killed Colonel Williams "opened in his breast the crimson sluice of life,"[15] we should remember that we are reading of the death of a hero, and heroes are not simply shot down; they die heroically or spectacularly, for they are active. Weems's smaller touches are above all to express activeness, because in his view man is an agent.

Beyond this success with the epithet as a means of actualization (a further proof that rhetoric constructs the actual world for us), Weems was equally adept at creating scenes of distress and ignominy, for which he had a use in the larger pattern of his context. As a climactic example of this power I should like to reproduce his picture of the inebriate's last stage, taken from his temperance tract *The Drunkard's Looking Glass: Reflecting a Faithful Likeness of the Drunkard, in Sundry Very Interesting Attitudes, with Lively Representations of the Many Strange Capers he Cuts at Different Stages of his Disease: at First, When he has Only "A Drop in his Eye;" Second, When he is "Half Shaved;" Third, When he is Getting "a Little on the Staggers or So;" and Fourth and Fifth, and so on, Till he is "Quite Capsized;" or "Snug Under the Table with the Dogs" and Can "Stick to the Floor Without Holding on."*

> But alas! the cursed sorceress, Whiskey, like Sampson's Delilah, has shaved the bristles of his strength, and like a bleeding Jockey Pig, it is now all holiday with his sinking powers. His tongue trips and stammers—his eyes are heavy—his looks swinishly stupid—he reels—he staggers—at length, unable to bear up any longer under the weight of his own beastly carcase, down he comes with a squelch on the first chair or bench, and rolling himself against the next prop (no odds to him whether it be a tar barrel, a molasses hogshead, or a sop jar) there with his chin to his breast and his head swung on one

14. Weems, *Washington*, p. 70.
15. *Ibid.*, p. 109.

shoulder, he falls to snoring—the whiskey in the mean time oozing from his eyes, and the saliva dribbling from his wide opening mouth. Presently, sickening under the vile drench that's upon his stomach, he begins to make wry faces—he twists and turns—he grunts and groans, with constant hiccups and eructations, till all at once half starting up, and reaching forward with both arms outspread, and horribly squawling, up he throws the filthy torrent, flooding the floor around him; then pale and limber as a rag, and miserably groaning, like a dying calf, down he sprawls into the midst of it all, and sinks to sleep! not only a filthier beast by far than any in the styes, but with all so perfectly paralized and helpless, that he lies at the *mercy of every danger*, and is frequently destroyed by such trivial accidents as would not have injured a *sober pig.*[16]

The detail of the picture is so complete that whether one bases his conduct upon conventional morality, upon prudence, or upon aesthetics, one is susceptible. Every avenue of approach is covered. The adjectives and especially the characterizing verbs (which often perform successfully the office of epithet) create the effect of total realization.

This achievement of a style highly colored by epithets which do not seem casual or superfluous[17] (if one gives a sort of initial consent to his topics) will be encountered in everything that Weems wrote.

16. Mason Locke Weems, *The Drunkard's Looking Glass*, 5 ed., District of Pennsylvania [Philadelphia?]: printed for the author, 1816, p. 30.

17. Compare with this the regular occurrence of epithets in the following passage from John Milton's "Lycidas," lines 136–48, in Harris Francis Fletcher (ed.), *The Complete Poetical Works of John Milton*, Cambridge: Houghton Mifflin, 1941, p. 136:

> Ye valleys low where the mild whispers use
> Of shades and wanton winds, and gushing brooks
> On whose fresh lap the swart star sparely looks,
> Throw hither all your quaint enameled eyes,
> That on the green turf suck the honeyed showers,
> And purple all the ground with vernal flowers.
> Bring the rathe primrose that forsaken dies,
> The tufted crow-toe, and pale jessamine,
> The white pink, and the pansy freaked with jet,
> The glowing violet,
> The musk-rose, and the well-attired woodbine,
> With cowslips wan that hang the pensive head,
> And every flower that sad embroidery wears:

We have thus far been treating metaphor and epithet as the chief sources of his "enargia," or "lively representation," as the quality was conceived by Renaissance rhetoricians; but contrasts and figures of dissimilitude are also exceedingly common factors in the effect. As we found in Milton, so in Weems, sharp contrasts keep the conflict of moral opposites before our attention. Let us consider two of the shorter kind, occurring in the life of Franklin. Pointing out that Franklin had in his ancestry a long line of blacksmiths, Weems wrote that he was entitled to show as his emblems "not the barren *gules* and *garters* of European folly, but those better ensigns of American wisdom—the SLEDGE-HAMMER and ANVIL."[18] He was especially pleased whenever such figures could be combined with alliteration. Touching upon the subject of religious persecutions, he declared that "they were common in those dark and dismal days, when the clergy thought more of creeds than of Christ, and of learning Latin than of learning love."[19] Contrast is also his means of presenting Benedict Arnold:

> There was Benedict Arnold—while strutting a BRIGADIER GENERAL on the public stage, he could play you the *great man* on a handsome scale . . . he outmarched Hannibal, and out-fought Burgoyne . . . he chaced the British like curlews, or cooped them up like chickens! and yet in the *private walks of life*, in Philadelphia, he could swindle rum from the commissary's stores, and, with the aid of loose women, retail it by the gill!![20]

An elaborate contrast is contained in his pamphlet *The Philanthropist; or a Good Twenty-five Cents Worth of Political Love Powder, for Honest Adamites and Jeffersonians*. Here Weems offers a long argument for the equality of man, but he incurs the expense of several pages to make clear that he does not mean equality of gifts and powers. In these respects, men are freely contrasted, as follows:

> As to *activity,* some men swift footed as the roe-buck, can bound across the fields with the motion of the winds, scarcely injuring the tender grass in their rapid course; while others snail slow in progress, can scarcely drag their torpid limbs along. . . .

18. Weems, *Franklin,* p. 6.
19. *Ibid.,* p. 8.
20. Weems, *Washington,* p. 4.

As to *understanding*, some are so very dull that it is a hard matter to teach them a sum in the rule of three; while others quickly drink dry the shallow fountains of human knowledge, and then boldly strike out into the main ocean of the Almighty's works. . . .

As to *eloquence*, some, like our famous Patrick Henry, can lead the passions of men about, with as much ease as a countryman calls his pigs after him; while another hardly has utterance sufficient to declare his passion to a pretty milk-maid.[21]

Sharp contrasts of fortune were a favorite topic, especially where moral decisions could be pointed out as the sources of great misery or happiness. In *God's Revenge Against Adultery* he relates the history of an upright citizen who was driven to murder the seducer of his wife. The subject of his peroration is a contrast.

Where now is the gay Mr. Wiley that dressed so neat and walked so light, with health and joy ever smiling on his ruddy countenance? Lo! there he lies a haggard corpse—wrapped in an old great coat—with matted hair and long black beard deformed—his shrivelled lips but half cover his teeth, still hard clenched in death—while his face, though cold as the earth he lies on, yet retains the dark and dismal frown of the wretched spirit which has just forsaken it!

And where is the elegant Dr. Wilson—he who shone above all the youth of Lewistown, as the tall cedar of Lebanon above the trees of the forest? Alas! he is seen no more. Adultery, like the flash of vengeful heaven, has blasted his top, and dashed all his branching honours to the dust.[22]

The last feature we shall notice which seems to afford some insight into the mind of the man and the age is an unabashed use of the pathetic fallacy. This ancient poetic recourse, whereby the poet pictures nature as joining in man's feeling or his effort, or as responding in some way to scenes of human significance, has not indeed disappeared from verse, but its presence in biography or even in oratory is today so rare that we must recognize that

21. Mason Locke Weems, *The Philanthropist; or a Good Twenty-five Cents Worth of Political Love Powder, for Honest Adamites and Jeffersonians*, Dumfries [Va.?]: publisher unknown, 1799, pp. 5–7.

22. Mason Locke Weems, *God's Revenge Against Adultery, Awfully Exemplified in the Following Cases of American Crim. Con.*, Philadelphia: printed for the author, 1818, pp. 23–24.

something has happened to its assumptions. Weems's employment of the device at times seems consciously fanciful; but on the other hand he was too shrewd a rhetorician not to realize what would "go." In the *Washington* the ocean is represented as appalled at the display of British might on the way to subdue the Colonies.

> A few days after this, Lord Howe came upon the coast with a *forest* of men of war and transports, shading far and wide the frightened ocean, and bearing nearly 40,000 men, British, Hessians, and Waldeckers.[23]

But when the British are reduced to surrendering at Saratoga, the sun himself is delighted with the Americans' display of chivalry.

> . . . when the British were marched out to lay down their arms, there was not an American to be seen! They had all nobly retired for a moment, as if unwilling to give the pain, *even to their enemies,* of being spectators of so humiliating a scene! Worthy countrymen of Washington! this deed of yours shall outlive the stars, and the blest sun himself, *smiling,* shall proclaim that in the wide travel of his beams, he never looked upon its like before.[24]

In the *Marion* we learn that Baron De Kalb, who fell at the battle of Camden, was not given a hero's grave, but nature shows appreciation of his services to the cause.

> No sculptured warrior mourned at his low-laid head; no cypress decked his heel. But the tall corn stood in darkening ranks around him, and seemed to shake their green leaves with joy over his narrow dwelling.[25]

The remainder of this essay will try to account for the gulf which separates our world from Weems's. It is so great, this distance between ourselves and his rhetorical wonderland, that Weems could not today be considered a serious writer. Yet we have already noted the facts of his influence, which seems to have been made possible by two enabling conditions. As in the case of Milton again, we must see that his high rhetoric bespeaks a rhetorically sensitive audience, with the one responding to the other.

The first of these conditions was that Weems, with his readers, lived in a dualistic world. A principle of difference between good and bad, between

---

23. Weems, *Washington*, p. 81.
24. *Ibid.,* p. 98.
25. Horry and Weems, *Marion*, p. 107.

the spiritual and the material, was the ground of operation of contrast and of similitude. That ground above anything else explains the tenseness of the scenes he puts before us. Who can remain indifferent when Good and Evil are locked in mortal combat? There is, in every treatment of character by Weems, despite his dislike as a good Episcopalian for the harsher provisions of Christian theology, the belief that man in this life is on trial for his soul. We quickly see how this tenet gives the rhetorician, like the dramatist, his main chance, for any such concept necessarily involves conflicting sides of a dualism. In the body of thought which expresses our theology, such expression takes various forms. There is God against Satan (Satan meaning in Hebrew "adversary"); heaven against this world; the soul against the flesh; the man in whom spirit has triumphed against the man ruled by appetite. The Christian theological story itself constitutes a plot which mirrors the struggle of each man for his salvation. Once we have realized what is at stake, we follow any career with zealous interest to see whether a soul has won the greatest of all prizes or has gone to perdition. Of course we find all of Weems's characters so embattled. For him, there are not "conditioned" men, that figment of modern psychology. Whenever he talks of the early conditions of his hero, it is only to demonstrate how he defied and transcended them. And there are few if any neutrals. One learns early whether one is expected to attach sentiments of praise or blame to an actor in these dramas. The cleavage between good and bad which psychology tends to deny or transmute Weems, like Milton, from his standpoint as moralist, labored to preserve and to widen.

The world pictured by science, to look at the other side, is non-dramatic necessarily because it is monistic. Where the world is all of one piece, there are no true conflicts in it, all seeming conflicts being dissolved into descriptive phenomena; and everything is accounted for by an intermediate cause. This means that all the stories of this world have only reportorial significance. But Weems, as we have now abundantly seen, was so far from sharing this view that for him every story of a life constituted a sermon. The hero was a free agent[26]; the world with its selfish and deceiving men was the adversary; and the moral always was that success ultimately crowns the keeping of faith. A typical example of how evil is put to flight after a brief

26. Cf. his explicit statement: "Free agents can sin anywhere. And God will have none but free agents." Mason Locke Weems, *God's Revenge Against Duelling, or the Duellist's Looking Glass, Exhibiting that Gentlemanly Mode of Turning the Corner, in Features Altogether Novel,*

engagement may be seen in a passage from the *Franklin*. Young Ben had embraced the philosophical doctrine of utility, but was soon persuaded by his father to abandon it.

> But the old gentleman, who was a great adept in moral philosophy, calmly observed to him, that if one boy were to make use of this plea to take away his fellow's goods, another might; and thus contests would arise, filling the world with blood and murder without end. Convinced, in this simple way, of the fatal consequences of *"doing evil that good may come,"* Ben let drop the weapons of his rebellion, and candidly agreed with his father that what was not *strictly honest* could never be *truly useful*. This discovery he made at the tender age of *nine*. Some never make it in the course of their lives. The grand angler, Satan, throws out his bait of *immediate gain;* and they, like silly Jacks, snap at it at once; and in the moment of running off, fancy they have got a delicious morsel. But alas! the fatal hook soon convinces them of their mistake, though sometimes too late. And then the lamentation of the prophet serves as the epilogue of their tragedy—*"'Twas honey in the mouth, but gall in the bowels."* [27]

Almost as soon as his biographies open, the personages take opposite sides of the stage, like heroes and villains in a tragedy. From this point on it is the author's task to accentuate through the various forms of similitude and dissimilitude their divergent characters. All this explains largely why Weems could open the flood gates of metaphor and epithet in the easy confidence of satisfying expectation.

The second condition which enabled Weems to employ his devices on so wide a scale is that his age was a far more contextural age than ours, which has suffered in the intervening century from powerful disorganizing forces. What this means is that his world was a much more related one than ours, and that owing to this circumstance he could make far greater assumptions than are open to us, a point I intend to develop in a later chapter. For the present, let us consider briefly the demands made upon the reader's imagination by the widely recognized rhetorical devices of metonymy, synecdoche, and metalepsis. To review them quickly: metonymy is the employment of something regularly associated with the object for the object itself; synecdoche is the employment of part of the object to symbolize the whole,

---

and Admirably Calculated to Entertain and Instruct the American Youth, Georgetown, D.C.: Elijah Weems for the author, 1820, p. 25.

27. Weems, *Franklin*, pp. 12–13.

or of the whole to symbolize the part; metalepsis is the ascription of some event to a remote though conceivable cause. It will be apparent upon a moment's reflection that all of these demand a stable world, because only a stable world is a known world and only in a known world can such suppositions be made with any assurance of success. In other words, in order to use a metonym with effect we have to know that it is normally, if not indeed unvaryingly, associated with the thing we desire to name rhetorically. Likewise in order to use synecdoche, we need good assurance that the part will be recognized as belonging to the whole, or the whole as including the part. And in order to use metalepsis, we have to trust a recognized chain of causation which will not break because the two links cited happen to be some distance apart. Naturally this requires considerable common agreement about causation, just as the others demand considerable common agreement about parts and wholes.

Thus a world in which these devices can be used without risk is a world in which things are fixed and causes are reliable; or it is a world in which such community of mind exists that we can expect the reader to supply the thing signified by the metonym, to recall one of our examples, in the same way that we would expect him to supply the missing proposition of an enthymeme. But to return to the point on which we set out: our world has become so fractionalized in the last century that these contiguities and these nexus can no longer be safely assumed. So many things have been wrenched from their traditional contexts that a writer or speaker often feels safer in taking the road of literalism. A century or two ago, for instance, a sentence such as "The issue was settled by the arbitrament of the sword," in which "sword" functions as a synecdoche for military conflict, was a very common locution. It so happens that by repeated use this contexture of ideas has survived, but how many people today have any direct evidence that swords are associated with warfare? The modern equivalent would be "The issue was settled by the arbitrament of the bombing plane." Obviously a world characterized by change is a world in which forms are dissolving, and this is precisely the reason today why one may fear to risk metonymy and synecdoche and metalepsis except in closely knit cultural groups.[28] The metonym or the synecdoche which a more stable age freely conceded, as part

28. Metonymy and synecdoche find a haven today in the language of sports, trades, and professions, but precisely because these activities are more or less codified, and one has a "right of assumption."

of the conventional symbolism, may today be rejected as an impertinence. It makes a draft upon the imagination, if not indeed upon the faith of the reader, which he, standing on ground vouchsafed by the senses, may refuse to honor. The publicly recognized network of implication has become much smaller, as the imaginative foundations of culture wear away. Naturally an age which encourages change for the sake of change can neither recover an earlier network nor create one of its own, since networks of symbolism reflect some stasis in the perception of things.

Now the effect of using metonymy, synecdoche and metalepsis is to make a style perspicacious, for all of these are means to perspective. It seems accurate to say that the difference between simple or immediate representation and these forms of mediate representation is the difference between the world viewed without the residue left by our experience of its nature and the world viewed through memory. It has already been demonstrated that the devices under description require an exercise of mind, and this very exercise necessarily brings up a vista. The sense of enlightenment which such style brings—even though it is a type of enlightenment which will be resisted by many—proceeds directly from this process of viewing things in their wider circumferences. Weems's world then is very much the world as it is seen by mind, and this alone constitutes him an "antique" writer.

Before leaving the subject of effects we must say one word about Weems's use of the pathetic fallacy. Again here is a device which did not seem as "impertinent" in his day as it does in ours. Man's concept of nature makes a greatly varied story; here it may be enough to point out that Weems lived in a world still anthropocentric, and that, as we have proved, his characters were conspicuously free agents. Now if the drama of man is the most important thing in the universe, as surely a majority in his time believed, it is no great step to have nature looking on with signs of approval and disapproval. It will be found that his characters are focal for things about them just as are the characters in the Old Testament and Plutarch. Therefore when Weems occasionally goes beyond these great models and has nature join with a smile or a tear, we may say it is an excess imputable to his ardent temperament, but it is not philosophically forbidden to him. Such things are implied in the setting he has prepared.

Finally, the question of whether Weems's biographies are true, which chiefly concerns a certain type of reader, is best included in the larger question of their purpose. If they are not true in the sense of fidelity to fact, neither are they false in presenting a misleading picture. They are pictures of the *moral* man against a background of some facts of his life. Weems was very shrewd at guessing the integrating principle of a man's character; and it is doubtful whether the most plodding scrutiny of the career of Washington, aided by all the apparatus of modern scholarship, has changed the impression of ingrained honesty which Weems sought to convey with his pretty tales and invented speeches. It would be hard to improve upon the judgment of Simms: "If a small fact suited not his great fact, he shoved it aside as unfitted for his purpose."[29] The great fact was always perspicuous.

What we have endeavored to show in this analysis is that Weems's high rhetoric was dependent upon the spirit of his time. That in his day such work was thought not funny, but dreadfully earnest, is the key to the difference we set out to examine. Weems had at his command certain leverages which have since been largely taken away. These included, to repeat briefly, a dualism, an unquestioning acceptance of free agency—at least by the multitude—determinate wholes and established causalities. The statement does not imply that we are today without rhetorical leverages, for that is a condition of man quite impossible to conceive. But it is fair to say that we have fewer, and that these are more wobbly and less understood in their operation than those of Weems's more ordered world. That world was, despite the novelty of a new continent, and despite the recent French Revolution, consubstantial with the world which had produced West European civilization. Consequently, there were vast resources of "settled" things upon which he could call to give his writing impulse. His lives of eminent Americans are for that reason more readable than the average biography today; but whether they can ever be recovered, except historically, will be answered along with all the other questions about the future of value and belief.

29. Simms, *Views and Reviews*, p. 127.

Responsible Rhetoric[1]

My discourse this morning is not so much about "Great Issues" as it is about "How to Think and Talk About Great Issues." And if that title seems a little presumptuous, I can only hope that what I have to say will bring it down to earth and show that there are issues also in how we choose to talk about issues.

Most Americans today accept it as an axiomatic truth that we live in a

1. A version of this speech edited by Thomas D. Clark and Richard L. Johannesen was published in the Winter 1976–77 issue of *The Intercollegiate Review* (12/2, pp. 81–87) under the title "A Responsible Rhetoric." An accompanying "editorial note" states that the speech was delivered at a "'Great Issues' seminar of senior undergraduates at Purdue University, March 29, 1955," and that the text was "taken from a transcription of a tape recording" of that presentation. That transcription, which also includes Weaver's responses to student questions after the speech, had been circulating in mimeograph form for some years and is reproduced in its entirety in Gerald T. Goodnight, "Rhetoric and Culture," unpublished Ph.D. dissertation, University of Kansas, 1978, pp. 488–508. Clark, Johannesen, and Goodnight apparently did not know that Weaver's handwritten manuscript of the speech had been donated to the Weaver collection at Vanderbilt University. An examination of the manuscript shows that the Purdue speech was a revised and shortened version of an earlier speech entitled "Responsible Rhetoric" that Weaver presented at a meeting of the Nineteenth Century Woman's Club in Oak Park, Illinois, on February 28, 1955. (Other evidence, especially the chronology of several of Weaver's examples, suggests that the speech was first delivered before an unknown audience in the late 1940s.) More important, a comparison of the published and manuscript versions shows that the published version incorporates numerous significant errors, some attributable to misstatements in Weaver's delivery but most the result of inaccurate transcription. Accordingly, the text presented here is a new version edited by Ted J. Smith III from the manuscript entitled "Responsible Rhetoric" in Box 3, Folder 3, of the Richard M. Weaver Papers at Vanderbilt University. In several places extemporaneous transitions missing from the manuscript but preserved in the published transcription have been included in the text. Weaver's original title has been retained both for the sake of accuracy and because of his claim (in a letter to Mrs. Alice C. Propst dated May 27, 1954, located in File C7 of the Polly Weaver Beaton collection) that the title "names the subject exactly."

free society. I often wonder, however, how many of us realize that a free society is by definition a pluralistic society. A pluralistic society is one in which there are many different centers of authority, influence, and opinion, competing with one another, arguing with one another, trying by various means to expand their spheres of influence, and producing a great variety, richness, and animation. In such a society there is no single voice, governmental, cultural, ethical, religious, or social. There are many voices, each speaking from its point of view and striving to maintain itself in the general competition for belief and support. In direct contrast stands the monistic ideal of society, experienced by many millions of persons in other lands, which does have only one voice, and which works by many means toward effecting a unanimity of opinion, belief, and sentiment on all the issues of this life. That system bears the name totalitarian, and it is by now an obvious fact that these two are engaged in a gigantic rivalry to capture the imagination of the world.

Having described in outline this situation, I now wonder a second time: of the Americans who realize that a free society means a pluralistic society, how many realize the special demands that a pluralistic society imposes upon its members? I am not referring to paying taxes, which you do anyhow, or to voting, which some people do without thinking. I am referring to just this: a pluralistic society by its very nature tolerates propaganda from all kinds of individuals, groups, organizations, institutions—from practically anything that is capable of articulation. And it does this on the strength of two suppositions. The first is that there are many subjects in regard to which we do not think that we have arrived at definitive truth. These subjects are still under study and investigation; not all the evidence is in; not all the opinions have been expressed; and therefore debate must go on. Hence the activity of our newspapers, magazines, public meetings, legislative assemblies, and so forth. We accept the fact frankly that most issues, including some of vital relation to our welfare, are still in the realm of deliberative forensics. The second supposition is that there exists among our people enough good sense, education, and reflective intelligence to assure us that in this deliberative process we will come up with the right answer. Not always at once, not always without friction and expense, but in the long run, it is felt that we will arrive at more sound conclusions than would a council of commissars or some other group delegated the exclusive authority to think and to decide. In brief, it is a principle of our society that we can listen to propaganda from all the special interests—including that of an incumbent administration—and do a pretty fair job of sifting the true claims from the false.

I begin then with these preliminary considerations: that a free society is a pluralistic society, that a pluralistic society is one which must countenance propaganda from many sources, and that coping with propaganda requires a widespread critical intelligence, which is largely the product of education. It is the last of these points that I wish to deal with directly. Does our educational system prepare people to deal with the vast amount of opinion, argumentation, and special pleading addressed to them today through all the channels provided by modern technology?

I am inclined to think it does not prepare them because we have largely ceased to teach rhetoric. If democracy means anything, it means that every person is an active advocate of policies. He must listen to many arguments, and he must make arguments in refutation. He cannot do either of these well—he cannot make his honestly held views acceptable to others, and he cannot disarm an opponent in an argument—unless he has some under-standing of the probative value of statements.

What I propose to talk about in the next few minutes I like to refer to as responsible rhetoric. Responsible rhetoric, as I conceive it, is a rhetoric re-sponsible primarily to the truth. It measures the degree of validity in its statements, and it is aware of the sources of compulsion which it employs. As such, it is distinct from propaganda, which is a distortion of the truth for selfish purposes. In this connection I always like to think of Francis Bacon's statement: "Rhetoric no more teaches man to support bad causes than logic teaches him to reason fallaciously."

The concepts which are involved here have their foundation in philoso-phy, and as we open this subject with our students at Chicago we say simply that there are four basic ways in which you can talk meaningfully about the world. This is the same as saying that there are four basic ways of thinking about reality, or four basic ways of interpreting experience. They are, in the language of philosophy, being, cause, relationship, and the fourth, which has a different kind of basis—authority. You can say that a thing is of such and such a kind, or that it is the cause of a certain effect, or that it has significant resemblance to something else, or that its truth is vouched for by an authority which everybody ought to accept. The first argument is based on definition, the second on cause and effect analysis, the third on resemblance or comparison, the fourth on the prestige of some authority.

What I have just stated, in rather abstract language, is actually a commonplace, recognizable by everyone. For these are the ways that we talk about things in our everyday discourse. If we say, "All good citizens are voters," we make a statement of the first kind. If we say, "War is a cause of inflation," we make one of the second. If we say, "Life is like a voyage," we make one of the third. If we say, "The Bible discloses that the greatest of gifts is charity," we make one of the fourth. You will recognize, I am sure, that assertions like these are the staple of our ordinary expression. Whenever we set out to prove anything to anybody, we find ourselves affirming that a certain thing exists as a member of a class, or that it is known to be connected with a certain cause or a certain effect, or that it has significant points of resemblance with something we already know, or that it is stated by some authority that everybody who is anybody respects. This is but an analysis of our actual modes of argument.

I should like to spend more time on the theory of this, but owing to my limited period I feel I had better turn to some concrete examples and show how these techniques of persuasion have been employed in arguing positions on the great questions of our history. Because they *are* the basic means of persuasion, you may expect to find one or more of them whenever men are pleading for a cause or a course of action. And to place this in a realistic context I should like to follow an historical order and take up certain issues according to their appearance in the development of our nation. If this seems permissible, I am going back to 1776 and the Declaration of Independence.

The Declaration of Independence is essentially an argument. Jefferson was presenting to a candid world a case for the independence of the American colonies. The argument is in the logical form known as the syllogism, but we are here interested in its content. Where did Jefferson go for his matter, for the kind of thing that would supply the rhetorical push? An inspection shows very clearly that he went to the second item on our list of four, namely consequences or effects. The great bulk of this document is made up of a detailing of these consequences. He listed a large number of particulars in which the colonies had suffered by the policy of the King of

Great Britain. Most of us will recall the tenor if not the substance of these: "He has refused his Assent to Laws, the most wholesome and necessary to the public Good. . . . He has dissolved Representative Houses repeatedly, for opposing with manly Firmness his Invasions on the Rights of the People. . . ." And so on. These constitute the celebrated "long Train of Abuses," and they are, as you will recognize, all consequences.

Now the argument from consequence rests upon this theory: a grave effect implies a grave cause, and conversely, a grave cause implies a grave effect. Jefferson was pointing to these facts as grave effects. The grave cause, as he saw it, was a desire to reduce the colonists under an absolute despotism. And this cause was regarded as reason enough to justify a separation of the colonies from the mother country, which was announced at the end of the Declaration. If Jefferson could prove the cause, he could prove the right to American independence.

For my next example I go forward about two generations to the period 1830–1860. It was during this period that a tremendous debate raged in the Senate over the nature of the American union. It was a time of growing national friction, in which great issues depended on how the Constitution was to be construed, and the focal point of the debate was whether or not the Constitution was a *compact*. It was this question that drew forth those famous speeches of Webster, Calhoun, and Haynes, which, taken with the *Federalist Papers*, probably represent the highest levels of American political thinking. I scarcely need point out that this was an argument involving definition—the first item on our list. If it was possible to define the American Constitution as a compact, certain things would necessarily flow from that definition, with important, though of course different, results for the contending parties. If it was possible to define it not as a compact, but as something more binding, another set of results would ensue. As it was, these oratorical giants and their successors wrestled for three decades to decide whether the Constitution belonged in this or that genus—in the genus of compacts, or outside this in some other genus. And you will find Abraham Lincoln resuming the argument in his First Inaugural Address.

I pass on now about fifty years to the period before our involvement in the First World War. This was a period of mounting national armaments accompanied by growing anxieties. There was also a growing resentment against war as a means of settling international differences. One of the most vehement spokesmen against war, and specifically against competitive armaments, was William Jennings Bryan, three times Democratic candidate for the presidency and Secretary of State under Wilson. In one of his speeches against competitive armaments, Bryan made use of the following illustration. Two neighbors have gotten into a disagreement and have become angry at one another. One of the neighbors goes out and buys a shotgun, "for defense." Word of this is soon conveyed to the other neighbor, who goes out and buys a better shotgun, for *his* defense. News of this, along with much talk about his neighbor's hostile intentions, is soon conveyed to the first neighbor, who decides to add more to his defensive equipment, and to be on the watch for menacing acts. This series of actions goes on and on until one of the neighbors shoots the other, "in self-defense." In this analogy the neighbors are any two nations of the world, the shotguns are armies and navies, and those reports sent back and forth are the rumors and statements which create international tensions. It would be tedious for me to point out how closely this analogy fits the relationship today between the West and the Soviet Union. But our interest in it as an example of argument lies in the fact that it derives its force from a comparison of two instances. If the two instances resemble in all important respects, and if the first instance produced an armed conflict, then it is probable that the second instance also will produce an armed conflict. It is a principle of logic that arguments based on comparison never produce anything more than probability. And probability is a matter of degree. We may hope that the probability in our case is a good many degrees short of certainty. But we would not be warranted in treating that probability as negligible.

We now come down to the present time for an example of the last source of argument, which is authority. One of the great controversial questions of our time has been whether the United States should become involved with other nations in treaties and alliances supporting this or that policy. Those persons who are sometimes described as isolationists have frequently invoked the name of George Washington in support of their position that we should not become so involved. Often they quote this sentence from Washington's Farewell Address: "Why, by interweaving our destiny with that of any part of Europe, entangle our peace and prosperity in the toils of European ambition, rivalship, interest, humor, or caprice?" You will recognize at once that this is an appeal relying for its force upon authority. Now the appeal to authority—and we all make appeals of this kind—is neither necessarily good nor bad. It all depends on the authority. Those who think this is a weak argument say that Washington did well enough in his time, but that was a century and a half ago. He had no conception of America as an imperial world power, and no knowledge of the forces that operate in the modern world. He is, in their eyes, a poor authority on these matters. The other side regards Washington as the father of this country, a pure patriot and a farsighted statesman, and a man who, because he was present at the birth of this nation, had a deep insight into its essential character and its real mission in the world. Washington believed that this nation would serve mankind best by remaining free, by rejecting the devious methods of power politics, and by setting an upright example to the world. In their eyes, therefore, he is a good authority.

By now the question may be forming in your minds, what have these things to do with responsible rhetoric? Granting that they are useful matters for a man to know when embarking on an argument, in what way do they make him more responsible?

Of course, he will never be responsible unless he is willing to be intellectually honest. But granted that, they are means of showing him the relationship of what he is saying to the truth. Or, expressed in another way, they are means of estimating the real truth value of any assertion or argument. The best way to see this is to turn things around for a few moments and look at matters from the other side—to look at some of the tricks that are employed by propagandists. As I said near the beginning, the chief reason people today are baffled and befooled by propagandists is that they have such a poor understanding of the arts of persuasion. For the tricks of propagandists are nothing more than perversions of the devices of rhetoric. The propagandist is a rhetorician, but a base one, because he is using an accepted machinery of persuasion to deceive and not to enlighten and edify. This use is an abuse. To prove this, let's inspect a few examples.

One of the commonest tricks of the propagandist in any age is namecalling. If he desires us to accept something, he applies a good name to it; if he desires us to reject it he applies an evil one. Name-calling is nothing on earth but the argument from definition, because the name is used to define the thing, or put it in a class. If the name given is a true one, then the definition is correct and the argument honest. But the propagandist applies a name which is speciously good. That is to say, it looks good to the uncritical, but actually is not. To cite one example, such an abuse occurs today when the Taft-Hartley Act is called a "slave labor law." This is a name supposed to put it in a class. Is there any legitimate sense in which those who work under the provisions of the Taft-Hartley law can be called "slaves"? I cannot see it, and apparently the sober sense of the community has rejected the notion. The propagandist is taking this law and trying to put it into a category where it does not belong. He is calling a false name. This is a perversion of the argument based on definition.

For the next example I will go not to political controversy but to advertising—a great field, I regret to say, for the abuse of rhetoric. A year or so ago there appeared in magazines eye-catching full-page ads by the manufacturer of a certain metal. The burden of these advertisements was that this metal had *won the war*. The argument ran about as follows: Without the metal which this company produces, it is impossible to make steel of a certain degree of hardness. And without steel of a requisite hardness, it is impossible to make airplane motors. Without airplane motors it would have been impossible to win the war. Therefore this company, or at least its product, won the war. What we have here is ostensibly a piece of cause-and-effect reasoning. But as soon as we analyze it, we see that it is a distortion. For what it actually does is confuse cause-and-effect relationships by insisting that there is one cause when in fact multiple causes exist. Granting that this metal was one of the causes producing the effect victory, still there were many, many others. No honest inquiry into the causes of the phenomenon would make it appear *the* one. Short-circuiting cause-and-effect reasoning is one of the easiest ways to deceive people. We must always be on our guard when great effects are claimed for a certain cause, or when a certain effect is ascribed to a single cause—as in ascribing the Great Depression altogether to Herbert Hoover. Causal reasoning is difficult even under the best circumstances. When a propagandist begins to tinker with it, strange results may appear.

Another type of abuse occurs when people are led along by false analogies. These are arguments based on seeming rather than real similarities. As soon as you begin to examine the points of correspondence, you find that the differences are more numerous or more important than the likenesses. Therefore the two things being compared are different in a more

fundamental way than they are alike, and different things ought to be done
with respect to them. I am expressing a personal opinion here, but to my
mind one of most misleading analogies being offered today is the one that
usually turns up in arguments for giving the vote to 18-year-olds. This argument asserts that if 18-year-olds are old enough to fight, they are old
enough to vote. True, only if you believe that fighting and voting are the
same kind of thing, which I, for one, do not. Fighting requires strength,
muscular coordination, and, in a modern army, instant and automatic response to orders. Voting requires knowledge of men and of history, reasoning power, wisdom. It is essentially a deliberative activity. Army mules and
police dogs are used to fight, but nobody has yet suggested giving them the
right to vote. This argument rests upon a false analogy, upon treating as the
same, things which are quite different.

People may be misled by arguments based on authority when they are
not sufficiently critical of the authority being used. But they can be misled
in a more subtle way when an argument is expressed in language that distinctly echoes some famous and revered document—say the Declaration of
Independence or the Gettysburg Address or the Bible. The language then
"sounds right"; it reminds them vaguely of something they have been taught
to regard with respect, and they may subconsciously "go along." Neither
politicians nor advertisers are above trying to get people on their side by
borrowing phrases and other stylistic elements from authoritative documents. The ethical question here involves whether the audience realizes the
kind of pressure that is being brought to bear on it.

Thus an understanding of these elementary principles of rhetoric is not
only helpful in the making of arguments, it is also most helpful in the criticizing of arguments. And beyond this, it is a surprisingly effective means of
reading the character and intentions of the man behind the argument.

"As a man thinketh in his heart, so is he" says the Bible. In the realm we
are now dealing with, we may translate this, "As a man frames his arguments when he wants to persuade others, so is he morally and intellectually." Once this truth is appreciated, you find that you can judge a man not
only by the specific thing he asks for, but also by the *way* in which he asks
for it. And the latter insight is sometimes very revealing.

There is one final question lurking in the background which I would like
to dodge, though I recognize that ultimately it cannot be evaded. This is

the question of whether any of these sources of argument—definition, cause, and so on—is better than another, or whether it is possible to arrange them in some rational scale. Personally, I think it is possible to rank them and say that one is better than another, but the reason I am tempted to dodge the question is that it leads straight to one's metaphysics. And that, of course, would be a very long argument. Instead of pronouncing upon that question, therefore, I am going to make a suggestion which may start you reflecting upon the matter yourself. Follow the utterances of some public figure, past or present, in whom you have a strong interest, and note what he prefers as the basis of his appeals. Does he like to define things and argue deductively? Does he like to dwell upon results? Is he fond of analogies? Or does he like to fall back upon authority and argue from the prestige of some great name? You will find this examination entertaining and instructive, and it may give you an understanding of the figure you did not have before. It will show you what term he considered most persuasive when he came to talk about great issues.

Propaganda[1]

Propaganda may be defined as the conscious attempt to create attitudes and induce actions with reference to some predetermined end. The term is employed to include both the process of propagandizing and the things that are propagated, which are ideas, opinions, and policies. The propagandist always has some end in view; he seeks to attain the end by means that are often devious and sometimes concealed; and this end is not the good of the person or group to whom the propaganda is addressed when all things are taken into consideration. Propaganda which is emitted by an entire nation, as in times of war, must be regarded as selfish in the sense that the nation is judging its own cause.

It is of primary importance to distinguish propaganda from education. These two are confused in the minds of many people because both are concerned with communication. Education imparts information and also seeks to inculcate attitudes. Propaganda frequently contains information, and it is always interested in affecting attitudes. A good part of modern propaganda, furthermore, tries to parade as education. The critical difference appears only when one considers the object of each. The true educator is endeavoring to shape his audience for the audience's own good according to the fullest enlightenment available. In doing so he erects and strives to follow a standard of objective truth. The propagandist, on the contrary, is trying to shape his audience according to the propagandist's interest, whether that be economic, political, social, or personal. For example, if a dietician should try to induce children to drink more milk by presenting facts and by exhortation because milk is needed for their growth, this would be education. But if a milk company sought to do the same thing for the

1. In William T. Couch (ed.), *Collier's 1955 Year Book.* New York: Collier & Son, 1955, 517–21. Copyright © 1955 Collier Newfield, Inc. Reprinted by permission of the publisher.

purpose of getting rid of a surplus, this would have to be regarded as milk company propaganda. Even though its presentation might contain some truthful information, the welfare of the children would in this case be subordinate to the end of selling more milk. The use by educators today of all the means of communication, display, and excitation on the one hand, and the attempt, on the other, of propagandists to work through educational institutions makes it imperative to keep in view this distinction of ends.

All propaganda must be regarded as cynical in some degree toward those to whom it is addressed, since it has in mind something less than their welfare. It seeks not to improve them but to manipulate them by presenting matter which is untruthful, exaggerated, or incomplete in significant particulars. Sometimes propagandists claim that while their propaganda may not represent the truth accurately, it keeps the public from succumbing to the even less truthful propaganda of the opposition. But in this case the question of truth is merely being deferred.

The issue of whether there can be such a thing as unconscious propaganda must be determined by this principle that all propaganda is deliberately tendentious. There can be no doubt that people constantly perform acts which have the effect of influencing others, but do so without design. To buy a certain make of automobile, to subscribe to a certain magazine, or to maintain membership in a certain organization will have some effect in persuading others to do the same through the familiar "bandwagon" source of appeal. But if these were classifiable as propaganda, scarcely any of our actions could be regarded as innocent. If a man decides to buy car B rather than car A, his example may induce someone else to buy car B, and thus it may have the same result as the company's advertising. Yet he is without ulterior motive; he has decided on simple grounds that car B is better suited to his needs than car A, and he cannot be charged in any rational sense with propagandizing. No one can foresee all the results of an action that he takes; some of them may further ends that he is ignorant of or out of sympathy with. The tropical natives who buy colored beads are hardly engaged in making propaganda for the glass manufacturer. It seems more accurate to regard the unconscious transmitters of propaganda as among the results of propaganda than as propagandists themselves. The proper definition therefore restricts propaganda to those acts which are deliberate, aware of both their ends and their means and carried on in the interest of the propagandist's objective.

History of Propaganda

In recent decades the word "propaganda" itself has become a term of strong emotional loading, but to see its meaning in perspective, one needs to realize that propaganda, or the tendency to propagandize, is very close to human nature. We cannot conceive of a normal person who does not wish to influence someone else to think in a certain way or to take a certain line of action. Although the term itself first came into use following the creation of the *Congregatio de Propaganda Fide* by Pope Gregory XV in 1622, propaganda itself certainly begins with the history of the race. Every period has used it according to the means available, and in connection with the religious, social, and political passions that existed. The early narratives of the Bible contain instances of attempts to gain ends through what can be recognized as propaganda. One writer, with some show of truth, has called Herodotus, the first historian, a propagandist for the Athenian state. Julius Caesar addressed propaganda to the Roman masses, and the style of his *Commentaries* has been cited as one of his means of gaining favor. During the great struggles over the Reformation both Catholic and Protestant sides produced large amounts of propaganda, in the form of exaggeration, distortion, false imputation of motives, and the atrocity story. By the time of the English Civil War public opinion had become so important in Europe that John Milton was hired by the Cromwell government for many years to conduct an incessant propaganda warfare on its behalf. Milton spared nothing in the way of exposure, denunciation, and abuse which might discredit the enemies of the political party he served. By the time of the American Revolution, journalism had become a considerable force, and the propaganda sheets issued by the Americans foreshadow modern methods. The Boston Massacre, for example, was played up in the Colonial press in much the same fashion as that used in recent world wars. Thomas Paine's sixteen papers entitled *The Crisis* were credited by Washington with a very great effect in sustaining the morale of the American troops. During the American Civil War both sides put considerable effort into propaganda. The Confederate government, very conscious of the influence of European opinion upon Southern fortunes, established in London a paper called the *Index*, the purpose of which was to present the South's side of the conflict. The Federal government took the propaganda struggle seriously enough to suppress more than 300 Northern newspapers at one time and another which were thought to be impairing Union morale. Atrocity stories were featured very freely by both sides, the South playing up the ravages of Hunter, Sheridan, and Sherman, and the North dwelling on the horrors of Southern prison camps for Federal captives. Andersonville, in Georgia, was used as a symbol of the enemy's heartlessness much as Dachau and Buchenwald have been in our own day. It is generally admitted by historians that Lincoln timed the Emancipation Proclamation in such a way as to have a maximum effect upon public opinion.

But in the First and Second World Wars the art of propaganda reached a development far beyond anything known before. This development may be traced to the invention of many new means of production and dissemination, such as photography, the motion picture, the radio, and the leaflet carried by air. Of great consequence also was the intensive study which had been given to psychology in the preceding decades. The latter contributed especially by making the appeals more subtle and more varied and thus harder to resist once the subject had been exposed to them. This period saw also the first real attempts to correlate and systematize the whole work of propaganda. Offices of propaganda, usually disguised by some euphemism, were set up and were given ample means to carry on the work of bolstering the nation's own morale while seeking to break down that of the enemy. And while these offices were busy concocting stories, issuing posters, and printing leaflets, the heads of states were conducting propaganda on a somewhat more lofty level. Here perhaps the most successful effort was President Wilson's Fourteen Points. This proclamation amounted to a promise of a judicial settlement instead of a settlement purely by force, wherein no distinction would be made between victors and vanquished. The proposal is credited by historians with great effect in weakening the morale of the German home front and turning the people against the Kaiser's government. Near the beginning of the Second World War much the same thing was repeated by Churchill and Roosevelt in the form of the Atlantic Charter, a grandiose pledge of a settlement fair to all and a rededication of the world to peace and progress. The fact that neither of these promises was honored has undoubtedly helped to give propaganda its present sinister connotation.

During the First World War especially the propaganda campaigns were carried on with such zeal and with such disregard of standards of truth and ethics that the strong revulsion which set in during the next decade appears to have followed naturally. A feature of the period was the publication of books exposing the practices of wartime propagandists, of which Arthur Ponsonby's *Falsehood in War Time* and Philip Gibbs' *Now It Can Be Told* were perhaps the best known. Such books were written in a "never again" spirit, which was destined not to last, as the enormous propaganda efforts of the thirties, of the Second World War, and of the present struggle with the Soviet Union make clear.

This struggle has assumed the form of an ideological contest between West and East to capture the imagination of the world. The West, and the United States in particular, have utilized radio programs beamed to the rest of the world, including Russia and her satellites, plus information services and libraries established abroad. The Soviet Union has utilized, in addition to its state-controlled publicity machine, a system of infiltration by agents abroad which is not available to the West because of the rigid exclusion enforced by the "Iron Curtain."

It has to be recognized that the Western democracies labor under the dis-advantage of having to sell the relatively abstract idea of freedom to peoples facing urgent economic problems. Moreover, the concept of respect for the individual, on which so much Western policy is predicated, is unknown to a number of foreign cultures. Finally, Western democracy has never meant a strict equalitarianism, but moral equality and freedom of opportunity.

The Soviets have had their greatest success by playing on the sense of frustration felt by many minorities and by most colonial peoples. They have had agents and sympathizers in many parts of the world, who have created dissension, helped to obstruct policy, and injected tendentious ideas into various channels of publicity. Many of these are nationals of the countries in which they operate; some are impassioned converts to the communist philosophy and bring to their work a sense of dedication. In comparison with them, many spokesmen and leaders of opinion in the Western nations seem to suffer from confusion or boredom. When one adds to this the philosophical naivete even of many educated Americans, one understands why the West has scored to date so few successes in the huge battle of propaganda.

In the United States the sympathizers with the Russian system have per-sistently employed the rhetorical technique of identification, maintaining that those policies which lead toward communization are most in line with traditional American ideals and in some instances undertaking to rewrite American history.

Propaganda and a Pluralistic Society

The West is more or less bound to its methods by a theory of pluralistic society. From the Soviet standpoint there is no such thing as propaganda in the sense employed in this article: the state is the sole judge of its own actions and of the welfare of its individual citizens, and it controls all the means of publicity. All of its propaganda is therefore viewed as a propagation of state-endorsed truth.

But the people of the West, with their tradition of individual freedom, have never admitted the right of a single voice to prevail exclusively. Liberal societies are made up of many different centers of knowledge, opinion, and influence. It is assumed that each of these, whether political, business, social, or cultural, will have its own case to plead and in doing so will be guilty of certain excesses which can be correctly labeled propaganda. But it is assumed also that man's progress toward truth is evolutionary, and that this progress is facilitated rather than impeded by allowing every responsible group to try to win adherents. This is the competition of ideas in the market place upon which the theory of philosophical liberalism largely rests. Untruths and partial truths will frequently be offered, but eventually, at the cost of some time and expense, they will be driven from the market by the true article. And a truth acquired in this way is possessed more fully and securely than one which is adopted without having to meet the test of competition.

It would be possible theoretically to unite society into a monolithic whole guided entirely by a group of the supposedly wisest men placed in charge of all matters. They would supervise what might be said on every subject and would apportion the amount of influence permitted to every group with special interest. In such a society there would be no room for propaganda because propaganda would be viewed as pure waste or excess. This is the kind of social scheme that totalitarians espouse.

The West, generally speaking, regards this ideal as abhorrent because it feels that man has not finally made up his mind about many matters, with which he must still deal in a deliberative way. Therefore it regards propaganda as the price that is paid for a free society, which is in form a pluralistic society. Among the innumerable free utterances which will be made in such a society are some which are more or less injurious, but it is believed that the social body will handle these in much the same way that the physical body handles poison, building up resistance to them and ultimately disposing of them. Meanwhile it is assimilating from all that it ingests whatever proves nourishing. In this light propaganda appears not as a prohibitible evil, but as part of the social process. It is educational in that area where right solutions are still a matter of opinion and not yet a part of the society's organic law.

HARD-TO-RECOGNIZE TYPES OF PROPAGANDA

Most systematic investigations have shown that propaganda is most effective when it catches people dormant, or not much concerned about the issues involved. It is least effective and sometimes it is not effective at all when people are aroused by an interest in the issue and have tried to define their own opinions. Moreover, propaganda seldom makes headway against bare facts. Careful studies of the results of World War I experience indicate that a propaganda campaign will add something to a nation's morale when things are going well but is relatively powerless to check discouragement when the military situation turns bad. There have been several striking examples of political candidates elected in the face of overwhelming newspaper opposition; and it is a fairly common thing for an individual to read a newspaper of a certain political persuasion regularly and to vote the opposite. The facts strongly suggest that the real check against harmful propaganda is the liberal intelligence of the citizen.

However, there are certain methods of distortion and emotional appeal which are likely to go unrecognized by any except the most reflective minds. Of these, the most effective is the simple device of suppressing alternatives. All rational choice is a process of sorting over two or more alternatives and taking the one which seems to promise best; and democratic government rests upon a premise that the common man is capable of doing this. Propagandists long ago discovered that no such process can occur if only one alternative is supplied. By this method freedom of choice is stifled almost as completely as if coercion had been used. Thus a people may be told by their government and by that arm of the press which practically every government has at its beck and call that the country has but one choice: it must

fight, or it must inflate the currency, and so on. If all the alternatives had
been canvassed and this one had been put forward as the special recommendation, the conditions of free choice would have been met. But when there
exists a practical monopoly of channels of information and communication,
it is next to impossible to put another alternative before any sizable part of
the population. Furthermore, there are varied and subtle ways of suppressing alternatives; sometimes effects are described and their causes are withheld; or causes are described and their effects are ignored; an action may be
narrated and its agent purposely be left unmentioned. These and many
other such partial renderings are alike in that they keep from the public a
true picture of a situation with alternatives. The more cynical users of propaganda take the view that the common man dislikes the labor of thinking,
and that he loves to be given a single course to follow, if his vanity can be
soothed in the process. Dr. Goebbels, the propaganda chief of Nazi Germany, declared "the ordinary man hates nothing more than two-sidedness,
to be called upon to consider this as well as that." This audacious pronouncement contains a certain amount of psychological truth inasmuch as
a choice causes one to hesitate and hesitation may contribute to the sense
of insecurity. Fear of insecurity being one of the dominant impulses of an
age of war and revolution, the selfish manipulators of mass opinion have
had an important circumstance on their side.

Closely connected with this method is that of taking some doctrine or
opinion and treating it as if it were a universally accredited dogma. The
single alternative referred to above is often presented in this guise. By
this means of misrepresentation the propagandist assumes either boldly or
blandly that everyone in his right mind accepts the opinion as a necessary
presupposition, and then he proceeds to build his case upon it. The effect
of this maneuver is to keep the proposition which is essential to the argument away from public criticism. Known in logic as "begging the question,"
it often succeeds in deceiving those who have little skill in analyzing the
implications of statements. For example, the idea that the profit system is
the foundation of all our prosperity often appears as a dogma underlying
the propaganda of business corporations. But the opponents of capitalism
use the same method by proceeding from a contrary dogma, which is that
the profit system is pernicious and can never be defended in principle. It
appears in the kind of statement to which the maker prefaces "of course."
Thus we hear "Of course the profit system is a passing phenomenon"; or

"Of course all Germans are warlike," and so on. The very form of the statement sometimes induces the timid or unwary to concede it the status of dogma. Commercial advertising makes use of the device when it implies that of course everyone buys a new car every year, or of course everyone takes vitamin pills, the suggestion being that if one acts in a contrary way, one has not caught up with enlightened opinion and practice. There has been an increasing tendency among people of the Western nations to propagandize for democracy in just this way. It is assumed that democracy is the dogma of all society, and that anyone who reasons about society at all must start with this in the place of first premise. The question left open is not the merit of democracy, but by what means shall democracy be attained.

Like the suppression of alternatives, reasoning of this kind narrows the range of choice. The unwarranted dogmatic assumption is one of the means of short-circuiting thought.

Another short-circuiting device which often eludes notice is the telescoping of a cause-and-effect sequence. Known to rhetoric by the technical name of "metalepsis," it takes the form of attributing a present effect to a remote cause or of citing a present cause as producing a remote effect. More specifically, the result of this operation is to confuse causal reasoning. Often it results in the supposition that there is only one cause whereas in fact a plurality of causes exists. The well-known story which undertakes to prove that the battle was lost for want of a horseshoe nail is perhaps the classic example of this mode of reasoning. In a modern instance, the manufacturer of a certain metal tries to gain public favor by asserting that this metal won the war. The line of argument, if fully expanded, would run something like this: without this metal steel of a certain hardness could not be produced; without steel of a certain hardness, airplane engines could not be made; and without airplane engines the war could not have been won. Therefore this manufacturer deserves credit for winning the war. The case is distorted by ignoring or de-emphasizing the intermediate steps of causation and by leaving out other causes. Political propagandists sometimes claim that the great prosperity of the United States is owing to its form of government. A rational case could be made out certainly by showing that the form of government has helped by encouraging initiative, and so forth, but it would be most unfair to leave out of account such factors as our tremendous endowment of natural resources and the advantages of our geographical position.

Obviously presentations of this kind defeat the careful analysis that is required to predict effects of causes. Yet it has a wide appeal because it ministers to the desire for simple diagnoses and easy solutions.

One of the most difficult types of distortion to recognize is that which practices a deliberate weighting while professing to give a full and judicious review of the subject. No newspaper is wholly free from this kind of propaganda. Moreover, the controversial question of propaganda in our schools and universities cannot be studied without some notice of this practice. A textbook in American history, for example, can greatly influence the subsequent thinking of its students by presenting a certain group as the chief founders of the nation or a certain section as the chief contributor to its culture while scanting the claims of other groups and sections. Again, if a reading course in economics includes a large number of thinkers who subscribe to a certain economic theory, the impression is inevitably given that most of the serious and effective thinking on this subject has been done by members of this school. In this way the book may not be representative while professing to be so. Even keeping the student's attention centered on certain sets of ideas to the exclusion or eclipse of other sets has the effect of propagandizing in their favor because the natural processes of repetition, identification, and unconscious absorption will inevitably do their work. The college of education in one large American university lists a course entitled "Philosophy of Education." The description of this course declares that it is "based on a careful and critical reading of selected chapters from John Dewey's *Democracy and Education.*" This is an example of complete distortion, with the effect of propaganda on behalf of a special theory of the subject. It has even been asked by one authority whether *McGuffey's Readers,* used throughout the Middle West in the latter half of the nineteenth century, were not purveyors of propaganda inasmuch as they directed the attention of school children to certain moral, social, and political ideals to the exclusion of divergent or competing ones.

Obviously educational curriculums as a whole are liable to this kind of distortion, and there is no completely neutral body of teaching material. The degree to which education can be kept free from the more reprehensible forms of propaganda depends little upon outside supervision, but a great deal upon the information, alertness, and conscience of the teachers themselves.

Name calling would not be a difficult device to recognize were it not for the fact that most people think critically about a name only the first time they hear it. Then they assign it a value and tuck it away upon a mental shelf. Political and other propagandists know this well, and one of their favorite tricks is to take the name down and use it with the value originally attached. The propagandist is thus making use of a certain force of inertia, created by the ordinary man's unwillingness or lack of time to re-examine terms. In our day, such terms as "Tory," "radical," "copperhead," "aristocrat," and "red" are used in just this way, without reference to their rational content. It is said that the farmers of the Middle West were kept in opposition to free trade for many years by being told that it was the "British policy." Free trade would unquestionably have been to their advantage economically, but the word "British" stiffened them into an unthinking resistance. The active mind is constantly engaged in inspecting and revaluing such names in the light of new happenings and enlarged historical perspectives. The propagandist who works in this manner is practicing deceit upon persons who put their trust in the epithets as originally used.

THE CONTROL OF PROPAGANDA

Although these and many other devices are used to mislead people in greater or less degree, a free society does not seek an end to propaganda as such. From the point of view of its basic philosophy, many of the subjects of propaganda are still in the field of deliberative forensics. In other words, society has not made up its mind about them to the extent of suppressing or censoring expressions of opinion. However, there are two criteria which may be applied in determining whether a given piece of propaganda exceeds the tolerance permitted in free public discussion. One of these is a judgment of the source. If the group issuing the propaganda is of extremely low ethical standards, so that it is reckless of results as long as it succeeds in its selfish objective, society may be justified in restraining or even prohibiting its attempts to influence. Certain forms of pseudo-medical advertising, for example, are dubious from the standpoint of ethics; and society cannot remain indifferent to these just as it cannot ignore advertising and other propaganda which lures youth along known paths of danger. All attempts to influence, including speeches, are judged somewhat in relation to the source; and some degree of control seems necessary for those who have proved themselves ethically irresponsible.

Another criterion is made necessary by the enormous efficiency of technology in the field of communication. Modern means of dissemination are so great and so effective that propaganda fed into one of these machines may get out of hand, producing results even beyond the intention of the authors. Technology itself becomes a kind of second force, aiding and abetting the spread of the doctrine. For this reason the public has become justifiably sensitive about the kind of thing that is propagated by means of the radio. The radio brings its message into the inner sanctum of every home, so that there are actual physical difficulties in avoiding exposure to its influence. Furthermore, motion picture technique has become a potent means for the instilling of attitudes. Many cities of considerable size have been reduced to having a single newspaper, or two newspapers under a single ownership. Whoever controls huge media like these has at his disposal an engine whose mere efficiency is potentially a public danger. Totalitarian states have recognized this plainly and have responded by making these means the tools of the state, on the theory that whatever has such extensive power to influence ought to be conducted by the government. The Western democracies are awake to the problem but have as yet formulated no clear-cut policy.

It is tempting to say that the only final protection against propaganda is education. But the remark must be severely qualified because there is a kind of education which makes people more rather than less gullible. Most modern education induces people to accept too many assumptions. On these the propagandist can play even more readily than on the supposed prejudices of the uneducated. It is the independent, reflective intelligence which critically rejects and accepts the ideas competing in the market place. Education to think rather than mere literacy should be the prime object of those seeking to combat propaganda.

Bib.: Edward L. Bernays, *Propaganda*, Horace Liveright, 1928. Arthur Ponsonby, *Falsehood in War Time*, George Allen and Unwin, 1928. George Sylvester Viereck, *Spreading Germs of Hate*, Horace Liveright, 1930. Aldous Huxley, "Notes on Propaganda," *Harper's Magazine*, Vol. 174, December, 1936, pp. 32–41. William Albig, *Public Opinion*, McGraw-Hill, 1939. Philip Davidson, *Propaganda and the American Revolution*, University of North Carolina Press, 1941. Leonard W. Doob, *Public Opinion and Propaganda*, Henry Holt, 1948.

The Best of Everything[1]

Culture is to a great extent a response to images that people carry around in their heads, and in past times most of these images have come to us from an assimilated religion and literature. Today, with advertising taking a good share of time and attention away from these, it is tempting to speculate on the effects of the imagery it tends to substitute. Granted that the mission of advertising is the practical one of selling, and granting moreover that the public has been educated to a certain good-humored skepticism regarding it—the *caveat emptor* the world over of the man being sold something—there still remains the possibility of definite effects upon outlook and mores. In brief, do certain advertising practices seriously interfere with the representation that man needs to have of himself and his society?

This is not a fresh criticism of advertisers for appealing to such base motives as wanting to get rich or be socially prominent, or for playing upon fear and hypochondria. These aspects of the institution are well-known and have been rather amply canvassed; they seem, however, to be more superficial—or at least more easily coped with—than certain deleterious effects which a great deal of advertising has upon the mind and the personality.

Reality Misconstrued

It requires a strong and active intelligence to resist any picture of the world which is constantly and studiously held up to the attention. One has to be an inventor to read well, said Emerson. The average consumer of newspapers and popular magazines is too passive a creature to invent something to put alongside the world which advertising sets before him. This is saying nothing of the unpleasantness involved, because what does one place alongside a world with the best of everything?

1. *National Review,* 1/11, February 1, 1956, 21–22. © 1956 by National Review, Inc., 215 Lexington Avenue, New York, N.Y. 10016. Reprinted by permission.

The bulk of present-day advertising comes as a consistent and unremitting misconstruing of reality. There are three areas in which it seems especially pernicious: its treatment of work, its treatment of history, and its jugglery of cause-and-effect relations. In these it faithfully reflects the modern "liberal" self-deceiving mind, which has brought the world to a chaos of contradictions.

The first of the three areas shows an especially telltale trend, which serves to illuminate the way things are going. Even twenty years ago most advertisers who had some product that involved use were satisfied to show a picture of someone using it. If it was laundry soap, there was an illustration of somebody laundering; if a saw, of somebody sawing; and so on, with no qualms about the dignity of labor. The postgraduate school of advertising which seems in charge today has got beyond crudities of this sort. Now pictures that might recall labor or strain have been largely banished, and what one sees is the end product, with the happy buyer looking on in relaxed satisfaction. If it is a laundry soap, the shining clothes are depicted; if it is a saw, the sawn logs, and thus it goes.

The principle seems to be that anything suggestive of struggle or fatigue or any kind of strenuousness is interdicted from the best of all possible worlds. In keeping with the pushbutton existence we are threatened with, everything somehow gets done without effort. The captain of his fate and master of his soul has only to look on. In a broad description of the trend, the whole motif has been shifted from achievement to relaxation and enjoyment, or passive attitudes.

The personality gets a wrench when one has to turn away from this dream world—labor absent, death denied, old age in the background or banished from view altogether—and confront the world that is ours. It is generally idle to dispute with those who believe that this is really "the height of the times" in the sense of being the age of fullest happiness and fruition. Without arguing conclusions, it can at least be noted that we live in the presence of the following facts.

History Bowdlerized

Never before have so many persons of learning and responsibility felt that the very survival of the race is a contingent matter—and contingent upon things that are not going very well. A monstrous fanaticism, based upon a perverse reading of history and accepting force as a legitimate weapon, is abroad in the world. Labor, while more productive in a material way, is for the millions increasingly divorced from natural rhythm. Mental illness has almost reached plague proportions. And popular culture, as measured by reading and entertainment, is on a toboggan slide toward cheapness and vulgarity. Set this world beside the one the advertiser depicts and says he is helping to create, and you have cause for a disturbance that looks like schizophrenia. Perhaps the disorder shows itself in the illogical policies of modern governments, which go unrebuked by the people, and in the zest with which peoples enter upon destruction when unleashed by war.

It is not surprising to find the same fixation upon unreality when history becomes the subject. Historical themes and scenes are popular with advertisers, but even the casual reader can detect a curious transfiguration. The means of presentation are now rich beyond compare, yet history somehow always gets presented as something that didn't really happen. The advertiser takes a cute attitude toward it, pulling out whatever is exotic, sensational or amusing, while suggesting by arrangement and tone that it could not occur with real people like those reading the advertisements. (After all, history has been defined as unpleasant things that happen to other people.) History in its true lineaments is too gloomy, too full of monitions, too fearful a commentary on the nature of man, to be compatible with the principles of advertising. So this bowdlerized version is constantly fed to a public which is historically almost illiterate anyhow. It cuts them further off from the past than before, diminishing their responsibility and their capacity to predict. From "it couldn't really have happened" it may be only a step to "It Can't Happen Here." It is a miseducation with serious potentialities.

Reasoning Confused

The unwary reader may be further disoriented with reference to the world he lives in by a persistent undermining of cause-and-effect relations.

One of the commonest methods of propaganda is to confuse cause-and-effect reasoning by insisting upon one cause where there exists in fact a plurality of causes, or by connecting remote causes and effects while ignoring the important intermediate ones. Everyone has seen examples of this kind of weighting: a romance goes on the rocks because a certain party neglected to buy a certain kind of cosmetic; or, the nation's armament is now invincible because some company has perfected a certain gadget. We are familiar with the kind of illustration which shows together two extremely disparate things; the contrast is an effective eye-catcher, and we are driven to read the print below to discover how in the dickens they ever got into the same picture. The connection will be expounded in the manner described above, and with those made credulous by Sunday-supplement science and the believe-it-or-not type of feature, it may pass as unobjectionable. So far has this gone that the full-page displays in our magazines of widest circulation may remind one of Dr. Johnson's famous description of metaphysical poetry, where "the most heterogeneous ideas are yoked by violence together." The difference is that the architecture of cause and effect which the poet most carefully thought out is here apt to be no more than a flimsy facade.

The establishment of causal relations is a difficult enough matter under the best conditions. Nothing is helped when people are habituated to make these essentially illogical connections. How much bombardment of this kind the mass mind can stand without showing degenerative symptoms is perhaps a subject for the psychiatrist.

Stemming from this same practice of taking logic lightly are some of the weird operations with language. As Charles W. Morton has pointed out, there has developed what might be called the "antonymous" school of advertising prose, by which modifiers of opposite meaning are blandly applied to the same article. The object apparently is to broaden the appeal until the product is all things to all men. Consequently we are assured that this wine has a "dry, sweet flavor" and that tobacco will delight with its "mild, rich aroma." If the article can be described as "ruggedly delicate," it stands a chance to catch both masculine and feminine fancy. The style has already spread to politics, and we seem to hear increasingly of the "liberal—conservative" faith of so-and-so or of the "conservative—liberal" policy that is going to please everybody. Elsewhere we have reached the point where making war is called "restoring peace" and each new engine of destruction is written up as a further pledge of our pacific intentions.

This is, of course, only one phase of the debauchery of language by advertising and the looser kind of journalism. The everlasting attempt to prostitute the word, to harness even its resonances to the work of selling or ingratiating, is a large and depressing subject in itself. Language as an indispensable convention suffers from such tampering, to say nothing of the esthetic impairment.

It is sometimes said, half humorously, that the public is king today, or that the common man is royalty. I would suggest that this comparison contains more truth than humor, and that the art of advertising, with its auxiliary professions, is but the ancient art of the courtier in modern dress and setting.

It was a precept of courtiership always to flatter the king, and some weak-headed monarchs were flattered into a state where they lost all perception of reality. The suitors of the public today are well up on this principle of success at court. It was likewise a precept that no one should ever be a bearer of bad news to the king if he could get out of it. There was too much human tendency to identify the bearer with the news. So our advertisers always manage to be bearers of good tidings, and if evil has to be reported, it is in connection with the king's enemies, which in this case are work, self-denial, boredom, disappointment, and the like. Thus the incessant effort of flattery and the withholding of the unpleasant news of life builds up insulation against a world which everyone is destined to come to terms with. At some point a reorientation has to occur, and where it has been painful, monarchs have been known to look for scapegoats. The old courtier generally understood that his was a risky business.

Few will deny that the proliferating products and gadgets of an industrial economy need to be introduced and sometimes explained to a potential consuming public. There is a core of information in all but the silliest advertising. The real question is whether such need carries a license for these excesses. Even though the times are in no mood for a self-denying regimen, and even though some doctors of the science of society are busy elevating the consumer to the pedestal occupied by the erstwhile man of achievement, there is a minimum below which realism cannot safely fall.

It was one of Napoleon's acid observations that cannon had killed the feudal order of society and that ink would kill the modern social organization. The prophecy continues to reverberate. The art of advertising and its allied crafts go too far toward substituting dream and wishful thinking for reality. Man's conception of life is changed importantly when you expel the idea of tragedy. When you expel history also, you create a vacuum into which almost anything can rush.

Concealed Rhetoric in Scientistic Sociology[1]

This inquiry concerns some problems posed by the use of rhetoric in the dissemination of a professedly scientific knowledge of man. It assumes that rhetoric in its right character is one of the useful arts and that knowledge about the nature and behavior of man can be gained and should be propagated as widely as possible. The question of what things should precede and enter into that dissemination, however, continues to raise real perplexities. Many of us who read the literature of social science as laymen are conscious of being admitted at a door which bears the watchword "scientific objectivity" and of emerging at another door which looks out upon a variety of projects for changing, renovating, or revolutionizing society. In consequence, we feel the need of a more explicit account of how the student of society passes from facts to values or statements of policy.

I would reject at the outset any assumption that the man who studies social phenomena either could or should be incapable of indignation and admiration. Such a person, were it possible for him to exist, would have a very limited function, and it is hard to see how he could be a wise counselor about the matters with which he deals. It seems probable that no one would ever devote himself to the study of society unless he had some notion of an "ought," or of the way he would like to see things go. The real focus of this study is on the point at which social science and rhetoric meet and on the question whether this meeting, in the case of what will here be labeled "scientistic" sociology, has resulted in deception rather than in open and legitimate argument. To begin the inquiry, it will be necessary to say a few things about the nature of rhetoric.

1. In Helmut Schoeck and James W. Wiggins (eds.), *Scientism and Values*. Princeton: Van Nostrand, 1960, 83–99.

1. Rhetorical and Scientific Discourse

Rhetoric is anciently and properly defined as the art of persuasion. We may deduce from this that it is essentially concerned with producing movement, which may take the form of a change of attitude or the adoption of a course of action, or both. This art, whether it presents itself in linguistic or in other forms (and I would suggest that a bank or other business corporation which provides itself with a tall and imposing-looking building is demonstrating that there is even a rhetoric of matter or of scene), meets the person to whom it is addressed and takes him where the rhetor wishes him to go, even if that "going" is nothing more than an intensification of feeling about something. This means that rhetoric, consciously employed, is never innocent of intention, but always has as its object the exerting of some kind of compulsion.

Defining rhetoric thus as the art of persuasion does not, however, divorce it entirely from scientific knowledge. My view is that the complete rhetorician is the man of knowledge who has learned, in addition to his knowledge, certain arts of appeal which have to do with the inspiring of feeling. Indeed, the scientist and the rhetorician both begin with an eye on the nature of things. A rhetoric without a basis in science is inconceivable, because people are moved to action by how they "read" the world or the phenomena of existence, and science is the means of representing these in their existential bearings. People respond according to whether they believe that certain things exist with fixed natures, or whether they accept as true certain lines of cause-and-effect relationship, or whether they accept as true certain other relationships, such as the analogical. One might, speaking as a scientist, define man as an animal, or one might assert that government spending is a cause of inflation, or one might assert that war and murder are similar kinds of things. But one could also make these statements as a rhetorician. How, then, can one distinguish between the two kinds of statements?

The difference is that science is a partial universe of discourse, which is concerned only with facts and the relationships among them. Rhetoric is concerned with a wider realm, since it must include both the scientific occurrence and the axiological ordering of these facts. For the rhetorician the tendency of the statement is the primary thing, because it indicates his position or point of view in his universe of discourse. Rhetorical presentation always carries perspective. The scientific inquirer, on the other hand, is merely noting things as they exist in empirical conjunction. He is not passing judgment on them because his presentment, as long as it remains scientific, is not supposed to be anything more than classificatory. The statement of a scientist that "man is an animal" is intended only to locate man in a biological group as a result of empirical finding; but the rhetorician's statement of the same thing is not the same in effect. For him the term "animal" is not a mere positive designation, but a term loaded with tendency from the wider context in which he is using it. He is endeavoring to get a response by identifying man with a class of beings toward which a certain attitude is predictable. He has taken the term out of the positive vocabulary and made it dialectical, a distinction I shall take up presently.

It may now be suggested that if the sociologists whom I am here calling "scientistic" had been true scientists, they would have asked at the beginning: What is the real classification of the subject of our study? And having answered this, they would have asked next: What is the mode of inquiry most appropriate to that study? I am assuming that the answers to their questions would have told them that their subject matter is largely subjective, that much of it is not susceptible of objective or quantitative measurement, and that all or nearly all their determinations would be inextricably bound up with considerations of value. This would have advised them that however scientific they might try to be in certain of their procedures—as in the analysis of existing facts—the point would be reached where they would have to transcend these and group their facts in categories of significance and value.

But what some of the more influential of them did was to decide that the phenomena which they were engaged in studying were the same as those which the physical scientists were studying with such impressive results, and that the same methods and much of the same terminology would be appropriate to the prosecution of that study.

2. The Original Rhetorical Maneuver

My thesis is that in making this decision they were acting not as scientists, but as rhetoricians, because they were trying to capitalize on a prestige and share in an approbation, in disregard of the nature of the subject they were supposed to be dealing with. Sociology took this turn at a time when the prestige of physical science was very great, possibly greater than it is even today, since certain limitations had not then been encountered or fully considered. Physical science was beginning to change the face of the earth, and it was adding greatly to the wealth-producing machinery of mankind. It was very human for a group engaged in developing a body of knowledge to wish to hitch its wagon to that star. F. A. Hayek, in *The Counter-Revolution of Science*, has related the case as follows:

> Their [the physical scientists'] success was such that they came to exert an extraordinary fascination on those working in other fields, who rapidly began to imitate their teaching and vocabulary. . . . These [subjects] became increasingly concerned to vindicate their equal status by showing that their methods were the same as those of their more brilliantly successful sisters rather than by adapting their methods more and more to their own particular problems.[2]

Accordingly, the founders of scientistic sociology did not so much arrive independently at a definition of sociology (in doing which they would have been scientists) as seek identification, for external reasons, with another field of study. In proceeding thus, they were not trying to state the nature of their subject; they were trying to get a value imputed to it. That this was their original rhetorical maneuver can be shown in the following way.

Rhetoric can be visualized as altogether a process of making this kind of identification. The process is simply that of merging something we would like to see taken as true with something that is believed to be true, of merging something we would like to get accepted with something that is accepted. Such an operation can be seen in the most rudimentary of all rhetorical devices, which is sometimes termed "name-calling." To something that we wish to see accepted, we apply a name carrying prestige; to something that we wish to see rejected, we apply a name that is distasteful. Rhetoric thus works through eulogistic and dyslogistic vocabularies. It is the thing-to-be-identified-with that provides the impulse, whether favorable or unfavorable. The honest and discriminating rhetorician chooses these things with regard to reason and a defensible scheme of values; the dishonest or unthinking one may seize upon any terms which seem to possess impulse, just to make use of their tractive power.

2. F. A. Hayek, *The Counter-Revolution of Science* (Glencoe: The Free Press, 1952), pp. 13–14.

If the foregoing analysis is correct, the scientistic sociologists applied a prestige-carrying name to their study. They were not classifying in the true sense; they were instigating an attitude. In brief, "social science" is itself a rhetorical expression, not an analytical one. The controversy over their methods and recommendations which goes on today continues to reflect that fact.

3. Positive and Dialectical Terms

Having thus assumed the role of scientists, they were under a necessity of maintaining that role. And this called for further "identifications." Perhaps the most mischievous of these has been the collapsing of the distinction between positive and dialectical terms. Since this distinction is of the first importance to those who would deal with these matters critically, I shall try to make clear what is meant by it.

Practically everyone grants that not all of the terms in our vocabulary refer to the same kind of thing. The difference between those which refer to positive entities and those which refer to dialectical ones is of decisive significance for the investigator. "Positive" terms stand for observable objects capable of physical identification and measurement. They are terms whose referents are things existing objectively in the world, whose presence supposedly everyone can be brought to acknowledge. "Rock," "tree," and "house" are examples. Positive terms thus make up a "physicalist" vocabulary, inasmuch as they represent the objects of sensory perception (even when these have to be noted by dials and meters). Properly speaking, there cannot be an argument about a positive term; there can be only a dispute, which is subject to settlement by actual observation or measurement.

"Dialectical" terms come from a different source, because they take their meaning from the world of idea and action. They are words for essences and principles, and their meaning is reached not through sensory perception, but through the logical processes of definition, inclusion, exclusion, and implication. Since their meaning depends on a concatenation of ideas, what they signify cannot be divorced from the ideological position of the user as revealed by the general context of his discourse. A scientist, as we have noted, locates things in their empirical conjunction, but the user of dialectic must locate the meaning of his entities in the logical relationships of his system, and hence his discovery of them cannot be an empirical discovery. For this reason we say that the meaning of "justice" or "goodness" or "fair play" is not "found," but rather "arrived at." It is implied by the world of idea and attitude with which the user started. A dialectical term does not stand for "motion," as the positive term out of science might do, but for "action," which cannot be freed from the idea of purpose and value.

The scientistic sociologist has tried to maintain his scientific stance by endeavoring to give the impression that all the terms he uses are positive and hence can be used with the same "objectivity" and preciseness as those of the physical scientist. I say he has endeavored to give the impression, because even an impression that this can be done is difficult to induce for any length of time, as I believe the following examples will show.

Let us take for illustration an expression fairly common in sociological parlance today: "the underprivileged," and ask ourselves how one determines its meaning. We see at once that it is impossible to reach the meaning of "the underprivileged" without reference to the opposed term, "the privileged." Evidently one has first to form a concept of "the privileged," and this will be in reference to whatever possessions and opportunities are thought of as conferring privilege. The one term is arrived at through logical privation of the other, and neither is conceivable without some original idea frankly carrying evaluation. "Privilege" suggests, of course, something that people desire, and hence "the privileged" are those in whose direction we wish to move; and "the underprivileged" constitute the class we wish to escape from. But where is the Geiger counter with which we could go out into society and locate one of the underprivileged? We would have to use some definition of privilege, arising out of an original inclination toward this or that ideal.

Or let us take the more general expression, "social problem." How is one to become aware of the supposedly objective fact or facts denoted by this expression? According to one sociologist, a social problem is "any situation which attracts the attention of a considerable number of competent observers within a society and appeals to them as calling for readjustment or remedy by social, i.e., collective, action of some kind or other."[3] At least three items in this definition warn us that a social problem is not something that just anybody could identify, like an elephant in a parade, but something that must be determined by a dialectical operation. First of all, the observer must

---

3. Clarence M. Case, *Outlines of Introductory Sociology* (New York, 1924), p. 627.

be competent, which I take to mean trained not just in seeing objective things, but in knowing when ideas or values are threatened by their opposites. This perception appeals to him for an attitude to be followed by an action, and moreover this action must be of the putatively most beneficial kind, "social" or "collective."

The point I wish to make here is that the scientistic sociologist is from the very beginning caught up in a plot, as it were, of attitude and action, and that he cannot divorce the meaning of the incidents from the structure of the plot. The plot is based on a position which takes facts out of empirical conjunction and places them in logical or dialectical constructions.

He is therefore not dealing in positive words that have a single fixed meaning when he uses terms that depend on a context for their signification. Another way of expressing this is to say that the terms in his vocabulary are polar, in that their meaning changes according to what they are matched with. And since the sociologist has the opportunity to match them with almost anything, he is not dealing with scientific invariables when he talks about "the underprivileged" or "a social problem." He is being an ethical philosopher from the beginning, with the responsibility which that implies.

The conclusion comes down to this: Things which are discriminated empirically cannot thereafter by the same operation be discriminated dialectically. If one wishes to arrive at a dialectical discrimination, one has to start from a position which makes that possible.

4. Other Forms of "Identification"

This ignoring of the nature of dialectical inquiry is the most serious perversion committed by the scientistic sociologists in seeking to maintain their identification, but there are other, perhaps more superficial, procedures, whose general end is the same kind of simulation. One of the more noticeable is what might be called pedantic analysis. The scientistic sociologist wishes people to feel that he is just as empirical and thoroughgoing as the natural scientist and that his conclusions are based just as relentlessly on observed data. The desire to present this kind of façade accounts, one may suspect, for the many examples and the extensive use of statistical tables found in the works of some of them. It has been said of certain novelists that they create settings having such a wealth of realistic detail that the reader assumes that the plot which is to follow will be equally realistic, when this may be far from the case. What happens is that the novelist disarms the reader with the realism of his setting in order that he may "get away with murder" in his plot. The persuasiveness of the scene is thus counted on to spill over into the action of the story. In like manner, when a treatise on social science is filled with this kind of data, the realism of the latter can influence our acceptance of the thesis, which may, on scrutiny, rest on very dubious constructs, such as definitions of units.

Along with this there is sometimes a great display of scientific preciseness in formulations. But my reading suggests that some of these writers are often very precise about matters which are not very important and rather imprecise about matters which are. Most likely this is an offsetting process. If there are subjects one cannot afford to be precise about because they are too little understood or because one's views of them are too contrary to traditional beliefs about society, one may be able to maintain an appearance of scientific correctness by taking great pains in the expressing of matters of little consequence. These will afford scope for a display of scholarly punctiliousness and of one's command of the scientific terminology.

At the opposite extreme, but intended for the same effect, is the practice of being excessively tentative in the statement of conclusions and generalizations. The natural scientists have won an enviable reputation for modesty in this respect: they seldom allow their desire for results to carry them beyond a statement of what is known or seriously probable. This often calls for a great deal of qualification, so that cautious qualification has become the hallmark of the scientific method. It is my impression, however, that a good many modern sociologists do their qualifying, not for the purpose of protecting the truth, but of protecting themselves. There is a kind of qualification which is mere hedging. I offer as an example a sentence from an article entitled "Some Neglected Aspects of the Problem of Poverty." The author begins his definition thus: "It would seem that it is nothing more nor less than a comparative social condition depending on a relative control over economic goods, the standard of comparison being a group possessing a maximum of such control, called the rich or wealthy."[4] There appear at the very beginning of this sentence two important qualifiers:

---

4. Merton K. Cameron, "Some Neglected Aspects of the Problem of Poverty," *Social Forces*, VII (September, 1928), 73.

(1) the verb is thrown into a conditional mode by the use of the auxiliary "would," and (2) the verb is not the categorical "is," but the tentative "seem," with its suggestion that one may be dealing only with appearances. This is followed by "nothing more nor less," which is a purely rhetorical flourish, evidently intended to make us feel that the author is going to be definite, whereas he has just advised us that he is not. What looks like carefulness is mere evasiveness; this writer does not want to assume the risk of saying what poverty is. Instances of such unwillingness to make a firm declaratory statement are so numerous that they almost constitute the style of a type of social science writing. With the unwary reader, unfortunately, this style may encourage confidence, whereas it should lead to challenge.[5]

5. Appeals to Authority

In addition to a language simulating that of science, the scientistic sociologists make use of an external means of persuasion in the form of an appeal to authority. A common practice with some of these writers when they are dealing with a subject that is controversial or involved with value judgments is to cite an impressive array of authorities. There is nothing improper in itself, of course, about the invoking of authority. But when we look at the method of certain of these authors, we are likely to find that the authorities are other social scientists who happen to share the particular view which is being presented. What looks like an inductive survey of opinions may in fact be a selection of *ex parte* pronouncements. Still, such marshaling of authorities, often accompanied by a quotation from each to heighten the sense of reality or conviction, can easily give the impression that all authority is behind the view being advanced. Thus many textbooks on social problems bristle with the names of persons whose claims to authority may be quite unknown to the reader, but whose solemn citation may be depended on to exert a persuasive force.[6] One suspects that it is the appearance rather than the real pertinence of the authority which is desired.

5. T. H. Huxley has such admirable words of advice on this subject that I cannot refrain from including them here: "Be clear though you may be convicted of error. If you are clearly wrong, you may run up against a fact some time and get set right. If you shuffle with your subject and study to use language which will give you a loophole of escape either way, there is no hope for you." Quoted in Aldous Huxley, *The Olive Tree* (New York, 1937), p. 63.

6. For examples see F. Stuart Chapin, *Cultural Change* (New York, 1928), p. 203; and Martin H. Neumeyer, *Social Problems and the Changing Society* (New York, 1953), p. 48.

Along with this there is another, and a more subtle, kind of appeal to authority which takes the form of a patter of modern shibboleths. These may be taken from everyday language, but they will be words and expressions associated with leaders of opinion, with current intellectual fashions, with big projects, and with things in general which are supposed to have a great future. Professor A. H. Hobbs, in his *Social Problems and Scientism*, lists among others: *modern, rational, liberal, professional, intergovernmental, objectivity, research, disciplines, workshop, interrelations, human resources,* and *human development.*[7] I would suggest that this language represents an appeal to the authority of the "modern mind." These are expressions carrying a certain melioristic bias, which one will have difficulty in resisting without putting oneself in the camp of reaction or obscurantism. The repeated use of them has the effect of setting up a kind of incantation, so that to sound in dissonance with them is virtually to brand oneself as antisocial. The reader is left with the alternative of accepting them and of going along on assumptions he does not approve of, or of rejecting them, which would entail continuous argument and would involve taking a position almost impossible to explain to a "modern."

6. Sociology as Deliberative Oratory

The use of appeals based on authority brings up again the role of the sociologist as advocate.

At the beginning of his treatise on *Rhetoric* Aristotle divides the art into three kinds: deliberative, forensic, and epideictic. Epideictic rhetoric is devoted to celebrating (as in the panegyric); forensic rhetoric is concerned with the justice or injustice of things which have already happened; and deliberative oratory is concerned with the future, since the speaker is urging his audience to do, or to refrain from doing, something or other. "The end of the deliberative speaker is the expedient or the harmful; for he who exhorts recommends a course of action as better, and he who dissuades advises against it as worse; all other considerations, such as justice and injustice, honor and disgrace, are included as accessory in relation to this."[8] By the terms of this definition a considerable part of sociological writing must be

7. A. H. Hobbs, *Social Problems and Scientism* (Harrisburg: The Stackpole Company, 1953), pp. 51–52.

8. *Rhetoric*, 1358b.

classified as deliberative oratory, and the practitioners of it as rhetoricians. When one sets up to advise concerning alternative social courses, one does exactly what the ancient orator in the Areopagus or the forum was doing, however much the abstractness of one's language may tend to conceal that fact. As Kenneth Burke has pointed out:

> . . . when you begin talking about the optimum rate of speed at which cultural change should take place or the optimum proportion between tribal and individualistic motives which should prevail under a given set of economic conditions, you are talking about something very important indeed; but you will find yourself deep in matters of rhetoric, for nothing is more rhetorical in nature than a deliberation as to what is too much or too little, too early or too late. . . .[9]

A good many current texts on sociology are replete with this kind of deliberation. Martin Neumeyer, in his *Social Problems and the Changing Society*, while discussing numerous opinions on the topics with which he deals, often steps into the role of judge and advocate. Thus we read:

> Homicides, suicides, illegitimate births, deaths due to venereal disease and the like seem to be more prevalent where there is low integration in cities. The more adequately a city provides for the health and welfare of its citizens, the greater the chance of preventing or controlling deviations. Well integrated cities are likely to have a better chance of survival and growth than poorly integrated urban areas.[10]

It might be contended that this passage is merely descriptive of certain laws of social phenomena. Still, the presence of such phrases as "more adequately," "health and welfare of its citizens," and "a better chance of survival and growth" show plainly that the passage is written from a standpoint of social meliorism.

The same kind of thing is done by George Lundberg, in his *Foundations of Sociology*, when he becomes a pleader on the subject of language itself. He argues that we ought to give up those terms created by the original myth- and metaphor-making disposition of the human mind in favor of a different "symbolic equipment." That he is entirely willing to utilize traditional rhetoric in making his point may be seen from the following passage:

9. Kenneth Burke, *A Rhetoric of Motives* (New York, 1950), p. 45.
10. Neumeyer, *op. cit.*, p. 107.

Untold nervous energy, time, and natural resources are wasted in warfare upon or protection against entirely imaginary monsters conjured up by words. Widespread mental disorders result from constantly finding the world different from the word-maps upon which we rely for guidance and adjustment. Social problems cannot be solved as long as they are stated in terms as primitive and unrealistic as those which attributed disease to demons and witches.[11]

A feature of another kind indicating that a good many sociologists are engaged in more or less concealed deliberative oratory is the presence in their work of a large amount of enthymematic reasoning. Reasoning in this form is a rhetorical kind of convincing, and the enthymeme is actually described by Aristotle as the "rhetorical syllogism."[12] In the textbooks of logic it is defined as a syllogism with one of the propositions withheld. In the argument

All who are patriots should be willing to sacrifice for their country.
You should be willing to sacrifice for your country.

the minor premise, "You are a patriot," is missing. It has been omitted because the maker of the argument has assumed that it is granted by the hearer and will be supplied by him to complete the argument.

This type of argument is rightly described as rhetorical because the rhetorician always gets his leverage by starting with things that are accepted. By combining these with things he wants to get accepted ("identification" again) he moves on to the conclusion which is his object. In other words, because the rhetorician can assume certain things—because he does not have to demonstrate every proposition in his argument—he can work from statements which are essentially appeals. He studies beforehand the disposition of his auditors and takes note of those beliefs which will afford him firm ground—those general convictions about which one does not have to be deliberative. Hence the enthymeme is rhetorical, as distinguished from the syllogism, because it capitalizes on something already in the mind of the hearer. The speaker tacitly assumes one position, and from this he can move on to the next.

11. George A. Lundberg, *Foundations of Sociology* (New York, 1939), p. 47.

12. *Rhetoric*, 1356b. Strictly speaking, in the Aristotelian enthymeme all the propositions are present, but one of them, instead of resting on proof, rests upon "signs" or "probabilities." See George Hayward Joyce, S. J., *Principles of Logic* (London, 1916), pp. 253–255.

A number of contemporary sociologists, as I read them, use the enthymeme for the purpose of getting accepted a proposition which could be challenged on one ground or another. They make an assumption regarding the nature or goals of society and treat this as if it were universally granted and therefore not in need of explicit assertion. I refer again to Neumeyer's *Social Problems and the Changing Society*. This work seems to rest its case on an enthymeme which, if expanded to a complete syllogism, would go as follows:

> If society is democratic and dynamic, these prescriptions are valid.
> Society is democratic and dynamic.
> Therefore these prescriptions are valid.

What the author does in effect is to withhold his minor premise apparently on the ground that no man of sense and information will question it. Therefore he does not take seriously those who would ask "Is society really democratic and dynamic?" or "In what ways is society democratic and dynamic?" (What is to take care of societies which are aristocratic and traditional, or do they have no social problems?) Having thus assumed the premise he needs in order to get his conclusion, he can proceed to describe the techniques which would be proper in a democratic and dynamic society, as if they were the only ones to be taken into account.

There is nothing illicit about enthymematic arguments; they are to be encountered frequently wherever argumentation occurs. My point is that something significant is implied by their presence here. Even if we are clear about why the sociologist must argue, why is he employing a form of argument recognized as "rhetorical"?

This takes us back to the original question regarding his province and specifically to the relationship of what he does to the world of value. A good many current writers in the field seem rather evasive on the subject of values: they admit that the problem of value has to be faced; but then they merely circle about it and leave specific values to shift for themselves. Occasionally one takes a more definite stand, as when Francis E. Merrill declares that the values of a social scientist are the values given him by virtue of his membership in a democratic and progressive society.[13] Even so re-

---

13. Francis E. Merrill, H. Warren Dunham, Arnold M. Rose, and Paul W. Tappan, *Social Problems* (New York, 1950), pp. 83–84.

spected a thinker as Max Weber seems less than satisfactory on the two roles of the social scientist. His position is that

> the distinction between the purely logically deducible and empirical factual assertions, on the one hand, and practical, ethical, or philosophical judgments, on the other hand, is correct, but that nevertheless . . . both problems belong within the area of instruction.[14]

Obviously the problem is how to encompass both of them. What Weber does is to lay down a rule for academic objectivity. The teacher must set

> as his unconditional duty, in every single case, even to the point where it involves the danger of making his lectures less lively or less attractive, to make relentlessly clear to his audience, and especially to himself, which of his statements are statements of logically deduced or empirically related facts and which are statements of practical evaluations.[15]

My question would be how the sociologist can in good conscience leave the first to embark upon the second without having something in the nature of a philosophy of society. His dilemma is that he is perforce a dialectician, but he is without a dialectical basis. He must use dialectical terms, but he has no framework which will provide a consistent extra-empirical reference for them, though we may feel sometimes that we see one trying to force itself through, as in the concept of society's essence as something "democratic and progressive." It seems to me that the dilemma could be faced with more candor and realism. No practical man will deny that the student of society can make use of many of the findings of positive science. Things must be recognized in their brute empirical existence; we are constantly running into things of which we were unaware until they proclaimed their objectivity by impinging upon our senses. And there are some things which must be counted. A pure subjective idealism is a luxury which a few thinkers can afford, but it is not a prudential system. I for one can hardly believe that science is purely ancillary in the sense of finding evidence for what we already believe or wish to believe. The world is too independent a datum for that.

---

14. Max Weber, *The Methodology of the Social Sciences*, tr. Edward A. Shils and Henry A. Finch (Glencoe: The Free Press, 1949), p. 1.

15. *Ibid.*, p. 2.

On the other hand, a large part of the subject matter of the student of society does consist of the subjective element in human beings. This has to be recognized as a causative agent. History shows many opinions, highly erroneous or fantastic, which have been active influences on human behavior. This factor has to be studied, but it cannot be simplistically quantified. Here at least there must be room for speculative inquiry.

Finally, the student of society should realize that he is a man writing as a man. He cannot free himself entirely from perspective. His view of things can have a definite bearing on what is regarded as a fact or on how factual units can be employed. To argue that the social scientist should adopt no perspective on matters is perhaps in itself to adopt a perspective, but a far less fruitful one than those in which, with proper regard for objective facts, a viewpoint is frankly espoused.

In view of these considerations, why does not social science call itself "social philosophy"? This would widen its universe of discourse, freeing it from the positivistic limitations of science and associating its followers with the love of wisdom. At the same time it would enable them to practice the art of noble rhetoric where it is called for, without unconscious deception and without a feeling that they are compromising their profession.

The Lincoln–Douglas Debates[1]

Just one hundred years ago Abraham Lincoln and Stephen A. Douglas were stumping Illinois for the office of United States Senator. They made a total of eighty-three appearances before the voters of that state, seven of which were in the form of joint debates. Now, on this anniversary of that famous contest, the University of Chicago Press has performed a service in bringing these debates to the public in a new and scholarly edition, *Created Equal? The Complete Lincoln–Douglas Debates of 1858* ($7.50). In addition to complete texts, the volume contains an introduction by its editor, Paul M. Angle, and many illuminating sidelights from newspaper accounts of the time.

The prospective reader should be cautioned, however, not to raise his expectations too high. Despite the important place they hold in American political history, these clashes are not of uniformly high forensic quality. A large amount of time was taken up with incrimination and recrimination. Each candidate charged the other with being party to a "conspiracy." Lincoln claimed that Douglas had entered into a conspiracy to make the institution of slavery national, by inserting a provision in the "Nebraska Bill" which would remove the restriction imposed by the Missouri Compromise and eventually make it unconstitutional for any state to prohibit slavery. Douglas claimed that Lincoln had entered into a conspiracy with certain leaders to dissolve the old Party and the Democratic Party by "abolitionizing" them, in return for which he was to get a seat in the Senate. These charges were aired and parried at nearly every meeting.

There is no doubt, however, about the real issue, which was what to do about slavery. And though he won the election, there is no doubt that Douglas got the worst of the argument. In the final debate he was reduced

---

1. *National Review*, 6/1, June 21, 1958, 18–19. © 1958 by National Review, Inc., 215 Lexington Avenue, New York, N.Y. 10016. Reprinted by permission.

to the demagoguery of attacking Lincoln's record in Congress on the Mexican War ten years earlier. In intellect Douglas was not even a little giant. Lincoln, on the other hand, was a master of argument, and his method was one that Douglas was peculiarly unfitted to cope with.

I would suggest that it is from the methods of the two men that the philosophic historian and the student of public affairs can learn most. It is apparent from the first that Lincoln was primarily a dialectician, engaged in trying to define certain terms. Douglas was replying to him as a rhetorician, and a rather poor one at that. In this role Douglas allowed himself to be caught doing one thing which the student of logic or any person with a good logical mind is most studious to avoid: he allowed himself to be caught playing around in the excluded middle.

The law of logic says that between two contradictories there is no middle ground. And Douglas kept trying to steer away from any commitment. The question was: what is the Negro? Is he a man? Is he a slave? Is he a free and equal citizen? Douglas would never say. As far as argument goes, any one of these alternatives would have been better than the position he took, which was that every state and territory had the right to answer the question in its own way, and that there the matter must rest. The nature of the Negro was therefore for him purely a matter of political determination.

Lincoln, on the contrary, took a stand, though it was a very limited one, and I do not doubt that many of his admirers will be surprised to learn how conservative he was on the race question. In replying to Douglas in the debate at Ottawa, he declared: "I have no purpose to introduce political and social equality between the white and black races. There is a physical difference between the two which in my judgment will probably forever forbid their living together upon the footing of perfect equality, and inasmuch as it becomes a necessity that there must be a difference, I, as well as Judge Douglas, am in favor of the race to which I belong having the superior position." Earlier in a speech at Springfield he had said: "What I would most desire would be a separation of the white and black races."

Lincoln's definition was simply that the Negro was a creature entitled to the fruits of his own toil. That, he argued insistently, was the definition implied by the Declaration of Independence, and his object was to place slavery where he thought the Founders of the Republic had placed it, namely, in a position pointing toward ultimate extinction.

Since Lincoln was willing to say what he thought the Negro was, and Douglas was not, the argument as argument could have but one outcome. Minimal as his definition was, it gave Lincoln a position from which he could attack and defend. Douglas had no defense except rhetorical appeals to a vague abstraction called "popular sovereignty" and to the prestige of the Supreme Court, which had just handed down the Dred Scott decision. The apostrophes of Douglas to this as "the law of the land," to be regarded as final and unquestionable, sound curiously like those being used today to protect the "desegregation" order from attack. Lincoln had no such reverence for this "law of the land" and said expressly that he expected to get it changed. "Somebody has to reverse that decision, since it is made, and we mean to reverse it," he asserted.

Lincoln did provide Douglas with one opening which the latter exploited with a degree of success. This was his famous statement to the effect that a house divided against itself cannot stand. Douglas was quick, if not very skillful, in pointing out that such doctrine, if pushed to its logical limit, is the principle of despotic government. "Uniformity is the parent of despotism the world over, not only in politics but in religion," he answered. Lincoln had to spend a lot of time in subsequent speeches digging himself out of that one, explaining that "it would be foolish for us to insist on having a cranberry law here in Illinois, where we have no cranberries, because they have a cranberry law in Indiana, where they have cranberries."

The issue was a potent one, of course, because it involves the idea of nationalization and the extent to which a state composed of many units should centralize its laws. Despite his disclaimer, Lincoln never made a very convincing case for states' rights. Douglas, on the other hand, never sounded very convincing in his real or pretended moral indifference to slavery, which he expressed by saying that he did not care whether slavery "was voted up or voted down." And furthermore Lincoln was protected by the very limited claim he made for the Negro, which would allow the states to make about any regulations for him they chose as long as his bondage was removed.

No case of course is a hundred per cent one way, and if Lincoln was the better controversialist, Douglas was the better prophet. I believe, moreover, that these facts are very closely related to their respective characters as dialectician and rhetorician. It is the work of the dialectician to form definitions and to work out their logical implications. It is the work of the rhetorician to take cognizance of prevailing values and of the urgency of historical forces. Douglas had said in a speech at Chicago: "Mr. Lincoln advocates boldly and clearly a war of sections, a war of the North against the South, of the free states against the slave states—a war of extermination—to be conducted relentlessly until one or the other shall be subdued. . . ." Lincoln said that anything like that was very far from his conception. Yet it was only a few years until the prophecy was fulfilled. If Lincoln was the better logician, Douglas had the better intuition of the situation.

What if Lincoln had been opposed then and in 1860 not by a third-rate rhetorician, but by a great one (who must by definition be also a pretty fair dialectician)? What if he had been opposed by someone of the caliber of Patrick Henry or Daniel Webster, who might have realized for the people with irresistible vividness the danger in the explosive forces which had built up? It is only speculation, but Lincoln might have polled considerably less than the forty per cent of the vote he received nationally, and the United States might have missed having its most mythogenic president.

The Cultural Role of Rhetoric[1]

One of the most ominous trends of our time is the tide of prejudice that is currently running against the traditional art of rhetoric. Almost everyone is aware in some degree of this feeling. Almost everyone is aware that the orator of the old style is no more, and that even those speeches which suggest traditional oratory are apt to arouse skepticism and suspicion. At times, indeed, in moments of great crisis, people will listen to a Churchill, a MacArthur, or a de Gaulle, but when the crisis is past, they lapse again into their dislike of the rhetorical mode, labeling all discourse which has emotional appeal as "propaganda." The kind of speech that is favored today is comparatively without feeling and especially without resonance, so that one hardly exaggerates in saying that eloquence itself has fallen into disfavor. Eloquence in disfavor signifies a crisis of the human spirit. In attempting to account for this phenomenon, I shall be speaking not as a professional teacher of rhetoric but rather as a social critic concerned over what the development indicates for our future.

In this loss of accreditation by rhetoric, we are witnessing one of the chief phases of modern disintegration, and those who aid and abet it are among the leading saboteurs of our culture. The effect of their work is to dissolve the cohesiveness that holds a culture together and to collapse the necessary hierarchy of values. In doing this they are preparing us for a defeat by those who have not thus lost sight of the human condition.

My thesis will be quite simply that a healthy rhetoric is essential to a harmonious society and to that attachment to values which assures the survival of a culture.

1. This essay is a variant of the chapter of the same title in Weaver's *Visions of Order*. It was clearly prepared as the text of a speech, quite possibly the one he presented at the University of Arkansas on November 8, 1961. Edited by Ted J. Smith III from a corrected typescript located in Box 3, Folder 1, of the Richard M. Weaver papers at Vanderbilt University.

The question of whether we ought to go on living as we do is not a scientific question. Neither is the question of whether we ought to maintain our state, do this or that, follow that policy or another one. All of these are historical and philosophical questions, which can be dealt with only in a world of discourse much wider than that of science because it contains science as one of its parts. Any assumption that such questions can be answered scientifically, or even that answers can be put in purely scientific language, is subversive of social ordering, which has to have its sanction from elsewhere. Those questions can be answered, certainly in the stage of final resolution, only in the language of rhetoric, for that language takes into account history and circumstance, belief and aspiration, and all those things "felt along the heart" which are decisive in the actions of men.

The phenomenon we are confronting today is not being seen for the first time. It has indeed a very old if episodic history, reaching back at least to Grecian times. The Greeks have in fact left the most instructive lesson in what I shall be referring to from this point on as the struggle between rhetoric and dialectic. Anyone who has dipped into the wonderful dialogues of Plato must have become aware, once he passed beyond their charming surface of play and fancy, of a steady contest going on between two forces. One of these forces is logic or reason, of which Socrates is of course the great protagonist and exemplar. The other is somewhat more difficult to name; it could be called common opinion or established belief or the conventional body of ideas about life and the world. This is represented by those whom Socrates overthrows in debate, one after another. The upshot of this contest is that logic, or dialectic, becomes the supreme guide to life; and in fact Plato declares in the *Phaedrus* that the philosopher king, to whom the governing of men is given, must be primarily if not exclusively a dialectician. The sympathies of posterity have been with Socrates, and the more intellectual type of people have tended to accept this proposition as a political truth, never more so than today. But it is precisely this proposition that I desire to hold up for examination: is logic or dialectic, however brilliant, sufficient without the aid of rhetoric, for dealing with *res publicae,* with the things of common concern?

The first feature that strikes us about pure dialectic is that this mode of thinking is neutral toward the bearing of its reasoning upon actuality. The dialectician is interested in drawing out the implications of propositions.

He says: "If you accept this proposition, you must logically face these inferences," and so on. His work is thus with logical implicativeness, not with historical discovery. Hence if we define dialectic in this pure form, we are compelled to say that it is indifferent toward existential truth, because the only truth that it recognizes is the product of its own operation. Professor Mortimer Adler has made an observation on this point which will stand. He writes: "Truth when it is taken to mean an extrinsic relation of thinking to entities beyond the process of thought cannot be achieved by dialectical thinking."[2] In different language, an exclusive reliance upon dialectical thinking does not allow one to arrive at the truth of existing situations; it allows only the consistency of logical demonstration. This explains precisely why one can become too committed to dialectic for his own good and for the good of those whom he influences.

Because social situations are historical situations, dialectic alone is disruptive. The widespread overturning of institutions in recent history and the frustration man now feels over his inability to guide his destiny, begins, at the most profound level, with an uncritical commitment to this belief, the belief that logical inquiry alone, unaided by rhetoric, is sufficient for human counsels. The belief appears among us sometimes in a guise that is not penetrated. We hear it contended by many leaders of opinion that if men will only avoid emotional entanglements and will utilize science in coping with their problems, they will be able to conduct affairs with a success hitherto unknown. That is to say, if they will rely upon dialectic, which is the counterpart to science, in arriving at decisions, they will have the advantage of pure knowledge, whereas in the past they have tried to get along with a sorry mess of knowledge and feeling. My contention is the direct contrary: to give up the use of rhetoric, which deals in historical consciousness and feeling, is the straight road to that skepticism and paralysis which today affects so much of the thinking of the West.

No better illumination of the contrast between the two modes can be found than in the trial of Socrates himself. Certain aspects of this extraordinary incident show in clearest outline the relation of dialectic and rhetoric, and of both of these to practical policy.

The reflective portion of mankind has wondered for centuries how so brilliant and civilized a people as the Greeks could condemn to death this

2. Mortimer Adler, *Dialectic*, New York: 1927, p. 31.

famous philosopher. It would be blasphemous to suggest that the Athenian assembly did not commit a dreadful injustice. But since the condemnation occurred, there must have been some cause; and I think that the cause lies much deeper than the fact that some of the men with whom Socrates associated turned out badly, or the resentment of a few Athenians whose vanity he had wounded through his questioning. The people of Athens had a certain case against Socrates which can be understood and elucidated. Set against their own attitudes and behavior, the case may not look very good to us, and we can still say that they put to death the most virtuous man in the city. Yet something very interesting and important can be discovered through analyzing in a fresh way the lines of force that brought about the result.

Socrates has come down to us as one of the greatest ethical teachers of all time. But by the Athenians who indicted him he was charged with being a subverter and a corrupter. Before we set down these two ascriptions as wholly incompatible, let us remember that Socrates was also the greatest dialectician of his time. We who study him at this remote date are chiefly impressed with the ethical aspects of his teachings, but those who listened to him in Athens may have been more impressed by his method, which was that of dialectic. By turning his great dialectical skill upon persons and ideas, Socrates could well have engendered the feeling that he was an enemy of the culture which the Greeks had created. He was in one sense of course the highest expression of it, but the kind of skill he brought to a peak of development needs harmonizing with other things. As I have previously stressed, when a dialectic operates independently of the facts of a concrete situation, it can be destructive. A dialectic which becomes irresponsibly independent shatters the matrix which provides the basis of its operation. In this fact must have lain the real source of hostility toward Socrates. Indeed, Friedrich Nietzsche seems to have arrived at this profound perception in a passage of *The Birth of Tragedy*, where he writes:

> From this point onward Socrates conceives it his duty to correct existence; and with an air of irreverence and superiority, as the precursor of an altogether different culture, art, and morality, he enters single-handed into a world, to touch whose very hem would give us the greatest happiness.[3]

---

3. Friedrich Nietzsche, *The Birth of Tragedy* (trans. Clifton Fadiman), in *The Philosophy of Nietzsche*, New York: Modern Library, 1937, vol. 5, p. 253.

Socrates sometimes goes out of his way to call attention to his own apartness. We recall that he begins the *Apology* by telling his hearers that they are not going to hear a speaker of the clever kind; that is to say, they are not going to hear an orator of the kind they are accustomed to; if Socrates is a good speaker, it is not in the style of his accusers. They have said nothing that is true; he proposes to speak only the truth. Further along, he professes to be "an utter foreigner to the manner of speech here." Obviously this is not the way in which a speaker consolidates himself with his audience; it betokens alienation rather than identification. Socrates has said in effect at the beginning: "Your way is not my way."

Thereafter he gives an account of the origin of his unpopularity. He had gone around to men reputed to be wise and had questioned them about matters of which they were supposed to have knowledge. He found it easy to prove, through his method, that they were not wise, but ignorant, or that their knowledge was so confined that it could scarcely be termed knowledge. Among those who underwent this examination were public men or political leaders and poets, along with rival philosophers. Socrates offers a candid relation of how his peculiar method had irritated and angered these persons. But it is to the role of that method in the trial itself that I wish to direct chief attention; for Socrates, when his life was at stake, could not or would not give up the instrumentality by which he had been offending.

Let us look at the literal charge which has come down to us: "Socrates is a transgressor and a busybody, investigating things beneath the earth and in the heavens, and making the worse appear the better reason and teaching these things to others." Added to this was the further charge that Socrates did not recognize the gods but insisted on introducing a new idea of spiritual beings. Probably there are several ways in which this latter charge could have been answered. But the way in which Socrates chose to meet it was exactly the way to exacerbate the feelings of those whom he had earlier offended. It is significant that he feels compelled at one point to say to the assembly: "Please bear in mind not to make a disturbance if I conduct my argument in my accustomed manner." Here is the passage which follows that request.

SOCRATES: You say what is incredible, Melitus, and that, as appears to me, even to yourself. For this man, O Athenians! appears to me to be very insolent and intemperate, and to have preferred this indictment through downright insolence, intemperance and wantonness. For he seems, as it were, to have composed an enigma for the purpose of making an experiment. Whether will Socrates the wise know that I am jesting, and contradict myself, or shall I deceive him and all who hear me. For, in my opinion, he clearly contradicts himself in the indictment, as if he should say, Socrates is guilty of wrong in not believing that there are gods, and in believing that there are gods. And this, surely, is the act of one who is trifling.

Consider with me now, Athenians, in what respect he appears to me to say so. And do you, Melitus, answer me, and do ye, as I besought you at the outset, remember not to make an uproar if I speak after my usual manner.

Is there any man, Melitus, who believes that there are human affairs, but does not believe that there are men? Let him answer, judges, and not make so much noise. Is there anyone who does not believe that there are horses, but that there are things pertaining to horses? or who does not believe that there are pipers, but that there are things pertaining to pipes? There is not, O best of men! For since you are not willing to answer, I say it to you and to all here present. But answer to this at least: is there anyone who believes that there are things relating to demons, but does not believe that there are demons?

MELITUS: There is not.

SOCRATES: How obliging you are in having hardly answered, though compelled by these judges! You assert, then, that I do believe and teach things relating to demons, whether they be new or old; therefore, according to your admission, I do believe in things relating to demons, and this you have sworn in the bill of indictment. If, then, I believe in things relating to demons, there is surely an absolute necessity that I should believe that there are demons. Is it not so? It is. For I suppose you assent, since you do not answer. But with respect to demons, do we not allow that they are gods, or the children of gods? Do you admit this or not?

MELITUS: Certainly.

SOCRATES: Since, then, I allow that there are demons, as you admit, if demons are a kind of gods, this is the point in which I say you speak enigmatically and divert yourself in saying that I do not allow there are gods, and again that I do allow there are, since I allow that there are demons? But if demons are the children of gods, spurious ones, either from nymphs or any others, of whom they are reported to be, what man can think that there are sons of gods, and yet that there are not gods? For it would be just as absurd if anyone would think that there are mules, the offspring of horses and asses, but should not think that there are horses and asses. However, Melitus, it cannot be otherwise than that you have preferred this indictment for the purpose of trying me, or because you were at loss what real crime to allege against me, for that you should persuade any man who has the smallest degree of sense that the same person can think there are things relating to demons and to gods, and yet that there are neither demons, nor gods, nor heroes, is utterly impossible.[4]

This shows us in a clear enough way the weapon Socrates had wielded against so many of his contemporaries. It is, in fact, a fine example of the dialectical method: first the establishment of a class; then the drawing out of implications; and finally the exposure of the contradiction. If one believes that there are human affairs, one must believe that there are men. If one believes there are things pertaining to horses, one must believe that there are horses. If one believes that there are things relating to demons, then one must believe in the existence of demons, that is to say, gods or spirits. As far as pure logic goes, this may be impeccable. But after all, this is *not* the way one affirms one's belief in the gods. The very rationality of it suggests some lack of organic belief. It has almost the look of an exercise, or a trap or a trick, and one can imagine hearers not very sympathetic to the accused saying to themselves: "There is Socrates up to his old tricks again. That is the way he got into trouble. He is showing that he will never be different." We may suppose that the mean and sullen Melitus, his accuser at this point—and nothing good is intended of him here—was pleased rather than otherwise that Socrates was conducting himself so true to form. It underscored the allegations that were implied in the indictment.

This is not the only kind of argument offered by Socrates in his defense, it is true. In fact this particular argument is followed by a noble one based on analogy, in which he declared that just as he would not desert the station he was commanded to guard while he was a soldier, so he would not give

4. Plato, *Apology* (trans. Henry Cary), in *The Works of Plato*, London: G. Bell & Sons, 1858, vol. I.

up his duty of being a gadfly to the men of Athens, which role he felt had been assigned him by the gods. Yet there is in the *Apology* as a whole enough of the expert dialectician—of the man whose main concern is with logical inferences—to bring to the minds of the audience that side of Socrates which had aroused enmity.

The issue comes to a focus on this: Socrates appeared to be a teacher of virtue, but his method of teaching it did not commend itself to all people. Now we come to the possibility that they had a share of justice on their side, apart from the forms which the clash took in this particular trial. I have mentioned that Socrates had derided poets and politicians and rhetoricians. The result of this was to make the dialectician appear to stand alone as the possessor of wisdom and to exclude certain forms of cognition and expression which historically have a part in holding a culture together. It is not surprising if to the practitioners of these arts his dialectic looked overgrown, even menacing. And in truth it requires an extreme stand to rule out politics, poetry, and rhetoric. The use of a body of poetry in expressing the values of a culture will hardly be questioned except by one who takes the radical view presented by Plato in Book III of *The Republic*. But Socrates says in an early part of the *Apology* that when he went to the poets, he was ashamed to find that there was scarcely a man present "who could not speak better than they about the poems they themselves had composed." But speak how? Poets are often lamentably poor dialecticians if you drag them away from their poetry and force them to use explicit discourse; however, if they are good poets, they show reasoning power enough for their poetry. And they contribute something to the mind of which dialectic is incapable: feeling and motion.

The art of politics, though it often repels us in its degraded forms, cannot be totally abandoned in favor of speculation. Politics is a practical art. As such, it is concerned with man as a spatio-temporal creature; hence some political activity must take the form of compromise and adjustment. There is a certain relativism in it as a process, which fact is made inevitable by the human condition. We need not question that Socrates was an incomparably better man than most of the politicians who ruled Athens. The great and, if you will, tragic error made by him lay in assuming, as some of our rationalists and liberals today like to assume, that society is a debating club. Society is not a debating club, but a going concern. It cannot debate at once all the postulates on which it is based, as if nothing had ever been decided.

Certain issues it has to bring up and resolve from time to time of course, but to assume that none of its problems are any nearer solution than they were at the beginning is to confess total failure and invite chaos. Certain questions have to be regarded as settled questions, and certain policies with a great weight of tradition behind them have to be regarded as above the impertinence of rationalistic games. Here is where the rhetorician brings the resources of his art to bear.

The fact that Socrates had aroused the rhetoricians against him lends significance to this. We have seen how he loved to indulge in raillery against speechmakers. Now it is one thing to attack those who make verbal misleading their stock in trade, and it is another to attack rhetoric as an art.

Rhetoric is designed to move men's feelings in the direction of a goal. Therefore it is concerned not with abstract individuals but with man in being. Moreover, these men in being it has to consider in relation to forces in being. Rhetoric begins with the assumption that man is born into history. If he is to be moved, the arguments addressed to him must have historicity as well as logicality. To explain: when Aristotle opens his discussion of rhetoric in the celebrated treatise of that name, he asserts that it is a counterpart of dialectic. He then distinguishes the two by saying that dialectic always tries to discover the real syllogism in the argument whereas rhetoric tries to discover the real means of persuasion. From this emerges a difference of procedure, in which dialectic makes use of inductions and syllogisms whereas rhetoric makes use of examples and enthymemes. Indeed, Aristotle explicitly calls the use of example "rhetorical induction," and he calls the enthymeme the "rhetorical syllogism." This bears out the idea that rhetoric must be concerned with real or historical situations, although dialectic can attain its goal in a self-existing realm of discourse. Now the example is something taken from life, and the force of the example comes from the fact that it *is* or *was*. It is the thing already possessed in experience and so is the property of everyone through the sharing of a common past. Through examples the rhetorician appeals to matters that everybody has in a way participated in. These are the possible already made actual, and the audience is expected to be moved by their historicity.

The relation of rhetoric to "things-in-being" appears even more closely in the "rhetorical syllogism." The enthymeme, as students of logic discover, is a syllogism with one of its propositions missing. The reason the missing proposition is omitted is that it is presumed to exist already in the mind of the one to whom the argument is addressed. The rhetorician simply recognizes the wide acceptance of this proposition and assumes it as a part of his argument. Propositions which can be assumed in this manner are settled beliefs, standing convictions, and established attitudes of the people. These are the "topics" to which he goes for his sources of persuasion.

Thus through the employment of the enthymeme the rhetorician enters into a solidarity with his audience by agreeing with one of its perceptions of reality, and this step of course enables him to pass on to his conclusion. If a speaker should say, "The magistrate is an elected official and must therefore heed the will of the people," he would be assuming a major premise, which is that "All elected officials must heed the will of the people." That unsupplied, yet conceded, proposition gives him a means by which he can obtain force for his argument. Therefore, quite as in the case of the example, he is resorting to something already acknowledged as "actual."

Dialectic is left with a different though adjunctive function. The mere demonstration of logical connection is not enough to persuade; every speaker of experience knows this. People must be approached through certain "topics" or common perceptions of reality. It is these, as we have now seen, that rhetoric assumes in its enthymemes, taking the ordinary man's understanding of things and working from that to something that needs to be made evident and compulsive. Dialectic lies behind the rhetorical argument, but is not equivalent to it.

In sum, dialectic is epistemic and logical; it is concerned with discriminating into categories and knowing definitions. While this has the indispensable function of promoting understanding in the realm of ideas, by its very nature it does not tell a man what he must do. It tells him only how the terms and propositions he uses are related. It permits him to use the name of a species as a term without ever attending to whether the species exists and is therefore a force-in-being. That might be sufficient if the whole destiny of man were to know, but we are reminded that the end of living is activity and not mere cognition. Dialectic, through being rational and intellectual merely, does not heed the imperatives of life, which help give direction to the thought of the man of wisdom. The individual who tries to make his approach to life through dialectic alone does violence to life through his abstractive process. At the same time he makes himself anti-social because his discriminations are apart from the organic feeling of the community for what goes on. From this it follows that the dialectician is only half of a wise man and something less than a philosopher king, inasmuch as he leaves out the urgent reality of the actual, with which all wise rulers and judges know they have to deal.

Now to look at the other side for a moment, one of the complaints we recurrently hear against the rhetorician is that he is always going over old ground, reiterating familiar things, dressing up old values, and reminding us again of common sentiments. In a large measure this must be true, though if he does this in an obtrusive or irksome way, he is an inferior master of his art. For the duty of the rhetorician is to take into account the consensus, to recall us to our partnership in belief—in short, to remind us of what we are before he goes on to considerations of policy. Let us remember for a moment how glowingly Pericles dwells upon Athens as "the school of Hellas" to inspire the Athenians to renewed effort in the Peloponnesian War. Without some comparable feeling a commonwealth does not exist, for people will act in a common cause only while they are conscious of an identity of sentiment.

The conclusion to which we are drawn is that a society cannot exist without a social bond, nor a social bond without rhetorical impulse. There are some things which the community needs to believe, and these beliefs come to us couched in rhetorical terms, which tell us what attitudes to take. To put them to the test of dialectic alone, leaving out the accumulated pressure of history, is to destroy the basis of belief and thus to remove the source of cohesiveness. The crucial defect of dialectic alone is that it ends in what might be called social agnosticism. The dialectician knows, but he knows in a vacuum; or, he knows, but he is without knowledge of how to act. Unless he is sustained by a faith at one end or the other—unless he embraced something before he began the dialectical process or unless he embraces it afterward—he remains this inassimilable social agnostic. Society does not know what to do with him because his very existence is a kind of satire or aspersion upon its necessity to act. Or, it does know what to do with him in a very crude and unpleasant form: it will put him away. Those who have to cope with passing reality feel that neutrality is a kind of desertion. In addition to understanding, they expect some motive for action, and we must concede them some claim to this.

In thus trying to isolate the pure dialectician, we have momentarily lost sight of Socrates. We must recognize that he did not in all his acts evince this determination to separate himself from the life of his culture. He served the state loyally as a soldier, and he refused the opportunity to escape after the state had condemned him. His reasoning, in some of its lines, supports the kind of identification with history which I am describing as that of the whole man.

Still, the indictment "too much of a dialectician" has not been quashed. The trial itself can be viewed as a supremely dramatic incident in a far longer and broader struggle between rationalism on the one hand and poetry and rhetoric (and belief) on the other. This conflict reappears in the later battle between Hellenic philosophy, with its rationalistic bias, and Christianity, which ended after centuries in a sweeping victory for the latter. Christianity provided what Greek dialectic had left out. It spoke to the feelings and, what is of paramount significance, it had a background of historical fact. The Christian always had the story of Jesus with which to start his homilies. This was the great *exemplum,* or example; he could argue from a fact, and this at once put him on grounds to persuade. Aristotle observes in his *Rhetoric* that in conversing with the multitude we do not aim at fresh scientific demonstration; we rest our arguments on generally accepted beliefs and principles, or broadly speaking upon things received. Practically, the victory of Christianity over Hellenic rationalism bears out the soundness of this insight. The Christians have always worked through the poetry of their great story and through appeal to many facts as having happened; for example, the lives of martyrs and saints. Dialectic has been present, for it is never absent from rational discourse, but poetry and rhetoric were there to make up the winning combination.

Hellenic rationalism waned before man's need for some kind of faith and before a pessimism about human nature which deepened as history lengthened. It is interesting that Nietzsche refers to Socrates as an "optimist," and indeed there is something optimistic about all rationalism. This idealization of reason is the Achilles' heel of Greek philosophy. If there is one thing that the Judaic and Christian faiths have been fiercely positive about, it is man's proneness to fall. And as for the darker side of man's nature, what can set this forth but a powerful rhetoric? Dialectic may put it before us in a conditional way, but it is up to the elaboration and iteration of rhetoric to make it real and overwhelming. Plato may have provided some of the reasoning behind Christian doctrine, but Paul and Augustine supplied the persuasion, and what emerged from this took over the power of Rome.

There seems little doubt that the weakening of this great source of Western culture and the present decline of rhetoric are linked together. At the beginning I spoke of a resentment against the orator as a man who engages in hortatory discourse. This resentment arises from an awareness that the orator is a teacher and a moral teacher at that. Anyone who uses words which he hopes will move men in a direction which he has chosen must wade boldly into rhetoric and morality. But here is where a chief point of contention arises. There are persons today, some of them even holding high positions in education, who pretend to believe that it is improper for one individual to try to persuade another. A curious name which has been invented for the act of persuasion is "psychological coercion." The users seem not to recognize that the term itself is a highly loaded rhetorical phrase, designed to sway people in the direction of their doctrine, which is a kind of "hands-off" policy. Do not meddle with people's beliefs; only teach them to think. Teach them to think and they will set the right course for themselves. This is unmistakably a fresh eruption of the old optimistic rationalism.

The student of language finds this insistently being put forward in the form of what is called semantics. The advocates of the semantic approach propose to ascertain definitely the relation between words and the things they stand for with the object of making signification more "scientific." They believe in general that traditional speech is filled with terms which stand for nonexistent things, empty ideas, and primitive beliefs which get in the way of man's adaptation to environment. For them the function of speech is communication, and communication must be about things that really are. (One cannot read their literature very long without sensing the strong political motivation that inspires their position. A considerable part of their writing is a more or less open polemic against those features of speech which they regard as reflecting or upholding our traditional form of society.) At any rate, they argue that unless we can establish that what we are talking about exists objectively, then we had better not talk at all. They want a vocabulary purified of all terms that are tainted with the subjectivity of the user, or at least they want to identify all such terms and place them in a quarantine ward. Hence, teach people to speak in uncolorful language and they will communicate only the truth. It is a dialectic cut down to primitive referents.

The great and evident error of the semanticists lies in their failure to perceive that language is by its very nature sermonic. Words are very close to volitions; speaking and willing go hand in hand. Rarely do we open our mouths except to enunciate something which is either action or attitude. And there is much of ourselves in this, inevitably and properly. Language is not a mere geography of the external world. The connections between a word and what it stands for cannot be determined in the way that they seem to believe. They go on the assumption that there is some extra-linguistic way of deciding what a word should mean, some point outside language from which one can judge the appropriateness of any choice of words for expression. Yet the effort to get around language thus and to apply extra-linguistic yardsticks is doomed to failure even in the case of words symbolizing physical objects. Some words stand for things, but they do not stand for them in the shape of the things. Language is a closed system, into which there is only one mode of entrance, and that is through meaning. Furthermore, what a word means is related also to context, with all the inter-modification which can be involved. A word does not get into the system through its objective fidelity to an object—this would indeed give us an "other-directed" world—but through its capacity to render what the object means to us.

The position of the semanticist is further weakened by a supposition that all words stand for things that are classifiable with phenomena. Here they are ignoring the immensely important role of the subjective in life. There are numberless ideas, images, feelings, and intuitions which cannot be described and classified in the same way as data of the senses, but which have a great effect upon our decisions in conduct. A rhetoric can take these into account, modify, direct, and use them, because rhetoric habitually deals in depth and tendency. A dialectic in the form of semantics cannot do this, because it is interested only in defining words as reflections of an outside physical order; for as I have pointed out, their prime concern is with whether a referent really "exists."

On first thought this might seem to give them the kind of respect for the actual order that is shown by believers in history and rhetoric. Yet a distinc-

tion is necessary: history is not the simple data of the perceptive consciousness; it is the experience of men after that has been assimilated and worked
upon by the reflective consciousness. The appeal to history is an appeal to
events made meaningful, and the meaning of events cannot be conveyed
through the simple positive references that semantic analysis elevates as an
ideal. Hence the semanticist is condemned by his own theory to be a neu-
tralist, who must say, "Here is the world expressed in language which has
been freed from tendency and subjective coloration." What is to be done
with the world is, as it were, postponed until the next meeting. Or, there is
nothing for this agnostic of values to do, even when it has been decided that
the referent of the word does exist, except to turn matters over to others
whose horizons are not bounded by logical positivism.

Socrates was saved from trivialization of this kind by his initial commitment to the Beautiful and the Good. He is also saved in our eyes by the
marvelous rhetoric of Plato. These were not enough to save him personally
in the great crisis of his life, but they gave high seriousness to the quest
which he represents. Modern exponents of positivism and semantics have
nothing like these to give respectability to their undertaking or persuasiveness to their cause. But both are in the long view victims of supposing that
definition and classification are sufficient for the ends of speech.

In a summing up, we can see that dialectic, when not accompanied by
historical consciousness and responsibility, works to dissolve those opinions
and feelings and evaluations which hold society together. It is even contumacious toward the "given," ignoring it or seeking to banish it in favor of a
merely self-consistent exposition of ideas. It is without commitment to
practical realities and is therefore essentially revolutionary.

In our own time and country we have had occasion to witness the disruptive effect of a dialectic not regardful of the rhetorical situation. The nation
is still torn over certain famous court decisions aimed at revolutionizing
established traditions and regimes. The effect of these decisions, in the
words of a writer as cautious as Judge Learned Hand, is to "set up racial
equality as a value that must prevail over all conflicting interests." How did
the Justices arrive at that doctrine? Two possibilities suggest themselves.
Either they were proceeding as legal dialecticians and were indifferent to
the bearing of the conclusion upon realities. Or, they were not indifferent
to the bearing of it, in which case they were setting themselves up as a third

legislative chamber and re-valuing the legislation of states. I am more struck with it as a dialectical gambit, a playing with words such as "equal," "unequal," "separate," and "inferior," with dogmatic equalitarianism as a starting premise. Whatever may be true in the realm of mathematics, it plainly is not true in the realm of the actual that equals are identicals. As soon as we pass from the mathematical–logical sphere to the world of the concrete, this truth becomes evident. The American people have always accommodated the idea of equality to certain historical facts and traditions, one of which could be called the fact of freedom, which includes individual and group choices and rejections. Under the influence of these decisions, many kinds of restraints are being attempted in various parts of the country which look for their sanction to the idea that racial equality is paramount over all other considerations. But absolutism in social and moral affairs is a kind of dialectical extravagance which cannot be harmonized with many facts of cultural life.

If this analysis is correct, what we see sometimes is an attempt to reach through a dialectical operation something which the country as a whole— that is, the consensus of the people—would very doubtfully approve were the question thrown open so that the rhetoric of experience might have its part in the determination. It is a confirming instance of how dialectic as the manipulation of ideas can outreach and subvert an existing civil order.

A civil order is a going concern; it is neither produced nor preserved merely by theorizing from absolutes. Its guardians must take constant recognition of that circumstantial world which is extrinsic to simple logical processes. To assume that we can readily correct existence by dialectical extrapolation is a form of presumption, not to say madness. Plato expressed the belief that God forever geometrizes. One might add in following that God forever dialecticizes, but that it is up to human beings to rhetoricize. To suppose that we should think and expect others to think in purely dialectical terms is to expect man to think as a god, and one of the precepts of ancient wisdom is that we should think as mortals. Whom the gods would destroy they entice into believing that they can think as gods—this might be a commentary upon that famous saying.

The divergence today between conservative and traditional policies and the policies of totalitarian radicalism can be well marked out by this line. The one attempts a full cognition of the realities before deciding how far a principle is applicable. The other looks upon the principle as self-vindicating and tries, usually at great cost and loss, to impose it upon a resisting world. Rhetoric, from its very nature, begins with a respect for the facts, and for feelings, which are also facts. It is therefore properly entitled to be called humane.

Indeed, there is ample ground for saying that rhetoric is the most humane of the humanities. This fact goes far toward explaining why today it is on the defensive. It is curious but true that man himself is presently under attack from many quarters. So many of our intellectuals and experts seem not to like man anymore. They are busy drawing his image anew. The materialists would reduce him to a whorl of molecules. Some psychologists would reduce him to a set of reflexes. The advocates of scientific socialism see him as a creature dragged along by ponderous historical forces. We can recognize some features of him in each of these caricatures. But only rhetoric continues to see him steadily and see him whole; only rhetoric continues to deal with the historically verified man, who is all these and much more—continues to deal with him and continues to like him. But this is not sentimentality; it is the wider vision accompanied by what the Christians called *caritas*—"charitable love."

If man himself is under attack, it is no cause for surprise that the most humanistic of the humanities should feel the same pressure. But that rhetoric will survive these scientistic disparagements there is hardly any question. The pity is that the attacks should ever have been made at all since, proceeding from contempt for history and ignorance of the nature of man, they produce confusion, skepticism, and inaction. In the restored man dialectic and rhetoric will go hand in hand, in a harmonious regime of the human faculties. That is why the recovery of value and community in our time calls for a restatement of the role of rhetoric in maintaining a society and a culture.

Language Is Sermonic[1]

Our age has witnessed the decline of a number of subjects that once enjoyed prestige and general esteem, but no subject, I believe, has suffered more amazingly in this respect than rhetoric. When one recalls that a century ago rhetoric was regarded as the most important humanistic discipline taught in our colleges—when one recalls this fact and contrasts it with the very different situation prevailing today—he is forced to see that a great shift of valuation has taken place. In those days, in the not-so-distant nineteenth century, to be a professor of rhetoric, one had to be *somebody*. This was a teaching task that was thought to call for ample and varied resources, and it was recognized as addressing itself to the most important of all ends, the persuading of human beings to adopt right attitudes and act in response to them. That was no assignment for the plodding sort of professor. That sort of teacher might do a middling job with subject matter courses, where the main object is to impart information, but the teacher of rhetoric had to be a person of gifts and imagination who could illustrate, as the need arose, how to make words even in prose take on wings. I remind you of the chairs of rhetoric that still survive in title in some of our older universities. And I should add, to develop the full picture, that literature was then viewed as a subject which practically anyone could teach. No special gift, other than perhaps industry, was needed to relate facts about authors and periods. That was held to be rather pedestrian work. But the instructor in rhetoric was expected to be a man of stature. Today, I scarcely need point out, the situation has been exactly reversed. Today it is the teacher of literature who passes through a long period of training, who is supposed to possess the mysteries of a learned craft, and who is placed by his very speciality on a height of eminence. His knowledge of the intricacies of Shakespeare or

1. In Roger E. Nebergall (ed.), *Dimensions of Rhetorical Scholarship.* Norman: University of Oklahoma Department of Speech, 1963, 49–63.

Keats or Joyce and his sophistication in the critical doctrines that have been developed bring him the esteem of the academy. We must recognize in all fairness that the elaboration of critical techniques and special approaches has made the teaching of literature a somewhat more demanding profession, although some think that it has gone in that direction beyond the point of diminishing returns. Still, this is not enough to account for the relegation of rhetoric. The change has gone so far that now it is discouraging to survey the handling of this study in our colleges and universities. With a few honorable exceptions it is given to just about anybody who will take it. The "inferior, unlearned, mechanical, merely instrumental members of the profession"—to recall a phrase of a great master of rhetoric, Edmund Burke—have in their keeping what was once assigned to the leaders. Beginners, part-time teachers, graduate students, faculty wives, and various fringe people are now the instructional staff of an art which was once supposed to require outstanding gifts and mature experience. (We must note that at the same time the course itself has been allowed to decline from one dealing philosophically with the problems of expression to one which tries to bring below-par students up to the level of accepted usage.) Indeed, the wheel of fortune would seem to have turned for rhetoric; what was once at the top is now at the bottom, and because of its low estate, people begin to wonder on what terms it can survive at all.

We are not faced here, however, with the wheel of fortune; we are faced with something that has come over the minds of men. Changes that come over the minds of men are not inscrutable, but have at some point their identifiable causes. In this case we have to deal with the most potent of cultural causes, an alteration of man's image of man. Something has happened in the recent past to our concept of what man is; a decision was made to look upon him in a new light, and from this decision new bases of evaluation have proceeded, which affect the public reputation of rhetoric. This changed concept of man is best described by the word "scientistic," a term which denotes the application of scientific assumptions to subjects which are not wholly comprised of naturalistic phenomena. Much of this is a familiar tale, but to understand the effect of the change, we need to recall that the great success of scientific or positivistic thinking in the nineteenth century induced a belief that nothing was beyond the scope of its method. Science, and its off-spring applied science, were doing so much to alter and, it was thought, to improve the material conditions of the world, that a next step with the same process seemed in order. Why should not science turn its apparatus upon man, whom all the revelations of religion and the speculations of philosophy seemed still to have left an enigma, with the promise of much better result? It came to be believed increasingly that to think validly was to think scientifically, and that subject matters made no difference.

Now the method of scientific investigation is, as T. H. Huxley reminded us in a lecture which does great credit to him as a rhetorician, merely the method of logic. Induction and deduction and causal inference applied to the phenomena of nature yielded the results with which science was changing the landscape and revolutionizing the modes of industry. From this datum it was an easy inference that men ought increasingly to become scientists, and again, it was a simple derivative from this notion that man at his best is a logic machine, or at any rate an austerely unemotional thinker. Furthermore, carried in the train of this conception was the thought, not often expressed of course, that things would be better if man did not give in so far to being human in the humanistic sense. In the shadow of the victories of science, his humanism fell into progressive disparagement. Just what comprises humanism is not a simple matter for analysis. Rationality is an indispensable part to be sure, yet humanity includes emotionality, or the capacity to feel and suffer, to know pleasure, and it includes the capacity for aesthetic satisfaction, and, what can be only suggested, a yearning to be in relation with something infinite. This last is his religious passion, or his aspiration to feel significant and to have a sense of belonging in a world that is productive of much frustration. These at least are the properties of humanity. Well, man had been human for some thousands of years, and where had it gotten him? Those who looked forward to a scientistic Utopia were inclined to think that his humanness had been a drag on his progress; human qualities were weaknesses, except for that special quality of rationality, which might be expected to redeem him.

However curious it may appear, this notion gained that man should live down his humanity and make himself a more efficient source of those logical inferences upon which a scientifically accurate understanding of the world depends. As the impulse spread, it was the emotional and subjective components of his being that chiefly came under criticism, for reasons that have just been indicated. Emotion, and logic or science, do not consort; the latter must be objective, faithful to what is out there in the public domain and conformable to the processes of reason. Whenever emotion is allowed to put in an oar, it gets the boat off true course. Therefore emotion is a liability.

Under the force of this narrow reasoning, it was natural that rhetoric should pass from a status in which it was regarded as of questionable worth to a still lower one in which it was positively condemned. For the most obvious truth about rhetoric is that its object is the whole man. It presents its arguments first to the rational part of man, because rhetorical discourses, if they are honestly conceived, always have a basis in reasoning. Logical argument is the plot, as it were, of any speech or composition that is designed to persuade. Yet it is the very characterizing feature of rhetoric that it goes beyond this and appeals to other parts of man's constitution, especially to his nature as a pathetic being, that is, a being feeling and suffering. A speech intended to persuade achieves little unless it takes into account how men are reacting subjectively to their hopes and fears and their special circumstances. The fact that Aristotle devotes a large proportion of his *Rhetoric* to how men feel about different situations and actions is an evidence of how prominently these considerations bulked even in the eyes of a master theorist.

Yet there is one further fact, more decisive than any of these, to prove that rhetoric is addressed to man in his humanity. Every speech which is designed to move is directed to a special audience in its unique situation. (We could not except even those radio appeals to "the world." Their audience has a unique place in time.) Here is but a way of pointing out that rhetoric is intended for historical man, or for man as conditioned by history. It is part of the *conditio humana* that we live at particular times and in particular places. These are productive of special or unique urgencies, which the speaker has got to recognize and to estimate. Hence, just as man from the point of view of rhetoric is not purely a thinking machine, or a mere seat of rationality, so he is not a creature abstracted from time and place. If science deals with the abstract and the universal, rhetoric is near the other end, dealing in significant part with the particular and the concrete. It would be the height of wishful thinking to say that this ought not be so. As long as man is born into history, he will be feeling and responding to historical pressures. All of these reasons combine to show why rhetoric should be considered the most humanistic of the humanities. It is directed to that part of our being which is not merely rational, for it supplements the rational approach. And it is directed to individual men in their individual situations, so that by the very definitions of the terms here involved, it takes into account what science deliberately, to satisfy its own purposes, leaves out. There is consequently no need for wonder that, in an age that has been influenced to distrust and disregard what is characteristically human, rhetoric should be a prime target of attack. If it is a weakness to harbor feelings, and if furthermore it is a weakness to be caught up in historical situations, then rhetoric is construable as a dealer in weaknesses. That man is in this condition religion, philosophy, and literature have been teaching for thousands of years. Criticism of it from the standpoint of a scientistic Utopia is the new departure.

The incompleteness of the image of man as a creature who should make use of reason only can be demonstrated in another way. It is a truism that logic is a subject without a subject matter. That is to say, logic is a set of rules and devices which are equally applicable whatever the data. As the science of the forms of reasoning, it is a means of interpreting and utilizing the subject matters of the various fields which do have their proper contents. Facts from science or history or literature, for example, may serve in the establishment of an inductive generalization. Similar facts may be fed into a syllogism. Logic is merely the mechanism for organizing the data of other provinces of knowledge. Now it follows from this truth that if a man could convert himself into a pure logic machine or thinking machine, he would have no special relation to any body of knowledge. All would be grist for his mill, as the phrase goes. He would have no inclination, no partiality, no particular affection. His mind would work upon one thing as indifferently as upon another. He would be an eviscerated creature or a depassionated one, standing in the same relationship to the realities of the world as the thinking technique stands to the data on which it is employed. He would be a thinking robot, a concept which horrifies us precisely because the robot has nothing to think about.

A confirmation of this truth lies in the fact that rhetoric can never be reduced to symbology. Logic is increasingly becoming "symbolic logic";

that is its tendency. But rhetoric always comes to us in well-fleshed words, and that is because it must deal with the world, the thickness, stubbornness, and power of it.[2]

Everybody recognizes that there is thus a formal logic. A number of eminent authorities have written of rhetoric as if it were formal in the same sense and degree. Formal rhetoric would be a set of rules and devices for persuading anybody about anything. If one desires a certain response, one uses a certain device, or "trick" as the enemies of the art would put it. The set of appeals that rhetoric provides is analogized with the forms of thought that logic prescribes. Rhetoric conceived in this fashion has an adaptability and a virtuosity equal to those of logic.

But the comparison overlooks something, for at one point we encounter a significant difference. Rhetoric has a relationship to the world which logic does not have and which forces the rhetorician to keep his eye upon reality as well as upon the character and situation of his audience. The truth of this is seen when we begin to examine the nature of the traditional "topics." The topics were first formulated by Aristotle and were later treated also by Cicero and Quintilian and by many subsequent writers on the subject of persuasion. They are a set of "places" or "regions" where one can go to find the substance for persuasive argument. Cicero defines a topic as "the seat of an argument." In function they are sources of content for speeches that are designed to influence. Aristotle listed a considerable number of them, but for our purposes they can be categorized very broadly. In reading or interpreting the world of reality, we make use of four very general ideas. The first three are usually expressed, in the language of philosophy, as being, cause, and relationship. The fourth, which stands apart from these because it is an external source, is testimony and authority.

One way to interpret a subject is to define its nature—to describe the fixed features of its being. Definition is an attempt to capture essence. When we speak of the nature of a thing, we speak of something we expect to persist. Definitions accordingly deal with fundamental and unchanging properties.

2. I might add that a number of years ago the Mathematics Staff of the College at the University of Chicago made a wager with the English Staff that they could write the Declaration of Independence in mathematical language. They must have had later and better thoughts about this, for we never saw the mathematical rendition.

Another way to interpret a subject is to place it in a cause-and-effect relationship. The process of interpretation is then to affirm it as the cause of some effect or as the effect of some cause. And the attitudes of those who are listening will be affected according to whether or not they agree with our cause-and-effect analysis.

A third way to interpret a subject is in terms of relationships of similarity and dissimilarity. We say that it is like something which we know in fuller detail, or that it is unlike that thing in important respects. From such a comparison conclusions regarding the subject itself can be drawn. This is a very common form of argument, by which probabilities can be established. And since probabilities are all we have to go on in many questions of this life, it must be accounted a usable means of persuasion.

The fourth category, the one removed from the others by the fact of its being an external source, deals not with the evidence directly but accepts it on the credit of testimony or authority. If we are not in position to see or examine, but can procure the deposition of some one who is, the deposition may become the substance of our argument. We can slip it into a syllogism just as we would a defined term. The same is true of general statements which come from quarters of great authority or prestige. If a proposition is backed by some weighty authority, like the Bible, or can be associated with a great name, people may be expected to respond to it in accordance with the veneration they have for these sources. In this way evidence coming from the outside is used to influence attitudes or conduct.

Now we see that in all these cases the listener is being asked not simply to follow a valid reasoning form but to respond to some presentation of reality. He is being asked to agree with the speaker's interpretation of the world that is. If the definition being offered is a true one, he is expected to recognize this and to say, at least inwardly, "Yes, that is the way the thing is." If the exposition of a cause-and-effect relationship is true, he may be expected to concur that X is the cause of such a consequence or that such a consequence has its cause in X. And according to whether this is a good or a bad cause or a good or a bad consequence, he is disposed to preserve or remove the cause, and so on. If he is impressed with the similarity drawn between two things, he is as a result more likely to accept a policy which involves treating something in the same way in which its analogue is treated. He has been influenced by a relationship of comparability. And finally, if he has been confronted with testimony or authority from sources he respects, he will receive this as a reliable, if secondary, kind of information about reality. In these four ways he has been persuaded to read the world as the speaker reads it.

At this point, however, I must anticipate an objection. The retort might be made: "These are extremely formal categories you are enumerating. I fail to see how they are any less general or less indifferently applicable than the formal categories of logic. After all, definitions and so on can be offered of anything. You still have not succeeded in making rhetoric a substantive study."

In replying, I must turn here to what should be called the office of rhetoric. Rhetoric seen in the whole conspectus of its function is an art of emphasis embodying an order of desire. Rhetoric is advisory; it has the office of advising men with reference to an independent order of goods and with reference to their particular situation as it relates to these. The honest rhetorician therefore has two things in mind: a vision of how matters should go ideally and ethically and a consideration of the special circumstances of his auditors. Toward both of these he has a responsibility.

I shall take up first how his responsibility to the order of the goods or to the hierarchy of realities may determine his use of the topics.

When we think of rhetoric as one of the arts of civil society (and it must be a free society, since the scope for rhetoric is limited and the employment of it constrained under a despotism) we see that the rhetorician is faced with a choice of means in appealing to those whom he can prevail upon to listen to him. If he is at all philosophical, it must occur to him to ask whether there is a standard by which the sources of persuasion can be ranked. In a phrase, is there a preferred order of them, so that, in a scale of ethics, it is nobler to make use of one sort of appeal than another? This is of course a question independent of circumstantial matters, yet a fundamental one. We all react to some rhetoric as "untruthful" or "unfair" or "cheap," and this very feeling is evidence of the truth that it is possible to use a better or a worse style of appeal. What is the measure of the better style? Obviously this question cannot be answered at all in the absence of some conviction about the nature and destiny of man. Rhetoric inevitably impinges upon morality and politics; and if it is one of the means by which we endeavor to improve the character and the lot of men, we have to think of its methods and sources in relation to a scheme of values.

To focus the problem a little more sharply, when one is asking men to cooperate with him in thinking this or doing that, when is he asking in the name of the highest reality, which is the same as saying, when is he asking in the name of their highest good?

Naturally, when the speaker replies to this question, he is going to express his philosophy, or more precisely, his metaphysics. My personal reply would be that he is making the highest order of appeal when he is basing his case on definition or the nature of the thing. I confess that this goes back to a very primitive metaphysics, which holds that the highest reality is being, not becoming. It is a quasi-religious metaphysics, if you will, because it ascribes to the highest reality qualities of stasis, immutability, eternal per-durance—qualities that in Western civilization are usually expressed in the language of theism. That which is perfect does not change; that which has to change is less perfect. Therefore if it is possible to determine unchanging essences or qualities and to speak in terms of these, one is appealing to what is most real in so doing. From another point of view, this is but getting people to see what is most permanent in existence, or what transcends the world of change and accident. The realm of essence is the realm above the flux of phenomena, and definitions are of essences and genera.

I may have expressed this view in somewhat abstruse language in order to place it philosophically, yet the practice I am referring to is everyday enough, as a simple illustration will make plain. If a speaker should define man as a creature with an indefeasible right to freedom and should upon this base an argument that a certain man or group of men are entitled to freedom, he would be arguing from definition. Freedom is an unchanging attribute of his subject; it can accordingly be predicated of whatever falls within the genus man. Stipulative definitions are of the ideal, and in this fact lies the reason for placing them at the top of the hierarchy. If the real progress of man is toward knowledge of ideal truth, it follows that this is an appeal to his highest capacity—his capacity to apprehend what exists absolutely.

The next ranking I offer tentatively, but it seems to me to be relationship or similitude and its subvarieties. I have a consistent impression that the broad resource of analogy, metaphor, and figuration is favored by those of a poetic and imaginative cast of mind. We make use of analogy or compari-son when the available knowledge of the subject permits only probable proof. Analogy is reasoning from something we know to something we do not know in one step; hence there is no universal ground for predication. Yet behind every analogy lurks the possibility of a general term. The general term is never established as such, for that would change the argument to one of deductive reasoning with a universal or distributed middle. The user of analogy is hinting at an essence which cannot at the moment be produced. Or, he may be using an indirect approach for reason of tact; analogies not infrequently do lead to generalizations, and he may be employing this approach because he is respectful of his audience and desires them to use their insight.

I mentioned a moment earlier that this type of argument seems to be preferred by those of a poetic or non-literal sort of mind. That fact suggests yet another possibility, which I offer still more diffidently, asking your indulgence if it seems to border on the whimsical. The explanation would be that the cosmos *is* one vast system of analogy, so that our profoundest intuitions of it are made in the form of comparisons. To affirm that something is like something else is to begin to talk about the unitariness of creation. Everything is like everything else somehow, so that we have a ladder of similitude mounting up to the final one-ness—to something like a unity in godhead. Furthermore, there is about this source of argument a kind of decent reticence, a recognition of the unknown along with the known. There is a recognition that the unknown may be continuous with the known, so that man is moving about in a world only partly realized, yet real in all its parts. This is the mood of poetry and mystery, but further adumbration of it I leave to those more gifted than I.

Cause and effect appears in this scale to be a less exalted source of argument, though we all have to use it because we are historical men. Here I must recall the metaphysical ground of this organization and point out that it operates in the realm of becoming. Causes are causes having effect and effects are resulting from causes. To associate this source of argument with its habitual users, I must note that it is heard most commonly from those who are characteristically pragmatic in their way of thinking. It is not unusual today to find a lengthy piece of journalism or an entire political speech which is nothing but a series of arguments from consequence—completely devoid of reference to principle or defined ideas. We rightly recognize these as sensational types of appeal. Those who are partial to arguments based on effect are under a temptation to play too much upon the fears of their audience by stressing the awful nature of some consequence or by exaggerating the power of some cause. Modern advertising is prolific in this kind of abuse. There is likewise a temptation to appeal to prudential considerations only in a passage where things are featured as happening or threatening to happen.

An even less admirable subvariety of this source is the appeal to circumstance, which is the least philosophical of all the topics of argument. Circumstance is an allowable source when we don't know anything else to plead, in which cases we say, "There is nothing else to be done about it." Of all the arguments, it admits of the least perspicaciousness. An example of this which we hear nowadays with great regularity is: "We must adapt ourselves to a fast-changing world." This is pure argument from circumstance. It does not pretend, even, to offer a cause-and-effect explanation. If it did, the first part would tell us why we must adapt ourselves to a fast-changing world; and the second would tell us the result of our doing so. The usually heard formulation does neither. Such argument is preeminently lacking in understanding or what the Greeks called *dianoia*. It simply cites a brute circumstance and says, "Step lively." Actually, this argument amounts to a surrender of reason. Maybe it expresses an instinctive feeling that in this situation reason is powerless. Either you change fast or you get crushed. But surely it would be a counsel of desperation to try only this argument in a world suffering from aimlessness and threatened with destruction.

Generally speaking, cause and effect is a lower-order source of argument because it deals in the realm of the phenomenal, and the phenomenal is easily converted into the sensational. Sensational excitements always run the risk of arousing those excesses which we deplore as sentimentality or brutality.

Arguments based on testimony and authority, utilizing external sources, have to be judged in a different way. Actually, they are the other sources seen through other eyes. The question of their ranking involves the more general question of the status of authority. Today there is a widespread notion that all authority is presumptuous; "Authority is authoritarian" seems to be the root idea. Consequently it is held improper to try to influence anyone by the prestige of great names or of sanctioned pronouncements. This is a presumption itself, by which every man is presumed to be his own competent judge in all matters. But since that is a manifest impossibility, and is becoming a greater impossibility all the time, as the world piles up bodies of specialized knowledge which no one person can hope to command, arguments based on authority are certainly not going to disappear. The sound maxim is that an argument based on authority is as good as the authority. What we should hope for is a new and discriminating attitude toward what is authoritative, and I would like to see some source recognized as having moral authority. This hope will have to wait upon the recovery of a more stable order of values and the re-recognition of qualities in persons. Speaking most generally, arguments from authority are ethically good when they are deferential toward real hierarchy.

With that we may sum up the rhetorical speaker's obligation toward the ideal, apart from particular determinations. If one accepts the possibility of this or any other ranking, one has to concede that rhetoric is not merely formal; it is realistic. It is not a playing with counters; its impulses come from insights into actuality. Its topic matter is existential, not hypothetical. It involves more than mere demonstration because it involves choice. Its assertions have ontological claims.

Now I return to the second responsibility, which is imposed by the fact that the rhetorician is concerned with definite questions. These are questions having histories, and history is always concrete. This means that the speaker or writer has got to have a rhetorical perception of what his audience needs or will receive or respond to. He takes into account the reality of man's composite being and his tendency to be swayed by sentiment. He estimates the pressures of the particular situation in which his auditors are found. In the eyes of those who look sourly upon the art, he is a man probing for weaknesses which he means to exploit.

But here we must recur to the principle that rhetoric comprehensively considered is an art of emphasis. The definite situation confronts him with a second standard of choice. In view of the receptivity of his audience, which of the topics shall he choose to stress, and how? If he concludes that definition should be the appeal, he tries to express the nature of the thing in a compelling way. If he feels that a cause-and-effect demonstration would stand the greatest chance to impress, he tries to make this linkage so manifest that his hearers will see an inevitability in it. And so on with the other topics, which will be so emphasized or magnified as to produce the response of assent.

Along with this process of amplification, the ancients recognized two qualities of rhetorical discourse which have the effect of impressing an audience with the reality or urgency of a topic. In Greek these appear as *energia* and *enargia*, both of which may be translated "actuality," though the first has to do with liveliness or animation of action and the second with vividness of scene. The speaker now indulges in actualization to make what he is narrating or describing present to the minds' eyes of his hearers.

The practice itself has given rise to a good deal of misunderstanding, which it would be well to remove. We know that one of the conventional criticisms of rhetoric is that the practitioner of it takes advantage of his hearers by playing upon their feelings and imaginations. He overstresses the importance of his topics by puffing them up, dwelling on them in great detail, using an excess of imagery or of modifiers evoking the senses, and so on. He goes beyond what is fair, the critics often allege, by this actualization of a scene about which the audience ought to be thinking rationally. Since this criticism has a serious basis, I am going to offer an illustration before making the reply. Here is a passage from Daniel Webster's famous speech for the prosecution in the trial of John Francis Knapp. Webster is actualizing for the jury the scene of the murder as he has constructed it from circumstantial evidence.

The deed was executed with a degree of steadiness and self-possession equal to the wickedness with which it was planned. The circumstances now clearly in evidence spread out the scene before us. Deep sleep had fallen upon the destined victim and all beneath his roof. A healthful old man, to whom sleep was sweet, the first sound slumbers of the night held him in their soft but strong embrace. The assassin enters, through a window already prepared, into an unoccupied apartment. With noiseless foot he paces the lonely hall, half-lighted by the moon; he winds up the ascent of the stairs, and reaches the door of the chamber. Of this, he moves the lock by soft and continued pressure, till it turns on its hinges without noise; and he enters, and beholds the victim before him. The room is uncommonly open to the admission of light. The face of the innocent sleeper is turned from the murderer, and the beams of the moon, resting on the gray locks of the aged temple, show him where to strike. The fatal blow is given! and the victim passes, without a struggle or a motion, from the repose of sleep to the repose of death! It is the assassin's purpose to make sure work; and he plies the dagger, though it is obvious that life has been destroyed by the blow of the bludgeon. He even raises the aged arm, that he may not fail in his aim at the heart, and replaces it again over the wounds of the poniard! To finish the picture, he explores the wrist for the pulse! He feels for it, and ascertains that it beats no longer! It is accomplished. The deed is done. He retreats, retraces his steps to the window, passes out through it as he came in, and escapes. He has done the murder. No eye has seen him, no ear has heard him. The secret is his own, and it is safe!

By depicting the scene in this fulness of detail, Webster is making it vivid, and "vivid" means "living." There are those who object on general grounds to this sort of dramatization; it is too affecting to the emotions. Beyond a doubt, whenever the rhetorician actualizes an event in this manner, he is making it mean something to the emotional part of us, but that part is involved whenever we are deliberating about goodness and badness. On this subject there is a very wise reminder in Bishop Whately's *Elements of Rhetoric:* "When feelings are strongly excited, they are not necessarily over-excited; it may be that they are only brought to the state which the occasion fully justifies, or even that they fall short of this." Let us think of the situation in which Webster was acting. After all, there is the possibility, or even the likelihood that the murder was committed in this fashion, and that the indicted Knapp deserved the conviction he got. Suppose the audience had remained cold and unmoved. There is the victim's side to consider and the interest of society in protecting life. We should not forget that Webster's "actualization" is in the service of these. Our attitude toward what is just or right or noble and their opposites is not a bloodless calculation, but a feeling for and against. As Whately indicates, the speaker who arouses feeling may only be arousing it to the right pitch and channeling it in the right direction.

To re-affirm the general contention: the rhetorician who practices "amplification" is not thereby misleading his audience, because we are all men of limited capacity and sensitivity and imagination. We all need to have things pointed out to us, things stressed in our interest. The very task of the rhetorician is to determine what feature of a question is most exigent and to use the power of language to make it appear so. A speaker who dwells insistently upon some aspect of a case may no more be hoodwinking me than a policeman or a doctor when he advises against a certain course of action by pointing out its nature or its consequences. He *should* be in a position to know somewhat better than I do.

It is strongly to be suspected that this charge against rhetoric comes not only from the distorted image that makes man a merely rationalistic being, but also from the dogma of an uncritical equalitarianism. The notion of equality has insinuated itself so far that it appears sometimes as a feeling, to which I would apply the name "sentimental plebeianism," that no man is better or wiser than another, and hence that it is usurpation for one person to undertake to instruct or admonish another. This preposterous and, we could add, wholly unscientific judgment (since our differences are manifold and provable) is propagated in subtle ways by our institutions of publicity and the perverse art of demagogic politics. Common sense replies that any individual who advises a friend or speaks up in meeting is exercising a kind of leadership, which may be justified by superior virtue, knowledge, or personal insight.

The fact that leadership is a human necessity is proof that rhetoric as the attempt through language to make one's point of view prevail grows out of the nature of man. It is not a reflection of any past phase of social development, or any social institution, or any fashion, or any passing vice. When all factors have been considered, it will be seen that men are born rhetoricians, though some are born small ones and others greater, and some cultivate the native gift by study and training, whereas some neglect it. Men are such because they are born into history, with an endowment of passion and a sense of the *ought*. There is ever some discrepancy, however slight, between the situation man is in and the situation he would like to realize. His life is therefore characterized by movement toward goals. It is largely the power of rhetoric which influences and governs that movement.

For the same set of reasons, rhetoric is cognate with language. Ever since I first heard the idea mentioned seriously it impressed me as impossible and even ridiculous that the utterances of men could be neutral. Such study as I have been able to give the subject over the years has confirmed that feeling and has led me to believe that what is sometimes held up as a desideratum—expression purged of all tendency—rests upon an initial misconception of the nature of language.

The condition essential to see is that every use of speech, oral and written, exhibits an attitude, and an attitude implies an act. "Thy speech bewrayeth thee" is aphoristically true if we take it as saying, "Your speech reveals your disposition," first by what you choose to say, then by the amount you decide to say, and so on down through the resources of linguistic elaboration and intonation. All rhetoric is a rhetoric of motives, as Kenneth Burke saw fit to indicate in the title of his book. At the low end of the scale, one may be doing nothing more than making sounds to express exuberance. But if at the other end one sits down to compose a *Critique of Pure Reason*, one has the motive of refuting other philosophers' accounts of the constitution of being, and of substituting one's own, for an interest which may be universal, but which nonetheless proceeds from the will to alter something.

Does this mean that it is impossible to be objective about anything? Does it mean that one is "rhetorical" in declaring that a straight line is the shortest distance between two points? Not in the sense in which the objection is usually raised. There are degrees of objectivity, and there are various disciplines which have their own rules for expressing their laws or their content in the most effective manner for their purpose. But even this expression can be seen as enclosed in a rhetorical intention. Put in another way, an utterance is capable of rhetorical function and aspect. If one looks widely enough, one can discover its rhetorical dimension, to put it in still another way. The scientist has some interest in setting forth the formulation of some recurrent feature of the physical world, although his own sense of motive may be lost in a general feeling that science is a good thing because it helps progress along.[3]

In short, as long as man is a creature responding to purpose, his linguistic expression will be a carrier of tendency. Where the modern semanticists got off on the wrong foot in their effort to refurbish language lay in the curious supposition that language could and should be outwardly determined. They were positivists operating in the linguistic field. Yet if there is anything that is going to keep on defying positivistic correlation, it is this subjectively born, intimate, and value-laden vehicle which we call language. Language

3. If I have risked confusion by referring to "rhetoricians" and "rhetorical speakers," and to other men as if they were all non-rhetoricians, while insisting that all language has its rhetorical aspect, let me clarify the terms. By "rhetorician" I mean the deliberate rhetor: the man who understands the nature and aim and requirements of persuasive expression and who uses them more or less consciously according to the approved rules of the art. The other, who, by his membership in the family of language users, must be a rhetorician of sorts, is an empirical and adventitious one; he does not know enough to keep invention, arrangement, and style working for him. The rhetorician of my reference is thus the educated speaker; the other is an untaught amateur.

is a system of imputation, by which values and percepts are first framed in the mind and are then imputed to things. This is not an irresponsible imputation; it does not imply, say, that no two people can look at the same clock face and report the same time. The qualities or properties have to be in the things, but they are not in the things in the form in which they are framed by the mind. This much I think we can learn from the great realist–nominalist controversy of the Middle Ages and from the little that contemporary semantics has been able to add to our knowledge. Language was created by the imagination for the purposes of man, but it may have objective reference—just how we cannot say until we are in possession of a more complete metaphysics and epistemology.

Now a system of imputation involves the use of predicates, as when we say, "Sugar is sweet" or "Business is good." Modern positivism and relativism, however, have gone virtually to the point of denying the validity of all conceptual predication. Occasionally at Chicago I purposely needle a class by expressing a general concept in a casual way, whereupon usually I am sternly reminded by some member brought up in the best relativist tradition that "You can't generalize that way." The same view can be encountered in eminent quarters. Justice Oliver Wendell Holmes was fond of saying that the chief end of man is to frame general propositions and that no general proposition is worth a damn. In the first of these general propositions the Justice was right, in the sense that men cannot get along without categorizing their apprehensions of reality. In the second he was wrong because, although a great jurist, he was not philosopher enough to think the matter through. Positivism and relativism may have rendered a certain service as devil's advocates if they have caused us to be more careful about our concepts and our predicates, yet their position in net form is untenable. The battle against general propositions was lost from the beginning, for just as surely as man is a symbol-using animal (and a symbol transcends the thing symbolized) he is a classifying animal. The morality lies in the application of the predicate.

Language, which is thus predicative, is for the same cause sermonic. We are all of us preachers in private or public capacities. We have no sooner uttered words than we have given impulse to other people to look at the world, or some small part of it, in our way. Thus caught up in a great web of inter-communication and inter-influence, we speak as rhetoricians affecting one another for good or ill. That is why I must agree with Quintilian that the true orator is the good man, skilled in speaking—good in his formed character and right in his ethical philosophy. When to this he adds fertility in invention and skill in the arts of language, he is entitled to that leadership which tradition accords him.

If rhetoric is to be saved from the neglect and even the disrepute which I was deploring at the beginning of this lecture, these primary truths will have to be recovered until they are a part of our active consciousness. They are, in summation, that man is not nor ever can be nor ever should be a depersonalized thinking machine. His feeling is the activity in him most closely related to what used to be called his soul. To appeal to his feeling therefore is not necessarily an insult; it can be a way to honor him, by recognizing him in the fulness of his being. Even in those situations where the appeal is a kind of strategy, it but recognizes that men—all men—are historically conditioned.

Rhetoric must be viewed formally as operating at that point where literature and politics meet, or where literary values and political urgencies can be brought together. The rhetorician makes use of the moving power of literary presentation to induce in his hearers an attitude or decision which is political in the very broadest sense. Perhaps this explains why the successful user of rhetoric is sometimes in bad grace with both camps. For the literary people he is too "practical"; and for the more practical political people he is too "flowery." But there is nothing illegitimate about what he undertakes to do, any more than it would be illegitimate to make use of the timeless principles of aesthetics in the constructing of a public building. Finally, we must never lose sight of the order of values as the ultimate sanction of rhetoric. No one can live a life of direction and purpose without some scheme of values. As rhetoric confronts us with choices involving values, the rhetorician is a preacher to us, noble if he tries to direct our passion toward noble ends and base if he uses our passion to confuse and degrade us. Since all utterance influences us in one or the other of these directions, it is important that the direction be the right one, and it is better if this lay preacher is a master of his art.

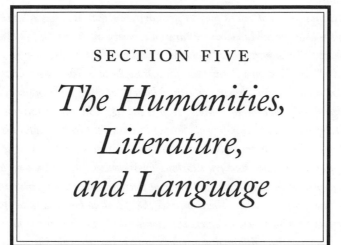

SECTION FIVE

The Humanities, Literature, and Language

In addition to his extensive work on rhetoric, composition, and Southern literature, Weaver occasionally turned his attention to contemporary poetry and fiction and the status of language and the humanities in the modern world. These writings are collected here in three groups—the first and second ordered conceptually, the third chronologically.

The first group includes three items that deal, respectively, with the effects of modernism on the humanities, poetry, and language. "The Humanities in a Century of the Common Man" is the text of a speech (originally entitled "The Humanities in a Common Century") that was delivered to an unknown audience sometime in 1948 (most likely in early August). First published in the New Individualist Review in 1964, its analysis of the corrosive effects of mass society is similar in tone and content to Ideas Have Consequences. It is followed by "Etiology of the Image," an extended book review from the June 1948 issue of Poetry. Although the journal was edited for a time by his good friend and colleague Henry Rago, this is the only work Weaver ever published there. Finally, "Relativism and the Use of Language" offers an extended analysis of the nature of language and meaning and their degradation in the modern world. Originally written for a September 1959 conference on "Relativism and the Study of

Man," it was published two years later in a similarly titled volume of conference proceedings.

The second group of essays focuses primarily on the responses of authors and poets to the changes in American culture and society in the century following the Civil War. "The Importance of Cultural Freedom" was first presented at a conference on "The Necessary Conditions for a Free Society" held in Princeton, New Jersey, in June of 1961. It was published later that year in Modern Age and again in a 1963 volume of conference proceedings. An important essay, it is noteworthy both for its summary of Weaver's views on culture and for his trenchant defense of modern art and literature. The "Introduction" to Logarhythms (1956), a book of poems and translations by Weaver's former student James L. Weil, weaves an analysis of the problems of contemporary poetry into an assessment of the author's work. "Realism and the Local Color Interlude" is a brief essay or essay fragment that depicts the "local color" writing of the last third of the nineteenth century as an "unconscious protest" against the changes in American society engendered by the Civil War. Probably written while Weaver was a doctoral student at Louisiana State (1940–43) or shortly thereafter,[1] it was first published in 1968 in a version edited by George Core.

The third and final group of writings is a miscellaneous collection of book reviews on language and literature, most of which were published in the Commonweal and Modern Age. In addition to evaluations of nonfiction works by George Orwell, I. A. Richards, Randall Stewart, and C. S. Lewis, it includes three early reviews of novels, a genre Weaver avoided in later years in the belief that "my reviews of fiction have never been very successful."[2]

---

1. As Core points out in his "Editor's Note" to the article, a chapter in Weaver's dissertation deals with individual local color writers. Another indication of his interest at the time in this kind of writing is a paper he wrote for a course at LSU entitled "A Frontier Gallery: Some Types in the Sketches of Joseph G. Baldwin." The most likely possibility is that the essay is the beginning of a longer work begun in 1943 or 1944 and intended for submission to the Sewanee Review but never completed.

2. Letter from Richard Weaver to Eugene Davidson dated September 5, 1961. Located in the correspondence files of the Intercollegiate Studies Institute and quoted by permission.

The Humanities in a Century
of the Common Man[1]

The current defense of humanities does not take into account the depth of the tide running against them, probably because it is politically unsettling to do so. But if we wish to acquaint ourselves with prospects we shall soon be grappling with as pressing realities, we shall have to look more candidly at what is undermining this historic body of study. If certain forces continue unabated, humanistic training as we have known it is not likely to survive another generation.

The first point to take into account is the paradoxical fact that the humanities are a discipline. I say paradoxical because there is a certain anomaly in asking the human being to undergo a regimen in order to become more human, or more *humane*, if we may give a focused meaning to the latter word. For the humanities are not the spontaneous, loose, and thoughtless expression of the human race, but on the contrary a highly difficult, concentrated, and directed expression which aims at a center—man at his best, not man transmuted into an angel, which is the proper study of divinity, but man incarnate, which is today, man in this world, making the best of his estate as he responds to its colors and configurations. That is why we can today admire the humanism of Greece and Rome, with indifference to the other tendencies of this civilization. Like every humanism, theirs was an achievement in sensibility and expression, and their brilliance was such that the modern world has up until now been glad to emulate. But it has always been accepted as a starting point that this emulation required education and effort, so that he who engaged in it sought to make himself over in accordance with an ideal superior to his untutored self. That would

1. *New Individualist Review*, 3/3, Autumn 1964, 17–24.

seem to be the premise of all humanistic study: the best which has been thought and said in the world was not uttered in a babble, but came slowly and often at the cost of self-torture, or at least of the mortification of passing desire. Education in the humanities has always meant a study of the classics, and a classic is a sort of cultural leader, to whom we submit ourselves out of our faith in edification.

Those who have been brought up on a humanistic education assume that there is something in the monuments of humanism which compels a respect. I fear that they are only taking a constant of their own lives to be a universal constant, which does not exist. Once before a long night descended upon these monuments. They were there to plead their case, but you cannot plead to those who will not hear. I should like to echo Whitman here, and say that if to have great poets, there must be great audiences, to have a victorious humanism, there must be a humanized audience. Enough has been said elsewhere of the dehumanizing pressures under which we labor; and acute observers have long detected in modern men, and not solely among those who are low-placed, an impulse to reach for the metaphorical pistol when the word culture is mentioned. There seems to be growing up an attitude of truculence, and nothing is more fatal to an appreciation of past accomplishment. There are plenty of signs that the traditional respect for artistic and intellectual distinction is being displaced by reverence for political power and institutions. The first of these requires a belief in personality, and the second tends to require a disbelief in it. That may prove the fundamental difference between them.

It is a commonplace of recent history that about 1930 our age turned sharply political. The impulse has been so strong in the 30's and 40's as to carry along with it, like some engrossing wave, a large part of all artistic expression. Artistic work came to be judged by whether or not it contributed to a conception of progress, and the term progress implies, of course, a direction. If we had to give a name to that direction, we would not have to seek beyond "social democracy." This is a quite elastic term which covers, on the one extreme, the palest social amelioration, and on the other the strictest type of state-managed economy, requiring total regimentation. But whatever the form, social democracy exhibits two tendencies which are serious for the future of the humanities. One of these is a change in the structure of society, and the other a disposition of society's income.

The first tendency works to break down the categories which have hitherto existed in favor of an undifferentiated mass. Without raising the question of whether these classes which have been privileged in the past have deserved their fortune, it can be asked whether society is not thereby sacrificing its strength. It seems to be incontrovertible that all progress in the higher meaning of that term—the progress which is the carrying out of an enlightened moral ambition—has not come from society fused as a mass, but from society held in a kind of counterpoise. Aristotle has illustrated this truth through an analogy with music. A state ceases to be a state when what is harmony is allowed to pass into unison. Now the mass seems to be this state of unison, which is without the principle of counterpoise. In the other type of society, which has proved creative, we have numberless arrangements in which men are functionally placed against men, since this is in very fact its integrating principle. There is a substratum of unity, of course, for without that even our definition would collapse. The principle of counterpoise works in such a way that one element plays its part and gets its living by being poised against another element. The one is commissioned to get as much as it can out of the other, more than would ever be granted without the pressure of its demand. The requirement is always made in the name of some higher order, or liberty, or degree of enlightenment. For example, in this functional counterpoise we have teachers against students, policemen against citizens, buyers against sellers, managers against employees. It is the pluralistic kind of arrangement, in which one group stands for and enforces an ideal of performance like a competitor in a contest, viz., especially teachers and policemen, and the rest of us profit by their necessary though at times irksome office. The effect of this arrangement is to make society vertebrate, if we may vary the figure. I do not see what social democracy is going to substitute for this structure. What has been suggested or exhibited thus far is a more simple and more rigid pattern, which is without the flexibility of the healthy organic body. Now the humanities have in the past exerted their authority from a kind of limited autonomy; they have been one of the weights holding us in a counterpoise. In the new state, what is going to "enforce" the humanities? It is becoming clear that if the state does not do it, it will not be done; and yet if the state does it, it will likely be done in a way that will prove fatal.

This brings us to the second tendency, which is the economic transformation accompanying the process we have just sketched.

Everyday observation brings home to us that as the modern state expands its power, it becomes more jealous of the rights of individuals. It grows more rigorous in the exercise of the authority it owns; and secretly, one fears, it determines to extend its reach. It is inevitable that in this development it should become more curious about what individuals do with their incomes. Its level of understanding here is pretty low; expenditures for food, clothing, and shelter it can grasp, but as it seeks to placate the greatest number, things beyond these will be sold to it with increasing difficulty.

Let us consider for a moment the way in which it has brought the individual's economic life under surveillance. First, the state somewhat timidly lays an income tax, applied at the outset to the wealthy, who are few and conspicuous. Next, on a plea of emergency, or extended social welfare, it increases the rates sharply, making them virtually confiscatory on the upper levels. This fact is not presented in defense of an unregenerate capitalism; its relevance to the argument appears when one recalls what has happened in this country to private donations to universities. As someone has remarked, you cannot eat up your millionaires with taxes and have them too.

The state finally adopts the withholding tax, which has the practical effect of putting everyone on the government payroll, since the government first looks at the salary, decides what fraction of it the individual shall have, and then passes on the remainder. Thus the private company becomes in effect a kind of disbursing agent for the government. This circumstance, which seems to have gone largely unnoticed, is symbolic in the highest degree of the trend even in "free" countries toward state collectivism. The bearing upon the case of culture is just this: what is going to happen to the supernumerary, non-utilitarian part of our activity when every individual is virtually on a government expense account? The inescapable conclusion is that the sum which goes for "brave, translunary things" is going to be politically determined—and inspired.

The modern world is creating an ideology whose hero is the satisfied consumer. He is the common denominator, and the offices of the state are to serve him, and not some imponderable ideal. This state serves, moreover, with an ever-increased efficiency. Today, everything is under control; nothing slips through; there is less chance than ever before that the state will fail of its announced aim. Populations have been numbered; incomes have been listed; techniques have become machine-like. We must therefore consider the chance of the humanities in a social democracy whose policies will be efficient, as far as its light goes, but whose ideals encounter an insistent pull downward.

At this certain point objections arise. "Culture," which in common parlance stands for the humanities, is still a word with a great deal of prestige; it yet has associations of value which would induce politicians to sponsor it even if they felt no attachment to it. It is frequently seen that social democratic parties are more liberal than others in recognizing the claims of culture. They pledge large outlays for education and a better deal for the artists and intellectuals under their regime. The promise is fair, but it has to be distinguished from the performance for the plain reason that it is uttered as part of the ideal, and does not reflect the forces which will mold the actual. It is one thing to promise in the name of the people reverence for great art and intellectual distinction, but this is a situation in which the will, or it might be more accurately described, the impulse, of the people is going to determine. After all, one of the chief aims of social democracy is the removal of those barriers which in traditional or formalized societies stand between the people and an immediate fulfillment of their wishes.

What is likely to happen is this: in the primitive or heroic days of social democracy we would very likely get commissars or administrators who believe genuinely in the humanities and who would put up a battle for them. One is compelled to suppose that they would be battling as individuals, against indifference from above and poorly educated taste from below. For a time they might do much, but it would be foolish to mistake in this case accident for essence. For these men would be individualists, and sooner or later they would be supplanted by others closer to popular sympathy. It is likely that their very success would be held against them, so refined are the arts of political detraction. They would be described as aloof from the people, or as thwarters of the popular will; for, in fact, they would be representing an "undemocratic" force. Their successors would be the political type, who know all too well how to commit a murder while concealed under the cloak of popular sentiment. They will give the public what it wants and provide the rationalization. This is the fate in store for all state-controlled culture.

Anyone who thinks this is a fanciful alarm should reflect upon what has been done to public education in the United States. The boast of the innovating "progressive" schools is that they prepare the youth for a changing world. *Would it not be incomparably more sensible to prepare the youth to understand why the world is changing?* This is what the humanities do. There is little appeal here to the exponents of progressive education because they have no desire to rise above the confusion. If they did, they would soon be at odds with the weight and mass of general opinion. Consequently, in our present educational system, popular pressure and specious doctrines have almost extinguished the idea of discipline. Yet I am inclined to think that this system has been better protected than one could expect the humanities to be in a pure social democracy.[2]

There are further reasons for saying that we have reached a point at which these dangers are not purely speculative. We are able to examine three years of socialist rule in Britain, which indicates that we have not been expressing undue alarm. I shall cite two passages from a "Letter from England," by D. S. Savage, appearing in the Spring, 1946, issue of the *Hudson Review.* "A Labour government is in power and, so far from fostering the arts and subsidizing artists as some of its more gullible adherents among the intelligentsia had hoped, it is proving on the whole inimical to cultural values; an implicit doctrine of 'bread alone'—that is, bread and guns—prevails." Mr. Savage ventures a prediction of his own. "It seems possible that as the social order hardens into shape we shall witness the emergence of two cultures—an official and an unofficial, the one well-paid, flashy, and sterile, drawing upon the talent of debauched artists and intellectuals, and the other surviving only through extreme enthusiasm and devotion."

It is an historic truth which holds good for the past several centuries of our life that culture has developed from the liberty of the superior individual to love superior things. Whether these individuals established foundations, or whether they merely sustained a market for works of distinction out of their earned or unearned surpluses, the result was as we have seen. The essential condition was that the individual had a power of decree. We have observed that the new social regime does not permit the individual much

---

2. Let us look at a special example which should serve to define the issue. Will anyone reasonably contend that the money which has been expended by the Rockefeller Foundation on education and research would have accomplished as much if it had passed through the hands of publicly elected officials? The fact that it was a privately managed corporation able to define what it wanted and, above all, able to wait for long-term results has made possible its great contribution.

power of decree, and it is very jealous of these surpluses. Its present humor is to describe them as theft and to appropriate them on one pretext and another. We arrive then at a state in which the single, sensitive, imaginative person cannot project his will in this fashion. As Paul Valéry has suggested, liberty in the modern "free" state is simply a liberty to be like the masses because political control is vested in them. They feel "free" because what they will is made law. The more one resembles the mass man, the freer he is because his impulses run the same channel as theirs. And if he is antipathetic to the idols of the mass, he may be very unfree, because mass law and mass ethos are enforced with peculiar rigor, and there is no court of appeal. Traditional forms of government now in disfavor provided a better haven for the individualist because they felt some distrust of their own power and often relaxed it in administration. It is the special mark of the mass that it has not such feeling about its power, and is exhilarated to see it brutally exercised. For its attitude toward the non-conventional, see our daily tabloids.

In summary, we face a future in which the mass is going to determine with increasing power what is done with the total productivity of the nation. There is little chance that it will devote a substantial part of that productivity to the development of pure science (unless science can be hitched to some wagon like preparation for defense in war), or to the creation of works of art which baffle or offend it.

It is now time to look at one or two aesthetic difficulties which will prove handicaps in an age dominated by this new mentality. I shall consider the first of these as the aesthetic plebeianism. There is an aesthetic of common life and an aesthetic of noble life, and the two are far from meeting. To find a principle that distinguishes them it is only necessary to point out that they correlate closely with optimism and pessimism. The noble view of life, which is the view that has conditioned art in the past, tends always to be pessimistic for the plain reason that life "does not measure up." It is not satisfactory when compared with that clear pattern which the believer in excellence has in his soul. This is clearly proved by the fact that the art of tragedy and satire have flourished in ages which were predominantly aristocratic, that is to say, ages which accepted as a reality the distinction between good and bad men, or actions. It could not be otherwise, for the reproof of man, and the very plot of tragedy depends upon man struggling in a net of evil. Whoever thinks he knows how the world ought to be feels a certain melancholy that it is not so. In all great art therefore there is a certain pessimistic overcast. Art is a kind of protest, a transfiguration. It has been remarked that if one looks below the surface of two of the most dazzling periods of creativeness in history, the Greek and the Elizabethan, he finds a well of melancholy. Shakespeare's plays deepened in gravity as the man matured.

But what occurs when life is made not the subject of a critique, but an occasion for relaxed joyousness and animal abandon? There have been signs for years that we are passing out of one climate of belief into another. A significant witness is that tragedy has all but disappeared. And if this is but a beginning, it may be no exaggeration to say that the new climate is to be anti-artistic and anti-cultural. We may be faced with a time when the root-idea of standards, which is the anchor of all humanistic discipline, is to be eradicated. Indeed, our expression here may be too cautious, for the extent to which knowledge has been displaced by opinion makes this almost now an actuality.

The aristocratic view of life is waning because the mass everlastingly insists that the world be represented as *pleasant*. One quality which the crowd is never able to acquire is a hardheadedness sufficient to accept the realism of the world. For this reason it falsifies whatever it touches, and there is no hope for true art where the principle at work is falsification. To foretell the kind of art expression which the mass is going to demand, and demand effectively by reason of its economic power, one has only to look at today's media of mass circulation. The preferred themes are romantic love (this seems to be a modern version of the Aphrodite Pandemos, which is distinct from the Aphrodite Ouranios of the ancients, and from the courtly love of the mediaevals), success stories, fantasies, comedy with elements of violence and sadism. I suspect that the truest index to this mentality is the comic strip, whose offenses against taste and aesthetic theory it would be impossible to number. But present in all of them is the unrelenting demand that the world be subjectivized to accord with our humor. The herd man never grows reconciled to the fact that life is a defeat, and that this defeat is its story. He wants instead a pleasing fiction by which his hopes are ingeniously flattered. It is not pressing the matter too far to say that what he *deception*.

What we are actually contending with in these aesthetic plebeianisms is the mass's deep-seated and enduring hostility to the idea of discipline. It does finally require some discipline of mind to accept the fact that life is not a triumphal progress, but a sadly mixed affair with many a disenchantment. When Arnold talked of seeing things steadily and seeing them whole, he must have had reference to just this evasiveness and flabbiness of mind which it is the function of culture to remove—where it can. It will never do that where the ideal is the thing made easy.

The psychological springs of this hostility are not far to seek. The mass can never grant that there is something superior to its *habitus* and its way of conduct. For as soon as it grants the existence of such, it is under a theoretic discipline. The mass is a jealous sovereign. Those who challenge it from a superior level it seeks to destroy with the *ad hominem* attack. It is daily verifiable that in a culture so maintained, the best rewarded of those who work in the arts are soothers and entertainers.

A secondary problem posed by the aesthetic plebeianism is the impossibility of maintaining a meaningful criticism. Obviously this aesthetic can never circumvent the criterion of popularity. It finds itself always in the tautologous position of saying that because a thing is popular, it is good; and because it is good, it is popular.

Art criticism is here in the same dilemma as political democracy when the latter sets up the voice of the people as the voice of God. Either it must accept its own proposition and say that the people is infallible, and can never for one minute, or in one action, go wrong; or else it must yield its whole position. If one admits that the people can even for a minute be deluded; that is to say, that one man or one minority can be right for a minute and the people wrong, then he admits the existence of a right that is not determined by the people. I feel this to be so important that I shall try to put it in another way. The moment one grants that the people can sometimes err, even temporarily, even when bamboozled by demagogues or the press, he has scuttled the thesis of the popular determination of truth. For he has already admitted that the people may be one thing and the truth another, and this could never be if popular opinion were the sole determinant of what is true.

Now when we apply this finding to the humanities in a mass society, the same interesting thing is revealed. Either popular impression is infallible, and the people are the only judge of what they should have, or else one must admit the existence of an independently grounded aesthetic. As soon as the latter is admitted, however, the beautiful and the non-beautiful become constants, and there is something superior to the popular taste, which may be applied to it. But I fear the mass is too intractable an animal to grant these existences after it has sensed the way they are tending.

Put into language, its denial seems to take this form: it does not matter if we disdain the moral earnestness of Christianity; it does not matter if we refuse to think with the clarity of the Greeks; it does not matter that we cannot dramatize with the success of the Elizabethans; it does not matter if we fall below the eighteenth century in elegance of manner. It does not matter? I suppose one can argue here only by begging the question and saying that it is blasphemy not to prefer the good and obey its commandments. And possibly it is as much as we can do about the condition of modern man to say that he is blasphemous. In the past he has blasphemed idols that were set up for him; and now he blasphemes those which he set up for himself when he repudiates the humanities.

The second difficulty may be, at some deeper level, the source of the first. As a teacher of humanities, I have grown disturbed over an attitude which is appearing in students, including those with some endowment of sensibility. I could describe it briefly by calling it a distrust of all rhetoric. The great passages of the past, the flights of Milton, of Burke, of Arnold, are lost upon them; and they show an active distrust of contemporary matter which is rhetorically presented. The power of language to stir, or to direct the feelings of man, seems only to provoke them to an antagonism. This has gone so far that the once-familiar rhetoric of pulpit and platform is beginning to seem an anachronism. Two different interpretations can be put upon this development.

The first is that the new generation has become scientific-minded and is insisting upon pure notation in all discourse. That is to say, it has accepted the advice of the semanticists and has resolved to have no traffic with words whose objective reference is dubious. They are impatient of anything which lacks the objective correlative, and so when language passes from a sort of literal correspondence with what is signified, to metaphor, as all rhetoric must, they simply cease to accept. Since they cultivate the scientist's detached outlook upon the world, emotion is for them mere disturbance in what ought to be clear communication. Pure notation will give them knowledge in the same way that mathematics does, or nearly so. And as for making up their minds about how to feel about a thing, well, that can wait—perhaps upon the development of yet another science.

The second interpretation, which I believe to be the true one, is that our generation is losing faith in the value of value. It will appear on a moment's reflection that this is the same as losing faith itself. Ours is not so much a generation of vipers as a faithless generation. Since the whole of humanistic study is based upon the acceptance of value, here is where the decay has its source. People have suffered much in the past decades, and they have not often been told the truth by their political leaders. It may be that there has set in as a defense a kind of psychic numbness. Since all feeling brings imposition in its train, there is a will not to feel. (I have noted among more than one student a kind of shrinking from propaganda as though it were a dreaded plague loose in the world—which in a way it may be.) Now we approach the ultimate in disenchantment.

Here would be cause for rejoicing if it were possible for man to live in a devalued world, but man is simply not that kind of animal. He has got to show his inclinations. And with the death of value there is every possibility that he will do it in grotesque, unintelligible ways, in fetishism and explosions of hard feeling, in demonism and vandalism. There is not the slightest possibility that he is less a creature of feeling than before. But the old gods have gone and the new gods have not arrived. It may be that in the interim he will turn into an idol smasher. The humanities seem high on the list of the things he will rudely reject, or allow to drift into obscurity. I fear that this is the meaning of the hatred of the old spacious rhetoric, with its tendency to elevate all that is described.

Most surveys of the plight of the humanities I have seen fall into wishful conclusions.

One supposition is that the colleges will be able to save them by a reform of curriculum. In response to this we see the inauguration of courses in general education. But this seems to be in essence only a streamlining. The courses are recast, made more compact and better integrated. The new conception, however, is hardly a discipline in the humanities such as used season the graduates of our universities. It may easily degenerate into other requirement like the ubiquitous English composition. The inte is good, of course, but the hope is not great. There was a time when a cultural education was income-producing for the legions that take it, and that means inevitably a different kind of education. Statistics on what the returned veterans have studied in our universities will prove the point.

Or it is supposed that larger grants to this and that will restore the balance. These will be gratefully received, and they will help, but it is sanguine to suppose that they will restore the balance in a displacement so huge as the one taking place before our eyes. I have already shown that public sources of such grants have a very limited independence and could not long survive political attack. A grant to the humanities today is like a contribution to a church whose doctrines we have no thought of honoring with practice. I doubt that anything large and vigorous can be sustained on this.

Teachers of the humanities are going the way of teachers of Latin and Greek and elocution unless we have something like a Second Coming of faith in the values.

Etiology of the Image[1]

It is not often that one encounters a work of the depth and scope of Rosemond Tuve's *Elizabethan and Metaphysical Imagery*. The author has performed an enormous labor of scholarship, and to this she has added some critical insights which must be taken into account from now on by those who judge modern poetry.

The greater part of the research is intended to correct an habitual misreading by moderns of Elizabethan and Metaphysical imagery. To accomplish this the author has to rehabilitate the image, or to show that according to Renaissance poetic it had a nature and a function quite at variance with those ascribed to it by some influential modern critics. Such imagery was not merely sensuous and decorative, but "imitative," logical, and functional according to a clear purpose.

The argument is that poets of the Renaissance always used the image to imitate a supersensible reality, although to avoid over-simplification it proves necessary to discriminate levels on which such imitation was achieved. The lowest was that of formal excellence; here the image appeared as an artifact, the success of which was measured by perfection of artistic form. On a second level the image functioned in the poet's ordering of nature; and here, since a pattern of coherence was sought, some standard of appropriateness to the subject or intention of the poem was involved. On the highest level images were "truth-stating" or "didactically concerned with the conveying of concepts."

All of the criteria by which Elizabethan and Metaphysical imagery has been judged—sensuous vividness, delightfulness, significancy, rhetorical efficacy, and decorum—are shown to be means either overt or covert by

1. *Poetry*, 72/3, June 1948, 156–61. Copyright © 1948 by The Modern Poetry Association. Reprinted by permission of the Editor of *Poetry*.

which the imagination was directed toward the world of the supersensible. From this emerges the ever-present didacticism of Renaissance poetry.

> The didactic theory operates to lessen the emphasis upon the sensuous function of images and to subtilize and multiply the logical functions they are capable of performing. Both these habits of thinking run counter to what Romantic criticism and Symbolist poetic have taught us to expect of poetic imagery.

It was essential of course to show that both Elizabethan and Metaphysical poets were working within a single poetic. The latter differed merely in preferring another genre, inasmuch as they "explored rather the possibilities of the short reflective lyric, and pressed them to their limits." But apart from this the Metaphysicals "stood with their predecessors in using images whose significancy committed them to generalized interpretations of experience or to evaluations with general implications." Because in its didactic function poetry was licensed to make use of the kindred disciplines of logic and rhetoric, the well-turned poem finally embodied an excellence of form, a strict logical concept, and a rhetoric which carefully kept the reader in mind.

The divergence between Renaissance and modern poetic, according to the analysis, is to be traced to differing conceptions of the end of poetry, and, ultimately, of the nature of the world. The Renaissance poet, confident of the existence of a "rationally apprehensible order," was interested in communicating his perception of that order as truth, and felt no compunction over using bare statement where that seemed most efficacious. His concern was with message, though not in the banal sense. The distinction rests upon a premise that "it is basic to Renaissance understanding of the didactic theory that poetry is concerned with truth, as carefully and sensitively as may be, and not with the Favorite Truths of the age."

The modern poet, on the other hand, having lost belief in the existence of that order, confines his interest to experience: what he desires is to convey the history of his conception, or to portray "his own process of interpreting or feeling." It is this difference which is responsible for the modern's delight in a logical language, and for his theory of the metaphor as a starting point for the exploration of consciousness. The modern poet then—when he is characteristically modern, as is not always the case—is left with something like the presentation of histories of unique psychological experience.

Inevitably such an article of poetic results in an impoverishment of imagery. The Renaissance principle that an image should be read as synecdoche, or as a window through which we obtain a large view of the beyond, rather than as description, gave the poets of the period a demonstrable advantage.

> The belief that the smallest particular is significant of ideas as large as the mind can inclose, and the constant habit of seeing the universe thus, helped to produce images of such profound reach that our own more self-conscious attempt to "be suggestive" cannot rival them in penetration.

If the end of a poem today is the communication of a quality of experience rather than a meaning, obviously something serious has happened to our belief in the accessibility of truth. The author indicates the situation by saying that "Elizabethans wrote and read images not like nominalists, but like realists." The force of that observation is that the modern poet, having become infected with the relativism of the age, is doubtful of truth and is therefore unable "to call unwisdom roundly by its name and expel its proponents from the domain of poetry."

> One supposes that this is not because we have more than the Elizabethans had of that kind of immaturity which resents wholesome doctrines, but rather because we have honestly become skeptical of man's capacity for attaining to and dispensing such wisdom. The whole business looks arrogant to us.

That the change which has produced modern poetry is a change of world-view is thus an underlying thesis of the work. The Renaissance poet lived at a time when the universe was thought to have a moral structure. For this reason he was capable of conceptions "which are both more daring and more humble than modern conceptions." They were more daring because they said more, and they were more humble because they were less egocentric. Naturally the poet who inhabits a world of meaning sees things not apparent to the one who inhabits a world of mere sensation. The belief of the Renaissance poet in an intelligible world behind the visible allowed him to think of poetry as a form of proof; indeed metaphor took a station among the Aristotelian predicables. Current assumptions related metaphor-making "to the logical place *similitude*," whereas the modern assumption relates it "to the play of association and to subconscious prepossessions for certain contents."

It becomes plain therefore that the modern world-view has undermined the image, both with respect to its power to signify—that is, to present what is apprehensible only through the intellective faculty—and its power to place a thing or an action in a scale of value. As the author reminds us, the modern poet

> can no longer range subjects in an order of elevation or importance, certainly not in an order of importance for which he would dare claim a validity defined by reference to the nature of things, rather than by reference to himself as honest observer of appearances. The seventeenth-century poet could still suit his style to the "essential" or true "greatness" of his subject.

The most rudimentary perception must grant that all poetry is a kind of affirmation, if only an affirmation that one thing bears resemblance to another. The timidity of our age in the face of simple predication, our hesitancy about saying one thing of another thing, thus saps at the root of poetry. And so the image which operates rhetorically or logically has been declared out of bounds. If there is no hierarchy of values, the image cannot "elevate"; if there is no truth, the image cannot "communicate." The only thing remaining for the image is the role which modern poetry has assigned it, the setting off of trains of association.

It is but an extension of this conclusion to say that poetry of the modern kind suffers from the anthropocentric delusion, since "the arrogance of the man who tries to expound what he can glimpse of the order imposed by God or 'Nature' cannot hold a candle to the arrogance of him who thinks there can be no order but that imposed by man, or by successive groups of men." And when the author declares at the end of her work that "to the Renaissance, the presumptuous man is still he who will not learn, not he who teaches," she shows, in keeping with the doctrine here urged upon poets, that she is unafraid to express her findings as wisdom.

Probably there will be debate over small points, but the case is, in the estimation of this reviewer, substantially proved. The evidence is mountainous, and a wide variety of objections has been anticipated. Finally it should be said that the author's mastery of the apparatus of scholarship has not prevented a clear, vigorous, and at times witty style.

Relativism and the Use of Language[1]

Nor do I think it a matter of little moment whether the language of a people be vitiated or refined, whether the popular idiom be erroneous or correct. . . . It is the opinion of Plato, that changes in the dress and habits of the citizens portend great changes and commotions in the state; and I am inclined to believe that when the language in common use in any country becomes irregular and depraved, it is followed by their ruin or their degradation. For what do terms used without skill or meaning, which are at once corrupt and misapplied, denote but a people listless, supine, and ripe for servitude? On the contrary, we have never heard of any people or state which has not flourished in some degree of prosperity as long as their language has retained its elegance and its purity.

—Milton to Benedetto Bonomatthai,
September 10, 1638 [2]

The epigraph from Milton is included here to represent a rather general feeling that a society cannot remain harmonious and healthy unless its use of language remains pure. "Pure" in this sense means stable, because fixed with respect to semantic references. More precisely, the feeling is that people cannot express the same idea or take the same attitude toward the same thing or agree on a policy which all will follow alike unless there is a certain minimal identity in the signification of the signs they employ, and the most common of these signs are linguistic. Confusion and conflict may result when the people engaged in any enterprise, which would include, of course, the maintaining of a state, find that their words are no longer reliable communicators of ideas and feelings. In such cases, where words have ceased to be a fixed medium of exchange, each party that feels misunderstood because its meaning was not received in the form intended may react with passion, and this can be the beginning of internecine strife. It will be

1. In Helmut Schoeck and James W. Wiggins (eds.), *Relativism and the Study of Man*. Princeton: Van Nostrand, 1961, 236–54.

2. *The Prose Works of John Milton* (London, 1806), I, xi–xii.

recalled that the United States Senate debated for thirty years whether the term "constitution" could be translated "compact." This difference was eventually settled by a bloody civil war. In our own time we have had ample occasion to notice how words of critical importance are used in varying and even conflicting senses. For the people of most Western countries, "democracy" means "government by the people"; for those in the communist world, it means "government of the people" by an elite presumed to be wiser than they are. "Liberalism" has been so twisted and perverted that it may be beyond any hope of rehabilitation in our time. Even a term like "peace," whose referent used to be a certain idea of order, now seems hard to match consistently with any idea. "Peace" and "war" have become hard to disentangle, and there seems to be a rather widespread mentality today that understands "peace" as the successful imposition of one's will upon resisters.

In opposition to this is another view, generated by the popularity of modern relativism, which is that semantic reference must be a relative affair. It is not easy to state this in the form of a precise theory, but the general sense seems to be that language, like every other phenomenon, has to be viewed as part of a changing world. There are, accordingly, no fixed significations. The meaning that a word has will depend upon the time and place in which it is used and the point of view of the user. Meaning is thus contingent and evolving. There is no absolute position from which the application of a word can be judged "right" or "wrong." There can be only shrewd estimates as to what the majority of men will accept. As the world changes, meaning changes too, and we can only hope that the two will proceed *pari passu*. The relativist is, of course, pleased rather than otherwise that language offers no exception to, or way of escape from, his world of relativity.

An awareness of the problems growing out of man's dependence upon words for communication is at least as old as the Greeks. It led Plato, in the *Cratylus,* to ask, with the typically Greek direct approach, whether there is not a natural rightness to the names of things. Does every object that bears a name have a kind of proprietary right to that name because of a definite (and possibly iconic) relationship between the two? Cratylus appears in the dialogue as the upholder of a doctrine that "everything has a right name of its own, which comes by nature, and . . . a name is not just whatever people call a thing by agreement, just as a piece of their own voice applied to a thing, but . . . there is a kind of inherent correctness in names, which is the same for all men, both Greeks and barbarians."[3] After a long discussion in which Socrates puts this theory to a number of tests, the idea that names have an essential rightness because they are imitations of the realities named is given up as inadequate, and the necessity of some element of convention is admitted. I believe that no serious student of language today, with the exception of a few advocates of "semantics" who are not very well grounded in language study, argues as a general thesis that there is some aboriginal iconic connection between a word and what the word stands for. (A few indisputable examples of onomatopoeia may have to be excepted.) Plato could not prove it for the Greek language, in spite of many ingenious attempts in this dialogue, and the immensely greater knowledge of linguistic variety that we have today seems to remove the problem from consideration.

The obscurity of the whole matter of semantic relationship, however, continues to create illusions. Some of these are due to the work of popular writers offering easy solutions, most of whom seem to take vaguely relativist positions. The sum of their doctrine appears to be that if we will simply adjust our vocabulary to changing external reality, most of the world's ignorance and prejudice will be removed. This might do no more harm than other nostrums, except that it finds reception among people whose use of language has a very practical bearing upon society. For in addition to permeating the public mind to an appreciable extent, it seems to have influenced some of our jurists, whose very prerogative makes them "definers," and whose definitions are, of course, binding in a legal sense. Here are two examples. Mr. Justice Holmes is on record as saying, "A word is not a crystal, transparent and unchanged; it is the skin of a living thought and may vary greatly in color and content according to the circumstances and time in which it is used."[4] Chief Justice Vinson observed: "Nothing is more certain in modern society than the principle that all concepts are relative: a name, a phrase, a standard, has meaning only when associated with the considerations which gave birth to the nomenclature."[5] The first of these pronouncements stresses the relationship between a word and the circum-

3. *Cratylus,* 383 b.

4. Quoted in Clinton Rossiter, *Conservatism in America* (New York, 1955), p. 4.

5. In his opinion upholding the conviction of eleven Communist leaders. See *New York Times,* June 5, 1951.

stances under which it is used. The second states outright that all names and phrases are relative to the situations that gave birth to them and introduces a further difficulty by maintaining that this principle has special application to modern society. I would not deny that some element of truth could be extracted from both observations, yet it would have to be hedged about very cautiously. Taken as a philosophy of language without careful interpretation, such statements are insufficient and misleading. In these instances, the source causes them to pass readily into popular thinking.

The difficulty of the whole problem makes us wonder whether some help cannot be found by investigating the ultimate origin of language. Yet this turns out to be a subject of the utmost perplexity. None of the theories of language thus far propounded impresses us as convincing, and some of them appear almost childishly naive. Attempts have been made to show that man first learned to speak by imitating the sounds of nature. Other attempts have been made to trace language to instinctive cries. Still other attempts have been made to show that the roots of words found in cognate languages express certain temporal and spatial relations. But why these root forms were chosen for these particular perceptions, why they are not found in all languages as well as the Indo-Germanic, and how they were elaborated upon to produce words capable of complex signification are questions that go unanswered.[6]

About all that can be affirmed with confidence is that language is a very ancient creation of man. Edward Sapir is of the opinion that it "antedated even the lowliest developments of material culture, [and] that these developments, in fact, were not strictly possible until language, the tool of significant expression, had itself taken shape."[7] He furthermore believes that not even interjections are merely instinctive; he thinks that they express some feeling about the occasion molded or transformed by a mentality that is qualitatively human.[8]

It therefore seems impossible to arrive at any theory of the "rightness" of the meaning of words by studying their first origin and by tracing their early evolutionary development. The origin remains wrapped in mystery, and there are those who will say that language is a divine gift to man, like his

6. For a survey of theories regarding the origin of language, *see* Mario Pei, *The Story of Language* (Philadelphia, 1949), pp. 18–20.

7. Edward Sapir, *Language* (New York, 1921), p. 23.

8. *Ibid.*, p. 4.

soul. The best resource left to us is to look at its constitution and function to see what light these shed upon semantic change and upon the social and cultural problems connected with this.

Language, as I conceive it, is a social and cultural creation functioning somehow within the psychic constitution of those who use it. The scope of the reference of words is accordingly determined by forces within the psychic constitution and not outside it. The question of stability in language cannot be considered apart from the psychic stability of the cultural group. And by the same inference the reason for changes in language, whether of the kind we approve or disapprove, will have to be sought in that prime source. All this may seem to border on a mystical account of what, after all, is an empirical fact, subject in several of its aspects to direct observation. Yet the problem of meaning remains elusive after observations of this kind have been made.

I am inclined to agree with W. M. Urban, in his *Language and Reality*, that the situation is the reverse of what is usually conceived.[9] It is not that things give meaning to words; it is that meaning makes things "things." It does not make things in their subsistence; but it does make things in their discreteness for the understanding. Extramental reality may itself be a nameless flow of causality, but when we apperceive it, we separate it into "discretes" such as "house," "tree," "mountain." And naming follows hard upon this, if, indeed, it is not an essential part of the process itself. Communication and cognition thus seem very closely related. To know a thing is not to arrive finally at some direct perception of a property, as Locke suggests, but to form some ideal construct of it, in which meaning and value are closely bound. Theories of meaning that include only the symbol and the thing symbolized leave out of account the interpreter. But there can be no such thing as meaning, in the sense of understanding, unless there is a third entity, the human being, who brings the two together in a system of comprehension.

The central point of this essay is that language cannot be viewed as a merely naturalistic phenomenon, subject only to forces that have their source in the objective world and, therefore, varying simply according to time and place.

As a starting point for the analysis of language, a statement which Shelley

9. W. M. Urban, *Language and Reality* (New York, 1939), pp. 105–106.

makes, in his "A Defence of Poetry," seems better than anything I have found in the writings of the scientific linguists. In the course of a passage dealing with the relationship of language and poetry, he says: "Language is arbitrarily produced by the imagination and has relation to thoughts alone." [10] This is equivalent to affirming that language is a humanistic creation, whose function cannot be understood except with reference to the realm of the mind. I shall qualify this later on, but taken as it is, it leaves us in position to deal with one of the paradoxes about language, which is (1) that there is no "natural" relationship between a word and the thing it stands for, and (2) that, nevertheless, the meanings of words cannot be changed by an individual on his own motion. An effective change cannot be made unless it is endorsed by that part of humanity to which one belongs linguistically. But since change is a fact of language, this leaves the question of who the real arbiters of a change are when it is made. I would answer that they are those who share most fully in what Shelley referred to as the imagination. I would here borrow an analogy that Croce uses in speaking of art when he says that all men are artists, but that some are great and some are small ones. In the same way, all men are "imaginers," but some men are small ones and some are great. Those who have the greatest insight into what words should mean are those with the greatest imaginative power.

Imagination in the sense used here is an absolute faculty. Not in actual cases, but ideally, it is commensurate with humanity itself. It is capable of telling us theoretically exactly what every word must mean because it is the imagination that holds in contemplation all the various meanings that have to remain discrete and yet have somehow to function together in coherent discourse. Just as those who have the best judgment in art approximate absolute taste, so those who have the best judgment in words approximate absolute imagination. All of us have had the experience of finding a particularly felicitous phrase in poetry and of feeling: "This is what the word really means; he has hit it closer than anyone has ever hit it before." I assume that we could not have this feeling unless two things were present: (1) our everyday, more or less obtuse understanding of the word, and (2) an awareness that there is a meaning beyond this, which our own imagination had not permitted us to attain. It is the man of greater imagination who helps to raise our imagination toward the absolute correctness of meaning.

10. Percy Bysshe Shelley, *Prose Works* (London, 1888), II, p. 6.

The problem of deciding upon the correct meaning of words, then, is not one of external measurement, but one of internal receptivity or capability. If we share to a large extent in that mutuality of spirit which makes meaning possible, we are receptive to true meanings; if we do not, we may accept wrong or perverted ones. And since there is no way of getting outside the human imagination to decide otherwise what a word should mean, we are compelled to realize that the most imaginative users of language are those who are going to have the greatest influence upon vocabulary in the long run. We realize further that the ones who name things in this way have a great influence in determining how the things will be regarded by our customs and laws. This is why Shelley, in that famous concluding sentence of "A Defence of Poetry," could call poets "the unacknowledged legislators of the world," a claim which might seem a bit of chauvinism in a poet, but which is capable of the most sober kind of defense.

Some such concept of language is required by the undeniable fact of its conventional function. And since words do function conventionally, they must function as deductive instrumentalities. Let us note here that one type of critic today tends to attack language as a means of communication on this very ground—the ground that words are conventional in their meaning and are therefore falsifying. The point of the criticism is that a convention is something abstracted and, therefore, untrue, a generalized sign of the thing itself, which we use because we are unable or unwilling to render the thing in itself in its fullness. A word in this conception is nothing but a stereotype, and "stereotype" is here an expression of disparagement, because it is felt that "typing" anything that is real distorts the thing by presenting it in something less than its full individuality and concreteness. Let us suppose that I make reference to a tree standing in my yard. The term "tree" does not designate the object with any degree of particularity. It does not tell whether the tree is young or old, low or tall, an oak, pine, or maple. The term is, therefore, merely a utility symbol, which I employ in communicating because in my laziness or incompetence I cannot find a fuller and more individualizing way of expressing this tree. If I were really communicating, the argument goes, I would reject the falsifying stereotype and produce something more nearly like the picture of the tree.

But if the analysis I have offered earlier is correct, these critics are beginning at the wrong end. They are assuming that individual real objects are carriers of meaning, that the meaning is found in them as redness is found in an apple, and that it ought to be expressed with the main object of fidelity to the particular. What they overlook is that meaning does not exist in this sense, that it is something that we create for purposes of cognition and communication, and that the ideal construct has the virtue of its ideality.[11]

Hence it appears that they misconceive the function of the word as conventional sign or "typifier." For if it is true that the word conveys something less than the fullness of the thing signified, it is also true that it conveys something more. A word in this role is a generalization. The value of a generalization is that while it leaves out the specific features that are of the individual or of the moment, it expresses features that are general to a class and may be lacking or imperfect in the single instance. What "tree," therefore, expresses is the generic nature of the tree, and so with "house," "city," "man," and all other such terms. In order to make statements that will have applicability over a period of time or in the occurrence of many instances, we have to avail ourselves of these classifiers. Obviously there are many

---

11. The author is aware that in these paragraphs he is going over ground that was well trodden in the Middle Ages. The great controversy over the status of universals, in which Abelard, Aquinas, and William of Ockham were prominent contenders, concerned questions with which the modern student of language and semiotics still has to deal. The position taken in this essay, which perhaps comes closest to that of Abelard, represents an attempt to answer the following question: What is the relationship between words and the extramental order that they symbolize? It is impossible, for reasons we have already seen, to assume a simple correspondence between the two. But, on the other hand, if we say there is no relationship, we abandon the objectivity of knowledge and leave the door open for pure subjectivism or skepticism. This is where Shelley's dictum has to be emended: words do not have relation to thoughts alone; they have relation to the real world *through* thought. The relationship between a word and whatever it stands for is thus an *imputed* relationship, which is the same as saying a relationship in thought. According to Abelard, what is expressed by a general term is in the thing symbolized (and hence the term has objective reference), but it is not in the thing in the form in which it is conceived by the mind. This distinction enables one to affirm that words do have relation to the real order, but that this relation can never be explained by simple analogies based on correspondence, contiguity, or other ideas involving that order. When I say that meaning creates things, I am saying that the mind conceives things in its own way for purposes of communication. It is the logical content of a word that is predicated of a percept, and this brings us back to the fact of language as a closed system, into which the extramental world has no direct mode of ingress. Prior to a more definitive epistemology and metaphysics, it seems impossible to say anything more definitive about the nature of reference.

situations in which we wish to say more about a thing than a specific image would convey. To do so, we abstract the common features of many such images (i.e., we arrive at a general meaning) and use the result as an index to a class of things. I repeat that if something is sacrificed in this process, something is also gained. Those who object to the word because it "stereotypes" are refusing to consider what may be the prime reason for the invention of language. They are forgetting that oftentimes we need to refer to a class of things, to those now out of sight as well as those before our eyes, to those that are past as well as to those that are now existing, and especially to those of the future.

At stake is nothing less than the whole body of general ideas. If we insist upon a point-by-point resemblance of word and particular thing signified, language would have to limp along at a very slow pace. Even ideographs are not really pictures of the things they represent; they are generalized depictions of objects and actions. It must be clear that the very business of a people and the continuity of a cultural tradition depend upon an acceptance of the agreed-upon sign in its extensive application. It is the imagination that sets the bounds of that application and has the privilege of widening and narrowing them.

One of the most interesting criticisms of the conventionalizing property of language, which I desire to notice at length, was made by the late Benjamin Lee Whorf. Whorf became interested in linguistic problems as the result of work he was doing as investigator for a fire insurance company. It was his duty to find out and report the circumstances surrounding the outbreak of fires. In the course of this work he became impressed by the way in which people are misled by what he calls "verbal analogies." He found that accidents sometimes resulted from the fact that people behaved in response to the conventional meanings of words when attention to the actual conditions would have produced a very different kind of behavior. Behavior dictated by the actual circumstances would have prevented an accident.

Here are two incidents he uses to illustrate his point. A group of men were employed around some gasoline drums which they had been told were "empty." Now "empty," just because it conventionally signifies the absence or privation of something, suggests at the same time an incapacity to cause harm (as it would if applied to a gun). But actually "empty" gasoline drums, because they contain vapor, are much more likely to explode than filled ones. Acting on the assumption that these drums were empty and therefore harmless, the men were careless about lighted matches and burning cigarettes and so allowed an explosion to occur. They had been betrayed by the general meaning of "empty" into misinterpreting the actual situation. The second example involves a wood distillation plant, where metal stills were insulated with a composition made from limestone.

> No attempt was made to protect the covering from excessive heat or contact of the flame. After a period of use the fire beneath one of the stills spread to the "limestone," which, to everyone's great surprise, burned vigorously. Exposure to acetic acid fumes from the stills had converted part of the limestone (calcium carbonate) to calcium acetate. This, when heated in a fire, decomposes, forming inflammable acetone. Behavior which tolerated fire close to the covering was induced by the use of the name "limestone," which, because it ends in "—stone," implies incombustibility.[12]

Now these seem to me very interesting, if unfortunate, exceptions to the utility of the generic sense of terms. But my point is that they can be regarded only as exceptions. For every occasion on which the use of a term like "empty" or "stone" leads to misguided action, there must be hundreds or thousands on which it guides the action correctly. In other words, the "class" meaning saves us incomparably more often than it harms us or causes us to have accidents. The analogizing function that these instances are used to deprecate is something we are unable to do without. Numberless necessary actions of our lives are predicated upon assumptions that "empty" does not mean "more dangerous than ever" but less dangerous and that "stone" means "fire-resistant." To the extent that these situations have to be faced as practical problems, I would merely point out that the user of the language had not been as specific as the language easily permits one to be. What was said was true up to a point, but beyond that it was not qualified in the right way. The gasoline drums were empty of liquid, but they were not empty of vapor, and the insulating material was stone in a sense, but it was stone in the process of chemical transformation. This is a problem that arises at every turn in the use of language. It does not call for denying the predictive "analogizing" function of words, but for making the prediction

12. Benjamin Lee Whorf, *Four Articles on Metalinguistics* (Washington, D.C.: Department of State, 1950), pp. 75–76.

a little fuller by expressing additional meanings. The meanings that were given needed to be supplemented by other meanings. But these meanings are no more physically attached to the objects than were the other "erroneous" ones. The real task is always to find the right construction for the real order in the logical order.

Believers in the value of language as a convention (and in the connection of this with preserving cultural tradition) are, for such reasons, suspicious of those who take a complacent attitude toward semantic change. They feel that change of meaning is somehow a sign of ignorance or laxity. It represents to them a breaking away from some original standard of "rightness" owing to the user's failure to inform himself fully about the word or to irresponsibility. They wish language to remain pure, and "pure" means in accordance with the old standards of signification. I share the moral impulse that makes them take this stand, but I believe some way will have to be found to take into account more of the realities involved. It seems an irrefragable fact that meanings do shift over a period of time, with a movement hardly more to be resisted than a glacier's. Is there any way of reconciling the ideal of semantic purism with this fact? Is it possible to visualize a kind of gold standard of semantic reference, from which illegitimate departures could be detected? I think it might be possible if we could find some basis for distinguishing between those changes which are "natural" and therefore must be conceded and those which are perverse and should be put down in the interest of intellectual and cultural integrity.

We can begin by noting what some students of language call "linguistic drift." This is a change, occurring usually over a long span of time, which affects such features as inflection, syntax, and usage. "Drift" suggests some kind of irrational, directionless change, whereas the striking thing about this change is that it seems to manifest direction. It is not an accumulation of random divergences, but a change occurring according to a pattern, which will accept some innovations and reject others. Sapir observes that "linguistic drift has direction. . . . The drift of a language is constituted by the unconscious selection on the part of its speakers of those individual variations that are cumulative in some special direction."[13] In brief, the change is selective and not simply accidental.

13. Sapir, *op. cit.*, pp. 165–166.

Now, there seems to be something corresponding to this that might be denominated "semantic shift." Over a long period of time words will change their references in ways that are not haphazard but are consonant with changes in the general mind. Just what the ultimate cause of the change is seems difficult to ascertain. Perhaps it is the result of an aging of the cultural group that speaks the language, of a sophistication or an assimilation of experience, of the accumulating of past history that inevitably brings with it a change of perspective. Nor do we understand the law of this change. The changes may follow our insights into reality, or they may reflect epiphanies of experience. Usually as the word changes, the meaning keeps polarizing around some idea. The word "dress," in the earliest meaning that can be traced, meant "to make straight." (Hence, "to dress food"; "to dress hides.") It is apparent that something of the core meaning survives in our phrase "to dress oneself." The word "write" traces back to an earlier word meaning "to cut, scratch." Since writing, after its many metamorphoses, is still a process of making an impression upon a surface with a pointed instrument, I would say that the original denotative meaning survives. These are examples out of ordinary vocabulary showing that while processes may change, the essential idea of the process may be conserved in the word used to signify it. This sort of change does not play havoc with codes of behavior or institutions.

But I think we can recognize two types of semantic change that are inspired either by false reasoning or by motives that are objectionable. The first of them I shall call "rhetorical substitution"; the second, "rhetorical prevarication." (I leave out of account those changes that are the result of simple ignorance of lexical meaning on the part of a few, such as the use of "fortuitous" to mean "fortunate" or of "thus" to mean "therefore.")

The first of the improper changes keeps the old word but applies it to a new thing (the user not being aware that in the world of language words create "things"). Evidently, this has its source in the old iconic fallacy. One finds in the writings of modern semanticists a persistent tendency to refer to language as a "map" of what it stands for.[14] I say that this seems to go back to the iconic theory of meaning because a map is a small-scale configuration of the territory it plots. Language, on this supposition, must fol-

14. Irving J. Lee, *Language Habits in Human Affairs* (New York, 1941), pp. 17–22.

low the outline of what it symbolizes. Now if a territory changes (e.g., if a river alters its course), the map has to change too. Otherwise, there will be a growing disparity between map and terrain, between language and the realities of the world, and we shall end in hallucinations. Words whose referents no longer exist are of no more use than outdated maps. Always, of course, the referent, as a shaper of meaning, is supposed to be something "out there." But since the word continues to exist (and since it may have agreeable overtones), the trick is to take it and apply it to a new situation. One writer revealingly calls this adjusting language to "life facts." [15]

I believe it can be demonstrated that this is what has happened to the word "liberalism." In the nineteenth century, this word referred to an ideal of maximum individual liberty and minimum state interference, to put it generally. Today, it is being used to refer to something like the ideal of the welfare state, which involves many restrictions upon liberty. Now if those who use the word thus could be brought into a semantic disputation, I think they would argue that the new meaning is justified because the old meaning is no longer possible. And if we pushed them to explain why it is no longer possible, I think they would answer that "circumstances have changed." I would want to ask them next what changed circumstances have to do with an ideal construct. What they have done is to take the old term "liberalism," whose meaning polarized around a concept of personal liberty, and to use this to mean something like philanthropic activity through the machinery of the state. The two ideas are manifestly discrete, but they have used the word for the second idea because it carries with it some of the value connotations of the old one. The second idea is, according to them, the only context in which a benevolent man can now operate. In fact, however, liberalism in the old sense is still there as a viable ideal if the mind is disposed to receive that ideal. When they say that the old meaning is no longer possible in the circumstances, what they are really indicating is that they prefer the new circumstances. Then they make the substitution, in disregard of the transcendental basis of language.

I believe that this is a very general truth. When a person blames a change of meaning upon changed facts, he is yielding to the facts and using them to justify a change that should not be made except by "ideal" consent. He is

15. *Ibid.*, p. 83.

committing the fallacy of supposing that the reason for such change can lie outside the realm of discourse itself—that meaning must somehow tag along after empirical reality. All of this seems to reflect a purely materialist or "physicalist" view of the world. But if one believes that physical reality is the sole determinant of all things, including meanings, one collapses the relationship between what is physical and what is symbolic of meaning and value. It is another evidence of how the modern mind is trying to surrender its constitutive powers to the objective physical world.

The second kind of improper change, rhetorical prevarication, does not allege the excuse that the world has changed. It is a simple attempt to impose a change in the interest of an ideology. (I here use "ideology" in contradistinction to "philosophy." A philosophy, having a much wider circumspection, will have something to say about a word's meaning that connects with the larger work of the imagination. An ideology works to serve particular ends, and therefore the changes in meaning that it produces will not be circumspective and must result in a degree of injustice.) For example, when the modern leftist applies the term "reactionary" to everyone who will not accept the Marxist concept of economic and social organization, I would regard this as an ideological perversion. The Marxist is using the word to ascribe an impulse to "go backward" to people whose political views may reflect nothing more than a nonmaterialistic concept of man.

My next example is a more insidious and, therefore, more dangerous instance of prevarication. We mark a growing tendency among certain groups of people to refer to alcoholics, moral delinquents, and even criminals as "sick" people. The violence that this does to the legitimate meaning of "sick" is easily seen. We have always thought of a sick person as a man who is a victim of things beyond his control and who, therefore, deserves sympathy and assistance from his family and perhaps from society. If he becomes exposed to bacteria, which, of course, he cannot see, and contracts a disease, or if he suffers from some degeneration of tissue or bone, we regard him as undergoing a misfortune to which he did not in any conscious way contribute. He may become more or less a burden to his family and society, but not through any act of will.

Now the attempt is being made through this rhetorical prevarication to edge the delinquent and the criminal into this category. The result, it is almost too obvious to point out, is to remove the idea of moral responsibility from delinquency and crime. It has always been thought that society is the victim of the criminal. But now it is being implied, through a tendentious use of language, that the criminal is the victim of society, which did not take appropriate steps to keep him from getting "sick." By this verbal trick, what was formerly considered worthy of punishment is held up for indulgent sympathy.

This line of false reasoning probably begins with sentimentality. It certainly ends by denying the power of self-discipline. For what it says is this absurdity: Every man is conditioned, but the criminal is more conditioned than others; as a result, we are supposed to pity him and show him more solicitude than the person who is behaving himself and working hard at his job. Society has not agreed, and it cannot agree and maintain its own health, that those who have willfully done wrong belong in the same category and should be treated with the same commiseration as those who are afflicted with physical illness. It is, therefore, nothing less than scandalous to spread the view that alcoholics, criminals, and others who have adopted evil courses are merely "sick" people.

But to return to my earlier characterization: this is a designing shift, a deliberate misapplication in the interest of a special program. The users do not fall back on the excuse that reality has changed and that verbal usage must change with it; they simply take the word out of one context and put it in another in order to advance an ideological point of view. The ideology that is seeking to advance this prevarication is utterly hostile to the idea of freedom and the concomitant fact of responsibility. Such perversions have to be fought by a noetic and dialectical examination of the contents of the words involved.

This essay has attempted to relate the modern concept of relativism to language and, more particularly, to semantic reference. I shall emphasize, in closing, that the findings must be read in the light of one very important distinction. There is a difference between saying that language is relative because it is a convention and saying that because it is a convention it may be treated or used relativistically. If language is a more or less local convention, then its meanings are relative to those who use it. It clearly does not follow from this, however, that those who speak it may use it with unrestricted license. Here one might usefully paraphrase a statement that Burke makes about civil government: "If language is the product of convention, then that convention is its law." Now, when we say that that convention is its law, we accept the idea of prescriptive meaning. I would prefer to describe the fact with a word of stronger implication: language is a covenant among those who use it. It is in the nature of a covenant to be more than a matter of simple convenience, to be departed from for light and transient causes. A covenant—and I like, in this connection, the religious overtones of the word—binds us at deeper levels and involves some kind of confrontation of reality. When we covenant with one another that a word shall stand for a certain thing, we signify that it is the best available word for that thing in the present state of general understanding. The possibilities of refinement toward a more absolute correctness of meaning lie within and behind that convention. But as long as the convention is in effect, it has to be respected like any other rule, and this requires that departures from it must justify themselves.

Language, therefore, must be viewed as nonrelative in two ways. Meanings cannot be judged as relative simply to time and place; hence, in our dialectical vocabulary there is a theoretical absolute rightness of meaning. (Another distinction, which I owe to the members of this Symposium, is the difference between knowing an absolute and knowing an absolute absolutely. We posit, without knowing, an absolute correctness of meaning; how we attain toward that I have indicated in my remarks on poetry and imagination.) In the second place, the convention or covenant of language must be treated as absolutely binding upon us, as far as our human condition permits, until a change is authorized by right reason. These two considerations prevent the anarchy which an unconditional permissiveness—itself a pernicious absolute—would allow. They are all the defense that is needed for those who believe that both effective and right ways of saying things can be taught the student who is entering the universe of linguistic discourse.

The Importance of Cultural Freedom [1]

Culture in its formal definition is one of the fulfillments of the psychic need of man. The human being is a focal point of consciousness who looks with wondering eyes upon the universe into which he is born a kind of stranger. No other being, as far as we can tell, feels the same amount of tension between himself and the surroundings in which he must pass his existence. His kind of awareness is accompanied by degrees of restlessness and pain, and it is absolutely necessary, as we must infer from the historical record, that he do something to humanize his vision and to cognize in special ways his relation to these surroundings. This he does by creating what is called a culture.

A culture nearly always appears contemporaneously with the expression of religious feeling. However, the two expressions must be distinguished as follows: religion is man's response to the totality and to the question of his destiny. Through religion he reveals his profoundest intuition regarding his origin, his mission on earth, and his future state. Culture is sometimes auxiliary to this expression, but characteristically it is man's response to the various manifestations of this world as they impinge upon his mundane life. He alters these to forms that reflect meaning; he fills interstices which appear unbearable when left void; he dresses with significance things which in their brute empirical reality are an affront to the spirit. In doing this he makes extensive use of symbolism, and because symbolism is supra-natural, we can say that cultural expression is a vestibule between man's worldly activities and the concept of a supra-nature which lies at the core of most religions. Anyone who engages in cultural activity, however unconscious he may be of this truth, is testifying to a feeling that man is something more than a part of nature. And only when man has begun to create a culture does he feel that he has found a proper way of life. [2]

1. *Modern Age*, 6/1, Winter 1961–62, 21–33.

2. It may be asked whether in the following discussion I am dealing with cultures empirically, recognizing any formalized and elaborated human activity as a culture, or whether I am

II

Little more needs to be said about the value of culture (a value which has on some occasions been challenged). But something does need to be said about the right of a culture to its self-constitution and self-direction. In surveying the history of cultures, we may be tempted to describe any given culture as a perfectly spontaneous and unregulated expression of the human spirit which can know no law except delight in what it creates. But when we study the phenomenology more critically, we become aware of a formal entelechy. A fact strikingly evident in the history of cultures is that any given culture is born, rises, and flourishes as an integer; that is to say, an entity striving to achieve and maintain homogeneity. It is this cohesive wholeness which enables us to identify it as different from other cultures, to give coherent descriptions of it, and to make predictions on the basis of these descriptions. Culture by its very nature tends to be centripetal, or to aspire toward some unity in its representational modes.

The reason for this is that every culture polarizes around some animating idea, figment, or value, toward which everything that it produces bears some discoverable relation. Everyone perceives that cultures are marked by characteristic styles; and the style will have its source in some idea, feeling, or projection that exists as a fountain feeding the various streams that flow down even into those areas where cultural expression is but slight. A culture lives under the aegis of an image, almost a tyrannizing image, which imposes something of its form upon all the numerous and varied manifestations of its activity. This but underlines the truth that a culture is a shared thing, which cannot exist without consensus. The members of a culture are in a manner of speaking communicants of that culture, and they look toward the center as to some source of authority for an imperative. Thus

---

supposing a normative, axiological definition. An attempt to define the limits of cultural freedom naturally implies the second approach. Every marked development of formal activity is a sign that the cultural impulse is present; in this sense the first datum is anthropological. But it is ridiculous to maintain that all cultures are equal and of infinite worth; whether a culture or a cultural activity is better or worse must be judged by the amount of satisfaction it provides for the higher faculties. That judgment can be reached only on the basis of a true philosophy of the human spirit. The point of view in this essay is, therefore, cultural pluralism but not cultural relativism. It is inevitable and right that there should be different cultures, but any culture may be viewed critically if the viewer has a definition of man.

culture always appears as a creation integral and self-forming, which maintains a coherency amid things which may be neutral, foreign, or distractive.[3]

The above feature deserves stressing because today culture is being threatened by some who do not understand—and who would oppose if they did understand—this principle of cultural integrity. A chief danger to cultural freedom in our time comes from certain political fanaticisms which are trying to break down this cultural integrity by assuming or attempting to prove that it has no right to exist. Sometimes this proceeding is against cultures which have existed independently under one political sovereignty; sometimes it is against the traditional or naturally evolved culture within one nation because it is argued that the institutions of that culture are obstacles to "progressive" reform. In the first case the movement is against culture pluralism, out of a hostility to independent centers of influence; in the second it may be this also, but it may be more directly interested in subordinating culture to ends of the state which have been conceived out of speculation rather than out of consultation with history.

The fomenters of such movements are trying to make political schemata prevail, and they are prone to regard anything that stands in the way of these—even cultural creations of the highest power to gratify artistically—as "reactionary." Both would deny to culture its rightful measure of autonomy, the one trying to pour it into the mould of the supervening national state, the other attempting to bring it into line with political abstractions which may have no relation to the spirit out of which the culture was born. Both are opposed to culture as expressive of a region, but there is ample ground for asserting that all cultures are necessarily regional.

We are not equipped to oppose their attempts without a fuller understanding of the essential nature of culture. For this reason I return to the point that a culture has to retain a high degree of integrity in order to survive, and that in order to maintain that integrity it has to practice a principle of exclusiveness. A culture is born expressive of a place and a time, and a mood which says implicitly "We hold these values." It is these particularities which give it character, and as a matter of nature character and integrity go together. A culture is like an organic creation in that its constitution cannot

3. Even anthropologists concede the impulse of a culture to integrate itself. For a discussion of this subject from the anthropological point of view, see Ruth Benedict, *Patterns of Culture* (New York: Houghton, Mifflin, 1934), Ch. III.

tolerate more than a certain amount of what is foreign or extraneous. Certain outside values may be assimilated through transformation or reworking, but fundamentally unless a culture can maintain its own right to its own choices—its own inclusions and exclusions—it will cease. It may be simply suppressed, or the cessation may take the form of a decline into eclecticism, cosmopolitanism, Alexandrianism, or those politically fostered modes which have been an emergence of our time—all of which conditions are incapable of profound cultural creation.

For the freedom of cultures as wholes, two rights must be respected: the right of cultural pluralism where different cultures have developed, and the right of cultural autonomy in the development of a single culture. In a word, cultural freedom on this plane starts with the acknowledgement of the right of a culture to be itself. This is a principle deduced from the nature of culture, not from the nature of the state. Culture grows from roots more enduring than those of the political state. It also offers satisfactions more intimate than those of the political state; and hence it is wrong to force it to defer to political abstractions; the very fact that it has not chosen to embody those abstractions is evidence that they are extraneous. Culture emerges out of climatic, geographical, ecological, racial, religious, and linguistic soils; a state may have to deal with all these factors, but it does not deal with them at the level where they enter into cultural expression. That is the reason for saying that the policy of a state toward the culture or cultures within it should be *laisser faire,* except at those points where collisions may be so severe that they imperil the minimum preservation of order with which the state is charged.

Abstraction in the form of the political dictate is the great foe of what must develop physiognomically. Cultural freedom is in special danger today because so much of our life has been politicalized in recent decades. We need not concern ourselves with the repression which was practiced in National Socialist Germany and is being practiced in Soviet Russia today. We know these forms for what they are; they are part and parcel of such regimes, and the case against them is largely one with the case against those regimes. It is otherwise with governments which are popular and free, but which allow political sanction to pressures building up against types of cultural expression. Sometimes we do not find it easy, in these cases, to distinguish between society and government; but we can be clear as to the direction of the pressure. It moves to condemn on grounds which are social and political, and its desire is for uniformity, standardization, consolidation, and all the other features of *Gleichschaltung*, as it moves to protect from criticism and even from realistic depiction something over which people have become politically excited. In our American experience, these pressures have been social largely, but sometimes they have been sufficient to manipulate local official bodies, such as boards and legislatures, to effect their will. Moreover, the occurrences have been occasional rather than systematic, but if they are allowed to happen often enough, the occasions could harden into a precedent.

A current trend which throws into clear relief this danger is the practice of condemning books because they give an unflattering picture or apply supposedly derogatory terms to minority groups. Ethnic groups have been especially militant against this kind of expression, and even that American classic *Huckleberry Finn* has been challenged and actually withdrawn from circulation in some places because the author applied to the Negro a form of the name widely used in his time. But the principle if accepted could be invoked by any minority which had had its feelings hurt or which merely happened to be politically or socially ambitious. Applied in extreme form it could require us to remove Boswell from the shelves because of Dr. Johnson's derogatory remarks about Scotsmen and Americans.

I hope there is no need to argue that it would be culturally fatal to regard in this way any individual or group as being above artistic intuition or critical evaluation. I call this an example of political fanaticism invading the realm of culture because the primary role of culture is neither to carry into effect the specific laws of the state or to give force to political ideologies which have won a temporary ascendancy. In these instances it is being asked to bow before a dogmatic equalitarianism. The truth to be recognized is that the cultural mission is to symbolize reality as this is reflected in men's attitudes, and there can be no *a priori* dictation to it to flatter or disparage. Creations that do one or the other must come out of honest perceptions and feelings, which are at some point in time expressive of a consensus. An artist may use as his subject matter attitudes of a past time, of a present time, or of a future time.

There exist, and I hope there will always continue to exist a large number of minorities of different kinds. Inevitably these will be the objects of varying attitudes, and the attitudes themselves will undergo changes. Whatever the level of expression, any such restraint of treatment would cut artistic effort off from the possibility of doing what it is supposed to do, and the situation would be far worse if the minority were allowed to prescribe the treatment. In short, it is wholly unpermissible to censor work of culture for presenting a subject as less attractive than one would like it to be. The right to represent freely is an inherent prerogative of culture; corrections will have to be left to change of attitude, to improvement of taste, to supplementation—or to better art.[4] The principle is simple: an artist cannot be bound to present only images of the innocuous. If he is a profound artist, he may be presenting images of what the majority will like a generation hence, for what the artist sees and what the generality of men see are at times two different things.

III

These forces of repression raise the question of whether there exists any significant relation between the various forms of government and the liberty of culture to flourish. Many would like to assume that there is a steady relation between the degree of democracy and the degree of cultural freedom, but this assumption is open to historical challenge. The most brilliant phase of Greek culture occurred indeed under a democracy, but a democracy which, according to Thucydides, was a "rule by the first citizen." The Augustan age of Rome, in the first century of the Empire, was by no means culturally poor. Nor would one call England in the latter half of the sixteenth century a period in which culture was stifled by a strong Tudor government. The high point of French drama was reached under Louis XIV, not to speak of the flourishing of many other arts at that time. Descending to later periods, we find that Imperial Germany in the latter part of the nineteenth century was enormously creative. Even Czarist Russia, despite its many repressions, was very productive of literature.

On the other hand, there have been governments of the monarchical kind which have been discouraging to cultural endeavor. George Savile,

4. A substantial part of American folklore has consisted of jokes about "the Irish." One may doubt that the Irish were ever done much harm by these, and today the situation has changed so that their application to the Irish seems to lack point.

Lord Halifax, in that remarkable political testament called "The Character of a Trimmer," while declaring himself biased in favor of monarchy, confessed that "in all overgrown monarchies reason, learning, and inquiry are hang'd in effigy for mutineers."[5]

Two extremes emerge from this examination. There are some despotic governments so filled with a feeling of insecurity that they regard the free life of culture as a threat to their existence (according to an informant of mine, contemporary Spain is an example). Others out of simple barbarousness or selfishness may do the same. A highly centralized government which is fearful of the structure of its power may be unfavorable to cultural activity except insofar as culture can be manipulated in the government's vindication.

On the other extreme is the kind of popular government which is so distrustful of all forms of distinction that it sees even in the cultivated individual a menace to its existence. Such states are likely to maintain a pressure which discourages cultural endeavor, although the pressure may be exerted through social channels. But apostrophes to universal enlightenment and culture do little good if the state renders odious or impossible the forms in which these have to manifest themselves concretely. Everyone recognizes that there has been a strain of this in American life, although we have been spared the harshness of Jacobinism. Democracies tend to be jealous of exemptions from their authority. Yet there is certainly something to Machiavelli's statement that a popular form of government elicits more of the energies of the people.

It is important to note that Jacobinism has always been hostile to culture.[6] When the scientist Lavoisier was brought to trial during the French Revolution, his contributions to knowledge, which were of the first order, were pleaded as a reason to spare his life. The plea is said to have been answered by the President of the Revolutionary Tribunal with the statement: "*La République n'a pas besoin de savants*," and Lavoisier was sent to the guillo-

5. *Complete Works of George Savile, First Marquess of Halifax*, ed. Walter Raleigh (Oxford: The Clarendon Press, 1912), p. 63.

6. Matthew Arnold makes this point in his *Culture and Anarchy*, and he adds the further important consideration that Jacobinism has a fierce hatred of the past. This thought could be elaborated: no government and no ideology which try to cut a people off from its past can be friendly to culture.

tine. The extreme radical François Babeuf, in his "Manifesto of the Society of Equals," exclaimed, "Let all the arts perish if only we can have equality." The nihilist Pisarev declared that he would rather be a Russian shoemaker than a Russian Raphael. In Hitler's Germany, which was a pathological deviation of the right as this extremism was of the left, there was contempt for cultivation well epitomized for posterity in the saying, "When I hear the word 'culture,' I reach for my revolver."

The reason is simply that these are virulences, and that culture does not survive in the presence of a virus.

Modern communism is full of the spirit of Jacobinism; and its influence upon culture, wherever it has made headway, has been much the same. The story of Pasternak needs no retelling. Mikhail Sholokov is, I believe, under a kind of limited dispensation; he is allowed to portray the local and the traditional, but not to the point of impugning party doctrine. Communism is by its very nature intolerant of independent projections of reality. And there is the further consideration that no one can take culture seriously if he believes that it is only the uppermost of several layers of epiphenomena resting on a primary reality of economic activity.

IV

These are political interferences, but no discussion of cultural freedom would be complete without some notice of the right to moral censorship claimed by the political state. Whatever its form, virtually every state has at one time and another used its apparatus of coercion to forbid certain cultural expressions on the ground of their pernicious moral tendency. This is essentially an intrusion, to be distinguished from that cultural coercion which the spirit of a culture exercises in defense of its integrity. The ever latent temptation to invoke the right of moral censorship makes it desirable to study the question in principle.

The idea that a society can be absolutely open either politically or culturally seems to be untenable. But it can be more open culturally, and the reason for saying this is that cultural or artistic creation exists in the province of the imagination. That is not a completely isolated province, but since cultural works are not immediately translated into moral consequences, they should get the longest hearing before it is determined whether—'nature imitating art'—they are going to prove deleterious.

Usually, it seems to me, we approach the problem from the wrong end. Granted that an ultimate right of censorship is defensible, still a society which is culturally or physically in good health will not often need to invoke it. This does not mean that in the life of such a society cultural expression will never touch upon matters of obscenity or depravity. On the contrary, in such societies these subjects may receive quite frank treatment, as they did in the comedy of Aristophanes, the poetry of Chaucer, the plays of Shakespeare, some eighteenth century novels, and many other forms. The point is that in such artistic expressions these matters are not the dominant foci of interest; they are there simply as filling out the normal range of human activity and interest. The culture is healthy enough to take them in its stride, to incorporate them, to hold them in their place, and to pass on to more important matters. They are not offered to excite pruriency; they are present rather because their absence would be an evidence of the infidelity of the artist to the complete artistic picture.[7] The Elizabethans and Jacobeans, for example, did not grow worried over "indecent" allusions; they saw no reason why one should not be frank about all the facts of life. They had a vision which was steady and whole, and they were interested in serious themes, which become less serious in proportion as things are suppressed because they might incite the perverse or the immature to harmful acts. Frankness is of course allied in meaning with freedom, which connotes maturity and poise.

The conclusion is that a society will not feel the need for much censorship unless it is somehow out of joint itself. The exploitation of cultural media for purposes which could be called morbid shows not that there are naughty people around but that the society itself has developed weaknesses. (I cannot deal here with the problem of how the state should protect minors from things they are not yet ready to cope with.) There may be occasions on which a society shows itself to be in such poor health that too many people are going to obvert things—are going to turn the products of culture toward ends that supply a different sort of gratification. Then some public

---

7. Sir Herbert Read has stated the principle (*Truth Is More Sacred: A Critical Exchange on Modern Literature*, by Edward Dahlberg and Sir Herbert Read [New York: Horizon Press, 1961], pp. 216–217): "No censorship can be imposed on the imagination, and the truth we should hold sacred . . . is truth to the divine promptings of the Muse—promptings which may take a poet into a lady's bedroom or a brothel as easily and as frequently as into the vernal woods or the market place."

restraint on the principle of *salus rei publicae suprema lex* may be necessary. Yet this is a stopgap procedure; the real reform must come from the other end, with the symmetrical development of the individual, so that he is his own sufficient guardian.

Our situation in the United States is complicated by a special historical inheritance. We are still suffering from the Puritan gnosis, which operates by rejecting totally certain parts of reality and then reacts hysterically when these parts come slipping back in in the forms of artistic representation. Unless it could be established that Puritanism is the consensus of our culture, we can only say that in the various rebellions against Puritanical suppression we are witnessing not a tendency toward evil, but a normal effort of the cultural spirit to express itself without crippling hindrance. The remedy for this situation is educating more people to see life and art in their true relations.

V

The question of the freedom of the creator in relation to his own cultural tradition is of special interest to our time. No other period has seen so many instances of artists in apparently violent revolt, of creative workers of all kinds departing radically from the tradition or seeming to attack its deepest presuppositions.

In modern poetry, in painting, in music, in sculpture, and in other forms, the story has been much the same: the new artists are new in a sense which could imply total dissociation from the past. If modern culture has produced some works which are aesthetically gratifying (and I for one would contend that it has) how can this wholesale revolt be explained meaningfully within a pattern of consensus and freedom?

Here one has to proceed with additional circumspection, because it is not given to us to lay down laws to poets, regarding either their subject matter or their forms. Still, we can insist that they be judged against a requirement that cultural creation must satisfy certain psychic needs which we have earlier connected with the birth of culture.

Within the fairly recent past the matter of artistic goals has become complicated by circumstances which artists in other ages have not had to face, at least in anything like such severe form. In most of the recognizable periods of art in the world's history, we can see clearly enough how the artist was held to performance in a tradition by an overriding *mythos*—a story about man or creation which provided the basic themes for his creations. The classical world had its mythology; the Islamic world had its religion; and our culture until recent times had the Christian story of man's life on earth and the Christian eschatology. This was a constructive symbol which gave the artist a starting point and a resolution of his values, even when the latter was only implicit.

But in the last century or two there has occurred a fragmentation of belief which has largely swept away this resource. In consequence, the artist of modernity has been faced with a true dilemma. He could choose on the one hand to symbolize the traditional values in the traditional forms for a public which no longer had a live belief in those values and thus suffer the fate of being regarded as merely quaint; or he could attempt to revitalize the tradition, beginning with audiences sophisticated and serious, who are aware of what has happened to man and to art. The most likely way to kill a tradition is to over-formalize it, which is to carry it on in the same way after everyone has ceased to defer to it. The way to revive it is to show that it has grown out of and is still related to our most cherished values. But this requires radical insight and the stripping away of many things which are mere accretions.

It is a mistake to suppose, as some apparently do suppose, that all modern artists who have employed highly novel forms have been in revolt for revolt's sake. The truth is that they have been in revolt against some of the products of our civilization. The past century has seen such an increase in popular education, with accompanying accent on the peripheral, such availability of printing, so much cheap reproduction and growth of the means of communication that there has been introduced into our culture a factor of vulgarity which touches many things and which works powerfully against the discipline of respect. The dominant trend of journalism and popular art has been in the direction of non-serious. However, true culture and art cannot flourish unless people believe that life presents some issues which are momentous. The tide of the trivial has been overwhelming, and it has seemed impossible to artists to oppose the sweep through its own channels; that is, by fighting back through the very media that have engulfed them. It has seemed equally impossible to oppose it by chanting the old values in the old ways, for this would truly be incantation. No one today can write a successful Shakespearean tragedy because our age in general does not possess a sense of the tragic ambivalence of man. No one today could produce a *Paradise Lost* because the paradigm on which this epic depends does not exist in the minds of the people. This is the kernel of truth in Walt Whitman's remark that "To have great poets there must be great audiences too." The only remaining strategy is to recover for man that sense which tells him that he needs this kind of play and this kind of poem. In his effort toward revivification of this sense, the modern artist has not infrequently retired into himself; he has accepted isolation or even alienation. We hear much complaint about the self-alienation of the artist from society, yet we must ask ourselves whether this is not sometimes defensible or even necessary. Sometimes the good has to go underground, as it were. C. S. Lewis points out that in the time of Domitian humanity itself had to become an underground movement.

At any rate, the "revolutionary" artist of whom I speak has had the aim of saving himself from the surrounding forces of sentimentality and vulgarity. In the nature of the case it is impossible to make a deal with these forces, and we should not be surprised if in striking back the artist has done so in ways even intended to be offensive. He has sometimes shown defiance and contempt toward those who would deny his level of seriousness.

All of this can be pointed up by remarking that we live in a post-1914 world. Most of the problems which men thought had been buried by two centuries of progress and a century of peace have been resurrected into life, some of them with a more frightening power to produce violence and chaos than ever before. As W. E. Hocking has observed: "The world-turmoil cannot fail to bring with it so wide a loss of order and predictable circumstances that *no art today can bear to speak simply in terms of beauty and affirmation.*" [8] That is why much modern art is signalized by an offensive warfare against the complacent and the stereotypical. The artist with his superior insight has perceived that we cannot *afford* such addictions.

And art, with its usual prescience, anticipated 1914 somewhat. The new movements were stirring by the beginning of the nineteenth century (in limited forms somewhat before), but the one which I select as an illustration

8. "The International Role of Art in Revolutionary Times," *Modern Age*, Vol. IV (Spring, 1960), p. 132.

erupted rather suddenly around 1912, the date conventionally taken for the beginning of modern poetry.

The modern poet, at war with the complacent and the stereotypical, has been spoken of as a revolutionary, but for reasons that will appear it would be just as meaningful, and it would better enable us to understand the object he has in view, to call him a reactionary. He is reacting through revolutionary means toward a vision of the world which earlier epochs, not affected by the kind of degradation ours has been through, possessed more fully. Not all poets of course have done this in equal degree, but it is safe to say that no poet today can get a hearing among serious readers of poetry unless his work somehow reflects the torturing experiences, with the resulting complexity of attitude, which distinguish our age.

Looking over the characteristics of the genre, we see the poet trying to break through superficies of falsehood and inadequacies of sensibility by avoiding all stock devices and patterns—of imagery, of phrasing, and sometimes of syntax, which might be expected to evoke a complacent response. He has spoken boldly through symbol and metaphor, avoiding the more leisurely simile and full predication; through unexpected combinations, violent antitheses, juxtapositions of the colloquial with the traditionally poetic or literary, and other means of surprise and shock which he hoped would awaken the reader into an awareness that there is a reality to be intuited aesthetically behind the sentimental, romantic, and often vulgar encrustation of the last century or so.

As a leading example of this, and an example very instructive on points which lack general understanding, I shall use T. S. Eliot. If we follow Eliot through "The Love Song of J. Alfred Prufrock," "The Waste Land," and "The Hollow Men," and then on through his later poems, we shall see what might be called the evolution of a conservative, or a conservator of our tradition. He has pursued this evolution while remaining one of the most experimental of our creative writers.

The first of the works named, which appeared in 1915, has been subjected to varying interpretations; but I am satisfied to regard it as an extraordinary intuition of the frustration, lack of direction, and helplessness which can be felt by a modern man at the height of our materially flourishing civilization. Space will not allow me to support this proposition with texts, but those familiar with the poem will recall enough of its method. They will realize that for a reader brought up in the preceding tradition of poetry, which means roughly the Victorian tradition, the poem teems with images which are vivid, but which shock, tease, or puzzle by their incongruity.

The wonder created by "Prufrock," however, was exceeded by that which met "The Waste Land" upon its appearance in 1922. This is admittedly a difficult poem, with its ransacking of legend and literature for images, its sudden breaks in surface continuity, and its odd juxtapositions of the noble and the beautiful with the cheap and the tawdry. Now, after the lapse of half a century, when the poetry of Eliot and some others has to some extent passed into the public mind and has itself become a tradition of a sort, the novelty of the method does not seem as striking as it did then. But then such affronts to the established idea of what a poem should be were taken as proofs positive that the poet had deserted his office, that he had contemptuously alienated himself from the whole tradition of poetry, that he was a man talking to himself, and so on. The feeling was not lessened by the appearance of "The Hollow Men," where the poet pursued the theme of emptiness through images of the barren and the repulsive.

But with the later appearance of "The Journal of the Magi," "Ash Wednesday," and "The Four Quartets," it began to be seen that Eliot was doing something very nearly the opposite of what had been alleged. He was in fact working to restore the tradition insofar as that depends upon a positive and coherent belief about man and his duty or destiny. "Prufrock" could indeed be called negative in the sense that its emphasis is upon a theme of deprivation. But "The Waste Land," for all its images of chaos and its mood of resignation to the breakdown of modern society, in fact prepares us for a turning toward affirmation, so much so that it has been described by one critic as "the rehabilitation of a system of beliefs."[9] "The Hollow Men" presents some of the philosophical difficulties, or difficulties of re-integrating the sensibility, which will be encountered in the work of this rehabilitation. With the publication of "Ash Wednesday" (1927–29) it became evident that Eliot was perhaps the foremost Christian poet of our time, who had won his way through a dark night of the soul to an affirmative position very much in line with our tradition. For this poem, in

9. Cleanth Brooks, *Modern Poetry and the Tradition* (Chapel Hill: University of North Carolina Press, 1939), p. 171.

the words of one interpreter, "describes stages of despair, self-abnegation, moral recovery, resurgent faith, need of grace, and renewal of will toward both world and God." [10] His beautiful "The Four Quartets," coming somewhat later, has been called a meditation upon what it means to be a Christian.

I am not here supposing that art has to be Christian in order to be good; my point is that Eliot through his "revolutionary" techniques (still revolutionary in "The Four Quartets") is not simply presenting a picture of fragmentation or anarchy or supplying an impulse toward antinomianism; but is arriving at something like the consensus which underlay the mythic structure of Western culture. What needs stressing is that he could not have done this in any other way; at least he could not have done so as a creative poet. Only by bringing the elements of our modern experience together in these arresting combinations could he have given the reading public a feeling that here is something momentous which must be heard seriously.

Much the same lesson can be found in the career of another great modern poet, William Butler Yeats. Yeats was of course writing before the outburst of modern poetry, but then these movements should not be too neatly periodized. While not as outwardly revolutionary as Eliot, he felt increasingly as he grew older an impulse to make an overt rejection of modern nihilism and to give his poems continuing reference to a system of belief. Conscious in a similar way that the old system had fallen into disbelief, he went the length of inventing his own system of mythology. This was published in 1925 as *A Vision*. An elaborate construction, it gives "a picture of history, an account of human psychology, and an account of the life of the soul after death." [11] Now there is hardly anything more radical than to invent a mythology, but the use to which this one was put was orthodox and traditional: it was to supply a unifying framework for the creations of the artist. Images from the system constantly recur in his subsequent poems and give them a depth of meaning they would not have otherwise.

Both of these poets have produced most affecting pictures of the maladies of modernism; but they are not breaking the world in pieces; rather

10. George Williamson, *A Readers' Guide to T. S. Eliot* (New York: Noonday Press, 1953), p. 184.

11. Brooks, *op. cit.*, p. 177.

they are at least striving to put it back together again. Their method is a response to the condition of the modern sensibility. A poet who cannot show that he has felt the disillusionments of his own time as poignantly as other people cannot speak to his time. This is the point from which the poet must begin the road back to more humane traditions.[12] F. O. Mathiessen notes that James Joyce, faced with a similar artistic difficulty, used the narrative structure of the *Odyssey* to give his novel *Ulysses* a framework.[13]

The only conclusion possible is that a cultural worker must remain free whether he is giving expression to his cultural tradition or seeking by some strategy to recover it. Experimentation and innovation on the part of the artist are not necessarily signs of ignorance or irresponsibility. "An art that merely reports or re-enacts the human load of footlessness, dismay, or despair—as what we call modern art tends to do—may be a loyal art, refusing romantic honors to the headless powers of the time."[14] It is true that inadmissible heresies will sometimes arise, but the policing of these will have to be left to the forces of the culture itself.

Finally let us bear carefully in mind that art is a form of cognition of reality; one of its functions is thus epistemic, and the epistemic is almost never bound or limited except to our loss. True, the consensus speaks to the artist, but it does not tell him exactly what he must do. Or, if he allows it to tell him exactly what he must do, he is not an artist of the first rank. It

12. I wish that the same hope could be expressed for architecture, which seems the most disoriented of the modern arts. Bruno Zevi has made an apt statement of its situation (*Architecture in America: A Battle of Styles*, ed. William A. Coles and Henry Hope Reed, Jr. [New York: Appleton-Century-Crofts, 1961], p. 133): "The moment of ostentatious novelty and avant-garde manifestoes has passed and modern architecture must now take its place in architectural tradition, aiming above all at a critical revision of this tradition. It has become evident that an organic culture cannot, in dealing with the past and specifically with architectural history, use two standards of judgment, one for modern and another for traditional architecture, if it is, as it must be, designed to provide modern disoriented and rootless man with a base and a history, to integrate individual and social needs which manifest themselves today as an antithesis between freedom and planning, theory and practice. Once we are able to apply the same criteria in evaluating contemporary architecture and that of previous centuries, we shall be taking a decisive step forward in this direction."

13. F. O. Mathiessen, *The Achievement of T. S. Eliot* (New York: Oxford University Press, 1947), p. 45.

14. Hocking, *op. cit.*, p. 129.

rather says, "Tell the story, but tell it in a new way." The Greek tragedians, bound as they felt themselves to be to the traditional stories, felt the need of this second injunction. That is all the coercion we can allow in the case of the artist. He is a man deeply affected by the momentousness, uniqueness, and truthfulness of various aspects of the pageant of existence. He must be culturally free to do what he can do with his own special gifts and insights. Where the sanction descends, it descends in the name of art, identifying but not forcibly suppressing, the faulty, which may be meretricious, didactic, or ideologically inspired. What is true for art thus narrowly conceived is true for culture as a whole regarded as an art, up to the limits where physical and moral survival raise problems of a more immediate kind.

In brief, cultural freedom as an integral part of the free society requires that distinctive cultures be allowed to preserve their homogeneity; that creators of cultural works should not be hobbled by political and sociological dogmas; and that in a given culture a tradition should be left free to find its own way of renewing itself. Violation of any of these shows a fundamental ignorance of what culture is and of how it ministers to the life of the spirit.

Introduction to James L. Weil, *Logarhythms*[1]

Everyone should realize by now that this is a peculiarly difficult age for the individual of poetic sensibility. The awareness which is part of a poet's true being causes him to feel a cross-pull between the ideal appeal of the great poets of the past, with their style and measure, and the excitement of the radical experimentation being carried on by the present generation. At the same time he must face a constant and sometimes truculent opposition to the very idea of poetry on the part of some scientists and their many journalistic camp-followers, who seem bent on bringing everything under the rule of a bleak positivism. Add to this the widespread distrust of values and of critical discriminations based upon them, and one can grasp the heroism that is involved in being a poet at all in our shaken world. As Frank S. Meyer has written, "This has been an era where by and large the man of sensitivity has been forced into a posture of private resistance if he wished to preserve his integrity."

When James Weil first became my student at the College of the University of Chicago in 1947, I knew that he was one upon whom the burden of this kind of consciousness rests. His strong seriousness, his resolution in pursuing ideas that attracted him until he found their justification, and his almost predictable fondness for the poet's poet, John Keats, marked him as a person who would be a bearer of our culture and a creator, with or without the recompense of sympathy and applause.

This judgment was vindicated when, a short time after his graduation, he published a small book of verse with a prefatory essay discussing some important aspects of the poet's dilemma. He brings out in the present volume a fresh group of poems, with a few translations from the German of Frank Muth. He has carried on this composition amid the distractions of a career in business. It will be a day of improved well-being for our culture

1. In James L. Weil, *Logarhythms*. New York: Poetry Library, 1956, 9–13.

when authors present themselves not as specialized "writers," but as "men writing," or men who write when they have something to say. This Weil does in his work to date, which derives part of its quality from his independence.

Weil began writing verse as a lover of the poetic line who was tortured, as so many humane spirits are today, by a dissociation of sensibility. The result is that states of pure feeling are not allowed to continue long; soon they must give way to disruptive urgencies, born of what the poet knows and fears. In his verse the reader will find this in the form of a deliberate breaking away from the mellifluous style. From Keats he learned the charm of poetry that is lush and flowing; but disinherited of Keats' more innocent world, he must bring into his poetry a sense of sudden emergence and violence. In "The Song of Lot," for example, the subdued beauty of "My name is Lot, akin to Abraham," is roughly jarred by the second line "I've nothing but my sins to sell," suggestive of the syncopated style of modern journalism and commerce. The pattern continues as the elegant passage beginning "I was a wolf, not shepherd to the lamb" is ended on a modern note of impatience and compression with "Come! Salt thy meat and chew thy knell!" Such attempt to get two worlds into the statement of a poem is almost the hallmark of the modern poet. Whether it is by the ultimate criterion a good practice has been argued hotly; but no one who is acquainted with the body of modern verse will deny that it has produced novel and brilliant effects. The impulse of the poet to assimilate all he knows forces him to be a realist about this world as well as a lover of the more human world that seems past.

This very awareness of alternative courses causes some of Weil's poetry, as it seems to me, to suffer from a preoccupation with technique. When an art is sick, or in transition, there will occur a temptation to see whether health cannot be restored by doing something about method, rather than by asking questions about the nature of the vision. This is perhaps a special lure to the beginning poet who has not learned how deep a draft upon the personality artistic expression makes. In "Metered" and also perhaps in "Saltersgate Moor," there appears some effort to accomplish by technique what can be created only through the whole process of artistic intuition. Such poems arrest us for a while through their virtuosity, but in the final rating they are more likely to be regarded as exercises than as achievements.

If there is a mood which characterizes a significant portion of Weil's better poetry, it might be described as a pessimism which is mildly ironical about itself. Thus a statement which might seem to prepare for the traditional romantic melancholy is suddenly confronted with a perception which brings one back to the world of things and facts and intellectual relationships. The pessimism is therefore never permitted to become sentimental; it is always checked by an *aperçu* which delivers from sheer feeling. This is the way in which I would interpret such poems as "The Peach: to W. H. Auden," with its planned anti-climactic close. In "Eve of the H-Bomb" we find a kind of apocalyptic feeling offset by an artful use of the technical vocabulary in which such matters are scientifically described.

These poems have their virtues, but it appears to me that Weil has given best evidence of the poetic talent that is in him in the sonnets "To Wilfred Owen" and "On the Death of Albert Einstein." These are works of what I consider a third stage; after a desire to follow the romantic lyric, there comes an engagement with the moderns and their acute consciousness of the present; but finally the conviction forms that poetry, while excluding no kind of subject matter, has to succeed as *poetry*.

The first of these sonnets deceives with its causal beginning, "How one surrounded by the noise of war," and then proceeds to build up an acute clash between the traditional calling of the Muse and the hardened attitudes induced by the mechanized killing of modern warfare. "Otosclerosis of a poet's ear" is one of those rapid shifts at which Weil shows unusual expertness; here it is a dip into the scientific jargon of the present, forcing the non-poetic locution into the mode of poetry, in the style of Tate, Ransom, and others. The "hero bombardier" is a finely ironic phrase, evoking as it does the difference between the hero of yesterday's mortal combat and the aviator of today, who neither knows nor sees his victims. The last lines of the octet carry us far into the world of barbarity and vulgarism, whose problems the poet overcomes in a sense by naming, while the sestet falls into critical musing about the cause and moral of it all. Again we perceive delicacy and crisis, and an effort to bring something out of the mood of ironic contemplation.

The other sonnet, with its variety of resource, is in my estimation Weil's highest achievement. The irony of allusion is here rich: Einstein is placed in a frame of reference with Brutus, Cain, and Romeo, and then is ingeniously distinguished with reference to the special nature of his achievement. The theme will recall the dichotomies often present in the poetry of Eliot and of Robert Penn Warren: the past of legend, beauty, and feeling contrasted with the impersonality of scientific formulations. The last few lines, while continuing the mood of the first part, bring in this other world with striking effect. I feel that the lines

> Then under stress of tensile and of tense
> Passed—from particle—to E from M C squared

constitute one of the most brilliant examples I have seen of weaving a specialized idiom into a tone set by a different sort of language. This is one of the effects most jealously sought by modernist verse, and Weil here shows his ability to achieve it while preserving the attitude he has established as his own. There is in this poem also a notably successful use of pairs, in "region or regime" and "that man's neck nor this man's bow," which suggests the kind of vista that good poetry opens for us.

In his translations from the German I should say that Weil has achieved a marked fidelity of statement while adhering closely to the pace of the poems. This will be seen especially in the lyric "Gedichte sind Gebete," where the translation follows the movement of the original and also manages to maintain a similar reverential tone. "Mutterschaft" offers a more difficult challenge, and the result seems not to have achieved the unity of the original, although it has conspicuous success in rendering the strangeness and violence of the metaphors. In "Selbstbildnis" I am not sure that Weil has captured the inner—or is it the peculiarly Germanic?—meaning of the words, and the English may be felt as a little halting and stiff in form. But taken as a whole, these are thoughtful translations, which, instead of ignoring or overriding the aesthetic problems involved in all translation, show an awareness of them and a willingness to deal with them on honest terms. All who have studied the German lyric know that it is an art form capable of peculiar poignancy, and although Weil may not have been triumphantly successful in his first effort at translation, he has conveyed important qualities while declining the dubious rewards of "free translation."

Looking back over *Logarhythms*, one sees a young poet writing a verse of sophistication and serious content. Weil shows his conviction that there is no good poetry without an "argument," in the Miltonic sense of that term. And there is always present a hard core of intelligence, ready to reject the external and the specious.

It is characteristic of the present generation of poets to seek out a title of subtle meaning, and it behooves the reader to give some thought to these "logarhythms" before putting the book down. These poems are exponent powers; they look at the contemporary world, but they carry us from it as Pegasus has always winged his way above the earth. The fact that "rhythms" forms the second half of the compound advises us as to which world the author believes will ultimately prevail. It is not a title of empty cleverness, but a clue to the poet's inner struggle.

Beyond this, it is my impression that Weil has not yet written enough poetry to define clearly his thematic line. For this reason it is risky to suggest with very much preciseness the direction of his potential development. I shall express the feeling, however, that Weil will reach his poetic fulfillment when the sophisticated technique of the moderns, in which he has trained himself with discretion, is used not only to express bewilderment and shock, which are right enough, but also compassion for the lot of man. As has been observed before, modern man has lost his innocence; he can never re-enter the Garden. The question before him is the one that T. S. Eliot so hauntingly puts: "After such knowledge, what forgiveness?" His knowledge is a burden; yet the knowledge can be used, and it is difficult to see how it can be better used than in expressing insight into man's comic and tragic status. Weil is gaining in resourcefulness for such a task, and I believe that he can make himself one of the significant poetic voices of a complex age.

Realism and the Local Color Interlude[1]

Editorial Note: "Realism and the Local Color Interlude" is one of several manuscripts written by Richard M. Weaver which had not been published when he died quite unexpectedly in early April of 1963. Although the paper is probably not as carefully wrought as Weaver would have eventually made it, the controlling idea is clearly and cogently articulated, and the author has characteristically said something new and important: in this case, about a subject which has been investigated almost too much—and on the whole with relatively little insight and sympathy. It should also be remarked that Weaver's *The Southern Tradition at Bay,* a study of the mind and culture of the South, contains a chapter entitled "Fiction across the Chasm" which deals in part with individual local color writers. The book will soon be published, and it will contain a foreword by Donald Davidson.

I have edited this essay from an original typescript which has generously been made available to me by Kendall F. Beaton, Richard Weaver's brother-in-law and literary executor. It is printed in the *Georgia Review* through the kind permission of the late Mr. Beaton and his wife, Polly Weaver Beaton, to whom I wish to record my gratitude.

—George Core

In a distinct period which extends from the close of the Civil War until about 1900, American literature was dominated by the local color movement. At first glance it seems anomalous that an era which saw almost total victory for the concepts of Union and centralization should produce the greatest expression of localism in literary work. But the anomaly is explainable: the United States, which had taken one road at such cost and with such determination to overthrow the opposition, was looking longingly down the road not taken. In going the way of Union and consolidation, it had to give up something; this is of course inherently true of all major

1. *The Georgia Review,* 22/3, Fall 1968, 301–5.

political decisions. The promise was held out naturally that the gain would greatly overbalance the loss; but then there were doubters, and in the American mind north as well as south and west there remained a desire to recover somehow what had been so ruthlessly written off as "wrong" by the civil conflict. The artists, always the first to sense a mood, supplied what was wanted. Local color was a cognition of the diversity of life which had been ended, or at least had been consigned to eventual disappearance by the cataclysm of the 1860s. The politically condemned half of our nature was kept alive for another thirty years by the local colorists.

There is no difficulty in showing that the local color writers were interested in the very things that the prophets of nullification and national glory rejected.

They were interested in the local, which is to say the limited, and opposed to the gigantic and the featureless. That is, an individual character in Indiana had more reality for them than a citizen of the new nationalized republic, unparticularized as he must remain in "national" political thinking. It is an opposition of abstract and concrete, of specific and general, of natural and hypostatized.

These writers were interested in characters for their charm or their peculiarity, and not for their power or efficiency, or capacity to stand as a type that some institution would find useful. Indeed, if we think of the type which emerged victorious and on top for the future from the Civil War, say the man who has served in the Federal Army, who will soon become a member of the GOP and who has ahead a successful career in politics and business, we note that the characters preferred by the local colorists are almost exactly the opposite. They are people both local and limited: they have no power and they know they are not likely to obtain any; they are generally simple and unambitious, and it never occurs to them to think in "national" terms. But they had one thing which is a perennial source of interest for art: their humanity. It was the depiction of this humanity, with a charm nourished through local conditions and attachments, that gave the writers of this school a chance to counteract the spirit of uniformity which was now abetted by so many powerful forces.

It may be further suggested that this interest in local color, limited as it was in its artistic achievement, was the real beginning of aesthetic sensibility in America. (Poe stands as too isolated a phenomenon to connect with any general movement.) For when we plumb the deepest springs of the artistic impulse, we find a source much akin to that of philosophy. All philosophy, Aristotle declared, begins with wonder, and it appears equally true that the artist is a wonder-struck being. What he intuits with a clair-voyant vision impresses him as unique, momentous, or important for what it is. No doubt he has its importance out of all practical proportion, yet this serves only to prove the point, for his interest is not a practical one. It is the product of a feeling of wonder in the presence of a manifestation of reality. The most irrefragable principle of aesthetics tells us that the artist does not wish to lay hands upon the object of his art, to possess it or use it in any way. Whenever that desire intrudes itself, the trance in which artistic intui-tion takes place is broken and more elemental forms of the spirit take over. Now just to the extent that local color writers passed by those subjects which were "important" and fixed their attention upon things "interesting" because of their indigenous nature and self-arrangement, they were culti-vating the aesthetic response. The interest attached to the thing itself, not to what it signified in some moral or political scheme. Hence the interest was innocent, and this is the pre-condition of true art.

By this token, whether the local colorists painted life in the mining camps of the West, or the old seaport towns of New England; whether he found his figures among the mountaineers of Tennessee or the impover-ished aristocrats of Virginia; whether the setting he described, with fond attention to detail, was the bayou country of Louisiana or the red clay hills of Georgia, the artistic aim was identical: it was to render with fidelity some segment of unspoiled reality. By "unspoiled" I mean here untouched by those considerations now thought to be overriding since the United States had taken the road of power. That was the fact; this was the indirect protest; the liberty of aesthetic presentation was being cultivated in the shadow of that triumph.

A question may be anticipated about the comparatively poor artistic quality of that literature. No one would contend that it represents one of the highest levels even of the American achievement. It is frequently marked by sentimentality, weakness of plot or even virtual absence of plot, over-reliance upon dialect as a source of interest, and the depiction of char-acters who do not have a great capacity for good or evil even in their limited *milieux*. No local color artist has won a position of front rank among American writers with the exception of Mark Twain, and he really holds his by virtue of his other achievements. The explanation is that the local color artists, like the remainder of their generation, were affected by the lowering of the American intellectual level between 1865 and 1900. In one way, as has been pointed out, they opposed the trend of things, but in the more pervasive matter of how strenuous an effort was expected of artists and thinkers in general, they showed the outlook of their time and took advantage even of the general relaxing of standards. When a story which showed little more than cuteness of characterization could really be sold to the *Atlantic* or to *Scribner's Monthly*, they wrote and sold it.

The Civil War left the United States in a prolonged cultural recession, and complacency with the second and third rate was one of its obvious features. The uncompromising aesthetic demands of Poe had dropped from sight; the profound symbolism of Melville was not even understood; and few in this period even knew where to place Henry James. It was not, therefore, an age prepared to cope with depth, and the local colorists gained the majority of attention. For these simple reasons they are more important historically and culturally than they are aesthetically, but their cultural significance could easily be underrated; they were creative artists of limited capacity doing what they could to fill a need actually greater than they could visualize—the need to counteract the business and technological supremacy growing out of 1865.

That the local colorists were right in the direction they took can be affirmed in another way. There is a demonstrable connection between the local color genre and the ensuing realism which began to predominate about the end of the century. For part of the artistic creed of the local color artists was fidelity to actual detail. The concrete facts which they observed in the various cultural regions of the United States they reported with fond attention. They did not, of course, always report it objectively; not infrequently they used it with the object of idealizing or romanticizing or sentimentalizing, and they did not stop to ask themselves serious questions about the nature of what they were doing. Accordingly, we have to acknowledge the intellectual limitations of their work. But after all has been allowed, the fact remains that they saw, and they got down in some form, a great deal of the concrete dimension of the American scene. Their pictures of setting and character in that scene may be idealized or romanticized, but they are neither abstract drawings nor unrecognizable portraits. The characterizing detail is there, and with it the assurance of some substratum of reality.

It was a natural passage from this to the realism of the next generation. The realists had but to take the same look, to avoid emotional surcharging, and their subject matter was found. As an actual example of the relationship, we may note that Hamlin Garland finds a place in both schools with his *Main-Travelled Roads*. Ellen Glasgow, in her early novels, is both local colorist and realist. Early in the next century came the works of Dreiser, Anderson, and others who dealt with local scenes, although their skill in reporting went far beyond that of the local colorists, and they undoubtedly set a higher standard by which fiction could be appreciated.

Local color literature may therefore be viewed as an unconscious protest which preceded the fully conscious protest of realism. Realism had a different focus, yet the taproot of both is the same. The local colorists strove to present what was human in character and setting, and this means what was individual. The realists presented what was in process of becoming dehumanized in character and setting. The lowly, drab, and frustrated types which they portray, and the dull, ugly, and monotonous which they describe are parodies of the great promise. If America claimed to have taken the way to wealth and happiness in 1865, well, the wealth and happiness had not been realized for large numbers of people, and environments had not been redeemed by the messianic oratory of the political nationalists.

As Matthew Arnold was to say in the course of an American tour in the 1880s, the human problem there had not been solved. This is what the local colorists were saying also in a kind of gesture, and what the realists were to say directly in their treatment of unlovely figures and ways of life.

The local colorists were not scientists, and they had no desire to dominate an environment. The realists likewise had no desire to dominate but to render with that fidelity which grants to the fact its status. The latter were filled with the greater passion, which sometimes led them into extravagances which the more mildly protestant local colorists were able to avoid. It is evident, however, that the reaction of both was against that spirit of Puritan origin which would impose itself upon the natural.

Review of *The Larger Rhetorical Patterns in Anglo-Saxon Poetry*[1]

This work is a judicious attempt to appraise certain artistic features of Anglo-Saxon poetry. In leaving out those historical and philological considerations which have hitherto been the staple of most Anglo-Saxon study the author announces that it is her purpose to study the poetry "for what it is worth." This is important, for however sure we may feel that Anglo-Saxon poetry bears the ineradicable stamp of the primitive, we must recognize that its best attainments, such as the *Wanderer* and *Beowulf,* present distinct aesthetic qualities.

The selection of the larger rhetorical patterns for treatment involves a discrimination both as to the nature of the patterns and to the circumstances of their occurrence in the poetry. The author has classified the envelope, parallel, incremental, and rhythmical pattern, and has distinguished the decorative inset and the conventional device. The suggestion that the incremental pattern is a specialized extension of the parallel pattern indicates that the Anglo-Saxon poet proceeded with more art than appears at first glance, and that he could rise to the challenge of technical difficulty. Six types of the decorative inset, a principal means of ornamentation, are discussed. The interesting view that the speeches are rhetorical devices because of an outstanding characteristic of formality is open to question. Anglo-Saxon poetry as a whole is a very formal body of writing, and it appears dubious to base much upon putative degrees of formality.

The author declares that if the poetry were arranged in a way to exhibit its "tapestried nature" it would present an appearance not unlike that of Eliot's *The Waste Land* or Benet's *John Brown's Body.* The study is a welcome supplement to the already exhaustive treatments of the material made with other objectives.

1. *The Vanderbilt Alumnus,* April 1936, 9.

Review of Robert Rylee,
The Ring and the Cross[1]

Robert Rylee has written a novel about high finance, politics, and the class struggle in coastal Texas during the boom period occasioned by World War II. The dominant character of this story is Adam Denbow, entrepreneur and politician, whose activities contributed largely to the building of a city, and who goes to the United States Senate. He represents power and privilege, as does the even more sinister oil millionaire, Wesley Clayton. Opposing them is Vaiden MacEachern, an idealist who dreams of freedom and opportunity for the individual.

In a sense this novel is a debate over the future order of society in the United States. Wesley Clayton makes the point that "the world has known two places of grace and security. One was the manor of medieval Europe, the other the plantation South of the 1850s. We have the chance to attain a state of equal grace. But with this difference: those two weren't founded on a stable material base. Today we have that base. We can make our state permanent." His means to this end, however, is a rigid authoritarian order imposed from above, such as might be achieved by freezing the politico-financial structure of which he is master. MacEachern, on the other hand, stands for a pluralistic society, free from the curse of nationalism, in which the individual will enjoy respect and have freedom of movement. "I want a unity derived from the tensions of opposites and nourished by conflicts, but one which recognizes that man's final loyalty is to no single nation."

In the end, MacEachern is assassinated by the entrenched powers he has fought. To the question of why his kind is cut off while the Denbows and Claytons go marching on, the answer is given that humanity will rise to avenge its own. Although the novel provides a forum for these exciting ideas, it is weak in realization. An astonishing proportion—I should esti-

1. *The Commonweal*, 47/2, October 24, 1947, 46 and 48.

mate nearly one-third—is generalized narrative. Perhaps this was thought necessary to introduce the extremely variegated populace present in a war manufacturing center. But generalized narrative, however indispensable at certain points in a novel, is not the kind of story-telling that makes us see things. There is too much synoptic presentation, and I fear that in description Mr. Rylee has not educated himself far past the cliché. Finally, because the characters tend to be embodiments of points of view rather than divided men, their struggles fail to touch us with poignance. The background is tense, but the reader who takes his delight in craftsmanship will not find much satisfaction here.

Review of Ward Moore,
Greener Than You Think[1]

The bare story of Ward Moore's *Greener Than You Think* is so far removed from the ordinary that a summary seems unavoidable.

Albert Weener, a nondescript salesman, lands the job of selling a substance called the Metamorphizer, which is a tonic for plant life. He unsuspectingly makes the first application to the front yard of Mrs. Dinkman in Los Angeles. It soon develops that the inventor has overlooked the matter of how to check the growth of metamorphized vegetation. Within twelve hours the grass is a foot high; within a day, six feet; after a few days it has reached the roof tops and is beginning to spill over into contiguous areas. The fire department is summoned; flame throwers are used; tanks are called into action. But to no avail; after a few weeks Los Angeles has to be evacuated. This is the beginning of humanity's battle against the Grass. As the phenomenal spread continues, incendiary bombs and even the atomic weapon itself are employed in futile attempts to stem the encroachment. The Grass gradually swallows up the West Coast, then all of America, then South America; and finally, leaping the Pacific, it begins an attack upon the Eurasian land mass. The last time we see Albert Weener all continents have been covered, and he is a fugitive upon a ship in the Atlantic, fatuously trusting that some means will yet be found to halt the noxious growth which his ignorance unloosed.

One might read *Greener Than You Think* for a good many pages and feel that it is nothing more than an ingeniously written farce. The author has an extraordinary inventiveness: to follow the progress of the Grass for three hundred and fifty pages without falling into patterns of reference, as he succeeds in doing, might tax the resources of the best narrator. He has also

1. *The Commonweal*, 47/7, November 28, 1947, 179–80.

a talent for the comedy of situation, and there is some fine irony at the expense of the hand-me-down ideas of this generation.

These are proofs of the author's skill, but they are not all. Mr. Moore writes as one well versed in the handling of concepts, and there are, amid the hilarity, unmistakable passages of reflective probing. If the story is taken as parabolical, the novel becomes a deadly satire.

What then is the Grass? There is much to indicate that it is scientific materialism and the amoralism which must be its accompaniment. Once science is advertised as the means of access to truth, its history becomes dynamic. Like the Grass, it presumes to feed on anything; it has no more thought of confining itself to a province of experience than the Grass had of remaining in Mrs. Dinkman's front yard. And like the Grass again, it promises to run us off the planet unless means are found to set it bounds.

The inventor of the Metamorphizer confesses in testimony before the Committee to Investigate Dangerous Vegetation:

> The authority I have flouted, in my arrogance as you call it, is that authority all scientists recognized in the days when science was scientific and called itself, not boastfully by the name of all knowledge, but more humbly and decently, natural philosophy. That authority is what theologians term the Will of God; others, the life force, the Immaterial principle, the common unconscious, or whatever you will. When I, along with all the academic robots whom you admire, denied that authority, we did not make ourselves, as we thought, men of pure science, but, on the contrary, by deposing one master we invited in a horde of others. Since we could not submit to moral force we submitted in our blind stupidity—we called it the rejection of metaphysical concepts—to financial force, to political force, to social force; and finally, since there was no longer any reward in itself for our speculations, we submitted to the lust for personal aggrandizement in fortune, in notoriety, in caste-bound irresponsibility, and even for the hypocritical backslapping of our fellows.

And further:

> In a word, it was the aimlessness and falsity of the nineteenth century coming back in the window after having been booted out the door. . . .

Since this is a typical investigating committee, such testimony is not understood, and the witness is advised to see a psychiatrist.

There can be no doubt that Mr. Moore has written an unusual novel and a significant one.

Review of Hermann Broch,
The Sleepwalkers[1]

Hermann Broch's *The Sleepwalkers* is a trilogy presenting the disintegration of modern European society. The first part studies a landed aristocracy imbued with militarist traditions and a defined sense of family and public responsibility. The second part takes one into the world of the worker, the entrepreneur, and the bourgeoisie of the years preceding the First World War. The last shows wide areas of German society crumbling under the impact of that war.

Judged by the standards which are ordinarily applied to fiction, *The Sleepwalkers* can hardly be accounted successful. Of the narrative portion one must report that much is tedious and much is ponderous, and one never finds in characters that tantalizing combination of uniqueness and universality which is the mark of true creation. One misses above all an organic unity of development in the story as a whole. The author, by styling his work "an essay in philosophy," seems to have shown more sense than some of his critics.

It cannot be denied that *The Sleepwalkers* is philosophically exciting. Mr. Broch has had the boldness to interpolate long passages of philosophical disquisition, including one on epistemology. He should be recognized for whatever success can be credited to this audacious maneuver. The result does not, in the opinion of this reviewer, make a good novel of ideas, but a novel within which important and essentially interesting ideas are sandwiched.

The author sees modern man as victim of what might be termed the Demon of the Abstract. This demon appears in the form of a logic divorced from content. An unconditioned logic is a force of extreme virulence, for

1. *The Commonweal*, 47/25−26, April 9, 1948, 620−22.

the effect of this force is to set up separate autonomies, each of which, at the dictate of its logic, drives ruthlessly toward a delimited goal. Periods in which the human being possessed spiritual anchorage tolerated no such exclusiveness of aim and operation. The medieval merchant knew nothing of the adage, "Business is business," for it was obvious to him that business impinged upon all areas of experience. The medieval artist knew nothing of art for art's sake, and the medieval soldier did not think of war as being justified by its own technical brilliance. The acknowledgment that each activity was in the service of something larger gave the era its style, and style is a sign that logic and content have achieved a balance.

The disintegration of a society is always foreshadowed by this split between reason and content. Among its consequences is the appearance of an autonomous reality which is no longer capable of submitting to the deductive system. We have witnessed this in the major alteration of our own cosmogony, since now "cosmogony no longer bases itself on God, but on the eternal continuance of inquiry, or the consciousness that there is no point at which we can stop." In other words, our age has substituted for truth an endless inquiry predicated on the assumption that truth is unattainable. The emerging anti-deductive reality turns out to be a reality of death.

Mr. Broch sees the salvation of mankind in a peculiarly difficult ideal of freedom, a freedom in which the rational and the irrational come together under the sanction of an "over-arching and majestic Being." It is the quest of this freedom which justifies the continued rebirth of humanity.

Such paraphrase scarcely does justice to the richness with which the concepts are developed. Even though the author failed to make a highly functional use of his ideological passages, one may admire the magnitude of his conception and the profundity of his reach. *The Sleepwalkers* is the work of an intellect of the first order.

Review of George Orwell,
Shooting an Elephant and Other Essays[1]

The special quality of George Orwell as an essayist may perhaps be conveyed through a series of approximations. He is a sensitive modern spirit not too demoralized to strike back, or, he is a humanist who admits the idea of progress, or, he is an eighteenth-century essayist with a modern sense of the urgency of problems. In these roles his forte is a kind of intellectual reportage, in which a hard basis of realistic observation is followed by a point.

The variety of subjects treated in this volume enables one to see that Orwell writes best when he is emotionally involved through some personal experience. The title essay, which goes back to the days when he was a police officer in Burma, is an outstanding accomplishment in using the frame of an episode to bring out the status of the white colonial in Asia. "How the Poor Die" and the light pieces "Good Bad Books" and "Thoughts on the Common Toad" are specimens of the same deft talent employed on widely dissimilar subjects.

On the more academic and controversial essays, such as "Lear, Tolstoy and the Fool," "Politics vs. Literature," and "Second Thoughts of James Burnham," judgment must be tempered. Here Orwell is very resourceful at exploring issues and at turning up hitherto overlooked par... ; but one does not always feel that his conclusions, even when they s... inviting, are deeply founded. "Politics and the English Language," t... recognizing the faults of modern malpractice, does not reveal t... owledge of the nature of language which would be required for a ... rse of correction. The comparison of Tolstoy to King Lear himse... Jonathan Swift to modern opponents of totalitarianism are to s... east stimulating; and

1. *The Commonweal*, 53/11, December 22, 1950, 2...

the denomination of Swift as a "Tory anarchist" seems to me an acute perception. Yet one may have the reservation, in following these more extended hypotheses, that the author makes use of shaky scaffolding, and that he occasionally runs along a pretty narrow plank to get from one point to another.

What Orwell has left us is what we rightly expect of every good humanist, a renewed sense of the proportion of things. This sense does not require, and indeed it can be hampered by, recondite learning or subtle reasoning. In *Animal Farm* and *Nineteen Eighty-Four* he showed the political mania of our age in proper perspective; and in this collection of essays he speaks, not of cabbages and kings, but of equally disparate subjects in the same humanizing spirit. Let me conclude with a sentence from "Thoughts on the Common Toad":

> I think that by retaining one's childhood love of such things as trees, fishes, butterflies, and—to return to my first instance—toads, one makes a peaceful and decent future a little more probable, and that by preaching the doctrine that nothing is to be admired except steel and concrete, one merely makes it a little surer that human beings will have no outlet for their surplus energy except in hatred and leader-worship.

Language and the Crisis of Our Time[1]

In *Speculative Instruments* I. A. Richards brings together a group of papers and addresses prepared over the past fifteen years. The pieces he has chosen for inclusion follow three main lines of inquiry: the nature and resources of language; specific problems of interpretation; and education and the future of the humanities, with special reference to language teaching.

His earlier works were brilliant technical treatises; this one might be viewed as the distilled wisdom of a life spent in the study of expression and communication. More than thirty years have passed since his *Meaning of Meaning* (written in collaboration with C. K. Ogden) appeared, with the effect of divorcing the world of utterances into "emotive" and "referential" terms. He now believes that "this bandying about of 'emotive' has done more harm than good," since it "encapsulated its topic, protecting it from further inquiry." The difficulty which prompted the distinction, however, is still there, though conditions have changed so that referential meaning now seems to be the aggressor. "Science is still animated by a revolt against centuries of oppression and frustration from the emotive functions, which have enjoyed privileges and usurped power beyond their due. If reference now aspires to become the world government and to put them in their place or reform them, that is not surprising. But a self-governing community of studies has to ask whether reference is able to say what the place of poetry and religion is, whether it is able to reform them or only able to destroy them."

The chief danger is that language will be viewed as a mechanistic activity, to be studied by some subbranch of behavioral science. The failure of the linguistic scientist is that he "thinks of it as a *code*, and has not learned that it is an organ—the supreme organ of the mind's self-ordering growth."

1. *National Review*, 1/13, February 15, 1956, 27. © 1956 by National Review, Inc., 215 Lexington Avenue, New York, N.Y. 10016. Reprinted by permission.

Such objections arise from Richards' conviction that language is inescapably normative. And the same position, it might be claimed, determines his general defense of humanistic education. I have yet to encounter a better formulation of the goal of humanistic training than his phrase "the discernment of relevancies." As soon as value-bearing terms are introduced, the user of language is finding his relevancies with reference to "hierarchical organizations of choices." With that admission, metaphor, myth and religion are again established in the real world.

The most urgent practical need is to find more capable teachers of the humanities. Francis Bacon boasted that he was instituting a kind of knowledge to which even ordinary intellects could make contributions. Today quite ordinary intellects *can* teach most branches of science, and carry forward research on some levels. It is otherwise with literature and philosophy. In teaching the humanities, as in writing poetry, one is not permitted to be second-rate. Otherwise the humanities suffer. "They are the hardest to teach because wisdom, which they exist to cultivate, cannot be cut and dried. Much in other subjects can."

Speculative Instruments thus throws light on some special aspects of the cultural crisis of our time.

Christian Letters[1]

In this unusual and important book a profound student of literature comes to grips directly with the question of whether literature needs to face the fact of value. Too many of our literary specialists seem to have taken the easy road of the social scientists, conceding in a general way that values have to be considered, but avoiding the hard and responsible task of saying what values and how. It is therefore not merely refreshing, it is exciting to find one of the most noted authorities in the field of American literary studies affirming that there is a distinct correlation between the presence of Christian religious concepts in our literature and the excellence of the literature in which these are found.

According to Professor Stewart, there are three ways in which American literature has gone wrong, and by this he means has run off into shallows where a great literature cannot be created. The first way was to rely exclusively upon the rational faculty. Man is not a rational being simply, and moreover the rational faculty cannot penetrate into the depths of intuition and of experience. Jefferson, by giving his blessing to the reason as the sole oracle, created a rationalistic bias in American thought which has been a strong influence for sterility. Not only the terrible experiences of recent decades but also the course of our literary development call for a critical look at the Jeffersonian deification of reason.

The second way was to postulate the natural goodness of man and thereby to remove evil from the sphere in which the literary artist has always worked. In this connection, perhaps the greatest disaster that ever befell American literature was Ralph Waldo Emerson. This may seem an astonishing assertion to those who have learned American literary history from conventional textbooks, yet it will cease to astonish when one begins to study the facts. For if it be allowed that Emerson did achieve a good deal

1. *Modern Age*, 3/4, Fall 1959, 417–20.

for himself, he foreclosed the possibility of achievement to those who subscribed to his doctrines. Why? The reason is simply that one cannot produce great literature in a world of fatuous optimism, which is the world to which Emersonism directly leads. Professor Stewart is severe upon Emerson, but in the opinion of this reviewer justifiably so. What is done here has long needed doing. Emerson was not a great philosopher; he was not the sort of man who could lay the philosophic groundwork for a vital literature; he was a local sage uttering aphorisms, most of which stemmed from the curiously unreal Transcendentalist view of man and of nature.

Professor Stewart's courtly style does not permit the type of assault that is popular in some quarters today, but the point is effectively made: ". . . the fact remains that Emerson is the arch-heretic of American literature, and Emersonism the greatest heresy. By no dint of sophistry can he be brought within the Christian fold. His doctrine is radically anti-Christian, and has done more than any other doctrine to undermine Christian belief in America." For Emerson "Good is positive. Evil is merely privative. . . ." From this it inevitably follows that Emerson's system is a monism. "There is no conflict, in the strict sense, between good and evil because evil is a mere negation, a minus quantity; no struggle between God and the Devil because the Devil is a 'nonentity,' that is, he does not exist."

Emerson ended by deifying man. Now a deified man cannot have any of the problems faced by a literary protagonist. If both he and the world are divinely good, all he has to do is express his natural impulses, and doubt, conflict, and evil all fade out. Accordingly nothing is left for literary depiction. The denial of evil is not only a profoundly un-Christian view, it is also a view which removes tragedy and eliminates the possibility of heroism.

How a great literary creator reacted in fact to Emerson's optimism may be seen in a letter written by Herman Melville after the latter had listened to Emerson lecture. "These men," he said, "are cracked right across the brow. . . . But enough of this Plato who talks thro' his nose." But when Melville wrote of a great creative artist, who in his Puritanical pessimism stood at the opposite pole from Emerson, he recorded, "Now it is that blackness in Hawthorne . . . that fixes and fascinates me."

The third way in which literature can go wrong is simply to evade the problem of good and evil through naturalism. In a chapter entitled "The Amoralists," Professor Stewart discusses Frank Norris, Dreiser, and Farrell in an exposition of this thesis. Through their labored documentation of setting the naturalists do achieve results that are impressive in a way. But the "stories" which they present amount to little more than tedious assurances that man is but a product of material forces, a cork bobbing on a surface whose undulations he has no way of controlling. Apart from the fact that our intuitive sense rejects this conception of man, however insistently it is recommended for our acceptance, such stories must of necessity lack that prime ingredient of epic and tragedy, the hero. There can be nothing tragic about a character who is merely passive, that is to say, who merely suffers. The author puts the case in these words:

> Being a puppet of forces, man can hardly appear in a heroic light, and it is a question whether the term "hero" can properly be applied to the protagonist, or chief actor, in a work of naturalistic fiction. The term hero suggests a morally responsible actor, and suggests, too, that certain adverse forces are being overcome by willful endeavor. The heroic actor becomes himself a force to be reckoned with. If the conflict is internal, then his better nature is capable of asserting itself, and often does assert itself.

Thus whether you regard man as supremely competent through his rational faculty, or as divinely good and therefore without internal conflict, or as a helpless "chemism" buffeted about in a world of purely material forces, you cut the ground out from under literature. The author quotes Allen Tate to the effect that where there is no tragic fault there is no drama in human character. From here one must go on to recognize that where there is no drama of human character, there is nothing about man that deserves treating by the method of literature.

American literature had arrived at such an impasse by the early twentieth century (allowing for the brilliant exception of Henry James, who was of course concerned with nothing but the moral consciousness and so steered well clear of the Scylla of Emersonism and the Charybdis of naturalism). Professor Stewart then shows that the extrication has come mainly through such modern writers as William Faulkner and Robert Penn Warren. Eliot must be included, of course, for obvious reasons, and his conversion to Anglicanism is an important datum in Professor Stewart's evidence. Eliot's poetry has shown a steady progression toward Christian belief, and *Ash Wednesday* "is perhaps the chief Christian poem of our time." It is in Faulkner and Warren, however, that the author finds the most interesting evidence of what an ethical and religious orientation can do for creative literature. For these two authors, alone among American writers today, have recaptured tragedy for the novel, and this may be tantamount to saying that they have saved the novel.

If there is one thing that can be affirmed with confidence about both of these writers, it is that they take as a basic premise in their presentations a concept very much like that of Original Sin. In Warren it is apparent in the handling of vivid characters like Percy Munn in *Night Rider* and Willie Stark in *All the King's Men,* and it enters as a dominant theme in his long poem *Brother to Dragons,* which is a repudiation of Jeffersonian optimism regarding the natural goodness of man. It even appears explicitly, for it is the title of one of his finest short poems. In Faulkner, I would suggest, the theme is less visible on the surface but is perhaps even more pervasive below surface. And I would point out as a sign of this the ubiquity of violence in his fiction. Such violence is but the recurring evidence of man's natural sinfulness, a fact which this author—"poetically the most accurate man alive," according to the *Times Literary Supplement*—could not have left out of his observation. The fact that Faulkner has been widely accused of exploiting violence for melodramatic or sensationalistic effect shows how little prepared the modern audience is to grasp this dimension of his work.

Professor Stewart's point is, then, that by returning to the truth that "All have sinned, and come short of the glory of God" (which he labels the most "democratic" because the most widely applicable of all propositions) these two powerful novelists have reclaimed man for literature. That is to say, they have rediscovered his capacity for good and evil, his need to struggle, and his need to assert himself against temptation and circumstance. As writers of a Christian outlook they can of course accept neither pure rationalism, nor the gnostic heresy of man's natural divinity, nor the scientific dogma of strict materialistic determinism. And it is precisely these rejections which leave them in a position to bring our literature "back to the tradition of Hawthorne and Melville, of Milton and Shakespeare."

As must appear by now, this is a very brave book. It brings into a field where there has been perhaps too little thinking in proportion to research a principle of interpretation which enables us to see the reason behind greatness. I would admit that not all of Professor Stewart's evidence carries equal power to convince, even with those favorably disposed. I have some difficulty, for example, with the line of reasoning by which he brings Hemingway into the fold of the writers of Christian proclivity. Moreover, I think his thesis will have to be interpreted as saying not that Christianity is the necessary cause of a great literature, but that something like it is the necessary condition. In other words, being a Christian does not entail being a great writer, but being a great writer does entail having the Christian-like view of man, which sees him as a dual creature, possessing the capacity for glory and damnation.

But in the face of a bold thesis like this, resting upon varieties of evidence, minor dissents and questions are only to be expected. They are indeed but ways of showing respect for the intellectual courage with which the case is argued. As for the case in general, I predict that few will venture to attack it, for the refutation would be too difficult and the failure to refute too embarrassing to those who might have an interest in trying it.

A Moral in a Word[1]

Anyone reading the literature of modern semantics with a reflective mind must conclude that many of those who pontificate about the relation between words and their referents actually have the smallest insight into the matter. But at the opposite pole stands a student like C. S. Lewis, who traces what words of multiple signification have meant at various times and do mean in various contexts, and illustrates what he says out of a vast erudition. His *Studies in Words* is a series of disquisitions upon *nature, sad, wit, free, sense, simple, conscious,* and *conscience.*

There does exist in language the fact of semantic shift, a process by which words over a period of time widen, contract, or otherwise change their roles. Of course not all words are affected or are affected equally. But since the present meaning of a word is often vaguely swayed by past meanings which have dropped into the subconscious, a knowledge of particular semantic historie can increase our facility and sometimes save us from inadvertent error.

It s rvealing, for example, to know that *frank* at one time meant the same thig as *free*. Hence the present use of the term as a social–ethical upgrae. "The frank person is unencumbered by fear, calculation, an eye to the un chance; he also shows the straightforwardness and boldness of a noble ture." In a comparable sense Aristotle could speak of *free* studies (for hi e word was *eleutheria*). Here is the root idea of our "liberal" educatic The free study seeks nothing beyond itself and desires the activity c wing for that activity's own sake. That is what the man of radically character—give him what leisure and what fortune you please—w er understand. He will ask, 'But what is the use of it?' And finding tha not be eaten or drunk, nor used as an aphrodisiac, nor

made the instrument of increasing his income or his power, he will pronounce it—he has pronounced it to be—'bunk.'"

Conscious and *conscience* were once so near in meaning as almost to excuse the college freshman's habitual mistaking of the one for the other. To
have *conscience* meant originally to be *conscious* of what you know—to pull
yourself together in an act of recollection. The meaning is present in the
Latin *conscire:* "to know together." Only later did the noun come to mean
something like "the lawgiver" or "the fear of hell." ("Thus conscience does
make cowards of us all.")

For readers of this journal the author's most valuable revelation may well
be the following. Commenting on the changes which overcame the meaning of *wit* in the eighteenth century discussions of literature, he has this
to remark: "However little the new poetry resembled the old, those who
claimed excellence for it claimed that it showed *wit.* As new shopkeepers
who have 'bought the goodwill' of their predecessor's business keep his
name for a while over their door, so the literary innovators want[ed] to
retain the prestige, almost the 'selling power,' of the consecrated word."

And precisely so in the field of politics. Here, I suggest, is the principle
that we need to explain what has happened to the term *liberalism.* How is
it possible that nineteenth century and twentieth century *liberalism* can
mean virtually opposite things? Under statism and collectivism the shop-
keeper and the wares have changed, but the name is still being used over
the door as a bait, because the old liberalism, with its frank acceptance of
liberty, created a great reservoir of good will.

Modern Letters Con and Pro[1]

Truth Is More Sacred is a fascinating duel between heart and head over the basic value of modern literature. Edward Dahlberg, author of *Bottom Dogs* and *Can These Bones Live,* leads with the case for the negative, and the indictment is severe indeed. Introducing himself as "rough and feral," he presents sweeping condemnations of the major writers of our time. And whatever one may think of his opinions, one must concede Mr. Dahlberg to be a master of literary invective. "I regard James Joyce, André Gide, Cocteau, Rimbaud, Verlaine, Eliot, Pound, as the bawds in the beauty parlor on Mount Ida." Of the novel which has been most revered by the *avant garde* he has this to say: "The *Ulysses* of James Joyce is the story of the scatological sybarites of the business world; it is a twenty-four hours' journey through ordure; a street urchin's odyssey of a doddering phallus." With reference to D. H. Lawrence: "It seems to me that the modern novel about love is all dross and no Helen." "Lawrence only cared to do nude figures; he put clothes on the men and women in order to remove them." Of Henry James, who is a special trial to Mr. Dahlberg's patience: "Henry James was as debilitated in his books as Pope was in his life. . . . the former, perspiring over his syntax, sends those he tortures to Egyptian ideographic writing in which a pair of legs going denotes a transitive verb." James was "the sovereign of the enervated phrase." ". . . he cared more for propriety than he did for the universe. Everything he did was governed by taste, and it was impossible for him to be clear because he wanted to be sure and tactful." "James was the canniest peeping male that ever observed feminine habits." On T. S. Eliot: "I blame Eliot for nothing except the books he has written." "Why leave the United States to be rid of its vulgarities in order to be a bad

1. *Modern Age,* 5/4, Fall 1961, 426–27.

St. Louis poet abroad?" "A thief may go to Paradise with Christ, but not a traitor to his own native speech. Eliot, Pound, Joyce, and Wyndham Lewis are matricides who have slain their native tongue." These are the judgments of a writer who would see our literature recover the vein of Homer, Hesiod, Chaucer, Shakespeare, and Swift.

Sir Herbert's response to this may seem somewhat patronizing because of a difference in style. But it is realistic, for it is based on a true theory of the relation of the artist to his world. The artist does not make his world; he depicts it, in the root sense of that term, which is to say, he paints it. Wholeness and simple affirmation are not aspects of our world. If much of modern literature is brilliant but fragmented and even tortured, that condition is not wholly the result of the perverse wills of artists. Art is both universal and relative, and the relative dimension is always the spirit of its particular milieu. With us, "the mirror is broken," and there is no prospect of having a whole and symmetrical image again, short of a recovery that would include much more than art. Accordingly Sir Herbert can reply in the exchange over Eliot and Pound: "The charges that you bring against Eliot and Pound could with the same doubtful cogency be brought against Joyce and Faulkner, Picasso and Klee, Stravinsky and Bartok—indeed against every representative artist of the past fifty years.

"I do not defend the age. I am a fatalist and believe that what has happened in the art of our time had to happen, as a logical reflection of what was at the same time happening in society at large." One may rail against *The Waste Land* and the *Cantos* as "symbols of our spiritual impotence," yet they are authentic just because they could not have been produced by any other age than ours.

As much as we may deplore the course of the time, we can still find aesthetic satisfaction in those artists whose loyalty is to truthful expression, regardless of whether that leads us into the vernal woods or a brothel. Therefore Sir Herbert can take pleasure in Joyce because "his words are doing good work, communicating his impressionistic vision of the world of reality." Lawrence was the greatest writer of his generation because he "held strongly to one half of the truth about beauty and about love." As for Henry James, it is easy to allow the preciosity of the man to obscure the great achievement of the writer. James had the most uncompromising ideal of all authors of fiction: "to create a fictional form as intense and as moving as the form of the classical drama," and as subject to rigid laws. "He worked relentlessly beneath these laws, and there is no fiction anywhere else in the world that comes near to the formal perfection of his." He defends Eliot as the true voice of our inner experience. "Eliot was the prophetic poet of his time, projecting the images of our guilt and remorse, accusing our consciousness of corruption, and recalling us to 'the Peace which passeth understanding.'"

It is difficult not to sympathize with Mr. Dahlberg, for his heart is in the right place, and his stance is heroic. He forces us to think of times when there were giants in the earth. But Sir Herbert has the juster view of the role of the artist. He confirms the prophecy of Jacob Burckhardt that "the utmost effort and self-denial will be necessary . . . if art and science are to remain *creatively* independent in view of the relation in which they stand to the daily press, to cosmopolitan traffic, to world exhibitions. All of these menaces have since Burckhardt's time increased a thousandfold, and to them we have added deterrents of which he could have no conception—air traffic, radio, and television." This is why we must save what we can from the "demotic jargon" of the mob, from "consolidated ignorance," and from the ideal of comfort which is supplanting that of glory, without expecting our artists alone to effect the miracle of renewal.

SECTION SIX

Politics

At a very early stage in his academic career, Richard Weaver repudiated his youthful commitment to the political Left, embraced the labels of "agrarian" and "conservative," and began devoting his energies to building the conservative intellectual movement. In December 1942 he wrote to his old friend John Randolph that "I now subscribe to the basic tenets of agrarianism" and noted: "I do not call myself a 'liberal' any more."[1] *By the fall of 1946, he was acting as faculty adviser for a University of Chicago student organization called the Conservative League, and on December 4th of that year he delivered a public lecture on "creative conservatism," his first of many speeches on the subject.*[2] *In the last eight years of his life, through his contributions to* National Review *and* Modern Age, *as well as numerous campus lectures (often at functions organized by the Intercollegiate Society of Individualists [ISI], of which he was a trustee), he became a prominent spokesman for the movement. This section presents the rather extensive body of his explicitly political writings, most of which were addressed to popular audiences. They are divided into five groups, each ordered chronologically.*

1. Letter from Richard Weaver to John Randolph dated December 27, 1942. Quoted by permission of Mrs. Esther Randolph.

2. Letter from Richard Weaver to Cleanth Brooks dated November 22, 1946. Located in Box 15, Folder 320, of the Cleanth Brooks Papers in the Beinecke Rare Book and Manuscript Library at Yale University.

All of the items in the initial group seek to define the nature and status of modern conservatism. The first is the published transcript of a University of Chicago Round Table discussion of the question "Who Are Today's Conservatives?" Broadcast nationally on the NBC radio network in February 1955, it features comments by Weaver, S. G. Brown, and Aaron Director. The remainder of the group consists of five speeches, four of which are published here for the first time. "The Prospects of Conservatism" is the text of an untitled address to a meeting of The Conservative Society of Yale Law School on May 16, 1955. It is followed by "Conservatism and Libertarianism: The Common Ground," a speech delivered on April 30, 1960, at an ISI seminar in Chicago and subsequently published in The Individualist, *an ISI newsletter. "Conservatism and Liberalism" was presented to a group of seminarians at Holy Name College in Washington, D.C., on October 15, 1960. Reconstructed from Weaver's handwritten notes and a partial tape recording of the event, it is noteworthy because it explicitly links conservatism to religious belief. "On Liberty" is the text of Weaver's untitled acceptance speech for an award he received at a massive Young Americans for Freedom rally in Madison Square Garden on March 7, 1962. The last speech, "How to Argue the Conservative Cause," was presented at an ISI function in Chicago on September 22, 1962, less than seven months before Weaver's death. Based on an earlier version delivered at the University of Wisconsin on April 22, 1959, it is notable both for its endorsement of capitalist prosperity and for its detailed critique of international communism.*

The second group of writings is made up of Weaver's reviews of what might be called "conservative" books. This includes books written by conservatives such as Russell Kirk and Frank Meyer, as well as those which express views compatible with conservatism, regardless of how their authors might choose to label them. Most notable among them is the review of the Letters of H. L. Mencken *from* Modern Age, *which offers Weaver's only extended discussion of an author he greatly admired.*

The next two groups are composed of, respectively, Weaver's six essays and five book reviews on liberalism and the Left. The essays, all published between 1956 and 1960 in Human Events *and* National Review, *are among his most polemical writings. Although most elaborate themes addressed in other works, the 1957 review essay "Integration Is Communization" is of special significance because it constitutes his most extensive public statement on forced integration and its effects on private property, the "last metaphysical right" on which he based his hopes for recovery in* Ideas Have Consequences. *Of the reviews, three appeared in the* Commonweal *and one in* Modern Age. *The fifth, an evaluation of Daniel Bell's* New American Right, *was submitted to the* Chicago Tribune *in February 1956, but there is no evidence that it was ever published. It is reproduced here from a typescript copy found among his papers.*

The final group is composed of six reviews of books dealing with a variety of political topics and leaders, all but one of them published in the Commonweal *between 1948 and 1951. They are worthy of special attention because most discuss contemporary international affairs, an area Weaver seldom addressed in his other writings.*

Who Are Today's Conservatives?[1]

STUART GERRY BROWN, AARON DIRECTOR,

AND RICHARD M. WEAVER

Mr. Director: I think there would be a general agreement on the observation, but in the last few years there has been a reversal of the trend
toward collectivism, at least in the Western world. This is seen in a very
marked way in a country like Germany; but it is seen, also, in Great Britain
and, I think, to some extent in the United States. If it were not for the fact
that the word "liberalism" has been corrupted so that it now is a synonym
for "collectivism," we might have been inclined to call this reversal a revival
of liberalism. Our next choice, in that event, might be to adopt the word
"conservative" as a description of the new tendencies. Unfortunately, we
dislike the idea of going back to anything. We seem to forget the observation that was made by a famous lawyer that there are ancient truths as
well as ancient prejudices. As a consequence, some people have adopted the
phrase "the new conservatism" to describe this general tendency.

To discuss this topic of the new conservatism, we have Stuart Gerry
Brown, professor of citizenship and American culture in the Maxwell
Graduate School of Citizenship and Public Affairs, Syracuse University;
and Richard Weaver, associate professor of English in the College, University of Chicago.

Perhaps it would be best to begin our discussion in an attempt to find
out what is covered by the phrase "the new conservatism," and maybe
Brown would like to enlighten us a little bit on his understanding of what
this phrase connotes.

Mr. Brown: I would be glad to say what it connotes to me. It seems to

1. *The University of Chicago Round Table*, #881, February 27, 1955, 1–11.

me that there are really two important meanings of conservatism now in common currency of American speech. I am not sure that they are always too closely related, but perhaps we'd better get them both out before us. One, I think, is the kind of conservatism which very frequently in American history has followed wars, or internal crises, or long periods of internal tension, where there grows up spontaneously a desire for something more stable, some anchors to windward, and some sense that we should now take stock of where we are; that we look back and see whether we have come too far in the immediately preceding period. I think this kind of conservatism is prevalent now, and I think it is a natural phenomenon.

Then there is, perhaps, a different kind of conservatism sometimes called "neo-conservatism" which is very much discussed, especially among intellectuals and students, and which is an attempt, I think, to revive some of the great ideas of the past and perhaps to apply them to the present time. This is a conservatism which speaks of a substitution for the bewilderments and anxieties of the present with a kind of renewing of faith in a divine order and plan in the world, in which individual human beings can find a status and a security with reference to that status which involves some restudying of American history as well as earlier history. It involves the introduction into our discourse of figures of thought not in recent years popular, such as the great English constitutionalist and parliamentarian Edmund Burke, or, in America, a new emphasis on John Adams as opposed to Jefferson; the reading of figures like John C. Calhoun or John Randolph of Roanoke.

Mr. Director: Now I think it might be appropriate to ask Weaver for his conception of the content of the new conservatism.

Mr. Weaver: In offering a definition of what is now being called a new conservatism, I think it is very important to distinguish between temperamental conservatives and reflective conservatives. The writers today who are being termed the "new" conservatives are, as I see them, reflective conservatives; and their conservative position is, therefore, a matter of conviction. They are convinced, with reference to certain concepts of good, with reference to certain means that should be taken toward realizing those concepts of good. It seems to me that the center of their position is the conception of society as a structural thing. This does not mean a monolithic corporate state, on the one side, and a mass of people, on the other, but rather a contrary kind of thing—a structure, a structure made up of many centers of authority and influence. These centers of authority and influence arise more or less naturally, spontaneously, in response to what people like to do; and, although they are not engendered by the state, they are protected by it as legitimate expressions and legitimate activities. I think this conservative I am describing is deeply impressed with the necessity of respecting the human personality. He regards the human personality as finally an ethical entity, and he thinks that the limitation of that by anything like state control or interference is an unwarranted exercise of state action or authority.

MR. BROWN: I would like to ask my colleague, Director, what conservatism means to him?

MR. DIRECTOR: Well, you see, I operate on a very much lower level of discourse than you, my colleagues, and conservatism to me is really, as I indicated at the outset, a new word for what used to be called "liberalism." And this position is fairly concrete. It puts the emphasis on maximizing individual freedom; but, unlike some liberals of the present day, it puts the emphasis on maximizing individual freedom not only in the field of civil liberty but in the field of economic activities as well. It puts the emphasis specifically on the social framework which will accomplish this objective. One of the things it emphasizes is that state activity should be minimized; that, before state action is undertaken, there must be submitted a specific reason for that action; otherwise, if there are no such reasons, individuals are to be left free to engage in voluntary exchanges. The reason which justifies state action is to accomplish objectives which individuals would like to accomplish on a voluntary basis but cannot do so because of technical conditions, and these specific circumstances can usually be specified. Moreover, this liberal conservative position is really not negative at all, because it relies on individual activity only on the assumption that it will be carried on in a free market; and, if it so happens that the market for one reason or another is noncompetitive in character, then it is the function of the liberal state to see to it that the market should be made competitive.

MR. BROWN: This is a kind of demonstration, it seems to me, that wh I said at the outset is true—that there are two kinds of conservatism volved here. Your reference, Director, to individualism and to liberalis the old sense raises in my mind a question whether the advancem technology, the increase of population, the overwhelming industrial of the Western world, particularly of the United States, in recent y not rendered even the possibility of the kind of individualism that you want something very, very doubtful.

MR. DIRECTOR: On the contrary, Brown, I would say that these are precisely the conditions which make it important that the system should be a competitive system. There are not any great problems to solve in a society which is not changing rapidly or in a society which is not growing rapidly. The real problems arise in a society which has growth of population and many technological changes; and, since the state is really not competent to deal with these complicated situations, the results, I think, will be much better if they are left to be worked out by the voluntary effort of individuals. So that what you consider as argument for departing from the old liberalism I consider as an additional reason why liberalism is much more important today than it was a hundred or two hundred years ago.

MR. BROWN: I would seize, if I might, on the phrase that "the state is really not competent" to handle these things. I proceed on the assumptions of democracy—and I am a liberal in the twentieth-century sense of the term, not in the nineteenth-century sense—and I would argue that the state consists of the expression of the will of the people through certain forms and institutions and that, if the people cannot manage their affairs and are not competent to do so through the forms of democratic government, there is scarcely any likelihood that they will be able to manage them on an atomistic basis, as mere individuals, without the help of government as an instrument of power. I do not know what Weaver thinks about that.

MR. WEAVER: I would like to say something about that phrase "the will of the people." I think one of the great distinctions between the conservative, on one hand, and the liberal and radical, on the other, lies in the diverse reading of human nature. The conservative thinks that there are situations in which man needs to be protected against himself, and men need to be protected against themselves. Therefore, a simple expression of majority will is not always a good thing; is not always a final verdict on matters. For that reason, he tends to set a great store by traditional usages, and also by formulations such as constitutions, which represent settled opinions and, n a sense, directives. In doing this, he, too, is interested in freedom; but I ink the difference lies, as I mentioned a moment ago, in a different con- tion of human nature and a different evaluation of means.

Ir. BROWN: Well, but when you raise the question about whether men lways able to manage for themselves, or whether they need to be pro-

tected against themselves, this seems to me to get you into a logical difficulty with reference to the democratic way of life, because, if men are not
able to protect themselves against themselves, who is going to do the protecting? Now, your answer to that is the institutions—the constitution and
the institutions set up under it. But these are carried out as processes by
men, and it seems to me the gamble has always got to be that in the long
run men will protect themselves against themselves, unless you want to set
up some kind of authority outside the will of the people.

Mr. DIRECTOR: Precisely. My reason for hesitating or being negative
about indiscriminate extension of a state activity is not because I do not
believe in the democratic principle, since, as you well know, there is a very
close relationship between the growth of the democratic tradition and the
growth of liberalism; but, nevertheless, these liberals recognize that. . . .

Mr. BROWN: You are speaking of the "older kind of liberals"?

Mr. DIRECTOR: I am speaking of the "older kind of liberals." These
people recognize that, while the democratic method is preferable to other
alternative methods, nevertheless the majority decision involves a substantial amount of coercion; and it seems to me, as a consequence of that, if we
are interested in maximizing individual freedom, we must keep those activities which are taken on the majority principle to a bare minimum and
leave as much as possible—and to me that includes a great deal—to be
decided by the voluntary decisions of individuals, singly or in relations with
other individuals and groups.

Mr. BROWN: This gets us into the problem of the extent to which individual decision-making is a possibility—what the limits to such decision-
making may be as a result of the kind of world we live in. I am thinking
now of a man who works on the assembly line in an automobile plant. What
kind of decisions can he make?

Mr. DIRECTOR: It is very simple. He makes the decision whether he is
to work on this assembly line or whether he is to work on a different assembly line. He makes the decision whether he is to work on his own or
whether he is to work for anybody else. He makes the decision whether he
is to engage in agricultural activity or whether he is to engage in some urban
activity. And what greater choice can you possibly offer to such a person
under an alternative system?

Mr. BROWN: I think that some of these choices which you attribute to
hypothetical individuals are fairly specious. I suspect that, if you grow up in

the environment of Detroit, you do not have much option to be a farmer in Iowa.

Mr. Director: On the contrary, you find a place like Detroit has a tremendous amount of mobility. New people are constantly coming in because they have decided that, given the alternatives that are open to them, they prefer to live in what you call the uninteresting assembly line as against getting much smaller incomes and having a quiet and peaceful life on the farm.

Mr. Brown: My concern is that they should get higher incomes and work less hours on the assembly line.

Mr. Director: Of course it is always desirable that people should have higher incomes. The issue is what kind of a system will give them higher incomes? You know we cannot just manufacture incomes. Incomes are produced by the people who are engaged in some activities. If you have some very interesting way by which you can raise the level of income, that certainly would be an interesting point to suggest.

Mr. Weaver: Brown, would you be willing to force a higher standard of living upon those who seem to be indifferent to it?

Mr. Brown: I have not run across anybody yet who is really indifferent to a higher standard of living. This seems to me one of the sort of stereotypes that occurs in the literature of the new conservatism, and it suggests to me that perhaps one of the difficulties with conservatism at the present time—at least of the intellectual sort—is that it is in an ivory tower. It is very easy to talk about people not wanting to raise their standards of living if you do not know any people, but I have yet to run across such.

Mr. Weaver: Nevertheless, there are different conceptions of the good life.

Mr. Brown: I agree with that.

Mr. Weaver: As some people see it, the good life requires the Cadillac. According to others, it can be lived without the assistance of any kind of automotive apparatus. I think that, when we use the state in order to force people to standardize their way of living, according to some, oh, shall we say centralized conception, we are violating what I tried to define a moment or two ago as personality and its right to be respected and deferred to.

Mr. Brown: It seems to me that it is precisely conservatism that wants to do that by imposing a scale of values and a place in society on people. I am just trying to recognize what seems to me an elementary fact about the world we live in: that we have to make a living in some way or other and that, as technology advances, the ways of making a living become, in one sense, less various. Consequently, if we want to realize the values of personality with which the conservatives are concerned, it seems to me we need to minimize the mechanized economic activity required to support life and maximize the amount of leisure.

MR. DIRECTOR: You cannot have it going and coming. I admit that you could minimize the amount of mechanization in the society, providing you already impose some values on the society, that is, the value that a larger amount of goods is an undesirable phenomenon. But, as long as you leave individuals free to decide that they prefer higher volume of goods instead of greater leisure, I do not see what objections you can possibly raise to that.

MR. BROWN: This, it seems to me, again, is really beside the point. I do not think the liberal of our time is concerned to have people work more. I think his gamble is that the advances of technology—under some kind of systematic planning, if you like, with the forms of property (I am not trying to determine whether they should be public or private, but with some kind of planning)—will increase the advantages to be gained by technology, so that he gets greater production with less labor. I mean, it seems to me, that that is the history of the American industrial revolution.

MR. DIRECTOR: Yes, but planning for what? Do you think that anybody can sit down and decide that we can have some better inventions than we now have? It is very easy to say that, if we just turn it over to somebody to plan, the results will be fancy and phenomenal. But the fact of the matter is that we do not know anything at all about the kind of changes that take place, which invention will be made, and which will not be made. To talk about planning out a society in which people will have to work less strikes me as planning out for living on the moon. And if you talk about who is realistic, I suspect that I, as a pure theorist, am the realist, and you are just living in a dream world of your own.

MR. BROWN: No. On the contrary, I think that the liberal of the twentieth century wants to start where he is; whereas, I think, the conservative wants to ignore where he is and go back to somewhere that may or may not have existed in the history of the world. Let me ask Weaver what it is that he wants to go back to?

MR. WEAVER: Well, the conservative, I should say, wants to conserve history.

MR. BROWN: History will conserve itself.

MR. WEAVER: He wants to conserve it in the variety and multifarious-ness of its reality; and this is a different thing from introducing some ab-stract design of society and imposing that by a national fiat. Our appeal is rather an appeal to what has been, in all its variety; and yours, it seems to me, is some kind of engineering blueprint.

MR. DIRECTOR: Of course, I might help you out, Weaver, by saying that what these liberals really want to do is to go back to a much older period. They really want to go back to a period when society was regulated by a central authority. So they need not feel so comfortable in saying that con-servatives want to go back to something as though that, in itself, is a term of abuse. As a matter of fact, they want to go back much further than that.

MR. WEAVER: I think I would agree with that.

MR. BROWN: Clearly the liberal does not want to go back anywhere. Clearly the liberal wants to move ahead. The difficulty with the analysis that you gentlemen are making at the present moment is that you are leav-ing out the processes of democracy. No liberal that I know of, of my time, has any desire to impose a blueprint from above. What he wants to do is to reflect, in some kind of co-ordinated and systematic way, the desires, the will, and the purposes of the great majority of the people, which clearly are for a better life.

MR. DIRECTOR: Yes; but, specifically, what do you want to do in order to create a better life?

MR. BROWN: What I want to do is to regulate the economy to the extent necessary to make it orderly and productive. What I want to do is to use the forces of government to prevent cyclic depressions; to use the resources of the federal government for investment in creative and progressive enter-prises which private capital has not the power or the stamina to manage for itself.

MR. DIRECTOR: What makes you think that the state can do all these things and at the same time bring about a larger volume of economic output?

MR. BROWN: I think the record is very clear on that.

MR. DIRECTOR: Where? In Germany? In Russia?

MR. BROWN: Neither of these countries has been democratic, except per-haps West Germany in recent years. I would point to such an example as the Tennessee Valley Authority, which seems to me to show exactly what I mean. This has brought far greater opportunity for individuals to develop their personality than ever existed in that area before. And it has involved huge quantities of public investment under some sort of government regulation.

MR. DIRECTOR: Why certainly you can always take money away from some people and benefit some other group of people. Are you in favor of a large system of subsidies in order to advance the good life? The good life of whom—the people who receive the subsidies, or the people who pay the subsidies?

MR. BROWN: I wish we had time to pursue the question of TVA as an example, further, but I think it could be quite readily shown that the prosperity brought to the Tennessee Valley has been reflected all over the country in such a way that all taxpayers, regardless of their region, have benefited from it.

MR. DIRECTOR: You would have a very difficult time to prove it to me; but, as you say, this is not a topic on which we can enter into any discussion at this moment.

MR. WEAVER: And even if that could be proved, Brown, what about the ultimate tendency of those measures once they are put into operation? Don't you have to think about where this may wind up? Granting that, if you can prove that it is a good thing within the limited area, still this is a step in the direction of state monopoly, and where will it stop?

MR. BROWN: I would challenge that; I do not see any state monopoly involved in it. It seems to me that the people who have operated under the Tennessee Valley Authority and similar kinds of developments in the last twenty or so years have been given far larger opportunities of choice than they ever had before, in addition to raising their standard of living. I would suggest that you ask the people in the Tennessee Valley.

MR. WEAVER: But if this is followed by a Missouri Valley Authority . . .

MR. BROWN: Which I hope it will be.

MR. WEAVER: . . . and that by another one, what is to keep the eventual merging of all those from taking place? And that, it seems to me, would be a step very close to a completely socialistic government.

MR. BROWN: This seems to me a bogeyman. I see no evidence that it points in that direction at all. In fact, the central principle that is involved—

I do not mean a contradiction in terms—is a decentralization, actually; and, when you are talking about regions you are not talking about running everything from Washington. You are talking about the people taking control and charge of their own affairs and managing them for the first time in their lives, in many cases.

Mr. Director: Of course you draw a distinction which has some significance, but not too much, between a set of regional monopolies instead of a central monopoly. But I regret to say that a monopoly is still a monopoly, even if it is carried on, on a regional basis.

Mr. Brown: I am quite content with the Tennessee Valley Authority's monopoly of electric power if it encourages, as indeed it does, a great variety of individual and smaller enterprises which could not have existed before.

Mr. Director: Well, why not extend it to the steel industry? Why not say that that, too, should be set up into a system of regional or national monopolies?

Mr. Brown: If, as is possible, Director, a time should come when the steel industry was producing inadequately. . . .

Mr. Director: What does "inadequate" mean? "Inadequate" can surely mean only that you want it to produce more.

Mr. Brown: In terms of an expanding economy.

Mr. Director: But who decides whether you need more or whether you need less?

Mr. Brown: I think ultimately the people do.

Mr. Director: The majority of the people?

Mr. Brown: All the people, in the terms of their desires.

Mr. Director: Oh, no; you are mistaken. In a free system, all the people decide whether they want to produce more steel or whether they want to produce more power. In your system, it seems to me, the majority decides that the other people ought to have more steel even though they do not want any more steel.

Mr. Brown: No. The wellspring of motivation is the same. It is the desire for the Cadillac, of which you spoke a moment ago, that calls for a greater production of steel.

Mr. Director: But you are going to preclude that by saying that somebody else is going to decide instead of the consumer.

MR. BROWN: No. I am saying that the private owner decides in terms of whether the manufacture of steel is profitable.

MR. DIRECTOR: And what will you decide on?

MR. BROWN: I will decide on the need for steel in meeting the desires of the people.

MR. DIRECTOR: How do you know how much steel is wanted except by finding out what the people are willing to buy in the form of steel?

MR. WEAVER: Yes. How does he decide whether it is profitable?

MR. BROWN: He decides whether it is profitable on the basis of whether he sells it at a profit. I think that is clear enough.

MR. DIRECTOR: Is that what the state is to do, to decide whether to produce a given amount of steel?

MR. BROWN: The democratic state, it seems to me, is responsive to the will and the needs of the people. Consequently, it is not a matter of somebody at the top deciding how much steel is to be produced, but it is the problem of getting as much steel as is demanded.

MR. DIRECTOR: If that is the case, it seems to me, we have an ideal system, since our society produces exactly the amount of steel, the amount of coal, the amount of textiles, the amount of power which people want to purchase.

MR. BROWN: In that case, I do not see how we can account for some three and a half millions of unemployed.

MR. DIRECTOR: If I may make a summary observation I would say that, as the discussion proceeds, it becomes very clear that there is really only one difference, and that is the difference between liberals, liberal-conservatives, and collectivists, and that what is introduced by the new conservatism does not really add very much. The real issue is really what kind of a society will promote values which, as I take it, are values we all hold in common.

The Prospects of Conservatism[1]

It was an exciting thing to me to be asked to join you at this dinner. I have been reading about your activities with growing admiration, and I had even hoped for some opportunity for an exchange of thoughts. Let me acknowledge at the beginning, however, that any outsider discussing conservatism before a school which has known the footsteps of John Calhoun and Robert A. Taft may well feel overcome with presumption.

It is a curious fact about individuals and nations that the closer they approach to the brink of some catastrophe, the more reckless and oblivious they become. The nearer they are to the downfall, the less able they seem to read the signs which are apparent to everybody else and to take the ordinary precautions. There seems to be a self-induced blindness which helps to hurry the victim on to his fate.

Anyone viewing our society from the outside in recent years might have supposed that this is the case with us. It must have been plain to such a viewer that this country could not continue long in its path without undergoing some great transformation—a change of form so great that its earlier identity would be a thing of the past, and what we have known as the United States of America would become an archaic memory. I feel no hesitation in referring to this as a catastrophe because, as I understand the forces at work, it would involve the total destruction of all the sanctions which have redeemed life—religion and morality and honor and distinction of mind alike would be rejected. The communist, with his hatred of all human affections, would win the day, and that "emancipated international atheistic democracy" of which Santayana once spoke would be a practical reality.

1. An address delivered to a meeting of The Conservative Society of Yale Law School in New Haven, Connecticut, on May 16, 1955. Edited by Ted J. Smith III from a corrected typescript located in Box 3, Folder 5, of the Richard M. Weaver papers at Vanderbilt University. In order to provide a sense of Weaver's style as a speaker, comments directed to his audience have been preserved.

The blindness appeared in the fact that no one seemed disturbed by the onrushing calamity. Or at least no one who was able to make his voice heard. There have been indeed occasional protests, but the makers were promptly put in their place by being called eccentrics, or primitives, or tories, or conservatives—men not interested in "keeping up with the times." It had all the looks of one of those heedless marches to disaster.

In the last few years, however, there have been real signs that eyes are being opened and that this course is going to be seriously challenged. A number of books have been published which take issue quite squarely with what the liberals imagined they had got everybody to accept as dogma. A fair number of men in the academic world have been willing to stand up and be counted for a political program which can only be described as conservative. And not the least important of these signs of awakening is the Conservative Society meeting here tonight. I feel we are now safe in saying that this battle is not going to be settled by default, that serious thinking in a direction not seen in decades is under way, and that new political alignments are impending.

When your chairman invited me to speak for a few minutes on this occasion, I decided that the best thing I could offer would be a view of some of the problems and difficulties—and opportunities—facing a nascent conservative movement.

I pretend to no great qualifications for this task. I am anything but a practical politician, and my contacts with other people of the conservative persuasion are not so wide as they might be. But I have been a reader of the conservative literature to which we can now point with some pride, and I believe I can see certain things emerging.

First it seems necessary to say something about the number and deployment of the enemy. Truly, his number seems almost beyond counting. He is in education, in government, in the church, in entertainment; and he seems almost to have taken over the newspapers and popular publications. Starting some thirty years ago with a couple of thin and often derided organs, the *Nation* and the *New Republic*, these liberals and collectivists have come as near as anything to making their views the official philosophy. And one of the features of this conquest is that many good people who would never have arrived at this position through their own thought processes have picked it up from the general tone of public discussion. It has been made to appear that this is "the way you think about things." Every political aspirant now feels he must qualify himself by making a public profession of liberalism. These prophets of the new order have made so much headway that now they are not afraid to attack those things which our forefathers regarded with deepest veneration—the concept of truth, the feeling of patriotism, the idea of personal loyalty, the belief that there are great men. I recently heard one of them who teaches "citizenship" in a prominent university declare that he is interested neither in religion nor morality. What his rule was for distinguishing between "good citizenship" and "bad citizenship" I never found out.

Any group confederating today in the name of conservatism may feel like a small band of Christians in a world loudly and defiantly pagan.

I hardly need remind you that the changes they have effected in our social and political organization have been proportionately great. A few weeks ago my friend W. C. Mullendore gave a speech in Los Angeles in which he enumerated twelve major situations which the radicals have brought about in the last quarter of a century. It was a bill of particulars, showing how far we have been led along this road.

Under the new dispensation the Federal government is vested with power to

1. support and defend one billion non-citizens and their lands wherever located on this globe;
2. convert public debt into irredeemable currency, to control and manage the credit of all the people and thus to expand the supply and to change the value of the American dollar;
3. dictate the level of wages, the relations between employer and employee, the hours of work, the ages between which people may engage in gainful employment, and to require employees to submit to the dues, discipline, and control of labor unions;
4. impose criminal penalties or deny access to the courts to those who attempt to choose social and economic groupings disapproved by the government.

The other eight are about equally frightening.

And this says nothing about what they have done in the all-important field of education. Proceeding there on a wholly fallacious theory of man and in open contempt of history, they have reduced education in our public schools almost to the level of a farce. With John Dewey as their prophet and their avatar they have undermined the basis of discipline and disparaged the authority of knowledge. No man can estimate the ravages that have flowed from this misguided philosopher.

Many other evidences could be brought forward to show how enormous have been the strides toward statism in government, toward materialism in social theory, and toward anti-intellectualism in education. But these are enough to show the size of the task that is cut out for us.

As I look over this dispiriting scene, I sense most of all the need for a counter program which shall be positive. I have never subscribed to the idea, apparently held by some, that conservatism is only a brake on somebody else's engine. Such persons seem to think that a conservative has done his job when he has issued a warning against going too fast. It is always somebody else, under this theory, who is the driver and has the plan of the trip; the conservative is only a sort of nervous backseat driver. He really doesn't know where he wants to go, but he doesn't like fast driving and moreover sudden turns make him dizzy. I say this is altogether wrong. We do not admit that the other side has all the motive force and we have only the retarding one. Conservatism would not be a political philosophy, and it could never have held together a political following if it were nothing more than this. There are periods of crisis, times of passion, when it is possible to make some political progress with a platform which is merely "anti" this and that. But these times pass, and the hour comes inevitably when people begin saying, "We understand well enough what you are against, but what are you for?"

Consequently, I feel it is of supreme importance to offer some alternative to the things we are opposing. In support of this idea, one might appeal to the nature of man. It is the nature of man to want to do something, to accomplish, to create, to bring forth. Destructive activity may satisfy him for a little while, but in the long run he wants to feel that he is bringing something into being. If the other side has a policy, with definite objectives—even though those objectives are outrageous—and you have none, you are at a disadvantage that cannot be overcome. The only way to combat his efforts is to set up an alternative of your own—something that people will turn out and work for with their own native zeal. Simply drawing attention away from his alternative and toward yours is the first step in weakening him. In politics as in other forms of competition, it is necessary to take the initiative away from the opponent. And sometimes it is necessary to make use of the opponent's own weight to throw him.

For these reasons, I hope that when a conservative program is put before this country, it will be positive and will contain elements of boldness. You don't win confidence in politics or in anything else by feeble imitation or by promising to do timidly what the other fellow is willing to do boldly. This is the trouble with all middle-of-the-roadism. Middle-of-the-roadism is too often nothing more than a shying away from all logically clear alternatives because the acceptance of a logically clear alternative exposes you to criticism. Of course it does, but it also provides you with means of meeting the criticism. You have a position. Tocqueville points out that all great political parties have resulted from adherence to basic principles. A great party that tries to substitute compromise for this, or that tries to find its stay in glamorous personalities, is on the way out. That policy proved fatal to the Whig Party in this country and to the Liberal Party in England, and I leave you to your own surmises about the present Republican Party.

This is naturally not the place to talk about specific issues. I have only given some reasons for believing that the conservative program when it comes should represent a positive alternative and should be asserted with boldness and conviction.

I will make one more point, however, in this connection. It could be inferred from these remarks that I only propose to offer the citizen a bigger price in the name of conservatism. That, however, is not my meaning, because I do not believe that bribery is the only means of getting people on your side. There is a widespread feeling that this is so, but I suspect that it comes from that crude simplification of human nature which liberals have so successfully purveyed. But contrary to what they seem to assume, human beings can be appealed to through things other than cupidity. They can be appealed to through duty, through self-sacrifice; they have even responded to appeals to "be hard on themselves." In the past the power of ideas to rally people has been practically unlimited. Today, it is true, there are an immense number of technological blandishments, and how successfully an ideal can work against them remains to be seen. But there exists here a moral resource which a conservative movement certainly should not leave untapped.

In spite of the great number and strength of the opposition, to which I was alluding a moment ago, there are some who think that the conservative movement may develop into a bandwagon before long. I find this thought a little overly optimistic; nevertheless I have heard it expressed more than once, and we ought at least to consider the possibility. If conservatism should become a popular thing among intellectuals, academics, and others, if it should become the fashionable line to take, the leaders of the movement would certainly face some vexing problems and they would have to survive some disillusionments. If the bandwagon should start rolling, it is certain that some would climb aboard whose only purpose would be to thrust things between the spokes of the wheels. We have already been served notice by some of our liberal friends that they would welcome a conservative movement—but our good sense tells us that it would have to be a nice tame one, one guaranteed not to create trouble or to accomplish anything. Any conservative who desires to be something more than a convenient foil for the liberals will decline this game. The more specific problems which might appear if we should ever assume bandwagon proportions will of course have to be met in their own forms and on their own merits.

The last matter I wish to examine in this brief survey could prove the most serious of all because it involves the potentiality of a split in conservative ranks over theory—a doctrinal division, that is to say. As I continue to read the growing literature of the subject and to study pronouncements by one person and another—pronouncements which are interfused with a large measure of idealism and loftiness of mind—I think I see developing two schools of thought which could come into conflict unless we have fortunate leadership. It seems necessary to define these broadly, so I will say that on the one hand are those who tend to identify conservatism with tradition and habit, who propose to take all their cues from settled institutions and old ways of doing things. In their view, conservatism is not something you reduce to a body of theory; least of all is it an ideology. This type of conservative gets his conservatism by inheritance, by imitation, by a decent respect for those forces and institutions that are in being. Like Burke, he believes that it is best to draw a veil over the origin of governments and over their philosophical foundations too. He seems to find most that he needs in instinct, in social discipline, and in the molding power of tradition.

On the other hand are those conservatives who tend to be much more speculative about matters. They like to examine the roots of things. They like to formulate consistent theories. They are respectful of precedent or they would not be conservatives, but they philosophize more than others about where precedent is leading. Some of them think that conservatism is capable of being just as intellectually rigorous as radicalism in another direction. Their position might be summed up by saying that while they think practice is good, they believe that in the final analysis there is no such thing as practice without theory.

In my own writing I feel that I have inclined to the speculative side. I am ready to admit that this may be a bent which stands in need of correction. I will pause here long enough, though, to offer a brief explanation of my position. It seems to me that a conservative must be something of a definer. He believes that there is a "nature of things" which can be found out. He looks for essences, and in argument particularly he starts from original definitions. His method, consequently, is much like that of a lawyer. When I hear a man basing his argument on nothing more than circumstances and results, I am inclined to suspect him of having succumbed to one of liberalism's most serious fallacies. Going back to my original distinction, we would not want to see developing a group of mere traditionalists on one side and a group of "radical" conservatives on the other—radical in the sense of following a theory to some extreme and getting out of touch with life. They might find it increasingly difficult to work together and even to communicate.

Now I feel very sure that this split does not have to occur, and I think I can demonstrate this by examining what appears to me the real conservative's attitude toward religion. Certainly no conservative with any depth at all respects religion merely because it is a tradition. It is a tradition all right, but this is only part of the reason he respects it. And on the other hand, no conservative respects religion merely because it looks like an ingenious explanation of the universe. It is a partial revelation of the universe; but its appeal is not intellectual merely; it has behind it the weight of tradition and prescription, which gives it the quality of compulsiveness. I should say the conservative respects religion because it is a combination of authority and insight. It comes recommended by the subscription of many generations of men, whose collective wisdom is much greater than that of any individual, as Russell Kirk properly reminds us, and at the same time it undoubtedly teaches.

This test can be taken out of the realm of religion and applied to social and political institutions. Or it can be applied to the conservative concept of man. Conservatism is nothing if not historical-minded; of course the conservative is interested in tradition because tradition tells us what man has been. But alas, he has not been enough, has not achieved enough. To find out what he can be, what he can accomplish, we have to invoke another kind of inquiry. Here is where the imagination, the theoretic faculty, and even intuition come into play. I am not frightened by those who wish to express conservatism in the form of prophetic ideas. They are the ones who can reconcile conservatism with progress, in some acceptable sense of that term.

We should recognize then that one conservative, because of his temperament or his training or his occupation, will feel more comfortable in appealing to the authority of usage, of precedent, of time-honored solutions. Another conservative, because of his temperament or training or occupation, will delight in showing the insights revealed by these very same things. He has learned the truth of Goethe's saying, "A deep thought lies in an old custom." I do not feel that these two are in opposition; they are only emphasizing different aspects of one cogent consideration.

There exists in every country a kind of primitive conservatism, which is largely rooted in agrarian life, which articulates very little, and which hardly rises to the discernment of issues. This is a valuable force, which cannot be left out of account. But because of its very nature, it cannot furnish leaders in the battle of ideas. It needs spokesmen always, and these spokesmen must come from people trained more or less like yourselves; that is to say, people who know something of dialectic, rhetoric, and the rival ideals of the good life. We require this kind of reflective conservative to offer a continuous criticism of the ends and means urged on the public by the radicals, and to visualize the conservative alternative. Whether we as individuals incline to be eulogists of tradition or whether we delight in uncovering the laws and principles that illuminate the conservative path—we in *this group* are fated to be this reflective kind of conservative. We have to make our force felt in the area of debate, where we will disprove the absurd claim of liberals and radicals that all serious thinking is conducted on their side.

It is certain that a mighty work of rectification is due. When you recall how little our opponents started with 30 years ago and what they have effected, it is challenging to think what may lie in prospect for us. The tone of this gathering tonight makes me feel that there may be some dramatic successes ahead.

Conservatism and Libertarianism: The Common Ground[1]

The subject of this paper is the common ground between conservatism and libertarianism—not the *possible* common ground, for I am convinced that they already, or naturally, share the same place on the political arc even though sometimes they are found eyeing one another rather uneasily. Among the theorists in both groups, it is true, we sometimes sense an unwillingness to come into a common front, apparently out of a feeling that this would require some fatal concessions. I hope to show that this is not so. It can be demonstrated that while the positions of the conservative and that of the libertarian may not overlap exactly, they do have an overlapping and they certainly are not in necessary conflict.

The modifier which has been most frequently applied to my own writings is "conservative." I have not exactly courted this but I certainly have not resented it, and if I had to make a choice among the various appellations that are available, this is very likely the one that I would wind up with. I must say that I do not see any harm in it, and in this I am unlike some of my friends, unlike some people with whom I agree on principles, but who appear to think that the term is loaded with unfavorable meanings or at least connotations.

And there is, in fact, a concept of conservatism filled with disparagement which needs to be fought by everyone who believes that a conservative philosophy is useful and constructive. There are some people who appear to think that conservatism means simply lack of imagination. The conservative, unable to visualize anything else, just wants to sit down with the status quo. There are others who seem to think that conservatism means timidity. The conservative is a person who has a sneaking presentiment that things

1. *The Individualist*, 4/4 (old series), May 1960, 5–8.

might be better but he is simply afraid to take the risk of improvement. There are some who seem to think that conservatism is a product of temperamental slowness. If your mind or reflexes don't work as fast as other people's, then you must be a conservative. In these conceptions, the conservative is always found behind, whether from mental or physical deficiency, or just plain fearfulness. Naturally, nobody looks to that kind of person for leadership.

But this is very far from my image of the conservative. A conservative in my view is a man who may be behind the times or up with the times or ahead of the times. It all depends on how you define the times. And this brings us at once to the matter of an essential definition.

It is my contention that a conservative is a realist, who believes that there is a structure of reality independent of his own will and desire. He believes that there is a creation which was here before him, which exists now not by just his sufferance, and which will be here after he's gone. This structure consists not merely of the great physical world but also of many laws, principles, and regulations which control human behavior. Though this reality is independent of the individual, it is not hostile to him. It is in fact amenable by him in many ways, but it cannot be changed radically and arbitrarily. This is the cardinal point. The conservative holds that man in this world cannot make his will his law without any regard to limits and to the fixed nature of things.

There is in Elizabethan literature a famous poem entitled "A Mirror for Magistrates." It contains stories of a large number of rulers, kings, princes and others who got into trouble and came to untimely and tragic ends. The story from these that I remember with special vividness concludes with this observation as a moral—and it is a kind of refrain line throughout the account: "He made his will his law." And that has stayed with me as a kind of description of the radical: he makes his will the law, instead of following the rules of justice and prudence. Fancying that his dream or wish can be substituted for the great world of reality, he gets into a fix from which some good conservative has to rescue him. The conservative I therefore see as standing on *terra firma* of antecedent reality; having accepted some things as given, lasting and good, he is in a position to use his effort where effort will produce solid results.

Radicals and liberals sometimes try to knock the conservative off balance by asking, "What do you want to conserve anyhow?" I regard this question as by now substantially answered. The conservative wants to conserve the

great structural reality which has been given us and which is on the whole
beneficent.

I might make this a little more precise by saying he wants to respect it,
although of course respect must carry with it the idea of conserving. There
is a famous saying of Francis Bacon which can be applied with meaning
here. Bacon does not seem the most likely figure to be brought into a defense of conservatism, but then every great thinker will say some things of
general truth. Bacon declared that man learns to command nature by
obeying her.

The same holds for the moral, social and political worlds. One does not
command these by simply trying to kick them over. One commands them
as far as it is possible to do so or appropriate to do so by obeying them—by
taking due note of their laws and regulations and by following these and
then proceeding to further ends. Of course, the conservative does not accept
everything that is as both right and unchangeable. That is contrary to the
very law of life, but the changes that he makes are regardful of the forms
that antedate, overarch and include him. The progress that he makes, therefore, is not something that will be undone as soon as his back is turned.

The attitude of the radical toward the real order is contemptuous, not to
say contumacious. It is a very pervasive idea in radical thinking that nothing
can be superior to man. This accounts, of course, for his usual indifference
or hostility toward religion and it accounts also for his impatience with
existing human institutions. His attitude is that anything man wants he
both can and shall have, and impediments in the way are regarded as either
accidents or affronts.

This is very easy to show from the language he habitually uses. He is a
great scorner of the past and is always living in or for the future. Now since
the future can never be anything more than one's subjective projection and
since he affirmed that he believes only in the future, we are quite justified
in saying that the radical lives in a world of fancy. Whatever of the present
does not accord with his notions he classifies as "belonging to the past," and
this will be done away with as soon as he and his party can get around to it.
Whereas the conservative takes his lesson from a past that has objectified
itself, the radical takes his from cues out of a future that is really the product
of wishful thinking.

As a general rule, I am opposed to psychoanalyzing the opposition,
knowing that this is a game both sides can play. But here we have a case so

palpable that one is tempted to make an exception. So many of these radicals seem to be persons of disordered personality. There is something suspicious about this impassioned altruism. They often seem to be struggling to cover up some deep inner lack by trying to reform the habits or institutions of people thousands of miles away. Something like this becomes thus an obsession, almost to the point—or maybe to the point of irrationality. Not that I regard all desire to reform the world as a sign of being crazy. Even more than that I would go along with Plato and say that some forms of craziness may be divinely inspired. But here we come to an essential distinction, and a parting of the ways. There is a difference between trying to reform your fellow beings by the normal processes of logical demonstration, appeal and moral suasion—there is a difference between that and passing over to the use of force or constraint. The former is something all of us engage in every day. The latter is what makes the modern radical dangerous and perhaps in a sense demented. His first thought now is to get control of the state to make all men equal or to make all men rich, or failing that to make all men equally unhappy. This use of political instrumentality to coerce people to conform with his dream, in the face of their belief in a real order, is our reason, I think, for objecting to the radical. As an individual he may think about molding the world to his heart's desire. He may even publish the results of his thinking. But when he tries to use the instrumentality of the state to bring about his wishes then all of us are involved, and we have to take our stand.

Here, as I see it, is where conservatives and libertarians can stand on common ground. The libertarian, if my impression is correct, is a person who is interested chiefly in "freedom from." He is interested in setting sharp bounds to the authority of the state or other political forms over the individual. The right of the individual to an inviolable area of freedom as large as possible is thus his main concern. Libertarianism defined in this way is not as broad a philosophy as I conceive conservatism to be. It is narrower in purview and it is essentially negative, but this negative aspect is its very virtue.

It took the study of John Calhoun to wake me up to a realization that a constitution is and should be primarily a negative document. A constitution—and we may think primarily of the Constitution of the United States in this connection—is more to be revered for what it prohibits than for what it authorizes. A constitution is a series of "thou shalt nots" to the government, specifying the ways in which the liberties of individuals and of groups are *not* to be invaded. A constitution is a protection against that kind of arbitrary interference to which government left to itself is prone. It is right therefore to refer to our Constitution as a charter of liberties through its negative provisions, and it is no accident that in our day the friends of liberty have been pleaders for constitutional government. I think conservatives and libertarians stand together in being this kind of constitutionalist. Both want a settled code of freedom for the individual.

This is a shared *political* position, but we can show that their agreement has a philosophical basis. Both of them believe that there is an order of things which will largely take care of itself if you leave it alone. There are operating laws in nature and in human nature which are best not interfered with or not interfered with very much. If you try to change or suspend them by government fiat, the cost is greater than the return, the disorganization is expensive, the ensuing frustration painful. These laws are part of what I earlier referred to as the structure of reality. Just as there are certain conditions of efficiency for operations in the physical world, so there are conditions for efficient operation in the social and economic worlds.

There is a concept expressed by some economists today in the word "praxeology." Praxeology, briefly defined, is the science of how things work because of their essential natures. We find this out not by consulting our wishes but by observing *them*. For example, I believe it is a praxeological law that a seller will always try to get as much as he can for what he has to sell, and a buyer will always try to pay as little as he can to get it. That is a law so universal that we think of it as part of the order of things. Not only is this law a reliable index of human behavior; it also makes possible the free market economy, with its extremely important contribution to political freedom.

The conservative and the libertarian agree that it is not only presumption, it is folly to try to interfere with the workings of a praxeology. One makes use of it, yes, in the same way that a follower of Bacon makes use of nature by obeying her. The great difference is that one is recognizing the objective; one is recognizing the laws that regulate man's affairs. Since the conservative and libertarian believe that these cannot be wished away through the establishment of a Utopia, they are both conservators of the real world.

My instincts are libertarian, and I am sure that I would never have joined effort with the conservatives if I had not been convinced that they are the defenders of freedom today. This fact is so evident in the contemporary world that one hardly needs to point out examples of it.

It requires only a little experience in politics or publishing for one to learn that the enemies of freedom today are the radicals and the militant liberals. Not only do they propose through their reforms to reconstruct and regiment us, they also propose to keep us from hearing the other side. Anyone who has contended with Marxists and their first cousins, the totalitarian liberals, knows that they have no intention of giving the conservative alternative a chance to compete with their doctrines for popular acceptance. If by some accident they are compelled physically to listen, it is with indifference or a contempt because they really consider the matter a closed question—that is, no longer on the agenda of discussable things.

The conservative, on the other hand, is tolerant because he has something to tolerate from, because he has in a sense squared himself with the structure of reality. Since his position does not depend upon fiat and wishfulness, he does not have to be nervously defensive about it. A new idea or an opposing idea is not going to topple his. He is accordingly a much fairer man and I think a much more humane man than his opposite whom I have been characterizing. He doesn't feel that terrible need to exterminate the enemy which seems to inflame so many radicals of both the past and the present.

This can be shown by relating an incident from the career of George Washington, who figures in my mind as the archetypal American conservative—a man versed in the ways of the world but uncorrupted by them, a man whose unshakeable realism saved our infant republic. Washington, for example, had the very ticklish job of maintaining relations with radical, revolutionary France during both of his administrations. In 1793 there arrived in this country one Citizen Genet, new minister from the French Republic, whose commission it really was to stir up trouble. He tried to involve the United States in a new war with Great Britain, and he even threatened to appeal to the American people over the head of their government. He was the sharpest thorn in Washington's side for some while.

But the next year, 1794, came the fall of Genet's party, the Gironde, and the accession to power of Robespierre and his radical Jacobin government. Genet was replaced, and Washington was requested to send him back to

France, where he undoubtedly would have faced the guillotine. But, and I here quote the words of a recent biographer: "Washington would take no agency, even remote, in the bloody business of the French terror; whatever Genet had done or tried to do, the President did not intend to order the young man to his doom. If Genet wished, it was agreed, he might have political asylum in America." So Genet became an American citizen and lived peacefully for forty years in our conservative republic. This impresses me as a classical instance of conservative tolerance and essential humaneness.

But thinking back to this period may remind us that Washington was himself a revolutionist, and this to my mind refutes any notion that a conservative must be distinguished by timidity and apathy. When the time is out of joint, he can be an active exponent of change. The difference is that he does not have the inflamed zeal of his counterpart, the radical revolutionist, who thinks that he must cut off the heads of his opponents because he cannot be objective about his own frustrations. It is interesting to know in taking leave of this subject, that Washington's Farewell Address was noticed by the London *Times*. What it had to say was this: "General Washington's address is the most complete comment upon English Clubs and Clubbists, upon factions and parties and factious partisans. The authority of this revolutionist may be set up against the wild and wicked revolutionists of Europe, if not as an altar against an altar at least as an altar against sacrilege."

In conclusion, I maintain that the conservative in his proper character and role is a defender of liberty. He is such because he takes his stand on the real order of things and because he has a very modest estimate of man's ability to change that order through the coercive power of the state. He is prepared to tolerate diversity of life and opinion because he knows that not all things are of his making and that it is right within reason to let each follow the law of his own being. A rigid equalitarianism is to him unthinkable because he appreciates that truth so well expressed by the poet Blake: "One law for the lion and the ox is oppression." I therefore can see nothing to keep him from joining hands with the libertarian, who arrives at the same position by a different route, perhaps, but out of the same impulse to condemn arbitrary power.

palpable that one is tempted to make an exception. So many of these radicals seem to be persons of disordered personality. There is something suspicious about this impassioned altruism. They often seem to be struggling to cover up some deep inner lack by trying to reform the habits or institutions of people thousands of miles away. Something like this becomes thus an obsession, almost to the point—or maybe to the point of irrationality. Not that I regard all desire to reform the world as a sign of being crazy. Even more than that I would go along with Plato and say that some forms of craziness may be divinely inspired. But here we come to an essential distinction, and a parting of the ways. There is a difference between trying to reform your fellow beings by the normal processes of logical demonstration, appeal and moral suasion—there is a difference between that and passing over to the use of force or constraint. The former is something all of us engage in every day. The latter is what makes the modern radical dangerous and perhaps in a sense demented. His first thought now is to get control of the state to make all men equal or to make all men rich, or failing that to make all men equally unhappy. This use of political instrumentality to coerce people to conform with his dream, in the face of their belief in a real order, is our reason, I think, for objecting to the radical. As an individual he may think about molding the world to his heart's desire. He may even publish the results of his thinking. But when he tries to use the instrumentality of the state to bring about his wishes then all of us are involved, and we have to take our stand.

Here, as I see it, is where conservatives and libertarians can stand on common ground. The libertarian, if my impression is correct, is a person who is interested chiefly in "freedom from." He is interested in setting sharp bounds to the authority of the state or other political forms over the individual. The right of the individual to an inviolable area of freedom as large as possible is thus his main concern. Libertarianism defined in this way is not as broad a philosophy as I conceive conservatism to be. It is narrower in purview and it is essentially negative, but this negative aspect is its very virtue.

It took the study of John Calhoun to wake me up to a realization that a constitution is and should be primarily a negative document. A constitution—and we may think primarily of the Constitution of the United States in this connection—is more to be revered for what it prohibits than for what it authorizes. A constitution is a series of "thou shalt nots" to the government, specifying the ways in which the liberties of individuals and of groups are *not* to be invaded. A constitution is a protection against that kind of arbitrary interference to which government left to itself is prone. It is right therefore to refer to our Constitution as a charter of liberties through its negative provisions, and it is no accident that in our day the friends of liberty have been pleaders for constitutional government. I think conservatives and libertarians stand together in being this kind of constitutionalist. Both want a settled code of freedom for the individual.

This is a shared *political* position, but we can show that their agreement has a philosophical basis. Both of them believe that there is an order of things which will largely take care of itself if you leave it alone. There are operating laws in nature and in human nature which are best not interfered with or not interfered with very much. If you try to change or suspend them by government fiat, the cost is greater than the return, the disorganization is expensive, the ensuing frustration painful. These laws are part of what I earlier referred to as the structure of reality. Just as there are certain conditions of efficiency for operations in the physical world, so there are conditions for efficient operation in the social and economic worlds.

There is a concept expressed by some economists today in the word "praxeology." Praxeology, briefly defined, is the science of how things work because of their essential natures. We find this out not by consulting our wishes but by observing *them*. For example, I believe it is a praxeological law that a seller will always try to get as much as he can for what he has to sell, and a buyer will always try to pay as little as he can to get it. That is a law so universal that we think of it as part of the order of things. Not only is this law a reliable index of human behavior; it also makes possible the free market economy, with its extremely important contribution to political freedom.

The conservative and the libertarian agree that it is not only presumption, it is folly to try to interfere with the workings of a praxeology. One makes use of it, yes, in the same way that a follower of Bacon makes use of nature by obeying her. The great difference is that one is recognizing the objective; one is recognizing the laws that regulate man's affairs. Since the conservative and libertarian believe that these cannot be wished away through the establishment of a Utopia, they are both conservators of the real world.

man needs help, and to the extent that he is engaged in combating the disintegration—in conserving what otherwise might be lost or dispersed—his is an activist program. Here I suggest lies the germ of the movement of the "new conservatism" in this country and elsewhere.

Our second word is "liberalism." How does its content compare and contrast with what has just been said? Almost everyone is aware of certain pleasant connotations in "liberal" and "liberalism." One of the meanings associated with "liberal" is "generous," and no one likes to think of himself as "illiberal" in the sense of "ungenerous." But we are now talking about the political focus of these terms, and there is special reason for noting the history of the word "liberalism." The word "liberalism" as employed in politics and journalism today means almost precisely the opposite of what it did a century ago. If a "liberal" of a century ago were to be confronted with some of the programs that are today put forward in the name of liberalism, he would certainly stare in surprise.

Nineteenth century liberalism was broadly synonymous with individualism and liberty. It taught minimum interference by the state and maximum opportunity for the individual to do what he could for himself. On grounds of reason, politics and ethics, it preached the rule of "let alone." The individual is happiest and society is most creative when the individual is freest to order his own affairs.

I shall offer a few evidences that this was formerly the creed of liberalism. One of the greatest of the nineteenth century liberals was John Stuart Mill. In his celebrated essay "On Liberty," he offered the following reasons for *not* extending the scope and activity of the state. (1) There are many things which are likely to be done better by the individual than by the government. (2) There are other things which an individual may not be able to do as well as an office of the government. Nevertheless, it is better to allow him to do these things as a means *to his own mental education and self-development.* (3) It is dangerous and in the long run evil to keep adding to the power of government. He has then to say:

> If the roads, the railways, the banks, the insurance offices, the great joint-stock companies, the universities, and the public charities were all of them branches of the government; if, in addition, the municipal corporations and local boards, with all that now devolves on them, became departments of the central administration; if the employees of all these different enterprises were ap-

Conservatism and Liberalism[1]

I begin with two words: conservatism and liberalism. People who are willing to accept the name "conservative" are not infrequently asked, as if it were an overwhelming question, "What is it that you wish to conserve?" The more I meditate upon this, the more it seems to me that the answer is an obvious one: the conservative wishes to conserve man—the human being. The implications of that answer, however, are not so obvious, and perhaps that is why the question is so often raised.

When one says that he wishes to conserve man, he signifies, for one thing, that he knows what man is. That is to say, he believes that man has an essential being, a definable nature, and a proper end. The program of conservation must seek to know that being better, to understand the capacities and limits of that nature, and to help man attain that end. I shall repeat this, for I think it is a cardinal point for any intelligible conservative position. The conservative thinks that man has a definable nature, that he is happiest in the true sense when he is following the laws of that nature, and that he has a unique and transcendent destiny.

In second place, the conservative believes that there are forces in this world which are inimical to these and which militate against all of them. There are forces which tend to confuse him about the reality of his being, voices which tell him that he has no nature except what is exhibited historically from day to day, and there are theories which deny the idea of a destiny. These forces and ideas are disintegrative in the sense that they leave man puzzled and at loose ends. The thinking conservative feels that this

1. The text of a lecture delivered to a group of seminarians at Holy Name College in Washington, DC, on October 15, 1960. Edited by Ted J. Smith III from Weaver's handwritten text of the lecture and a preliminary typescript prepared by Carla Dehmlow. Both documents are located in Box 2, Folder 6, of the Richard M. Weaver papers at Vanderbilt University.

pointed and paid by the government, and looked to the government for every rise in life; not all the freedom of the press and popular constitution of the legislature would make this or any other country free otherwise than in name.[2]

Then he closes the essay with this ringing affirmation:

The worth of a State, in the long run, is the worth of the individuals composing it; and a State which postpones the interests of their mental expansion and elevation, to a little more of administrative skill . . . ; a State which dwarfs its men, in order that they may be more docile instruments in its hands even for beneficial purposes—will find that with small men no great thing can be accomplished; and that the perfection of machinery to which it has sacrificed everything, will in the end avail it nothing, for want of the vital power which . . . it has preferred to banish.[3]

I am not submitting this as the final argument for individual liberty. Mill rests his case frankly upon utility, which I believe to be shortsighted and wrong. I am still speaking historically here: This is what the nineteenth century liberals thought. But it seems to me that they had at least a good argument from consequences.

Now what do we find when we turn to present-day liberalism? As I suggested a moment ago, it is virtually the reverse of this. I cannot follow the semantic degeneration which would account for this change, but everyone knows that the self-professing liberals in politics and journalism now are nearly all statists—that is, people who believe in widening the power of the state for the presumptive good of the individual. They believe in more state ownership of things, more state control of what remains private, state interference in education, with all the centralization of power which this makes inevitable.

A senator who comes from not very far from here recently defined liberalism in a leading magazine as the use of all the levels of public authority to spread property and increase the common welfare. How he gets "liberalism" out of that is the semantic puzzle just referred to. Etymologically "liberalism" derives its meaning from the root idea of liberty. Somehow these people have got "liberty" and state-achieved security all confused.

2. John Stuart Mill, "On Liberty," in Stefan Collini (ed.), *On Liberty; with the Subjection of Women and Chapters on Socialism,* Cambridge: Cambridge University Press, 1989, p. 110.
3. *Ibid.,* p. 115.

And indeed we find that they have very little to say about liberty in the old sense. Last spring I noticed on our campus the announcement of a lecture which was going to discuss whether individual liberty was any longer a tenable ideal in modern industrial society. I did not get to that lecture, but it was clear from the source and from the way it was stated that this lecturer proposed to argue that liberty is now one of those outmoded ideals in which we can have at best but a sentimental interest. I was shocked to see the boldness with which an idea so heretical in terms of our traditions and historical ideals was being suggested. Still, when you think about it, it is only a gathering up of many propositions which are being widely received today. These are my reasons for saying that modern "liberalism" is a screen for statism and collectivism.

Now all differences of the kind I have been describing trace back to differences in world-views. Sometimes the world-view is not very consciously formulated by the holder; nonetheless, it can be deduced from the things he says he believes, even about very specific topics. I wish to give the discussion a turn here and look at the implications of the two opposed positions and also note what I perceive to be the impact of these views upon certain areas of thought and action. It is necessary to begin at the profoundest level, with theology, or religion. How do these two groups divide when the matter of religion is brought in? It certainly behooves me to proceed very cautiously before this audience. I am not learned in theology, I was not brought up to discuss religion, and I shall now rush in where wise men would fear to tread. But if you will permit me to broach the matter in broad terms, I think I can give you a religious difference between the conservative as I define him and the modern-day liberal.

To begin with, and most importantly, the conservative believes in the existence of a non-self. This is but a way of saying that he believes in a creation. He does not believe that the world began with him or will end with him. There is a creation, older than himself, greater than himself, which has ontological status. This creation is essentially good and is not infinitely subject to his will. His position thus is really one of modesty. Perhaps the surest mark of the conservative is this willingness to respect or venerate something other than himself. He believes in the uniqueness of man, but he does not translate this uniqueness as supremacy or omnipotence. He sees rather that this unique creation is limited and is subject to restraints. Accordingly, the conservative has a perspective on man himself which the liberal is characteristically unwilling to take. This is why we often find the conservative saying: 'Before you embark on this scheme you had better measure it against history, and also against that external reality which we know to exist. They are bigger than you and your wishes. And you had better count in also, as one of those forces, human nature.' In sum, conservatives believe that there is a structure of reality which cannot be changed by wishful thinking, and cannot be easily changed at all.

Now when we turn to the modern liberal, we find a person who increasingly places man at the center of things—indeed, not only at the center, but in potentially unlimited control. This liberal does not concern himself much with whether this world is a creation. Generally, he seems to think it isn't, and in any case he appears indifferent toward finding out whether the creator had designs. The world appears to him a brute, empirical fact, which man has got to subdue and manage. And since he fights more and more against the idea of teleology even in philosophy, he is often silent upon the question of the way the world should go. Yet this is a question which has to be answered even in the intermediate run, and hence we usually find him operating from the postulate that the world should go the way men want it to go, without consultation with any other source and without any feeling of humility.

It scarcely needs pointing out—for it has been pointed out many times—that this has the effect of divinizing man. If he is the only source of direction in the universe, and the only source of value, then his will is the supreme will, and there cannot be any ground for criticizing it or impeding it—though I leave out of the account here the difficult problem of how that will is to be determined. In a figure that may evoke the modern mind, man is now Chief Engineer of the Universe, and he is not really accountable to anybody but himself.

This attitude is actually the confluence of a number of things which have developed over the past few centuries: the disbelief in revealed truth, secularism, scientism, romantic and sentimental theories of human nature, and that seductive brand of optimism spread by the sages of New England under the name of transcendentalism. All of these have added their impetus in varying measures, but there is one more which I think needs an especially careful scrutiny. This is a simple-minded form of evolutionism which we often find emerging as a philosophy: the idea that man is constantly evolving and that whatever he is evolving into is what he is supposed to be. This, as you will see at once, places him beyond all criticism. It is idle to question what nature is doing with man; whether or not she has a conscious purpose, the last stage is the most fulfilled stage in terms of what is going to happen. I have found this basis of thinking showing up even in political and historical works, where "historical forces" play the role of "natural forces" of evolution. To conclude, the modern liberal has tended to embrace a cosmological view which deifies man. The wishes of man are the last court of appeal and nothing that he wants to do can really be repudiated.

Views as far-reaching as these cannot fail to have a decisive effect upon the way one thinks about specific and practical things. And so it is when we pass on to consider how these broad groups differ in their political and economic objectives. Here one sees at once that the heady wine of management has deeply influenced the politics of the modern liberal. But even without the intoxication, there is a logical progression from what I have called his cosmological outlook to the omni-competent state. If the world is infinitely malleable to man's will, the only criterion is efficiency: What means will get the job done best or fastest? Now it is very generally admitted, even by the friends of liberty, that centralized and dictatorial forms of government are more efficient in many respects than others. It is the principle of military organization. A dispersal of power is not conducive to quick or maximum effort. For that one needs a central command and obedience all down the line. Now the liberal, positing a secular security as the highest goal of man, can't find any reason why this power should not be invoked. If we can solve all our problems by feeding, clothing, and sheltering, then why not convert the state into a gigantic enterprise and get on with the job efficiently? Of course, there is grave doubt whether the state can actually do this job, but you sense the appeal of this theory to some minds. This is why we hear increasing talk of "the planned economy" and "the welfare state" and security against this and promises for the other—all on the assumption that the collective means will be the most successful. But we should note very carefully that this depends on another assumption, which is that the public authority has the right and even the duty to manipulate man for his own good. Individual privileges and desires are more and more left out of the equation of statism.

The other night I was looking into a recent book by the well-known Swedish sociologist Gunnar Myrdal. I found him talking very complacently about how individuals can be got over their liking for individualism. After a certain amount of state regulation, he says, people discover that they don't mind it at all and even begin to like it. As if it were anything new that people grow to like things that are not good for them!

Here is where the conservative meets the liberal in head-on opposition. With his definition of the essential nature of man, he cannot accept any such proposition. For the conservative, man is a creature destined to be free—even at his peril. He needs a certain range of liberty in order to be himself—a being who derives his dignity from the very fact that he must make precarious decisions. According to my understanding, this is a Christian concept. If there is one thing Christianity brought into the thinking of the world about the individual person, it is that the individual is an opposing force—an opposing force to governments, institutions and circumstances which would distort his essential nature. Our very systems of ethics and politics rest on an idea of sacredness in the personality. This is not something for an engineer's manipulation. Yet everywhere in the literature of liberalism, socialism and communism, one finds attacks upon the *persona*—upon the private being of the individual.

This concept of the dignity and the rights of the individual lies at the bottom of the conservative belief in private property. A man needs something he can call his own—he needs a scope for his free choices—in order to realize himself as a person. To say that no man shall own anything is to put his will at the disposition of the collective will in a way that precludes his own growth and responsibility. Of course, I am not speaking here of consecrated orders, which have a special vocation. I am speaking of the ordinary laymen who do the work of the world and who need a proving ground for their ability and responsibility. Private property, which he cultivates, improves and perhaps increases, according to his industriousness and talents, is the proper theater for this. The conservative recognizes that some inequalities appear, but inequalities always result from differences in native endowment—in intelligence, energy, stamina—as well as acquired things like character, habits and education. It is absurd to deny opportunity to these on the ground of a doctrinaire egalitarianism.

For the rest of the argument in favor of individual liberty and initiative,

I think the conservative might well go along with Mill. There are some things the individual can do for himself better than the state can do them, despite large theoretical claims to the contrary. And there are other things it is best for him to do for himself, even though he cannot do them as well—for his own education, development and sense of fulfillment. Even here I suspect that a double standard is being employed. Say the individual does *not* do them as well by the abstract measure of engineering efficiency. Still he may be doing them better if we think of the kind of intensity and intimacy of the effort that goes into them and the sense of reward that he gets from applying his own faculties. The net result might be less, but the feeling of accomplishment would be greater. And the man has been involved personally. In brief, it would be richer and more meaningful for him. If we believe, as historically the people in this country have done, that the final end is the individual and not the state, we must stand the cost of this kind of enrichment. In the long run it is certain to be made up for, and more than made up for, by the maintenance of creativity.

I turn now to the area of education. The differences between modern liberal and conservative philosophies show up strikingly in the current clashes over educational theory. Of course, no theory of education makes sense unless it is based on some consistent view of the kind of creature who is to be educated and of the kind of life he ought to be educated for. If one believes that man is and can be only an animal, he should be trained as an animal—not really "educated" at all, for this word has higher connotations. If one believes that he is a spiritual being with a soul and an eternal destiny at stake, these must be guiding concepts in the design of his education. If one believes that he is by nature wholly good, a certain kind of educational regimen is indicated. If one believes that he has aspirations toward the good but serious liability to error and wrongdoing, a proper education must take this into account. Metaphysics comes into the picture too, for it has decisive things to say about the nature of what is knowable.

Everybody should be aware that in this country there has existed for the past half-century a powerful movement called "progressive education." The assumption of the name has been impudent, because whether it has any rightful claim to be considered "progressive" is, to put it mildly, a very moot point. But if one accepts the liberal credo, it can be made to look progressive. It is compounded of large elements of pragmatism, optimism and romanticism about the nature of man, rejection of the idea of enduring truth, and a politics based upon an expected triumph of collectivism. As such it represents a very radical departure from the traditional Judaic-Christian-classical concept of man and the world and the nature of knowledge. In supporting that charge I will go into some detail. I may claim to speak from research at this point, because I have recently been doing some work on this problem. Here is a list of some of the chief assumptions and tenets of so-called "progressive" education.

1. First, as to knowledge, there is no such thing as a body of knowledge which reflects the structure of reality and which everyone therefore needs to learn. Knowledge is viewed as an instrumentality which is true or false according to the way it is applied to concrete situations or the way it serves the purposes of the individual. Since most of these educators have embraced the notion that the essence of the world is change, there is no final knowledge about anything. The truths of yesterday are the falsehoods of today, and the truths of today will be the falsehoods of tomorrow.

2. This being so, the object of education is not to teach knowledge but to "teach students." What this means is that everything should be adapted to the child as child, to the youth as youth and to the particular group according to its limitations. There are no ideals or standards of performance which these are bound to measure themselves by or to respect.

3. As a corollary of the above principle, the child should be encouraged to follow his own desires in deciding what he should study, and what aspects of what subjects, and at what times.

4. The teacher must not think of himself as being in authority, because the very idea of authority is bad.

5. The student should never be made afraid of anything connected with the school. Marks and competition are evil because they result in feelings of inferiority and superiority, which are "undemocratic."

6. The mind is not to be exalted over the senses: democracy requires that sensory and "activist" learning should be valued on a par with intellectual learning. The mentally slow or lazy are not to be made to feel that they are lacking; it is better to impugn the whole tradition of intellectual education than to hurt the feelings of the less bright and the indolent.

7. Consequently there should be less education through symbols like language and figures and more through using the hands on concrete objects. It is more important to *make* maps than to learn them, said John Dewey, the grand prophet of this revolutionary movement.
8. The general aim is to train the student so that he will adjust not to the now-existing society, as is sometimes inferred from their words, but to a society conceived as a thoroughly secular social democracy.

A few other propositions equally startling can be deduced from the writings of the new educationists, but these should be enough to show how radical the break with tradition has been. However, lest the meaning of this be too revolutionary to reach the consciousness all at once, let me rephrase two or three of the central ideas. Knowledge, which has always been the reason for instituting schools, does not exist in any absolute or binding sense. The mind, which has always been regarded as the distinguishing possession of the human race, is now to be viewed as a tyrant which has been denying the rights of the body as a whole. Discipline, that great shaper of mind and body, is to be discarded because it carries elements of fear and compulsion. The student is to be prepared not to save his soul, or to inherit the wisdom and usage of past civilizations, or even to get ahead in life, but to become a member of a Utopia resting on a false view of both nature and man.

In trying to understand an apostasy from our traditions so great as this, I have cast about for some historical parallel. The most correspondent thing I have been able to find—the search in this direction being suggested by Professor Eric Voegelin's brilliant book *The New Science of Politics*, which I hope you will all become acquainted with if you don't know it already—is the Gnostic movement of the first and second centuries. There are in fact some extraordinary resemblances between modern educationism and ancient Gnosticism. Like the modern "progressivist," the ancient gnostic ended up by divinizing man. He looked upon creation as incomplete and as needing to be completed by man. He largely ignored history and based his thinking on psychologizing. He was antinomian in his dislike of discipline and restraint. If he had prevailed, he would have destroyed the Christian movement, as the progressivists, so called, are destroying education today where they prevail. Not all political liberals, of course, have accepted these educational fallacies. Still, it is curious how many of them are sensitive to attacks upon "progressive education." These they often construe to be attacks upon the idea of public education or attacks upon democracy, or both. However, I cannot help feeling that the battle against these false progressivists has been basically won. They have been refuted in theory, and a nation which is facing a test for survival is not going to go on putting up with educational fantasies.

I hope my words have implied that the conservative's view of education is just about the antithesis of this. He believes that man is a body, a mind and a soul, prone to error but capable of glory. He believes that there is a corpus of universally valid knowledge which is not simply at the mercy of time. It is important to note that he believes in the value of history. I think his point of view on this subject was never put more felicitously than by the eminent Catholic historian, Lord Acton, who said: "If the past is an obstacle and a burden, knowledge of the past is the safest and surest emancipation." The conservative believes that education is disciplinary in its very nature, and that without the idea and practice of discipline, neither the body nor the mind can be trained. He does not preach the socialist commonwealth, but he does believe that without some moral consensus societies cannot endure.

Now, in this running contrast of two outlooks, I have said many things in favor of conservatism and little if anything in favor of liberalism. Does this mean that conservatism holds a monopoly, that there is nothing at all to be said in favor of liberalism? I would not put it in that way, but rather in this: If I had stood here and given you an objective, impartial description of the two and had said, "Now take your choice," it would have been a swindle. Every speech involving politics and morals ought to have an inclination, and my inclination is toward the conservative point of view. Still, I am little disposed to fight over the term "conservative" itself. The term does bear certain handicaps which are difficult to shake off. Some persons, I know, who would agree with nearly everything expressed here do not like to be called "conservatives." It might be better if we could use the simple term "realism." This seems to beg the question in favor of my side, but to explain why I think it is just, I am going to put the whole matter in a broader framework and then close.

There is no doubt that we are in a crisis where we have to determine in what form our culture and civilization are going to continue. Many voices can be heard telling us that what we have inherited from Judea and Greece and Rome and the Christian Church is no longer workable or tenable. These people envision a world resting upon science and technology and material progress, upon centralized states and a regimented mankind. It is a world in which man has no real dignity; he simply goes along with what are sometimes called "historical forces." This is the prophecy of the new future, which is to be very unlike the past.

The conservative creed which I have outlined is a protest and a remonstrance against this. But it is not such merely at the level of political opposition. It is not inspired simply by the desire to differ politically with people we don't like. Rather the conservative protest rests upon a belief that this new prophecy is erroneous. Instead of being more realistic than the tradition, it is less so. It leaves out too much that is known and true about man himself and substitutes half-truths and sometimes mere wishes. Delusions nourished by superficial study mate with uncritical enthusiasms to produce all kinds of vagaries. Values are left without foundations and the most eloquent lessons of history go unheeded and unheard. Conservatism deserves to be called realistic because against all this sort of thing it is holding a dike. It believes that "Man will prevail"—not through his prideful knowledge of science, and not through himself alone, but by the help of an intuition of something greater than himself.

On Liberty[1]

The sincere friends of liberty, a great historian has said, have been few in any age. We are living at a time when the very idea of liberty, upon which our nation was founded, is threatened by open forces abroad and by insidious forces at home. There has never been a moment in our history when the sincere friends of liberty more needed to consult together and to publish to the world the real nature of that which most makes life worth living.

It is our traditional belief that man was given liberty to ennoble him. We may infer that those who would take his liberty away have the opposite purpose of degrading him. Too much is being said today about the dignity of man without realization that the dignity of man means the *worth* of man. There can be no worth of man unless there is an inviolable area of freedom in which he can assume the stature of a man and exercise choice in regard to his work, his associates, his use of his earnings, his way of life. Little by little this area has been traded away in return for plausible gifts and subventions, urged on by slogans. Now we are at a point where regimentation, which used to be suggested with apologies, comes couched in the language of prerogative.

The past shows unvaryingly that when a people's freedom disappears, it goes not with a bang, but in silence amid the comfort of being cared for.

That is the dire peril in the present trend toward statism. If freedom is not found accompanied by a willingness to resist, and to reject favors, rather than to give up what is intangible but precious, it will not long be found at all.

It therefore gives me great pleasure to accept this award from hands that have joined to win back and to secure our heritage of freedom.

1. The text of Weaver's acceptance speech for an award bestowed on him by the Young Americans for Freedom at a rally held in Madison Square Garden in New York on March 7, 1962. Edited by Ted J. Smith III from a typescript of a final draft acquired from Weaver's sister, Mrs. Polly Weaver Beaton, and currently in the possession of the editor.

How to Argue the Conservative Cause[1]

At the kind invitation of this Conservative Club I am here to offer a few observations on the present state of the Conservative cause. Some while ago I read a remark in a newspaper, attributed to a Republican Congress-

1. The origin of this speech has been a matter of some confusion, largely because at least seven versions of it have been preserved, some of which have been misidentified. The versions include one holograph and three typescript texts of varying lengths in the Richard M. Weaver Papers at Vanderbilt University, two audio recordings of one presentation of the speech (cassettes 7B:59–8A:236 and 9A:275–10A:17 in the Weaver collection at Hillsdale College), and a transcription of one of the audio recordings in a 1978 doctoral dissertation. Based on letters from Richard Weaver to Donald Lipsett dated May 9, 1959, and from Louis Dehmlow to Donald Lipsett dated October 10, 1962, both in the Hillsdale College collection, a poster for an April 22 speech preserved in the Polly Weaver Beaton collection, and evidence from the audio recordings, it is possible to establish the history of the speech with some certainty. Weaver first presented it as a public lecture sponsored by the Wisconsin Conservative Club at the University of Wisconsin on April 22, 1959. On that occasion it was entitled "The Conservative Cause." The audio recordings in the Hillsdale College collection are from that presentation, as is the holograph version of the text in the Vanderbilt collection. A transcription of one of the recordings of the speech—retitled "Rhetorical Strategies of the Conservative Cause" and misdated April 26, 1959—is included in Gerald T. Goodnight, "Rhetoric and Culture," unpublished Ph.D. dissertation, University of Kansas, 1978, pp. 575–608. Weaver then presented the speech again (as was his common practice) at an event in Chicago sponsored by the Intercollegiate Society of Individualists on September 22, 1962. On that occasion it was apparently entitled "How to Argue the Conservative Cause." Immediately after the event, Louis Dehmlow acquired Weaver's typewritten speaking notes and had one or more typescripts prepared from them. Of the three typescripts in the Vanderbilt collection, the 22-page version is apparently the one Weaver used to deliver the speech and the 19-page and 11-page versions are ones prepared by Dehmlow. The audio recordings of the 1959 presentation and the various typescripts of the 1962 presentation show that the two speeches were quite similar in content, although the 1962 presentation was shortened and updated. The text presented here is a version edited by Ted J. Smith III from the 19-page typescript entitled "How to Argue the Conservative Cause" in Box 3, Folder 1, of the Richard M. Weaver Papers at Vanderbilt University. That typescript carries the following erroneous notation in an

woman, to the effect that while in fact the conservative position was being presented from a number of sources in this country, somehow "the line was not selling." More recently I read a newspaper reviewer who alleged that the New Conservatives, as they are sometimes called, had not made a very convincing case. Like all remarks which contain a modicum of uncomfortable truth, these have proved a troubling consideration. This is more especially true because I feel that the battle between conservatives and liberals is now fully joined, and that in this battle the conservatives are the upholders of freedom. I say I cannot deny some justice to the remarks, for I have seen too many occasions where it appeared to me that the most solid and cogent arguments, the most American positions, the most patriotic kinds of appeals, were not getting the kind of acceptance we have every right to expect. But if one should infer from this that the Conservative cause is essentially weak and foredoomed to inconsequence, I would say that he is misreading the situation. I intend to focus my talk tonight upon this particular anomaly—upon the fact that a strong and forcefully appealing case has had some difficulty in getting across to its natural market. The emphasis in what follows therefore will be upon how we should argue the Conservative cause.

The first step in any such undertaking is a candid analysis of the situation. And candor need hold no terrors for us, because I am convinced that in this fight the majority, and probably the very great majority, of the American people are on our side.

Recently I sat down and tried to estimate what things the people of this country, in a real showdown, would be willing to fight for. When I say fight for, I mean work for, sacrifice for, defend as things they have no intention of ever giving up. These are things so ingrained in our way of living, so essential to liberty and the pursuit of happiness, that we would never, short of a national collapse, think of surrendering them. I arrived at a list of three, arranged in the order of their power to evoke passionate defense.

1. The right to practice a religion.
2. The right freely to choose one's own type of work.
3. The right to privacy, including the right to hold private property.

---

unknown hand (not Weaver's): "U. of Wisconsin/April 22, 1959." Some of the changes introduced in the present version were derived from Weaver's annotations to the 22-page typescript in the Vanderbilt collection.

Despite certain winds of doctrine that blow from this and that suspicious source, I am convinced that the majority, and probably the very great majority, of Americans cherish these rights. I need not point out to you that all of them are under heavy and systematic attack from international communism. The situation then shapes up as follows: the majority of the American people are committed to a set of preferences which are in direct opposition to the ideology of communism. There is plenty of reason to believe that the further one goes down toward the grass roots, the stronger one finds that adherence to be, and the greater the impatience with communist and socialist overtures. It is always heartening to discover support among those who are closest to the earth, closest to the daily necessity of work, who *make* their living in the literal sense of that phrase. When the time comes, these people are usually the true fighters.

It is the intellectuals, or a good many of them, sad to say, who have been corrupted. How this came about would probably make a complicated story, which there is no need to go into at this point. But stand near the campus of almost any large American university—and especially the large *and* famous ones—and you feel yourself impelled to exclaim: "I had not thought miseducation had undone so many!" Most of our students come to college from plain and naturally patriotic homes. But when they get there, they find that "liberalism" is the hidden premise of many if not most of the courses that are there for them to take. That is to say, their studies are predicated upon an assumption that liberalism is now the official national assumption, and any serious disagreement with this is looked upon as idiosyncratic deviation. The chances are that three out of every four of the student's teachers will be professing liberals. Now many of these are good, well-intentioned people, some of them with a very strict sense of personal obligation. But knowingly or unknowingly they are part of a process of softening up their country for conquest by alien and, to my mind, inhumane ideas. (I once defined a liberal as a person who is not a communist but who cannot give any good reason for not being one.) This makes him all the more dangerous as an unconscious instrumentality. He can appear as a humanitarian and an idealist at the very time that he is being used by those who have the most cynical ends in view. Indeed, the academic liberal sometimes has the gentleness of the dove. But what he lacks is the wisdom of the serpent. And it is the latter, I very much fear, which is going to prove necessary in our battle for survival.

The criticism I make here cannot of course be confined to professors and teachers. If you look in the pulpit, in the press, in the editorial offices of our widely circulated magazines—especially it seems to me the leading women's magazines—you find much the same situation. The liberals of whom I speak have captured the means of communicating and disseminating ideas to such an extent that they are now practically a self-perpetuating group; and if their notions are taken up by the oncoming generation, it is because the oncoming generation has little or no access to alternative philosophies.

This is a brief exposition of the present lines of force. There is at the top a group composed of the academic, professional, and managerial classes who have imbibed and who tend to pass on the ideas of collectivism. Why our best, or rather our *most*, educated classes have succumbed to this is, as I suggested before, a curious problem. One probable answer is that a great deal of modern education is half-education—just enough to make the individual vaguely dissatisfied with his tradition and his inheritance and not enough to make him strike down and find an anchorage in something that will really hold. Below this group is the great body of plain people, who are waiting for someone to speak their piece. How they have been able to stay in the main uncorrupted is also an interesting theme. Certainly they have been assailed by printed matter in enough forms to turn them in the direction of totalitarian liberalism. I have a theory that the printed word is like some of these bacteria and toxins, which have the property of building up resistance to their own power to injure. Expose people to them enough, and these people develop sufficient immunity to survive. As in the case of other self-protecting devices in the body, there is an in-built system of psychology which prevents ravages. At any rate, there are times when we have to give thanks for whatever generates this healthy skepticism about things that appear in print.

Now, the first step in planning a rational program is to distinguish our friends from our enemies. I have given reasons for believing that in the present and pending contests the greater part of the people are our friends. They are neither atheists nor materialists—that is certain. They do not believe that the government either could or should do everything for them. They do not believe that individual liberty is passe. They are sometimes deceived by the rhetoric of the other side into voting for things that weaken the supports of a free society. But talk to the man in the street, and you will find that he is still a pretty solid citizen. I do not desire to sentimentalize him or to credit him with extraordinary powers and virtues. But there are times when it is an achievement just to retain sanity.

So, the conservatives are in the position of speaking for a majority against a minority.

Now when the members of this disaffected minority see that they are going to meet conservative opposition, they are prone to ask: "What do you wish to conserve?" My answer to that is that we wish to conserve Western civilization, including emphatically the American contribution to it. And I do not think that anything less than this is threatened by the movement of international communism. We are the heirs of a civilization that goes back three thousand years. The gift of the Hebrews and the Christians for religion, the genius of the Greeks for art and philosophy, the genius of the Romans in law and government—all of these are in our antecedents. With many later additions and increases in insight, these have given us the support of a belief in transcendental reality, a tradition of free inquiry into the constitution of nature and of man, and a system of representative government which, when it is rightly used, can hold off all forms of despotism. These things we have from the Old World. To them the New World has added perhaps a new and practical concept of the brotherhood of man. Not a mass society, not an artificial leveling, but a concept of regard for the individual and a welcome for native ability regardless of where it appears. A respect for freedom, initiative, and enterprise has given us the most wonderful productive system in the world. And we may note that this American trust in individual ability and incentive goes back to the first days of our settlement. Recently I was reading that early American classic, William Bradford's *History of Plymouth Plantation*. The Plymouth Colony, you may remember, was instituted among somewhat communal lines. Property was held in common, work was collectively organized, and each was to receive "according to his needs," as the modern socialist formula expresses it. It took the colonists just three years to find out that such a system had serious limitations. By 1623, this grave historian tells us, the colony was languishing in want and misery. At this point I give you his own eloquent words:

> So they began to think how they might raise as much corn as they could, and obtain a better crop than they had done, that they might not still thus languish in misery. At length, after much debate of things, the Governor (with the

advice of the chiefest amongst them) gave way that they should set corn *every man for his own particular,* and in that regard trust to themselves; in all other things to go on in the general way as before. And so assigned to every family a parcel of land, according to the proportion of their number, for that end . . . and ranged all boys and youth under some family. This had very good success, for it made all hands very industrious, so as much more corn was planted than otherwise would have been by any means the Governor or any other could use, and saved him a great deal of trouble, and gave far better content. The women now went willingly into the field, and took their little ones with them to set corn; which before would allege weakness and inability; whom to have compelled would have been thought great tyranny and oppression.

The experience that was had in this common course and condition, tried sundry years and that amongst godly and sober men, may well evince the vanity of that conceit of Plato's and other ancients applauded by some of later times; that the taking away of property and bringing in community into a commonwealth would make them happy and flourishing; as if they were wiser than God. For this community (so far as it was) was found to breed much confusion and discontent and retard much employment that would have been to their benefit and comfort.[2]

Later he adds the sober reflection: "And [it] would have been worse if they had been men of another condition."[3] Which is to admit that even in a community strongly committed to and permeated with the spirit of religion, the incentive of reward was found indispensable, and the "conceit of Plato's" exposed as a delusion.

This is the kernel of the American success story, and it has had many splendid sequels and parallels.

Some of our liberals and socialists can see in this only the germ of the "robber baron." But I do not see why anyone should be frightened into losing a just perspective on things by that rhetorical phrase. That the successful men who have amassed large fortunes in this country have done more *harm* than good would be very difficult to prove. But why let theorizing turn our eyes from the fact that we have the highest popular standard of living in the world by far? We have so much foodstuff that we are looking for means to give it away. We produce so much cotton fiber, tobacco, and

2. William Bradford, *Of Plymouth Plantation* (ed. Samuel Eliot Morrison), New York: Alfred A. Knopf, 1952, pp. 120–21, Weaver's emphasis.

3. *Ibid.,* p. 121.

what not that we have to contrive schemes to hold down the annual crop. We have so many automobiles that the streets of even small towns are clogged, and we wonder where on earth the next five or six million that roll from the factories are going to be put. We are so prolific in appliances and gadgets that the makers of these are seeking new ways to put them in the hands of people.

It is hard to believe that in the midst of this plenty some people feel called upon to apologize for our failure.

One explanation for this curiosity is that it may be possible for a system to decline in favor because of its very success. People somehow lose their bearings and forget what a splendid thing they have got. Or, they are bored with having too much and become restless; they decide they do not want what they have. They turn to the other thing, whatever it is, in the hope that it will give them something different. But what this points to is spiritual malaise, not economic breakdown. Capitalism has delivered the goods, and it is absurd to think of going on the defensive about that.

Now furthermore, as we move into this fight to win, it is well to remember the military maxim that the best defense is a good offense. It is high time to stop feeling guilty and condemned because our system has given us so much that other peoples are poor in comparison. It is time to look behind iron and bamboo curtains and bring the sins of the other side into this debate.

The feature of communism which damns it irrevocably is that it is profoundly unethical. This can, of course, be proved historically. Its use of deceit, terror, and violence, its brutal liquidation of dissenting elements among its own population and among its own officials, its rape of nearby countries, its savage suppression of popular uprisings, as in Hungary, its use of forced or slave labor, and its cynical disregard for international agreements when they have ceased to serve its ends—these are all parts of the known record. There is no need to rehearse the tale further. All we need to do is note that they illustrate the working of the communist principle that the end justifies the means. There is a certain deceptive look of idealism about that principle, yet analysis and experience both will show that it is one of the most vicious and immoral rules of conduct ever formulated. The truth is that the ends and the means cannot be separated in the way that this suggests. The ends and the means have a mutual bearing; means always condition the ends, and it is entirely possible for means to swallow up ends. Once you begin a thing with improper means, you are already estopped from attaining your real goal. More especially, when ethical restraints are thrown aside, the means tend to supplant the ends. In the everyday sphere we would not think of trusting a man who told us he was going to be pretty bad now so that later he can be completely good. But this is what we are witnessing in communist nations on a colossal scale. The Soviets claim to look forward to some kind of Utopia. Toward the achievement of that Utopia, anything is allowable—torture, the taking of life, deceit, the substitution of systematic falsehood for history. Of course the Utopia recedes infinitely. One of the things Marxism had in mind originally was the "withering away of the state." But now in the process of pursuit, the state becomes greater, more omnipotent, more arbitrary than ever—communist China being a particularly horrifying example. Another has been fashioned out of bullets and suppression in Cuba, on our very doorstep. We are justified in concluding that the people who tell us that the end justifies the means are really interested in means, to the obscuring of all rights. On this ground alone we may say that a communist state cannot belong to the comity of nations.

There is another, though it is a connected, way in which the communist philosophy is profoundly unethical; and this lies in the disregard it has for the human personality. Under a communist regime personality is definitely on the list of proscribed things. I shall always remember something a well-known American writer told me about his experience during the twenties and thirties when he was thrown into contact with a good many communists. He noticed that regularly the first thing the communists tried to do was *invade* the personality. In my very limited contact with these people I have found the same thing. A communist is very impatient with anything that suggests personality—first impatient, then hostile. Personality is to him something "reactionary." Here is where the clash between the traditional civilization of the West and the militant fanaticism coming out of the East is most evident. For when we reflect upon it, we see that our most cherished institutions are built upon respect for the personality. Personality is the final ethical tie-up of the individual. It is the evidence, if you will permit the expression, that he has a soul. Christianity won its great triumph in the ancient world by introducing a respect for the singular, unique, invio-

late person—for the personality. It had been up to that time something not
fully recognized. And this enabled it to do something that even Greek philosophy had not been able to do—to identify in the *persona,* the individual
person, an internal center of force invested with certain rights. Our ethical
systems, our literature, and our institutions since that time have reflected
this new valuation of man. Now all this is being denied. To the communist
personality is so much moonshine. His view is certainly consistent with,
and is in fact made necessary by, his materialism. If one starts with a premise of simple materialism, one cannot derive any meaningful idea of personality. Respect for personality has to mean that one believes in forces other
than the material. When our Western statesmen refer to the communistic
regimes as materialistic and atheistic, this is not simply name calling. These
are logical descriptions of an order where the very idea of personality is
systematically combatted.

Even if communism had proved overwhelmingly successful in the practical sense, these would be reasons enough to condemn it outright. We
would still prefer the Judeo-Christian image of man, the ideal of freedom,
and the concept of transcendent right, to a mere surfeit of goods. But if
communism cannot win in a court where religion and ethics are recognized, you would expect it to make a very strong case in another court. Now
where is the evidence that it is a successful economic system? Most of the
evidence today indicates that a socialist system can neither deliver the goods
nor insure their equitable distribution. It cannot produce the goods because
government planning is no substitute for the free market and the incentive
of private gain. It cannot distribute them equitably because bureaucratic
dispensation is no substitute for the flexible practices of adjustment and
accommodation that exist under free choice.[4] There are even signs that
nations which have adopted socialism in greater or less degree are having to
confess this truth. We hear people recently returned from Russia saying that
whatever it is they have over there, it is not equalization of income, or income according to need as laid down by the communist prescription. Nor
is it a condition of abundance in any form. An acquaintance of mine who

---

4. Weaver's speaking notes include at this point the marginal notation "The Berlin Wall."
See page 12 of the 22-page corrected typescript in Box 3, Folder 1, of the Richard M. Weaver
Papers at Vanderbilt University.

spent several weeks in the Soviet Union just this last summer told me that the impression he brought back was one of bleakness and scarcity. To get things done at all, they have had to harness the motive power of self-interest.

The free enterprise society, for all the abuse that is heaped upon it, is a natural growth in response to durable human nature. This means that it has more of the resiliency of an organism, and that means, in my judgment, that it will survive. The communist system is something imposed from above in the name of a pseudo-metaphysic. All systems which rest only on theory and abstraction are life-denying. There is a brittleness to them which will not survive real impact. In the long term that augurs well for us. But we do not wish to live under the shadow of this threat any longer than we have to.

There is a great deal of reason to believe that our poor success on the world front has been owing to default. Some of our World War II policies were predicated on the worst of illusions. Some of our international state-craft since then has been misguided or inept, with here and there a decision in our favor when the chips were down. This is far too long and complicated a story to review here. What concerns us as a group is to continue the fight on the domestic front with more effectiveness than in the past. And this turns the discussion to some limited but highly important features of strategy and tactics. What is the best way to stay on the offensive here?

A very important tactic is correct aiming. A fair number of conservative articles and pamphlets which come to my attention appear to shoot too high or to one side. They have not defined the vulnerable targets. They attack things that do not need attacking or they make assumptions which are vulnerable themselves. One of the effective procedures in debate is to start from an area of agreement. I am not talking here about making concessions or pretending that conflicts do not exist. Compromises are often ruinous, and I am convinced that the middle of the road is the road that leads out of the picture for any political party or movement that takes it. One has to decide clearly what one wants and then stick by it. What I mean is that we should start from fundamentals on which it is hard to disagree. For example, we can ask the opposition directly whether they agree with us in believing in freedom—a question which seems innocent enough but which is loaded with dynamite against the other side. I notice that even on

college campuses where liberal and communist groups are to be found, the
people who move with these groups are great praters about freedom. They
want freedom, all the freedoms; they eulogize nonconformity and act as if
the *status quo* were a conspiracy to take away their individuality. How in the
name of logic can they find their supreme sanction in freedom and their
spiritual home in Moscow? There one does not have even the freedom to
choose between two political parties, to say nothing of buying a house, or
writing a novel which is unsympathetic toward the regime, or traveling
abroad. They have no right to indulge in these contradictions; it is really an
impudence. They ought to be exposed in them. We can begin with such
simple questions as: Where do you expect to find freedom in a communist
order, which regards even individualism as a sign of bourgeois reaction?

The same people, we notice, are fond of the word "rights," and a similar
question can be asked about these. What rights are guaranteed or even recognized by an order which makes general social utility the absolute criterion
for every decision? Our own political tradition is based on the concept that
every person has certain inalienable natural rights. Such rights are not the
gift of the state. They are anterior to the state, and the violation of these
rights, as the Declaration of Independence makes plain, may be just cause
for overthrowing a state. There is one good reason why a communist state
of the Russian type can never recognize such rights. The rights depend on
something greater and more enduring than the state. In the all-powerful
state which allows no allegiance to anything but itself, what are rights today
may be forbidden tomorrow. When the liberal tinctured with communism
talks about rights, he really means something like policies—policies that
are in line with a projected communist attainment of power. Thus the
"right of free speech" can be a right or not a right, depending on how they
view its political tendency. With them rights are not essences but instrumentalities. This is another deception they should not be allowed to practice. If one believes in rights as a God-given area of inviolate freedom, that
is one thing. If they give the impression that they believe in this, they can
be invited to show where such areas are protected in states that follow the
communist ideology.

We have another area of presumptive agreement in preferring a flourishing economy to one where scarcity is the rule. Here again, which has consistency of theory and performance on its side? It is the communist states,

not the capitalist ones, which have been offering pie in the sky. And, in my opinion, we have been too liberal about supplying them with pie until they can get theirs out of the sky. But to return to the point: even upon the ground of material achievement the opposition should be asked what it really has to demonstrate. Its regimes are still struggling with the most elementary problems of production and distribution. Once more we have started with a seeming agreement about ends, but when we come to the subject of means, a most radical disagreement emerges, and the burden of proof is on them.

This in brief is what I mean by aiming to hit where it hurts. There is no need for us to set up straw men to knock down. All we need to do is ask the opponent, what is your *real* reason for espousing this system or even for wanting to coexist with it? We don't want to hear "window-dressing" reasons. A good deal of liberal and leftist propaganda impresses me as "good" or plausible reasons masking real reasons, though I am not quite sure what the real reasons are. Behind the plausible reasons there must be some kind of formless discontent, some irrational desire to destroy, or some kind of soul-sickness which makes them rush to embrace the very thing they should be concerned to destroy. In a recent issue of *National Review*, Mr. Forrest Davis described contemporary liberalism as "pragmatic, disdaining the moral quotient, ignorant of history, and emotionally biased toward the totalitarianism of the Left."[5] This may well say about all that can be ascertained about the real reasons that impel these people. If the liberals are pragmatists (and I would agree that generally they are), they have lost faith in principles; if they are disdainful of the moral quotient, they are of course not interested in the moral aspect of the new order; if they are ignorant of history, they really do not care about the facts of the case; and if they are emotionally biased toward the totalitarianism of the Left, they are driven by some feeling they don't care to express. Maybe they just *don't like th'* great, beautiful, *successful* country of ours.

Thus far I have been conducting a kind of imaginary argument wit' communist or liberal leftist. But obviously this kind of mentalit' above characterization is correct, is difficult to argue with. Where

ɪɪ,

5. Forrest Davis, "Liberal Mandarin in Moscow," *National Review* 1959, 654.

brought to face reality, of course, it ought to be. I have named some issues on which it should be forced to take a stand when there is opportunity for a direct confrontation.

But this opens up the whole question of *where* our arguments can be directed for greatest effect. There is a school of thought which says that when you are out to preach a gospel you should aim your arguments and appeals neither at those who agree with you nor at those who directly disagree with you. You ought to aim them at those in between, at the waverers, the fence straddlers, or the ones who have not yet made up their minds. You thus try to bring over to your side the uncommitted individuals. Although this idea has a certain aspect of correctness to it, I want to suggest a reason for believing that it may be a mistake.

First of all, it is hard in *this* case to determine what this group is. It seems very indefinite in extent and composition. I cannot see any large group in the United States really poised between freedom and communism, though some people out of ignorance may act as if they were. Most of the people, I continue to believe, are actually on our side. On the other side there is a much smaller, but very noisy, and rather articulate and practically influential group. What lies in between is hard to describe. I doubt that it is very numerous or politically of much consequence. People who have not already made up their minds as to whether they prefer freedom and individualism or communism seem to me not to count for very much.

But even if you seek them out, there is danger that in appealing to those in the middle we will weaken our case. There will be a temptation to make concessions and to blur distinctions that ought to be kept sharp—in a figure of speech, to dilute the dose for a queasy stomach. And this can sometimes take on the look of losing faith in your own philosophy. For every one in the middle who is won over by tactics of appeasement, one confirmed and solid supporter may be disillusioned or even antagonized. And one confirmed supporter is likely to do more for the cause than half a dozen who are merely induced to listen and to say, "Maybe."

I believe rather that our case can be most advantageously addressed to our own side. What is necessary to win any political victory, according to my reading of history, is a hard core of determination and enthusiasm. If these are lacking, the movement cannot make headway. If they are present, the movement has a dynamism which urges it on. Enthusiasm is something that spreads by *contagion*, not so much by logical argument. I hope this does not sound unduly cynical, but I have sometimes felt that we hold political rallies for the same reason that the Indians held war dances. The rally does not convince the other party. But it does arouse the enthusiasm of the members to a fighting pitch. And as soon as the news gets around that a group of people is really hot on some issue, interest tends to pick up by this contagion. This is when the uncommitted person begins to open his ears and wonder whether he has not been missing something. Interest and devotion invite more of the same, and soon the movement is snowballing. A few men heartily dedicated to a cause will draw more attention than a large number who are conspicuously without zeal. There is no reason why we should not recognize that our strength lies in our own element. And anyone who does not play his strength, plays against his strength.

Of course, the figure of the war dance can be pushed too far. We are certainly not going to confine ourselves to emotional appeals and the raising of blood pressure. There is a good deal of educational work to be done among our sympathizers, and this seems to me to be work of a special kind. It involves reasoning about the relationship between means and ends, or better say, the exposition of these. Among the conservative groups in which it has been my privilege to move, I have felt that the greatest lack took the form of a misunderstanding of what means were adapted to produce what ends. This seems, moreover, to be a pretty wide misunderstanding among the American people as a whole. It often shows up in the curious results of elections. The people say they want one thing, but they vote for measures and for men almost certain to bring about the opposite thing. We need to school people, even some of our avowed conservatives, to see that you don't approach a goal by marching in the opposite direction. And a series of little marches may add up to a long one. You don't preserve freedom by turning and appealing, as if automatically, to the federal government every time you want something done. There are people of avowedly conservative conviction who have been guilty of these contradictions. That is my reason for saying that we need more education as to what means can be expected to produce what ends. This education is partly political, but it is also partly philosophical, since there is need for better synthesis of beliefs and resulting actions.

The reference to political and philosophical education in a sense returns us to the beginning, since it involves the question of where the conservative stands. There is some difference among well-known spokesmen for our side as to whether the conservative is necessarily a traditionalist. Edmund Burke was of the opinion that tradition throws a veil over the origin of many of our institutions, and he was rather glad that it was so. I am very doubtful on this score—so doubtful that I do not think I can go along with those who say that we must find our chief reliance in tradition. For one thing, I find a certain timidity in the thinking of those who are mere traditionalists, and that is one weakness we cannot afford. We have got to be just as willing to face ultimates, to see things in their ultimate natures, as the opposition. We have got to say in language that goes to the root of things why we believe that liberty is better than captivity to the state, why private property is basically a good thing, why it is best to reward intelligence and effort. Anything less will mean failure in the forensic argument. It will not be enough to defend them by merely saying that we have inherited them along with our system. We must show why we prize them in essence. That is what I mean by facing questions in an ultimate light.

The problem can be met by stating a distinction. Conservatives are traditionalists in the sense that they value the power of tradition as a great stabilizing force in society and as a means of effecting many things which laws could never effect or would effect more harshly. But they are not bound to tradition as the final arbiter of right and wrong. For that we will go to philosophy, in confidence that it will give ample support to the conservative view of man and of institutions. This is but a way of affirming that we should not run from arguments over essential ideas by taking refuge in traditions.

A certain timidity about going to the bottom of things may explain why conservatives in this country have overlooked one very important source of impulse and strength. The desire to have more, to enjoy more, to become more comfortable is not the only driving force in human nature. There is alongside this, though sometimes buried, a desire to sacrifice, to be hard on oneself. This may sound paradoxical to some, but then human nature is not a simple equation. In our very great material success, we have largely forgotten this other reservoir of force. It is an indisputable fact that people can be appealed to on the basis of self-sacrifice. Many persons get a greater thrill or sense of reward out of this than out of anything else in their lives. There is a strong psychological attraction in the idea of strenuousness and self-discipline. The very popularity of athletics and sports is a simple reminder of that truth. You do not have to promise every man a featherbed at the end to get him to do something that requires vigorous and disciplined effort. The sense of achievement and of good accomplished may be quite enough.

In this respect I think the communists have been ahead of us in psychological realism and consequently in some forms of result. They have not held back from the idea of sternness and self-subordination for the promotion of an end. In so doing, they have drawn upon a motive power that we have largely disregarded. It is one we have got to think much more about, as we address the conservative appeal to youth. Contrary to what might be gathered from some sources, youth does not always want to be bribed by promises of easy living. Youth wants the experience of achievement, the sense of distinction, the feeling of being able to prevail in the world. And for this it is quite willing to expend itself. Therefore, I am not at all disturbed to think that in the future of this struggle we might have to tell people to be hard on themselves. Cut out complacent thinking, easy solutions, comfortable temporizing and show your fitness to win a real battle as the generations before you did. This kind of appeal, I am convinced, reaches far deeper than any mere promise of something for something. And when it is responded to, the response produces a solidarity you do not get in any other way. The communists have now for a long while been exploiting this impulse to self-sacrifice for the attainment of a spurious ideal. We should not do any less for the attainment of a real and a patriotic one.

Review of Bertrand de Jouvenel, On Power: Its Nature and the History of Its Growth[1]

Everybody knows that the number of books on social and political theory published today is so vast as to present a problem of selection. It is safe to say, however, that Bertrand de Jouvenel's *On Power* will find a place in the most select library of the subject.

I should like to introduce *On Power* by saying that it is free from the vices characteristic of books produced by a crisis. We rarely open a contemporary work on public affairs without getting at least echoes of wartime bombast, evidence of fashionable enthusiasms and resentments, or topical applications which are certain to date the book presently. *On Power* is historical, perspicacious, universal in outlook, and hortatory only after long passages of analysis. It was written by one who has acquired the detachment not to believe that the revolution he has been through is *the* revolution, or that the war he has witnessed is *the* war. Machiavelli complained that men are wont to read history "as though heaven, the sun, the elements, and men had changed the order of their motions and power, and were different from what they were in ancient times." M. de Jouvenel has perceived, not without some dismay, that all history is cut from the same cloth.

Essentially this book is a study of the rôle of power in human communities. One almost could say that it is a study of power as a malignant growth. I have been a little disturbed by the author's tendency to hypostatize power—that is, to treat it as something actually apart from the human beings through whom it is wielded, but if one takes the concept as figurative—and he calls it "the Minotaur"—one can avoid the fallacy of assumption.

* * *

1. *The Commonweal*, 50/19, August 9, 1949, 466–68.

The thesis of the book is that power is a thing whose nature it is to grow; and that it has grown virtually in proportion to the so-called progress of civilization. Changes in terminology have only served to keep people from discerning this alarming and perhaps fatal fact. The most stubborn misconception of the modern era is that liberty can be enlarged by transferring power from one group to another. But this transference has no necessary effect on power, and in the actual event has but augmented it. In support of that conclusion the author cites facts which every considerate man should reflect upon. One begins with the discomfiting realization that "there goes with the movement away from monarchy to democracy an amazing development of the apparatus of coercion. No absolute monarch ever had at his disposal a police force comparable to those of modern democracies." (Is not our FBI said now to number over 13,000?)

Next he is faced with the modern phenomenon of total war. A survey of a thousand years of warfare reveals that "there has been a steady rise in the coefficient of society's participation in it, and that the total war of today is only the logical end of an uninterrupted advance toward it." Obviously it is far harder today to hide from the state, or to withdraw from its programs of action. And whoever thinks that has no bearing upon the matter of liberty is himself the victim of terminological confusion. The most shocking development, however, is the way in which today men of intellect are dragooned into the service of the warlords. I recall reading that at the height of the Napoleonic Wars a scientific congress sat at Paris, attended alike by British and French savants, to whom the bloody contest for Europe was something occurring in a world apart. Contrast that with the present situation: "Even Thought itself, in former times contemptuous of these brawls, has now been roped in by the devotees of conquest to proclaim the civilizing virtues of gangsters and incendiaries." In proportion as statism grows, any kind of apartness from it is regarded as treasonable.

* * *

One is tempted to quote many of M. de Jouvenel's apothegms, so realistic are they and so richly supported by history. I must content myself, however, with directing special attention to the substance of two chapters. "Totalitarian Democracy" is an explanation of why, amid what looks like an irresistible onward march of democracy, real liberty is withering away. This has occurred because democracy, which began as a conception of liberty and

law—or better say, of liberty guaranteed by law—has passed into a conception of the absolute sovereignty of the people. These two things are
incompatible, as every contributor to the foundations of democratic theory
knew. Rousseau understood it; the American Constitution is an embodiment of it. But the evolution of democracy has been a drift away from belief
in the necessary character of the laws to an exaltation of the will of the
multitude. Devices laboriously set up to keep popular passion within
bounds are now derided as little better than superstitions. "The life of
democracies has been marked by a growth in the precariousness of laws.
Kings, chambers of peers, senates, anything that might have checked the
immediate translation into law of whatever opinion is in vogue, have everywhere been swept aside or rendered powerless." The American Senate persists, it is true, but one need only recall how in large sections of the
American press Congress has been consistently impugned and the chief
executive as consistently pictured as the champion of the people. As the
author remarks, quoting Proudhon, the popular instinct grasps the simple
notion of power much more easily than the complex one of constitutional
liberty. In this way the totalitarian wave of the future rolls on, unaffected by
rhetoric about freedom.

How right then is M. de Jouvenel to say that it is disastrous folly to give
"one and the same bland admiration" to every leader who "espouses the
popular cause," without distinguishing the two ways of serving it!

*   *   *

"Liberty's Aristocratic Roots" is a more detailed analysis of the passage from
liberty to Caesarism. Liberty of the personal kind has never been the goal
of plebeian masses, but rather of independent freemen, who have done
battle for their privileges against kings, emperors, and even parliaments. So
it was with the Roman patricians against the emperors, with the barons
against the monarchs aspiring to absolutism. We might remember that it
was the imposition of taxes by a *parliament* which inspired the American
colonists to armed rebellion in the name of liberty. The plebeian masses do
not want liberty, but participation in power, and of course the wages of
power, which are to them sometimes considerable. Alliances between king
and commonalty; between the modern dictator and the classless populace

seem adequate proofs of that. Caesarism is quite anxious that "those who are oldest in liberty within the society should lose their moral credit."

One is now prepared for the author's exclamation near the end of his work: "Where the idea comes from that men hold despotism in detestation I do not know. My own view is that they delight in it."

Of course the thing people delight in is often the thing they should not have. Is there any way in which rational beings can oppose the trend toward the omnipotent state? Here M. de Jouvenel is not original, for wisdom on this subject is not new wisdom. He believes that our only hope is the acceptance of a code of right which is neither relative to contemporary interests, pressures, and passions, nor dependent on this party or that piece of governmental machinery. It means respect for law as an expression of the nature of things; and it certainly requires that we get over our infatuation with Power, even when it comes bearing gifts.

Battle for the Mind[1]

That Russell Kirk's *A Program for Conservatives* is an event as well as a heartening book will be recognized by all who have followed the battle for the mind in this country.

For a generation we have been taught from many sources that there is but one way for us to go, and that is to follow after the Gadarene swine. Mr. Kirk is a young man, high minded, eloquent, learned in history, and filled with the conviction that these things need not be. His work is a brave retort to the disorganizing heresies of our time.

* * *

The author demonstrates that conservatism is no novelty in America. The American Revolution was a conservative movement, resisting centralized usurpation from abroad. Some of our greatest political thinkers have been profound conservatives, and the average American clings to his basic institutions with a tenacity which impressed Lord Bryce and other foreign observers. To equate the American with the radical is ignorant when it is not tendentious, as often seems the case today.

* * *

The true conservative, Kirk declares, is not a child of fortune. He may appear anywhere, but in America he is perhaps less likely to be found in Wall Street than in some modest home in the Mississippi valley. This is so because he is defined essentially by belief in the following principles:

There is an order higher than that devised by man which it is our duty to find out and to respect.

Civilization shows itself in variety and complexity and individual attachment; and standardization is the death alike of vitality and interest.

1. *Chicago Sunday Tribune Magazine of Books*, October 24, 1954, Section IV, page 3.

There is no social justice through mechanical leveling, but rather the reverse.

Society thrives on distinctions so long as they are distinctions of natural ability, earned leadership, and sympathetic attachment.

History is a storehouse of wisdom, whereas the abstract designs of collectivist reformers are the fancies of an overheated brain.

Society must be receptive to change, but change is most likely to be gain when it is the work of private endeavor and sagacity.

Doctrinaire breaks with the past are costly failures because they take too little account of the substance of history and human nature.

All of these thoughts, so discerning of the nature of man in society, he develops into a program for order, community, loyalty, and tradition.

* * *

For many years anyone raising his head above the level of current chaos has been in danger of having it struck down by a malevolent crew who saw their profit in dissolving our institutions. I predict that this is not going to happen to Mr. Kirk. He knows how to fight his battle; and his natural allies, who are legion, are beginning to awaken.

A Program for Conservatives[1]

It is refreshing in these times to hear someone discussing an alternative to materialistic socialism. Two years ago Russell Kirk in his *The Conservative Mind* showed that quite a number of men had been profound thinkers in spite of the disadvantage of having been born before Marx, and that a number who came after him rejected his doctrines. In his recent work, *A Program for Conservatives,* he offers some practical guidance to those who are alienated by the two modern forces of materialism and political abstractionism.

The wisdom of Conservatism appears especially in its avoidance of the presumptuousness which characterizes so much social thinking today. In drawing up a kind of credo for conservatives the author lists first the following requirement: "A belief in an order that is more than human, which has implanted in man a character of mingled good and evil, susceptible of improvement by an inner working, not by mundane schemes of perfectability." The conservative stands in contrast with the radical by acknowledging the duty of veneration. He is not spiteful toward the past or the world around him. He believes that if these had nothing to teach us, they would never have been. He knows that not all problems can be solved in and by the present, and likewise he knows that not all problems can be solved with reference only to this world. "Politics moves upward into ethics, and ethics ascends to theology. . . . And the religious man, whatever his party allegiance or outward politics, in some considerable degree is at heart a conservative, for he appeals to an authority beyond the vanity of Demos or Expediency, and he trusts in the wisdom of our ancestors and in enduring values." He knows that there is no substitute through economic plenty or anything of that kind for "the unbought grace of life"—a bonus of happi-

1. *Faith and Thought,* January 1955, 4–5.

ness which is given to us when we have shown respect, observed measure, and done our duty.

A Program for Conservatives is valuable in at least two ways. It provides a clear statement of principles for a great many people who have felt intellectually homeless but who have known that they could never find a home in dialectical materialism, or in any materialism. Second, by its references to a large number of cogent thinkers in political science and philosophy it proves that no one need be intellectually ashamed of the Conservative position.

Review of Arthur A. Ekirch, Jr.,
The Decline of American Liberalism[1]

In this stimulating book Professor Ekirch undertakes to show that American liberalism has been in steady decline since the founding of our republic. What he means by "liberalism" may be inferred from his statement that the eighteenth century was its "classic age." This classical liberalism had as its central doctrines "the concept of limited representative government and the widest possible freedom for the individual—both intellectually and economically." Such characterization must be kept clearly in mind, since "what frequently passes for liberalism today is too often an opportunistic philosophy which, by its extreme relativist definition of terms, effectively conceals the disintegration of the liberal tradition."

According to his analysis, the American Revolution was the grand triumph of liberalism. It brought to a climax the idea of a liberal society which had been developing in the colonies for a century and a half, and at the same time it fanned the hopes of European liberals who were struggling for a more humane society. The Constitutional period, with its movement toward centralization, represented something of a retreat, although the Bill of Rights crystallized into law a number of important guarantees of freedom. Since then, however, the liberal tradition has taken one buffeting after another, and now its future is problematical.

For example, Jacksonian democracy, although it professed to champion the welfare of the masses, does not appear to Professor Ekirch to have advanced the cause of liberalism. What the party of Jackson did was work out an alliance among southern slaveholders, western expansionists, and urban immigrant masses which sacrificed liberal values to national unity and territorial aggrandizement. Even the Progressive movement, which dominated politics around the turn of the century, gave no reprieve to lib-

1. *Mississippi Valley Historical Review*, 43/3, December 1956, 469–70.

eralism. It fought against many domestic abuses, but it was strongly na-tionalistic, and it deserted entirely the philosophy of natural rights for a kind of political instrumentalism. Professor Ekirch finds it characteristic that Albert J. Beveridge, who was a leading Progressive at home, was at the same time one of the most blatant overseas imperialists. Essentially American Progressivism was a move away from Jeffersonian liberalism to-ward a German type of statism.

The Second World War and its aftermath have generated even greater pressures against the freedom of the individual. On the one hand, there are the real or supposed demands of national security, and on the other there are the proposals of the new "totalitarian liberals," which tend toward ex-changing the old area of freedom for economic security through socialism.

Thus in the space of a hundred and fifty years, "liberalism" has practically reversed its meaning and is now used to sanction a statism potentially more absolute than anything seen in the past. The author's forecast is frankly pessimistic; he thinks that classical liberals today can do little more than keep alive the memory of liberalism's past achievements and hope for some break in the iron ring that seems to be closing around.

Obviously this is a thesis history, whose argument will stand or fall with the original definition. Professor Ekirch seems to wobble a little himself on the matter of definition in the final chapter, where, in looking for a ray of hope in the present situation, he equates liberalism with "process not sys-tem, movement not finality." Some readers may feel, moreover, that he has not delved deep enough into the psychological and moral causes of the change he traces. But that he has given the true history of a decline seems to me indubitable. The eighteenth century may not have had a special reve-lation about liberty, but it left in writing some formulations and observa-tions which the lover of liberty still does well to consult. Perhaps that is why constitutionalists and others who hark back to the early days of the republic are often labeled "reactionaries" by the modern "liberal."

Which Ancestors?[1]

Russell Kirk's importance in the conservative renascence became evident with the publication of his *The Conservative Mind*. This brilliant history of conservative thought reminded the public that not all profound thinking veers to the left, and that past ages at least have seen no essential conflict between conservatism and benevolence. Since then Mr. Kirk has produced a steady stream of articles and reviews testing by the touchstone of his conservatism a wide variety of men, movements and institutions. The present work brings these together.

What is the touchstone that he applies? It consists principally of a respect for the wisdom of our ancestors and a veneration of tradition. Using these as his ultimate appeals, he attacks incessantly the spirit of innovation, politics based upon abstractions, what he well terms the "defecated liberalism" of our day, and that program for diminishing the mind which is called "progressive education." The objects of attack are certainly chosen with sound instinct, and no one is more gratified than I by his effort to make the public aware that the past contains some achievements superior to the present, and that presentism can never be a measuring rod where values are concerned. It is because I want this awareness to be wider and more irresistible that I mention a few difficulties which seem to be showing up.

The danger in erecting the wisdom of our ancestors as the standard is that it invites the question "Which ancestors?" After all, Adam was our ancestor, and so were many who have spoken radically, irresponsibly, or superficially. If we add the voices of our ancestors together, we get the same sort of melée of opinion that fills the air today, and it may be questioned whether the wiser voices would not be drowned out by others. If we have

1. *National Review*, 2/10, July 25, 1956, 20–21. © 1956 by National Review, Inc., 215 Lexington Avenue, New York, N.Y. 10016. Reprinted by permission.

an ancestral legacy of wisdom, we have also an ancestral legacy of folly, and the ground for choosing between them is still to seek.

Essentially the same objection applies to a general embrace of tradition, plus one further difficulty. Traditions grow up insensibly and, as it were, vegetatively; they are adaptations and include strong emotional preferences. These facts in themselves may be good, yet they certainly create problems when traditions come into conflict and have to be reconciled. Since they are not rational creations, they are not susceptible to rational adjustment unless one is willing to isolate intellectually their elements of value and of truth. Yet this is a process disrespectful of tradition in the sense that it transcends tradition and looks for some higher guide. The only way a traditionalist can object to this is by saying that tradition expresses something not in the arguable realm, which is itself a grave commitment.

I am glad to say that I agree with practically every position on issues that Mr. Kirk takes in this wide-ranging collection of essays. I only wish to see his learning and persuasive rhetoric reinforced by a different kind of artillery—a kind that will prevent the conservative from being at a disadvantage in armaments. I do not want to see the conservative reduced entirely to arguments based on authority. Actually, he has on his side some of the greatest masters of theory, which is why the Liberal usually looks silly when, with the use of their methods, he is pushed back to his primary assumptions.

Distinctions in terms of principle are especially needful at a time like this, when quite preposterous persons are seeking to apply the name "conservative" to themselves, and in some cases are getting away with it.

Review of Forrest McDonald,
We the People: The Economic Origins of the Constitution[1]

This book could be described simply as a scholarly evaluation of Charles Beard's famous thesis of the economic origin of the Constitution. But viewed in its broad implications, it may be regarded as a refutation, deserving to be cited often, of the general concept of economic determinism.

The publication in 1913 of Beard's *An Economic Interpretation of the Constitution of the United States* touched off a *cause célèbre* in American education. The author, an associate professor of politics in Columbia University, filled with zeal for the new doctrine that men's attitudes are simple reflections of their economic interests, tried to account in those terms for the framing of our Constitution. The resulting shock was so great that it led eventually to his departure from the faculty of Columbia and his adopting the role of free-lance historian for the remainder of his life. Beard lived to reverse his views on the matter in his *Basic History of the United States* (1944), and now Professor McDonald provides unassailable proof that Beard's original position is untenable.

Beard's argument was, in brief outline, that the movement for the Constitution and the ensuing battles over its ratification were an economic class struggle. As it came to be written, then, the Constitution was "an economic document drawn with superb skill by men whose property interests were immediately at stake; and as such it appealed directly and unerringly to identical interests in the country at large." The impulse behind its adoption was the fact that "important groups of economic interests were adversely affected by the system of government under the Articles of Confederation, namely those of public securities, shipping and manufacturing, money at interest, in short, capital as opposed to land."

1. *Freeman*, 9, May 1959, 58–62.

Accordingly, the entire campaign for the Constitution was begun and pushed forward by "a small and active group of men immediately interested through their personal possessions in the outcome of their labors. . . . The propertyless masses were . . . excluded at the outset from participation (through representatives) in the work of framing the Constitution. The members of the Philadelphia Convention which drafted the Constitution were, with a few exceptions, immediately, directly, and personally interested in, and derived economic advantage from, the establishment of the new system."

The amount of labor which Professor McDonald performed in order to determine whether these assertions have any basis in fact was evidently enormous. First, he analyzed the delegates elected to the Philadelphia Convention with reference to the areas from which they came and the political factions with which they were identified in their home states. Next, he investigated the economic circumstances of every one of the fifty-five delegates who actually attended to determine whether, and in what sense, they were men of property. Next, he analyzed their conduct in the Convention to see whether there was any correlation between their economic interests and their attitude toward the new system of government which was being drawn up. Finally, he studied the battle over ratification in every one of the thirteen states to determine whether any inferences can be drawn regarding the economic status of those elements opposing and those favoring ratification.

His conclusion is what every man of sense would have anticipated. There is hardly a shred of evidence for Beard's thesis to rest upon; it was all spun out of a theoretical prejudice in favor of economic determinism. But let Professor McDonald announce the finding in his own words: "Beard's thesis—that the line of cleavage as regards the Constitution was between substantial personalty interests on the one hand and small farmer and debtor interests on the other—is entirely incompatible with the facts."

Here is a sampling of the facts which his research uncovered. Let us bear in mind that Beard had represented the Constitution as a kind of capitalist "plot" against farmers and debtors. "Five of the men who either refused to sign the finished Constitution or who walked out of the Convention (Gerry, Randolph, Mercer, Lansing, and Luther Martin) were among the largest holders of securities in the Convention. Had they sold their securities in Philadelphia as the Convention opened, the proceeds would have been sufficient to buy all the securities owned by forty-five of the remaining fifty delegates."

Delaware was the first state to ratify, the vote being 30-0. Its convention was largely made up of small farmers, of whom sixteen had annual incomes between $40 and $267. Only five of the thirty held public securities.

New Jersey was the next to ratify, and it also voted unanimously. "The convention was a fairly representative cross section of the economy of the state." About twenty-five of its thirty-eight members were farmers and landowners.

Pennsylvania was one of the states in which there was sharp conflict over ratification. The investigation showed that the delegates on both sides of the issue held about the same amounts of the same kinds of property. The slight difference was that the anti-Federalists were a little *better* endowed with personalty, especially public securities, than proponents of the Constitution. That is, of course, the exact opposite of what Beard would have had us believe.

The conflict in the critical state of Virginia was a fierce one. But here, too, the author's data tell the same tale. For in this state "the property holdings of ratificationists and antiratificationists were virtually identical, except that more small farmers from the interior supported ratification than opposed it." To this he adds the telling item that "if there was a debtors' faction in Virginia, it was largely identical in personnel with the proratificationist group."

The great state of New York came as near as anything to rejecting the Constitution, the final vote being 30-27. There, the struggle over ratification was a complicated and bitter affair between two distinct parties, one led by Governor George Clinton and the other by Hamilton and John Jay. But their respective positions cannot be explained in terms of the Beard thesis of economic cleavage. "In the showdown over ratification neither party to the conflict had a monopoly of economic interest of any kind. . . . The ranks of both parties included approximately equal numbers of large and small landholders and speculators in various forms of property." Beard had argued that in New York the struggle was a clear one between security holders (Federalists) and advocates of paper money (anti-Federalists). But Professor McDonald's research shows that in this state "security holders" and "paper money advocates" are but two names for the same group of people.

There remains the general question of whether the American people at this time can be grouped into any significant categories with reference to their enthusiasm for or against the Constitution.

In attempting to answer this, Professor McDonald divides the states themselves into three groups: those favorable to the Constitution (Delaware, New Jersey, Georgia, Connecticut, and Maryland), those divided over the Constitution (Pennsylvania, Massachusetts, South Carolina, and New Hampshire), and those more or less opposed to the Constitution (New York, Virginia, North Carolina, and Rhode Island).

The only thing that can be deduced from this comparison is that those states which wanted the Constitution were states which were not able to cope with their own problems, those which were divided on the issue were states which felt somewhat more able to do so, and those which opposed it were states which felt that they were getting along well enough as sovereign entities.

But these feelings themselves depended on a great variety of factors. Delaware felt that she was simply too small to go it alone. Georgia felt unable to cope with the Indian menace on her frontier. New York might have gone it alone had not the City of New York threatened to secede. North Carolina, economically and culturally the most isolated of the thirteen, seems to have proceeded out of a general indifference.

So it comes down to this: the states were eager to ratify according to whether or not they felt a need for national union. The role of economic interests remains indefinite, indecisive, and unpredictable.

It is to be hoped that this painstaking piece of scholarship will contribute much toward exploding the theory that human beings act and vote merely according to their anticipations of economic gain. The sensible part of mankind has never embraced anything so narrow and unrealistic. Historians can thus provide important help to philosophers and others in re-educating people to know that "economic man" really doesn't exist. Man acts sometimes selfishly, sometimes unselfishly, but more often out of varying combinations of these motives. This means that man is a free agent in a sense no economic determinist would allow, and in that fact lie our challenge and our hope.

A Great Individualist[1]

Henry Louis Mencken may fairly be accounted the most consistent cham-pion of individual liberty this country has ever seen. Coming to the fullness of his powers at a time when the nation first ventured into the role of inter-national Messiah, and when it was giving, not the first, but probably the most extraordinary, exhibition of its capacity for fantasy thinking in na-tional Prohibition, he laid about him with a zest which no one who lived through the twenties can forget. And now that we are beset with equally great if not greater political grotesqueries (a phrase which I believe would have met his approval), those who long for an order of sanity and liberty may well echo the famous line of Wordsworth and cry, "Mencken, thou should'st be living at this hour."

The recently published *Letters of H. L. Mencken* give an opportunity to refresh our memory of this vivid personality. What the reflective reader will discover here is another source of proof that Mencken was essentially a conservative critic of life and letters. Such estimate could amaze those who mistake his sweeping diatribes as evidence of a radical temper. But it is necessary to see things in the right relation: the features of American life which he attacked were radical aberrations from conservative common sense; his frequently violent criticisms showed a zeal, traditionally pardon-able in any apostle of fairness, to expose folly, pretense, imposture, and self-promotion.

I have said common sense because it can reasonably be argued that Mencken was not a philosophical conservative. He never formulated a creed; he was skeptical of general truths; and the very notion of metaphysics was often the butt of his wit. In this department he was lacking, but there is a conservative of taste and temperament, and of this type he is an easily recognizable example. Taste and temperament bred a sure judgment for

1. *Modern Age*, 6/2, Spring 1962, 214–17.

what is right in conduct and good in literature. Still, even the most instinctual conservative has some need of reliance upon ideas, and where Mencken does allow himself to express general views, he is conservative even by the philosophical test. He had definitive convictions about the limited capacity of man, and a real personal humility, for which his purposely inflated rhetoric was but an ironic mask. The *Letters* abound in evidence on these points. He confesses in writing to Charles Green Shaw in 1927:

> My belief is that happiness is necessarily transient. The natural state of reflective man is one of depression.
>
> I have little belief in human progress. The human race is incurably idiotic. It will never be happy.
>
> I hope to write at least one good book before I die.

If Mencken had what could be termed a political philosophy, this could be summed up as a belief in natural aristocracy. Such belief had not the slightest connection with snobbism; he felt sincerely that the maximum of liberty will prevail when the better element is in control, for they will effectively preserve a decent minimum of order, while allowing the remainder of mankind to be fools in their own way. Democracy to him meant plebianism, which is the rule of the masses in the name of their vices. This is why he could write:

> All appeals to any intrinsic love of free speech are futile. There is no such passion in the people. It is only an aristocracy that is ever tolerant. The masses are invariably cocksure, suspicious, furious, and tyrannical. This, in fact, is the central objection to democracy: that it hinders progress by penalizing innovation and nonconformity.

To that state of affairs anything was preferable, and in this light one must understand his occasional postures of indulgence toward societies that today would be called reactionary or authoritarian. Oddly enough, Mencken at one time became a contributing editor to the *Nation*, whose political reformism and crusading spirit were completely out of line with his convictions. A letter written to Louise Pound on the occasion contains a few political observations:

> I have joined the *Nation* as a contributing editor. This is a joke, the significance of which rather escapes me. . . . My politics are anything but Liberal. I am a *kaiserliche-königliche* Tory, believe in slavery, and await pa-

tiently the restoration of the Hohenzollerns and the new Vormarsch upon Paris.

Every reader of Mencken will remember that among the liberties for which he contended most strenuously was that of imbibing stimulants, and many of his merriest sentences are on the subject of alcohol. On one occasion he rejected a manuscript sent in by Upton Sinclair with the following note:

> I like the Jack London chapter very much, but its onslaughts upon alcohol make it impossible for us. We are committed to the revival of the saloon exactly as it was. America misses it and is much worse off for the lack of it. London, sober, would have written nothing worth reading. Alcohol made him.

And at the conclusion of the note:

> Twenty barges in tow of five tugs set out from the Bahamas for Baltimore last Tuesday. It will be a Christian Christmas. God's hand is in it!

But reverting to the more serious, one must remember that no sampling of this correspondence would be complete without some notice of his literary *dicta*. Here, for example, is a shrewd appraisal of Sherwood Anderson, expressed in a letter to Theodore Dreiser:

> Anderson's short stories often give me a great kick (as Scott Fitzgerald would say), but his novels usually seem a bit confused and muddy. I doubt that he has the sheer power to swing a long book. But his details are often superb.

His judgment of Thomas Wolfe, written at the time of the latter's death, is now virtually the canon:

> If he had lived five years longer, he'd have got rid of many of his defects.

The great vogue of Steinbeck's *The Grapes of Wrath* inspired an acid note to H. L. Davis:

> I have been reading Steinbeck's "The Grapes of Wrath." It seems to me to be a very poor job. It is full of pink hooey, and contains some very stilted and ineffective writing. . . . Steinbeck of course is getting encomiastic notices in the pink weeklies, but that is of no significance. They always praise any book that blames every bellyache on Wall Street.

It has been said many times that a humanitarian is one who loves humanity in the abstract, but hates it in the form of individuals. Of this type Mencken was the exact opposite; he despised the abstractions of humanitarianism, but he was always quick to go to the assistance of underdog individuals. No one can say how many struggling young authors he helped to fame, while jeering at the critical consensus. If men are to be judged by their deeds rather than by their professions of philanthropy, his accolade will be immeasurably greater than that of social doctrinaires, who have never learned the truth of William Blake's saying that he who would do good to another must do so in "Minute Particulars." The accumulation of these particulars was in Mencken's case so great that he must stand as one of the greatest and the most helpful of this country's rugged individualists.

Anatomy of Freedom[1]

In an essay brilliant with destructive analysis, aimed on the one side at Liberal collectivism and on the other at a dangerous strain he sees in some of the New Conservatives, Frank Meyer re-opens the great conversation which humanity will always be ready to engage in, we hope, about the nature and scope of freedom. Mr. Meyer writes as a man who has gone over the ground in conscience; and what he has found is that the individual, the irreducible person, is the primary reality and the sole repository of virtue. He has found further that the state is much more likely to impede the realization of virtue than to assist it; and that the more monopolistic the state becomes, the greater obstacle it is to those who desire to live rational lives in freedom. And finally he argues that even those who deprecate the overgrown state and place their trust in the smaller organic community are relying too much upon external forces and even disguised coercion to be true friends of freedom. These are findings that deserve to be searchingly appraised.

Mr. Meyer, while attacking widely, is actually defending a rather small perimeter, from which it would be very hard to dislodge him. A few citations will convey the extent of it. His intention in writing the book, he announces in the opening sentence, "is to vindicate the freedom of the person as the central and primary end of political society." No room is left here for a spurious egalitarianism. "The only equality that can be legitimately derived from the premises of the freedom of the person is the right of all men to be free from the coercion of power exercised against their life, liberty, and property." Social and political organizations can do nothing more than furnish the antecedent conditions for the striving of the individual man. "At best the proper social and political circumstances, like a rich and well tilled seed-bed, can provide felicitous circumstances in which a man

1. *National Review*, 13/22, December 4, 1962, 443–44. © 1962 by National Review, Inc., 215 Lexington Avenue, New York, N.Y. 10016. Reprinted by permission.

may work out his fortune or misfortune, his good or ill." Yet this truth has been lost sight of so far that "Our humanitarians of the welfare society take as their maxim: treat no person as an end, but only as a means to arrive at a general good."

By all odds the chief enemy of freedom and virtue (and the inseparability of these constitutes his chief affirmative point) is the Liberal-collectivist dogma, which is summed up in a brilliant paragraph: *Emotionally, it prefers psychoanalysis to the dark night of the soul, "adjustment" to achievement, security to freedom. It preaches "the end of ideology," admires experts and fears prophets, fears above all commitment to value transcending the fact.*

I wish it were possible to give space here to the many striking passages of historical interpretation. One which must be mentioned, however, with the highest recommendation, is Mr. Meyer's account of the contemporary form taken by Rousseau's General Will. The Liberal-collective theory of the state, he points out, is but a concept of the state "as the embodiment of the General Will." And it has been used and is being used by every modern revolutionary movement, Communist, Fascist, nationalist, and welfarist. The dialectic of it is very simple; and it is irresistible if one makes the initial surrender, which is to admit that this will expresses what all would will if they knew what was good for them.

Rousseau forged a weapon more destructive than he knew, for the "General Will in a curious way combines positivist glorification of power with the appearance of a value-based justification of that power." A merely positivistic theory could never have survived; he offset that weakness by providing a value system, which, however, lacked any specific content—only what the people will. What do the people will? This is hard enough to determine under most circumstances; but just here arises the opportunity of the élite theorists, whether Communists, Fascists, or totalitarian Liberals. They will step in and make the people's will known to it. This will is—it goes without further explication—the will of the élite, dressed out to suit the lineaments of the occasion, but always presented as expressing the desire of the mass for their own welfare. The one thing indispensable to the success of such an arrangement is possession of the power of the state. Whether this is obtained through a *Putsch* or through a "landslide" in time of crisis, the élite identifies itself with the state, and hypostatization is now complete: the General Will is always what it should be, and the state can do no wrong.

In this analysis Mr. Meyer has done a service of first importance, for he has made it easy to understand the separation that has often existed between the thoughts and feelings of the body of the citizens (yes, even in Nazi Germany) and the attitudes and pronouncements of a ruling clique, able to maintain itself in power by all the strategies and tactics that the modern technological world makes available.

Although I have only unstinted praise for Mr. Meyer's attack upon such perversions, I must express doubt about one or two of his collateral theses. One of these comprises the essence of his attack upon the New Conservatives as represented by Kirk, Nisbet, Hallowell, and others. The point of Mr. Meyer's criticism is that these spokesmen follow a dangerous theory of community, which traces back to the classical concept of the *polis*. The Greeks, he argues, for all the brilliance of their analysis, were limited in their thinking by the idea of the *polis*, against which they were only rarely able to see ground for any individual rights. And these New Conservatives, thinking within that limitation, and influenced by Burke's theory of organic growth and tradition, have erected the community into some kind of prior institution, full of potential harm to the individual person.

Yet if these New Conservatives go too far with the idea of community, Mr. Meyer does not concede some of the benefit which is plainly there. His position is a long step in the direction of Thoreau's anarchic individualism, which is one of the most anti-conservative positions ever taken. Thoreau always saw the community as something hovering about in a threatening way, yet his solution was simple: if the community got in your way or vexed you, you simply seceded from it. But the situation is far from that simple. You did not join your community as you might join a musical society or a chess club; you were born into it, and it has been a part of your nurture since long before you started thinking as a political animal. That community is a figment, without any grade of ontological standing, I am therefore not at all sure. A mere compresence of men together is not a community; but when a group of men start acting accordingly to certain psychic and moral lines of force, something else has come into being. Still, it would be a far-fetched inference from this that "Total state and 'plurality of communities' . . . are variants . . . of the same denial of the primary value, on this earth, of the individual person." Again, I fear that Mr. Meyer is attacking not an entity of the New Conservatives but a straw man of his own set-ting up when he speaks of "the subtler, quieter tyranny of a 'customarily' imposed community, in which no one can escape from the deadly environ-ment of hereditarily or geographically imposed association." Political ar-rangements for the dispersion of power are liable to be upset, as we are witnessing all too often today, but the circumstance of plural communities is a constant factor on its side.

The other thesis involves a point far more perplexing. Mr. Meyer rejects as untenable the thought that freedom is "freedom for." To him, this is a mockery; freedom is freedom unqualified; it must therefore be freedom to do evil as well as good. It is only in the school of choice between things good and evil, so to put it, that virtue can be developed.

When this issue is raised, profound arguments are heard on both sides. The one side says with Mr. Meyer that freedom which is in any way pre-determined or conditioned is a contradiction in terms. Freedom to do good only would be a slavery to the good. The answer comes back that freedom as an end in itself is simply vacuous. Man's destiny does not stop with "being free"; it is something positive, a fulfillment, and in a teleological world view, this can only be a fulfillment of a good. Freedom is therefore not an ulti-mate but a means, and a means is subordinate to its end. Moreover, to set up freedom as an ultimate could lead to the doing of some atrocious things in the name of freedom, and where would be the net gain in that? The question penetrates to the metaphysical, and the present reviewer prefers to remain reticent on it, at least a little while longer.

But whether or not Mr. Meyer has established freedom as the sufficient end of political society, he has struck hard at those who are interested nei-ther in good nor freedom.

The Middle of the Road: Where It Leads[1]

When you drive your car, do you drive in the middle of the road? This seems a silly question to ask because you don't, of course, if you want to stay alive and get somewhere.

But a lot of people have been sold on the idea that the middle of the road is the safest place in politics and on all sorts of controversial questions. They have been led to believe that in the middle position you are out of harm's way and you are more likely to be right than those who are on either side of a question. A little thought will show that this idea is born not of wisdom but of confusion or fear or both.

Properly speaking, middle-of-the-roadism is not a political philosophy at all. It is rather the absence of a philosophy or an attempt to evade having a philosophy. All great movements in the past have grown out of and have depended upon some self-consistent view of man and society. They have presented a program embodying clear principles, and people have gotten behind the movements because they wanted the principles to triumph. In no case did they labor and fight to see the principles bartered away for a few concessions by the opposition. If they felt they were right, they were not willing to settle by splitting the difference between themselves and the enemy. The great sacrifices of history have not been inspired by political trimming and unmanly compromise. Try imagining the figure that Washington would cut in history today if he had decided on a compromise settlement with the British.

Middle-of-the-road policies have a false attraction for some people because they keep them from having to think a position through. All they have to do is borrow a little from the parties on either side of them, add this up, and tell themselves that this is the "sound" position. But a position half way between right and wrong is not a sound position. It only postpones and

1. *Human Events*, 13/12, March 24, 1956, 5–8.

makes more difficult the eventual decision. And there are different views of man's destiny which can never be made compatible.

Middle-of-the-roadism is seldom anything more than short-sightedness. It is not an insight into political matters because it is wholly dependent upon what other parties say, or stand for. It takes its bearing from them. And far from being safe, it is just the spot to catch brickbats from both sides.

When you ask people why they have adopted a middle-of-the-road position, you nearly always discover that they fall into these two groups. The first group has been deceived into believing, as we have just noted, that you find the right by averaging right and wrong. If this were true, there would never be any use for intelligence and moral conviction.

The second group is usually fearful of taking a position which an enemy might characterize as "extreme" in spite of the fact that many ideas are attacked as extreme for no other reason than that they express clear-cut principles. Nearly all advocates of principles have been attacked at one time or another as "extremists." But if the principles were sound, the leaders generally prevailed. It does take some intestinal fortitude to champion an idea that has powerful enemies. But people who are frightened by this kind of criticism are usually afraid to stand up for any principle.

There is a third group of middle-of-the-roaders which is even less admirable than these two. These are the opportunists, the believers in pure expediency, who think that the best chance is to take a middle position and play off both sides against each other. Then while the parties on either side are fighting they try to run off with the bacon. These are the ones who believe that you cannot really stand for something and win an election. They are generally afraid of all ideas because their sole object is to get into office. They are politicians in the worst sense of the word. Everybody recognizes this type of political "leader."

History, however, shows that they are dead wrong even about the matter of winning. Occasionally dodging about in the middle of the road does lead to a temporary victory. But these are fleeting successes for the simple reason that you can't fool all of the people all the time. In their hearts people despise a trimmer and, as soon as they find him out, they leave him. The great causes which have triumphed and the leaders which have led them have never been found in the middle of the road. They have set their course by some ideal and have resisted all temptations, which have sometimes been many, to come halfway to the other side. And the parties which have played the game of compromise on vital issues have seen their glory and their power vanish. For proof of this, let's go to history.

A century ago this country had an important and powerful party called the Whigs. Its leader was the attractive Henry Clay and he had support from the best elements in all parts of the country. But his party made the fatal mistake of trying to straddle the fence on major issues. As a result, it was not Clay, "the Great Compromiser," who went to the White House, but the hard-hitting Andrew Jackson. By 1856 the Whig Party was dead. Stephen A. Douglas tried the same trick, looking for the middle of the road between issues that were in direct conflict. He lost to Abraham Lincoln, who had taken a definite stand on one side. Even when the Democratic Party has won, on issues that many do not approve of, it has done so in taking a decisive stand for something. Better an opponent whose position you are certain of than a supposed friend whose only interest is in dodging the crucial issues. Such has generally been the judgment of the American voters on those who were merely looking for the line of least resistance.

We find that the story has been the same if we look at British politics. Two generations ago there was a powerful party in England called the Liberal Party. It was able to win elections at times and name the Prime Minister. Today it is little more than a ghost, a negligible element in British political life. The explanation of its demise is the same as that of the American Whigs. It tried to be a middle-of-the-road party, a party of compromise. But as always, the more pressing issues became, the more impatient people became with temporizing and half solutions. The result was that the Liberal Party was squeezed to death between the Conservative Party and the rising Labor Party. These represent with considerable distinctness a right and a left. That is to say, they offer the people reasonably clear alternatives. The poor Liberal Party, interested solely in being tepid on all matters, has virtually ceased to exist.

So much for the claim that the middle of the road is the path to success. Dodging issues and watering down solutions is not merely the way to failure; it is the way to extinction.

All great political parties owe their vitality to the importance of the things they stand for. And this is never truer than in periods of defeat which, in the normal alteration of political circumstances, must sometimes occur. A beaten party with a real issue has an excellent chance of coming back. A beaten party without an issue is a dead duck. And those parties which have tied their fortunes to some personality who happens to excite the masses are only setting a term to their effectiveness. When he goes, as he must, the wind is out of their sails. A party which has abandoned issues for personalities cannot overnight make itself a party of principles again.

These considerations have a melancholy bearing upon the situation in our country today. There is one group, not clearly distinguished by a party name, but quite definite about what it wants and expects to bring about in this nation. Most accurately speaking, it is the party of collectivism. It works on various fronts and under various labels, but there need be no confusion about its objectives. It wants an America, new-modeled according to the Soviet Union.

There are two ideas in the philosophy of collectivism of which every American ought to be aware. One of them is a thorough-going materialism, which insists that man is merely a natural animal, which repudiates religion and all belief in the Divine Providence, and which maintains that happiness is purely a matter of gratifying this animal's appetites. The other idea is that the state is supreme and the individual nothing, that society should be managed down to the smallest details by a centralized authority, and that there is no higher power—no human tradition, no conscience, no precept of religion—by which this control can be criticized. An all-powerful state, designed along engineering lines to satisfy the physical wants of the masses, is their aim and goal, although often it is their method to admit only part of it at a time. In the writings of their prophets, Marx, Engels, Lenin and Stalin, however, it is revealed without any squeamishness.

You would think that in this country of ours, with its heritage and its achievements, there would be a tremendous outcry and opposition to anything so one-sided in its interpretation of history and man's nature and so chilling to human instincts.

There is a great segment of our population to the right of collectivism and morally committed to fight it. Strange as it may sound, however, a good many of its leaders have adopted the policy of appeasement. Instead of issuing a direct challenge, in terms of principle, they have tried to see how many concessions they could make without being accused of surrender.

They have tried to see how closely they could approach the position of collectivism while still paying lip service to what they are supposed to be defending.

Logic and duty call for them to stand up for their side, not to fight the battle by retreating from it. They have sought a middle-of-the-road position between a militant collectivism and our tradition of freedom and individualism. Historical examples show that the next step is capitulation, or liquidation of the party which is so cowardly.

If this should come about, it will certainly be recorded by history that no people ever gave up so much for so little. We possess a great, beautiful, inspiring country. In our comparatively brief history we have created some traditions that any people would be proud to sustain; we have borne leaders and heroes to match those out of Plutarch; we have accomplished many things which by previous standards were thought impossible. We have combined equality with a method of rewarding success and distinction which has no parallel in history in its ability to produce social satisfaction and incentive to achievement.

Best of all, we have created a spirit of kindness and helpfulness which mitigates the lot of life's failures without trying absurdly to place them in the driver's seat. Every candid foreign observer is struck by this, and we feel intuitively that it is a very American thing. "Nowhere is cruelty more abhorred," Lord Bryce wrote admiringly of the America he saw. Now it is proposed to exchange this for the regimentation, the directives, the penalties, perhaps even the forced labor camps and executions of an alien and inhuman philosophy.

There is little doubt that the middle of the road today leads in this direction. The radicals know what they want; too many of the rest of us only temporize and hope. Already a good many people are behaving as if their conscience hurt them over being American, so they give a little here and a little there in the hope of not being too offensive to the truculent enemy.

This is the reason that even the election of 1952 did not halt creeping socialism. Because no influential leader drew the line in terms of clear principle, the immense bureaucracy of the New Deal was allowed to consolidate itself further. This and that clamorous group has been able to extort state aid according to New Deal methods. All candid observers realize that the trend toward statism has not yet been reversed.

The need of the time is for a leadership willing to face the facts. Complacency toward what is happening is a betrayal of the America we have inherited. The kind of leader that people are willing to stay with, and to sacrifice personally for, is the kind that says, "I'm going to fight it out on this line if it takes all summer." Wavering and self-defeat through compromise where vital points are at stake never yet held a following. To win this struggle we have got to get on the right side of the road and keep it with resolution.

The Middle Way: A Political Meditation[1]

The return of the Eisenhower party to office makes inevitable a fresh look at the "middle of the road" as a viable political philosophy. Whether the espoused doctrine of moderation, rather than special circumstances, was responsible for either of its victories is, of course, highly arguable. Yet there are many who see in it the cause of success, and the recent elevation of Arthur Larson, who sounds the official philosophy of moderation, to a post of influence will doubtless lend countenance to their claim.

All this is profoundly troubling to those who believe that keeping midway between the two sides of a basic debate has grave theoretical liabilities, and that in the long run theory is going to assert its claims. The question is not whether but *when* a party which has no guide line except "moderation" is going to meet an issue from which there is no refuge in the middle of the road.

Everyone notices that the middle position is sought by those who are uncomfortable with ideas and the oppositions which these entail. They try to get as far as possible from the two sides of an issue. To comfort themselves with, they have an old saw, not respectable logically, but useful to temporize with: "The truth is always found somewhere in between." But in between what?

The assumption, to the extent that it ever gets clarified, seems to be that when two sides are engaged in a clear-cut controversy, each one must be approximately half right and half wrong. The wise man therefore takes a portion of what each has and with these constructs a middle road of wisdom. This is not only safe, it is also easy, for one never has to undergo the sometimes arduous work of defining a position independently. That labor can be left to "extremists," of whom the conservative is pictured as one. The

1. *National Review*, 3/3, January 19, 1957, 63–64. © 1957 by National Review, Inc., 215 Lexington Avenue, New York, N.Y. 10016. Reprinted by permission.

Moderate fancies that in keeping away from clearly defined and deeply anchored views, he is keeping away from errors.

But this involves a dangerous misunderstanding of the nature of alternatives, as was pointed out by a great thinker two thousand years ago. Plato
had occasion to face this question in the *Euthydemus*, and his analysis is well
worth calling to the attention of present advocates of the in-between course.

> All persons or things which are intermediate between two other things and
> participate in both of them are thus: if one of these things is good and the
> other evil, the participant is better than the one and worse than the other; but
> if it is in a mean between two things which do not tend toward the same end,
> it falls short of either of its component elements in the attainment of these
> ends. Only in the case when the two components which do not tend to the
> same end are evil is the participant better than either.

Plato says in this passage that he is talking about "people who do not
understand the nature of intermediates." They are the ones who have not
analyzed reality enough to see that the middle position is not necessarily
the best one.

The Liberal's Dilemma

Within the frame of this analysis, the dilemma of the Liberal "middle-
of-the-roader" emerges as a true one. Let us put him to the test in a
choice concerning the most fundamental conflict dividing the world today,
whose sides may be denominated "individual freedom" and "collectivist
dictatorship."

If he admits that the first of these is good and the second evil, he takes a
position inferior to the first when he chooses a position between them. If
he maintains that both are good but have different objectives (and this
seems to be the philosophy behind coexistence), then his middle position is
inferior to both, since it cannot achieve either end as well as the two defined
positions. He has the remaining choice of saying that though they tend
toward different ends, both are evil, so that the middle position is a means
of keeping away from either end. Obviously if he chooses this alternative,
he discloses what he really thinks about freedom.

Some imagine that this problem is solved in favor of "moderation" by
Aristotle's doctrine of virtue as a mean found between two extremes. But
Aristotle is talking about positions which *do* lie between two evils, one of

excess and one of deficiency. Thus "resoluteness," lying in a mean between "rashness" and "cowardice," is better than either of them; and "generosity," lying midway between "prodigality" and "niggardliness," is likewise. But Aristotle goes on to point out that there are some things whose badness is implied in their names, so that one can never be right with regard to them. There is no happy medium in doing a thing which is essentially wrong. There is no time, occasion, or manner which justifies it. For those who believe that collectivist dictatorship invades an area of inviolable liberty, collectivist dictatorship is this kind of thing. There is no right measure of this invasion; it is not justified even through invoking the modern talisman "security."

The prophets of the New Republicanism, as pointed out in a recent editorial in *National Review*, insist that the Republican Party keep moving to the left behind (but not far behind) the Democratic Party. They assume that the desirable middle ground is to be found just to the right of wherever the Democratic Party happens to take its stand. They do not bother to ask whether the leftward drift is not toward something essentially bad, so that there is no happy intermediate with regard to it. It is a curious piece of political servility and blindness.

The blindness comes from ignoring the fact that just as some things are bad in themselves, others are good in themselves, and these derive their whole force from their existence as clear-cut ideals. Try lowering them ever so little, and they are vitiated. The fact that they are never wholly realized in the world is not a reflection upon them, but upon the infirmity of man. The essential freedom of the individual is this kind of thing, not wholly realizable at any time, but not to be bartered away by concessions to a wholly different kind of thing.

In one of the satires of Anatole France, there is a story about a girl who is charged with having an illegitimate child. Her defense is that it was "only a tiny one." This seems a fair parody of the Liberal rationalization. For the philosophical bankruptcy of modern Liberalism comes from a confusing of categories, from supposing that what is wrong in principle can be made right by a little quantitative balancing. Most Liberals have in fact imbibed large doses of positivism, and this seems to have effectually destroyed their faith in ideas. They tend increasingly to derive their political philosophy from physical analogies, of which "the middle of the road" is a fair example.

As a result of this, the Liberal arrives at the notion that there are no truths, but only accommodations of physical forces. Facts can exist together: it is ideas which are irreconcilable. Therefore he tries to get rid of ideas as things deriving ultimately from metaphysics and therefore without significance. The right plan is to harmonize forces, and stop worrying about ideas, which in a positivist's world are only epiphenomena.

The Vector of Forces

Hence most of the Liberals are impressed with the bulk and force of the Soviet Union. But impressed in this way: the Soviet Union is a force to be accommodated, if not indeed to be imitated. Already we have had sly suggestions that we ought to revise our educational methods with an eye to Soviet "achievement." Circumstance is not only the last, it is the *only* refuge of those who have given up faith in ideas.

Such loss of faith explains the progressive abandonment, in education and elsewhere, of the criteriological sciences, like logic and ethics. So we witness attempts to dissolve logic into psychology, psychology into biology, biology into chemistry, and chemistry into physics. This is, as Professor R. G. Collingwood pointed out years ago, "the propaganda of irrationalism." Where physics is the sole matrix, elements cannot be in logical opposition, but only in physical union and equilibrium. In a world so reduced, what one looks for is the vector sum of forces. And the vector sum of forces is the middle of the road. If this should become the predominant world view, it is evident that the whole moral and dramatistic picture of life as a struggle between good and evil would have to go, for these concepts are determined only through logical discourse. Where the vector of forces is the supreme object of search, there would be no need for deliberative assemblies. All you would need is a reasonably good mathematical physicist.

Descent into Mindlessness

So New Republicanism looks very much like a typical product of the "operational thinker." The "operational thinker" does not really think; he senses. Like an insect with its antennae, he can detect the impingement of circumstances and the drift of things. The real question is whether his goal can ever be anything more than insect living. On the human plane, the goals of life have to be arrived at dialectically; that is, through investigating and comparing the implications of propositions. That kind of thinking never rests halfway between contradictories. It may not be able to carry out a proposition completely and at once, but it does not therefore discard all propositions. That, again, is the act of irrationalism.

It seems clear that "the middle of the road" is one of the guises worn by relativism. And relativism is the means by which Liberalism is descending into mindlessness. Somewhere in its course Liberalism succumbed to a sentimentalism which caused it to ignore the structure of reality. Sentimentalism always allows feeling undisciplined by intelligence to obscure the nature of things. The more it ignored the structure of reality, the more it went into debt, so to speak, for its extravagances. Finally, the only way out was to repudiate the debt by denying the creditor. This it has done by saying that courses do not have to be justified by theory. That may do well enough until someone comes along who has both a practice and a theory. Then, as Charles Péguy once said, "We shall learn metaphysics by the firing of rifles."

Roots of the Liberal Complacency[1]

That today's Liberal is marked by complacency will appear to some a paradoxical charge. Most Liberals may shrug it off as something which, in the nature of things, cannot be imputed to them. Does not the Liberal creed make criticism of any and all matters a cardinal point? Does it not invite the free competition of ideas in the market place? Has not the Liberal set up a kind of eternal restlessness of the mind as the only enlightened condition?

Until fairly recently one's answer to all of these might have been yes. But the question today is whether the Liberal has not succumbed to certain fallacies of unwarranted assumption, which is the father of complacency. It is not an unknown thing to have the very vices one is opposing slip up on one from the rear in some pleasant disguise. This the Liberal has done, it seems to me, by not being truly circumspect, and by giving in to certain weaknesses which may be in themselves neither liberal nor radical nor conservative, but are human. A fault cutting across all of these is graver than any a mere political *ism* can remove. This means, if true, that the Liberal is now beyond the ministrations of anything save logic and ethics.

To see this complacency, one has only to look at the present generation of academic Liberals. One marks the telltale signs of indifference, of arrogance, of pomposity in their attitudes and their literature. They are very confident of their rightness that nothing is permanently right. This does not keep them, however, from blandly making their dispositions on the theory that the conservative opposition has been permanently routed. Many of them would be surprised to learn that their attitude can be as maddening to the conservative who has found his conservatism the hard way as the incapacity of a Bourbon to learn anything once was to advocates of the rights of man.

1. *National Review*, 3/23, June 8, 1957, 541–43. © 1957 by National Review, Inc., 215 Lexington Avenue, New York, N.Y. 10016. Reprinted by permission.

The complacency of this new, and often well-healed, Liberal is fed by a number of roots.

The Liberal has become, to all intents and purposes, a materialist. I do not pretend to use the term "materialism" here in a strict philosophical sense. I mean simply that the Liberal is now inclined to accept wholly the objectives of an efficient material civilization and to judge policies in their relation to the "standard of living." One sees his willingness to carry statism to any length whatever to universalize this standard of living. Writing a few years ago in the *Atlantic Monthly,* Joseph S. Clark, Jr., graduate of Harvard *magna cum laude,* then Mayor of Philadelphia, and now United States Senator, offered this curious definition of the Liberal:

> To lay a ghost at the outset and dismiss semantics, a Liberal is here defined as one who believes in utilizing the full force of government for the advancement of social, political, and economic justice at the municipal, state, national, and international levels.

Nowhere else have I seen so naked a profession of new Liberalism, or one which shows better how far this has gone toward embracing the statism to which nineteenth-century Liberals were, in the name of liberty, most opposed. (The confusion at which Mr. Clark hints is not one of semantics, but one of historical about-face.) The last phrase of the definition leads of course to Point Four thinking, to the materialist illusion that envy, hatred, and violence can be removed from the globe by handouts, by "economic assistance," and by making the "underprivileged" nations of the world urban, industrialized, motorized, and sanitized in an equal degree with Detroit and Los Angeles.

A natural consequence of this is the Liberal's idealization of comfort. He shows a definite antagonism toward all strenuous ideals of life. The code of the warrior, of the priest, and even of the scholar, denying the self for transcendent ends, stands in the new lexicon as anti-Liberal. The working day of a Thomas Jefferson or a Theodore Roosevelt would actually be an affront to the Liberal code. "For they are moderate also even in virtue—because they want comfort," says Nietzsche in *Thus Spake Zarathustra.* He goes on to add that the noble man does not want anything from life gratuitously. But today popularity is substituted for greatness and conformity for heroism. The Liberal preaches an altruism that is sentimental, and he is therefore hostile to all demands that the individual be something more than his natural, indolent, ease-loving, and complacent self.

More damage has resulted from this materialism and its attendant attitudes than from anything else the Liberal has spread. In the first place, it falsifies reality for the masses by leaving out of account the world of ideas and telic concepts which are alone capable of giving to societies a lasting cohesion. In the second place, by setting up comfort as the highest good, it leaves shut up the greatest of all reservoirs of strength, the will to sacrifice for the advancement of some noble good. Thus by its unwarranted assumption it misleads on the one hand, and on the other it stultifies.

Quite likely the Liberal has been betrayed into this by his scientism. Scientism is itself an unwarranted assumption which lends a plausible kind of support to the attitudes described above. Since it is derived from certain propositions about the nature of the world, it requires a little introducing.

Science exists in the form of a set of methods. That the application of these methods has wrought transformations in the outward world is the most ubiquitous fact of our time. What is not so well understood, however, is the effect of this practical success upon the more general theory of reality and knowledge. Until rather recently it was generally held that subject matter is prior to method. But in the last few decades, this position has been reversed, and it is now being said, or assumed, that method is prior to subject matter. This comes from the premise that nothing which cannot be found by the scientific method is real, which is of course the position of modern positivism. What happened in the process of this shift was that methodology became the ontological absolute; things are real in proportion to their capacity for being discovered by the scientific method. Here is a complete victory for instrumentalism whereby, in effect, a methodology makes reality as it proceeds with the act of discovering. So John Dewey could argue that the instruments of inquiry not only inquire, they also determine what can be inquired into. In the old order of knowledge, this latter was a datum provided by God, or at least by the empirical fact of creation.

The effect of this on man's attitude toward the world can be nothing less than revolutionary, and in some quarters it has already been disastrous. For what it does is rule out the given, the contingent, the inscrutable—in sum, all that is greater than or independent of man. The ground for that humility which all the great ethical systems have inculcated is thereby withdrawn.

Man, with his Method, leaps into the seat of the Creator, which, in the wisdom of poetry and religion, is the ultimate act of pride.

Hence it comes to be believed that there are no problems which cannot be solved by the methods of science because, in terms of the concept itself, such problems cannot exist. A problem to be conceived at all has to be conceived as something which this ontologically prior set of methods could solve. From this now widely held assumption comes the Liberal's complacent belief that all the situations produced by selfishness, ill will, and violence can be removed once science, with its omnicompetent methodology, gets around to them.

Nowhere has the effect of this belief been more manifest than in "progressive" education, which was the first practical victim of the heresy. There, as every observer of the movement knows, subject matter, representing the antecedently real, has been virtually retired in favor of methodology. The teacher is not a man who knows facts and ideas but a man trained in method. It is assumed that there is nothing which the method cannot do. When stubborn facts of the given world—such as inequalities of aptitude or the human tendency toward delinquency—stand in the way of the triumph of the method, they are either ignored or misleadingly reported. For these educational positivists there is no nature of man, but only some pliable stuff which can be kneaded into any desired shape by the principles of a materialist psychology.

The Liberals' Alogism

Despite the seeming sophistication of this theory, most Liberals today are not real intellectuals, and their lack of real intellectualism leaves them complacent where wiser men are alert and discerning. When one considers the extent to which they preponderate on college faculties and the extent to which they control the means of publishing ideas, this may appear an audacious statement. But a study of this literature will show that an alogism has turned the Liberal unavoidably down the road toward anti-intellectualism. By alogism I mean a rejection of logical rigor and a complacency in the face of contradiction.

One of the chief directives of Liberalism is to deny the existence of "either-or" choices. The Liberal insists on substituting the "both-and" choice, which keeps him from ever having to accept or reject flatly. This is why he ends up in the "middle of the road." A desire to squeeze in between two contradictories keeps the Liberal from seeing anything with clarity. At the same time, it leads to a breaking down of categories, so that in the final result he has nothing to think with. It leads to a politics of truces, compromises, and even sellouts. There is a difference between saying that there are no clear-cut principles of right and wrong and saying that a principle cannot always be applied with rigor in a world that is concrete and various. The latter is the policy of all men of sense and experience, but it is prudence, or what the Greeks called *sophrosyne,* not "liberalism."

It is the sentimentality of the new Liberal which leaves him incapable of accepting rigid exclusion. He does not like to think that God and the devil are irreconcilable. He thinks that with a little patient explaining and some of his famous tolerance, each could be brought to see some good in the other. In brief, he does not contemplate a right and a wrong.

This propensity to moral and intellectual flabbiness on the part of the Liberal leads to an inordinate fear of a certain type of man, of whom Taft and MacArthur are good examples. Such men reveal, by the very logic of their expression, that they think in terms of inclusion and exclusion. Their mentality rejects cant, sniveling, and double-talk. When they speak, one knows that he is listening to a man, in the eulogistic sense in which Emerson and Thoreau used that word. There is, in fact, a great deal to be inferred from the almost hysterical reaction that the man of Plutarchan mold inspires in the Liberals. There must be present a hidden anxiety, born of a knowledge that they will be helpless when the leader of character and conviction comes along, as he must. Hence the voluminous outpouring, from supercilious dismissal to vituperation, whenever an individual of clear mind and strong personality appears on the scene and begins to gather strength. On these occasions, the Liberals' complacency is succeeded by, one might say, a fear for their complacency.

Despite these occasional disturbances of his peace, however, the Liberal feels most of the time that he is protected by an invincible dogma. I use "dogma" here in the etymological sense of "opinion." And the opinion is that today everyone must be a Liberal. This can be seen easily enough in the tone of the popular press, in the philosophy of Progress, and in the cult of scientism. But one finds it entrenched also in sources that are more decisive, in the sense that they furnish the reasoning behind the more popular expressions.

Here it appears in the form of a proposition that liberalism represents a new level of the human consciousness which will never be given up. It is the hidden premise of numberless college textbooks. It is evident in the judicial philosophy of Oliver Wendell Holmes, with its repudiation of "fighting faiths" and its belief that truth is something relative to the demands of the market place. It becomes mandatory, consequently, to oppose all fixed truths and traditional formulations—indeed, all universals—and this on the principle that humanity has found absolutely that they won't work. Even so otherwise discerning a philosopher as Ortega has declared that today all men are Liberals in the sense of sharing this opinion.

One striking result of the dogma in our country today is the complacent assumption that both political parties must be "liberal." It used to be felt that one political party was enough to represent the point of view that is Liberalism; now some of our political leaders say by their acts, if not by their very words, that a party must be Liberal to deserve consideration by the electorate.

Hence the astonishing efforts in the last few years to transform the Republican Party, which in the main has stood for a conservative approach to economic and political questions, into a second "Liberal" party in plain emulation of the Democratic. It is this carbon-copy Liberalism of the "new Republican" leadership which has led candid observers to point out that the American people today do not have a real choice on the major issues confronting them. One alternative is being deliberately withheld. So the American voter is left with the opportunity of voting "*ja*" for Democratic Liberalism or "*ja*" for Republican Liberalism. The engineers of this maneuver are assuming that Liberalism, like the Constitution, is antecedent to citizenship; you do not vote for it or against it; you vote only after you have taken a pledge to accept it. This is tantamount to assuming that Liberalism is something no longer within the area of debate, but is rather a part of our organic law. Almost needless to say, recent Supreme Court decisions seem to reflect the assumption.

So successful have the Liberals been in establishing this dogma through education, publishing, and politics that people today are literally unable to understand the language of the conservative point of view. They can conceive neither the meaning of its terms nor the spirit of it. No one has expressed this better, or with more ominous suggestion, than George Santayana.

> Modern civilization has an immense momentum, not only physically irresistible but morally and socially dominant in the press, politics, and literature of the Liberal classes; yet the voice of a dispossessed and forlorn orthodoxy, prophesying evil, cannot be silenced, and what renders that voice the more disquieting is that it can no longer be understood. When the prophets or apologists of the modern world attempt to refute those vaticinations, they altogether miss fire, because of their incapacity to conceive what they attack; and even in the exposition of their own case they are terribly confused and divided.

These are faults of the mind and the moral consciousness.

And Then the Bureaucracy

Finally one has to recognize a massive circumstance which has played into the hands of the Liberals. This is the bureaucratization of American life. It is a fact of paramount significance that our contemporary world is dominated by three large, and in some ways comparable, bureaucracies. They are the bureaucracy of government, the bureaucracy of business, and the bureaucracy of education. It is also of paramount significance that these bureaucracies are fed by our educational institutions. This means that most of the members, and certainly nearly all of the upper bureaucrats, will have received the proper indoctrination before they reach their posts. The government bureaucrats will have been taught that the state is destined to grow larger and larger and to gather to itself more and more of the national income. The business managers will have been given a pap which tells them that business is for "service" and not for profit, that owners and managers are only "trustees" of the employees, and so on. And the educational bureaucrats will have been taught that the main concern of education is with democracy and that its immediate task is to speed the evolution of society into a collectivized state. With this formidable apparatus for inculcating and enforcing an orthodoxy, it is little wonder that the Liberals do act as an Establishment. This is why anyone who speaks up in the name of individualism and privacy, and the right of men to win distinction through the exercise of intelligence and energy is likely to find himself solitary and forlorn.

This is a practical circumstance supporting the Liberal complacency, but its effects are far-reaching. The Liberals now operate the training schools for the managerial classes. When it is realized how much the advocates of "progressive" education have been able to do by compulsorily routing all future public school teachers through their highly tendentious curricula, we will not overlook what the Liberals are able to do in their indoctrination centers, which today seem to include most departments in most universities. Here the young person is taught an attitude toward the state which is not Liberal, but servile. He is thereby prepared for the further bureaucratizing of life.

If Liberalism stemmed out of some deeply anchored and coherent philosophy, if it expressed some compelling vision of existence, we could not apply the term "complacency" to the attitude it has engendered. We might speak instead of conviction and tradition and find some satisfaction in the prevalence of settled views. But "conviction" is just the word one must never use in connection with the modern Liberal. His conviction is that there are no convictions—or that convictions are "prejudices"—his belief that there are no enduring beliefs, and his truth a pervasive skepticism. Even his "dogma" has root only in the circumstance that he is now ascendant.

It is this non-committal attitude toward all the positive issues of life that keeps Liberalism from rising to the dignity of a philosophy which might unify an epoch and provide ground for constructive creations. With its lack of attachment to anything except its own relativism and tentative success, it cannot manage, with all its thousand tongues, anything better than superficial and often contradictory observations about its own chaotic world.

Integration Is Communization[1]

The Supreme Court's extraordinary dictate to the public schools promises to keep race relations inflamed for an indefinite period. It is therefore to be expected that there will be a continuing spate of books from "liberal" sources, filled with self-righteousness and preaching the funeral of what is pejoratively called "discrimination." At hand are three which suggest the range of treatment: *The Negro and Southern Politics*, by Hugh D. Price (New York University Press, $5.00); *Go South to Sorrow*, by Carl T. Rowan (Random House, $3.50); and *Passive Resistance in South Africa*, by Leo Kuper (Yale University Press, $3.50).

Mr. Price's book was originally a thesis done at the University of Florida. Dealing in the statistics and "trends" of social science, it surveys the role of the Negro in recent Florida politics and, with an occasional jab at conservatism, concludes that he is there to stay. *Go South to Sorrow* is low-grade political journalism. Declamatory, shrill, and containing wild misstatements (e.g., "No child in South Carolina gets the kind of schooling given to youngsters in Michigan," and "Everyone in Alabama is poorer than everyone in Pennsylvania"), it is a sorry specimen of Negro intellectual leadership. Mr. Kuper's book centers on the apartheid movement in South Africa and, at the expense of considerable jargon, comes to the conclusion that passive resistance is proving a useful political instrumentality.

If this were all, Mr. Kuper's book might be the most innocuous of the three. But this is not all, for it is Mr. Kuper who, unwittingly or not, opens the real issue. In his discussion of race relations in South Africa, he notes that Communism is there being progressively redefined in racial terms. That is to say, Communism is coming to be identified in racial integration. The blame for this he tries to shift to the apartheid laws themselves. But

1. *National Review*, 4/3, July 13, 1957, 67–68. © 1957 by National Review, Inc., 215 Lexington Avenue, New York, N.Y. 10016. Reprinted by permission.

surely this is artless. The Communist attitude toward race stems from Communism's positivistic representation of man, which has always had as one of its cardinal tenets the dogma that there are no real differences between people except economic differences. Remove the economic differences and all the others—racial, cultural, social, and moral—disappear. Thus the collectivizing of the economy can be depended on to obliterate the various differences that keep people from being "socialized."

Herein lies the clue to much that confronts us today. The Communists are skilled enough in warfare to know that their goal can be approached by different ways. They know that some nations are still too "backward" to look with an enthusiastic eye upon the collectivizing of their economy. These nations must be edged toward it by indirect methods. And the Communist tactic most aggressively used in this country now is the one hinted at by Mr. Kuper—the approach through the idea of "racial collectivism." This phase of the leveling or obliterating process can now be presented with a great deal of moral unction. Moreover, it has the tactical advantage of undermining our historic constitutional structure.

In every part of the United States the common people, who do not wear the blinkers that some politicians prefer to don, have understood this for a good long while. To them Communism has always signalized its advent by an ostensibly free and natural but actually self-conscious and tendentious racial mingling. This is the way the American public has intuitively spotted the emergence of Communism. And its reaction, despite the stream of propaganda and wishful editorializing from many sectors of the press, has been about 90 per cent in favor of our traditional American society and mores.

The common people often perceive elemental things which the overeducated cannot see. That they have been right in identifying this as the opening tactic of Communism in this country now seems beyond question. We can observe in a number of areas how "racial collectivism" is being used as a crowbar to pry loose rights over private property. There was a time when ownership of property gave the owner the right to say to whom he would and would not sell and rent. But now, with the outlawing of restrictive covenants by the Supreme Court (especially in *Shelley v. Kraemer*), this right has been invaded, if not effectually taken away. There was a time when owners had complete discretion as to whom they would and would not hire to work in their private businesses. Now that right is invaded by various kinds of FEPC laws, which tell him that he cannot consider differences of race in selecting his employees. There was a time when private educational institutions had the right to set up any standards they chose for the admission of students. Now at least one state has a law which forbids any institution even to accept applications with data relating to the race and religion of the student applying. Just recently there has come the decision of the Supreme Court in the Girard College case, in which the terms of a will which had stood for more than one hundred years were set aside because the charity it provided had been limited to white orphan boys. One must have a pretty sophistical education not to see in this a steady and indeed now far advanced eroding of rights over private property following a Communist racial theory. In most of the process the Supreme Court has been, as Mr. Frederic Nelson suggests in a contemporary article, the "running dog" of the Kremlin.

"Integration" and "Communization" are, after all, pretty closely synonymous. In the light of what is happening today, the first may be little more than a euphemism for the second. It does not take many steps to get from the "integrating" of facilities to the "communizing" of facilities, if the impulse is there.

To remove any doubt as to the impulse behind this Liberal line, let us turn back to *The Negro and Southern Politics* and look at the Introduction. This was provided by William G. Carleton, Professor of Political Science at the University of Florida; and here the terms of the new rhetoric emerge in all their audacity. Why, Professor Carleton asks, is the integration movement destined to prevail? And he replies: "Because it is in harmony with the integrated mass society that machine technology has produced, to which we are irrevocably committed." And why should this be accepted as inevitable? The answer lies in "the mass conformity and increasingly 'other directed' nature of all segments of American society." Now he is ready for the big admission. The specific cause of the whole movement, he owns, is "Communist competition on a world scale." So the professor is able to conclude grandly by declaring: "If democratic reformists were able to see themselves in historical perspective, they would paraphrase Voltaire and say, 'If Marx had never existed, we should have had to invent him.'" All this, it must be added, is said with perfect complacency, without a trace of suggestion that somewhere we ought to stand and fight against this submergence in massness. Here we have in a brief passage the reality that the Liberal journals have so industriously tried to deny: Moscow is piping the tune; the American professoriate is beating time; and we are beginning to dance to it.

While this surrender goes on, the Liberal publicists encourage it by representing every concession as a gain and every evacuation as a victory. We can expect no end to such demoralization until they and their followers calm down enough to see the truth of three propositions. 1) Integration is not an end in itself. 2) Forcible integration would ignore the truth that equals are not identicals. 3) In a free society, associations for educational, cultural, social, and business purposes have a right to protect their integrity against political fanaticism. The alternative to this is the destruction of free society and the replacement of its functions by government, which is the Marxist dream.

On Setting the Clock Right[1]

Isn't it curious that almost any serious social criticism today will be met with the retort that "You can't turn the clock back"? If one hints that atomic energy may not be a good thing for mankind in its present state of moral development, one is accused of turning his back on the future. If one suggests that the war of unlimited objectives really settles no more than previous wars have done but entails immensely greater destruction of life and property, one is charged with wanting to return to the horse and buggy days. If one remarks that both theory and observation prove that collectivism is fatal to individual liberty, one is blamed for being out of step with the times. If one hazards an opinion that the amount of noise and confusion prevailing today is perhaps not the best thing for the human psyche, one is branded an enemy of progress. In fact, I can't think of any objection to the present physical and moral order which will not likely be answered with some variety of the charge that the critic wants to turn the clock back.

This retort is heard so regularly and from sources so influential in the practical way that we need to make a serious examination of its argumentative basis. What is it that leads people who in other matters may exhibit good intelligence to suppose that they have an argument in the idea that "You can't turn the clock back"? What is it that allows them to imagine they have the clincher in any debate over conduct or social policy when they assert that the future dictates a certain line of action to which alternatives are only futile attempts to move back the hour hand?

As always in situations of this kind, one has to look for the hidden assumptions. But before entering upon an analysis of these, let us note that there is one fact upon which both sides must agree. This is that there is at least one important difference between the past and the future, which is

1. *National Review*, 4/14, October 12, 1957, 321–23. © 1957 by National Review, Inc., 215 Lexington Avenue, New York, N.Y. 10016. Reprinted by permission.

that the past has been objectified and the future has not. What this says is simply that the past has happened. The past exists in the form of history; it is something we in a sense possess, something we can examine and appraise. Within the limits imposed by historical reconstruction, we can know it for what it was. A statement about the past thus differs in nature from one made about the future; it is subject to a kind of testing (unless we have succumbed to a complete skepticism about the possibility of knowledge); whereas a statement about the future deals with something that does not exist, or to be as exact as possible, does not exist in the same way. Obviously if we regarded statements about the past and the future as equally and similarly provable, the whole character of human thinking would have to be radically altered, and horse races and Presidential contests would lose their interest.

Two Assumptions

What, then, is the assumption about the future of those who assert so peremptorily that "You can't turn the clock back"? Necessarily they are saying either 1) that there is an inexorable course of this future-which-has-not-happened, which has been disclosed to them but not to their opponents, or 2) that this future is their own subjective feeling, which they intend to transform into reality and to impose.

If they adhere to the first of these assumptions, they are determinists of one provenance or another. Many of them have imbibed consciously or unconsciously so much of scientific materialism and psychologism that they really believe man is "only an atom in the vast system of derived existence." For them, the way to predict any future event is to study the present lines of material force. These forces were set in operation back in some dark abysm of time. All we know is that the chain of causation is unbroken and unbreakable; one event follows another regularly and unavoidably as one billiard ball imparts its force to another. Even man's consciousness is but an ephemera cast up by this mighty stream of antecedent and consequent events. Man may think that he is influencing the course of things, but in fact he is himself totally conditioned, and his responses are but links in the chain of causation. As one of the cleverest of the nineteenth-century writers put it, "You may choose what you like, but what determines your liking?"

For persons of this outlook there is no possibility of avoiding the future indicated by these lines of force, however bleak and unattractive it may seem. The future will emerge inexorably out of the present, and there is nothing we can do if all the signs point to a further dehumanization of man. After all, it was never intended that man should be human—in fact, it was never intended that he should be anything at all.

In sum, the argument of the determinists is that the present constitutes a great cause, and that the effect cannot be very different from the cause. Those who expect a different effect are extrapolating erroneously from the data before us. This future which has been revealed to them, but not to humanists and religionists, is inferred from the present trend toward scientific materialism and collectivism. Therefore, the iron age is just around the corner, and they are disposed to scorn as nostalgic weakness any attempt to change the course to something nearer the heart's desire. Man must "face the fact" that he is only a part of nature and that he only deceives himself when he thinks he can transcend its blind purpose. First the biologists, then the sociologists, and even the physicists (for a while, but not now) added their bit to the depressing bill.

Even Science Cannot Predict

This line of argument can now be largely refuted by an appeal to science itself. Recent science, under the leadership of physics, is turning away from the former rigid determinism. For one thing, the translatability of matter and energy has made the old distinction between material and non-material essentially meaningless, so that there is no longer any scientific point in pluming oneself upon being a strict materialist. But far more important is the likelihood now looming up that the indeterminate, even in the material world, is a part of ultimate reality. Physical scientists have found that they cannot always predict what individual atoms will do, for they appear to "hop about." In large masses atoms do seem to obey statistical laws of probability, but a law of this kind does not foretell what an individual member of an aggregate will do. At this most profound level of physical reality, then, we are seeing what has been called a revival of "free will among the atoms." If matter at this level does not obey immutable laws of causation, we may infer *a fortiori* that the complex and mysterious organizations of substance called living matter do not obey them either.

Somewhat more difficult to deal with, from the standpoint of the argument for freedom, is the legacy of certain historians, political scientists and social critics who have brought in the term "historical forces" and who have treated these as uncontrollable absolutes which are hurrying man on his way. Indeed, this belief in mysterious "historical forces" has almost become the dominant view of the modern world, underlying learned works of history and philosophy and percolating down to become the inarticulate premise of men who could not rise to this level of speculation.

Such a postulate of immanent forces is in Hegel, it is in Marx, it is in Toynbee, and it provides the theoretical framework of many lesser attempts to explain the course of the world. In outline, it provides an absurdly easy solution to many problems, since anything you do not understand you may toss into the bin "forces of history" and have done with it. Those movements which have failed and those institutions which are moribund are contrary to these forces, whereas all victorious movements and all prospering institutions are in accord with them. The "forces of history" are thus only a reification of what we do not really comprehend. The net outcome, of course, is another degradation of man. As Frederick Wilhelmsen has pointed out in his brilliant essay "History, Toynbee, and the Modern Mind": "To ground the meaning of history within some law thought to be consubstantial with the flow of time is certainly a denial of the ethical and religious drama of the moment, but it is even more a denial of the unique dignity of the human personality."

If the other argument for the determinist position can be refuted through science, this one can be refuted, it seems to me, through simple realism. The force of the human personality is one of the things we most immediately and intuitively know. If we pretend we do not know it, we deliberately shut out large areas of comprehension, for the fact of personality will explain many things which "the forces of history" serve only to obscure. That dominant personalities have polarized and energized great historical movements is something that recommends itself as a truth to minds not sophisticated with the ingenuities of dialectical theory.

They Have a "Feeling"

For those who adhere to the second of the two assumptions, the future is not determined except in the form of their own feeling. When, therefore, they say that "You can't turn the clock back," they are saying that we cannot proceed contrary to their feeling of how the future ought to be.

One can sense this readily in the attitude of most Communists. And going further, one can see that the Communists have in fact inverted the order of reality. For them, the past—the only part of time that has been objectified—has no reality. The present is used by them only to promote the future—this accounting for their arrogance toward all existing institutions. Now since they have an eye only to the future, they must look only to their subjective feelings. To them, this subjective feeling is the world that truly *is*, and all of the stubborn inheritances from the past that stand in the way of its realization are so much illusion. When, therefore, the advocates of collectivism tell us that we can't set the clock back because collectivism is the wave of the future (to have a mixed metaphor forced upon one), they are really telling us that nothing can withstand their feeling, which they mean to make prevail. This is all there is to the argument; there is no necessity one way or another, there are only desire and will, and their confidence that these are stronger in them than in us.

This analysis accords with Professor Eric Voegelin's highly significant thesis in his *The New Science of Politics,* which is that the Communists are the modern Gnostics, who like the Gnostics of antiquity substitute wish fulfillment and a dream world for the structure of reality. The reason they accept ideas which are flatly denied by human nature and make outrageous proposals is given in a brilliant passage:

> In the Gnostic dream world . . . non-recognition of reality is the first principle. As a consequence, types of action which in the real world would be considered morally insane because of the real effects which they have will be considered moral in the dream world because they intended an entirely different effect. The gap between intended and real effect will be imputed not to the Gnostic immorality of ignoring the structure of reality but to the immorality of some other person or society that does not behave as it should behave according to the dream conception of cause and effect.

The other person, it might be added, is usually the wicked capitalist, or now even the individualist.

Now if these partisans who "live in the future" should admit that this future is only their subjective feeling which they are determined to objectify, they are bound to show that it is somehow better or more deserving of realization than that espoused by the other side. In this case they will have to abandon any argument based on our presumptive inability to turn the clock back. For they are now conceding that there is no order which will come necessarily with the passage of time; there are only contemplated and willed orders: we can have one or another, and our choice must take us back to some standard of values about which men can differ.

The argument thus becomes not one of historical necessity—which they might have won by mere postulation—but a controversy over axiological principles, in which our opponents are necessarily at a disadvantage since admission of axiology involves ideas of worth and propriety. Even argument for one type of society rather than another on the basis of man's "natural rights" involves implications disastrous for them. As Edmund A. Opitz has pointed out: "The idea of natural rights is not the kind of concept which has legs of its own to stand on; as a deduction from religious premises, it makes sense, otherwise not."

Blueprint for Confusion

So it is that those who wish to force us into acquiescence with a world increasingly secularized and dehumanized, must either confess themselves absolute determinists—a position that is no longer tenable on any ground save that of belief in mystical "historical forces"; or they must admit that they intend to shape the future themselves, which is not argument at all, but an announcement of intention.

That is, they must do either of these things if they are cornered in argument. But it is not often that they allow themselves to be cornered, and a large part of the success of the Communists and their Liberal aides in propaganda comes through their impudence in having the thing both ways. The steps are simple, but they have worked so well that they evidently need exposing.

The first step is to confuse and paralyze the opposition by sowing widely and ostensibly in the interest of "objective understanding" the idea of determinism. Once you have convinced a man that he cannot operate on any representation of reality but your own, you have him in a state of virtual impotence. The second step is to regard this as nonsense as far as your own

affairs go and to proceed to fashion the world according to your preferred concept of it. The claim "There is no citadel which Bolshevism cannot take" may be put forward as an expression of faith in an inexorable historical process. But as the Communists have effectively used it, it is an expression of their will to power and their determination to overcome everything which stands in the way of the actualization of their dream.

The Communists have wielded their two-edged sword in this way: one edge they have used to cut away the poor bourgeois' belief in the efficacy of his own will, and the other they have used to hack at the present moral and physical order with all the resolution and enterprise of the old-time entrepreneur.

In the former undertaking they have been assisted, as previously noted, by numbers of well-meaning scientists and befuddled academics, who have been carriers of the doctrine of determinism. Not all of these have been conscious forerunners of Communism, but when an individual lays a claim to intellectual leadership, he cannot easily be excused for ignorance of implications. If you sow dragon's teeth, you may expect to reap armed men; and if you teach a representation of man which pictures him as nothing more than a cork bobbing on the surface of forces he cannot control, you may expect him to default on his responsibilities. These innocents have done much to prepare the way for the seizure of power by men who know from experience that whether freedom of the will can or cannot be metaphysically proved, they can grab what they want if they are sufficiently determined and unscrupulous.

The immediate task of those who are resolved not to have a future which will be intolerable to the spirit is to attack both of the assumptions we have been discussing. A full equipment for doing this is now available. The determinists can be shown that the most advanced of the sciences no longer supports the idea of mechanical determination. Those who make reality identical with change or the flow of time must be persuaded that this idea can result only in the sanctification of force and the belief that "Whoever wins is right." Those who mistake their own subjective feelings for the future must be asked to show cause why their feelings should be considered nearer to reality than our own.

For the positive part, we must affirm that the spirit of man is unconditional and that he can, within limits wide enough for a humane civilization,

make the kind of world he wants to live in. (First, of course, he must search his heart about the kind of world he really wants to live in: many of our dilemmas proceed from wanting good things, but wanting bad ones more.) We must prove again that the rewards of civil living and imaginative culture are not things existing by accident in the interstices of an iron fate, but are the creations of ideas that transcend the flow of time. Thus we can show not only that the horrors of *1984* can be avoided but also that the high forms of human achievement in the past are, in essence, recoverable. Then our response to the old chestnut "You can't turn the clock back" will be "I'm not turning it back; I'm setting it right."

Mass Plutocracy[1]

In the course of some rambling about the country, and in response to the generally deteriorating news from the various political fronts, I have been moved to ask more than once, What *is* the matter?

My deepest suspicion is that the American people as a whole have now adopted (or perhaps it would be fairer to them to say they have been given) the qualities and the outlook of a plutocracy. Plutocracy is defined in its root meaning as the rule by those having wealth. Interpreted slightly, it means rule through the power of money. Some nations have at some stages in their history been ruled by classes whose chief claim to distinction was their wealth. The character of this kind of rule is viewed very skeptically by classical political science. When Solon was forced to undertake the reform of the Athenian state, things having arrived at an impasse, one of the significant steps he took was to ban luxury. He did not try to make everyone equally opulent; his reform was in the direction of insisting upon a certain plainness of life even among those who had it to spend. Luxury, we infer, he regarded as something politically harmful. His idea was to press down from the top, so that there would be no examples of extravagance and high living to excite the emulation of the commonalty.

The solution of our political wise men is precisely the contrary of Solon's. It is to make everyone a plutocrat and to enable everyone to engage in the display of luxury. They begin at the other end, not with the tempering of desire, but with the satisfaction and even the artificial inflation of desire. A principle that was inherited from Greece and was spiritualized by Christianity has been thrown to the winds. Evidently we are in a new world.

In looking for the root of our trouble, let us remember that a rich man is not necessarily a plutocrat. Plutocratism is a state of mind and a moral out-

1. *National Review*, 9/18, November 5, 1960, 273–75. © 1960 by National Review, Inc., 215 Lexington Avenue, New York, N.Y. 10016. Reprinted by permission.

look which in the past some men of wealth have evinced and some have not. A man of wealth need not be plutocratic in his thinking. The plutocrat is distinguished not by the possession of money but by belief in its talismanic power. To him money is the axis on which the world turns. He trusts it to bring security and happiness almost automatically. And trusting in it this way, he believes that little if anything else is needed. We must be clear upon the point that some men of wealth are too intelligent to be plutocratic in their outlook, whereas men of little wealth and little sense may easily be so. The existence of individuals of large private means can be a good thing for society, and even a few genuine plutocrats may do no very extensive harm. But the situation changes when the mentality of a whole society, from top to bottom, becomes plutocratic.

Postwar Delusion

There are many signs to show that the plutocratic mentality has spread tremendously in this country since the Second World War. Unless I misread the evidence here is the greatest danger to the American nation today. Its values and judgments, from the millionaire at the top to the little fellow at the bottom who is struggling to meet his monthly payments to the loan company, are to a large extent tinctured with plutocratism. This fact alone explains many of the discouraging aspects of our foreign and domestic politics.

The evil may well have begun at the top, for the most marked symptoms of a virulent plutocratism appear in our foreign aid programs. Since the Second World War, in one form and another, and often in response to statesmanlike-sounding appeals and propaganda campaigns and fanfare we have poured out many billions of dollars. It has gone all over the world, for this and for that, and the defense has been that it is buying peace and security. My complaint is not against the sacrifice to Americans, but against the main strand of thinking which seems to underlie the great donation.

Almost the whole of the lend-and-give-away program looks unmistakably like the reverie of the plutocrat, who feels sure that money will do all, so that the harder ways of effecting ends need not be bothered with. Money has been thrown up as a barrier against military menace and ideological penetration. Look at it as you will, the governing assumption has been that we can win friends and make the indifferent love us by the inducement

of money. Now it is perfectly true that loans, subsidies, and bribes have from ancient times been used effectively in diplomacy and war. They have been used to buy neutrality, to equip allies in need, to supply the sinew for struggle where that was wanting. But in practically all cases these were specific grants for specific purposes, which could be noted as fulfilled or not. It was hardheaded policy, which got the respect that hardheadedness receives in business and war.

Now the giving seems to be in the spirit of largesse. The money is bestowed not for doing something, but for doing nothing. It is conceived as a sort of blanket pacifier. Often the claim to the benefit is regarded not as something to be earned but as a right existing initially. The old axioms of statecraft that there is no such thing as gratitude between nations (*n.b.* Russia and China today fifteen years after their rescue from the Germans and the Japanese), that you cannot buy friends though you may buy services and that the real safety of a nation lies in its ability to command respect and not in its ability to buy off robbers and blackmailers have been surrendered in favor of the plutocratic delusion. A clique of post–New Dealers and New Republicans with great means at its disposal but out of touch with history, and therefore with reality, has inaugurated a new mode of insuring the nation's safety.

It is frightening to realize how many of our policies of the most important and far-reaching kind are being predicated upon a thinking which is thus narrow. Most of the "aid" phase of our foreign effort is based upon the supposition, and tends to further encourage at home the supposition, that if we will but feed, house, and clothe the world, the world will become amiable, and we will not even have problems to worry about. Of the exponents of this type of thinking Nelson Rockefeller seems to be the most fatuous. Now he has broached a scheme for an Inter-American Housing Authority, the object of which will be to provide every Latin American with decent housing in the North American sense. This is being put forward as a foundation for hemispheric solidarity. It is the politics of subsidy again, without the necessary element of knowledge and realism. Some years ago Professor William S. Stokes wrote a remarkable article entitled "The Drag of the Pensadores" in which he demonstrated that the reason the Latin American countries are behind the United States industrially is not that they are too poor or too illiterate or too unstable politically; it is simply that industrialism does not consort with the way of life which cultivated Latin

Americans—who are among the most cultivated people in the world—
envisage as the best for man. The whole trend and emphasis of their culture
is in more aesthetic, more hedonistic directions. There is no assurance in
history that industrialism and its kind of prosperity would make them any
happier or any more inclined to love us. I think of the expression of *want-
lessness* which I once saw in Mexico on the face of a peasant in from the
hills. There is dignity in that too. And I think of what Japan did with industrialism about fifty years after the Western nations had made her an
almost enforced gift of it.

Some while ago I was discussing a problem not unrelated to this with a
college professor, and a professor of English, of all people. Without flourish
or ado, he injected into the discussion this question: "Can you think of any
business class in history which has ever tried to do anything except pay off
when it felt itself threatened?" The question came like a judgment. When I
tried, I could not think of such a class, though I muttered something about
not everything having been seen yet and the possibility that businessmen
too could be educated. But the evidence was on the other side—the mass
give-away programs of the last decade and a half, and on the domestic front
the timidity of businessmen about putting up any kind of theoretical opposition to creeping socialization. Let the state take its 52 per cent of the
profits, the mood seems to be; we can live with that sort of arrangement
and still have a good bit left. The thought that a government which takes
52 per cent of the profits is in effect a 52 per cent owner is not raised in the
form of an issue of principle.

Political Thought Excluded

All of this is connected with the way in which at home issues have been
withdrawn from politics. The revealing character of the plutocratic mentality is that it avoids like the plague solutions which require other than
plutocratic thinking. It is a very current complaint, needing no reiteration
here, that there are no longer any real differences between the two major
parties. The old clashes over substantive alternatives are no more; both parties are so nearly for the same things that the voter looking for a reason for
his choice is lucky if he can find as much as a distinction of emphasis. The
explanation is that both parties are now dominated by a plutocratic element

(and this is the element which was so anxious to get rid of Taft) which has insisted upon retiring these matters from discussion so that both can try to win the electorate by the plutocratic method of bribery; that is, by promising every group everything right out of the federal treasury. What is being done on the international scene is thus being done on the domestic scene in other forms and guises. The sclerosis which has attacked political thinking and traditional party controversy has its origin in the belief that if enough money is offered, people will be placated, and this is the new science of politics.

I have many times read newspaper articles about candidates, frequently hundreds of words in length and obviously intended to describe and introduce the candidate to the public, in which there was not a single phrase to indicate what the man stood for or believed in. His parentage, his children, his education, his lodge membership, his hobbies, and perhaps his nominal Republican or Democratic affiliation, but as for what the man thought positively about policy in these days of complexity and crisis—nothing. As far as one could infer from the story, the writer considered that an irrelevance. Or perhaps he merely thought it would be boring to the readers. And indeed political candidates today are of the faceless type. A stencil has been prepared. The candidate must be "youthful" (why not older and presumably wiser?), handsome or at least personable (what has happened to the unhandsome, gnarled, or hardbitten type, whose very angularity of feature was thought to express character and firmness of conviction?), "forward-looking" (toward what?), and "liberal" or at least "moderate," which is the utmost concession made toward recognizing a conservatism of principle. It is an empty type, far more suggestive of the entertainment world than of that world where life and death problems furrow brows and through which geniality is not the passkey. Small wonder the writer of the story does not ask him his politics; it would be like asking a popular band leader to declare himself in the midst of a program. The plutocratic mind is not looking for issues, and the politician cannot afford to be a square.

The most insidious inroads of the plutocratic habit of mind, however, are in the world of education. Increasingly we have been propagandized to the effect that money is the cure-all for what ails our schools. Bigger and more elaborate plants, higher salaries, and more gadgetry seem to spell for educators and politicians alike the remedy for what are quite serious educational shortcomings. Now this has its evil fruit in the campaign to put education on the federal payroll. Once there, the problems of the educationists, as they visualize them, will be solved, for it will be impossible ever to get it off again. People have got to realize that federal aid to education is inevitable, one educator recently remarked smugly in a public address, because only the federal government has adequate taxing power. There we are in on a secret. The fact that a proliferation of what are called facilities is already in many instances getting in the way of true educational accomplishment makes no impression upon these brethren. Education too has learned how to featherbed.

Education's Purpose Missed

The same tendencies are showing up in the thinking of students, for it is no longer the style to look upon the period of education as a time when the body lives abstemiously so that the mind can be active. Recently an official of the University of Texas declared that while it would be possible to plan for a university that would accommodate 40,000 students, it would not be possible to plan for one that would accommodate 40,000 automobiles. Recently also I saw a study made in a high school showing the correlation between academic performance and ownership of or access to an automobile. The correspondence was perfect; the students who had little or no access to an automobile made the highest marks; those who had one at their disposal made the lowest, with the intermediate marks being distributed *pro rata*.

Then one thinks of the time much less than a century ago when in the colleges, and in the academies too, the students rose at six o'clock, made their own fires, washed in cold water, and marched off to face a curriculum composed of Greek, Latin, and mathematics, with English and history as the lighter subjects, and one begins to smell rottenness again. The idea that Mark Hopkins at one end of a pine bench and a student at the other can constitute a university is not part of the plutocratic consciousness.

Thus the educators are beginning at the wrong end just as are our social engineers. It used to be axiomatic that education concerns what inheres in the mind and the personality. The relationship of things to these was incidental and peripheral. The purpose of education was acknowledged to be the enlargement of the capacities of the individual, for which some discipline, self-regulation, and even self-denial were considered necessary. Now considered necessary is a mounting pile of things which obscure the true role of education as a regimen. Qualities may be a source of discomfiture in that they remind us that we do not have them or do not have them in enough measure. But it is treason to the very idea of education to be complacent toward the pupil as he is. I realize that much of this has come in via the road of progressive education, but not a little can be blamed upon the accumulation of material comforts and the belief that these somehow ought to take the pain out of education. Students have been encouraged to feel that there are many things of the material kind which have a rightful claim to large allocations of their attention. My simple query is, what can be the fate of discipline and concentration in these circumstances? The flabbiness which has overtaken so much of our cultural life has its source in the neglect of those matters which appertain most closely to character. Character develops in response to inner and outer checks, and a check is always in the form of a negative. But in the new climate of yea-saying to all wants, negatives are not popular.

"Well, it's no crime to be poor," I heard a lady observe a good many years ago. This proposition is now definitely dated. Only lately I saw in a leading woman's magazine an article which was one long commiseration with the people of the Southern mountains because their annual income is considerably below the national average. The author was going all out to be friendly and sympathetic, but it was evident that the crime of the Southern hillmen was being relatively poor, and of course something must be done about crime! When I thought of the traditional qualities of these people— their pride and independence, their dislike of being beholden to anyone and especially to the government, their sturdy love of country, their contempt for danger, and the contributions they have made to our martial history from Davy Crockett to Alvin York—and then thought of what he wanted to do to them, I felt a sense of outrage. The intention was well-meaning but the assumption was blind; a saccharine plutocratic Liberalism was out to conquer one of our last strongholds of virility and individualism. Jacob Burckhardt, who discerned in the nineteenth century so many things which have grown to plague us in the twentieth, summed it up this way: "Nobody knows how to be poor any more."

The Economic Obsession

It is odd how in these plutocratic dreams both at home and abroad we seem to have assimilated unconsciously one or more of the premises of our great enemy. Philosophically the most basic tenet of the Communists is that economic activity is the primary activity; ideas and institutions are little more than epiphenomena, bubbles cast up by the stream of economic process. Therefore all effective thinking about human affairs starts from this and in fact never leaves it. Any event is referable to an underlying economic situation, and is indeed contained by it and explained through it. Consequently if we attend to economic wants, all other things will be given to us. Our only difference is that we say capitalism, with the aid of a lot of state management, can achieve the same goal. The difference for the Soviets is that they have their perverted idealism to give them a perverse strength. They are not surfeited with goods, and the prospect of their world crusade produces tonicity instead of flabbiness.

The question becomes one of survival. The choice lies between assuming that a plethora of goods will prepare a nation for victory in struggle, and assuming that the development of qualities—what the Romans comprehended in their word *virtus*—is not and never will be dispensable. The oracles of secular Liberalism and statism have concluded that the simple broadcast of wealth is the answer to life's challenges. Our mastery of the physical world, they appear to reason, has caused us to pass a critical point, so that we need no longer be concerned with those forces which derive from physical vigor and character. *Virtus* like honor is now something for the museum.

But life has other challenges, and the testimony of history is against those who place their faith in a material sufficiency. My prediction is that the test of whether a people or a nation will survive still depends on the mettle that is in them and not on the appurtenances that they own. All possessions are in fact detachable. What is not detachable is the constitution of the man. His capacity to endure physical hardship and his ability to think clear and straight take precedence as gifts over his belongings. The former may insure the latter, but the latter cannot insure the former.

Plutocratic thinking begins by ruling out this unpleasant conclusion, which is that the man will have to stand a test as a man and not just as a possessor of outward means. At one time such thinking was characteristic of only a few persons, who had allowed their possessions to distort their vision. Now it is becoming characteristic of the masses, and as our leaders tend to become more and more followers, out of their fear of pressure groups, it is the line which they feed back to the masses. Is there any way of avoiding an epitaph which would read, "Here lies the world's greatest plutocracy"? It is too early to despair, but certainly a mountain pile of stuff and guff about progress and comfort will have to be swept away before anything can be done. Much of it has appeared with the imprint of universities and from the hands of professors attached to these. Much of it has been transmitted by politically motivated politicians. And journals of high and low opinions have contributed a mighty share. Until it is removed, we will not be able to see man as a creature of more than appetitive function, whose training must include the disciplines of rigor and denial. But it needs the word and the special power of a prophet to wake us up to the necessity. A prophet in a plutocracy is a rebel. Of course he would not have to be honored in his own country in order to save it.

Review of Leo Baeck,
The Pharisees and Other Essays[1]

This is a collection of studies of comparative religion and culture by a celebrated spokesman of European Jewry. It considers a wide variety of subjects, including Pharisaism, Jewish mysticism, Greek and Jewish preaching, and the influence of Judaism on Christianity.

The work as a whole is brilliantly and persuasively written, but one must call attention to the implications of certain ideas. If there is one lesson which the experience of our generation has underscored, it would seem to be the danger inherent in any program of separatism. Yet the title essay constitutes an apology for an historic program of this kind. Here we find the Pharisees praised for their "consciousness of being different and of belonging together in and through their religion." We read further that their sense of community rested upon a feeling that "the land was their land, its soil was holy in their eyes, and they wanted to make it a realm of purity, of 'separateness.'" This sounds oddly akin to some contemporary doctrines which have been censured for advancing the principle of exclusiveness. The author's argument that such voluntary isolation was a means toward universalism and a connection with humanity on a higher plane is seductive rather than solid and convincing.

Perhaps the most interesting essay of the group is "Two World Views Compared." In this the author employs a contrast of the predominantly esthetic world view of Hellenism with the predominantly ethical, activistic world view of Judaism to reveal his opposition to the idea of stasis in theological conception. The Greek ideal, he says, was something consummated and static; the Jewish ideal is creative. He gives large credit for the undermining of the Middle Ages, in which "statics . . . gave place to dynamics

1. *The Commonweal*, 46/20, August 29, 1947, 484.

and the consummated work of art to the function," to the philosophy of the Old Testament. The author is too complacent, it seems to me, in passing from this to an assertion of the superiority of the Hebraic deity as a living god who "creates in order to continue to create." This concept encounters on one level insuperable metaphysical difficulties. On another, through its doctrine of the endlessness of becoming, it would leave us in the morass of Dewey's instrumentalism. In fact, the author affirms in his concluding essay that Judaism, because of its undogmatic character, "can never be refuted— one can only live opposed to it."

Generally speaking, his position confronts us with all the dilemmas of "progressive" religion. It can be seen that Jewish liberalism, of which the author is a well-known exponent, does not differ materially from other forms of religious liberalism.

Baeck was a leading rabbi of Berlin. During the years of Hitler's ascendency he served as president of a council created to represent German Jewry. In 1943 at the age of seventy he was sent to Theresienstadt concentration camp, where despite conditions he was able to organize study groups and continue his life work as teacher.

Review of Beatrice Webb, *Our Partnership*[1]

From the time they became man and wife in 1892, Beatrice Potter and Sidney Webb worked together for half a century in the cause of social reform. *Our Partnership* covers the years 1892–1912, during which this indefatigable pair helped to guide the Fabian Society, wrote a definitive history of trade unionism, labored to reform the London County Council, and established, with the assistance of a few others, the University of London.

All of these are achievements of some magnitude, but it would be easy to exaggerate the interest of this book for the average reader. It consists primarily of extracts from contemporary diaries kept by the author, connected by brief passages of narrative and exposition. Much that is here related will appear dry unless one comes to the book with a special interest in the spadework of social reform.

There is one respect, however, in which it should bring delight to any reader of normal sensitivity, for it carries one back to that era of sanity ending in 1914 when it seemed that the patient collecting of fact, the writing of solid books, and the making of enlightened speeches might early bring about the millennium. We have had to revise our estimates since then, but it gives one the pleasant sense of innocence regained to return even for a night to a period in which such optimism seemed justified.

Mrs. Webb found time to set down, amid the statistics and endless records of meetings, a few sharp characterizations of the leading figures of her day. The work of the two, both in and out of politics, brought them into contact with every sort of notable, from labor leaders on one side to staunch conservatives on the other. It must be confessed that these little sketches are without regard to the political affiliation of their subjects. Britain was becoming acquainted back in the 1890s with prima donna-ism among labor leaders, and some of their portraits are done with an acid pen. John Burns,

1. *The Commonweal*, 48/7, May 28, 1948, 166–67.

to cite a single example, is characterized as "unscrupulous, incurably suspicious," and "a born leader of barbarians." Others appear in scarcely more flattering light.

It is doubtful whether many reformers have had less trust in the wisdom and capacity of the common man. The Webbs believed in government for him, but hardly by him. Here are a few typical observations: "We have little faith in the 'average sensual man,' we do not believe that he can do much more than describe his grievances, we do not think that he can prescribe the remedies." "I do not believe that the ordinary man is capable of prescribing for the diseases of the soul any more than they are for the diseases of the body." "We staked our hopes on the organized working-class, served and guided, it is true, by an *élite* of unassuming experts who would make no claim to superior social status, but would content themselves with exercising the power inherent in superior knowledge and longer administrative experience."

From this ideal of service they never deviated, and in a world plagued with selfishness and malevolence, their work must remain a monument of goodwill to men.

Review of Samuel H. Beer, *The City of Reason*[1]

In *The City of Reason* Professor Beer has attempted the kind of thing which academic people are often considered incapable of—an original contribution to thought instead of to learning. Or, if the achievement is not strictly original thought, it is an original application. He has taken the philosophy of A. N. Whitehead and has erected upon it a theodicy and a politics.

The publisher describes the work as a philosophy of liberalism; and it could well be regarded as an effort to find some solid content for that usually empty and deceptive expression. One may be sure that a few who have freedom at heart are dismayed by the shallowness of many who carry the liberal banner; and Professor Beer is trying to show that liberalism rests upon something more fundamental than the position from which certain liberal weeklies tend to argue. It is not easy to gauge his success.

I imagine that the reader will be first of all impressed by the amount of conservative or even "reactionary" doctrine that the author finds it necessary to put in his foundations. He quotes approvingly Whitehead's statement that "The theory of induction is the despair of philosophy"; he cites the presence of wholes in nature as proof that the world is neither chaotic nor purposeless; he even declares that the social scientist must take the soul seriously. His own liberalism rests on a principle that the world is creative, and his theodicy on the idealist premise that "nothing is lost."

He accepts Whitehead's basic picture of the universe as consisting of (1) an infinite conceptual realization, (2) the free physical realizations in the temporal world, and (3) the ultimate unity of the first two. These are described as equivalent to the Primordial Nature of God, the temporal world, and the Consequent Nature of God. Accordingly, through a process to

1. *The Commonweal*, 50/3, April 29, 1949, 73.

which Whitehead gives the name "concrescence" everything is developing toward a Saving Order.

The structure seems weakest to me in the doctrine of final cause. In order to leave the universe creative, Whitehead rejects the concept of a limited number of "forms" or "ends." This universe is realizing a pre-existent potentiality, yet its creations, which are actualizations of the potentiality, are "genuinely novel." There appears to me a contradiction here which is not entirely clarified by the quotation from Niebuhr to the effect that "eternity will fulfill and not annul the richness and the variety which the temporal process has elaborated."

After saying that this work represents a piece of independent thinking, I must add that it suffers somewhat from the scholar's inveterate habit of taking a text solemnly. When the author speaks of the doctrines of other men, there is a certain tediousness of elaboration which one associates with the study. He has moreover a tendency to corroborate his own points by appeals to celebrated names and celebrated systems. This is the way academic theses are substantiated, but it is not the way documents of deep insight are written.

Every generous man must applaud the intention the book represents, but it would be sanguine to prophecy a great influence.

Review of Daniel Bell (ed.), *The New American Right*[1]

This volume contains seven essays, most of them previously published, by historians and social scientists seeking to define and dissect what is termed "the new American right." Their differences in content, method, and tone are so great that it is difficult to characterize them, except by saying that they are all opposed to it, as preachers are opposed to sin. Some attack it by denunciation; others try to analyze it into thin air. An underlying but obvious purpose is to preach the funeral sermon of Senator McCarthy.

Daniel Bell writes a sober covering essay on "Interpretations of American Politics." But following him, Richard Hofstadter tries to demonstrate that only those who accept the Eisenhower brand of liberalism are true conservatives, all others being pseudo-claimants to the name. Peter Viereck goes through some spectacular gyrations in an effort to prove that "McCarthyism is not anti-Communist," and that the new push from the right is really a plebeian radical movement, with shocking historical antecedents. Professor Talcott Parsons argues blandly that McCarthy sentiment is only a symptom of emotional strains, which will disappear as soon as the nation has achieved a life adjustment to the international chaos.

David Riesman and Nathan Glazer interpret the new right as an alliance between certain "demi-intellectuals" and "the discontented classes." This essay is an amazing tissue of presumption and innuendo. The complacency with which these writers assume that the East is the depository of all wisdom and virtue whereas the West is inhabited only by sons of the wild jackass has to be seen to be believed. The trouble with the discontented classes, they allege, is that they have not come to "the large civilizing cities," but instead have gone "to Wichita or Rock Island . . . to Houston or San

1. Submitted to the *Chicago Tribune* in February 1956 but no evidence of publication.

Diego." On the other hand "the Baptist Rockefeller, coming from Cleveland where he was educated, allowed Easterners to help civilize him." After this, one is not surprised by the categorical assertion that "New ideas have their headquarters in New York." Viereck chimes in on the same theme; to him the current rightist surge is mostly "a Midwest hick Protestant revenge" against Ivy League prestige and sophistication.

The most valuable essay in the group is Seymour Martin Lipset's "The Sources of the 'Radical Right.'" He avoids the wild swinging of Riesman, Glazer, and Viereck and gives a thoughtful discussion of the roots of the more extreme anti-leftist feeling.

The book is quite uneven, and the reader is advised to read at his own risk.

Illusions of Illusion[1]

The expanding conservative movement must expect to find a variety of works directed against its philosophical and political position. This is, among other things, a witness to its present importance and promise for the future. Furthermore, it is not impossible to think that some of these works will bring criticism which can be assimilated. Conservatives remain in this age almost the only believers in tolerance; in any age I think they will respect the spiritual admonition present in T. S. Eliot's saying: "One needs the enemy." The enemy helps one to define oneself: he can arouse conscience and bring chastisement for errors.

At least this is what I would have been willing to say before reading M. Morton Auerbach's *The Conservative Illusion*. Now I begin to doubt; unless the critics of conservatism can furnish something more real than this, there is little chance that the great conversation can be profitably continued very long. I have said "something more real" because I would indicate at the beginning the general nature of this work. *The Conservative Illusion* sets out to do a complete demolition job on a point of view and a philosophy which are older than Burke, older than Plato, older than the Bible, because they go back to the ancient time when people first began to reflect about the nature of man, the nature of creation, and the manifold relations between the two. The project is, to say the least, ill-advised, and the actual achievements are incidental. Still, as an example of the recourses the enemies of conservatism may try in their alarm, the book is worth examining.

One begins to understand the presumptuousness of the attempt after looking at the author's method. By a combination of dialectic and hypostatization he manages to create a definition of conservatism so artificial and so brittle that it shatters easily upon contact with historical circumstances,

1. *Modern Age*, 4/3, Summer 1960, 316–20.

which he is always ready to supply in abundance. According to Professor Auerbach, if the conservative steps one foot in one direction, he becomes a "reactionary"; let him step one foot in another and he is a "liberal"; one foot in another and he is an "authoritarian." And if he stays in the little corner that is defined for him, Professor Auerbach has a special set of postulates to belabor him with.

It is most revealing to note that although Professor Auerbach's great enemy is Plato, to whom he attributes most of the afflictions that come in the form of conservatism, he is thus constantly indulging in the worst, the least acceptable kind of Platonizing. Under his examination almost everybody turns out to be something less, or other, than a conservative because some of his beliefs do not square with the rigid, archetypal idea which has been set up. And such failures to measure up even in minor matters are used to pronounce conservatism an illusion. In its formal aspect the book is one long exercise in definition-chopping. Following out his method, he arrives at the absurdity of declaring that the Dark Ages and the Late Middle Ages have been the only conservative societies.

It is not easy to locate the real point of the author's attack. His argument is so bound up with these stipulative definitions and at the same time so reiterative that one can get lost in the mazes and repetitions. As far as I can make out, however, the case is approximately as follows: there may be conservative values, but they can never get themselves translated into reality, at least under the aegis of conservatism. The result is that the conservative must either abandon his attempt and become "alienated," contenting himself perhaps with writing a *Utopia;* or he must try by force to get them realized and so transform himself into an "authoritarian"; or else (note the crossing of boundaries of definition again) he must become a "liberal" by largely accepting the institutions and methods of the time, while wearing some conservative trappings. I must say that the conservative thinkers of my acquaintance know nothing of these inhibitions which he so pontifically lays upon them.

Still, conceding that all of these courses can be followed, there is no real ground for presenting them as inevitable. What makes them appear so in the author's exposition is a peculiar metaphysic of history which pervades the book from end to end. He sets up a concept of abstract, inexorable

historical forces which have no relationship to human will or purpose. In fact, there is no conservative principle that he is more vocal against than belief in the primacy of ideas and values. Consequently, whenever he wants to write *finis* to a political doctrine, all he has to do is invoke his conjuror's term and say that "historical forces" make it irrelevant.

But the reader still wants to know why historical forces, even of the kind he visualizes, make conservatism more irrelevant than other political philosophies. Here it becomes necessary to look more closely at the idea of conservatism which he has codified. The term which he uses most frequently in designating its essence is "harmony." I suspect that this may be an evasion of a more accurate word which would be embarrassing for the author to handle. The word is *order*. Order, or harmony as an expression of order, I would agree, is the goal which most if not all conservative thinking has in view.

Now the present author appears to believe that because ours has been increasingly an age of conflict, the conservative ideal of order must be abandoned as an impossibility. I quote from page 85: "Conservatism seeks 'community,' tradition, harmony, and quiescence. In this century it has found organization, violence, political powers, and revolutionary upheaval." If these two sentences are taken as premises, what conclusion is to be drawn? The conclusion I would draw is that however incompletely conservatism may be realizing itself, it offers the remedy for the major evils besetting our era.

No informed person will deny that conservatism, with its passion for an order reflecting a meaningful hierarchy of the goods, has been having a rough time for several decades. That is evidenced by the common admission that we are passing through a period of exceptional crises. But to pass from the presence of conflict to a conclusion that control and discipline and order have no place in the world is to reverse the process by which political judgments should be arrived at.

Any theory of political ordering has some difficulty in actualizing and maintaining itself in the face of empirical reality; and any such difficulty can be interpreted as a "tragic" limitation. It is highly characteristic of the author's militant secular liberalism that he is very impatient with the idea of tragedy. Anything containing an element of the tragic is repudiated by him for this reason, and if in some places he makes himself appear difficult to argue with, it is largely because he has left out this dimension of reality.

And correspondingly it is because he shies away from any such recognition that he can insist upon the unrealistic standards of complete consistency and triumph for the politically permissible. In his account, as previously noted, conservatives are always being "defeated" by adjusting themselves to the liberal trend, or by becoming alienated, or they are undone by the contradictions in their own doctrines.

He is a great one to find contradictions in everybody, and he rests so much of his case upon this kind of discovery that something must be said about it as a point of argument. To show that a political system or a political thinker exhibits contradictions is not nearly so serious a charge as he assumes his readers are ready to believe. I will hazard that such can be proved more or less about any comprehensive system which has ever been put forward. What the contradictions may, and certainly in many cases do indicate is that the author of the system is at grips with reality. The contradictions are not of course good things in themselves, but they are evidences of a referential relationship to the world, and they may be resolved on a higher level. Thus they are often signs of vitality.

I would take a position quite the contrary of Professor Auerbach's and say that the system which has everything perfectly blueprinted is far more to be suspected as to its origin and viability than the one which has not managed to solve a contradiction or two. The conservative believes in order, of course, but not in the perfectly rationalistic order which is a burlesque on what is attainable in the real world. The conservative order is one which encompasses ideals and facts, unity and diversity. It is neither merely natural nor merely intellectualistic; it is an order which seeks to bring together the existential world and a pattern of justice. For Professor Auerbach to suppose that turning up a contradiction in this and that person's position is to administer the *coup de grâce* merely underscores the rigidity of his own thinking.

I am prone to believe that this peculiar quality of the book (which originated as a Columbia University doctoral dissertation) results actually from Professor Auerbach's own isolation from his subject. Let me say here that he sounds throughout like a man who has learned everything that he knows about social orders from books. His understanding never seems to penetrate beyond the verbal representations of the things he is talking about. He appears to have no sense of the emotional factors which cause people to love

and to try to preserve their communities and sometimes to do "contradic-tory" things toward that end. Hence, for all his invocations to history, his own concept of it remains jejeune.

The only way he can maintain his curious thesis is to keep a wedge driven between conservative values and his version of reality. In his eyes, any revo-lution, any significant conflict, any decay of an aristocratic order is another proof that the conservatives have failed. Thus on page 254 we find him preparing what looks like a deadly trap for conservatism: "Unless we are to assume that ideology is an irrelevant construction of the mind, it is essential that values be grounded in history. *History is the real test of ideology,* because history is the critical battleground of the human values which ideology rep-resents." But anyone who recognizes this as nothing more than dialectical materialism can easily slip out of the snare. The truth Professor Auerbach refuses to take note of is that for those who reject positivist philosophies, history is not to be read in simple fashion from the phenomenology of events.

History does not become history until it has been interpreted, and then not merely in regard to preponderance of matter. There may indeed occur confused battle on a darkling plain, but this will not be simply a case of external facts and forces. For the conservative the battle is moral and spiri-tual. The function of the study of history is to heighten the conscience; and this teaches one to resist history as well as to accept it, for events do not legitimize themselves. No matter how many victories Professor Auerbach's historical forces win, he has not secured anything he can defend in terms of value. He leaves history at the level of reportage, whereas the conservative image of history arises out of primal affection and a desire to follow tran-scendental ideals of justice. And it is this that gives content to the philoso-phy of conservatism.

Considerations like these leave one wondering about the alternative he has in view. *The Conservative Illusion* is obviously intended to be destructive criticism, but even in works of the most destructive kind the author usually has somewhere in the wings, so to speak, an idea, a hint, a suggestion of what should appear in place of what he seeks to destroy. The nearest ap-proach to anything of the sort appearing in this polemic is a notion of free-dom which he is heroically rescuing from conservative control.

But the notion lacks clear exposition, and when we put together the vari-

ous pieces, it becomes nothing more than turning ourselves over to the blind historical forces which he has reified. He does, however, give us glimpses of what this kind of freedom will produce. On his own admission it issues in a society where there is more interest in weather control and space travel than in moral problems and political community, and in which "movie stars, crooners, and athletes" will have more prestige than men of thought and character. Such are the historical forces which render conservatism obsolete.

I am left with the feeling that *The Conservative Illusion* is itself a remarkably defeatist book. It is evident from beginning to end that the author cannot abide the idea of a source of order or center of control. Having erected, as he thinks, a heavy tombstone over those who have taught the desirability of such a center, what has he left to offer? It is a politics of infinite dispersion. Everything goes flying off in its own direction; liberalism becomes ever more liberal; hierarchies are toppled so that there is no longer any means of judging one thing as better or worse than another. Moral order is collapsed into something like the universe of modern astrophysics, with everything moving away centrifugally, nobody knows where or why. And this goes on forever, because if at any point one stops and tries to pull back toward a position of value, he becomes a conservative. After more than three hundred pages of tiresome insistence, the author comes to rest with this statement:

> But to offer mankind Conservative harmony as its supreme goal, on the assumption that social and moral forces are decisive in history, is to offer an illusion; and to burden man with a superfluous sense of guilt for failing to achieve an illusion is to make a grim joke of history which has too long borne unnecessary tragedies.

That is a lot of toil to arrive at a conclusion the first half of which is untrue and the second empty rhetoricism.

Review of *The Diary of Pierre Laval*[1]

The publication of the *Diary of Pierre Laval* is one of several signs that the public is growing weary of discussion of the war which is but a churning of epithets, and is ready to begin inquiry into circumstances and motives.

The present work, which in the strict sense is not a diary, but Laval's notes for his own defense, provides a useful occasion to raise some questions about the general nature of collaboration.

The author's case for himself may be quickly summarized. Laval wrote that he believed the French people would suffer less with some shrewd and stubborn negotiator to fend for them against the Germans who had invaded and seized their country than they would in the absence of such an intermediary. "In brief, would it have been in the greater interest of France to abandon it to disorder and to the cruel domination of the conqueror rather than to make the attempt which, in fact, was made to hold off the conqueror by negotiation, thus alleviating, to some extent at least, the load of suffering and hardship." The argument is that even an overthrown France had to have a government, and that he accepted a prominent part in the spirit of self-sacrifice.

It is very important to guard against the mood in which "to understand all is to forgive all"; yet it is none the less true that the practical difficulties of a conquered people are sometimes overlooked. What is the proper role of a citizen when his country has been seized by an invader, and when he is told by his government that resistance is no longer practical? The Anglo-Saxon countries, which have not faced this dilemma in modern times, are prone to give smug and thoughtless answers to that question. After all, in a country of forty millions, not everyone can flee overseas; not everyone can live in the bush. The millions who remain must stand in some sort of rela-

1. *The Commonweal*, 49/5, November 12, 1948, 122.

tionship to the unwelcome guest. Should they be inarticulate as well as overthrown?

In actual cases, whether one who enters into engagements with the victorious enemy is to be regarded as a traitor to his country, or as a patriot called upon to perform an onerous duty seems to have turned upon a purely pragmatic point. If the enemy is destined to be ousted soon, he is the former; if the enemy is there for an indefinite stay, resistance is but intransigence and may do the country more harm than good. And while this standard applies, one's political virtue depends on his skill as a military forecaster. In 1940 Russia was a German ally, and Britain appeared falling. A Frenchman who at that moment knew that the United States would enter the war and turn the tide either must have had power of clairvoyance, or have been in unusually close contact with Washington. As long as the war was but a European war, which the Germans seemed certain of winning, Laval was "right"; later, when it had turned into a war of a Grand Alliance against Germany, he was "wrong." History is replete with cases more or less comparable. Which were the more patriotic, the Filipinos who collaborated with American forces in 1900, or the Moro tribesmen who fought them? Should the Boer General Smuts now be despised as a collaborator with the British? And what of the Germans in Berlin today who are collaborating with the Americans? If the Americans remain, they are "right"; if the Americans withdraw either voluntarily or involuntarily and Germany goes communist, they will be "wrong," probably to the extent of Laval and lose their lives. Laval seems to have been aware of this pragmatic standard when he wrote, "Call in question if you will my good sense, my political sagacity or statesmanship, but not my patriotism."

But if one looks at this problem morally, and not pragmatically, it will appear that what a man is finally judged by is his loyalty to an ideal of justice. If he allies himself with unjust powers, he is a traitor, regardless of whether they come from without or from within. A question of far more general concern then is, what should be the response of a citizen to his own government when it comes to him with unclean hands? Does obedience to a guilty government make the citizen guilty? The upshot of the Nazi trials is that one must place his conscience above his formal allegiance to the state. After this verdict, obviously there is nothing left to the divine right of national sovereignty. It will be interesting to see whether the nations which have made this a principle of international law are willing to admit its application at home. By such a test, to employ a well-known example from our own history, Henry David Thoreau is vindicated for having refused to "collaborate" with the United States in the Mexican War; and any conscientious objector who says that he regards war as the sum of all crimes has an excellent case at law.

The truth about Laval is that he was incapable of rising to such a conception. He was such a *little* man. It is perhaps unfair to base conclusions solely on a document composed in distress, but there is nothing whatever in these notes to indicate imagination, breadth of mind, elevation of sentiment, or even skill in argumentation. Everything that is said is miserably *ad hoc*. His horizons were incredibly narrow. I will cite what seems to me the prime illustration of this. "Honor," he wrote, "is there wheresoever and in whatsoever form the interests of our country can best be defended." He speaks slurringly of ideologies. For him, politics was but trading, carried on in a somewhat more exalted sphere. The modern world seems more and more to thrust these pettifogging souls into positions of highest responsibility. Their very shortsightedness is often a factor in their popularity. But the world, it is the old world yet in the sense that tragic mistakes are paid for in tragic consequences. When Laval was led out to be shot after his judicial farce of a trial, he can hardly have looked like an arch villain. He too much resembles a little man who guessed wrong, and who was sacrificed to the pent-up passion of men who were no bigger than he was.

Review of Herbert Feis,
The Road to Pearl Harbor[1]

The defeat at Pearl Harbor will remain a salient of American history, one of those outthrusts of events which close one chapter of a nation's story and open another. Such events are always interesting to explore historically; and Pearl Harbor, because it is politically controversial, makes an especially rewarding study. Mr. Herbert Feis' *The Road to Pearl Harbor*, written while the author was a member of the Institute for Advanced Studies at Princeton, is a careful chronicle of the movements in Tokyo and Washington which led up to the overt action of the Japanese.

I can think of several ways in which the usefulness of this book might be conceived. It might be regarded simply as a detailed story of how one war came about. It might be considered a case book for diplomats in times of international tension. It might be regarded as an inquiry into the problem of what constitutes an aggressor. In the present posture of affairs, perhaps the third is the best focus of our interest.

The basis of conflict between Japan and the United States in the Orient is well known. The Japanese, probably reasoning from historical analogy, considered themselves entitled to hegemony in East Asia. They contemplated a hierarchy of countries in this wide area, with Japan at the top as leader and protector. The United States, for its part, insisted that East Asia remain a group of politically equal countries, and that no change be made in the *status quo* except through peaceful means. Actually the American position was another "containment" policy. As Mr. Feis puts it: "The terms offered by the American government would have meant that Japan accept defeat; give up the gains of past effort, and the prospect of future expansion."

1. *The Commonweal*, 53/1, October 13, 1950, 20–22.

When two powers find their policies irreconcilable, they go on the defensive. This sounds innocent enough until one begins to examine the nature and content of defense. Soldiers have understood from the beginning what the public has been told only in recent times, namely, that the best defense is a good offense. But under the new code of international ethics, an offense is a crime. Now if the best defense is a good offense, and an offense is a crime, it follows that the best defense is a crime. This dilemma, posed by the different avenues of diplomatic military thinking, faced Japan in 1940 – 41, and will continue to face all those who toy with the notion of preventive war. In Japan, after much casting about among alternatives, in which there seems to have been real appreciation of the dangers involved, the military conception of "best defense" prevailed and led to the disabling raid upon Pearl Harbor. This is the course of political and military affairs which Mr. Feis has laid out in detail.

It is always pertinent to estimate the degree of objectivity in a work of this kind. If the measurement of objectivity is the amount of fact, direct quotation, and documentary evidence supplied, then *The Road to Pearl Harbor* is objective and may be considered a work of scholarship. But more than this is needed to make a narrative, and when one looks at the connecting links, the interpretations and characterizations, one finds it anything but objective. Thus when Mr. Feis is less than a third of the way through, one finds him writing: "In this act Matsuoka and the men he served showed themselves most clearly as they were: displaced villains out of nineteenth-century American melodrama, advancing upon the obstinate object of their affection with white words and black hearts." What kind of political science is this? And what does it do, except excite feeling, to say of a Japanese Imperial Conference: "The tail of the serpent wound round to its mouth"? Many more instances could be cited. This work pretends to be an impartial examination of evidence, but outbursts like these are pleadings.

In the author's long report of diplomatic maneuvers, cabinet discussions, and official communications, one human incident stands out. The incident is reported in Prime Minister Konoye's *Memoirs*. In a general conference, the Emperor was questioning the heads of army and navy about the probable length of a Japanese-American war.

> . . . the Emperor recalled that the General had been Minister of War at the time of the outbreak of the China Incident, and that he had then informed

the Throne that the incident would be disposed of in about one month. He pointed out that despite the General's assurance, the incident was not yet concluded after four long years of fighting. In trepidation the Chief of Staff went to great lengths to explain that the extensive hinterland of China prevented the consummation of operations according to the scheduled plan. At this the Emperor raised his voice and said that if the Chinese hinterland was extensive, the Pacific was boundless. He asked how the General could be certain of his three months calculation. The Chief of Staff hung his head, unable to answer.

Review of Ferdinand A. Hermens,
Europe Between Democracy and Anarchy[1]

It would be a loss if the generality of Professor Hermens' title were allowed
to obscure the well-defined issue he discusses. In the work itself the issue is
perfectly focused: it is the question of whether democracy can be maintained under conditions of proportional representation, a system of election
which has won wide support in modern times, especially in Europe.

At first glance it might seem unrealistic to augur the success of a democratic government from so formal a thing as the system of choosing representatives; but the extensive evidence collected by Professor Hermens
shows the contrary. And here let it be said that this is an inductive study.
The author presents to his readers a thoroughgoing survey of representative
governments in various parts of the world in an effort to find some correlation between their stability and power to govern and the means by which
their parliaments are chosen.

This survey leads him to characterize the majority system of election
as "positive democracy" and the system of proportional representation as
"negative democracy." The advantage of the majority system is that it places
in power a single cohesive group, which has declared its intention, and
which has been chosen by the voters to carry out a definite program. The
disadvantage of the system of proportional representation is that it leads to
the "fractionalization" of political life; that it thus renders the formation of
a government with a single will very difficult; and that such governments as
it leaves possible usually totter from crisis to crisis as they bid for support
from minor parties in the effort to keep up their voting strength. This circumstance often leads to a condition of "parliamentary paralysis," and in
such conditions the appeal of direct action may become very strong.

1. *The Commonweal*, 54/11, June 22, 1951, 266.

Nowhere does the problem of reconciling democracy with authority and action come out more clearly than in this difference. In theory, democracy provides a *pro rata* representation of every group, force, or unit of opinion large enough to be counted. Yet if it does nothing more than this, it may not provide a government which can govern. Somehow there has to be an institutional arrangement whereby the preponderating force can take over and constitute itself the government. The vanquished minority may remain vocal, but it must not be allowed to put a spoke in the wheel at every opportunity to impede the work of the governing party.

Few have understood this better than Abraham Lincoln, whose observations on majority rule made in the First Inaugural Address are appropriately quoted on Professor Hermens' title page. In this very connection it is interesting to recall that in the election of 1860, Lincoln polled only 1,866,000 votes out of 4,680,000 cast, or a plurality of hardly 40%. Had a system of proportional representation been in effect in this country, it seems questionable whether a vigorous policy could have been pushed in that crisis.

I have emphasized that this is an inductive study, and let me say further that the author carefully traces the role of proportional representation in the rise of Italian Fascism and German National Socialism. In regard to the former, he notes that after the election of 1921 "there were in the Chamber . . . fifteen Communists and thirty-five Fascists, including Mussolini, none of whom would have been elected under the majority system." With reference to Germany, he writes that after 1930: "Hopelessness and despair spread all over the country, in particular among the young generation, and the extremists used the ample opportunities given them by PR [proportional representation] to exploit it to the full." Within three years Hitler was Chancellor of the Reich.

Such are the facts; as to the generalization to be made upon them, I think it would be hard to improve upon that of the Italian scholar whom Professor Hermens quotes: "The majority system asks the voter to do something which he can do, namely, to give an answer to the concrete question concerning political leaders and the measures they propose. PR demands something from him which he cannot do: he is asked to exercise an option between different political world outlooks which he is not able to understand."

Professor Hermens' book is a valuable document for contemporary political science, but I would not seem to take it for granted that he will convince everyone. Actually there are vexing questions at the heart of the problem he discusses. How much should one concede to the expediency of workability? Surely some governments which have been admired for their efficiency or for their survival value have contained dangers to the spirit. Is it well to try to get along without some conscious option between political world views? Is it right, after all, to suppress the "polar positions," as by his account the majority system tends to do? Sometimes the middle ground, which it appears to encourage, turns out to be a dead center. These questions will trouble some consciences, but it is all to the good to have a thesis made which will affect us at that level.

Nehru: Philosopher, Prophet, Politician [1]

No fact has been more disturbing to Western confidence than the refusal of India to side fully with the West in the Korean conflict. The long history of India as the spiritual leader of the East, together with widespread moral support of its independence movement, has given that country a kind of sanctuary, so that the rougher appellations applied to other nations in time of international disagreement have hardly seemed suited to it. We feel that India is a kind of prophet or sage among the nations, whereas the rest are but political hucksters or worse. I imagine that considerations of this sort led Mr. Cousins to seek his interview with Prime Minister Nehru, and to publish the recorded transcript of his two conversations in book form. (*Talks with Nehru.* Jawaharlal Nehru and Norman Cousins. John Day. $2.)

These sixty pages of question and answer are best studied for the glimpse they give of the Indian leader's mind. Not that they are greatly revealing; there are some indications that Nehru was trying to get through a dull occasion with the least wear and tear possible; and no doubt the head of a state soon comes to realize that the moment he steps beyond generalities, he is in trouble. Notwithstanding these limitations, the broad lineaments are there, and they have something to tell us about present and pending East–West differences.

Let me say before going further that the man looms large. Prime Minister Nehru seems to belong to a class elsewhere almost extinct, the political leader whose opinions have some basis in philosophy. He speaks with wisdom and prophecy, and it will be far better for us to try to understand what he is saying than to assume, on superficial evidences, that India is lost to our side.

For Nehru the prospects of civilization are darkened by what is happen-

1. *The Commonweal*, 54/18, August 10, 1951, 432–33.

ing to the individual man. As the mentality of the crowd everywhere gains ascendancy, the conditions necessary to his creative development are deteriorating. The result is a "de-individualization and brutalization" which leaves him irresponsible. Yet he admits that in many departments of life the forces making for centralization seem inexorable.

The view of democracy of one so situated is naturally of the utmost import to us. Democracy should cease to put so much faith in slogans. "The Communist lives on slogans. Some of the slogans are not bad, but I dislike most slogans. They prevent the person from thinking. All slogans, I think, are rather confusing, although they may contain an element of truth in them. So let us face this problem, certainly in a moral way, in a spiritual way, and, if I may say so, in a reverent way and, if I may also say so, with always the idea at the back of my mind that I may not be wholly right."

The key phrase in this passage, it seems to me, is "in a reverent way." In the last analysis of forces, probably the greatest enemy democracy faces is aggressiveness; but it is the height of unwisdom to suppose that aggressiveness shows itself only in the form of military force. There is a psychological aggressiveness, an industrial aggressiveness, a kind of aggressiveness nourished by vanity; and it would be tedious to point out that some nations which consider themselves democratic and peace-loving have been the chief bearers of these aggressive complexes. Military conflict is the final product, of which these are the breeders. We need therefore to attend closely to the following: "I would say that democracy is not only political, not only economic, but something of the mind, as everything is ultimately something of the mind. . . . It involves a certain contemplative tendency, and a certain inquisitive search for truth—and for, let us say, the right thing. . . . Ultimately it is a mental approach applied to our political and economic problems." "A certain contemplative tendency!" How seldom do we see this named as one of the components of democracy! But here are the two almost forgotten virtues, reverence and contemplativeness, placed at the base of democratic mentality. It is a counsel to resist the temptation of imperiousness (surely the psychological forerunner of imperialism) and to cultivate a willingness to let some things be. There is even more direct language on the point: "But I am terribly afraid of people who talk about morality or about crusading. The whole conception in India was built up, if you look at Indian history, on the principle of nonproselytization."

It must be understandable why a man for whom these are essential verities cannot go along with the clichés of thought that seem to fetter Western minds, even in high circles of government. To Nehru the United Nations is good in formal outline; yet a legal structure is not enough, especially if large bodies of the world's population are ignored. It will be an effective instrumentality only when "the organization itself begins to represent what might be called the will of the world community." He believes that communism and nationalism, although they have worked together in Asia in the last twenty-five years, are coming into increasing conflict. When conflict occurs, nationalism proves the stronger. For these reasons he does not believe that China is a puppet of Soviet Russia. The two are allied in various ways, but at every critical point "China decides for itself what it has to do and what it has not to do." He feels that the present Chinese government is "very representative of the large majority of the Chinese people."

Fears that Nehru and his followers may become adherents of Bolshevist communism seem groundless, largely because of the legacy of Gandhi. Gandhi taught the leaders of the independence movement that means should never be subordinated to ends. This lesson made a deep impression upon Nehru, and is here cited with approval.

One political fact which emerges with steady clarity in the Prime Minister's statements is the determination of India to maintain its independence. It appears that for the foreseeable future, independence is going to be a kind of political absolute for the Indians. The achievement of that independence cost them something, and nothing that threatens it is going to get a moment's consideration by them.

I suggest that this may be the prime factor in India's decision to go its own way. After all, the peoples of the Orient are said to have long memories, and it is certain that we of the West have short ones. A people like that of the United States, which not only forgets quickly but tends to make a virtue of forgetting, fails to understand the difference that can make. If the average American will turn back the pages of his country's history only fifty years, he will be amazed at the things that were being said in his national Congress. I should like to make this point through an example. Little more than half a century has passed since Albert J. Beveridge declared on the floor of the Senate, to the applause of the galleries:

God has not been preparing the English-speaking and Teutonic peoples for a thousand years for nothing but vain and idle self-contemplation and self-admiration. No! He has made us the master organizers of the world to establish system where chaos reigns. . . . He has made us adepts in government that we may administer government among savages and senile peoples.

Pray God the time may never come when Mammon and the love of ease shall so debase our blood that we will fear to shed it for the flag and its imperial destiny.

Now a convenient short memory may keep such facts from rising up to embarrass us, but fifty years is a short time to the peoples of the East, and we may not suppose that they have forgotten them. They are going to make assurance doubly sure that they are not again the victims of such sentiments, and a sufficient grasp of that fact will have to be the foundation of our dealing with them. The modest insistence of Prime Minister Nehru upon such realities may be one of the best contributions to world understanding.

Review of Edward Crankshaw,
Cracks in the Kremlin Wall[1]

This book is an attempt to place the USSR in a true perspective. Mr. Crankshaw's thesis, to cite it very simply, is that most people of the West are victims of their own fears in supposing the Soviet Union to be an enemy of immeasurable strength and cunning. He believes that ideologically, and perhaps otherwise, it is an enemy, but an enemy with motives different from those generally ascribed.

Like some other students of contemporary Russia, Mr. Crankshaw stresses the historic continuity of Russian policy. He thinks it is not Marxism but Russianism that is threatening the Western democracies; or, to put it in his own language: "We are faced no longer with a hostile group of Bolsheviks who happen to be Russians, but with a hostile group of Russians who happen to be Bolsheviks."

If we wish to understand Lenin, for example, we must take into account not only that he was a born materialist and conspirator but also that he was "a born Russian." This factor of national character he seems to regard as the most important in the equation, but there are others which go to explain the complexity of the Soviet government's behavior. One of them is the supreme difficulty of keeping the Soviet Union, with its economic backwardness, its political history and ethnic composition, together as a going political concern. Another is the prevalent fear of Western attack or of "capitalist encirclement."

The Soviet rulers of Russia have responded to this situation with a policy which is a compound of the peculiarly Russian intuition of reality, of Marxist dogma, and of simple gangster tactics. The result has been a course

1. *The Commonweal*, 54/24, September 21, 1951, 582.

highly devious, often contradictory, and very far from anything like a master plan carried out over the years. Mr. Crankshaw rejects the notion that Russia is, in any active sense, embarked upon world conquest as incompatible with Stalin's realism.

I am inclined to think that this is only another fairly good report on Russia by an historian and journalist who has spent time in Moscow. Mr. Crankshaw's analysis of the Russian character rings true, and one may feel profited by this part of the report. But his affirmation that there are cracks in the Kremlin wall because Russian foreign policy (and domestic policy too) is filled with contradictions doesn't say a great deal. Would not an analysis of British or American foreign policy over the past fifteen years show precisely the same thing?

The net effect of *Cracks in the Kremlin Wall* is to make the leaders of the Soviet Union look like human beings—albeit Russian human beings—and that is a proper corrective to the kind of thing we have been getting from less informed sources.

Review of Amaury de Riencourt,
The Coming Caesars[1]

The Coming Caesars may be described as an extended essay on historical patterns which makes some bold predictions about the future of the West. The author's thesis is that America is now well on the road to Caesarian government, and that, since American power will inevitably dominate the world, the age of Caesars is here.

The argument derives such force as it has from a grand historical analogy. In a long and detailed survey, Mr. de Riencourt maintains that Europe stands in the same relation to America in which Greece stood to Rome, and that just as Rome was fated to overcome Greece and master the world, so America is fated to take over Europe and dominate the world of tomorrow. This is supported by a concurring analogy, in which European culture is likened to Greek culture and American civilization to Roman civilization. In his analysis, culture and civilization are distinct stages; a civilization always follows upon a culture and, in a manner of speaking, lives upon the capital the culture has created. As Rome absorbed and to some extent maintained the culture of Greece, so America is absorbing and to some extent maintaining the European cultural heritage. On analogy with Rome, its civilization must end in "a universal state under the sway of a Caesarian ruler."

In developing this case, the author draws many specific parallels between Rome and America. But the decisive parallel for his argument was the adoption by both of the course of expansion and power. He recalls the time when the Americans stood at a crossroads: would they follow the decentralizing lead of Jefferson, or would they "embark upon the road to consolidation, centralization, and fusion, with all that is implied—territorial

1. *Freeman,* 7, October 1957, 61–63.

expansion, increasing national power, and eventual imperialism leading to a profound transformation of the political structure"?

The crucial turn came with the end of the conservative Virginia Dynasty and the beginning of radical democracy under Jackson, with its augmentation of the power of the President. Mr. de Riencourt does not fail to remind us that imperialism and democracy have too often been linked in history for their conjunction to be accidental: "the implacable expansion of vigorous democracy has often been blurred by ideological misconceptions; but it is a stark reality."

The story from this point on deals with the inevitable elevation of the President into a "tribune of the people," which fact has put an end to the original balance of power among the branches of the government. Even Lincoln, with his native democratic instincts, assumed virtually unlimited power during the Civil War and so established precedents which any future "strong man" could use for his own purposes. But it was in Franklin D. Roosevelt that the Americans found their first real "tribune of the people," and it was out of the Tribunitian office that Augustus created the imperial dignity. "Franklin Roosevelt was determined to establish a semidictatorial rule, a personal rule such as none of his strong predecessors would have dared to contemplate in their wildest dreams." And such was his success that when the New Deal was in full operation, "nothing could have been further removed from the parliamentary type of government." With the changes of structure effected by Roosevelt, it now seems almost hopeless to think of diminishing the powers of the President. Many will feel that Mr. de Riencourt hardly exaggerates when he writes: "Today he wears ten hats—as Head of State, Chief Executive, Minister of Foreign Affairs, Chief Legislator, Head of Party, Tribune of the People, Ultimate Arbitrator of Social Justice, Guardian of Economic Prosperity, and World Leader of Western Civilization. Slowly and unobtrusively these hats are becoming crowns and this pyramid of hats is slowly metamorphosing itself into a tiara, the tiara of one man's world imperium."

But skillful as it is in its delineations, the work suffers gravely from obscurity of purpose. In some places the tone suggests that the author wishes to put the Americans on guard against this approaching Caesarism. In other places, he seems to hold people culpable for not appreciating the necessity of Caesarism. In yet other places, he seems to regard Caesarism as one of those inexorable forces which it would be foolish to oppose and idle to try to assist.

To have real value, a book of this kind should isolate with some degree of clarity the cause of Caesarism, as Garet Garrett did so brilliantly in *The People's Pottage*. Then we would have an inkling of where to take hold if we desire to arrest the process. But Mr. de Riencourt's causal analysis is almost hopelessly confused and chaotic. He jumps wildly from the literal to the metaphorical, and from things that could be controlled to things that are by definition uncontrollable. In one place the cause is given as "historical evolution," in other places as "our hearts and minds," "biological laws," "inescapable destiny," etc. The reader may be pardoned if he throws up his hands in discouragement and says that although Mr. de Riencourt has described much, he has proved little or nothing that could be of use to those who hope to save freedom.

SECTION SEVEN

History

Although Weaver made his career as a professor of English, much of his work in politics, culture, and literature necessarily included a strong historical component. He was therefore quite pleased when he was asked in 1959 to teach the University of Chicago's year-long course in the History of Western Civilization. As he noted to Donald Davidson, he liked the assignment because "it will make appear less academically ambiguous the kind of writing I seem destined to do."[1] This section brings together in three small groups his miscellaneous historical writings.

The section begins with two discussions of Lord Acton. Preparation of "Liberalism with a Ballast," a 1954 review essay devoted to three books by or about him, first stimulated Weaver's interest in the man. Six years later he published his own study, "Lord Acton: The Historian as Thinker," in Modern Age. The next three items—a review essay, a review, and a speech, spanning fourteen years of Weaver's life—all address the question of whether, in the formulation of the first, "the American can be considered a political regenerate." The fullest answer is given in "The American as a Regenerate Being," the text of a lecture delivered to the fledgling American Studies Program at Whitworth College in Spokane, Washington, on April 27, 1962. One of the last of Weaver's major

1. Letter from Richard Weaver to Donald Davidson dated June 9, 1959. Located in Box 3, Richard Weaver correspondence file, of the Donald Davidson Papers (Addition) in the Special Collections of the Jean and Alexander Heard Library at Vanderbilt University and quoted by permission.

speeches, it was published posthumously in the Southern Review *in a version edited by George Core and M. E. Bradford. A group of six reviews of historical biographies of American political leaders completes the section. Published between 1956 and 1958 in* The Freeman *and* National Review, *they are of interest mainly because of the comments Weaver makes about their subjects: George Washington, Patrick Henry, James Wilson, John Quincy Adams, Henry Clay, and Abraham Lincoln.*

Liberalism with a Ballast[1]

Sir John Emerich Edward Dalberg-Acton, later Lord Acton, moralist and writer of historical monographs, has survived until now largely by virtue of a memorable aphorism. Writing in 1887 to Mandell Creighton, canon of Worcester cathedral, he remarked: "Power tends to corrupt, and absolute power corrupts absolutely." Then he went on to say, in a vein which readers of *Essays on Church and State* will come to recognize as characteristic: "Great men are almost always bad men, even when they exercise influence and not authority: still more when you superadd the tendency or the certainty of corruption by authority. There is no worse heresy than that the office sanctifies the holder of it."

This might be called the chief speculative concern of an original mind who had unusual advantages for viewing history, both through its books and monuments and as passing scene. Hereditary First Knight of the Holy Roman Empire, related to families of rank in England, Continental in training and to some extent in habit of mind, member of Parliament and advisor to Gladstone, Acton might be thought of as an historian peculiarly in the midst of things; and many have wondered why he left no work commensurate with the apparent opportunities. But it had been observed by Johann Döllinger, the German theologian who inspired and guided his youth, that if Acton did not write his great book before he was forty, it would never be written. The prophecy proved correct, and the "History of

1. *The Sewanee Review*, 62/2, Spring 1954, 334–41. Copyright 1954, 1982 by the University of the South. Reprinted with the permission of the editor.

Essays on Church and State. By Lord Acton. With an Introduction by Douglas Woodruff. New York: The Viking Press, 1953. 474 pages. $6.00; *Acton's Political Philosophy*. By G. E. Fasnacht. New York: The Viking Press, 1953. 247 pages. $4.00; *Lord Acton: A Study in Conscience and Politics*. By Gertrude Himmelfarb. Chicago: The University of Chicago Press, 1952. x, 251 pages. $3.75.

Freedom" (not to be confused with the title mentioned below) remained
only a project. A moralist's concern with the topical matters of his own
day absorbed much of his energy; and a conscientiousness about research,
which seemed to increase as his life went on, immersed him ever deeper in
materials but kept him away from the forge where the work of sustained
creation has to be done. In consequence, nearly all of his writings, apart
from his university lectures, took the form of essays and reviews for peri-
odicals of the fugitive sort. From these, two volumes, *The History of Freedom
and Other Essays* and *Historical Essays and Studies,* have previously been
compiled; and the present volume, consisting principally of thirteen essays
and eleven book reviews, constitutes a third from the same source.

It was therefore conscience, in a manner of speaking, which prevented
the writing of the great work, and it was conscience also which focussed
the subjects of his chief historical essays. Acton's lot was to unite in one
being the scientific historian, trained by the Germans—who were then pioneering the "new" history—and the pious Catholic, reverential toward the
Church; and if it is possible to generalize the interest which these two disciplines encouraged, one would perhaps have to say that it was the idea of
prerogative. The burden of conscience and knowledge kept turning his attention to the problem of defined rights and of the limits of office. As an
historian, concerned with the substantive things of the world, he found a
natural subject in questions of church and state.

The essay on "Ultramontanism," which opens the present collection, is
therefore a good introduction to Acton. Ultramontanism was historically a
movement within the Catholic Church which had resisted the secular state
and tried to push forward the bounds of Church authority. It had been
militant and predominantly illiberal, and Acton himself was to maintain a
warfare with the Ultramontanes during most of his career. Like a number
of good Catholics, he was distressed by the gulf between what Catholicism
was to some of its communicants and what it might be with the aid of
somewhat greater open-mindedness on non-doctrinal matters. This essay,
written for *The Home and Foreign Review* in 1863, was an extended *ad hoc*
definition, aimed to show what Ultramontanism could achieve if it took
into account modern learning and liberal sentiments.

He begins by pointing out that knowledge is essential to the Christian
Church and that the fact of progress is entailed by the divinity of her founder. The very preservation of doctrine implies its development, and Acton

regarded it as one advantage of Catholicism over Protestantism that the former was less dependent upon a collection of scriptures and more free to unfold doctrine in the light of new knowledge.

Ultramontanism stands in the same relation to Catholicism in matters of opinion as Catholicism stands to Christianity in matters of faith. It signifies a habit of intellect carrying forward the inquiries and supplementing the work of authority. It implies the legitimate union of religion with science, and the conscious, intelligible harmony of Catholicism with the system of secular truth. Its basis is authority, but its domain is liberty, and it reconciles the one with the other.

Ultramontanism had been perverted so as to become a party term for "the strict Roman system"; and this he felt obliged to oppose on two grounds: first, that it sought to bring an arbitrary kind of authority into the Church; and second, that it hindered Catholics from moving freely in the realm of inductive inquiry. The ideal which he held up tried to bring together doctrine and liberty of research in a harmony which is described as follows:

When a man has really performed this double task—when he has worked out the problem of science or politics, on purely scientific and political principles, and then controlled his process by the doctrine of the Church, and found his results to coincide with that doctrine, then he is an Ultramontane in the real meaning of the term, a Catholic in the highest sense of Catholicism. The Ultramontane is therefore one who makes no parade of his religion; who meets his adversaries on ground which they understand and acknowledge; who appeals to no extrinsic considerations—benevolence, or force, or inter- est, or artifice—in order to establish his point; who discusses each topic on its own intrinsic merits—answering the critic by a severer criticism, the meta- physician by closer reasoning, the historian by deeper learning, the politician by sounder politics and indifference itself by a purer impartiality. In all of these points the Ultramontane discovers a point preeminently Catholic, but also preeminently intellectual and true.

Ultramontanism was not, however, destined to be redeemed by a redefi- nition. Despite Acton's continuing protest that by its tendency to create new dogmas it added to the burden of the pious Catholic, the Ultramon- tane concept was the one which prevailed in Church policy. A crisis in his own relationship with Catholicism came with the general council convened at Rome in 1869 to consider the dogma of papal infallibility. Acton was in the city during most of the sessions of the council, and although he was not in official capacity, he was so placed as to learn many details of the proceedings. Under the pseudonym "Quirinus," he sent a series of letters to Döllinger, who, after a certain amount of editing, published them in the Munich *Allgemeine Zeitung.*

Döllinger had already taken the position, as historian, that the doctrine of infallibility was not consistent with the history of the Church; the "Quirinus Letters," telling of maneuverings and backstage movements, were calculated to discredit the means whereby the dogma was approved, in the summer of 1870. For the part he played in opposition, he was shortly afterward excommunicated; Acton was not excommunicated, but he was asked, at the instigation of Archbishop Manning, for a confession of belief. In the statement with which he replied Acton declared that he was, "in spite of sins and errors, a true Catholic." Thus his personal solution seems to have been that notwithstanding doubts and disagreements, it was best to yield to the authority of the Church, and that the rectification of mistakes could be left to the slow process of history. This decision can undoubtedly be related to his conviction that Christianity is not a system of metaphysics which borrowed its ethics elsewhere, but a system of ethics which borrowed its metaphysics elsewhere.

Acton had to face comparable issues in the field of purely secular politics, and no problem engaged him more earnestly than that of democratic absolutism. There was being enacted during the years in which he was publishing most regularly a great test of absolute majority rule in the form of the American struggle over national union and state sovereignty; and it is a fact of note that Acton was the only outstanding European intellectual who consistently upheld the cause of the Southern states. At the very time of secession he wrote for *The Rambler* a long essay on "The Political Causes of the American Revolution," thereby applying, incidentally, the name of revolution to the American civil conflict, just as Charles Beard and others were to do much later.

To understand Acton's view of Southern secession, it is necessary to know that he had a tremendous admiration for the original American Revolution, and that in his political theory this and the Civil War were conjoined events. In his judgment our Revolution was one of the great accomplishments of history because it had taken the idea of liberty and sunk its foundations in principle. Then its creators proceeded to a second great work when they set up a system of government popular in nature but protected against the evils of majority rule. He believed that America had attained the front rank in political science, and that at least six Americans deserved to be ranked with the foremost Europeans. Thus Acton, starting with this exalted view of the original structure of the Union, saw the South as the defender of its vital safeguards and the North as working to turn it into a democratic despotism.

The exposition of this essay shows an astoundingly intimate knowledge of documents and authorities—the kind of knowledge that made his contemporaries feel that, despite the paucity of his publication, he was the most learned historian of the age. Certainly it may be doubted whether anyone outside the United States had made himself more painstakingly familiar with the debates in the Constitutional Convention, the early alignment of American political parties, the slowly developing but ultimately potent tariff issue, and the impairment of the power of the states. He saw all these events, and the act of secession which appeared at that moment their culmination, as proceeding from an original defect of the Constitution, which had failed to set effective limits to the tyranny of majority will. It was natural that he should have an intense admiration for Calhoun, whose doctrine he termed "the very perfection of political truth." "Webster may have been the truest interpreter of the law; Calhoun was the real defender of the Union," he wrote; and it pleased him to show these two drawing together near the end of their careers in warning the abolitionists of the results of their disregard for laws and constitutions.

Here he found vindication of his belief that "The strict principle of popular sovereignty must . . . lead to the destruction of the state that adopts it, unless it sacrifices itself by concession." Indeed, the working out of this truth seemed to him to give to the history of the United States between the Constitutional Convention and the election of Jefferson Davis to the presidency of the Confederacy "an almost epic unity."

It is interesting to find Acton admitting to himself that his position on the question was due in part to his nurture as a Catholic, which made him hostile to all forms of political abstractionism. He felt that the wisdom taught by his religion called for more concession to concrete realities than the Northern reformers were making.

It is as impossible to sympathize on religious grounds with the categorical prohibition of slavery, as, on political grounds, with the opinions of the abolitionists. In this, as in all things, they exhibit the same abstract, ideal absolutism which is equally hostile with the Catholic and with the English spirit.

Here in a second major issue Acton was concerned with the idea of prerogative and of rights safeguarded by definition. Just as he had tried to find within the Church a viable freedom for the inquiring intellect, so he was trying to find in the political realm a viable freedom for the activity of the increased numbers who were now participants in government. In both instances he felt that success depended upon something antecedent and restrictive: in religion, an accepted but settled dogma; in government, an overriding law which would set bounds to majority will and make it certain that minorities would never be reduced to subjects.

The allegiances which he thus maintained may seem, on the surface, anomalous for a liberal; but it is necessary to understand that Acton arrived at his liberalism by a route different from that of most who claim this political position; indeed, by a route which carries most travelers into a different camp. He did not believe that liberalism was middle-of-the-roadism, or an amiable reconciling of opposed parties in the commonwealth. It was not an art of compromise or a calculation of results, and he deprecated Burke and Morley for tendencies in that direction. Such a course seemed to him an indifference to principle which would make political activity impossible for a man of ideals. For Acton, liberalism was always the force of ideas and ideals in politics, and his chief point against Toryism was that it represented not intellect or statecraft, but landed interest. Furthermore, his outlook was not based upon a belief in the natural goodness or perfectibility of man, which is the philosophic ground upon which the reforming liberal so often stands. He had a pessimistic, almost bleak view of human nature. Not only was it true that most wielders of power had been evil, it was even a mistake to connect good ideas with good men. Where liberalism made its entry into the picture was through the necessity of liberty to the salvation of man.

It would be far wrong, consequently, to think of Acton as the type of optimistic liberal we have come to know in recent decades, ignorant of history, incautious as to means, and inclined to the idolatry of the state. One sentence from the "Extracts" included in *Essays on Church and State* places this beyond doubt: "Neither paganism nor Christianity ever produced a profound historian whose mind was not turned to gloom by the contemplation of the affairs of men."

The reader of Acton who hopes to have his understanding illuminated by G. E. Fasnacht's *Acton's Political Philosophy* faces disappointment. The work professes to be an analysis, but the present reviewer finds it little more than a crude compilation of passages with rather pointless commentary. It is true that Mr. Fasnacht has had recourse to Acton's unpublished manuscripts in the Cambridge University Library in addition to the published works and works about him. He has made groupings of material under such chapter headings as "The Theory of Conscience," "Nationality and Power," and "Acton's Relations to Other Thinkers." But the whole volume is woefully lacking in just what the reader is led to expect, a kind of analytical clarity. The commentary is imperceptive, repetitious, clumsy in emphasis, and generally badly written. A good many times after reading Mr. Fasnacht's interpretation of a paragraph or two quoted from Acton, I found myself forced back to the original to avoid becoming confused. Some of the sentences in the latter part of the work repeat the substance of sentences in the earlier part without increment or fresh application. Poor transitions keep the reader fumbling for the continuity. As a publication which locates a good deal of source material for the student of Acton it is not, of course, without value. But as an analytical essay it is chaotic and dull.

Gertrude Himmelfarb, now a leading authority on the life and thought of Acton, describes her volume as the "biography of a mind"; and most readers will probably agree that she has been right in choosing to present Acton's ideas against the background of his career. If her subject was "an unsystematic but profound thinker," one courts trouble in trying to make a logically organized scheme of his thoughts, and this seems to have been the principal difficulty that Mr. Fasnacht succumbed to. It is easier and it is more intelligible to show his ideas developing with his personal maturity, with the course of world affairs demanding historical and moral judgments, and with the opportunities he had to test the validity of his conclusions. Therefore we find in her work the kind of sequential picture which shows Acton growing up with his interest in Catholicism and in history, carrying on his conflicts with Rome after he had begun to define his position, working with the British Liberal Party, and at the end filling the chair of Regius

Professor of Modern History at Cambridge. The amount of research is extensive, and her judgments, if they do not please all admirers of Acton, are supported.

The portrait allows us to see why Acton must now be considered "one of our great contemporaries." Most of the historians of his generation were writers before the deluge; that is to say, they wrote before two great world wars and the weakening of ethical controls showed how little our civilization is removed from primitive and barbarous impulses. The Catholic religion in which he was brought up; scientific history, which he learned from the Germans; and above all a willingness to study moral problems in their contexts, protected him against seductive assumptions. The man who could write the following was not floating with the main current of his age:

> Government of one, or of a minority is not a government of force, but in spite of force, by virtue of some idea. The support makes up for the inferiority of brute strength. This is aristocracy—which is not equivalent to simple strength.
>
> Democracy is government of the strongest, just as military despotism is. This is a bond of connection between the two. They are the brutal forms of government and as strength and authority go together, necessarily arbitrary.

Similarly, we would not expect the man who saw the introduction of representative government in Germany as a means to increase the power of the state and to facilitate military conscription to be deceived by slogans. Today he seems as unillusioned as Thucydides or Gibbon. He set an example of his own precept that "no historian thinks well of human nature."

What remains after such scrutiny and so much rejection must be of impressive toughness, and something does remain. Acton never abandoned his belief in the possibility of progress (in his own austere definition) and in the necessity of liberalism to its fulfillment. For him history, taken by itself, had no meaning; it acquired meaning only through such postulates; there had to be some fixed moral standard outside it, some pole star by which reckonings could be made. This is a view whereby knowledge and hope come together, the unhappy record of human affairs and our intuitive feeling that existence is not meaningless. "God in Nature [is] more manifest than God in History. Yet History leads to him and Nature away from him" was a kind of final verdict.

Lord Acton: The Historian as Thinker[1]

Reporting a conversation he once had with Lord Acton, James Bryce gave the following description: "He spoke . . . as if from some mountain summit high in air, he saw beneath him the far winding path of human progress from dim Cimmerian shores of prehistoric shadow into the fuller yet broken and fitful light of modern time." The eloquence was great; the penetration even greater. "It was as if the whole landscape of history had been suddenly lit up by a burst of sunlight." That now, after the lapse of nearly a century, Acton does not appear any less Olympian is testimony to his stature as historian and thinker.

To the work which was to make him famous Acton brought the gift of an extraordinarily cosmopolitan background. He was descended on the one side from an old Catholic family of English country squires. On the other he came from the ancient German family of Dahlbergs, whose members had been knights of the Holy Roman Empire. A branch of the English family had settled in France and later in Italy. His grandfather, John Francis Acton, so raised himself in the esteem of the Queen of Naples that he became prime minister of that kingdom, and it was in Naples that Acton was born, in 1834. His antecedents and the course of his later life combined to make him, it has been said, an expression "of German learning, of French thought, and of British and American experience."

After an early period of schooling in France, he was sent to England, to the Catholic school at Oscott, so that he might prepare for Cambridge. But Acton was not destined to become a part of Cambridge until more than forty years later, when he was made professor of modern history at that university. Legally he could have been admitted, but anti-Catholic feeling was still high, and he was denied entrance by three of its colleges.

1. *Modern Age*, 5/1, Winter 1960–61, 13–21.

This failure now looks providential, since it led to a favorable turning point in his life. He decided to continue his education in Germany, and by 1850 he was in Munich, settled in the household of Dr. Johann Ignaz von Döllinger, a priest and a famous theologian and church historian of the University of Munich. Döllinger proved the person to excite his idealism and his intellectual passion. What fired the imagination of Acton, who had come from an environment slack in comparison with this, was the enormous industry and learning of his new teacher, and the abstemious habits of life which seemed to mark these as a kind of dedication. But crowning even this was the fact that Döllinger was a leader in the Catholic Renaissance in Germany, which naturally made an immediate appeal to him because of his heritage, his own experiences, and a love of the church which never deserted him through many trials and disillusionments. Here in Munich he began the immense reading which was to make him, in the opinion of many, the most learned man of his time. One fact may convey an idea of his voracious appetite for print. During his first few weeks in Munich, he later told some one (and we may note that at this time he was sixteen years of age), he read through the fifty-five volumes of the *Biographie Universelle*.

The thing of greatest value and consequence which he learned from Döllinger was a concept of history and of what it means to be historically minded. Döllinger, along with other German scholars of his group, had become convinced that the meaning of Catholic Christianity was not to be found merely in the study of dogma and doctrine but also in the study of historical change and development. Acton was in close association with this master for the next eight years, although time was taken out for travels, which included one journey to the United States and another to Russia. Then in 1858 he returned to England, filled with determination to stir up English Catholicism.

The means he chose toward this end was magazine journalism. He was connected, either as editor or regular contributor, with four journals in succession, *The Rambler, The Home and Foreign Review, The Chronicle,* and *The North British Review.* In the course of his work for these he wrote articles on a wide variety of historical, political, and ecclesiastical subjects, which displayed in a man still in his twenties an extraordinary sense of historical fact and a feeling for the inner impulse of movements which other historians could but treat from a distance.

Among the things which made him distinctive as an historical writer and which continue to mark him as a prophet in his own time none was more compelling than the idea of freedom. "When Acton speaks of liberty, there is always a ring in his voice," G. P. Gooch was later to write. This was the dominant focus of his thinking, an intellectual and a moral preoccupation which never ceased to influence his way of looking at events. In his view the achievement of liberty was the thread of progress to be discerned in human history. That progress was not steady; it was not without dark nights of absolutism and oppression; yet it was there, and it justified the sacrifices that compose so much of the human story. Fairly early in his career Acton projected the writing of a "History of Freedom," a work for which he above all men seemed equipped by training and by temperament to attempt. But for one reason and another—partly because of the immensity of the task and partly because of his own conscientiousness about the method of execution—the book was never produced. Even so, we can be grateful that two essays, "The History of Freedom in Antiquity" and "The History of Freedom in Christianity," were completed, for these allow us to see how he was conceiving a problem at once so universal and so intricate as the realization of liberty.

Acton's concept of liberty grew originally out of his reflections upon religion and the state. It seems characteristic that the essay on "The History of Freedom in Antiquity" should begin with this sentence: "Liberty, next to religion, has been the motive of good deeds and the common pretext for crime, from the sowing of the seed at Athens two thousand four hundred and sixty years ago until the splendid harvest was gathered by men of our own age." Then he continued by way of further prologue: "It is the delicate fruit of a mature civilization. . . . In every age its progress has been beset by natural enemies, by ignorance and superstition, by the lust of conquest and the love of ease, by the strong man's craving for power, and the poor man's craving for food. At all times sincere friends of freedom have been rare, and its triumphs have been due to minorities that have prevailed by associating themselves with auxiliaries whose objects often differed from their own. . . ." Then he went on to note that liberty is the essential condition and guardian of religion. The greatest source of danger to liberty is the state, which sometimes injures it by doing too little and at other times by doing too much.

The idea of liberty, Acton held, was born among the Israelites, whose government was a federation founded upon voluntary consent. The Hebrew prophets constantly testified that the laws, which were divine, were paramount over sinful rulers. In doing this they set up the distinction between the nation and the higher law which has been the seedbed of freedom down to our own time.

In Greece the idea of liberty was born with the reforms of Solon. Solon gave the poorer classes a voice in the election of magistrates. This change, slight though it may seem to us, contained a principle that transformed the basis of the Greek state. "It introduced the idea that a man ought to have a voice in selecting those to whose rectitude and wisdom he is compelled to trust his fortune, his family, and his life." The revolution thus inaugurated by Solon was completed by Pericles, whose reforms, though right in essence, required a higher type of leadership than appeared after his decease.

The Romans in securing their freedom faced the same problems and went through the same experiences as the Greeks. There the struggle was between the aristocrats, who had wrested power from the kings and were determined to keep it, and the plebs, who demanded a share in it. But whereas the Greeks were able to reach their solution in a short while, the Romans required two centuries. The achievement itself, however, was much longer lasting. But in Acton's view the ancient free states had one radical defect: they were both state and church in one. Religion, morality, and politics were lumped together. The state did much for the citizen but little or nothing for the man. "What the slave was in the hands of his master," he wrote, "the citizen was in the hands of the community." It was inevitable that, lacking one vital element, the ancient governments should have collapsed into despotism. That vital element was introduced by Christianity. This was belief in the sacredness of the person and thus in a center of power distinct from the state. What the pagan philosophers in all their brilliance had not been able to do, that is, set effective barriers to the power of the state, was done in response to that injunction: "Render unto Caesar the things that are Caesar's and unto God the things that are God's." This instituted a basis of freedom upon which the world since that time has been able to build. It was to the working out of this principle that Acton turned in his second essay, "The History of Freedom in Christianity."

When the Roman Empire was subverted by Teutonic barbarians, civilization lapsed for a period of five hundred years. Yet even this catastrophe brought with it certain seeds of freedom which were destined to grow. The barbarian invaders had lived under a tradition of freedom. Kings they had

had at intervals, but sometimes these were elected and sometimes they were deposed. Their chief office was to lead the people in war. The supremacy of the popular will was in general acknowledged. These primitive peoples were rather rapidly converted to Christianity, and eventually there grew up in Europe side by side a political hierarchy and an ecclesiastical hierarchy. Out of the long struggle between the two arose the modern concept of civil liberty. This was not the object of either, as we know—and here one may recur to Acton's observation that liberty is sometimes won by minorities working with auxiliaries which have other objects in view. The historical fact was that each side called the nation to its aid in the name of liberty. "If the Church had continued to buttress the thrones of the kings whom it had anointed, or if the struggle had terminated speedily in an undivided victory, all Europe would have sunk down under a Byzantine or a Muscovite despotism." The weight of the church, especially that of the papacy, was thrown into the struggle against the indefeasibility of the right of kings. The growth of national states especially at the time of the Reformation placed liberty in jeopardy again by greatly increasing the scope of what the state thought it should do. And the trend in this direction was not arrested, in terms of political theory, until the American Revolution.

Acton was formulating these thoughts at a time when nationalism was proving the dominant force in Europe. The Italian risorgimento and the wars of unification which occurred at short intervals apart in Switzerland, in Italy, and in Germany were to show the force of the trend. An historical movement so widespread and so full of promise and of danger could hardly escape the attention of a philosophic historian—especially of Acton, always alert to detect those developments which bore favorably or unfavorably upon his cherished ideal of freedom. Here was a case in point, for nationalist movements usually arose under the banner of freedom and independence, but whether they actually resulted in the gaining of these or in their subversion was an arguable question. As early as 1862 Acton published in *The Home and Foreign Review* a sixty-page essay on the topic of nationality. Although this was a product of his early period, it represents the main stream of his political thinking, and it has been perhaps the most widely studied of all his writings. Of special interest is the fact that it brings together his philosophy of freedom and his view of the then rampant nationalisms of Europe.

The essay opens with some general observations on revolution and reform. Practical evils often give rise to theoretical systems which are designed to cure them. These systems frequently contain large errors because they do not conceive the problem in the right way or do not provide relief of the right kind or in the right measure. Nevertheless, they may contribute something, because they point out the direction in which reform needs to move. And hence, Acton declared, "false principles which correspond with the bad as well as with the just aspirations of mankind are a normal and necessary element in the life of nations." The modern period has witnessed the appearance of three of these in particular: equality, communism, and nationality.

The French Revolution constitutes a dividing line in history, before which the modern concept of nationality did not exist. "In the old European system, the rights of nationalities were neither recognized by governments nor asserted by the people." Frontiers were determined by the interests of ruling families. Absolutists cared only for the state and liberals only for the individual. The idea of nationality in Europe was awakened by the partition of Poland.

This event left, for the first time, a nation desiring to be united as a state—a soul wandering in search of a body, as Acton put it. The absolutist governments which had divided up Poland—Russia, Prussia, and Austria—were to encounter two hostile forces, the English spirit of liberty and the doctrines of the French Revolution. These two forces supported the nascent idea of nationality, but they did so along different paths. When the absolutist government of France was overthrown, the people needed a new principle of unity. Without this, the theory of the popular will could have broken the country into as many republics as there were communes. At this point the theory of the sovereignty of the people was used to create an idea of nationality independent of the course of history. France became a Republic One and Indivisible. This signified that no part could speak for the whole. The central power simply obeyed the whole. There was a power supreme over the state, distinct from and independent of its members. Hence there developed a concept of nationality free from all influence of history.

This was in contradiction to another concept of nationality, which maintained that certain natural and historical forces ought to determine the character and the form of the state. When the new nation of France embarked on a program of conquest, it was opposed by this second concept. Napoleon, by attacking "natural" nationality in Russia, by engendering it in Italy, and by governing in spite of it in Germany and Spain, called into being forces which were to make nationalism potent throughout the nineteenth century. Those ideas and institutions which had suffered most at his hands—religion, national independence, and political liberty—all contributed to movements directed against the French Revolution. The ensuing uprisings were essentially popular in nature because the people opposed French supremacy as hostile to their freedom.

But the spirit of nationality which had emerged received a hard blow at the Congress of Vienna. The liberals of the day were interested only in liberalism in the form of French institutions, and the powers which formed the Holy Alliance were interested only in restoring absolutism. "The governments of the Holy Alliance," he wrote, "devoted themselves to suppress with equal care the revolutionary spirit by which they had been threatened and the national spirit by which they had been restored."

The revolution of 1848, though unsuccessful, promoted the idea of nationality in two ways. Austrian power was restored in Italy in a more centralized and energetic form, and this produced a feeling among the people that there was no hope of relief except through national freedom. The second way was through the restoration of the democratic principle in France. This brought in again the notion of the sovereignty of the people, and to it the idea of unity and nationality seemed essential. A nation imbued with this notion cannot allow a part of itself to be owned by another state nor can it allow itself to be divided up. "The theory of nationality, therefore, proceeds from two principles which divide the political world—from legitimacy, which ignores its claims, and from the revolution, which assures them; and for the same reason it is the chief weapon of the last against the first."

At this point a distinction emerges explicitly which has been implicit from the beginning. Acton is here differentiating between the *theory* of nationality and the *right* of nationality. The two views correspond to the French and the English systems. The first sees the state as resting upon a unity which is in reality fictitious and which "crushes all natural rights and established liberties for the purpose of vindicating itself." It is capable of subverting governments, of oppressing minorities, of exercising what

amounts to a foreign domination over lesser national elements within the
state. The idea of the right of nationality, which is the English conception,
recognizes that national minorities are entitled to certain liberties because,
as a matter of empirical fact, they are united by language or race or geography, or culture or any combinations of these. It obeys the laws and results
of history and tends toward diversity. It sees the fact of nationality as an
essential but not the supreme element in determining the form of the state.
This view makes possible a union of nations, and "the presence of different
nations under the same sovereignty is similar in its effect to the independence of church and state."

The theory of nationality, as contrasted with the right of nationality, Acton regarded as a backward step in history. In explaining this point, he
reintroduced the thought with which he started. Nationality tends to arise
in opposition to something which should not have existed in the first place.
It must be seen therefore as a corrective; and it must contribute to that
which the theory itself condemns—the liberty of separate nationalities under one sovereign community. It is thus one of these "false ideas" or "extremes" which are able to accomplish what nothing else could accomplish.
But it becomes arbitrary and subversive because it surrenders the individual
will to the collective will and then makes the collective will subject to conditions which are independent of it. What can be said for nationality is that
it had a mission in the world and that in its period it worked successfully
against the two forces which are the worst enemies of civil freedom, absolute monarchy and the revolution.

In a period when the peoples of Asia and Africa, of various levels of
culture, are placing naïve hope in the power of nationalism to redeem them,
these sober words should be full of warning, both for those who are tasting
the heady wine of national independence for the first time and for those of
the West who are, with seemingly equal naïveté, urging them on.

It is of special interest that Acton brought these considerations to bear
upon the American crisis of 1861. He had made one visit to the United
States, and he possessed a detailed knowledge of, and—what was hardly
characteristic of the Englishmen of his time—a great respect for, American
history. His ecumenical point of view enabled him to take the story of
American sectional conflict and place it in the wider frame of French revolutionary nationalism and the ensuing movements toward unification. For

Acton therefore the great debate over the nature of the American union and the Civil War was not a unique event, but part of that political spasm, if the term be permitted, which was then affecting Europe and erupting in military struggles. (Although he does not mention it, the European struggle most closely analogous with the American one in the ideologies involved and in the nature of the two alignments was the Swiss Civil War of 1847.)

Acton addressed himself to the problem in a long essay on "The Political Causes of the American Revolution," which appeared in *The Rambler* in May 1861. Although this antedates by a year the essay on nationality, it is evident that both proceeded from the same course of thinking. By "the American Revolution" Acton meant the American Civil War, then on the verge of breaking out. His essay was a causal exposition of the forces which had made this a crisis of nationalism.

To appreciate the force of his reasoning, one should know that he had an almost unbounded admiration for the founders of the American government. He regularly spoke of them in superlatives. In political science, he declared, "there are at least six Americans on a level with the foremost Europeans." He knew in intimate detail the literature of the Constitutional Convention, which he regarded as having produced the most perfect form of democracy seen in the world. But it was admirable in a special sense which he stressed: it was "armed and vigilant less against aristocracy and monarchy than against its own weakness and excess." It was this thought that underlay his admiration for American federalism. "Whilst England was admired for the safeguards with which, in the course of many centuries, it had fortified liberty against the power of the crown, America appeared still more worthy of admiration, for the safeguards which, in the course of a single memorable year, it had set up against the power of its own sovereign people." Acton was thus clearly a constitutionalist, and he regarded the long sectional struggle which preceded the Civil War as a contest to decide whether the federal principle was going to be preserved.

He begins this essay also with a series of generalizations. It is the innate tendency of monarchy to become more free, but democracy has a similar tendency to become more arbitrary. The latter is true because power is already in the hands of those who seek to subvert and abolish the law. The real test of democracy, therefore, is whether it can remain law-abiding; that is, "whether it can adhere to the constitutional limitations laid down at the beginning." "The strict principle of the sovereignty of the people," he observed, "must . . . lead to the destruction of the state that adopts it, unless it sacrifices itself by concession."

"The greatest of all modern republics has given the most complete example of the truth of this law. The dispute between absolute and limited power, between centralization and self-government, has been, like that between privilege and prerogative in England, the substance of the constitutional history of the United States. This is the argument which confers on the whole period that intervenes between the Constitution of 1787 and the election of Mr. Davis an almost epic unity." Following this comes a long series of quotations from speeches made at the Constitutional Convention. Madison, Gerry, Wilson, Hamilton, Sherman, and others are cited to show the apprehension that was felt of an unbridled democracy.

He then proceeded to trace the history of the United States through Jefferson's embargo and the Hartford Convention, through the disputes over the tariff and nullification and other issues of sectional controversy. His deepest admiration was reserved for the ideas which Calhoun introduced into this debate. The arguments of Calhoun in defense of the nullifying ordinance he pronounced "the very perfection of political truth" because they took into account "the realities of modern democracy" and "the securities of medieval freedom." He reproduced a long quotation from Calhoun's *Disquisition on Government,* describing it as "so profound and so extremely applicable to the politics of the present day that we regret we can give only a feeble notion of the argument." "Webster," he declared, "may have been the truest interpreter of the law; Calhoun was the real defender of the Union." This judgment, which will sound very odd to some, must be understood with reference to Acton's view of a viable democracy. His approval of Calhoun centers really on one point: Calhoun had seen that the real essence of a constitution lies in its negative aspect, not in its positive one. It is more important for a constitution in a democracy to prohibit than to provide. The will of the majority would always be reaching out for more power, and unless this could be checked by some organic law, the end of liberty would come when the federal authority became the institute of the popular will instead of its barrier.

It has seemed strange to some that Acton, the great apostle of freedom, should have been a defender of Calhoun and Southern secession. But for him slavery was an unfortunate circumstance which did not touch the heart of the issue. What was being hammered out in the American quarrel was the ancient question of unrestricted power to rule. The American government, as he saw it at this time, was being destroyed by the "spurious democracy of the French Revolution," which was endeavoring to elevate simple majority rule to the status of divine right.

Running through all of these observations—the reflections on freedom, the account of nationality in modern European history, and the commentary on the course of democracy in America—is one consistent principle. It is the idea of political pluralism. Acton believed that the preservation of liberty depended on the maintenance of different centers of power, authority, and influence.[2] Of power Acton had a mortal distrust, and monolithic power was absolutist, whether it tried to sanctify itself by the name of church, monarchy, or democracy. The remark of Acton's which has been most widely quoted has to do with the evil effects of power. In an exchange of letters with Mandell Creighton, another English historian, he said: "Power tends to corrupt, and absolute power corrupts absolutely." Accordingly the contest for liberty was one long struggle against concentration of power. That is the ground for his insistence upon a free church in a free state. It explains his defense of the Southern states in invoking the principle of secession. The United States had originally been based as a nation upon federalism, which was, in Acton's own phrase, "the supreme political principle." This principle had been eroded away in the battle of contending interests and sections until the result was the threat of a centralized democracy operating by simple majority rule—the tyrannical principle of the French Revolution. It explains his defense of those traditions, institutions, classes, corporations, and nationalities which are barriers to uniformity and centralization. "Diversity," he noted, "preserves liberty by supplying the means of organization." It explains why he was often suspicious of those movements which appeared under the claim of "rights" and were ostensibly seeking the redress of wrongs. Nationality, which had been born of a wrong done to Poland and which was the major force in ending the domination of

2. This is the real meaning of his otherwise puzzling reference to "the securities of medieval freedom." The medieval world was organized into various corporate bodies with sharply defined and recognized areas of liberties.

Europe by Napoleon, became itself an irrational and domineering force, disinclined to respect rights which had a different but a real basis. Socialism and liberalism were pointed in the same direction. Setting out as programs to "liberate" people, they discovered that they were more interested in ruling them. Though Acton thought of himself as a liberal, some of his most severe strictures are directed against what he considered to be perversions of the liberal creed. "Foreign liberalism," he wrote, "demands not freedom but participation in power." And further: "No despotism is more complete than that of the modern liberals. . . . The liberal doctrine subjects the desire of freedom to the desire of power, and the more it demands a share of power, the more averse it is to exemptions from it."

Everything in Acton's thinking, therefore, tends to polarize around this conviction: absolute power is not to be trusted to any individual, institution, or form of government. The rights of minorities as centers of protest must be guaranteed. "It is bad to be oppressed by a minority, but it is worse to be oppressed by a majority." "Government by a majority is more likely to be a government of force. Government of one or a minority is not a government of force, but in spite of force, by virtue of some idea. The support makes up for the inferiority of brute strength." The ultimate principle of history is ethical, and this cannot be worked out in the absence of freedom, of which a pluralistic political organization is the only effective safeguard.

Acton's special quality as an historian arises from the depth of his insight and from his courage in making judgments. One might add that it also depends upon his recognition of a strain of tragedy in history. He was not, by the usual outward tokens, a great figure among historians. He never published a single outstanding work to make his name memorable. He was not a great narrator. Until his last few years he held no influential teaching post. He has not won and seems destined never to win a wide audience of readers as did Gibbon or Macaulay. But he has impressed posterity as having something profound to say in his own right upon the materials of history. In reading him, one encounters a reflective mind constantly casting flashes of illumination upon these materials, never deserting them long enough to go on speculative voyages, but on the other hand probing into their meanings, philosophical and moral. It seems fitting therefore to ask finally what Acton thought about the uses of history itself.

One might begin the answer by saying that for Acton history was a lesson in pessimism—or, if that is putting it a bit too strongly, history was a solid rebuke to sanguine presumptions about the nature and the future of man. Out of this vein of feeling, he could write: "No historian thinks well of human nature." And he recorded another somber observation: "Neither paganism nor Christianity ever produced a profound political historian whose mind was not turned to gloom by contemplation of the affairs of men." Moreover, he thought there were things in history which must remain unforgivable—that is, inexcusable by an appeal to the nature of the times or to temperament or to circumstance. What then was the purpose of studying the painful and often sanguinary story?

The purpose of the study of history, according to Acton, is to heighten conscience. Reflection upon what man has done makes sharper in us that faculty by which we distinguish between good and evil. Let me suggest in this connection that the word "conscience" signifies in its root meaning something very much like recollection. To have conscience is to remember what we are and what we have been; it is a presence of knowledge to the mind which tells us what we ought and ought not do—not in the form of simple precepts, of course, but through an accumulated awareness of the past reminding us that some kinds of actions have produced good and others harm. Nothing was more repugnant to Acton's thinking than the belief that historical events are self-justifying. Even Edmund Burke, whom Acton in his early period described as "the teacher of mankind" in politics, he later became uneasy with. Burke appealed too much to expediency. "Burke," he said, "loved to evade the arbitration of principle. He was prolific of arguments which were admirable but not decisive." Ranke also fell under his condemnation. "Ranke's dogma is impartiality," he wrote. "Ranke speaks of transactions and occurrences when it would be safe to speak of turpitude and crime." Thus history should arm conscience. The historian is not only the interpreter of the past; he is also in a sense the guardian of morality. It is his duty to trace all the currents of thought "which jointly weave the web of human history," to discern what strengths and weaknesses they possessed and to pronounce accordingly. Unless he does this, "... history ceases to be a science, an arbiter of controversy, a guide of the Wanderer, the upholder of that moral standard which the powers of earth and religion itself tend constantly to depress. It serves where it ought to reign; and it serves the worst cause better than the purest. . . ." For Acton, nothing could take the place of the sovereignty of the developed conscience. It was this which enabled the historian to contribute something to that advancement which he believed humanity had made and possessed the power to go on making. "If the past has been an obstacle and a burden, knowledge of the past is the safest and surest emancipation."

Orbis Americarum [1]

A recurrent question in the history of our people is whether the American can be considered a political regenerate. When the emigrant set out for these shores, did he bid good-by to Europe as the character in Hardy's poem bade good-by to sorrow, only to find that she loved him dearly and would not remain behind? Or did he actually emancipate himself from a past? The experiment of Europe had a cynical issue, but it was hardly the thought of the Pilgrim and the pioneer that this was the inevitable issue of the experiment of man. A new world meant for them, if not a heaven, at least a place for a new government and new ideals. As we now look upon a history which includes forays of imperialist expansion, a civil war, and the growth of monopoly capitalism, the thought may appear presumptuous, but we must remember that it animated a vast migration. America was promises, and the American was regenerated by his dedication to philosophical propositions of government. It seemed cynicism to deny that fact. From before the foundation of the Union until the debate over involvement in the Second World War, Americans stood upon a premise of splendid moral isolation.

Contrary to a belief now widely propagated, the upholders of this isolationism have not all been lowbrows. It is well known that Washington expressed it in the Farewell Address; but Jefferson and John Taylor of Caroline also publicized it; and later Emerson and Whitman gave it copious literary expression. It is unmistakably echoed at the beginning of the Gettysburg Address.

Now the note is sounded again. Henry Bamford Parkes, an English-born historian of the United States, takes the position that there has been a char-

1. *The Sewanee Review*, 56/2, Spring 1948, 319–23. Copyright 1948, 1976 by the University of the South. Reprinted with the permission of the editor.

The American Experience. Henry Bamford Parkes. Alfred A. Knopf. 343 pages. 1947. $3.50.
The Angry Decade. Leo Gurko. Dodd, Mead and Company. 283 pages. 1947. $3.00.

acteristically American experience which teaches a special lesson. It would be unfair to group Mr. Parkes with the cruder exponents of the doctrine, but there is no overlooking the fact that he accepts the existence of an ideology which can only be termed Americanism. It could virtually be formulated by taking the converse of Europeanism. It is anti-traditional, anti-hierarchic, anti-formal, anti-supernatural. Mr. Parkes goes to the point of implying that the American experience is so distinctive that European experience is not a profitable study for Americans; it can only provide them with inappropriate analogies and perverse ideals. To say of the Federalists that "Thinking in European rather than American terms, they had a wholly irrational fear of the mass of their fellow citizens" suggests the conclusion that the nature of man in America was somehow different from the nature of man in Europe. To say of John Taylor of Caroline that he "deduced his principles from American experiences and not from irrelevant European speculations" continues the distinction. Mr. Parkes can write of the most European section of the United States: "Unfortunately the social ideal of the South was of European origin, and insofar as it was based on slavery, it was hierarchical, undemocratic, and un-American." Here he draws a narrower conclusion than his premises entitle him to; he could have written that insofar as it was European it was un-American. In his final chapter he observes that "when America has failed, it has usually been because it has not been true to its own genius but has been too much influenced by the doctrines and precedents of Europe." The American government is styled a "unique creation."

I do not cite these passages to pin an America First badge on Mr. Parkes, who has written a careful, sympathetic, and generally intelligent appreciation of the American past. Yet it seems necessary to examine some of the consequences of this idea of American particularism. If it is true that European experience is irrelevant for Americans, what is to prevent one's saying that American experience is irrelevant for Europeans? And if that is true, what becomes of interventionism in Europe (this the author specifically endorses); what becomes of the "United States of Europe" or of world federation formed on the American model? What becomes of various schemes to reform the minds of former enemies through educational methods which have grown out of the American experience?

Mr. Parkes envisages, however, a different application of his theory. He seems to imply that the American experience is something new, but something new for the whole world; it is a revelation, a definite outpost of all progress. Yet if such is the argument, I fail to see an essential difference between the thesis of this book and Mr. Henry Luce's American Century, which means the domination of the globe by American organization and power. Is it possible that a *pax Americana* could be effected by some instrumentality other than that which won the *pax Romana*? Is it possible that through teaching, noble examples, and appeals to the imagination we could achieve this settlement?

The greatest value of Mr. Parkes's book lies not in its treatment of non-European aspects of American life, but in its presentation of a polarity within the American scene. This is the struggle between capitalism and agrarianism, which has been the source of our most significant political alignments. The conflict was present at the founding of the nation and continued active until the outbreak of the Civil War. The decisive victory of the industrial North appeared to expel agrarianism from the arena for good; but in another twenty years it was back again in the form of farmers' alliances. And in recent years the fight has been taken up vigorously by intellectuals resolved to make a fresh stand against a business civilization. Mr. Parkes is correct, it seems to me, in making this opposition a dominant motif of the American story, though his interpretation of agrarianism may be open to question. The agrarian is suspicious of cities and of politics in the service of business; he defends small-scale enterprise and the privacy of personality; he tends to think with Jefferson that the tilling of the soil is the most innocent vocation. But if he is a tiller of the soil he is too close to the reality of things to take much stock in the natural goodness of man. And if he believes in equality, as Mr. Parkes asserts, it is probably in some form distinguished from what goes by the name of egalitarianism. With these qualifications, it must be affirmed that agrarianism has a formidable case, that it has been more articulate than is commonly supposed, and that it seems to offer the third alternative needed to escape from the modern dilemma.

There is one judgment of American institutions, however, in which I hope Mr. Parkes is profoundly wrong. He argues at some length that the President of the United States should not be a leader, but should be merely a follower of mass sentiment. To fulfill this role he must have an "infinite flexibility" which is "incompatible with rigid principles and convictions." It has been said with an uncomfortable degree of truth that the American President is a demagogue *ex officio*. Mr. Parkes's formula would make him a demagogue also *de jure*. If we have reached a condition in which our chief magistrate is only a translator of mass feeling into executive action, our case is hopeless. Mr. Parkes is saying in effect that democracy cannot tolerate leadership.

In Leo Gurko's *The Angry Decade* one encounters a different purpose and a different mode of presentation. This work won the Dodd, Mead Non-Fiction Award for 1947. As a review of American experience from the stock market crash of 1929 to the Japanese attack on Pearl Harbor, it takes its place with a number of comparable works which have served to give us a more concrete possession of our past. Such undertakings are praiseworthy, for in an age dominated by journalism people need increasingly to be reminded of what they have been and what they have done—even within a preceding decade.

Mr. Gurko's interpretation avoids forthright political commitment. He appears mildly New Dealish, but he is too perceptive not to recognize that the New Deal was opportunistic, and that not one of the great problems it attacked was settled by the time the Second World War arrived to put an artificial quietus on all such problems. He too finds agrarianism a live issue. It is here presented as "one of the two principal theories of civilization" which engaged the attention of the Thirties. "Proletarians and Agrarians accepted the same premise, the growing iniquities of capitalism, and then proceeded to march briskly in opposite directions, one providing for the urban working classes, the other for the rural hinterland; one proclaiming the dictatorship of the mass, the other the oligarchy of the few; one embracing the attraction of a socialist future, the other wedding itself to the blandishments of the Eighteenth Century with its population of propertied independents."

For his key to the American mentality of this era he goes mainly to the work of creative artists, especially writers. One must therefore look at the literary assessments to discover his tendency. Something is told by the allocation of space: Thomas Wolfe gets a whole chapter to himself; Farrell, Faulkner, and Steinbeck get approximately half a chapter each; from there the range is on down to a sentence or two of honorable mention. That

Wolfe deserves such recognition for the attention he won and the influence he exerted seems probable; that he is the only American novelist of the period between two wars whose dimensions are comparable to those of Balzac and Dostoevski seems less so. Steinbeck, because of the thematic progression of his novels, is described as the period's "chief literary chronicler." The vogue of the historical novel is fully explored. Poetry gets rather short shrift from the author, who regards it as not having measured up to the attainments of fiction and drama.

What *The Angry Decade* presents in substance is a pleasantly written but not profound *Kulturgeschichte*. The chief limitation is that it remains merely descriptive; one misses the effort at penetration which might have given us a fuller sense of the form and pressure of the time. The author's style achieves at times a nice balance of imagination and restraint, but it is marred in spots by a journalistic superciliousness. He brings his period to an end with a fine apocalyptic paragraph:

> And so, with many protestations of unity and faith in victory over enemies now officially proclaimed, with feuds temporarily laid aside, and in the grip of that exaltation which comes when a die long agonized over is finally cast, the nation passed, not without restlessness, not without foreboding, into the great war, the war that was to beget the atomic bomb and change the face of the earth.

Both works close with the somber reminder that America not only has come of age, but that she is also learning some unpleasant truths about the expense of greatness.

Open All the Way[1]

In *The Americans: The Colonial Experience* (Random House, $6.00) Professor Daniel J. Boorstin has produced a frank "thesis" history. Underlying the entire work is the argument that nothing European has been successfully transplanted to America. Or, if this metaphor is a little too rigorous, nothing that has been transplanted from Europe to America has managed to survive very long in the original form.

He seems to find in America some special set of thick, stubborn circumstances which exert an irresistible evolutionary pressure upon anything transferred to its soil. Among the things that American soil will not nourish are *a priori* ideas and systems, institutions resting upon exclusive principles, and hierarchies of any kind, including aristocracies and intellectual elites. This is a way of affirming that the American is destined by his environment to be empiricist, pragmatist, and democratic. One is impressed from the outset by Professor Boorstin's strong feeling against the theoretic and the structural.

It must be confessed that he argues his case heroically. He examines the major colonial undertakings one after another and tries to show that they succeeded or failed according to their promoters' readiness to adapt their ways of thinking to American exigencies. The Puritans failed to establish a Zion in the wilderness, but they did establish a colony because they had sense enough to leave aside strictly theological disputes and concentrate on the practical problems of church organization and community life. Of all those who came to the New World for reasons of religion, the Quakers were the most ill prepared to make the necessary adaptation. "The curse of perfectionism" and "the unfitness of their dogmas" left them incapable of "the larger task of building a new society in a new world."

The biggest failure of all was the colony of Georgia, which was under-

1. *National Review*, 6/13, November 22, 1958, 339–40. © 1958 by National Review, Inc., 215 Lexington Avenue, New York, N.Y. 10016. Reprinted by permission.

taken as a completely blueprinted affair. And the most successful was Virginia. That was because the settlers of Virginia came without any rigid ideas of church or state and set about making the best adaptation they could to the circumstances of a tobacco-producing economy. The economy was wasteful in many ways, but it did subject the planter class to "an unrelenting test of alertness and enterprise." Hence the Virginia leaders of the Revolution and founders of the Union. Nowhere does the author's insistent anti-formalism show more clearly than in his statement about Virginia Anglicanism: "In their own peculiar way, and even without realizing it, Virginians were 'purifying' the English church of its atmosphere of hierarchy and its excessive reliance on ritual."

Almost the whole tendency of America has been, for Professor Boorstin, in the direction of particular adaptation, improvisation, differentiation by locale, and the like. Almost, but not entirely. For when he comes to his section on American speech, we find things marching in the opposite direction. Here he spends pages not merely narrating but celebrating the achievement by Americans of a uniformity of speech.

Why did not America, with its great variety of land, climate, and ethnic composition, produce numberless dialects, or at least wide differences in pronunciation? Here the author has to look for another kind of cause. It was a passion for equality and community which made the people embrace a standard vocabulary and pronunciation. Geographic and social aspects of uniformity "have been both symptoms and causes of a striving for national unity." Further, "the very idea that there was a single 'proper' speech which any person could learn from a recipe book was subversive of the old ways and the old caste. It is easy to see how this way of looking at language would suit the new world." If the Americans in their other actions had reveled in their power to engender variety, why in this case did they show an equal enthusiasm for uniformity? And whence the passion for learning things from a recipe book, which would seem to counteract their suppositious attitude toward book knowledge?

Professor Boorstin has erected as the cause of his much stressed American resistance to traditional ideas and disciplines that which he would like to see prevail in American life: egalitarianism (at least to the extent of totally rejecting the idea of an elite), empirical procedures, distrust of forms, systems, and even of principles, and a strong strain of anti-institutionalism.

This is a proceeding which is fairly common in some areas of contemporary thought. One describes the forces one would like to see predominant in a society, and then one "proves" that they are inexorable causes. Whether or not Professor Boorstin thinks of himself as a Liberal, it needs pointing out that this is one of the techniques of the Liberals. It is the means by which they can argue that the future is on their side, since the future must emerge from the past, and the desiderated causes are made to seem historically grounded.

What the author is arguing is, in sum, that the dominant impulse of American history is toward the completely open society. There is nothing to which this society is unequivocally committed. Like the typical Liberal, he is willing to postulate little more than the right to experiment. Formalism and intellectualism are viewed almost as blights, and the native American growths as blight-resistant.

To realize how much he is willing to discard to arrive at this, one must note certain passages in the section dealing with American culture. "American printed matter," he writes, "thrived on the absence of a strong literary aristocracy. It was diffuse. Its center was everywhere because it was nowhere. . . . It was the product and the producer of a busy, mobile, public society, which preferred relevant truths to empyrean Truth. . . ." Consequently, down to this time "Not the litterateur but the journalist, not the essayist but the writer of how-to-do-it manuals, not the 'artist' but the publicist is the characteristic American man of letters." This is well enough if what one means by "man of letters" is a person who succeeds in getting into print. It will not do if one is talking about literary value. But "value" is an aristocratic word.

It is pleasant to think of ourselves as a peculiar people, but there may be an element of self-congratulation in it. It is intoxicating to think of ourselves as defiers of traditional forms, though that may be both wasteful and perilous. I think that Professor Boorstin has exaggerated the American separation from Europe. After all, one can be an American—one could even be an American isolationist—without denying that we are the heirs of much of Western European civilization. Finally, one can share his feeling about "garret-spawned European illuminati like Lenin, Mussolini, and Hitler" without trying to make American society quite as mindless as it appears in his pages.

The American as a Regenerate Being[1]

EDITED BY GEORGE CORE AND M. E. BRADFORD

Editorial Note: Richard Weaver's essay is presented as edited by George Core and M. E. Bradford, who comment on the text as follows: "'The American as a Regenerate Being' was originally delivered as a lecture at Whitworth College in Spokane, Washington, on April 27, 1962. It is one of several unpublished manuscripts that Richard Weaver was apparently working on just prior to this death. This version has been edited from an annotated original typescript of the author's which is close to being a fair copy. Weaver's revisions have been incorporated into this text, and his suggested elisions have been followed as well. Obvious errors have been silently corrected, and in a few cases explanatory asides for the benefit of the audience have been omitted. The editors are grateful to the late Kendall F. Beaton and his wife Polly Weaver Beaton, Richard Weaver's literary executors, who kindly made the original manuscript available to them and permitted its publication."

———

Running continuously through American literature, from the records set down by early settlers to the immensely more sophisticated writings of our present day, is one insistent question, variously conceived and variously answered, which may be phrased in succinct form thus: Is the American a regenerate being? Regenerate means, of course, in its etymological and theological sense, born again or made new. Whether the question comes to us in a naïve form, or in a form circumspective and knowing, the problem it poses is essentially this: we know that the American is a man in a new world, but is he also a *new* man?

From the bare outline of our history we can say that "America is westering." American has somehow always meant going west. From the time

1. *The Southern Review*, 4/3 (n.s.), Summer 1968, 633–46.

when Columbus guided his caravels towards the West Indies to the present hour when thousands pour monthly into California, there has continued this huge Western trek, away from Europe, then away from the "effete East," towards regions vaster and somehow more promising. But beyond and above this simple physical migration there has occurred, in the opinions of many, a kind of spiritual migration, in the course of which the migrants transported themselves not merely from the British Isles and from Europe but also from one moral condition to another. Under this conception the new arrival to these shores was not merely a transported man, he was also a transformed man, who had entered into a new status, for which the term "regenerate" might hopefully be right.

As reasons for leaving Europe behind him, the departing voyager had not simply complaints of poverty, or lack of opportunity, or of oppression, he had also a moral case. Europe was a failure when measured by the practicable ideal of what might be, and America was the place where that ideal might be realized. Not even the rich and marvellous cultures of Europe were atonement for what she had become; they were undeniably admirable as forms, but they were restrictive upon something yet more precious: human dignity and freedom. Hence, in seeking a place that would make him free, the American was seeking at the same time to raise himself up to an ideal which is paramount because it takes cognizance of individual worth despite the weight and prestige of institutions which have long histories to consecrate them.

In Europe there is much of beauty but little of love; in America there is little of beauty, but much of love, George Santayana has said in one of his famous aphorisms. And this contains a key to the difference. Europe has produced much that gratifies the aesthetic and intellectual sensibility; yet something has been left lacking. There has not been that affinity between man and man which religious thought places even above the claims of beauty.

I do not suggest that so neat a premise was in the conscious mind of every newcomer when he disembarked. But in the form of latent premise, it guided the impulse of very many of the new arrivals. Even those who came with the crudest thoughts of gain had the feeling that something was not right back home; supposing rightly or wrongly that they had been deprived, they looked for redress in the New World, or at least for kinder treatment from others. As for those who came for religious and political reasons, the case is too clear to need stating: America was to be the New Canaan where they could establish a society under better sanctions than had been possible in the land of their origin.

The thesis of superior American purity owes a great deal, obviously, to our Pilgrim ancestors. Separatists in more than one sense of the term, they withdrew physically from Europe to set up their theocracy in New England. Later, however, this same feeling of moral superiority made appearance in our social and political writing. Thomas Jefferson was the strongest of all advocates of keeping America free from what he conceived to be European contamination. He would have prevented young Americans from going to Europe for their educations because he felt that on balance they brought back more evil than good. It is interesting to see his reasoning upon this subject.

> But why send an American youth to Europe for an education? . . . If he goes to England, he learns drinking, horse-racing, and boxing. These are the peculiarities of English education. The following circumstances are common to education in that and the other countries of Europe. He acquires a fondness for European luxury and dissipation, and a contempt for the simplicity of his own country . . . he returns to his own country a foreigner.

After our country had achieved its independence and had gained a degree of national self-confidence, the theme was continued quite as loudly as before, if with emphasis on other things. Throughout the first half of the nineteenth century there was a strong and well-articulated tendency to look upon the American as the "new Adam"—as a man in position to begin history afresh, without any debt to a sinful past. It would be surprising to some present-day Americans to learn how many acknowledged leaders of that period were "America Firsters" in the matter of our national culture. Ralph Waldo Emerson, delivering his "American Scholar" address, called upon his audience to cease to attend to the courtly Muses of Europe. Henry David Thoreau wrote: "I look upon England today as an old gentleman who is travelling with a great deal of baggage, trumpery which he has accumulated from long housekeeping, which he has not the courage to burn." Even the sober-minded Hawthorne chimes in, in the same tune. "The time will come, sooner or later," he said to W. D. Ticknor, "when John Bull will look to us for his salvation." Later he discovers a lack of sympathy with the French: "Their eyes do not win me, nor do their glances melt and mingle with mine." Noah Webster was announcing that "American glory begins at the dawn." Daniel Webster addressed himself to the theme in the Bunker Hill oration:

> Her obligations to Europe for science and art, laws, literature and manners, America acknowledges as she ought, with respect and gratitude. . . . But America has not failed to make returns. . . . America exercises influences, or holds out examples, for the consideration of the Old World, of a much higher, because they are of a moral and political character.[2]

Edward Everett summed up his prescription in one phrase: the health of America required *separation from Europe*. The *Democratic Review* affirmed that "our national birth was the beginning of a new history . . . which separates us from the past and connects us with the future only." And further: "The expansive future is our arena. We are entering on its untrodden ways . . . with a clear conscience unsullied by the past." James Russell Lowell aimed a diatribe at imitative writing by Americans and at the same time affirmed a belief in the native superiority of the American.

> Forget Europe wholly, your veins throb with blood
> To which the dull current in hers is but mud.

Somewhat later, Walt Whitman was to declare that "the priest departs, the divine literatus appears," meaning of course that religion with its long history and its traditions was about to leave the stage, and that in its place were to come creators of literature divinely inspired with messages of democracy and the future.

As R. W. B. Lewis has observed in his *The American Adam*, the image of this new Adam was practically an ethical polemic. It was the American retort against Europe, with its past of narrowness and oppression and political unrighteousness. The new Adam as celebrated here was not just regenerate man: he was man who had never known a fall. Orators and poets and men known as philosophers thus indulged in an apotheosis of the American.

Some of these pronouncements have about them, indeed, the blatancy of political chauvinism; others are more perceptive of real truths. What I am stressing at the moment is the persistence of the idea upon different levels,

---

2. The last sentence of the quotation is as Webster wrote it.—Editors.

the insistency of a feeling that in America something new had emerged. And now if we turn to a later generation of writers, men who have nothing about them sounding of rodomontade, we still encounter the sense of an American difference.

D. H. Lawrence was an unmannerly critic of American literature, but, as is apt to be true of one who has no need to apologize and no desire to ingratiate, he made some very penetrating judgments. Lawrence emphasized the thought that the American has a special kind of consciousness. This he attributed in part to the polarity of place—the American characteristically is the Westerner in his wide-open West. I do not think nearly enough has been said in cultural history about the effect of place upon a people's way of looking at things and of ordering their values. This does not mean that an Eskimo will have one kind of outlook by virtue of being above the Arctic Circle and a Congolese another in any easy and predictable way. It is not a doctrine of simple environmental determinism. Yet it does mean that place will enter in some formative way into the cultural constitution. To be in or of a place is a part of one's definition. Cosmopolitanism is a kind of privation. But only the artist or the philosophical critic is equipped to say how this being of a place moulds one. That is a task for insight. It is enough to note here that Lawrence, certainly no man to fall for easy or second-hand ideas, took stock in this proposition.

However, historical and other factors also enter into one's formation, and here again Lawrence has some interesting views. After the Renaissance, he says, Europe took the road into a liberal *cul de sac*. Not all Europeans found this path attractive, and those who were moved by ideological or spiritual reasons to make a change decided to go to America and abandon the old European consciousness entirely. They wanted neither its traditional order and rule nor the kinds of chaos and breakdown certain to result from post-Renaissance liberalism. A very speculative kind of diagnosis, one might say, and yet because of its coherence with some recognizable facts, one not to be ignored. What did these emigrants want, who were rejecting both the old and the new in Europe?

They wanted some new relationship with the world which would bring with it a positive gain in freedom. At the basis of the American consciousness, he says, lies a dictum: "Thou shalt not presume to be a master." This is what the American declares to all other Americans and to outsiders as well. "Thou shalt not presume to be a master." This does not mean, "Thou shalt not be a master." The key word is "presume." It announces that you shall not conceive in advance, without any ground or evidence, that you are entitled to mastership. Here appears the radical break with Europe. For there was in the old European tradition much of presumption, the feeling that certain men or orders were aboriginally destined to be lords of others.

In this regard, however, an important distinction is to be made. The American attitude is not to be taken simply as an attack upon aristocracy or upon the idea of superiority or upon any hierarchical ordering of society. It is an attack upon presumption, upon the claim without the deed, the aristocratic pretense without aristocratic fulfillment. What the American says in essence is, prove your title. Nor can this be regarded as a posture of simple pragmatism. It is rather a recognition of the principle that status cannot survive without function.

All existence wears the two great aspects of permanence and change. It is as idle to say that nothing ever changes as to deny that anything has a fixed nature. Without permanence there is no possibility of knowledge; without change there is no possibility of life. This broad truth is applicable also to society. Status there has to be; without some granting of rights, privileges, and conditions, it is not possible to conceive an orderly society. But unless society insists upon function or performance at some point as justification of these, it lapses into a caste system, and a caste system is by definition out of contact with reality.

It has been the distinctive American achievement to bring these together into a new balance—to affirm function while at the same time preserving status. But since for us Europe has generally stood for an over-balance of status—a too great reliance upon establishment—in our behavior and our culture we have more often expressed our faith in function as the wholesome corrective. It is the deed as opposed to the prerogative, the active man as opposed to the man invested with some aura or some reputation which has been our redress of the balance. If there is one accent heavier than others in American culture and literature, it is upon the redemptive virtue of this aspect of existence.

In many cases we have carried this too far; in some instances we have made it a shibboleth. But I feel right in saying that where the American is dramatized vis-à-vis the European or European type, we find stressed this justification by action, which carries with it a certain cleanness, as opposed to the encrustations of any kind of settlement—even of civilization as this has been known.

The air of it was detected in the confident look and the free ways of our pioneers. And we encounter it in the literary depictions of our most creative artists—Mark Twain and Whitman and Henry James. Huckleberry Finn, that extraordinary intuition of what is most American in the American, is a kind of super-separatist. He flees from the world of civilization as represented by the Widow Douglas and the various respectabilities of village life. He embarks on that drifting voyage down the Mississippi, which not only keeps him separated or emancipated from the shore, but also keeps him on a moving medium, which can be taken symbolically as a means of escape from an imprisoning past. When Huck declares at the end of the book, "I reckon I got to light out for the Territory ahead of the rest, because Aunt Sally she's going to adopt me and sivilize me and I can't stand it. I been there before," he is speaking the characteristic note of the American regenerate. I was sunk in civilization. Now I am redeemed. I shall not fall again. Twain returns to the theme in *A Connecticut Yankee at King Arthur's Court,* where he tilts his own kind of lance against the whole institution of chivalry. Since chivalry was probably the most remarkable formal development of European culture, it was for Twain the most logical target for attack from his premises, even if we must deplore some inadequate comprehension of it.

The distrust of Europe and its civilization is somewhat harder to document from Whitman. Whitman was not a good hater. That expansive, all-inclusive outlook of his inclined him to extend hospitality toward everything. Even the Old World, he admitted now and then, had to be counted in somehow. Yet on balance his note is clearly that of American regenerateness. And nowhere is it more finely expressed than in that fine line of "Starting from Paumanok": "Solitary, singing in the West, I strike up for a New World." Here is the regenerate American with all of Whitman's cheerful confidence.

A stanza from "Song of Exposition," written ten years later, gives a fuller inventory of his feeling, especially on the subject of American cultural destiny.

Come, Muse, migrate from Greece and Ionia;
Cross out, please, those immensely overpaid accounts;

That matter of Troy, and Achilles' wrath, and Eneas', Odysseus' wanderings;
Placard "*Removed*" and "*To Let*" on the rocks of your snowy Parnassus;
Repeat at Jerusalem—place the notice high on Jaffa's gate, and on Mount
    Moriah;
The same on the walls of your Gothic European Cathedrals, and German, French
    and Spanish Castles;
For know a better, fresher, busier sphere—a wide, untried domain awaits,
    demands you.

Two men more unlike in temperament and artistic method than Whitman and Henry James it would be difficult to imagine—though James once
confessed, with a consciousness of anomaly, that Whitman was his favorite
poet. Still, one finds in James in a singular way the American emerging as
an approvable type. James handled the problem, of course, in his own subtle
and probing style, yet the upshot is not very different. He himself had felt
the powerful pull which the more aesthetic civilization of Europe is likely
to exert upon an American of sensibility. The general pattern of plot in
more than one of his stories is for an American protagonist to go to Europe
seeking those sources of satisfaction which the older civilization has to offer. There he comes up against intrigue, dissimulation, and duplicity which
put his innocence to a severe trial. But somehow, in most cases, the American emerges in a superior light. In his novel entitled *The American,* to take
a significant instance, Christopher Newman, who has been treated haugh-
tily and shabbily by the aristocratic Bellegarde family, finally has it in his
power to retaliate. But instead of retaliating, instead of descending to the
level of their ways, he simply destroys that which had given him the opportunity for revenge. He turns away from the whole affair in an apparent
conclusion that this is not the kind of thing for him. It is a peculiarly
American magnanimity.

In one of his best, though regrettably one of his least known novels, *The
Bostonians,* there is a kind of a fortiori demonstration of this same difference. Here, interestingly enough, the setting is in his own country, but the
clash of forces is basically the same. In this instance a young Mississippian,
very solid, normal, and candid, whom business has brought to Boston, falls
in with Boston intellectuals and blue-stockings. Basil Ransom, the Mississippian, keeps his aplomb; and the Bostonians are exhibited with varying
degrees of caricature. The point is made plain in the course of the novel

that their sophisticated intellectual culture has somehow spoiled them or got them off balance; it has drawn them away from that standard of sanity and directness which is represented by Ransom. Here the conflict is not the American against the European, but the American of a traditional type against people in that section of America most oriented towards Europe. And while James would never dream of speaking of his hero in this novel as "wholesome," that is the aspect under which he enters and leaves, and this was one reason for the poor reception of the novel in Boston.

The identical polarity appears in the finest work of the figure with which I shall conclude this group, *The Great Gatsby*, by F. Scott Fitzgerald. This is a peculiarly affecting account of innocence in contact with an older, more sophisticated, and guilty kind of culture. Jay Gatsby is a Westerner in fact— from North Dakota, a part of the West with something of the frontier then remaining. Caught up in the wave of the First World War, he goes to an officers' training camp near Louisville, and there he meets Daisy Fay. Daisy is the only girl of wealth and social position he has ever known, and it is easy to see the extraordinary glamor which she held for him. They have a brief romance, but of course Daisy is not for Jay Gatsby. She soon marries Tom Buchanan, a fabulously rich Chicago heir, and they go off to live in luxury on Long Island. Still, Gatsby is like Petrarch having seen his Laura: he can never forget her or put her out of mind. After the war he becomes the head of a vast bootlegging enterprise and makes money in such amounts that he is able to become a neighbor of Daisy's on Long Island and to continue his worship from much nearer. In a distant sort of way they resume their affair, but the result of the new contact is to bring out the essential devotion, manliness, and idealism of Gatsby, so poor in his background and education, and the essential selfishness, callousness, and even corruption of Daisy and Tom and their group. Like rich and indulgent people of their kind, they make a mess and leave it for others to clean up—that is the judgment of the book. Gatsby has made his money in illicit traffic, but they are rotten compared with him. There can be no doubt that Fitzgerald is expressing in fictional form this archetypal idea: that when the honest, straightforward, and well-meaning West goes to the East, it finds itself in a different kind of moral atmosphere. This is not the innocence of the Garden any longer: it is something older and somehow depraved. What had been enacted in the America–Europe relationship can thus be acted out in the West–East relationship in America, and certainly Jay Gatsby is the one we would choose to call the American.

Interestingly enough, Fitzgerald made a pronouncement which shows that he had reflected upon this profound difference. He said: "France was a land, England was a people but America, having still about it that quality of an idea, was harder to utter." How quickly and truly that dissipates the notion that America has been merely the most successful real estate venture in history. Having about it the quality of an idea, it is hard to utter. But that is our next task, if we are to determine in what way the American is a new man.

The American *is* a regenerate being in the sense that "being an American is a moral condition."

The American is unregenerate in the sense that, like all other men, he has been born into history and lives in history. He has to work out "the awful experiment of time."

The question *has* to be answered both ways.

But on the other hand he is a man redeemed when you discover him showing a certain mercy of equality to those around him and keeping faith with his lofty yet sometimes vague aspirations.

Probably no other people has ever been able to bring together these modes so successfully. The American has done it by preserving a certain tension between his idealistic outlook and an unrivaled ability to come to grips with facts and master them to his advantage.

The tension that I speak of is writ large in our history. Let us think of the realistic or seamy side first. We came as settlers or invaders (mostly with good intentions) and took the land away from the original inhabitants. This process went on for 300 years, and involved just about every species of fraud and force. Beginning in 1619 we started importing African blacks and kept on until we had many millions of them working in the status of slaves. I say "we" because it is sometimes overlooked that those who transported this property to our country were chiefly New Englanders. The violent upheaval which put an end to the institution of slavery was the greatest war of the nineteenth century, excepting only the Napoleonic wars. A rough and ready kind of settlement, with many incidental injustices. Following this crisis came the "Great Barbecue," a hectic era of great fortune building, during which the agricultural West and South unquestionably got exploited, and partly through political means. Then quite unabashedly we indulged in a few bouts of imperialism and seized some parts of the moribund Spanish Empire. After the First World War we went through a boom-and-bust period of financial expansion and afterward picked ourselves up by methods that are still controversial. But we came to the Second World War strong enough, physically and morally, to assure victory for the side that represented free government.

I have tried to make this an unadorned tale, a kind of pragmatic view of the history of the American people, a *res gestae* or chronicle of things done one way and another. It is the sort of story that could be cited by our critics and enemies as proof of our aimlessness and immorality. It is in fact cited by some who think that the United States needs nothing so much as to live down its past.

Yet it would be a very prejudiced and tendentious commentator who would limit himself to this side. The other side, of aspiration and ennobling ideals and of native kindliness, has always been there to establish what I am calling the tension.

From the time of the Mayflower Compact there has been an orchestration of hopes, and again it would be a prejudiced historian who could not see that these have in fact exerted an upward pull upon the course of our activities. There is the pervasive idealism of Jefferson, from which we derive so many of our avowed (if not always invoked) political sanctions. "The principles of Jefferson are the maxims of a free society," Abraham Lincoln was to say. There is something in Jefferson's practicality about all kinds of physical devices and arrangements combined with a kind of visionariness which places him close to the generic American type—closer even than Franklin, who is sometimes thought of as the Aeneas of our tribe.

Right in the midst of the busy Yankees appeared the tracts of the New England Transcendentalists. No more eloquent sermons against materialism have ever been preached. Thoreau scorned the thought of possessions with a completeness which in another age might have established him as a saint. *I am rich in proportion to the things I can do without* was his constant theme. The philosophy of the entire group is distinctly otherworldly; it is precisely the kind of thing one would not expect to appear in America if one accepted the pragmatic picture—that is, the picture which reduces America to materialist self-seeking.

In the Civil War period Lincoln stands out as a striking embodiment of this tension of opposites. He was and always remained a politician, but he saw politics in the wider frame of morality. He was never an Abolitionist, and our "civil rights" advocates today will find very cold comfort in some of his utterances, yet he had his own position against the "peculiar institution." It was an accommodation to facts and an allegiance to principle at the same time. In the best of his speeches he showed a remarkable power to transcend immediate issues, however much they were working upon popular passions. Recall for a moment the Gettysburg Address. It is almost impossible to tell, from *internal* evidence, which side on the battlefield he is speaking for. Nearly all of the predicates can be applied to both sides. The most earthy of our presidents in his origin, he proved capable of the most sublimated thinking.

Descending to later times, we encounter another representative in Theodore Roosevelt. Roosevelt always seemed fascinated by the European idea of *Realpolitik,* of which indeed he made some use. But in this he always appears on the defensive. It is not an American mode; it did not sit on him well. He was at his most natural when he was "doing good" in those "man-of-action" poses which he liked to adopt.

Every epoch, Herder says, has its own relationship to the divine or the transcendent. If America is an epoch, why is this not true of her, and why should we not be loyal to that relationship? These are questions which get no answers from positivists and relativists, for the first will not recognize an ontological basis for values, and the second looks upon neither general truth nor tradition as weighing anything in a balance with the urgency of the moment. People who persist in denying the image of America are mostly found in these groups. We cannot depend on them to defend anything for us, because their view is too superficial to reach what is most valuable in our eyes.

The predicate "regenerate," to which this lecture has been keyed must of course be taken considerately and not too literally. What I feel justified in concluding is that the American is a new type, made new by the quality of his experience. What that experience has been the average man feels in his bones; but as I have endeavored to point out, our literary artists, who to the extent that they are artists speak the truth disinterestedly, have articulated it sometimes in rather subtle ways. And it seems to me that it is a complex thing, which has defied and will go on defying and resisting those "terrible simplifications" with which Europe has been experimenting for half a century. Communism, Fascism, Naziism, and other forms of totalitarianism are in fact ruthless simplifications, forced upon peoples who had lost their sense of direction or their moral health. We have shown high immunity to them through the very novelty of our attitude born out of that fructifying union of materialism and idealism. Much of our political genius has lain in saying "No" to propositions which would lead to uniformity and rigidity. Even the doctrines of Rousseau, the historian John Fiske noted, "found few readers and fewer admirers among the Americans." In the Old World from which we descend, the attractions of theory have been enough to produce many unbalanced and dangerous situations.

Not long ago I heard an American university president who was just back from Europe, where he had talked with scholars and intellectuals, say that to his surprise he had found the Europeans not at all interested in or impressed by American technological achievements. Their attitude was that we were here before you in this field, and we are just as capable in it today as you are, if not more so. What we want to hear about are the ideas that control your life. These are the unique American contributions. In my opinion, they were reading America right. What Europe can learn from America is not how to make a machine, but how to conceive values at once realistic and elevating, around which people will unite without coercion. We have not always done this, but characteristically we have sought to do it. And to the extent that this comprises the American's character, he has attained a new level, which can be described, without too much risk in the metaphor contained in the word, as a regeneration.

Anybody's Guess[1]

After all that has been written about him, the character of Lincoln remains an enigma wrapped in a mystery. The immense volume of partisan biography makes it risky to consult secondary sources, and the student who wishes a true picture is practically obliged to go to the man's own writings. From *The Collected Works of Abraham Lincoln,* recently issued by the Rutgers University Press, Paul M. Angle and Earl Schenck Miers have prepared this selection, ranging from Lincoln's first political announcement to the voters of Sangamon County in 1832 to his final documents envisaging the problems of Reconstruction.

One clue to "the man," perhaps, is his sense of style. From early maturity Lincoln possessed an extraordinary insight into the nuclear meanings of words. His mind was precise, logical and aristocratic; he had no patience with forms of pretentiousness like verbiage, and legal opponents dreaded his succinctness in argument. Nor was this style confined to official utterances; little gems like his suggestions to young men considering the study of law and the letters of advice he wrote to his ne'er-do-well stepbrother, John D. Johnston, are in the same vein.

A book such as this enables the reader to form his own opinion upon questions which can hardly be answered with any sureness. Was Lincoln a plain, homespun citizen who yielded to an imperative call to save the nation, or was he secretly ambitious? More than one of his close associates in Springfield believed that he was highly ambitious. And it certainly appears here that when Lincoln went after office, he left nothing practical undone to win it, and that his mind fed on politics.

Was he always a perfectly frank, open, guileless person who deserved the sobriquet, "Honest Abe"? The answer may depend on how one reads him.

1. *National Review*, 1/22, April 18, 1956, 20. © 1956 by National Review, Inc., 215 Lexington Avenue, New York, N.Y. 10016. Reprinted by permission.

Some of his utterances show a surface of complete candor and simplicity while possessing an inner deviousness that leaves one puzzled as to his intentions. His genius at language enabled him invariably to stop short of the politically fatal commitment.

Did Lincoln really hope to avert civil war? It is a standard schoolbook proposition that he did. But there is evidence here that as early as the Kentucky elections of 1849, in which every anti-slavery candidate was defeated, he gave up hope for a non-violent settlement of the slavery controversy. His handling of the Fort Sumter incident also supports the latter view.

Lincoln was by nature a moral philosopher, and he had a sense of the tragic that sets him off sharply from the optimists, strenuous extroverts, and believers in Progress who seem the only political timber available today. A half poetic pessimism accompanied him through life. Once after witnessing the cheerful, carefree behavior of some slaves who were being sold down the river, he observed that life leaves the worst of human conditions tolerable and the best little more than tolerable.

The commentaries of the editors are too much in the tradition of hero-building. But the selections themselves show one of the most complex minds ever produced by this country; and the reader may cease to wonder why Lincoln has been claimed with equal zeal by radicals, liberals, and conservatives.

Inglorious Exit[1]

This is the first biography ever written of James Wilson, described here as "one of the principal architects of our nation."

Wilson was born in Scotland in 1742, to poverty and the dour religion of the Scottish Covenanters. A bursarship enabled him to attend St. Andrews, where he spent five years living on the grim diet and in the unheated rooms of the St. Andrews "terner," while laboring at Greek, Latin, mathematics, logic, and ethics. Originally he had intended to enter the ministry, but already news of the Scottish Enlightenment was seeping through, with its promise to substitute earthly happiness for salvation. Wilson listened, and shortly after the death of his father he sailed for America.

Settling in the colony of Pennsylvania, he supported himself for a time by tutoring, but this held narrow prospects for a man of his ambition. A large proportion of the leaders of the early American communities were lawyers, because the settlement of land titles and the work of imposing form on the anarchical frontier gave them immense opportunity. For a fee, the famous John Dickinson took Wilson as apprentice, and before long he was one of the leading lawyers in the colony. When the debate over independence began to gather volume, Wilson entered it with his "Considerations of the Nature and Extent of the Legislative Authority of the British Parliament."

He was a member of the Second Continental Congress and a signer of the Declaration of Independence. In the long and often bitter controversies over the nature of state and federal constitutions, he took a mixed position. He fought "an unceasing warfare against the democratic elements of the Pennsylvania frontier," for which he was denounced, and once almost mobbed, as a "Tory" and "aristocrat." In the Constitutional Convention he

1. *National Review*, 2/13, August 18, 1956, 20–21. © 1956 by National Review, Inc., 215 Lexington Avenue, New York, N.Y. 10016. Reprinted by permission.

stood with Madison, Hamilton, and others for a stronger and more centralized form of government. On the other hand he opposed the filtering of the wisdom of the people through an elite of electors and favored the direct election of both Houses of Congress and of the President.

Along with many leading men of the period, Wilson had an insatiable appetite for land speculation. His share in the Illinois-Wabash Company entitled him to 400,000 acres, and this was but one of several holdings. He also acquired businesses which he hoped to pay for out of future profits. When the panic of 1797 arrived, all came down with a crash.

Wilson had hoped to be appointed the first Chief Justice of the Supreme Court, but rumors of his financial dealings, which, if not irregular, went far beyond prudence, caused Washington to pass him over in favor of John Jay. He was, however, named Associate Justice. It is startling to think of this member of the highest tribunal in 1798, in wild flight from his creditors, twice thrown into jail, and dying in hiding in a remote town in North Carolina.

Professor Smith seems to admire his subject as the prophet of a future nationalized democracy. The prophetic strain appears somewhat ominously in the statement that "Wilson knew quite well what the [Supreme] Court might become in time by the quiet but persistent accumulation of power." Credit must be given, however, for a fine piece of biographical research and execution. The facts are marshaled with judgment, and the style at times achieves literary distinction.

Review of Samuel Flagg Bemis,
John Quincy Adams and the Union[1]

John Quincy Adams was the last President to serve before the flood of Jacksonian equalitarianism permanently changed the tone of American political life. He was not a brilliant or a profound man; but he was an indefatigable worker who kept a diary of his activities for sixty years; a prodigious reader, learned in sciences other than politics; and he was a patriot of the Revolutionary school. Perhaps most important of all, he possessed a New England conscience, which means that he had character, however angular and lacking in charm. There were many uses for a man like this in the formative period of our republic, and history did not fail to match him with great events. "A boy tugging at his mother's hand, he watched from a distance the Battle of Bunker Hill," and he served his country until the age of eighty, when he was fatally stricken on the floor of the House while making a speech on the Mexican War.

The great contest of his life was with Andrew Jackson, whom he defeated for the Presidency in 1824 only after the election was thrown into the House of Representatives. It stands as one of the few times that a mere civilian has been able to triumph over a military hero in a rivalry for the chief office of the land. Even so, it was an uneasy Presidency; Adams' rather abstract program of "Liberty with Power" did not excite the popular mind, and the Jacksonians marked time until they could make their real power felt. After his term as President he was sent to Congress from the Plymouth district of Massachusetts in 1830, and he served faithfully in the humbler office for eighteen years.

During this period as legislator, Adams fought for an "equitable" tariff, supported the Bank of the United States as an instrumentality of Union,

1. *Freeman*, 6, June 1956, 62–64.

took a leading part in the anti-Masonic movement which at one time attained considerable political proportions, contended against the Southern "nullifiers" at every opportunity, and opposed the annexation of Texas as a nefarious scheme to increase the power of the slavocrats.

All of these matters the author relates in sober professorial style, with compendious footnotes. To say that the narrative is fresh or exciting would be unwarranted. It is a product of scholarly industry, with no aspect of Adams' mature life considered too dull for liberal quotations and citations. Adams' early career was similarly treated in Bemis' previous biography of him.

No experienced reader of biography expects a biographer to be wholly impartial; the very fact that he has chosen a certain life to chronicle shows that he cherishes some sentiment in regard to it. Nevertheless, it seems to me that in two instances Bemis has been unduly partisan and lacking in critical candor. The first of these concerns his subject's relation to the Texas Question. In his early years, Adams had been an expansionist himself, but when Texas entered the picture, he seemed to lose all perspective. He swallowed whole the current abolitionist view of the issue, which was that the annexation of Texas and the Mexican War constituted a gigantic plot on the part of Southern slave owners to add to their territory. Recent historical scholarship has proved that the facts are at variance with any such interpretation. On this matter Adams was parochial, shortsighted, and intemperate.

In the second instance, he seems most ungenerous to John C. Calhoun. Every stick is used to beat this American statesman. He chortles over Calhoun's about-face on the tariff issue. In a fashion hardly congruous with critical scholarship, he captions Adams "Defender of Freedom" and Calhoun "Defender of Slavery." It is just as if Adams had to have a "heavy," and Calhoun is it. The reader gets no inkling from what is said here that Calhoun, through his doctrine of the concurrent majority, is one of the most effective of all antitotalitarian spokesmen, and that as far as political theory goes, he erected a sounder scaffolding for liberty with power than did Adams himself.

The vast amount of research which went into this work leaves every reader in Professor Bemis' debt. But the execution as a whole leaves something to be desired. An excessive spirit of adulation rather frequently interferes with proportioning, and colors the author's expression.

The Western Star[1]

America has seen few political personalities as attractive as Henry Clay. Born in Virginia in 1777, he moved while a young man to that "spreading meadow whence the rivers flow," which is central Kentucky. He had the right combination of appearance, magnetism, audacity, and eloquence to please the card-, horse-, and politics-loving aristocracy which dominated that region, and his star rose fast. In 1806 he became United States Senator, and in 1850, forty-four years later, he was still a dominant political figure in his state and in the nation. In between political activities he lived the life of a gentleman-planter at his beautiful estate "Ashland," outside Lexington, and dispensed a convivial hospitality.

In *Henry Clay and the Art of American Politics* (Little, Brown, $3.50) Professor Clement Eaton surveys his career for the Library of American Biography series. Clay was one of the American commissioners sent to Ghent to negotiate a treaty following the well-nigh disastrous war of 1812. The contrast between his behavior and that of John Quincy Adams, who read five chapters of the Bible every day and retired at nine, has become legendary. But Clay was an expert poker player; and had he not brought to the treaty table what he learned at the poker table, it is doubtful whether the United States would have emerged so favorably from a war which it can hardly be said to have won.

He was the first to advocate recognizing the South American republics, then in rebellion against Spain, and his name today carries more prestige in Latin America than that of any other American statesman. In 1826, while Secretary of State, he suggested cutting a canal "across Mexico or Central America," to be free to the ships of all the world. In Congress he defended

1. *National Review*, 3/15, April 13, 1957, 358–59. © 1957 by National Review, Inc., 215 Lexington Avenue, New York, N.Y. 10016. Reprinted by permission.

the rights of the Southern Indians, who had been harshly wronged by Andrew Jackson.

A believer in tariffs, Clay tried to be a moderator between elements at the North who wanted a high level of protection and those at the South who wanted free trade. And two years before his death in 1852 he maneuvered through Congress the last of his great compromises, which postponed the issue of civil war for ten years and in so doing probably determined the outcome. It is not surprising that over in Illinois a gangling tyro in politics named Lincoln looked upon Clay as his idol and wondered how he could be like him.

Meantime Clay ran for the Presidency three times, more than any other man in history except Eugene Debs and Norman Thomas. But despite his art of politics and fervent supporters in every part of the Union, the dazzling prize eluded him. The reasons seem to have been both personal and political.

Clay was never a profound political thinker. His formal education was slight, and though he deplored this, he did little to repair the deficiency. When admirers sent him books, he glanced at them but did not read them. He attacked Calhoun, his great rival in the Senate, as a "metaphysician." For the persuasiveness of his speeches he relied upon topical interest, his own appealing personality, and what all contemporaries agreed was a wonderful voice.

His political position was seriously mixed. Kentucky has always been a border state, trying to explain the North to the South and the South to the North. In Clay's time it was also a border state between East and West, with the added task of trying to explain the older, more settled regions to the frontier and the frontier to them.

All this involved Clay in many political ambivalences. He owned slaves but did not believe in slavery. His famous compromises were designed not to solve the problem but to pacify the opposing sides. Though he came from an agricultural section, he stood for tariffs and so alienated large segments of Southern opinion. Though he delighted in being called "Harry of the West" and "the Western Star," he supported the National Bank, which was anathema to the Jacksonians and to the West in general. When issues became acute, his failure to take a consistent line cost heavily. A temporizing stand on the annexation of Texas in 1844 probably lost him the Presidency by alienating voters on either side of the question.

Then there was his Whiggery. The Whigs have left important lessons in how not to survive as a great party, and Whig policy seems to have been congenial to Clay's nature. No party, says Tocqueville, will endure long if it makes personalities rather than principles and ideas its main source of strength. This the Whig Party did regularly; in the campaign of 1840 it declined even to adopt a platform. The graver political issues became, the more inadequate the Whigs were, so that one could say that they prepared their own demise in 1856. Personality, popularity, and glamor could carry the party through minor crises, but could not carry it through a major one. This explains why Clay, with all his charm and with his impressive record of achievement, has not gone down in history as a seminal political thinker. He was not a political landmark, like Calhoun; he was a mentor of the art of politics, perhaps, but not of political philosophy.

Professor Eaton's final accolade for Clay is that by his tactics of compromise he saved the Union until it was able to save itself in the war of unification of 1861–65. Yet there is another side of this which biographers seem unwilling to stress: Clay is a kind of bridge stretching from the Virginia Dynasty to the Gilded Age.

Thence, in another span, the bridge reaches on to modern industrialism and centralized government. The author intimates as much when he says that in the critical decade of his life "Clay changed the emphasis of his political thinking from the preservation of human rights to the advancement of the material well-being of his section and the nation." Clay's nationalism inspired the nationalism of Lincoln. His devotion to tariffs and to federal-sponsored internal improvements played right into the hands of those who turned this country from a decentralized, agrarian, and somewhat libertarian republic into a plutocratic, nationalized state, in which the leaders of opinion were no longer ministers and lawyers, but businessmen. True, Clay did not live to see the Gilded Age. But the forces that created it were there, and he was their mouthpiece. All they needed was the political and economic right of way which the Civil War gave them. From their excesses sprang eventually a monster of different, but no lovelier mien, the New Deal.

One of the gravest temptations is to say that you love liberty but to show by your actions that you love other things more—to decide that "material well-being" is more important than "the preservation of human rights."

Clay was not profound enough to see the nature of this choice. Jefferson saw it and made it to the extent of adopting an almost anarchistic attitude toward the state. While Clay did a number of things that are admirable in themselves, he did not perceive that who sups with the devil needs a long spoon. His concessions to centralization and a burgeoning industrialism paved the way for some of the most onerous problems that our generation is heir to.

Trumpet-Tongued Foe of Coercion [1]

In *Patrick Henry: Patriot in the Making* (Lippincott, $7.50) Robert Douthat Meade undertakes a definitive biography of the man whose eloquence did much to bring about American independence. Although this volume, the first of two projected by the author, traces his career only as far as the Continental Congress, it is valuable for its account of his background and of his entrance upon the theater of the Revolution.

Henry's father, John Henry (of a family which earlier spelled its name "Hendrie"), was a product of the bleak northeast of Scotland. After attending the University of Aberdeen for four years, he decided to exchange the rigors of his native environment for the opportunities of America. Arriving in Virginia in 1727, he petitioned Governor Gooch for a tract of land in Hanover County. Here he married a widow, and here in 1736 was born a son, who was named Patrick after an uncle.

Young Henry's formal education was brief, but it was sound. After he had attended a common school until the age of ten, his education was taken over by his father, under whose tutoring he learned some Latin and Greek and became, according to a contemporary account, "well acquainted with the mathematics, of which he was very fond." We are also told that by the age of fifteen he was "well versed in both ancient and modern history."

After two failures as a storekeeper, Henry, in desperate straits to support a family, which he had started by the age of eighteen, decided to become a lawyer. His preparation consisted of reading law for considerably less than a year—by one account for only six weeks—and when he journeyed to Williamsburg for his license, the board was reluctant even to admit him to examination. One of the examiners afterward said "he was so ignorant of

1. *National Review,* 4/13, October 5, 1957, 307–8. © 1957 by National Review, Inc., 215 Lexington Avenue, New York, N.Y. 10016. Reprinted by permission.

law at the time, that he should not have passed him, had he not discovered his great genius." In this way Henry squeaked by to begin his real career.

The event which first stamped him as a remarkable orator was not the speech containing the famous peroration "Give me liberty or give me death." It was a courtroom performance twelve years earlier in which Henry suddenly rose to prominence as an advocate in the celebrated "Parson's Cause."

Since 1696 the clergy of the established church in Virginia had been paid in tobacco, the rate of their salaries being fixed at 16,000 pounds of the weed per annum. Owing to bad crop conditions in the 1750s, the Virginia General Assembly amended this rule to permit payment either in tobacco or in money at the rate of two pence per pound. As tobacco often sold much higher than this, the parsons felt that they were being cheated out of part of their salaries and began to file suits for unpaid balances. It was an issue involving conflict between the authority of the colonial assembly and that of the Crown, which never sanctioned the new rule.

In 1763 Henry was retained to defend the "collectors" of Hanover County against a suit for damages of the Reverend James Maury for arrears of salary. After a fumbling beginning which left his friends disconcerted, he suddenly caught fire and launched into that fervid style which was to make him one of the great orators of the age. By the end of the first twenty minutes the audience was hanging forward in "deathlike silence," and many afterwards testified to having felt "bereft of their senses" by the force of his eloquence. For two generations thereafter the highest compliment that could be paid to a speaker in Virginia was, "He is almost equal to Patrick when he pleaded against the parsons." The jury awarded damages of one penny, and Henry was immediately recognized as the boldest champion of colonial rights.

Two years later Henry, now a member of the House of Burgesses, offered a set of resolutions on the Stamp Act. The first four of these were relatively mild declarations, but the fifth, which branded anyone who denied the exclusive right of the General Assembly to levy taxes an enemy of American freedom, brought on a "most bloody debate." It was here that Henry, rising to heights in defense of the resolution, declared: "Tarquin and Caesar had each his Brutus, Charles the First his Cromwell, and George the Third may profit by their example." To cries of "Treason! Treason!" he made the famous reply, "If this be treason, make the most of it."

How great actually was Henry as an orator? Has the legend of his prowess merely mushroomed with time? Evidently not, for the impression he made upon the discerning of his time was deep and lasting. Jefferson, who was notably candid in such matters, wrote that "Mr. Henry's talents as a popular orator . . . were indeed great, such as I never heard from any other man. He appeared to me to speak as Homer wrote." And the widely read and philosophical George Mason could say: "He is by far the most powerful speaker I ever heard. Every word he says not only engages but commands the attention; and your passions are no longer your own when he addresses them."

Though not original or profound, Henry had the true rhetorician's gift of bringing abstract propositions into relation with the urgency of actual situations. A child of the eighteenth-century political enlightenment, he conceived it his chief duty to combat the coercions of church and state. Professor Meade often refers to his "liberalism," and he was a liberal in the old sense of placing freedom far ahead of security. That is good reason to renew his acquaintance today, and to hope that someone equally trumpet-tongued will arise to defy the newer and more omnivorous forms of statism.

First in Peace[1]

When Douglas Southhall Freeman, author of the definitive *R. E. Lee*, died in 1953, he was at work on a seven-volume life of Washington. Five volumes had been issued, and the sixth, which was near completion, was finished by his colleagues of the *Richmond News Leader*. The publisher then arranged for two of his co-workers, John Alexander Carroll and Mary Wells Ashworth, to write the closing volume of the series. This work, covering the period from the beginning of Washington's second Administration to his death in 1799, now appears under the title *George Washington: First in Peace* (Scribner, $10.00).

Admirers of Dr. Freeman will have no cause to be disappointed with the achievement of those who took over the task. In completeness, in scholarship, in judiciousness, and in style, this work compares favorably with the *Lee* and with the *Washington* volumes from Dr. Freeman's own hand. Here is biography in its highest conception—a narrative of balance and candor, free from the crudities, distortions, special pleading, and curious social assumptions which have plagued this department of literature in recent decades.

The reflective reader of this life may well wonder how it has ever happened that Lincoln has been elevated above Washington in the national pantheon, or even placed on a level with him. Washington gave forty-five years to public service in one form or another, and the problems which he faced when he became a national leader seem vastly more difficult and dangerous. Lincoln had on his side an immense superiority of resources: he could afford to make mistakes and simply charge them to surplus. Washington had no such surplus; one or two mistakes and all might have been lost. For seven years he led the almost forlorn hope of the American Revo-

1. *National Review*, 5/14, April 5, 1958, 329–30. © 1958 by National Review, Inc., 215 Lexington Avenue, New York, N.Y. 10016. Reprinted by permission.

lution. Perceiving, like an early Mahan, the influence of sea power on such struggles, he got the help of a French fleet to bottle up Cornwallis.

Once the nation was formed, he had to be the helmsman of an infant republic for eight years. The first of these were relatively untroubled, but the last four, with which this volume deals in great detail, were anything but so. With one arm he had to hold off Britain and France—Britain resentful, and France aggressive and filled with the idea that America owed her much for services in the Revolution; and with the other he had to hold off the Indians of the Northwestern and Southern frontiers, who were perennially being incited by British and Spanish agents. It was a triumph of realism and sound judgment.

The greatest share of Washington's troubles came from Revolutionary France. Just a few weeks before he entered upon his second term, Louis XVI had gone to the guillotine, and a few months later, a general European war broke out. Both Britain and France counted on making use of American produce, and France had high hopes of bringing America in on her side, the more so because there was in America a very large and vocal "French Party."

In April of that year Citizen Genêt, the new French Minister to the United States, arrived at Charleston full of boldness and intrigue, and at once set about commissioning ships for the service of France. Then he made a triumphal tour from Charleston to Philadelphia before bothering to present himself to the government. Angered by Washington's unshakeable determination to keep America neutral, he threatened to appeal to the people over the head of the President. This was too much; even the pro-French Jefferson had to back down and admit that Genêt was no longer *persona grata.* There was poetic reversal in the fact that before Genêt could return to France, his own party fell from power and he faced the prospect of the guillotine. Washington, who "would take no agency, however remote, in the bloody business of the French Terror," allowed him to remain in this country, of which he eventually became a citizen.

The following year brought the Whiskey Rebellion. The inhabitants of Pennsylvania's western counties, to whom whiskey was not a luxury, but "medicine and nourishment" and "the main source of livelihood," were offering violent resistance to the government's excise tax on liquor. There is something odd in the spectacle of Washington mounting his horse and accompanying the forces as far as Bedford, where 13,000 militiamen were collecting to put down the movement. There is no sign that he took joy in the mission, and the mildness of his response to an address from the citizens of Carlisle should have set the tone for subsequent Presidents: "In any case in which it may be indispensable to raise the sword of Justice against obstinate offenders, I shall deprecate the necessity of deviating from a favorite aim, to establish the authority of the laws in the affection of all rather than in the fears of any."

This is perhaps the place for a question about the nature of Washington's Federalism. It seems not to have been a highly conscious, defined, and articulate theory of politics, with premises and settled objectives, like that of Hamilton or Fisher Ames. Washington had given the best years of his life to making the nation a going concern, and he did not wish to see it dissolved at this early stage, especially for transient causes. Experience in the field and in office had taught him that a firm sort of organization would promote his end and that the opposite would not. It seems to have been little more complex than this.

There is the notion that his Federalist principles were somehow connected with his being one of the wealthiest men of the country. Readers will discover that although he may have been land-rich, he was almost money-poor. On one occasion the petitioner for a loan of $3,000 had to be informed that he had less than that amount in the bank. On another, he wrote a neighbor who had asked for help: "My friends entertain a very erroneous idea of my pecuniary resources when they set me down for a money lender. . . . My public allowance, whatever the world may think of it, is inadequate to the expense of living in this city. . . . To keep myself out of debt, I have found it expedient now and then to sell lands."

There is an ancient maxim that none should be allowed to rule except those who do not desire to rule. By this standard it would be hard to find a figure in history whose title to magistracy was clearer than Washington's. There is no reason to doubt the sincerity of an exclamation, made in a moment of anger over journalistic abuse, that he would rather be a farmer than emperor of the world. More plaintively he wrote to Edmund Pendleton near the middle of his second term: "I can religiously aver that no man was ever more tired of public life, or more devoutly wished for retirement than I do." He was destined to have less than three years of the kind of life he longed for.

From the time he joined his staff at the age of twenty-two, there was no man upon whom Washington relied more steadily than Alexander Hamilton. In important ways the two men complemented each other. "He is enterprising, quick in his perceptions, and his judgment is intuitively great," is how Washington characterized him after twenty years of association. Last year Columbia University celebrated the two-hundredth anniversary of Hamilton's birth, and included on the program was a group of three lectures by Professor Broadus Mitchell. These are now published, with a few of Hamilton's letters appended, as *Heritage from Hamilton* (Columbia, $3.75).

How one wishes that Professor Mitchell had learned something of style from the chief author of the *Federalist*. Filled with halting sentences and fumbling diction, many passages of this work are a torture to get through. Nor is one likely to feel that such faults are overshadowed by brilliance of content. There are many true observations about Hamilton's role, of course. But it is surely straining things to the limit to portray him as a father of modern socialist collectivism. How many would ever guess that Hamilton was a forerunner of Norman Thomas? But here we read: "It was by national action, for which Hamilton and his friends cleared the way, that Mr. Thomas' socialist program has been sensibly forwarded." Later he remarks with evident satisfaction: "His [Hamilton's] *reasoning* could have served as a model for Soviet planning a hundred and forty years afterward."

The left-wingism of the Liberal professors seems almost a madness, driving them to grab at anything which can be used to strike at conservative ideals of liberty and responsibility. The book is filled with sallies against opponents of the New Deal, of centralization, of administrative law. There are even a couple of sermons against the sin of opposing integration. It is all summed up in the prescription that if states and other groups insist upon local ways of doing things, "they must be aided or commanded to conform to national standards."

But as Washington said, Hamilton's judgment was "intuitively great." He would have made the distinctions that seem to lie beyond Professor Mitchell.

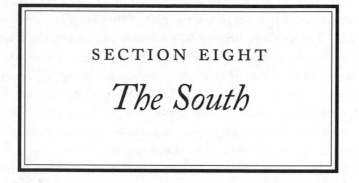

SECTION EIGHT

The South

Of all the things he thought and wrote about, it was the American South, that "last non-materialist civilization in the Western World," which most engaged Richard Weaver's attention and affections. He began his intellectual career with a dissertation on Southern letters in the postbellum period, and at his death he was "about half" finished with a new book contrasting the cultures of North and South.[1] In the twenty years between—from 1943 to 1963—he produced a steady stream of shorter works on Southern history, culture, literature, and politics. Most of these have already been anthologized in The Southern Essays of Richard M. Weaver *(1987) and so are not included here. But a substantial body remains, including two important essays not previously published. These writings are presented in two groups, both ordered chronologically.*

Six longer works make up the initial group. "The Anatomy of Southern Failure" is published here for the first time from a final manuscript copy found in a set of papers preserved by Weaver's family. It summarizes and somewhat extends the main arguments of The Southern Tradition at Bay, *but it is more harsh in tone—especially about the men of the New South—and more pessimistic in outlook. Given its content and style, it is almost certainly the article*

1. Letter from Richard Weaver to Randall Stewart dated May 19, 1962. Located in file C14 of the Polly Weaver Beaton collection and quoted by permission. There is no evidence that Weaver completed any substantial amount of work on the book in the period after this letter was written, although he did submit a chapter ("Two Types of American Individualism") to *Modern Age.*

"based on the epilogue to a dissertation which I completed last year at LSU" that was submitted to the Sewanee Review *in July of 1944. The editor, Allen Tate, rejected that manuscript, and there is no evidence Weaver ever tried to publish it elsewhere.*[2] *The next four items include an early and rather critical essay on Southern education published in* College English *in 1945, two review essays for the* Sewanee Review *on works of Southern history, and an aggressive defense of "The Regime of the South" from a 1959 issue of* National Review. *The last and most important of the group is "Two Diarists," which is also published here for the first time. Written in 1960 or 1961, it is the first of three chapters Weaver completed for his projected book on the disparate cultures of the American North and South. The other two chapters, "Two Orators" and "Two Types of American Individualism," have long been in print and are included in the* Southern Essays, *but for some reason this manuscript was overlooked. A polished essay in near-final form, it uses the diaries of Cotton Mather and William Byrd to show "near their source" the "philosophies of life which have done more than any others to produce in the United States two differing cultures."*

A miscellaneous group of seven book reviews from National Review *and the* Nashville Tennessean *newspaper completes the section. The most important are the two reviews of books by Donald Davidson, the trenchant critique of Hodding Carter's* The Angry Scar *(which Weaver chose to see as "Reconstruction: Unhealed Wound"), and his more measured but still quite negative assessment of* The Legacy of the Civil War *by Robert Penn Warren. Written with sadness and great care, the last of these, "An Altered Stand," marks Weaver's break with a man he deeply respected as a former teacher, a peerless writer, and one of the twelve contributors to the Southern Agrarian manifesto* I'll Take My Stand.

2. Letter from Richard Weaver to Allen Tate dated July 15, 1944. Located in the correspondence files of the *Sewanee Review* in the University Archives of the Jesse Ball duPont Library at the University of the South and quoted by permission. If this is the same article, it seems likely that Tate rejected it at least in part because of its rather fulsome praise of the Southern Agrarians.

The Anatomy of Southern Failure[1]

The Southern people have been the object of so many reproaches that to add one more might seem the work of supererogation. But I shall add one with the explanation that this is the reproach to end all others, to subsume whole categories of criticism and castigation. I propose to talk about the original sin of the South, which is today being visited upon a late generation.

For this broad region from the Potomac to the Rio Grande is a land of frustration, and no measuring stick has been brought forth which will make it appear an equal competitor in the arts and devices of modernism. The most hopeful comparisons end with apologies, reservations, and pleas to give us just a little more time. Yet there is a fair possibility that all such comparisons rest upon a false *a priori,* and that critics are in fact blaming the South for not violating the laws of its being. They expect of the South a faithful collaboration with the modern world, and when they fail to get it, they seek explanations in sloth, or ignorance, or willfulness. They are really proponents of a *Gleichschaltung,* and the most individualistic and uncooperative of the sections has caused them much concern.

The advocates of Southern autonomy have their disappointments too, and they have suffered the added disadvantage of not knowing exactly what they wanted. Since they have failed to visualize a clear end, they have not provided a very satisfactory analysis of Southern failure. They have allowed sentiment and a short-sighted view of history to becloud the picture so that

1. An essay based on the epilogue to Weaver's doctoral dissertation, almost certainly written in late 1943 or early 1944. It is apparently the text of an article Weaver submitted to the *Sewanee Review* in July 1944. Despite praise for it from Cleanth Brooks, Allen Tate rejected it for publication, a course required by modesty and recommended by prudence. Edited by Ted J. Smith III from a corrected typescript of a final draft acquired from Weaver's sister, Mrs. Polly Weaver Beaton, and currently in the possession of the editor.

their single proposals have appeared ridiculous. They have been slow to perceive that the South has never made itself respected—and this means, of course, also feared—because it has never known what it was. It has lacked a metaphysic, and in lacking this it has missed the very thing which would have given it self-confidence and won it the tribute of a different kind of opposition. So it has defended its weaknesses, remained silent on its real virtues, presumed where it had no ground, and apologized where it bore no responsibility.

We may begin by admitting that the South exhibits still a oneness which has puzzled other sections. Its history shows a pattern of synthesis struggling unweariedly, though oftentimes blindly, against forces of disintegration. The cultural forms which were built up in Europe during the Middle Ages, under whatever mysterious impulses lead to such creations, were brought to the South before the acids of modernism had eaten into them. This made easy the establishment of a Southern orthodoxy, which has inspired the remainder of the nation with mingled fascination and horror—fascination because it seems akin to the singular unity of mind which lies at the base of all high cultures, and horror because it tends toward an enfeebling conformity. The Old South was the Old World before the great upheavals. The social foundations of its life were laid prior to the French Revolution, which carried far, though it did not begin, the dissolution of Western Civilization. Its great battle against that Revolution was fought not in the eighteenth century, but in the latter half of the nineteenth, when it was an anachronism. It is by now a commonplace that when the French Revolution made man the measure of all things, it prepared the way for skepticism, rationalism, and relativism. By weakening the power of institutionalized religion, by destroying the principle of traditional right, by enthroning the pragmatic-minded middle class—in short, by impeaching all ancient authority and by denying supersensible reality—it set up the prerogative of egotism and the sanction of private advantage. A world of competing interests took the place of the old structural society, which had its final expression in some ideal of service to God, a single end to which king and peasant in due proportion contributed. Lenin's thesis that revolution and war are inseparable is wonderfully demonstrated by the quarter of a century of strife into which this movement plunged the world.

As it was the strange fate of the Southern people to fight this war half a century late, it seems that they might have gone into it with a superior understanding of the issues. In 1790 Edmund Burke provided the English with a remarkable analysis of their position in the struggle, and no one can read his *Reflections on the Revolution in France* without seeing that he sensed the character of coming events. Indeed, this great critic of Jacobinism correctly foretold the course of European liberalism for the next hundred and fifty years. First the intoxicant of freedom drowns out all considerations of responsibility. Then the work of wrecking long-established orders and usages goes forward in the belief that these things are only impedimenta. A jealousy of all distinctions sets in, and there follows a diminishing respect for morality and knowledge, the only bases, ultimately, for ranks among men. Having destroyed the various nuclei of power and authority, which are made possible by religion and a commonly shared code of ethics, society feels a sensation of helplessness. In reaction against this, it resorts to centralism, to the strong man, to "personal leadership"; democracy has now traveled the short road to despotism, and the state is at the end of the cycle described by Plato. Burke saw this, and the Southern theologians, who were profound men in their way, saw it also.

If one could demonstrate that all, or even most Southerners were fighting a heroic rear-guard action against tendencies which eventually mean collapse, he could assign them a role in history as honorable as that which they are usually given has been lacking in honor. But most Southerners, because of their defective orientation, cannot lay claim to the motives which would vindicate their course. As others have before remarked, they were doing good things for bad reasons. They put up one of the most stubborn fights for first principles ever witnessed without knowing what the first principles were. Instead of seeking basic grounds to defend a conservative order against irresponsible and nihilistic radicalism—as Burke, who knew history, had done three generations earlier—they brought in the political catchwords of the hour and confined themselves to the issues of American sectionalism.

On almost every point of difference with the North they had an excellent case, though one must admit that some years of experience were required to show how excellent that case was. In religion they clung to the hard God and the clear if dogmatic precept. A few decades of religious liberalism have shown that to deprive God of his thunder and to convert religion into a mild utilitarianism will not only confuse the flock but will also raise grave doubts as to the place of religion in life. While Ralph Waldo Emerson was wrecking the theocratic tradition in New England, he was also preparing the way for that wistful futility which seems to suffuse its consciousness today. The setting up of man, his impulses, his "self-reliance" as objects of worship can lead only to disillusionment and despair, as Albert Taylor Bledsoe and Robert Lewis Dabney declared. It was not through these things that Christianity achieved its wonderful hold over the imagination. It was rather through its great drama of wicked man on trial in this life for his future existence; its contrast between that which is spiritual and the world, the flesh, and the devil; the scale of perfectibility disclosed to man; the profound paradoxes lying at the heart of its morality. Any niggling rejection of these on grounds of literal difficulty, and any blurring of the distinctions which give the creed its vitality, however they may gratify doctrinaires, weaken the intrinsic power of religion. The rightist tendencies among churchmen today are an effort to atone for these errors.

In the matter of an agrarian class society, too, the South had an excellent case, and one wishes that she had known how to present it without exacerbating the militant American democracy. There is no escape from the problem of power and responsibility. If one makes war upon localized centers of authority, he must hand the power over to a central agency. The state thus centralized has a wider field in which to abuse its authority; it is less amenable to restraint; and if any lesson is to be learned from the history of the nineteenth century, it is this: that the large "nationalized" state finds the temptation of aggrandizement irresistible. It was no accident that as soon as our nation recovered, under this sort of dispensation, from the effects of civil conflict, it plunged into international imperialism. The Jeffersonian ideal of local autonomy, with its close relationship between the ruler and the ruled, and with its gradations reflecting the common-sense divisions of humanity, combined the maximum popular control with an opportunity for traditional values and the prestige of persons to exert their stabilizing influence. The secret of a healthy society is this difficult synthesis of fluidity and form, which prevents the individual from being sacrificed to extreme theories of either left or right. Society is not an iron law of equality; it is a structure in which the individual must feel that he can help determine the relationship between his capacity and his place. Such, at its best, was the aristo-democracy of the Old South.

Nor is it fanciful to say that the South's adherence to the code of honor reflected a sound instinct. The various theories of relativism which have swept the world in the last century have led through doubt to chaos and the desperate search for "values" which characterizes modern thinking. Beginning with the establishment of a sophistical utility as the supreme sanction, it has ended with the setting up of the bitch-goddess Success, so that today it is an accepted excuse of any action to say that it "will pay." The world would be in better moral health if instead of teaching that everything, including honesty, is a matter of policy, it had clung to the belief that the course of honor, because it is based on principle, is in the long run the course of expediency. But honor is treated as an old-fashioned prejudice, and an appeal to the *vox populi* is all that is needed to banish any scruples it may have suggested. The disappearance of the gentleman from political life, nowhere more visible than in Europe, is perhaps the most alarming development of modern times. There can be no effective restraint where self-restraint is lacking, and here is one of many signs that our age has lost the inner mastery and needs to be born again.

As for the education which the South chose to give its sons, one can easily presume too far, but he can say that within its limits it was of the right kind. It was education as the world had known it before the Great Betrayal; it had not made virtues of pandering and quackery; and if it succeeded only in giving a man "an elevated view of all subjects, particularly public affairs," as one antebellum writer expressed it, what better foundation for a free state can be envisioned? The desperate pleas heard today to reform a demoralized education, to get it back on the right track, contain phrases reminiscent of the schoolmen before 1865, and point to the bankruptcy of sentimental optimism.

No, the defender of Southern civilization must say that the struggle of the South against the North, however it was spoken of in its day, was implicitly a struggle for ideals which lay behind—and perhaps concealed by—the bid for independence. Most writers feel that they have demonstrated all that can be hoped for when they have proved that in the eyes of the Southern partisan it was a fight for civil liberties worthy to rank with the battle put up by the Colonists. But the issues were profounder than this; it was a battle against pervasive influences which have reduced the modern world to moral impotence.

The South felt intensely that it was right, a fact which explains much of the despair of the Reconstruction era, when it seemed to many an honorable man that truth had been crushed to earth without power to rise again. But it has never, except in a fragmentary way, arrived at a metaphysic of its rightness. It never became sufficiently coherent, and in consequence the work which might have dramatized the conflict for the South as the doctrines of the New England school did for the North remained unwritten. The same deficiency appeared in the political prolongation of the struggle after hostilities. Actually the opposition to Northern cultural hegemony assumed two aspects: an almost superhuman effort on the part of a few individuals to keep before the people the true nature of their cause; and an obstinate refusal on the part of the surviving gentry to open their minds to self-criticism. But one does not find the great informing impulse such as brought Germany back after her humiliation by Napoleon or Italy from her servitude to Austria firing the people and leading them to assert their identity. On the contrary one finds among the masses a tendency to be dazzled by material innovations—a portent of spiritual decay under any circumstances—a growing pragmatism, and a widening corruption in quarters where previously dishonesty had meant real disgrace and retirement from office.

Thus while some persons have wondered how the South was able to offer such firm resistance to the program which the North—a section which after 1865 could think of itself as "the nation"—drew up for the country as a whole, it would be more proper to ask why the South, with a case so strong, did not resist even more successfully. The question goes back to the diffusion of ideals. The mass of the Southern people were but meagerly educated in the values of their culture, and when those who had been sufficiently educated began to fall away, whether from ordinary misfortune, lack of adaptability, or sheer inanition, their places were taken by men from below who had received no such schooling. These men have shown rather too much adaptability, which takes the form of an appalling readiness to embrace the ways of commercial bounderism and to serve at the shrine of the bitch-goddess. The "little foxes" not only succeeded in a material way; they also persuaded much of the nation that they were the rightful representatives of the South.

It is not necessary to suppose that a little training in the analysis of values would result in the self-defeating liberalism which has left its mark upon so much of the North, and to which even the stagnation of the South, as a less positive evil, might be preferred. Liberalism, despite its present popularity as a nostrum, is philosophically weak. If anything, it is a policy which ought to accompany any set of positive beliefs—a policy of receptivity and open-mindedness without which doctrines grow blind and partisans fanatical. One may be the conscious heir of a tradition and still be "liberal," or we might say alert, to the point of admitting that the passage of time makes inevitable the discard of some old things, just as it does the incorporation of some new ones. This attitude gives society the regulative effect of good habits without denying the necessity of adaptation. Southern liberalism has been little more than a pragmatic acquiescence in whatever the national majority seemed in a mood to demand. But behind liberalism there must be a point of view and an intellectual clarity which can conceive a concrete program free from contradictions and illusions. The world of affairs demands a choice of alternatives, and it is a melancholy fact that since the Civil War the South has not possessed sufficient intellectual freedom to make even a clear-cut conservative choice. What survived the holocaust it preserved; what new things were offered its masses took; surely there is little mastery over fate in this passivity.

In effect, two mistaken courses were open to the people of the South, and both were followed. The gentlemen of the old order, with set minds and flinty determination, resolved to live on unchanged; the people who came up from the depths—and this word is used not without determination—flourished not only ignorant of the traditions of their culture but also indifferent to the value of any traditions. Wise conservatives like E. A. Alderman and wise progressives like Walter Hines Page were not the Southern oracles; the men chiefly listened to were huckstering politicians interested only in popular approval, whose doctrines seldom bore on the real problem of Southern improvement.

Immediately connected with this is the scandalous disregard which the South has always shown, and still continues to show, toward her men of literary and artistic gifts. The intellectual or artist who seeks recognition in this climate may well wonder whether the South's devotion to the ideal of the political soldier is any less exclusive than it was in Charleston in the 1850s, though there is reason for saying that the record of Southern cities is better than that of Southern universities. After the Civil War a surprising number of Confederate generals were at once elevated to the presidency of Southern institutions of learning. Though men of character and excellent intentions, they could not escape the limitations of their background, which caused them to encourage *ad hoc* studies, to discount intellectual pursuits, and to distrust free inquiry. Their legacy is strong in the Southern colleges today, where the intellectual student may find himself as friendless as he would in the world of commerce. With the exception of a few old institutions which have their roots in some solid antebellum tradition, Southern colleges have proved the easiest prey to educational heresies. As there is no Babbitt like a Southern Babbitt, so it must be recorded that there are no sadder travesties on the educational ideal than those Southern schools which have succumbed to presentism, scientism, and vocationalism.

The Southerner who rises to real intellectual stature knows that he must find his audience in the North or nowhere. And if he goes there to accept a position commensurate with his abilities, as he more often than not does, his compatriots exhibit no sense of loss. Page was writing out of experience when he said that for such a one the only salvation lay in immediate flight. It need cause no astonishment that the South after exporting its brains in this reckless fashion for three generations displays only mediocre ability from education on the one side to politics on the other.

The men of the New South are not the men their grandfathers were, nor can we allow the claim that they are better men of another kind. They have lost character. It is always a more hopeful sign to have sinned greatly than to have remained indifferent to good and evil. The sinner may repent, and with his vitality and the knowledge gained by his sinning, build anew. But the man who takes no cognizance of either virtue or vice cannot be approached on this plane: how can he be saved at all? This is the question to be asked about the present generation of Southerners. They have inherited serious difficulties which they do not care to think about; they sense an aggressive opponent in the North but do not know how to define their rights against him. One can sympathize more readily with the intransigents, like Bledsoe, fighting almost single-handedly against the whole tide of modernism; or with some member of the United Daughters of the Confederacy, who cherishes at least the memory of great aspirations and great sacrifices. The present-day Southerner has no sense of direction; he takes his cue from the North and then misapplies it; he will not be heroic enough to be a good Southerner nor energetic enough to transform himself into a first-class Yankee. He is a problem to the nation and he is a most vexatious problem to the Southern educator, who would like to see something positive emerge from his labors.

Significant of the philosophical blindness of the South is its failure to see how much of its inheritance is today needed for "the healing of the nations." This is not a matter of "restoring the Old South," which is a false conception of the issues; it is rather a matter of perceiving that its education and its traditions produced a moral type which needs to be re-created. Its allegiance to a spiritual ideal, sometimes admired as quaint, but more often scoffed at as barbaric or backward, emerges as the one power which may defeat the destruction of belief by scientific materialism and the corruption of society by money.

It may be doubted whether the heritage of Southern culture will ever again develop as a distinct pattern. The South is committed along with the nation in too many ways, and it has gone whoring after too many of the strange gods of modernism. There is always the possibility, of course, that the distinctly Southern values, because they are central values, will prove focal in any general world-wide re-orientation, but it is unlikely that this could start in the South, or that the South could get credit for having preserved the values that the world suddenly found itself in need of. All that has happened thus far indicates that the world, or such part of it as subscribed to the New Order, has sensed the deficiency, but has sought to supply it by means immeasurably crude and violent—another evidence, perhaps, that the original creative impulse has played out.

The vast majority of the Southern people at present appear content to be second-class Yankees. They failed to defeat modernism, and now that modernism itself has failed, they blithely embrace the failure. They are, as Robert Penn Warren has vividly expressed it, the tail of a kite that is going down. No independent political thinker has come out of the South since Tom Watson, and he, imperfectly educated and cursed by the old Defense-mindedness, ended his public life in bitterness and incoherence.

The dismal story is, in summary, that the South lost the initiative three generations ago and since then has failed to show the wish, much less the capacity, to regain it. One single exception must be noted in a brilliant group of university men who appeared in the 1920s. Consisting partly of

Rhodes Scholars, who in England discovered that the virtues of antebellum civilization were the virtues of any old and settled society, and partly of men whose study of history had led them beyond the journalistic nonsense which is the pabulum of the present-day majority, they restated the case for Southern civilization. Their historical and critical writings have constituted the first stream of creative thought to emanate from the South since the days of Jefferson. The wave of incredulity and outrage which met their proposals was a measure of the decline of the South. The collaborationists were horrified because here was some brilliant reasoning that challenged the wisdom of collaboration. And hardly a reader below the Potomac was able to see that here for the first time in a century was a group of Southerners talking about first principles instead of offering wretched evasions. It was perhaps too a measure of their rightness that the North, more experienced in the failures of modernism, better educated, and, as always, more receptive to new ideas, regarded their program with more respect and invited many of them to become its teachers.

The South has paid a heavy price for its indifference to ideas, and there is no sign that the end is yet. Its mind is still the mind of Charleston of the 1850s, insular and inflexible, but it is in worse plight, for it lacks a point of view. If its fate is less in its hands than ever before, that is not entirely the result of Yankee malice, as the Southern commonalty has imagined. Until it recovers the vision, and gives some evidence that it again desires the initiative, there can be little change in its present role of drift, indifferentism, and futility.

Scholars or Gentlemen?[1]

One of the persistent problems in American cultural history is the comparative absence of belles-lettres in the Old South. It is anomalous that a section which had developed a number of rather complex cultural patterns, which usually showed a certain taste in selection, and which considered itself the more civilized portion of the country, should have been indifferent, not to say hostile, to the cultivation of the arts. Several theories have been adduced to explain this condition: the South was primitive; it had no cities to serve as centers of activity; the climate was too hot to permit sustained effort; the men were too busy with politics to find time for literature. Without denying some measure of effect to each of these, I should like to mention a factor which I believe to have been of decisive influence in discouraging the professional littérateur: the Old South was developing a Spartan strain in its civilization, which led to a distrust, on principle, of the artist and the thinker. Basil Gildersleeve once drew a parallel between the American Civil War and the Peloponnesian War, placing the North in the role of Athens and the South in that of Sparta. His analogy can be extended; the South was Sparta not only in its position as combatant but also in its depreciation of the intellectual and commercial pursuits which throve at Athens.

It is well at the beginning to arrive at a clear notion of the southern social order. Despite the efforts of some modern researchers to prove that there was no aristocracy in the South or that the aristocracy was of negligible importance, it is one of the most obvious facts of the American past that the basic social organization of the Old South was aristocratic. The presence of Negro slavery made it inevitable that this should be so. The aristocrats were not numerous, and they never succeeded in perfecting themselves like the European orders with long heritages behind them, but they were

1. *College English*, 7/2, November 1945–46, 72–77. Published by the National Council of Teachers of English.

the leaders of the community, and those who aspired to rise in the social scale strove to be like them.

These aristocrats were destined never to enjoy the kind of stable condition which allows such a group to become a patron of the arts. From the time of their arrival they were engaged in battles—against the Indians, against the wilderness, against the mother-country. Hardly had rest from these troubles come, when the South saw slavery, the foundation stone of the plantation economy, threatened by a world-wide humanitarian movement; and from then on it looked forward to internecine war. It should not be remarkable, therefore, that the southern populace learned to revere the politician and the soldier and to look with positive disfavor on those employments which unfitted a man for the business of governing and fighting.

The plantation-owner might collect a fine library, and he might read Scott and Byron with pleasure, or even look into the Latin poets, but he was proud that his knowledge was that of an amateur. Indeed, all southern education rested on the classical assumption that specialization of any kind is illiberal in a freeman. King Philip's famous taunt to his son Alexander, who had performed skilfully upon the flute—"Are you not ashamed, son, to play so well?"—would not have required elucidation for the ante bellum southerner. Plutarch explains this attitude by declaring that "he who busies himself with mean occupations produces, in the very pains he takes about things of little or no use, an evidence against himself of his negligence and indisposition to what is really good." The southern theory of education, which can be traced to Aristotle by way of the Elizabethans, aimed not at any special proficiency but at "a catholicity of taste as well as of feeling, and an elevated view of all subjects, particularly public affairs." It was training for the gentleman-ruler, whose position in society would entitle him to look down upon any kind of specialization as *déclassé*. As early as 1699 a youthful orator at the College of William and Mary was sounding the southern distrust of the scholar type:

> For in such a retired corner of the world, far from business and action, if we make scholars, they are in danger of proving mere scholars, which make a very ridiculous figure, being made up of pedantry, disputatiousness, positiveness, and a great many other ill qualities, which render them not fit for action and conversation.

John Randolph of Roanoke, who typifies so much that was good and bad in the southern aristocracy, sneered at professors and at those whose "great learning, combined with inveterate professional habits," leaves them "disqualified for any but secondary roles anywhere."

These sentiments go reverberating down the years of southern history; and wherever we find a group of free spirits eager to promote some artistic or literary venture, we hear them complaining of the excessive attention given to politicians and men of affairs. The career of the *Southern Literary Messenger* is in itself a lesson in the struggle to win the southern mind from its Spartan addiction to politics and war. In its first issue the editor pointed out:

> It is folly to boast of political ascendancy, of moral influence, of professional eminence, or unrivalled oratory, when in all the Corinthian graces which adorn the structure of the mind we are lamentably deficient. It is worse than folly to talk of "this ancient and unterrified commonwealth"—if we suffer ourselves to be terrified at the idea of supporting one poor periodical, devoted to letters and mental improvement.

A list of letters saluting the first appearance of the *Messenger* reflects the frustration of those who had been wishing for literary activity in the South. Said one correspondent:

> With these sentiments you may be assured that I wish success to your endeavor to rouse the spirit of the South in the cause of literature; to draw its intellectual energies from the everlasting monotonous discussion of politics, which has run the same round of arguments and topics for forty years, and allure her favored sons and daughters to the kinder and brighter fields of science and letters.

Another expressed to the editor his fear that

> you may meet with some inaptitude or distaste to mere literary contribution from the educated of our citizens. This, however, cannot last long; you may feel it at the outset, but it will soon end; for I doubt not that the Messenger, as one of its best effects, will draw into literary exercise the talents which now lie fallow throughout the community, or which have long extravasated in politics or professions.

A third wrote enthusiastically:

> If the object of your labors be attained, of which there can be no reasonable doubt, posterity will be more grateful to you than to thousands of political

exquisites of the day, whose memory will last only so long as their ephemeral productions.

Despite some outward success, it is plain that the *Messenger* had to contend with much apathy and indifference in its regional constituency. Thus in 1843, nine years after the hopeful beginning just described, one finds the editor exclaiming: "How glad to us will be the day, when an ardent love of liberal learning shall have supplanted some of the hobbies of Southern intellect, have roused its slumbering energies and imparted a taste for purest joys and sweetest solaces." By 1857 it appeared that some progress had been made against the universal preoccupation with politics, and the editor could exult in the new-found glory of authors:

> The literary men are regarded with greater consideration than formerly, and are not now compelled to walk under the huge legs of politicians and peep about to find themselves dishonorable graves. It is getting to be thought that a man may, perhaps, accomplish as much for the South by writing a good book as by making a successful stump speech; and he who contributes to the enjoyment of his fellow citizens by a lofty poem or shapes their convictions by a powerful essay is not an idle dreamer merely and that the pen devoted to the treatment of subjects out of the range of political and commercial activities is as usefully employed as the tongue which is exercised in the wearisome declamation of legislative halls.

Such expectations, however, were soon mocked. Two years later, in connection with a pointless debate then going on in Charleston over whether William Gilmore Simms could write good English prose, there appeared this characteristic note of exasperation: "When will the people of the South learn to know and honour their worthiest literary men?"

We may now ask what the writers themselves thought of their situation. One of the first to deplore the strong anti-intellectual prejudice was John Pendleton Kennedy, who in a letter dated May 1, 1835, wrote to Washington Irving: "You have convinced our wise ones at home that a man may sometimes write a volume without losing his character." Philip Pendleton Cooke, circumstanced as few were in his time to court the literary muse, had the following illuminating incident to report:

> What do you think of a good friend of mine, a most valuable and worthy, and hard-riding one, saying gravely to me a short time ago: "I wouldn't waste

time on a damn thing like poetry; you might make yourself, with all your sense and judgment, a useful man in settling neighborhood disputes and difficulties."

There is evidence that Cooke himself became to some extent tinctured with the same attitude. Literature he regarded as an occupation for the middle years; after that, age and gravity called for statecraft. He wrote to a friend:

My literary life opens now. If the world manifest any disposition to hear my "utterances," it will be abundantly gratified. I am thirty: until I am forty literature shall be my calling—avoiding however to rely upon it pecuniarily— then (after forty) politics will be a sequitur.

Few were made more unhappy by the lack of understanding and appreciation facing the southern man of letters than Paul Hamilton Hayne. It appeared to him a "species of ignorance . . . invincibly blind and presumptuous." In a letter written to Margaret J. Preston shortly after the war he made the following bitter observation: "Touching the *Southern Public,* and those who from places of practical trust & toil lead,—generally its opinions,—we *artists*—may as well make up our minds to receive nothing—unless it be contumely, and a thinly veiled contempt."

The career of William Gilmore Simms is instructive in the fascination which the southern social order exercised upon men of strong and independent mind, even while it tormented them with frustration. Simms was the nearest approach to the professional man of letters in the ante bellum South, if we leave out the doubtful case of Edgar Allan Poe. Born outside the aristocratic class, he made a determined effort to gain entry into it by means of his pen; and if indefatigable industry and allegiance to the principles of his society had been measures of success, he would have gone to the top. For several years he deserted romance, in which his achievement had been best recognized, to attempt biography, history, and oratory, securing with his "The Morals of Slavery" a place alongside Governor Hammond and Chancellor Harper in *Pro-slavery Arguments.* He assumed the unrewarding editorship of the *Southern Quarterly Review* with the object of giving the South an organ comparable with New England's *North American Review.* But it was not to be; his considerable exertions in defense of the southern feudal order did not get him admitted to the magic circle; he discovered that in this milieu, proficiency in letters, even loyal service to the regime, was no substitute for political success or hereditary standing. In Charleston, if anywhere, aristocratic disdain for the mere man of letters was decisive, and no conceivable fame in the field of his choice would have been weighed in the scale with the successes of others in camp and senate. Although by some miracle of affection Simms remained a loyal Charlestonian to the end, he could not refrain in moments of despondency from admitting that celebrated city's indifference to his work. On October 30, 1858, he wrote in a personal memorandum:

> Thirty odd years have passed, and I can now mournfully say that the old man [his father] was right. All that I have ever done has been poured to waste in Charleston, which has never smiled on any of my labors, which has steadily ignored my claims, which has disparaged me to the last, has been the last place to give me its adhesion, to which I owe no favors never having received an office, or a compliment, or a dollar at her hands; and, with the exception of some dozen of her citizens, who have been kind to me, and some scores of her young men, who have honored me with loving sympathy and something like reverence, which has always treated me like a public enemy to be sneered at than a dutiful son doing her honor.

The bitter epitaph which he composed for himself "Here lies one who, after a reasonably long life, distinguished chiefly by unceasing labors, has left all his better work undone"—is a poignant testimony of defeat. The tragedy of Simms's career was that he expected something which this society was simply not prepared to give, and in the struggle he sacrificed too much. As compromises are often fatal, there is little doubt that the concessions he was compelled to make to be effective as a man account for his relative mediocrity as poet and romancer.

Richard Henry Wilde, whose delicate faculty gave the world "My Life Is like the Summer Rose," chose to leave the scene of politics and cotton-raising to lose himself amid the art and dreams of medieval Italy. How this act impressed a sober mind of the day may be seen in a few excerpts from Stephen G. Miller's *Bench and Bar of Georgia* (1858):

> The mission to which Mr. Wilde addressed his faculties and gave years of toil in Europe was not in harmony with his relative duties to mankind and with that position which his eminent talents and finished cultivation had secured from the world. He was qualified for extensive practical usefulness as a

jurist, scholar, and statesman. . . . In Europe there was delight to the senses, but mildew to the heart. The voluptuary, the man of fashion, the idler were gratified; but the moral hero, the public benefactor, the man of enterprise, the scholar of a just ambition, desirous to leave a record of popular utility, would turn with generous self-denial from such enchantments.

The author could not understand how Wilde could devote years to the study of Tasso, "to the sentimental details, to the fantasies of insanity, and that, too, not for the benefit of medical jurisprudence." In short:

> The task, with whatever success performed by Mr. Wilde, was below the merit which should have sustained itself in a better field,—at the forum, in the walks of political economy, in commerce, in constitutional law, or in the analysis of government, all of which admitted the classic beauties of style.

There is a long list of southern writers, less sensitive to the claims of pure art, who turned without apparent reluctance from an early period of creativeness to engage in practical affairs. William Wirt, whose *Letters of a British Spy* and *The Old Bachelor* reveal a talent for the genial essay, became attorney-general of the United States and gave to office that energy which might have made him conspicuous in letters, as his contemporary biographer noted. John Pendleton Kennedy himself, whose *Swallow Barn* is hardly surpassed in charm and deftness by the best of Irving, closed his life as a complacent functionary and businessman. Augustus Baldwin Longstreet, who with *Georgia Scenes* began the rich tradition of frontier humor, later spoke apologetically of his work as a mere bagatelle and soothed his conscience by hoping that it would one day be valuable as history. Having gained place and respectability, he wrote learnedly on the biblical justification of slavery. Joseph Glover Baldwin followed up *The Flush Times of Alabama and Mississippi*, one of the inimitable works of American humor, not with more writing of the imaginative kind, which the popularity of this volume should have encouraged, but with a series of political portraits of such men as Jefferson, Hamilton, and Clay. Nathaniel Beverley Tucker after writing *George Balcombe*, a novel described by Poe as the best which America had to that time produced, gave his time to political treatises. So the story goes until Appomattox and after.

Beyond a doubt this tendency to denigrate the work of the artist was increased by conditions leading toward civil war, but it was there all the while, deep-seated and conscious of itself. There are two grounds for the hostility with which an aristocracy may regard the thinker. The first is that his work necessarily leads to refinements of sensibility which leave a man unsuited to the brutish business of fighting. Wherever war and statecraft are held the chief offices of man, preoccupation with an art will be looked upon as a sentimental weakness. In the South this hostility was the contempt of a chauvinistic, military caste for those employments—commercial as well as intellectual, it should be emphasized—which demoralize the warrior. Its classic expression is Hotspur's retort:

> I'd rather be a kitten and cry mew
> Than one of these same metre ballad mongers

The second is that an aristocracy distrusts the intellectual because it wishes to minimize the conflicts in the established order. To make its position secure it wants a general sanction; it does not want a troublesome debate which might lead to disturbances. The intellectual and the artist, if they are disinterested in their reflections, upset the men of secure position by pointing to unwelcome essences.

The southern people have always prided themselves on being a preeminently sound, outdoor, unbookish people, never tormented by Hamlet's self-questioning because they accepted a few simple truths and refused to go in for sophisticated doctrines. It is not without significance that in the great journalistic battle preceding the Civil War, New England was constantly reviled in the southern press as the "land of notions." Southerners were proud of the fact that they were not bothered by ideological conflicts, just as they were of the fact that their wealth did not come by shopkeeping. One of the frankest statements of this point of view may be found in the *New Eclectic*, a southern journal published in Baltimore after the war. In attacking an English writer who had spoken critically of the South, the editor could declare:

> He was in search of *isms*, of which happily we have none. He was tracing the development of what in New England are called "ideas"—things which the healthy nature of our people loathes, and which we exorcise with bell, book, and candle, as we would the Devil from whom they come. Our faults, shortcomings, vices if you will, have at least this redeeming feature, that they

are natural. Our moral distempers are those of a constitution naturally sound and vigorous.

It is the judgment of history that the chief fault of the Old South was complacency. It was provincial, and it was becoming isolationist; it was indifferent about learning from the great world; and it was satisfied with second-rate achievements in all else as long as it could lead in the spectacular theaters of war and politics. It would cherish learning and the arts if they proved ornamental, but the actual work of creation, like the manufacture of the elegant things which went into its mansions, it preferred to have done elsewhere. A scholar must scorn delights and live laborious days. In the Old South a man could be a gentleman or a scholar, but he could not, except in a superficial sense, be both.

History in a Dry Light[1]

In the ninety years that have passed since there was stillness at Appomattox, something like eighty thousand books have been published about the Civil War, its political and economic origins, its campaigns, its leading figures, its social and literary consequences. The appearance of these two volumes, one treating the war in its military, economic, and social aspects, and the other presenting a comparative study of its interpretations down to the present day, provides further examples of the literature it continues to inspire. There seems no diminution in its power to attract the scholar, as well as the romancer; and it may be worthwhile to speculate on some of the reasons for its appeal to the serious mind.

In first place, the American Civil War is a wonderful field for those who have grown to love the chess game of military strategy. One can scarcely think of another war in which there were so many critical battles; that is to say, battles which, with a more decisive result, might have ended the war right there, or have thrown it in favor of the side which finally lost. Many wars have been decided by one or two major engagements. But in this bitter four-year struggle there were at least fifteen battles which must be rated major by reason of the numbers and resources involved. And of these, five or six could have determined the outcome one way or another. In consequence, both amateur and professional strategists continue to be fascinated by problems like the following. What if the Confederates had walked into Washington after Bull Run, as Stonewall Jackson is reported to have wished to do? The Union would have lost its capital at the beginning of the war—

---

1. *The Sewanee Review*, 63/2, Spring 1955, 280–86. Copyright 1955, 1983 by the University of the South. Reprinted with the permission of the editor.

A History of the Southern Confederacy. By Clement Eaton. New York: The Macmillan Company. 1954. 351 pages. $5.50. *Americans Interpret Their Civil War.* By Thomas J. Pressly. Princeton: Princeton University Press. 1954. 347 pages. $5.00.

a serious thing for any government engaged in combatting a "rebellion." Or, what if Grant had lost his entire army at Shiloh, as he narrowly missed doing? He would have lapsed into obscurity, and those battles in the West, which eventually proved the undoing of the Confederacy, might not have been fought. Or, what if Longstreet had attacked at dawn on the morning of July 2 at Gettysburg, while the Second, Fifth, and Sixth Federal Corps had not come up? He might have carried the famous ridges, and the Confederates would have been in position to menace the Eastern seaboard. Or, what if Braxton Bragg had attacked Rosecrans while he had him in a trap in the mountains below Chattanooga? There might have been no battle of Atlanta, no march to the sea, and Lincoln might have failed of reelection in '64, as at one time he feared. Winston Churchill has observed that many of the great decisions of history have been won "on the narrowest of margins." The possibilities in these and other situations explain in part why the war has been re-fought for three generations, and why it has furnished texts for army war colleges, both here and abroad.

Another continuing source of fascination lies in the fact that our Civil War was the last major conflict in which the ideals of chivalry, nurtured in Europe during the Middle Ages and deriving some sanction from the spirit of Christianity, exerted a visible influence. A good deal of nonsense has been uttered on this subject, and there have been exaggerated claims and denials. But if we go to the contemporary accounts, we discover that it was enough of a "horse and buggy" war to expect certain standards of conduct of those who took part. Imagine, if you can, the meeting between Grant and the Confederate General Leonidas Polk (also a bishop in the Episcopal Church) after the battle of Belmont, Missouri. Polk later wrote that he had asked Grant to join him in a truce, to discuss "the principles on which I thought the war should be conducted; denounced all barbarity, vandalism, plundering, and all that, and got him to say he would join in putting it down." Mr. Eaton, who has written a bourgeois sort of history and who apparently does not much relish this kind of thing, has nevertheless recorded it. Where would you go, outside a mediaeval tapestry, to find something like it? Yet it is almost equaled by the scene at Appomattox four years later when Grant, modest, and correct in all save dress, discussed old times with the impassive Lee before sitting down to write out the terms of surrender, which allowed Confederate officers to retain their side arms. When one compares this with the acts of ferocity by which recent wars have been closed, one is impelled to ask, what has happened to civilization? The modern style is to grant the enemy no terms whatever, to seize and execute his leaders, and then, as if in a frenzy to obliterate them or reduce them to ultimate atoms, to dispose secretly of the remains. Such is the logical consequence of all-outism, which the spirit of Christianity was chiefly concerned to prevent. One pardons something to the spirit of nostalgia.

For reasons connected with this, few can read the documents of our Civil War without feeling that he is meeting men of heroic mold. Study the pictures as they have come down to us in sketches and daguerreotypes; read the memoirs and testimonies. There arises an image both visual and aural; the sober, bearded faces, the magniloquence. I think especially of Johnston's *Narrative of Military Operations,* with its professional crispness; of Hood's *Advance and Retreat,* an account by a brave soldier given a hopeless assignment; of Richard Taylor's *Destruction and Reconstruction,* with its philosophic poise of the scholar gone to the wars. They discuss principles in resonant phrases; they argue strategy with combined assurance and detachment, sometimes writing to a former enemy in the field for confirmation of a fact or opinion. There is enough self-exculpation to leave them human, but almost nowhere is there self-pity. And the cries of the wounded do not get into the literature of the Civil War—not until two or three generations later. The manner is unsentimental; the mood is one of high seriousness. Compare these with the technicians, propagandists, and comedians who have been permitted to make the history of recent wars, and one feels another impulse to return to the more dignified drama.

Yet another fact of absorbing interest to many is that here we see a mighty struggle between democratic and aristocratic forms of society. There is no point in going into the social origins of Southerners, which do not affect the proposition anyhow. It is enough to recognize that the South had an aristocratic social organization. With this there seems to go a kind of historic mission, for it has always been the role of aristocracy to oppose the centralization of authority. So it was with the aristocratic families of Greece and Rome; and so it was with the nobles of Europe when the nationalizing monarchs undertook to gather more and more authority into their hands. It would seem that to fight centralized power is to join the aristocratic party, whether you happen to be aware of it or not. On the one hand are the plebs and the Caesars; on the other the defenders of local authority and self-determination. The Southern people, from the time of the presidency of Jefferson to the present-day Dixiecrats, have been distributists in regard to governmental power.

The aristocratic mentality influenced Southern policy in a good many ways. Ortega points out convincingly that no aristocracy anywhere has been able to rationalize anything. Its method, to the extent that it can be called a method, is that of the sudden and brilliant intuition. To a remarkable degree this theory is borne out in the conduct of the war by the two sides. The war conducted by the Confederate leaders was characterized by inspiration rather than calculation. And when affairs were in such a posture that success could be won by a brilliant intuition, the South was generally successful, as is witnessed by the campaigns of Lee, Jackson, and Forrest. When affairs were in such posture that success could be won by business-like calculation and logistical superiority, success generally favored the North, as in the campaigns of Grant, Sherman, and Thomas. The South's business management was wretched from start to finish and in almost every department. The one technology in which it outdistanced the North was the manufacture of gunpowder. But here the key to its success was the genius of General Josiah Gorgas. And he, as one may learn from Mr. Eaton's book, was a native of Running Pumps, Pennsylvania. After the North decided to devote its huge resources to the *business* of war, the contest grew unequal. It is an interesting sidelight on the connection of democracy and rationalism.

It is supposable that the very proliferation of historical interests and approaches has called forth Mr. Eaton's book. *A History of the Southern Confederacy* is evidently intended to be a "balanced" account. Adopting the emphasis that has come with social science, it tries to present its subject in a general setting of forces, economic, social, cultural, and so on. And given the premises, the aim is well carried out. It is conscientious, workmanlike, specific as to facts; and if a reader looks up something in the place where it ought to be, he will probably find it there. Even the language suggests a conscious effort toward discipline.

Yet the very controls imposed by this method allow one or more essential things to escape. There is an *Innerlichkeit* to Southern history which is hardly intimated by this book. To say in a few words what that is would be impossible; I will only add that I think W. J. Cash got something of it into his brilliant *Mind of the South*. It has to do with the all-important matters of value and motivation, of the bond that keeps the whole together. Only in the reductionist equations of science do you arrive at the whole simply by adding up the parts. A philosophic history must be written from the inside, with insight into what creates the historical entity. I do not believe that a reader of *A History of the Southern Confederacy* will grasp why Southern boys charged into the hail of fire at Shiloh, "bowing their heads as to a snowstorm," as Lloyd Lewis has written, or maintained their decimated ranks up Cemetery Ridge. Admittedly, these things are hard enough to render by report and commentary, but the idea of *élan* seems absent. And if it had been missing in the circumstances, the war would never have been fought at all. This is history in a dry light.

In a manner of speaking, Mr. Pressly's *Americans Interpret Their Civil War* has the same etiology as the foregoing work: there have been so many interpretations of the war that it is tempting to gather the more distinct ones into a single volume and see whether there is any trend toward unity on the subject. Mr. Pressly's patiently adduced evidence indicates that there is little if any. In fact, a reader uninitiated in this field may be shaken by the variety of opinion and estimate. There was the view that Southern secession was a heinous conspiracy on the part of a few politicians, who were willing to wreck the world's one free government in order to aggrandize their power. Extreme opinion of this kind produced works like Thomas S. Goodwin's *The Natural History of Secession: or, Despotism and Democracy in Necessary, Eternal, Exterminating War* (1864). There was the contemporary rebuttal, offered by A. T. Bledsoe and R. L. Dabney, that the South was the Vendée of the United States, not merely fighting for its existence, but maintaining the cause of the whole world against Jacobinism, with its atheistical leveling. There was the view of James Ford Rhodes, whose monumental *History of the United States from the Compromise of 1850* served as a major bridge between old and new interpretations. Rhodes believed that secession was not a conspiracy, but rather a mass movement on the part of a people unfortunately committed to the odious institution of slavery. Where he departed from his Northern predecessors most sharply was in saying that although the North had been right during the war, the South had been right during Reconstruction. There was the view of U. B. Phillips, who taught that the South's social structure cannot be understood without reference to a large Negro population, and that the unwillingness of the Abolitionists to recognize this factor drove the South to the recourse of secession. There was Charles Beard's interpretation, given in *The Rise of American Civilization,* which presented the conflict rather simply as a struggle between industrialism and agrarianism. There was the Marxist view, which conveniently saw the war as merely one of the stages in the rise and eventual collapse of capitalism. There was a group which argued that the conflict was irrepressible; and there was another group, about equally well furnished with learning and doctors' degrees, which argued that it was repressible, had a different line of policy been followed.

Mr. Pressly's scholarship would be worth all the effort if it made us feel that we know more certainly than did our fathers and grandfathers what actually caused the war. Mr. Eaton makes the sober observation: "It is highly probable that the typical soldier, Northern or Southern, had no clear idea why he was fighting." That sounds morally certain, and I have always admired the conciseness of General Beauregard's explanation of Bull Run, as given in *Battles and Leaders:*

> That one side was fighting for union and the other for disunion is a political expression; the actual fact on the battlefield, in the face of cannon and musket, was that the Federal troops came as invaders, and the Southern troops stood as defenders of their homes, and further than this we need not go.

Historical causation being a highly conjectural matter most of the time, this seems an excellent on-the-spot calculation. Since then, perhaps, our perspectives have widened somewhat, and a certain amount of reliable predication on a number of subjects comes through. At the very least, we have progressed to the point where neither side cites the total depravity of the other as the cause of the war.

There is another matter, however, about which Mr. Pressly can be much more certain, and he has the whole body of his collected material as the proof. This is that the issues of the Civil War, unlike those of the American Revolution, continue to live on and to affect political alignments. In this respect, as he explicitly points out, the Civil War bears much more comparison to the French Revolution. It left a legacy of social and political differences so deep that they bid to last indefinitely, and they are even capable of taking on fresh strength, depending on the course of affairs. Anyone who imagines that all the issues were disposed of when Grant and Lee had their interview in McLean's parlor is a provincial in this country. Some of the issues, like those which tore France apart in the 1790s, are too reflective of philosophies of life to be settled for good by a trial at arms. Southern spokesmen have known that they have on their side much of the Bible, and Aristotle, who believed that the ideal form of government is not a democracy but a constitutional republic. Restatements of the Southern position like those made during the 1930s by the Agrarians and others show the power of these basic viewpoints to reassert themselves. And in a way the South's case becomes stronger as technology increases, and men are more and more perplexed to know what is happening to the human spirit.

There is a final topic, somewhat tangential to the subject of these books, yet having to do with their value as contributions to learning, which I wish to broach. I put it in the form of a question: how can anyone who has studied the American Civil War, or any major civil war, be as naïve about the idea of world union as our globalists are today? Even if they should be granted their fondest wishes, say a world government with a world parliament, what is to prevent some terrible thing from arising in the future and destroying this by civil war? They seem to think that such an establishment would have an *a priori* guarantee of permanence. The study of history does not bear them out. Many empires, leagues, and alliances of the past which thought of themselves as one and indivisible forever have proved otherwise. In our own day, two or three civil wars have been won by the side fighting the established government. War is an intranational as well as an international phenomenon. Their plan for horizontal unification seems to take no account of that. It is a social science ideal, projected in contempt of history. To have any power of lasting, unions must be vertical as well as horizontal. And this calls for some harmonization at the level of philosophy and spirit, or perhaps better say, of the philosophy of the spirit. This consideration, like a good many suggested by current Southern writing, directs our attention to a universal moral circumstance.

The Land and the Literature[1]

There is a legend about a man who wrote a book on our Civil War and gave it the title "An Impartial History of the War Between the States from a Southern Point of View." I intend no derogation by suggesting that this is the kind of work Clifford Dowdey has written in *The Land They Fought For*. His history is impartial in the sense that it contains sharp and even merciless criticism of Southern blunders and shortcomings, including shortcomings of character. But it takes the Southern point of view of the good things the South stood for, and it demonstrates how the Southern people learned, as few other modern peoples, the meaning of *vae victis*. Also, it is continuous in its reprobation of those things done by the North which have left an unhealed wound in our body politic.

Critical power and narrative skill combine to make it one of the best accounts ever produced of the Confederate South.

Mr. Dowdey proves his historical insight by starting the story of the Confederacy with Nat Turner's rebellion, which precursed by thirty years the formal outbreak of hostilities. This grisly episode began on the farm of one Joseph Travis in remote Southampton County, Virginia. Travis himself was an obscure small farmer who kept a few Negroes but earned his living chiefly as a coachmaker. In Nat Turner he had a young slave whose unusual qualities had won him the position of overseer on the place. He had been taught to read and encouraged to study the Bible. He developed a great interest in portents and prophecies and before long was local preacher to the blacks. "He found portents in the sun and moon, particular hieroglyphics in leaves and suchlike and in general created of himself a mysterious figure of supernatural gifts." Gradually these began to spell out to him a

1. *The Sewanee Review*, 64/3, Summer 1956, 485–98. Copyright 1956, 1984 by the University of the South. Reprinted with the permission of the editor.

The Land They Fought For. By Clifford Dowdey. Doubleday and Company. 1955. $6.00. *A Southern Reader.* By Willard Thorp. Alfred A. Knopf. 1955. $7.50.

holy mission. In August of 1831 he gathered a small band of accomplices armed with guns, swords, and axes and fell upon one isolated farmstead after another. The trail of murder was not ended until more than fifty white persons had been killed, the majority of them women and children. The fear inspired by this massacre was magnified by memories of the slave insurrection in Haiti, whence a number of refugees had come to the South. There was no reprisal beyond justice executed upon the participants, but there was an aroused demand in Virginia for abolition and deportation of the alien race.

This was the year in which William Lloyd Garrison founded *The Liberator*. The collision of events was ominous. The North had the abstraction freedom, but the South had the concrete problem of 4,000,000 Negroes in various stages of cultural development. With this as significant backdrop, the author narrates the thirty-year cold war which led to the holocaust of 1861–65.

The chief merit of Mr. Dowdey's history lies in its boldly handled, and I believe accurate, analysis of the cause of Southern failure. That cause may be summed up in a simple proposition: the South was caught up in a revolution, and its chosen leaders did not know it.

There is a wonderful episode in Robert Penn Warren's "Cass Mastern's Wedding Ring" in which two Mississippi brothers are discussing prospects on the eve of hostilities. They happen to meet Mr. Jefferson Davis on a river boat shortly after his election to the presidency of the Confederacy. Mr. Davis makes a graceful little speech about how he had "always looked upon the Union with superstitious reverence," and so on. Later Cass, the wistful, dreamy idealist, ventures to his brother Gilbert that "Mr. Davis is a good man." But Gilbert, the "success" of the family, a hard, ruthless realist, destined to make a huge fortune during the Gilded Age, retorts, "What we want now they've got us into this is not a good man but a man who can win." This scene epitomizes perfectly the dual nature of Southern leadership, and it can be used to introduce two distinct types of mentality. The war effort of the South was divided between the politicians, who were largely of the Cass type; and the military men, or at least the ones that are best known, who were of Gilbert's outlook.

The first group believed, with what now seems an extraordinary lack of grasp of realities, that the impending conflict was just another political movement, or at most just another defensive war, to be concluded after a battle or two. Davis himself was a "moderate," who had been U.S. Senator and Secretary of War, and who behaved as if the only change were a geographical one from Washington to Montgomery and then to Richmond, where he carried the bureaucrat's love of apparatus. Into the post of vice-president came the effete Alexander Stephens, who was, if possible, even more self-deluded. If some Confederates thought that the Yankees could be beaten with corn stalks, Stephens thought that they could be beaten with a rolled-up copy of the Constitution. What a pity that neither of these ingénues had pondered the lines written by Andrew Marvell on a man who fared very well in a revolution.

> Though Justice against Fate complain
> And plead the ancient rights in vain
> (But these do hold or break
> As men are strong or weak.)

J. B. Jones, a Washington clerk who had transplanted himself from the Federal capital to Montgomery, looked at the first session of the Confederate Congress and thought that he was seeing the United States Congress "through a reversed opera glass." In such men was a well spring of folly which doomed the cause from the beginning.

The second group was made up of men who discerned correctly that, whoever was due the blame, a revolution had broken out in the United States, and that you do not survive in a revolution by being "good" in any priggish sense or by taking half measures. You try to find out the level at which revolutionary forces are running and plan your steps accordingly.

Among those who understood the true implication of affairs for the South was Col. R. E. Lee. I only wish that Mr. Dowdey had quoted, in further substantiation of his thesis, the letter that Lee wrote to his sister Anne about the time he resigned his commission in the United States Army. He advised her that "we are in a state of revolution" which "will yield to nothing." One of the Russian leaders—Trotsky, as I recall—is on record as saying that the true conservative always perceives the nature of a revolution better than the liberal or middle-of-the-roader. Realizing that the independence of the Southern states could never be made good by anything less than a hard and fast military decision, Lee took a dim view of all measures predicated upon the idea of a static defense. He knew that once the arbitrament of the sword had been invoked, the best defense (in this particular case the only defense) was a good offense. Defensive victories like the Seven Days, Fredericksburg, and Chancellorsville, which filled the South with jubilation, did not elate Lee. He saw only too well that, the disparity of forces being what it was, winning victories like these was only submitting yourself to the enemy's grindstone. The only solution was the destruction of the opposing army as an operating force, and this, it seems to me, explains the supreme gamble which he made in Pickett's charge at Gettysburg.

Another who had a clear understanding of the state of affairs was Thomas J. Jackson. Unlike Lee in many ways—growing up in poverty in the mountains of what is now West Virginia, and devoid of every social grace—Jackson had but "one calendar year" in which to win military immortality. But he possessed an insight into the nature of conflict which causes Mr. Dowdey to rank him as the supreme realist of the Southern side.

> At Harper's Ferry, Jackson, more than any other outstanding Southern leader, civil or military, perceived the true nature of the struggle into which they had been drawn. Completely opposite from the government at Montgomery, he dismissed all consideration of the abstract "rights" of the issue, the history of the issue, and the involved relations of the Confederacy to the United States. He applied himself solely and totally to the problem as it existed: to maintain the independence of the Southerners' land against an enemy trying to destroy that independence by force.

A third leader in the same category, with still a different kind of background, was Nathan Bedford Forrest. Born in the frontier society that was Mississippi in the 1820s, a self-made man in business and war, disliked by most of the West Pointers, Forrest has had to wait two generations for general recognition of his genius. Lee, during his years in Lexington, pronounced him the greatest soldier produced by the Confederacy. Moreover, testimony has come to light that Grant was sensing his quality as early as the summer of 1862. We find this indicated in the recently published *Three Years with Grant*, by Sylvanus Cadwallader, who covered the general's headquarters for the Chicago *Times*. The journalist noted in his diary that Grant never showed any concern if he heard that Joe Wheeler or Roddey was operating in his vicinity; "but if Forrest was in command, he at once became

apprehensive because the latter was amenable to no known rules of procedure, was a law unto himself in all military acts, and was constantly doing
the unexpected at all times and places. . . ."

This was exactly the kind of revolutionary mentality required by a desperate situation. But Forrest spent most of his time under the command of
the futile and self-defeating Bragg. It was a picture of the internal failure of
the South.

The civilian government was not wholly lacking in men of the "Gilbert"
type. The astute Judah P. Benjamin was one. James Seddon, who became
Davis's *fourth* secretary of war, was another. Secretary Stephen Mallory im-
provised a navy whose achievements were fairly remarkable in view of its
minuscule size; and Josiah Gorgas gave the Confederacy an effective ord-
nance department.

This was substantially the disposition of leadership with which the South
faced a struggle that before long eventuated in the first total war. There
were those who wanted to win the war and knew the measures that best
favored success. There were those who at least behaved as if they did not
want to win it. The "top policy" decisions, as the current phrase has it, were
in the hands of the latter. The facts, real and potential, were simply not
appreciated by Davis, the bumbling cabinet members, and the Confederate
Congress. These began by giving the North almost every precious advantage it could have coveted, short of a present of the Confederate capital.

An outstanding example was the policy which laid an embargo on cotton. Cotton was the one thing possessed by the Confederacy with which it
could have acquired that indispensable sinew of war, gold. But instead of
shipping out every possible bale before the Union blockade became effective, the government prohibited the export of cotton. The theory was that
England, in desperate plight for fiber, would break the blockade and recognize the new nation. The *reality* was that English cotton manufacturers,
with a big supply on hand, found a heaven-sent opportunity to raise the
prices of their textile goods and made money hand over fist. *Sancta simpli-
citas!* Mr. Dowdey draws the appropriate moral.

> This fateful and ruinous policy was caused by the lack of one true revolu-
> tionary who could conceive of *winning* independence. Nobody in Montgom-
> ery was psychologically disassociated from Washington.

That the people as a whole were in favor of the independence movement there is hardly room for doubt: out of a population of about 6,000,000, counting two border states, more than 600,000 volunteered for military service. But at the top there was always this divided leadership, a handful of realists looking at the concrete situation and trying to achieve a decision which would stick, and the Davis party, which included a few of the military figures, living in a dream world of "rights" and abstractions, and refusing to learn lessons even from reverses. As Mr. Dowdey aptly observes, Lincoln never kept a general who had the aura of defeat on him. Davis not only kept them but sometimes promoted them.

This is the thesis that the author propounds—one may be tempted to say rides—from the beginning of his narrative of the war to the end. As is often true of concepts which go to the root of things, it is accompanied in places by overstatement. Mr. Dowdey has a principle for distinguishing the sheep from the goats, and he employs it perhaps to make them seem a little further apart than they were in actuality. The villains of the piece tend to be unrelievedly villainous and the heroes tend to be without fear and without reproach. I do not mean to suggest by this that he stereotypes his characters; on the contrary his portraiture is individuating, and this is one of the qualities which keep the book alive throughout. I think no writer, for example, has captured the essence of Jackson's character better than he has in these two sentences. "To say that he made absolutely no effort to please would be an understatement. . . . The colonel's sole interest in any man was that he do his duty to the letter as his commanding officer saw it."

Here is Lee as he appears in 1861, a major-general in command of the state troops of Virginia.

> From the first Lee was deaf to loud-talking politicians and would-be Napoleons. He believed the war might last for ten years and he prepared for a long war. He also had to prepare for the opening invasion in a hurry, so that he was rushing defenses at the same time that he was building for the future.
>
> The reluctantly seceding state of Virginia, destined to become the battleground of the Civil War, was designed by nature to favor the invader. It was literally riddled with inviting avenues of entrance. Lee's immediate task was to place a block in each avenue.

In patient obscurity he worked at the task of "fortifying a state against invasion by a nation."

The style is equally incisive when the author turns his attention to those who are blamed for the defeat of the Confederacy. In this group Mr. Dowdey places General Joseph E. Johnston, who "ended the war as he began it, by retreating." General Johnston is pictured as follows.

> There is a legend that his soldiers loved him because, under his care, one said, "We never missed a meal and never fought a battle." It is certainly true that his shrewd estimate of the evil his enemy could visit upon him made Johnston extremely skillful at avoiding armed combat. Verbal combat was another matter. Where his dignity was concerned, his perquisites and prerogatives, the peppery and highborn Regular Army man was quick to bristle and, never counting the cost, to press home the attack.

The obloquy which he heaps upon the Davis-Bragg combination is similarly a work of art.

There is an ancient saying to the effect that you never leave a war by the same entrance by which you came in; the basis of the war changes as the war goes on. This truth can be illustrated with especial vividness from our Civil War, and Mr. Dowdey has made it another of the themes of his work. Shortly after First Manassas, Congress passed a resolution saying in effect that the war had nothing whatever to do with slavery, but was being waged against the doctrine of secession. But between the opening and the closing phases there occurred a profound change of spirit, method, and intention. The South, and evidently much of the North too, went into the struggle thinking that it would be fought much as the European wars—probably the Napoleonic Wars were chiefly in mind—had been fought for several centuries. Two armies met in the field and slugged it out; the side that got the worst of it accepted the verdict of the sword, or as much of it as it had to; the men dispersed; and life went on much as before. It is probable that the American Civil War would have followed this pattern had men like McClellan been left in charge of the Federal forces. McClellan believed in the old-fashioned code: when he found the Confederates leaving land mines behind them in their withdrawal up the Peninsula, he protested against "this barbarous mode of warfare." The Confederates saw the point and abandoned the practice. According to Mr. Dowdey, Southerners understood McClellan because he "fought to suppress the armed forces of dissident fellow countrymen whom it was his duty, and his desire, to return to a common Union. He did not consider it his duty, and it was certainly not his desire, to make war on those civilians among his countrymen who differed from him on the interpretation of the Constitution. He fought without hate, without cruelty, as if it were indeed a rebellion to suppress and not an alien people to conquer and despoil."

It surprises me that no one has pointed out a tradition quite strong in the South, created by the keelboatmen and the Southwestern frontiersmen generally, but diffused very widely, that the winner in a fair fight is entitled to be boss. That is what the fight is for, to decide which one "can whip" and is therefore "the best man." But the fight had to be a fair contest of strength and resourcefulness, even if considerably rougher tactics were allowed than one now sees in the prize ring. Defeat is always a bitter pill, but a chivalric code, even a rough one like this, makes it easier to take. Probably the South could have assimilated defeat on these terms as it never has on the other.

Before long, however, there appeared "the mystic soldier," the sort of man who finds some kind of obscure gratification in a pageantry on destruction and suffering. Kenneth Burke has described the type in a rare passage of his *Rhetoric of Motives*.

> There are those for whom war is a vocation, to whom the thought of the universal holocaust is soothing, who are torn with internal strife unless, in their profession as killers, they can commune with carnage. The imagery of slaughter is for them the way of mortification.

This characterization seems to fit General Sherman well, and probably also Sheridan and Hunter, though it would not fit Grant. Mr. Dowdey expresses it in this fashion.

> Once the United States Government released its powers of destruction on the subjugation of a people, the policy inevitably bred the type of man who was affected by unrestrained power as were the barbarous rulers of old. In Sherman's case, the power of destruction fed on itself as any power feeds. By his own gloating descriptions of the "desolation" he left in his wake, Sherman all too clearly revealed the hold that his own power of terror had on him.
>
> In his soldiers, violence likewise was self-feeding, and they regarded Southern families as no more than helpless victims. "Rebels have no rights," was said to a thousand defenseless women who protested at having their personal belongings stripped from them.

Lee's often quoted saying at Fredericksburg, "It is well this is terrible; otherwise we should grow fond of it" seems to me an indication that he knew this feeling but had mastered it.

Some readers are likely to resent the kind of psychological attention that Mr. Dowdey gives to important leaders on both sides, especially in certain dissertations upon psychomatic illness. This reviewer personally welcomes it as a distinct and realistic contribution to a subject which has been often rehearsed from too lofty a perch. Psychological incapacity seems to explain a number of events which cannot otherwise be accounted for. There was too much sickness among Confederate leaders for any Southern partisan to feel complacent about. Davis, for example, was ill or suffering much of the time; during some crucial periods he was actually confined to his bed. Emotional strain rather regularly erupted in physical symptoms. During the winter of 1858–59, as tension between North and South mounted, he had an attack of glaucoma which virtually blinded him in one eye, and he suffered recurrently from severe eye trouble during his whole administration. "This affliction can be closely associated with or related to emotional stress," Mr. Dowdey notes. (Referring once more to Warren's "Cass Mastern's Wedding Ring," we find Cass remarking that Mr. Davis "did not look well." Brother Gilbert replies, "A sick man, it is a fine how-de-do to have a sick man for president.") Vice-president Stephens was a semi-invalid. But possibly the most costly of all the psychomatic disorders to the Confederacy was that of Braxton Bragg. A constant sufferer from migraine headaches, actually unnerved by the thought of sending his men into battle, Bragg threw away the two greatest prizes that were offered the Confederacy, at Perryville and at Chickamauga. After his brilliant march into Kentucky, with the city of Louisville within his grasp, "General Bragg needed what did not then exist in America—a psychiatrist," writes Mr. Dowdey. At night in camp at Perryville, after his men had won the first day's fighting and pushed the enemy back a mile, Hardee and Polk "anxiously watched their general pace the floor, rubbing one hand with the other, his face revealing tormented thoughts that no one could imagine. Out of his bewildered anguish, the only decision that Bragg could reach was to withdraw." It seems less surprising that Davis and Bragg, who "both suffered ailments of psychogenetic origin when under stress," had such an affinity for one another. I feel that in some places Mr. Dowdey is guilty of excesses in language, but when he characterizes Davis's last orders to Hood and Forrest as "dementia," I go along. We may not need a psychologist to tell us that Davis and Bragg were crazy, but it is good to have the matter proved from this quarter.

There are two matters of substance, however, in which *The Land They Fought For* seems liable to criticism. Mr. Dowdey gives an unfair amount of space, it seems to me, to the Eastern theatre of operations. He is a native of Virginia, and in view of that state's great contribution to the Confederate cause, one understands his pride in the Army of Northern Virginia. Moreover, this is an area on which one of Confederate sympathies is prone to focus, since all the major Southern victories, with the exception of Chickamauga and the defense of Charleston, were won here. Nevertheless, there is an important school of thought which holds that the outcome of the war was determined by events in the West. There is some justice in the remark that South Carolina and Massachusetts may have started it, but Illinois and Georgia fought it out. In this respect I see some room for reproportioning.

Again, in the last two chapters he dwells too much on the aspect of debacle. Gloom gets thicker and thicker, and every event is related to an outcome already pronounced inevitable. The author may here be following his thesis too relentlessly, and I question how well it reflects the mentality of the period. I have read accounts by men who went through it all and who wrote more cheerfully than Mr. Dowdey does in this part. There was gallantry right up to the end, and gallantry is essentially a defiance of circumstances.

Though this is possibly but the reverse of one of the book's virtues, the style seems to me marked in a good many places by a kind of gratuitous asperity. It adds nothing to the quality of the work to refer to Joseph E. Johnston in half of a dozen or more places as "Retreatin' Joe," despite that general's penchant for retrograde movement. The same must be said of referring to Beauregard time after time as "Old Bory." "Old Bory did fine," he writes, in telling how he bottled up Ben Butler's army at Drewry's bluff. Describing a group of thirty volunteer nurses from Mobile as "self-yclept 'the Florence Nightingale Brigade'" is a lapse from taste. These things are below the dignity of his subject, and I should think that the color and energy of the style could have been well managed without them.

But when all has been said, Mr. Dowdey has written one of the most original, informed, and moving histories of the Confederacy, which ought to prove equally convincing to readers South and North.

Willard Thorp's *A Southern Reader* is a voluminous conspectus of the South presented through its literature. Readers may well find interesting the story of this book's inception. Mr. Thorp was born in Delaware County, New York, which makes him, as he says, "a sub-species of Yankee." He attended a village school where the teacher of history was a "black abolitionist," who taught the Civil War as a moral crusade against a land of iniquity. "For some reason," Mr. Thorp relates, "this seemed to me absurd. To the delight of my schoolmates I stood up for the Confederate cause, drawing my arguments from the files of *Harper's Magazine* and *Harper's Weekly* for the war years, which we happened to have at home." He embarrassed the teacher by pointing out that for a region that sat in darkness, the South had won a surprising number of battles. Knowledge kindled interest, and when he stood on Virginia soil the first time, he felt that he "had seen for a moment an enchanted land." Now, years later, after much travel and many contacts, he still finds the South "the most exotic and exciting region in America."

This is a preface to delight most Southerners, who have long felt that if they could be known in their concrete habitat, apart from the epithets and clichés of condemnation devised by abolitionists and political journalists, they would not be found so unreasonable, and moreover their deep attachment to the land they fought for would be understood.

Mr. Thorp has arranged his selections according to topical divisions, and within these he has chosen his material freely with reference to chronology, point of view, type of literary expression, and so on. There appear at the beginning "The Land" and "The Rivers"; later come "Education," "Sports and Pastimes"; "The Negro"; "Politics"; "Religion"; "Cities and Towns"; and similar groupings to the number of sixteen. One hundred and eleven authors (including a few outsiders who visited and wrote about the South) are called upon. (The most interesting thing in the entire collection, to my mind, is James Lane Allen's "County Court Day in Kentucky." It shows beyond reasonable doubt that the South was on the way toward developing an *agrarian* culture comparable to what one finds in, say, rural France.) The feast is a rich one, and even readers who know the South are likely to derive a fresh impression of the variety and multiplicity of this fabled region. No other area of the United States is more often referred to as a unit, yet no other shows so much particularity and individualism once you look inside. Perhaps this combination of unity in diversity is the real secret of its vitality, now making itself felt so strongly in the nation's literature.

So true is this that it is almost impossible to know the South in any thoroughgoing way without contemplating anomalies. It is the "rebel" section, yet it is the section which fought a terrible war for the Constitution as laid down in 1787. It is the land of violence, yet it is famed for that unbought grace of life which is courtesy. It is accused of indulgence and lasciviousness, yet its gods are the austere and self-denying Calhoun, Jackson, and Lee. It is always being publicly whipped for intolerance, yet it produced Jefferson, to whom every American libertarian runs for political ammunition. It is denounced in a selection given here from W. E. B. Dubois as "uncivilized"; yet it has generally claimed a civilization superior to those contiguous to it; and John Peale Bishop declares that "the South, whatever may be said, passed those two tests which the French have devised for a civilization, and to which they admit only themselves and the Chinese. It had devised a code of etiquette and created a native cookery." It is criticized as the land of greasy foods and pellagra-producing diets, yet the kitchens of South Carolina and Louisiana have long delighted epicures. To cap all the anomalies, it is the "aristocratic" section, yet there has been no more faithful adherent of the Democratic party. So much for the danger of taking hold of the South by a simple handle.

These contrasts are rather well represented, and there is little point in quarreling generally with the selections for the reason that one man's anthology is not another's. Mr. Thorp confesses that "nearly every selection in this book competed for its place with a half-dozen others just as good." This is disarming enough, but I find it mildly curious that there is not a single selection from *I'll Take My Stand*, the most explicit defense of the Southern tradition written in this century, and the most discussed one. By the same prompting, why is a brilliant Southern spokesman like Donald Davidson cited only to the extent of a single paragraph whereas "right thinking" liberals like Virginius Dabney and Hodding Carter are permitted to run on in two articles apiece? The editorial prefaces with which Mr. Thorp introduces the many selections suggest that there may be conscious outlook in such choosing. In fact I am amazed, considering the source, to find these inspired with a spirit of Rotarian uplift, or worse, filled with attempts to explain the South in accordance with "today's thinking." It is just as if the compiler had forgotten his earlier professions and were taking the attitude that despite a few exoticisms and archaisms, which serve only to add condiment to the national broth, the South is optimistic, forward-looking, and progressive just like Zenith. Granted that the region has produced some of the worst Babbitts and boomers to be seen in the country, and granted that these have to be represented in any catholic anthology, still, they are not the ones who have made the South a distinct (waiving the question of whether a distinguished) culture and a conscious political minority. To illustrate: in introducing a passage from Jefferson, he tries to editorialize away that worthy's opinions of the Negro as set down in the *Notes on the State of Virginia*. In discussing the group of selections on religion, he writes, "The ante-bellum South was even more a Bible belt than it is today." This is dubious in fact, but even if we grant it as a premise, what would be the conclusion? Presumably that it is not in accordance with "today's thinking" for a people to have a sacred literature. In discussing "Southerners at Home" he expresses himself as follows.

> Among Southern "Shintoists" conversation sooner or later gets round to the Confederate War, and Shiloh and Antietam are refought during the rest of the evening. (The Northern guest must remember to apologize for the depravity of the Union troops who carried off millions of silver spoons.)

There may be elements of Shintoism in the Southern interest in grandfathers, but a good many Southerners take stock in Burke's maxim that those who care nothing for their ancestors will care nothing for their descendants. As for the other matter, the theft of the spoons may have become a national joke, but as Southerners refer to it, it is a kind of symbol of the spoliation which kept the South weak for two generations. These are but a few of many examples which seem to slant the approach in the manner I have indicated.

Perhaps I am overlooking the good humor intended here, but it seems to me that Mr. Thorp would have done more for his readers if, instead of indulging in this kind of sniping all along the line, he had pointed out the connection that indubitably exists between these refusals to conform to the national pattern and whatever there is of interest and piquancy in Southern culture. It seems evident that if the South had embraced the modern program of liberalism and scientificism, it would have produced little to attract connoisseurs of cultures and ways of life. The fact that it has clung to its belief in the supernatural, that it has never abandoned the idea that man is a special creation, that it persists in seeing life as a drama (or at least as an anecdote), in which creatures of free will make choices and are saved or damned, and that it has never accepted a simple equalitarianism is very closely related to its present literary renascence, as well as to its conservation of certain values that have been pretty well leached out of other societies. If the South today increasingly draws the attention of those who continue to believe in literature, that is because the South remains, despite some terrible pounding from the outside and a good bit of betrayal within, a stronghold of humanism. There is a pronounced tendency today among many scientific-minded liberals to think that humanism is too expensive just because it stands in the way of this or that planned utopia. I would not charge Mr. Thorp with anything so uncomplimentary to a professor of letters, but it does seem to me, to repeat, that many of his *obiter dicta* are discouraging to the very things he admires. To want something but to object to its necessary cause may be a tempting indulgence, but it is not very philosophical.

The Regime of the South[1]

In the national controversy raging over segregated schooling, we often hear of "the Southern way of life." I suggest that this phrase is used with too little understanding both by those who wield it for defense and those who hurl it in attack. It is true that the South has a "way of life," but the point that is missed is that a "way of life" is a normal social phenomenon. "Way of life" is in fact our everyday translation of the old term, "regime." And "regime" is a word rich in social meaning.

Modern social scientists have a way of finding or coining words which only obscure their discussions. They could communicate better if they dropped a good deal of their special jargon, but now and then they bring forward a term which is really serviceable. One of the most interesting of these is *anomie*. This word comes from two roots which combine to mean "an absence or privation of custom and order." Interpreted more fully, it signifies a condition of society in which the guidelines of belief and behavior have largely disappeared, so that frustration and chaos reach dangerous levels. A society suffering from *anomie* is in a state of disorganization, from the lack of whatever has previously given it the power to unify and cohere.

Anomie is, in brief, a word for disintegration; and it is the judgment of many students that large parts of the modern world are suffering more or less acutely from *anomie*. If so, the most urgent task of social criticism is to diagnose the condition and find some remedy which will bring the disintegrated parts back into a unity.

The remedy will have to be "regime."

It is the nature of a regime to be much more than the sum of the government and the laws. It is these plus beliefs, traditions, customs, habits, and observances, many of which affect the minutiae of daily living. A regime

1. *National Review*, 6/21, March 14, 1959, 587–89. © 1959 by National Review, Inc., 215 Lexington Avenue, New York, N.Y. 10016. Reprinted by permission.

tells the individual from early days, through his nurture and education, what is expected of him, how he stands in regard to this person and that, and what kind of social response he can expect from the choices that are open to him.

Locations and Directions

Regime is, in substance, a complex of law, custom, and idiomatic social behavior, and it fills all the interstices of life. Described thus in outline, it might appear a set of imprisoning forces, but we must be careful to remember that walls support as well as obstruct. In actual fact a regime is a system of sustaining forms, and everyone who has been in contact with a regime recognizes its capacity to give every man, the high and the low, some sense of being at home. It tends, moreover, to diminish the sense of being "low" by sustaining the sense of belonging.

A regime is thus comparable to the rule of a household. There is a place for everybody, though the place cannot be the same for everybody. The very fact that we speak of "place" means that we envision a social whole, in reference to which there are locations and directions. The principle of the ordering may be more intuited than reasoned out. Yet this sense of inclusive ordering makes the individual feel that his presence is acknowledged in more than a perfunctory way. A regime is thus a powerful check against the sense of lostness, the restlessness, and the aimless competition which plague the modern masses and provoke the fantastic social eruptions of our era.

The idea of regime is thus an antidote to much that is complained of in modern life. It is, to tell the truth, what all of us except the lawless and the nihilistic are looking for. It is the richest and freest form of communal life because it does not depend on top-heavy government, but upon the voluntary preferences of many individuals, acting and interacting out of respect for some basic values.

There is no doubt, on the other hand, that a regime as a "way of life" is also a principle of exclusion. It is a way of rejecting what is inimical or foreign to the group's nature and of retaining what can be assimilated. Social and cultural groups, like organisms, must be able to fend off what they cannot accept without ceasing to live. To say that this is a law of life is almost superficial; it is rather a law of existence. Intolerance of what would be fatal is a necessity for survival. The difficulty of most people who have been conditioned by "modern thinking" is to interpret all exclusiveness as having its root in injustice. But this is so far from being true that one can affirm that some degree of exclusiveness is essential to self-identity and self-preservation.

Those societies which have a way of life have a distinctive culture. A culture is a body of forms organized about certain ideas expressing value, which gives structure to the life of a people. In so doing it satisfies psychic needs which cannot be met in any other way. Culture is inexplicable save through reference to this inner need for beliefs, forms, settled dispositions, rituals, and other defined patterns. If these things are somehow lost by a people or are suddenly taken away from them, the result may be so grave as to produce actual illness. A regime therefore is definitely hygienic; and we should look with suspicion upon those who oppose the very idea of regime.

There are many things compelling us to believe that Liberalism is the death-wish of modern civilization. In its incapacity for commitment, its nihilistic approach, and its almost pathological fear of settled principle, Liberalism operates to destroy everything and conserve nothing. The reason it hates the idea of regime is therefore not far to seek. A regime is sustained by the kind of self-definition and self-constitution which require a love of life and of the positive arrangements that enrich the employment of life. A regime therefore cannot be liberal about itself any more than a man can be "liberal" about his own existence. A regime can be generous, kindly, humane, even humanitarian, but it cannot be liberal in the sense of perpetually entertaining the question of whether it ought to continue. This does not mean that it cannot accept correction or make the empirical changes that are required by changes in the world. But a regime cannot live exclusively on a diet of self-questioning, to say nothing of self-hate. Liberalism has worked itself into an impasse where the only thing that it can postulate is the necessity for questioning what exists. Liberalism cannot postulate anything positive, because such affirmations will carry with them exclusions, and the only source Liberalism can recognize for exclusion is intolerance or "narrow-mindedness."

Some American Regimes

It follows inevitably that the Liberal is exacerbated by the sight of any independent and healthy growth. Such a growth can only remind him of his own hollowness. A regime holds the mirror up to the Liberal. He hates what he sees there, and strikes out in anger against the bearer of the unpleasing image. Those who know that the struggle of these times is neither sectional nor national but world-wide must be prepared to deal with this hatred of regimes as a struggle within the consciousness of the man afflicted by modernism.

Everyone knows that the regime of the South is under heavy assault by Liberalism. But before taking up this conflict in particular, I wish to call attention to the presence of other regimes in the United States. I am not asserting that the South is the only region which has created this form of cultural life. There is no doubt that New England had a regime during a period of its history, a real and a charming one, with its chaste ideals. Yet New England, despite the fact that it was on the victorious side in our civil struggle, does not seem to have been successful in preserving its "way of life." That way lingers north of Boston; and the New Hampshire celebrated by Robert Frost clearly has its appeal to the poet as regime. But the New England regime has certainly decayed in the centers of influence. The very idea of attachment to it is caricatured in the novels of John P. Marquand.

One might claim that even the Old West had a regime during the period when it was, more or less, as it is represented by our cowboy films. The rule by the man who was quickest on the draw, the rough and ready classification of people into good and bad, the figure of the cowboy with his horse and saddle, and the clear lines of social approval and disapproval—these probably add up to a regime, though one based on the transient circumstances of a frontier. The Old West had a structure and an ethos, and these are the essentials of social cohesion.

Today it is not uncommon to hear references to "the American way of life." Whether the American way of life is enough of a piece to be reckoned a regime can be argued one way and the other. If the definition is somewhat relaxed, and if the data are taken from certain areas of activity, perhaps it is. But the important thing about the phrase is that we hear it introduced when the object is to contrast the United States with Soviet Russia or, in some cases, with certain forms of Europeanism.

When we want to stress the way in which we are *really* different from the Soviets, we refer not to our government or the Bill of Rights, but quite properly to our regime, which is to say, our ingrained way of doing things, our habitual preferences, and the rest of what makes up the very fabric of living. This underscores the fact that a regime is not something abstract, like a written constitution, but a multiplicity of matters large and small, which are felt with varying degrees of intensity. It is also a clear warning to those who would attack a regime in the name of some deduced and doctrinaire theory. A regime evokes emotional responses at a thousand and one points. This is the sign of its capacity to make people feel deeply and peculiarly at home with it. When therefore I hear of "the American way of life," I take it as a sign that the Americans have as much natural desire for a regime as does any large group, although some accidents of their history may have kept them from developing more than regional regimes in the full sense intended here.

Three Reasons

Of all the regions of the country, the South has maintained a regime in the clearest and most enduring form. It has a society more unified by imponderables, more conscious of self-definition, more homogenous in outlook than any other region. This is not the place to rehearse the history behind that fact, but I can mention three things which seem to me to explain its persistence. One is the South's adherence to a structural form of society, known odiously in some quarters as "aristocratic." A second is its receptivity to the idea of transcendence, which has been referred to seriously as its religiousness and scornfully as its Bible Beltism. The third is its preservation of history, which by the modern mind is equated with "living in the past." All of these are strong barriers to *anomie*. A stable structural society creates the feeling of permanence because it provides the shelter of an accredited authority which cannot be overturned by tomorrow's vote. The idea of transcendence is the real source of symbolization in life, which persuades men that they have lived and are living for something more than things of the moment. And the preservation of history keeps tradition from seeming arbitrary, endowing it not only with reason but with grace.

It will be recognized that these are conserving forces. The effect of a regime is to conserve and to stabilize. No one has to believe that every particular thing conserved by them is valuable. No society has met that standard, and it certainly has to be granted that societies, like people, are properly subject to correction through appeals to logic and ethics. The South has had the enormously difficult problem of accommodating a large minority distinct in race and culture. But what I am talking about here is a cohesive social ordering, which the South has had in outstanding measure. The use of the term "Southern culture" is the popular recognition of this fact.

The South is the natural prime target of those who hate the very idea of regime. Anyone who looks beneath appearance to reality must see that the attack upon the Southern school system is but one front of a general attack upon the principle of an independent, self-directing social order, with a set of values proper to itself. It is the one pushed most vigorously now because for a variety of reasons it can draw the most publicity, and it is the kind of action for which the Liberal's sentimentalism makes him most gullible.

The Real Motive

No long memory is needed to recall other fronts on which the attack against the South has formerly been active. Not very long ago the issue was "fundamentalism," and the South was being crucified for holding a religious belief not terribly different from that of respectable contemporary neo-orthodoxy. Later it was the sharecropping system, which certainly brings great wealth neither to owner nor cropper, but which is nothing to get excited over from a distance, unless one starts with a strong initial prejudice. Still later it was the poll tax, again nothing to get excited over unless you believe that adding to the number of votes automatically adds to the amount of wisdom. Thus the attackers have said by their actions, "Any stick to beat a dog!" This is the reason we urgently need to look for the real impulse behind their militancy.

The modern Liberal has confused liberty with power, but the only use he has for power is to destroy. If these fanatical destroyers are allowed to have their way, the next thing to be challenged will be the basis on which the more general "American way of life" is forming. The same charges of inequity leveled against the Southern regime will be leveled against capitalism, private property, the family, and even individuality. The Liberal's rage is directed against all restraints which allow things to grow in their own native character. He has a verdict of guilty against everything that stands in the way of certain ideas which are themselves life-denying.

This issue goes back to ultimate concepts about the right not merely to be free but to live. The right to live in the proper sense of "live" means the right to follow the law of one's being. When doctrinaire liberalism is applied to societies, the choice is between rejecting it in favor of a natural regime, or accepting it in the form of an enforced Utopia sustained by the police state. The first prevents *anomie* through the traditional means of consent and organic growth; the other strives to prevent it through an imposed conformity which is without soul. The attempt is futile because spirit is the final integrating factor of a society.

Most of us readily admit that this nation owes both its independence and its happiness to the principle of self-determination. That principle is now in danger of being suppressed by a blind zeal for standardization and enforced conformity. To oppose that trend, we do not have to become sectionalists. We need only grant the right of distinct groups to exercise some liberty of choice in the ordering of their social and cultural arrangements. If that liberty is denied, there will be no ground left on which to assert any other liberty.

Two Diarists[1]

The philosophies of life which have done more than any others to produce in the United States two differing cultures can be appropriately studied near their source in two early diarists, Cotton Mather and William Byrd. Born but eleven years apart in the latter half of the seventeenth century, they mirror in their thinking worlds so opposed that a contrast of them goes far toward explaining basic conflicts and tensions in American culture down to our time. That both men represent in a sense extremes of their positions enhances rather than detracts from their value for the student of American culture. And most fortunately for him, both men left behind copious records, that of Mather covering the great majority of his adult life and that of Byrd covering with fullness three different periods.[2] Since the records will be studied here more for what they reflect than for what they report in the way of actual fact, a prior survey of the life of each will be useful.

I. Cotton Mather

Cotton Mather was born in Boston on February 12, 1663, the son of Increase Mather and the grandson of John Cotton, both eminent Puritan divines. Naturally he was reared amid the most intense Puritan piety. He entered Harvard at the age of twelve, the youngest student ever to matriculate, and in 1681 he obtained the degree of master of arts. A habit of stammering,

1. An essay probably written in 1961 or 1962 and intended as a chapter (most likely the first) in a book contrasting the cultures of the American North and South on which Weaver was working at the time of his death. Edited by Ted J. Smith III from a corrected typescript (evidently a final draft, although missing some footnotes) located in Box 2, Folder 1, of the Richard M. Weaver papers at Vanderbilt University.

2. Byrd's diaries cover the periods February 6, 1709–September 12, 1712; December 13, 1717–May 19, 1721; August 10, 1739–August 31, 1741.

present from his early youth, almost caused him to abandon his ambition of entering the ministry, but gaining control over it, he began assisting his father at the Second Church in Boston. Later he became pastor of this church, an overseer of Harvard, and in 1713 he was elected a member of the Royal Society following publication of his *Curiosa Americana*.

Mather was himself one of the great voices of the Puritan pulpit. As a writer his output was prolific in the extreme, more than 450 titles being credited to him. His career was heavily punctuated with trouble and loss. Two of his three wives and nine of his fifteen children died during his lifetime. The third wife became mentally unbalanced and during her fits of insanity made away with parts of the famous diary. His son Increase, of whom he seems to have been especially fond, grew up an incorrigible, went to sea and was lost from a vessel out of Barbados. He fell into financial difficulties, from which friendly members of the flock had to rescue him. He was violently criticized and attacked from a number of quarters, once having a live grenade tossed into his house. His *Wonders of the Invisible World* and his association with the witchcraft trials of 1692—in regard to which, however, he showed a degree of skepticism—have gained for him an odium among the foes of the old orthodoxy; and his lack of receptivity to contemporary changes has drawn scornful criticism from liberal historians like V. L. Parrington.

But we should not discount the reality of Mather for his time or ours. The causes which permitted him to become a grotesque flowering of the Puritan ethic had been alive and active for a century before his birth, and they continue, in forms that are often undetected, down to our own period. Mather remains indeed a very serious manifestation for us. Though certain of his features may be ascribed to the special conditions of his place and time, that which gave him power was a definite capacity for perversion of the human spirit which can show itself in any age. Mather has today more spiritual descendants than our average contemporary would suspect, and the forces of this heredity in their renewed forms continue to be important influences in American life.

He was a child of the extreme reformation, of that "dissidence of dissent" which was to transform and all but destroy the essence of historic Christianity. The story of the reformation is the story of a secession from the ancient, metaphysical, and humanistic church of Roman Christianity, whose creation stretched across a thousand years.[3] The withdrawal was inspired by a feeling that this institution had corrupted, and was now an obstacle in the way of, the divinely revealed Christian religion. The remedy for the situation seemed to be a recovery of that religion in its pristine purity, without the trappings which by the medieval period surrounded it. What emerged as the prime impulse in the reform was the rejection of the idea of mediation. Luther was to insist on justification by faith alone; Calvin on a salvation through grace awarded by God. When the Puritan spirit reached its extreme attenuation of doctrine in Quakerism, everything suggestive of the need of a means in the approach to God had disappeared. The feature of chief interest to the student of the impact of religious ideas on a culture is the steady shifting of agency in the direction of man. On the level of theory Calvinism might seem to contradict this: predestination is absolute, for God chooses, on a principle reflecting divine justice, to save a portion of mankind and to consign the remainder to perdition. There is no way of seeking or earning grace, and indeed no certain way of knowing whether grace has been given to one. But since men cannot actually live with this idea—cannot conduct themselves as if their actions were totally without significance in the drama in which they have been cast—the Puritan deserted the theory in his practice and made moral conduct the very sign of whether one is acceptable to God. Here the transferral to human agency becomes evident; man is now the captain of his soul and how he steers determines the outcome. There is no intercessor for him except the Savior Christ, with whom he must get into immediate and right relations. Man is on his own responsibility in a way which makes him more of an arbiter than he had ever been before in historic Christianity. In the later and more extreme development of this view (there were a few outcroppings of it in seventeenth century Massachusetts, as when the schismatic "Gortonists" taught that Christ was in everyone[4]) such captaincy had the effect of divinizing man as the true fount of goodness.

To make such doctrine possible, it was necessary that the Puritan take an

3. The extent to which Roman Catholicism contains and expresses Western civilization becomes evident if one reflects that it incorporated Judaic religion, Greek philosophy, and Roman government.

4. Edward Johnson, *Wonder-working Providence*, New York: Barnes and Noble, 1910, p. 224.

apocalyptic view of his place in history.[5] Under this view, the critical period is always now, the time when he is waging the battle for his salvation. The individual becomes far more active in the redemptive process and in consequence more focussed upon himself. An egocentric concentration upon the self is the first tendency we mark when we begin to look critically at the habit of mind of Cotton Mather. One of the essential drives of Puritanism, as noted, is separatism, the desire to break away from a larger, allegedly more corrupt group and to strike out along a new path of purism. Separatism may be justified by an existential situation, but on the other hand it may result from a kind of self-regard which is egotism. There are grounds for asserting that Puritanism began in response to the former, and there are ample grounds for saying that it succumbed to the latter. The preliminary picture now begins to fill out with completeness. The repudiation of the need for intermediate relations, the withdrawal from larger, more sinful bodies, and the emphasis upon the agency of the "I" in effecting what is projected issue in the peculiarly egotistic and self-righteous motive in the Puritan character.

The first characteristic one is struck with in reading the diary is Mather's feeling that he is a cynosure of God. God is looking with undivided attention upon everything he does, is following with jealous scrutiny the thoughts of his heart and is adding up by infallible calculation his merits and demerits. God is always available for him to walk and talk with. But this idea does not seem to be held upon any theological or metaphysical ground. It derives from some curious extrapolation of the importance of the self. At any rate, Mather appears consumed with the idea of his own personal importance to God.

The idea appears in the frequently expressed wish that he be allowed to perform some outstanding service for the Lord. In his eighteenth year, at a time when he was passing through a period of physical weakness, he recorded the following hope:

> Nevertheless, if it bee thy Will, I would *live,* to do some *special Service* for thee, before I shall *go hence and bee no more.*[6]

5. Alan Simpson, *Puritanism in Old and New England,* Chicago: University of Chicago Press, 1955, p. 19.

6. Cotton Mather, *Diary of Cotton Mather,* ed. Worthington Chauncey Ford, New York: Frederick Ungar, 1957, vol. 1, p. 9.

A few days later he was writing:

> This day also I received an Assurance from the Lord, that I should yett *live to do some great Service for him.*[7]

The thought of special service is recurrent.

> And in some of my further Prayers, the Lord, gave mee glorious Assurances . . . that Hee would employ mee to do peculiar Services for His blessed Name.[8]

For April 18, 1696, there appears an entry well expressing the self-abasement and egotistic aspiration which often emerged together.

> On this Day, prostrate in the Dust, on my Study-floor and melted into *Tears* of Joy, I received fresh *Assurances,* that the *Spirit,* of the Lord Jesus Christ, would fill mee marvellously, and gloriously, and that Hee would quickly employ mee in *eminent Services* for His Interests.[9]

In the entry for March 4, 1698, he reported that "the Spirit and the Angel of the Lord" appeared and gave to him, in a way that he could not utter, the following assurance:

> *That I shall serve my Lord Jesus Christ, yett exceedingly;* and, more particularly, that I am quickly to do a *special Service* of great Consequence for the Name of my Lord Jesus Christ, which, as yett I know not what it is.[10]

Two years later he entered an "Article of Thankfulness," in which he recorded his gratitude that "the Lord in sovereign Grace, hath called me forth to be signalized in the Service of His Churches and Interests"; and he concluded that "*as I now suffer with the Lord Jesus Christ, and for Him, so I shall one Day reign with Him.*"[11]

These are something more than the outpourings of a pious and humble man. The thematic trend compels us to see that Mather was ever conscious of himself as an instrumentality. There was nothing of the spirit of St. Francis in him. His very self-abasement is the concavity of his egotism. Almost

---

7. *Ibid.,* vol. 1, p. 11.
8. *Ibid.,* vol. 1, p. 18.
9. *Ibid.,* vol. 1, p. 192.
10. *Ibid.,* vol. 1, p. 254.
11. *Ibid.,* vol. 1, p. 379.

everything reflects a desire to be noticed and used, and to be used in such a way as will bring notice. Following one of the periods in which he was filling his mind with self-reproach and confessing his sins to God, he added at the end of an entry:

> But while I was thinking so, the Lord gloriously told mee, *that Hee would honour mee, and sett mee on High because I had known His Name.*[12]

An amusing exhibition of vanity precedes the section of the diary given to his thirty-eighth year. Here Mather reproduced a poem, which is captioned:

Ab Amico Satis Adulatore

on

Cotton Mather

The poem goes as follows:

> For *Grace* and *Act* and an Illustrious *Fame*
> Who would not look from such an *Ominous Name*,
> Where *Two Great Names* their Sanctuary take,
> And in a *Third* combined, a *Greater* make!

It is followed by the remark: "Too gross Flattery for me to Transcribe; ('tho the Poetry be good)." Worthington Chauncey Ford, editor of the diary, notes that Mather has struck out the four lines of verse, but in such a way that they can be easily read.[13]

If any doubt remains on the score of his self-importance, however, it should be removed by noting his vanity of authorship. If this learned divine had what amounted to a lust, it was for getting into print and being circulated. When he was but twenty-four a condemned murderer requested him, according to the custom of the time, to preach him a "suitable sermon" before the execution. Mather recorded that the people "greedily desired" the publication of this sermon, with the following result: "I, a *sorry Youth* . . . had an Opportunitie, most *publickly* to invite men, unto such *Closures with the Lord Jesus Christ,* as I myself had *privately* been practising for many years."[14]

12. *Ibid.,* vol. 1, p. 126, entry for March 20, 1686.
13. *Ibid.,* vol. 1, p. 335.
14. *Ibid.,* vol. 1, p. 122.

A similar occurrence took place seven years later. On this occasion Mather preached the sermon before two young women who had been condemned for murdering their bastard infants. He reported that this sermon, upon being printed, "was greedily bought up," and he noted (in the margin of the diary) that "T'was afterward reprinted in London."[15]

A more eloquent instance concerns one of his major writings. From 1693 to 1697 Mather was at work on what he refers to as *The Church History of this Country,* the germ of what later became his *Magnalia Christi Americana.* He despatched this to London for publication, where its fate remained a source of great anxiety to him. On the fourth of April, 1702, he devoted an entire entry to his fears.

> I was in much Distress upon my Spirit, concerning my *Church History,* and some other elaborate Composures, that I have sent unto *London;* about the Progress towards the Publication whereof, the Lord still keeps me in the Dark.

But in prayer that night he told the Lord that if this attempt to serve Him by writing the *Church History* were rejected, he would submit and go on loving and serving him.

> Thus did I resign unto the Lord; who thereupon, answered me, that He was my Father and that He took Delight in me, and that He would smile upon my Endeavours to serve Him, and that my *Church-History* should be accepted and prospered.[16]

In May of 1703 we find him exclaiming:

> No less than *six Books,* do I now publish, in about the space of *two months;* all of which will prove useful I hope, unto the Interests of my glorious Lord.[17]

Such frenetic publishing had not, however, proved agreeable to his flock. Not that they felt he was neglecting his duty; he was far too industrious for that. It is much more likely that they sensed a zeal for self-advertisement in this incessant recourse to the press. A diverting sidelight appears in an entry for March, 1699, where Mather took note of some public opposition to his continuous publication.

15. *Ibid.,* vol. 1, p. 165.
16. *Ibid.,* vol. 1, pp. 424–25.
17. *Ibid.,* vol. 1, p. 481.

. . . thro' the *Energy,* and *Subtilty* of *Satan,* Prejudices were like to prevail against mee, in the *apostatizing Generation,* unto such a Degree, as to take away almost all my Advantages of being serviceable: that whereas I had en-joy'd singular Advantages to do good, by the Way of the *Press* People were now prejudiced against mee for printing so many Books, and it will be nec-essary for mee to desist from the Printing of any more.[18]

As the date proves, he did not regard this resolve as binding.[19] As late as 1711 we find him writing that God had:

. . . made use of my Pen to write many Books for the Advancement of His Kingdome; Yea, and had strangely encouraged and fortified my Service-ableness, by such Marks of Respect from other Parts of the World, as no Person in *America* has ever yett received before me.[20]

The modernism which was in Mather in germ thus sensed the power of the press. To have access to general publication is to be "the voice" and to have the means to manipulate. It is a form of reaching out, of controlling, and of imposing the pattern of one's mind. It is the intellectual's way of striving for mastery over the environment. When we contrast it with Byrd's almost extreme reticence about publishing, we get one of the best views of the gulf separating the two men.

One episode mentioned in Mather's diary reveals to a striking degree an egotism deriving from a feeling that he was at the center of God's vision. On the second of January, 1699, his little daughter Nanny, while playing with her sisters in the father's study, fell into the fire and was "sorely burned" on the right side of her face and her right hand and arm. Mather immedi-ately interpreted this as God's way of punishing him for something he had

18. *Ibid.,* vol. 1, p. 340.

19. Barrett Wendell in his *Cotton Mather: The Puritan Priest* (New York: Dodd, Mead, 1891, p. 232) includes the following verses written by one John Banister upon Mather's recep-tion of the degree of Doctor of Divinity from the University of Glasgow:

On C. Mr's Diploma

The mad enthusiast thirsting after fame,

By endless volum'ns thought to raise a name.

With undigested trash he throngs the press;

Thus striving to be greater, he's the less.

But he in spite of infamy writes on,

And draws new Cullies in to be undone.

20. Mather, *Diary,* vol. 2, p. 129.

done: "Alas, for *my Sin*, the just God throwes *my Child* into the *Fire!*"[21]
It seems unnecessary to comment on the egocentricity of this thought
further than to say that Mather supposed himself to hold such a place in
the Almighty's scheme that God would use his children thus to prick his
conscience.

There was implied from the beginning in the Puritan vision of reality a
right to blame others when things went wrong. The logic of this is not far
to seek. Natural limitations do not exist for the Puritan in any compelling
way. The world is a stage which man directs. Agency having been transferred to the individual, what is done or is not done comes about through
his will, or his will perverted by Satan. Accordingly Mather was always
ready to characterize the actions of his foes as inspired "by the very energy
and management of Satan." Near the end of the century there had been
arriving in the colony a number of schismatics, preaching a version of the
Gospel that Mather felt would divide the churches. One of them was a
certain "S. May," whom he described as a "pernicious Incendiary."[22] Mather
was able to expose the newcomer as having plagiarized sermons, but some
of the people continued to follow him, and of them the diarist gave the
following description.

> I never saw a more sensible Energy of Satan, upon the Minds of a *Mob*, than
> in this Instance; and God, for Holy End's letting Satan loose, the wicked
> Incendiary, with the silly Drove, which hee bewitched, made it a main Part of
> their business, to ly and rail, and rage against mee, on all Occasions. . . .[23]

The establishment of a new church in Boston filled him with apprehension
and moved him to the usual ascription of motives.

> I see *Satan* beginning a terrible Shake unto the Churches of *New England;*
> and the Innovators, that have sett up a *new Church* in *Boston* (a new one in-
> deed!) have made a *Day of Temptation* among us. The Men are ignorant, ar-
> rogant, obstinate, and full of Malice and Slander, and they fill the Land with
> *Lyes,* in the Misrepresentacon whereof, I am a very singular Sufferer.[24]

21. *Ibid.,* vol. 1, p. 283.
22. *Ibid.,* vol. 1, p. 315. The "S. May" mentioned here was one Samuel May. Mather later
determined (see p. 351) that he had been known in England as Samuel Axel.
23. *Ibid.,* vol. 1, p. 323.
24. *Ibid.,* vol. 1, pp. 329–30.

No life that is reported fully can be without some comic aspects, and Mather included an amusing one in the story of how he was pursued by a young woman. The incident occurred in his fortieth year, immediately following the death of his first wife. He introduced the story by noting that "*February* [1702] begins with a very astonishing trial." How the young lady, whom he goes so far as to describe as "comely" and of "incomparable Accomplishments," prosecuted her suit is best told through his own report.

> This young Gentlewoman first Addresses me with diverse Letters, and then makes me a Visit at my House; wherein she gives me to understand, that she has long had a more than ordinary Value for my Ministry; and that since my present Condition has given her more of Liberty to think of me, she must confess herself charmed with my Person, to such a Degree, that she could not but break in upon me, with her most importunate Requests, that I would make her mine; and that the highest Consideration she had in it, was her eternal Salvation, for if she were mine, she could not but hope the Effect of it would be, that she should also be Christ's.[25]

The lady, seconded by her mother, proved extraordinarily persistent, to his mounting perplexity and anxiety. It is evident from what he declares that the relationship became a matter for public gossip. How the distracted minister suffered under this one of the "great Vexations from Satan"[26] may be seen from a series of entries.

> I am in the greatest Straits imaginable, what Course to steer.[27]

> My dreadful Distresses continue upon me.[28]

> . . . there is a Noise, and a mighty Noise it is, made about the Town, that I am engaged in a Courtship to that young Gentlewoman; and tho' I am so very innocent, (and have so much aimed at Conformity to my Lord Jesus Christ, and Serviceableness to Him, in my treating of her,) yett it is not easy presently to confute the Rumour.[29]

25. *Ibid.*, vol. 1, p. 457.
26. *Ibid.*, vol. 1, p. 468.
27. *Ibid.*, vol. 1, p. 467.
28. *Ibid.*, vol. 1, p. 469.
29. *Ibid.*, vol. 1, p. 470.

He rejected her advances, but the gossip continued.

> . . . the Divel owes me a Spite, and he inspires his People in this Town, to
> whisper impertinent Stories, which have a Tendency to make me Contempt-
> ible, and hurt my Serviceableness, and strike at, yea, strike out the Apple of
> my Eye.[30]

His predicament was ended when he decided to leave the widowhood
he had resolved upon and took as his second wife Elizabeth Hubbard, a
neighbor.

Such is Mather's treatment of what, in another age, would have been
called romance. Though he does speak in somewhat tender epithets of the
fair pursuer, it is plain that the important theme is his public reputation,
the subtlety of Satan in finding out ways to "buffet" him, and the malice of
those who made the affair a topic of conversation. Nowhere is there any
sense of joy, and least of all is there any awareness of the comic dimension
present in all sexual attraction. All is anxiety, fear, and self-accusation,
along with the imputation of the spirit of lying to others. The world of
human relations had been strained through a Puritan sieve.

Naturally a diarist implies much about himself by what he ignores or
chooses to leave out. A modern reader who has had contact with more than
one tradition may well be struck by the almost total indifference to nature
in this long and detailed record. Many features of Mather's style indicate
that he possessed a more than ordinary talent for description, but nowhere
is there a loving detail or a kindly perception of the world about him. The
"wondrous Works" of God in Creation and Providence are eulogized, but
they are not depicted. The beautiful North American continent, in which
they were pioneers, was but a territory into which the Devil had seduced
the Indians so that he could rule over them without interference. The land-
ing of the Pilgrims was an invasion of this part of the Devil's domain. King
Philip's War was the Devil's retort against them. So the unfolding continues
without the slightest affectionate response to the beauties and charms of
nature. The one moment when it appears that we might get such a perception is quickly diverted to theological reflection.

> The Time of the Year arrives for the glories of Nature, to appear in my
> Garden. I will take my Walks there, on purpose to read the Glories of my

30. *Ibid.*, vol. 1, p. 487.

SAVIOUR in them. I will make it an Emblem of a Paradise, wherein the *second Adam* shall have Acknowledgements paid unto Him.[31]

One other occasion occurs in which we might expect a glance at the countryside, or a human perception of some of his companions. Mather—noting in the diary that this was a very rare thing—took a day off to go fishing at a nearby pond with a group of neighbors. He lost his footing on a canoe and fell into the water. Had the canoe not been near the shore, he recorded, he might have drowned. He tried to understand the meaning of the occurrence and ended with this question: "Am I quickly to go under the Earth, as I have been under the Water!"[32] Nothing else is given which could visualize for the reader this venture into the out-of-doors. It is a bare-bones relation, without color or humor.

Again the derivation of this attitude from the rigor of the Puritan outlook is plain. If one starts from this cosmological framework, certain things must follow. The great sensible world loses its office of mediation, which it possessed even in the Scholastic philosophy. Despite the instance in the quotation above, nature was not regularly suggestive of God; neither were those artifacts and institutions in which man has always embodied his feelings. Not even cultural creations had a role to play in man's orientation toward his maker. Prayer, mortification of the flesh through fasting, and attention to the exposition of the word of God through appointed teachers composed the whole duty of man, for whom the world of nature was merely indeterminate background.

A strict Puritanism is thus pure of nature. The problem of what to do with it, however, remained, and the answer came in a way that has been very consequential for our cultural history.

If nature is regarded as something having no value in itself, it still may be regarded as infinitely usable for man's purposes. To the extent that it is used, it ministers to that exclusive priority that man has assigned himself in this radical view of the cosmos. In this way Puritanism lends powerful support to what is later to be known as the scientific attitude. For nature as something infinitely malleable and usable agrees logically with the notion that nature has no essential independence or meaning. If nature can be worked into any shape to assist man's supposed mission on earth, the way is

31. *Ibid.*, vol. 2, pp. 619–20.
32. *Ibid.*, vol. 2, p. 367.

open for the prying, experimenting, and controlling which come to their fruition in modern science. Now a paradox is enacted. Nature ejected from all consideration returns by a backstairs route and trips man's hand. From being nothing, nature becomes everything. That is to say, what was first banished from the ontological realm comes to constitute the whole ontological realm once man is preoccupied with dominating her. An indication of this is the fact that Mather was no mean scientist himself for the times. He was one of the first to become interested in the possibility of inoculating against smallpox, and this in the face of violent opposition from some of his flock and the townspeople. It was eloquent of things to come that Mather, an extreme manifestation of the Puritan spirit, turned in the crisis presented by a smallpox epidemic to a rudimentary experiment in science. And his kind of interest was characteristic of what was to follow: his concern was with how it works in *ad hoc* and applied ways. It was an interest in effects, not the interest of one who desires to know with an attitude of wonder and reverence. For the Puritan the exclusive consideration is with how nature can be improved through man's manipulation. The human will is at work on something in which God has no special interest.

It is commonly said that Mather and his kind lived in a world populated with demons. This we may accept in a sense more meaningful than that intended by many who make the assertion. The reason that demons were real to the Puritan worthies was that these existed in themselves. It is a truism that we are ready to ascribe to others what we feel in our own being. Our pictures of others are of necessity extrapolations of our own natures. If one has found in himself some insidious failing, he is likely to probe suspiciously for it in others. The reason therefore that the Puritans could believe so strongly in demons is that they were themselves the victims of demonic possession. In their own way of expressing it, these demons were minions of Satan; but we need not accept the doctrine that they were independently existing agents of the Evil One. They were creations of the Puritan mind. I would emphasize that this does not deny them existence; it is rather a way of accounting for their existence as a part of the totality. Much of what appears to a later day as incredible in the Puritan temper can be explained by a circumspect theory of demonism, if we are wholly realistic and not positivistic. Let us see how this accounts for the case under study.

Demonism is definable as that habit of mind which judges everything and apperceives nothing. If there is one thing which should impress the reader of this diary more than another, it is that all things are subjected to judgment. There are very few assertions which are not expressive, at least in the light of context, of imputation of evil or of righteousness, praise or blame. And here is seen the essence of Calvinism; Calvin, who had by the way been a student of law, judged the world for God, taking judicial recognition of the elect and the non-elect. To intrude human disposition into matters thus far is demonic, for it is the nature of demonism to be blind to everything except what it wants. No one has ever heard of a demon who loved the world or of one who showed mercy to a victim because that victim had some rights. The demon has one view of the world, and according to that he must make his will prevail. So in Mather and other representative figures of his sect we find a terrible, exclusive emphasis upon judging and legislating; the moral imperative becomes obsessive and shuts out from consciousness everything which exists by a different mode.[33] This total absorption with dominating the world according to a law makes the Puritan one of the most fatally unbalanced types in history. It is not merely that he was intolerant toward others; his intolerance was more destructive than this because it started with creation itself. If a man can see nothing that is good in the broad nature that is spread around him, it is to be expected that he will condemn and interfere. There is nothing to prompt him to be gracious toward other existences. This explains why they could, without any sense of being humorous, refer to the members of their congregations as "saints."[34] But this kind of sainthood must be regarded as demonism, for the sufficient reason that it assumed the right to condemn without measure. In their fierce concentration upon making the law, as revealed to them, prevail, they did not care for the knowing of being.[35] This is precisely the mood of demonism, and that is why the Puritan tradition down to our own day has

33. For example, there was no place in their scheme for the moral virtues, which take into account man in his setting, but only for the theological virtues, which are absolute and know no measure. There is no real grace for man because of his fallen condition, which must extend to him some form of mediation. Their intentness upon an immediate relationship with God swept out of regard natural order, and with it the idea of natural rights and laws.

34. The expression got abroad, and we find William Byrd referring with evident derision to "the saints of New England."

35. Barrett Wendell (*Mather*, p. 2) in a sympathetic portrait of Mather admits that "beyond doubt, like emotional people about us—abolitionists, nationalists, what not—he often saw things not as they were but as he would have them." But the attitude proceeds from more than emotion; it is founded in a basic world view.

been a narrowing and destructive, as opposed to the more genial and humane spirit, which sees man and creation under a different aspect.

II. William Byrd

William Byrd, the second of his name in Virginia, was born on March 28, 1674. His family, like most of those in the colony which at one time and another became illustrious, was not of noble extraction, his grandfather in England having been a goldsmith. His father, however, became wealthy through land ownership and a variety of business enterprises, and as was usual for one so circumstanced, he held a number of the highest posts in the colony.

The young Byrd was sent to England at the age of seven to be educated. At the Felsted Grammar School in Essex he received a good grounding in Latin, Greek, and Hebrew, which he continued to make use of throughout his life. Following this he studied business methods in Holland and later in England; and then, after three years spent at the Middle Temple he was admitted to the bar. His next few years were given to the pleasures of London society, during which he led the life of a typical man-about-town. He came to know the leading wits and writers of the time, among them the playwrights Wycherley and Congreve. In 1696, at the age of twenty-two, he was elected to the Royal Society, to which he later contributed a paper on an albino negro. In this year he returned to Virginia, but after a short stay he was back in England again, until 1704. During this period he served as agent for the colony, and his experience in dealing with the Board of Trade and the Privy Council gave him political background which was of great value in his later career.

When his father passed away in 1704, Byrd inherited the entire estate, comprising over 26,000 acres. He settled on the plantation named "Westover" and took to wife Lucy Parke. Thereafter he entered upon the career of a country gentleman, which was actually a far from idle one. The size and variety of his holdings called for constant alertness and continuing supervision. The famous secret diary was begun in 1709. Byrd continued the habit of reading which he had early developed, and by the end of his life he had accumulated a library of 3,600 volumes. Business interests caused him to go to England again in 1715, from which he did not return for five years.

During a part of this interval (December 13, 1717–May 19, 1721) he resumed the secret diary, and the entries he made at this time provide one of the most candid pictures available of the life of a man of estate and fashion in the London of the early eighteenth century. In 1728 he was appointed one of the commissioners to settle the disputed boundary line between Virginia and North Carolina. His account of this surveying expedition, *The History of the Dividing Line Betwixt Virginia and North Carolina Run in the Year of Our Lord 1728,* is a recognized classic of early American literature. It was followed in 1733 by *A Journey to the Land of Eden,* a description of a visit which Byrd made to his properties along the border of North Carolina. In the last year of his life he achieved the long coveted position of President of the Council of State. Byrd died in 1744, having fulfilled in many ways what was expected of an eighteenth-century landed proprietor, and having added to this some unique accomplishments of his own.

The record of his early existence which Byrd saw fit to keep is virtually as different as possible from Mather's. To begin with, it is a secret diary, written in a code shorthand, and intended, as far as can be presumed, for his own eyes alone. In second place, it shows no attempt at literary quality. Mather, for all his concentration upon himself, introduces no small amount of literary flair. Now and again he breaks out into the little essays, diatribes, expostulations, and even narratives, and it cannot be overlooked that he is an expert at wielding the metaphor. Modifiers often flow at a surcharged rate, and one can see that the art which he employed in preaching harrowing sermons carried over into the recording of his daily activities and soul-searchings. As a literary expression, Byrd's diary is nowhere close when compared with that of his Puritan contemporary. It suffers even when compared for variety of content. That he was a writer of skill we know only from his other productions.

There are certain kinds of things that Byrd mentioned with unvarying regularity, so that the topics of his record can be easily classified. He always mentioned what he read, and he usually read in the morning just after getting up. He noted what he had to eat, sometimes remarking on whether he had adhered to his rule of limiting himself to one kind of dish a day. He recorded, usually by name, the people he met and talked with. He alluded, though nearly always briefly, to the business transactions of the day. He recorded the disciplining of his servants and slaves. He mentioned the things happening to his neighbors and others which would be regarded as news. He reported sicknesses, his own and those in the community, and sometimes he went into considerable detail regarding the medications resorted to. He mentioned intimate relations with his wife and with the many mistresses and prostitutes with whom he consorted in London. Finally, he almost invariably recorded whether he said his prayers, even on nights following a bout of fornication. The four following entries may be regarded as typical, the first two being taken from the diary he kept at "Westover," the second from that of his London period.

> March 28, 1710. I rose at 6 o'clock and read a chapter in Hebrew and some Greek in Anacreon. I ate milk for breakfast and said my prayers. I danced my dance. About 10 o'clock Major Harrison, Hal Harrison, James Burwell and Mr. Doyley came to play at cricket. Isham Randolph, Mr. Doyley, and I played with them three for a crown. We won one game, they won two. Then we played at billiards until dinner, before which Colonel Ludwell came on his way to Mr. Harrison's. They all dined with us and I ate boiled pork. Soon after dinner the company went away and I took a nap. Then we walked to Mr. Harrison's, whom we found better. We played a game at cricket again. I took leave about 8 and returned home where I found Jenny better. I caused her to be cupped and then gave her [m-t-y] pills. This was my birthday, on which I am 36 years old, and I bless God for granting me so many years. I wish I had spent them better. I neglected to say my prayers but had good health, good thoughts, and good humor, thank God Almighty.[36]

> July 29, 1711. I rose about 7 o'clock and read a chapter in Hebrew and some Greek in Homer. I drank some warm milk from the cow and about 9 o'clock had some tea and bread and butter. About 10 came an express from Drury Stith to tell me he was sick of a fever and desired two bottles of cider, which I sent him. I gave Will Eppes leave to go see his mother. Moll at the quarters was sick of a fever for which I gave her a vomit that worked very well. Billy Wilkins was also sick. I ate boiled pigeon and bacon for dinner. In the afternoon we sat and talked till 3 o'clock and then ate some watermelon. Then wrote the entries of my journal and afterwards read some French till the evening and then we took a walk about the plantation. My wife and I had a small quarrel about the trial which made us dumb to each other the rest of the night.

36. William Byrd, *The Secret Diary of William Byrd of Westover, 1709–1712*, ed. Louis B. Wright and Marion Tinling, Richmond: Dietz Press, 1941, p. 158.

I said my prayers, and had good health, good thoughts, and indifferent good humor, thank God Almighty.[37]

* * *

May 30, 1718. I rose about six o'clock and read nothing because I prepared to go to Petersham to the Duke of Argyll's with Colonel Cecil. I said my prayers, and had milk for breakfast. The weather was cold and cloudy. About nine I called on Colonel Cecil and we went to Petersham through the King's Gate to the Duke of Argyll's who was just going to the [Fair?] with my Lady Duchess. However, he ordered Mr. W-s-c-m to entertain us with all the house afforded. We walked in the garden before dinner and ate some strawberries and about 3 o'clock went to dinner and I ate some boiled beef. We had Burgundy and champagne and Colonel Burgess dined with us. We stayed till 6 o'clock and then took leave and returned to town, where I picked up a woman in the street and lay with her at the Union Tavern and then went to the Spanish Ambassador's where I stayed till twelve and then went home in a chair and neglected my prayers, for which God forgive me.[38]

April 14, 1719. I rose about 8 o'clock and read a chapter in Hebrew and some Greek in Lucian. I said my prayers and had milk porridge for breakfast. The weather was cold and cloudy. My man gave me a warning. I received a letter from Virginia. I wrote a letter to Mrs. B-s to refuse to lend her fifty pounds. I wrote a letter likewise to my daughter. About 12 o'clock I went into the City to the Virginia Coffeehouse and from thence to Mr. Perry's and dined with the old gentleman and ate some roast beef. After dinner I went to visit Mrs. Perry and drank tea. About 5 o'clock I set Mr. Carter home and went to the play but stayed not there but went to Lady Powlett's and drank some caudle. From thence I went to Will's, read the news and had two dishes of chocolate, and about 10 o'clock went with Mrs. S-t-r-d to the bagnio and rogered her once.[39]

From the literary point of view it is a dull record. What he read—always without commentary on the reading; what he ate and drank; whom he saw or visited during the day; what the weather was like; and his sexual perfor-

37. *Ibid.*, p. 381.

38. William Byrd, "The Secret Diary of William Byrd of Westover from December 13, 1717 to May 19, 1721," in Louis B. Wright and Marion Tinling (eds.), *The London Diary (1717–1721) and Other Writings*, New York: Oxford University Press, 1958, p. 128.

39. *Ibid.*, p. 256.

mances. These are the staple, from which there is seldom deviation. As far as the content goes, when one has read a few entries, one has read the diary. Still, all human expression is selective, and Byrd was by no means an unimaginative man, as his other writings amply testify. These matters were regarded as memorabilia by an upper-class person of superior education, and of capacity, even tendency, to reflect about the world. Certain inferences regarding bent and emphasis, which will to some extent apply to his class, must be drawn. We note first of all that he lived in the external world and that he gave it a great deal of attention. Places, persons, the weather, and so on existed for Byrd as important features of the world. His interest in food for example—a subject never mentioned by Mather except in the most general reference—is indicative of a certain outlook, since it focusses upon an aspect of material being. What one eats passes into one, becomes a part of one, and this he apparently meditated upon to the extent of forming his rules of diet. It is not a materialism; it is simply a recognition, quite within the frame of belief of an Anglican and a humanist, of the material basis of life. A part of man is human, and to be human means to be participated in by the physical world. But at the same time that Byrd was recording his diet and the effect of various medicines he took, he was always remembering to mention whether he had communicated with God through prayer. This is the Christian dualism.

Moreover, the people who came into his diary appear in the flesh. They are not abstractions, like those who are in a state of blessedness because they have been elected for salvation or those who are in a condition of sin. They have the normal range of problems, economic, political, and domestic, as well as problems of health and of temperament. As Byrd reported these he almost never indulged in censure or blame. On those rare occasions when he does give way to criticism, this is likely to be an expression of irritation or displeasure, rather than of moral condemnation. His most common practice was to offer an explanation or a sidelight upon the subject. A good illustration appears in the entry under the date of March 2, 1709, in which he records a visit to "Commissary" James Blair.

> I was very much surprised to find Mrs. Blair drunk, which is growing pretty common with her, and her relations disguise it under the name of consolation.[40]

40. Byrd, *Diary, 1709–1712*, p. 11.

It is significant that he was more concerned to explain than to condemn. "To understand all is to forgive all" is indeed the abysm of sentimentality, but Byrd was protected against this extreme. There is usually present, if only in the tone of his expression, a distance from the act which denotes that he is not embracing it uncritically. Where judgment occurs, it is judgment without *hubris*. Very different is Mather's habit of intruding the judgment at once and making it the substance of the expression, which is the demonic prepossession. Byrd always tries first for a substantive penetration of the event.

Accordingly there was no disposition on Byrd's part to proclaim judgment as if from a Sinai; his habit was to see and report the world, which by and large he found a tolerable place to live in. Altogether it is a very earthy record which he left, and there is hardly a trace of embarrassment over being involved with the world. Such was the condition of created man. There is nothing, however, that can fairly be called coarseness, and it would be about as far wrong as possible to infer from his records of sexual promiscuity that he believed man to be an animal. Quite in accord with his dualistic picture of the world, sex had its place, but place, one might say, was the essence, which means that it had a definite and recognized role. He did not observe that place according to the rules of moral propriety, but neither did he allow sex to eclipse the other vocations.

The sexual adventures recorded in the London diary have naturally raised the question of whether such piety as he expressed must not be regarded as dishonest. To assert simply that Byrd was a man of sincere religious feeling may not be enough to settle the matter; the anomalies of his conduct justify a little further speculation. The reader of the London diary discovers that it was a common practice for Byrd to take his mistress or a whore whom he had picked up in the street to a tavern where rooms were let for what today is called "vice." Then he would go home and say a prayer before retiring, and sometimes he would ask God to forgive him for what he had just done. But the next day, or at the most a few days later, he would repeat the performance. One may regard this as simply comic, or if he is addicted to the psychological explanation, he may think of it in terms of schizophrenia. But an adequate answer must bring two considerations together: the position of the pre-Puritan church on the matter of sin, and the customs of the society which he frequented. Before the Reformation had introduced a new notion of asceticism, carnal indulgence by the layman was not regarded with superstitious horror. It was a lapse, but it was not irreparable. Man had been told that he was frail and that he needed support for his sinful nature. It was not right, but it was not entirely outrageous that he thus testified occasionally to this sinful nature.

Then the mores of the time could not have been without influence upon a man of fashion. The style of behavior inaugurated by the Restoration was still very much in vogue. The idea of the gentleman as the scholar-debauchee, although it was beginning to receive criticism from the rising middle-class journalism popularized by Addison and Steele, remained a force through much of the eighteenth century. Byrd was in London at a time when sexual morality was least restrictive, and he was not of an especially self-denying nature. That indulgence, prayers, and repentance should come so close together may seem absurd, but it is not impossible; one might say that Byrd was putting more strain on the Lord's willingness to forgive than is prudent, yet there is no reason for saying that he was insincere. There is much to indicate that he accepted faithfully the existence of a transcendental order. Sinning and repenting appear as a kind of counterpoint in his life, which gives, to say the least, a human tension.

Otherwise too the London dairy shows him very much a man of the world. His days were filled with visits to people of various ranks, to drink tea or chocolate, to dine, to play cards. The evenings were spent at coffee houses and taverns, and, in other kinds of company, at bagnios. Here again Byrd seldom judged those about him. He mingles and he notes facts and occurrences in a manner suggesting that they had some importance in themselves. Thus the world was part of the datum of reality, and he paid it due. An element of respect is contained in this, which suggests a basically friendly attitude.

But because Byrd's diaries are so lacking in imaginative quality, one cannot arrive at a full picture of the man without looking at some of his other writings. Luckily there exist the two other productions, already mentioned, which allow us to do this without shifting radically the genre under study. *The History of the Dividing Line* and the *Journey to the Land of Eden* may both be regarded as autobiographical narratives. Inasmuch as Byrd injects his feelings into these to a far greater extent, we may use them to test further what is indicated in the diaries.

That he was an observer of nature in an affectionate way is abundantly proved. Everywhere we sense his attitude that the manifoldness of the natural world is something to be admired and prized. A feeling that the world is out there to be cognized in its particularity may be deeply significant of one's philosophy. It is a recognition of another presence and it is a restraint upon egotism. In March of 1728 Byrd, in company with the other Virginia commissioners, was to meet the commissioners from North Carolina near Currituck Inlet on the coast to determine a boundary then in dispute between the two colonies. The following description of the locality shows the kinds of things his eye took in.

We also surveyed part of the adjacent high land, which had scarcely any trees growing upon it but cedars. Among the shrubs we were showed here and there a bush of Carolina tea called Japon, which is one species of the Phylarea. This is an evergreen, the leaves whereof have some resemblance to tea, but differ very widely both in taste and flavor. We also found some plants of the spired-leaf silkgrass, which is likewise an evergreen, bearing on a lofty stem a large cluster of flowers of a pale yellow. Of the leaves of this plant the people thereabouts twist very strong cordage.

A virtuoso might divert himself here very well in picking up shells of various hue and figure, and amongst the rest that species of conch shell which the Indian peak is made of. The extremities of these shells are blue and the rest white, so that peak of both these colors are drilled out of one and the same shell, serving the natives both for ornament and money, and are esteemed by them far beyond gold and silver.[41]

Here is his description of the cabin of a typical North Carolinian.

Most of the houses in this part of the country are loghouses, covered with pine or cypress shingles three feet long and one foot broad. They are hung upon laths with pegs, and their doors, too, turn upon wooden hinges and have wooden locks to secure them, so that the building is finished without nails or other ironwork. They also set up their pales without any nails at all, and indeed more securely than those that are nailed. There are three rails mortised into the posts, the lowest of which serves as a sill with a groove in the middle big enough to receive the end of the pales: the middle part of the pale rests

41. William Byrd, *History of the Dividing Line*, in Louis B. Wright and Marion Tinling (eds.), *The London Diary (1717–1721) and Other Writings*, New York: Oxford University Press, 1958, p. 541.

against the inside of the next rail, and the top of it is brought forward to the outside of the uppermost. Such wreathing of the pales in and out makes them stand firm, and much harder to unfix than when nailed in the ordinary way.[42]

A fine example of Byrd's genial appreciation of the different, or of what nature presents in her own diversity, appears in his description of the Indian women at "Nottoway."

> Though their complexions be a little sad-colored, yet their shapes are very straight and well proportioned. Their faces are seldom handsome, yet they have an air of innocence and bashfulness, that with a little less dirt would not fail to make them desirable.
>
> Such charms might have had their full effect upon men who had been so long deprived of female conversation, but that the whole winter's soil was so crusted on the skins of those dark angels that it required a very strong appetite to approach them. The bear's oil, with which they annoint their persons all over, makes their skins soft, and at the same time protects them from every species of vermin that use to be troublesome to other uncleanly people. We were unluckily so many that they would not well make us the compliment of bedfellows, according to the Indian rules of hospitality, though a grave matron whispered one of the commissioners very civilly in the ear, that if her daughter had been but one year older, she should have been at his devotion.[43]

How this contrasts with Mather's view of the Indians as, first, people seduced by the devil, and, second, as objects for conversion, hardly needs elaboration.

That Byrd had no expectation that all men would conform to a pattern of virtue is equally evident in these writings. The sight of people living in a state of nature aroused in him no feeling of indignation. His attitude was a combination of irony and joviality, usually tinctured with some play of the imagination which fits the picture into an aesthetic frame rather than a moral one. Near the beginning of the expedition he recorded this description of a pair of castaways.

> While we continued we were told that on the south shore not far from the inlet dwelt a marooner that modestly called himself a hermit, though he forfeited that name by suffering a wanton female to cohabit with him.

42. *Ibid.*, p. 566.
43. *Ibid.*, pp. 571–72.

His habitation was a bower covered with bark after the Indian fashion, which in that mild situation protected him pretty well from the weather. Like the ravens, he neither plowed nor sowed but subsisted chiefly upon oysters which his handmaid made a shift to gather from the adjacent rocks. Sometimes, too, for a change of diet, he sent her to drive up the neighbor's cows, to moisten their mouths with a little milk. But as for raiment, he depended mostly on his length of beard, and she upon her length of hair, part of which she brought decently forward, and the rest dangled behind quite down to her rump, like one of Herodotus' East Indian pygmies. Thus did these wretches live in a dirty state of nature, and were mere Adamites, innocence only excepted.[44]

On those few occasions when Byrd was moved to actual censure, it was by way of disparaging sloth or bad management. As the owner and actual supervisor of a large estate, we may imagine him alert to detect signs of this. His interest, as might be expected, was in the practical demands for productivity and health, rather than in the morality of labor. The indolence of North Carolinians—that colony then being notorious as a favorite refuge of runaways and outcasts—was a constant source of witty criticism. Here is a passage appraising the way of life in "Lubberland."

We observed very few cornfields in our walks, and those very small, which seemed the stranger to us because we could see no other tokens of husbandry or improvement. But upon further inquiry, we were given to understand people only made corn for themselves and not for their stocks, which know very well how to get their own living. Both cattle and hogs ramble in the neighboring marshes and swamps, where they maintain themselves the whole winter long and are not fetched home till the spring. Thus these indolent wretches, during one half of the year, lose the advantage of the milk of their cattle, as well as their dung, and many of the poor creatures perish in the mire, into the bargain, by this ill management. Some who pique themselves more upon industry than their neighbors will now and then, in compliment to their cattle, cut down a tree whose limbs are loaden with the moss aforementioned. The trouble would be too great to climb the tree in order to gather this provender, but the shortest way (which in this country is always counted the best) is to fell it, just like the lazy Indians, who do the same by such trees as bear fruit, and so make one harvest for all. By this bad husbandry milk is so scarce in the winter season that were a big-bellied woman to long for it, she would

44. *Ibid.*, p. 543.

lose her longing. And in truth I believe this is often the case, and at the same time a very good reason why so many people in this province are marked with a custard complexion.[45]

Nothing in these two works reveals Byrd's attitude more significantly than his spirit of gallantry in the face of the difficulties of nature. Instead of showing irritability, disgruntlement, or a suspicion that nature is somehow a tool of the devil, he shows only a rise of spirits and a play of fancy which humanize the situation. Obviously he was not looking for something to blame for the hardships. The explorer must expect this kind of thing because that is what a wilderness is like, and one takes it on its own terms without any sense of being persecuted by it. Hardships are in a way nature pushing back, and we have now sufficiently seen that Byrd granted to nature an independent basis of being. An expedition of this kind would even be incomplete without some experience of the frustrating powers of nature. Here is his description of the surveyors crossing a swamp.

> We ordered the surveyors early to their business, who were blessed with pretty dry grounds for three miles together. But they paid dear for it in the next two, consisting of one continued frightful pocoson, which no creatures but those of the amphibious kind ever had ventured into before. This filthy quagmire did in earnest put the men's courage to a trial, and though I can't say it made them lose their patience, yet they lost their humor for joking. They kept their gravity like so many Spaniards, so that a man might then have taken his opportunity to plunge up to the chin without danger of being laughed at. However, this unusual composure of countenance could not fairly be called complaining. Their day's work ended at the mouth of Northern's Creek, which empties itself into Northwest River; though we chose to quarter a little higher up the river, near Mossy Point. This we did for the convenience of an old house to shelter our persons and baggage from the rain which threatened us hard. We judged the thing right, for there fell an heavy shower in the night that drove the most hardy of us into the house. Though indeed our case was not much mended by retreating thither, because that tenement having not long before been used as a pork store, the moisture of the air dissolved the salt that lay scattered on the floor, and made it as wet within doors as without. However, the swamps and marshes we were lately accustomed to had made such beavers and otters of us that nobody caught the least cold.[46]

45. *Ibid.*, pp. 547–48.
46. *Ibid.*, pp. 548–49.

A passage of similar mocking appears in *A Journey to the Land of Eden*.

> We fixed his [Major Mayo's] eastern corner on Cocquade Creek, and then continued our march, over the hills and far away along the country line two miles farther. Nor had we stopped there, unless a likelihood of rain had obliged us to encamp on an eminence where we were in no danger of being overflowed. Peter Jones had a smart fit of ague, which shook him severely, though he bore it like a man; but the small Major had a small fever and bore it like a child. He groaned as if he had been in labor, and thought verily it would be his fate to die like a mutinous Israelite in the wilderness, and be buried under a heap of stones. The rain was so kind as to give us leisure to secure ourselves against it, but came however time enough to interrupt our cookery, so that we supped as temperately as so many philosophers, and kept ourselves snug within our tents. The worst part of the story was that the sentinels could hardly keep our fires from being extinguished by the heaviness of the shower.
>
> Our invalids found themselves in travelling condition this morning, and began to conceive hopes of returning home and dying in their own beds. We pursued our journey through uneven and perplexed woods, and in the thickest of them had the fortune to knock down a young buffalo, two years old. Providence threw this vast animal in our way very seasonably, just as our provisions began to fail us. And it was the more welcome too because it was change of diet, which of all varieties, next to that of bedfellows, is the most agreeable.[47]

Byrd thus appears in all his doing and thinking as a man who has come to terms with the world. Almost totally absent is the spirit of deprecation, except in those cases where his instinct as a manager was affronted by the sight of indolence or bad husbandry. There is a right way to do things, but we must not expect either nature or man to be brought under complete control. Both of these are to be used and enjoyed, in a sense, but without the compulsion of messianic mission. When Byrd encounters one or the other, he accepts it as having place—and place carries with it some investiture of status. In a new country, almost a wilderness setting, Byrd is urbane, and the hallmark of urbanity is a certain kind of respect for what presents itself in its own spontaneous way and form. Whether the outcome is finally judged good or bad, the secret of it is breadth of tolerance.

47. William Byrd, *A Journey to the Land of Eden*, in Louis B. Wright and Marion Tinling (eds.), *The London Diary (1717–1721) and Other Writings*, New York: Oxford University Press, 1958, pp. 609–10.

III. Conclusions

In assaying the basic difference between Mather and Byrd, we may begin by recapitulating the circumstances which they shared. They were contemporaries, of English extraction, born in America. Both were men of considerable education, with some interest in science, and both became members of the Royal Society. Each was an outstanding, perhaps the outstanding, member of his community: Mather a theocrat and "teacher" of Puritan Boston; Byrd a large landowner and a public servant in royal and Anglican Virginia. And both were interested enough in their lives to preserve long and intimate records.

But the difference in their thinking and their way of life remained extraordinary, and from this difference have flowed the two great streams of American radicalism and conservatism.

That difference has its taproot in their respective attitudes toward creation. For Mather, creation hardly existed as a beneficent fact. The world was there, but it was an essentially negative reality; it was prone to be used by evil spirits for their purposes, and the best to be said for it was that it could be made to yield to man. By the logic of this kind of thinking, "could" was at some point translated into "should." No purpose was served by letting the world stand as it was because the world had no claim to status. Now to use the world is to change it, and here appears the Puritan ethos of functionalism. The more man does with the world, the more he is showing his sense of duty in this life. To live virtuously is to concentrate everything for man's purposes under the aspect of that drama of salvation which was so vivid to the Puritan mind. Later the conviction of a transcendental reality fades out.[48] But what had been established does not. The impulse to domi-

---

48. As long as this impulse was under the discipline of a religious realism, certain tendencies that later became overwhelming were in check. But eventually, in the nineteenth century, when this realism had been abandoned, the real destiny of the trend emerged. It was against such destiny that Emerson, Thoreau, and other members of the Concord group spoke out. There have probably never been more eloquent sermons against materialism, engrossment in business, and indifference to nature. But Emerson and Thoreau were reacting against a tide which had been set flowing far back, and which they could not successfully resist from the positions which they took. To be aware of its destructiveness was of course to their credit, but to devise a protection against it was more than an eclectic philosophy and rhetoric could do. Puritanism lost its cosmological foundation, but retained its bias and its method, and these proved very strong throughout nineteenth-century America.

neer over creation and certain habits of concentrating interest were due to
serve the future institutions of business and science. The heart of the legacy
is a belief that nature has no purpose apart from man's will, in consequence
of which he is constantly called upon to judge and to reform her. Accompanying this is a dynamism: things must be changed in order to effect purposes, and finally change becomes a principle which is used to vindicate
itself. The culmination is a business civilization and an order based increasingly upon science, in which not the actualized past but the future becomes
the probative idea. Alienation and narrowness can be sources of power, and
they gave to the Puritan both his will and his strength to conquer.

Byrd's outlook, on the other hand, derives from an acceptance of stasis
and status. He was conscious of no driving imperative to change the forms
in which things had come from their maker. Acceptance of the pattern for
what it is was the major premise of his thinking. The things that were
around him shared in a substantial reality. Nature, people, the physical endowment of man, and the cultural creations of society and art were therefore to be contemplated, and contemplation requires intactness. There was
a Providence, and it was discovered through things; else why were they
there? Man was neither the creator of everything nor the sole agent of his
destiny. Byrd did not believe that the human part of man is reprobate. Man
was an incarnation, which represented a meeting of the natural and the
supernal. The natural and the divine were thus seen together in a body, and
this vision set bounds to the idea of dominion. The ideal is not a rejection,
but a proper distance from things, which prevents both an unnatural alienation and an undignified involvement with them.

The Puritans recovered one strain of the Hebraic spirit, but they added
a special conviction about what was material, which narrowed and one may
say fairly warped their view of what was before their eyes. The religious
tradition and the social class that Byrd represented, on the other hand, had
little of the spirit of condemnation and was far more receptive to the
Graeco-Roman part of the Judaeo-Christian heritage. This did not begin
by rejecting the material order, and it balanced the metaphysical idea of
becoming with that of being. Moreover, it contained another idea very dear
to the classical mind, that of measure. The maxim for human life must be
"nothing too much," and to imagine that one can think as a god is, in the
wisdom of antiquity, madness. Byrd's adjustment to the world is a display
of this ideal; it is an acceptance qualified by distance and measure, in re-

sponse to a sense of man's dual nature. Egotism is held in restraint by an awareness of other things. Hence his poise, his urbanity, his willingness to let live. He moved in a world which appreciated these virtues and rewarded them.[49] But when they met Puritanism in a wider struggle, it developed that the Puritan temper possessed a power of aggression which classical balance and tolerance could not withstand.

49. Philip A. Bruce in his *Institutional History of Virginia in the Seventeenth Century* (New York: G. P. Putnam's, 1910, p. 260) speaks thus of early Virginia: "The whole tone of that life was generous, liberal, abounding, at the very time that it was marked by reverence for religion and respect for law."

Misunderstood Man[1]

This is the first of two volumes in which Hudson Strode attempts to inter-pret anew the character of Jefferson Davis, termed by some "the most mis-understood man in history."

Whether or not this description is merited, there are facts about Davis' career that deserve to be better known, and Mr. Strode sets them forth in an appealing combination of history and biography. Many Southern leaders have been accused of insularity, but Davis had a relatively wide background. He was a student at Transylvania and a cadet at West Point; he served for five years on the then extremely primitive Northwestern frontier; he learned plantation management under the tutelage of his highly successful brother Joseph Emory Davis; he fought in the Mexican War and he visited Cuba; he knew official Washington well both as legislator and as a Cabinet mem-ber; and he spent a summer in New England. On comparison, it appears that he had seen a good bit more of the world than his opponent Abraham Lincoln.

Davis was never an ardent secessionist. On the contrary, he was, like Lee, a "Union man," though not at any price. He was among the last to abandon hope of compromise.

Wherever he went, his bearing attracted notice, and no one could make a more graceful speech. The careful reader of his rhetoric will hardly fail to detect a Wilsonian ring. An examination might show that the idealisms of the two men were much alike.

These facts have caused historians and biographers from James Ford Rhodes down to the present to say that Jefferson Davis was the best equipped man in the South for the post that devolved upon him. This is true if one assumes that the presidency of the Southern states was a routine

1. *National Review*, 1/7, January 4, 1956, 30. © 1956 by National Review, Inc., 215 Lexington Avenue, New York, N.Y. 10016. Reprinted by permission.

job, like being United States Senator or Secretary of War, which it definitely was not. He might have been a good helmsman for calm seas. But
Davis had thrust upon him the leadership of a counter-revolution. He was
neither bold enough nor creative enough to devise policies where strong
revolutionary currents were running. His mind handled large, abstract ideas
impressively well, but it lacked natural shrewdness. He did not have the
necessary realistic—one is tempted to say sardonic—grasp of human motives. His gentility seemed to encase him. Finally, there is strong evidence
throughout his record of a tendency to psychosomatic illness.

In this volume Mr. Strode has written an engaging narrative of his years
up to the presidency of the Southern Republic, but he seems not to have
penetrated to the weaknesses of one of history's tragic figures.

Person and Journalist[1]

"Marse" Henry Watterson, editor of the Louisville *Courier-Journal*, was the last great figure of "personal" journalism. Professor Wall has produced a distinguished account of his long and eventful career.

Henry Watterson was born on Pennsylvania Avenue in Washington while his father was Congressman from Tennessee. "At an age when most children are playing marbles, Henry was dining at the White House with Polk and Taylor." He knew personally every occupant of the White House from John Quincy Adams to Franklin D. Roosevelt, with the exception of William Henry Harrison. He took an active part in eleven Presidential campaigns, and his role quite possibly determined the outcome of the bitter Hayes–Tilden election dispute of 1876.

Kentuckians have always believed in personality; Watterson was an unregenerate if outwardly "reconstructed" one, and they loved him for it. From his editorial perch in the *Courier-Journal*, which he took over in 1868, he spewed fire and brimstone for fifty years. There was one exception: when Watterson deserted Bryan in 1896 for the "Gold Democrats," unprecedented wrath descended. Subscriptions were canceled by the thousands until the *Courier-Journal*, faced with bankruptcy, had to beg for mercy. It must be one of the few occasions when a major American newspaper has been brought to its knees by popular indignation.

There were other tergiversations in this career. A young man of twenty-one, Watterson stood at Lincoln's elbow as the latter delivered his First Inaugural Address, listening with seeming approval. But six months later he was serving on the staff of Bedford Forrest in Tennessee. Soon afterwar he became editor of *The Rebel*, the most widely read newspaper in the Co federate Army. But the war was scarcely ended when he was in Cincinn

1. *National Review*, 2/29, December 8, 1956, 19. © 1956 by National Review, Inc., ington Avenue, New York, N.Y. 10016. Reprinted by permission.

attached to a Republican paper, denouncing Southern leaders and toasting "the genius of Republicanism." A generation later, forgetful of how much his own section had suffered from the expansionist and imperialist forces behind the Civil War, he was one of the chief whooper-uppers for war with Spain and Manifest Destiny. In 1914 he was moralizing to Europe that "in strife there is neither glory nor gain." Two years later he was shouting editorially "To Hell with the Hohenzollerns and Hapsburgs" and demanding American intervention. But by 1919 he had become bitterly anti-Wilson and anti–League of Nations.

It is not easy to say what produced so many changes of side and of opinion. Watterson is here presented as a "New South" man, and it is an observation of mine of long standing that all "New South" men are pragmatists just beneath the skin. Yet it seems impossible to convict Watterson of pragmatism. He fought movements which had powerful forces behind them, like woman suffrage and prohibition. As the author points out, no government in power ever satisfied him, and if a President served one day longer than four years, Watterson was sure that he was conspiring for a third term. The Administrations of Franklin Roosevelt, had he witnessed them, would have unhinged his reason.

Perhaps the core of his personality lay in a great deal of personal courage and a belief that to tell the truth as you see it is to shame the devil.

Cotton Culture[1]

The history of King Cotton is indeed the story of a "romantic trouble-maker." It all began in 1793 on Mulberry Plantation near Savannah, when a young Connecticut Yankee, under the urging of local planters, invented a machine to comb the seeds out of "vegetable wool." Little did Eli Whitney realize that he had "stopped the slow dying of Negro slavery and stimulated it anew on a vast scale, started a westward cotton movement that is still in progress, founded a cotton plantation system that profoundly affected the culture and politics of a great region, fostered the controversy that ended in civil war, and fastened upon the United States a massive race problem."

Across the water, people in Birmingham and Manchester had already gone "steam mill mad," and soon the English factory system was ready to spin all the cotton the South could supply. Production increased enormously; between 1801 and 1859 it doubled every ten years, until it reached an annual figure of 4,500,000 bales. So dazzled were some by this circumstance that when a group of Southern leaders issued a manifesto in 1860, they got political theory all mixed up with cotton and called their defense *Cotton is King, or Proslavery Arguments.*

In the years since the Civil War, King Cotton has been often down but somehow never out. In 1931 a tremendous 17,000,000 bales was produced and the price slid to five cents a pound, "the price of a bottle of Cola." Yet despite the exhaustion of soil, the boll weevil, surpluses, and the competition of synthetic fibers, it marches on. And owing to the first of these causes, it marches westward. It will surprise some to know that California is now the fourth ranking producer in the nation, and that Arizona produces more than South Carolina. Wherever cotton culture has existed for

1. *National Review*, 3/11, March 16, 1957, 264–65. © 1957 by National Review, Inc., 215 Lexington Avenue, New York, N.Y. 10016. Reprinted by permission.

long, it has produced a tangle of stubborn problems, which are the real subject of Mr. Cohn's book.

Mr. Cohn has written largely as a social critic, and as far as his judgments go, they are informed and sometimes acute. But as Thoreau said of the State, the way it appears depends on the point from which you look at it. If you accept the premise of industrialism and the money economy, then you say that the evils of cotton culture and cotton manufacture had to be. The motives which sent New England shipowners to the Slave Coast, which led the Southerners to buy what they brought back for the cotton fields, and which led the English factory owners to work eight-year-old children sixteen hours a day are not greatly distinguishable. The Southerners depleted their lands and lodged an alien race in their midst; the English stunted several generations of workers and inspired a "grave, bearded" gentleman, as Mr. Cohn duly notes, to write *Das Kapital*.

This is the melancholy and inerasable history of the subject. But to my primitive notion, it is just one more chapter in the story of the machine's inhumanity to man and of the lust for abstract power through money. The real answer is neither socialism nor mammoth farm supports, but the distributive economics and agrarianism of a farmer named Jefferson.

VU Prof. Explores Basic Human Issues[1]

That Donald Davidson is a key figure in the brilliant Southern Renascence is known to all who have been inspired by his teaching and writing. In *Still Rebels, Still Yankees* he brings together a group of essays which have appeared over the past quarter of a century. To give an idea of the range and richness of this collection is not easy. The author deals with aspects of modern poetry, the role of tradition in prose fiction, the qualities of oral literature, the heritage of Southern culture, and the more general questions of regionalism and nationalism. But it is even less easy to give an idea of the passionate eloquence which informs these essays. Professor Davidson has the courage of his thought, and the courage of one's thought is conviction. It is this conviction, this belief in necessary truth, which gives his writing a quality unmatched by any other literary and social critic of our time.

No American writer has opposed more resolutely the sham values, the sickening standardization, and the general soullessness which a nationalized industrialized state has brought to this country in the names of Union and Progress. No one has worked more singlemindedly, in his critical as well as his creative writing, to keep the image of man humane. He has championed the essential place of religion in man's life, the sustaining value of tradition, the right of persons to be individuals, and the right of regional groups to cultivate the kind of art, including the art of life, which is suited to their regions and their temperaments.

Professor Davidson knows that the real clash in America today is not so much a clash between a geographical South and North as between regions which have preserved a culture, and the self-conscious, envious, and belligerent lack of culture which one finds especially in the large urban centers. In the memorable title essay, "Still Rebels, Still Yankees," he shows us a

1. *The Nashville Tennessean*, April 14, 1957, 7G.

Vermonter and a Georgian, each happy and flourishing in his own way, each tilling and loving his own land, and soundly proof against the radicalisms that emanate from New York and Hollywood. It is a heartening picture of opponents of the Leviathan state, North and South, who cannot see "social security plus television" as the end of the dream of the Founding Fathers and the pioneers.

There is no need to despair as long as there is one courageous voice among ten thousand. Professor Davidson is such a voice, and he ought to be heard by all who believe in value, in the dignity of true sentiments, and in the idea of loyalty to one's own tradition.

VU Prof. Describes Fugitive-Agrarians[1]

Southern Writers in the Modern World comprises the Lamar lectures, delivered by Donald Davidson last year at Mercer University. The reader whose eye is delighted, as it well may be, by the attractive format of this little volume can be assured that he will find within an even greater beauty and interest. Here, told in distinguished prose, is the story of one of those rare events which have a way of occurring at their own place and in their own time, the flowering of an indigenous literary culture.

I will hazard that the first lecture, "The Thankless Muse and her Fugitive Poets," is the best account that ever has been or ever will be written of the gathering of the Fugitives. Professor Davidson takes us back to the spacious days before the First World War when a group of young men at Vanderbilt discovered a common interest in the idea and practice of poetry.

We get revealing glimpses of those things which make the substance of a literary movement: John Crowe Ransom taking Davidson aside and timidly exhibiting his first poem—which was on the improbable subject "Sunset"; later, meetings at the home of James M. Frank on Whitland Avenue, where the air rang with high discussion and relentless criticism; and finally, plans to publish a magazine of verse, which was for esoteric reasons named "The Fugitive." It would take a long list to include the literary awards and fellowships, the distinguished professorships, and the editorships of literary journals which lay in the future for the group that assembled there to follow the unprofitable calling of poetry.

This phase of the history of the Fugitives was ended, according to Professor Davidson, by the Scopes "evolution" trial. The Scopes trial, though reduced by publicity and showmanship to the level of a vulgar carnival, presented an issue of the greatest moment: must the findings of positive science be accepted as the final word on all that is to be believed about the

1. *The Nashville Tennessean*, July 6, 1958, 8C.

education, culture, and destiny of man? No person committed to the realm of value, as poets must be, can properly remain indifferent to that question.

But as it happened, a little band in Tennessee, made up of a few of the Fugitives and some others, was almost the only force that challenged intellectually the presumptions of scientific positivism. From their opposition stemmed two of the seminal books of our time: *I'll Take My Stand,* by Twelve Southerners, and *God Without Thunder,* by John Crowe Ransom. These were directed, each in its own way, to related questions: (1) Is it possible for man to live a humane life in the presence of the industrial order? and (2) is it possible for him to live a humane life solely on the principles of science, which is the parent of that order? Both were powerful dissents from complacency with scientific materialism.

In the last of the lectures Professor Davidson addresses himself to the relation between the writer and the modern university. Can the university help the writer in any way except by giving him asylum in a world that seems increasingly to be run by barbarians? The question is difficult to answer precisely. Vanderbilt was very good for the writers who attended it in this period, but hardly through express provision by trustees or administration.

Perhaps the case of Vanderbilt and the Fugitives is too remarkable to permit much generalization. My own feeling is that Vanderbilt helped most by setting a standard high enough to attract those who wished to be challenged and then by leaving them to follow their own bent and their own passion. The result was a brilliant day in the life of the imagination.

Reconstruction: Unhealed Wound[1]

Reconstruction was a far greater failure than the Civil War itself. In suggesting that the Civil War was a failure I mean that, if one concedes that it had to come out as it did, there was no sense in its lasting so long. Considering the great disparity of resources between North and South, one may well ask why it was not ended like, say, Prussia's war against France—two or three well-executed decisive battles, and the military phase was essentially over. Instead, it turned into a struggle of some twenty major battles and a final war of attrition in the Eastern theater. The Lincoln Administration, though determined on its course, was ignorant of war.

But if the government during this period made, in this sense, a failure, the congressional leadership which assumed power in the ensuing period (and which fought and vilified Andrew Johnson at every step) made a fiasco. Lincoln had discussed the issue of union and secession in terms that were almost metaphysical. If the Union was indivisible, it followed that the states were never out of the Union, even during the war; there was then, in essence, no problem of "readmitting" them, even though certain practical circumstances had to be taken into account. However abstruse such reasoning may seem, it did provide a basis, in terms that were comprehensible, for continuing the Union.

The force of this logic was lost upon the leaders of Congress who took over after Lincoln's assassination. They saw in their section's victory an unparalleled opportunity for vengeance, economic exploitation, political domination, and the other attendant benefits of conquest. There was much malice, but what strikes one as appalling about this policy is its shortsightedness. One cannot imagine Churchill, even at the time when bombs were raining destruction upon Britain, losing sight of the fact that Britain might one day need the German people. But the plotters of Reconstruction seem

1. *National Review*, 6/20, February 28, 1959, 559–60. © 1959 by National Review, Inc., 215 Lexington Avenue, New York, N.Y. 10016. Reprinted by permission.

not to have realized that if the Southern people were to be forcibly kept in the Union, the rest of the Americans would have to live with them on some terms and might even one day need them. That shortsightedness left the bitter legacies that continue to poison our cup down to today.

In *The Angry Scar* (Doubleday, $5.95) Hodding Carter, well-known Southern Liberal, surveys the epoch in which these issues were fought out. The work is not presented as original history. It rests upon scholarly research, now quite extensive, which has been done in the field by others. It is, in his own words, an "interpretive synthesis," which tries to place Reconstruction in the mainstream of American history.

With much of Mr. Carter's retelling of the story I have little fault to find. He relates the Carpetbagger invasion, the story of the kangaroo governments which were set up in the Southern states, the fury of the Radicals in Congress, and the bleeding of a section already left bankrupt by the war. The oppressions, knaveries, thefts and debaucheries of Reconstruction were so numerous and so awful that even the unimpassioned historian must present a vivid set of facts.

But I question whether he is fair to those who recaptured home rule for the South. In his account of the internal politics of the Southern states during this period the terms "Redemptionists," "Conservatives," and "Bourbons" continually recur, with the last named getting the highest degree of his disapproval. One derives an impression from much of this account that there was a fair maiden called Progress, who was always about to be, but never quite was, rescued from some dragons bearing these names.

A special consideration that Mr. Carter seems to scant is this: people do not behave, nor are they expected to behave, under a state of duress as they do in a free and unforced condition. In times of war, even deception is recognized as a legitimate weapon, and Reconstruction was hardly different from a prolongation of the war. The Ku Klux Klan was a "lawless" organization, but it was the Confederate Underground; the "deal" which made Rutherford B. Hayes President was indeed a deal, but it was made to end a regime of force; the Southern "Bourbons" did indeed make arrangements with the victorious economic forces of the North, but as one of the Southern Agrarian writers has admitted, this was a left-handed way of winning a minor victory in a situation of otherwise unrelieved defeat. These may all have been regrettable episodes, but they were factors in the story.

This brings me to my chief point of criticism. A real sense of the tragedy of these events is just what I miss in Mr. Carter's book. In spite of considerable documentation evidently intended to convey it, nowhere does he give me a feeling of the stark entanglement of good and evil that characterized this sad chapter of our history. I derive more feeling of the essential tragedy of Reconstruction from one page of Lloyd Paul Stryker's great biography of Andrew Johnson than I do from the whole of *The Angry Scar*. Mr. Stryker was born in Illinois and was a Republican; Mr. Carter was born in Louisiana and is a Liberal—which prompts immediately the question of what a Liberal has to offer when he takes in hand a subject like this. And the answer begins to look like a minus quantity.

The problem has to do with point of view. It has been suggested from more than one quarter that a Liberal is unfitted by his presuppositions to understand the tragic aspects of existence and indeed really to deal with the problem of evil. *The Angry Scar* appears to me something of a confirmation of that hypothesis. Liberalism is a kind of abstractive process which takes out whatever is unmalleable and fashions the remainder into a dream world of wishful thinking. Politically this has long been evident, and now that the Liberals have captured so many of the channels of communication and publication, it is being proved in other ways.

To cite one particular example: on page 154 the author says: "Other Southerners, aware that their region had loitered well behind the rest of the nation before the war in economic and democratic aspirations and attainments, might have welcomed, save for the mass enfranchisement provisions, the progressive provisions of the new constitution."

Who were these other Southerners? According to my reading in the field, they hardly existed. Their existence would, moreover, have been incompatible with the image which the South had of itself and of the proper way of life. That was one of the potent facts in this battle of forces. But a Liberal has somehow to extrapolate them out of little or nothing. That is why I say that Mr. Carter's book, though a well-written narrative in the sense of being neatly formulated and agreeably phrased, has a systematic bias or a suppressed premise that tends to obscure the depths of the conflict.

The book does serve to remind us of a chapter of our past which should never be forgotten. But it does not remind us sharply enough—though it does faintly suggest this on the last page or so—that tragedy can always be re-enacted.

An Altered Stand[1]

The Legacy of the Civil War is a curious book to come from an author who began his career with *John Brown: the Making of a Martyr* and followed this with one of the most eloquent essays in the symposium *I'll Take My Stand*. A first impression could be that he had deserted what he knows (because no man, with the possible exception of Faulkner, has the South more in his bones than Robert Penn Warren) for the superficialities of modern Liberalism. This reviewer was amazed to find passages sounding almost like Mrs. Roosevelt: "Everyone agrees that the chronic poverty and social retardation of the South have, in fact, been a national liability. . . ." Again, there is sarcastic reference to the "constitutional theorizing" of a Southern governor. These things we expect from the more imperceptive leftwing journals; we do not expect them from a writer who was able to create the complexity that is Willie Stark and present the tangle of motivation that appears in *Brother to Dragons*.

Not all of the book is thus suggestive of the current crusade against the South. The author explores the theme of common guilt as expressed in the facts occurring both before and after the great military collision. But when he sums up the South's sin as reliance upon the "Great Alibi" and the North's as belief in its "Treasury of Virtue," we are back in the language of journalistic formulation. Moreover, the fact is hardly unique; no defeated people can go on living without an explanation of that defeat; and without a theory that virtue was on its side, no victorious people can well avail itself of the fruits of the victory. The real nature of the legacy of the Civil War is therefore still to seek; but a fault of the book is that it may tend to freeze discussion at this level.

Like most students who have speculated seriously about the subject and

1. *National Review*, 10/23, June 17, 1961, 389–90. © 1961 by National Review, Inc., 215 Lexington Avenue, New York, N.Y. 10016. Reprinted by permission.

who realize something of the thickness of it, Mr. Warren wonders why the South could have remained so attached to the memory of ante bellum society through a century of pressure to change. The true answer is that, although this culture was disfigured by an historical circumstance, it was based upon a paradigmatic ideal. And once a people have glimpsed that possibility, they are not easily beaten or bribed into giving it up. That is what the "nostalgia" is for. The cultural difference was deeper than the book allows, and belief in cultural pluralism is what keeps the contest going on, despite judicial ukases and decrees of a central government.

It is now conventional to refer to the Civil War as a tragedy, but we must keep in mind that in a tragedy something is lost. What was lost was a transcendent idea of community, and a kind of integrity of the personality. It was the latter which could lead Charles Francis Adams to say that if he had been in Lee's place, he would have done exactly as Lee did. Likewise it could cause Lee to say, with wry reference to his own nationalist sentiments (on an occasion when his forward brigades were being driven back), "I suppose it's up to us Union men to win this battle." Both felt somehow that their roles were laid upon them. Since then a more calculating type has come to predominate; and the book comes up with an odd verdict in favor of the pragmatic resolution, which is not very consistent with the apostrophe to tragedy in the closing pages.

Mr. Warren is right, and is in his usual felicitous vein, when he observes that the Civil War was the "mystic cloud from which emerged our modernity." But he shows a complacency toward some of the products of that modernity, material and human, which as a younger writer he would have spurned.

Bibliography:
Published Works of Richard M. Weaver

COMPILED BY TED J. SMITH III

1929

"Kentucky," in "A Panorama of Peace: A Symposium." *The Intercollegian*, December 47/3, 1929, 72.

1931

Clifford Amyx and Richard Weaver. "Looking over the Magazines." *The Kentucky Kernel*, July 24, 1931, 3; July 31, 1931, 2; August 7, 1931, 3; August 14, 1931, 4; August 21, 1931, 2.

1935

"Southern Agrarianism" or "Our Southern Agrarians." *The Commonwealth* (Lexington, KY), 1/3, July 1935.

1936

"Review of *The Larger Rhetorical Patterns in Anglo-Saxon Poetry*." *The Vanderbilt Alumnus*, April 1936, 9.

1943

"The Older Religiousness in the South." *The Sewanee Review*, 51/2, April–June 1943, 237–49.

1944

"Albert Taylor Bledsoe." *The Sewanee Review*, 52/1, Winter 1944, 34–45.
"The South and the Revolution of Nihilism." *The South Atlantic Quarterly*, 43/2, April 1944, 194–98.

1945

"Southern Chivalry and Total War." *The Sewanee Review*, 53/2, Spring 1945, 267–78.

"Scholars or Gentlemen?" *College English*, 7/2, November 1945–46, 72–77.

1947

"Review of Leo Baeck, *The Pharisees and Other Essays.*" *The Commonweal*, 46/20, August 29, 1947, 484.

"Review of Robert Rylee, *The Ring and the Cross.*" *The Commonweal*, 47/2, October 24, 1947, 46 & 48.

"Review of Ward Moore, *Greener Than You Think.*" *The Commonweal*, 47/7, November 28, 1947, 179–80.

1948

Ideas Have Consequences. Chicago: University of Chicago Press, 1948.

"Lee the Philosopher." *The Georgia Review*, 2/3, Fall 1948, 297–303.

"To Write the Truth." *College English*, 10/1, October 1948, 25–30.

"Orbis Americarum." *The Sewanee Review*, 56/2, Spring 1948, 319–23. (Review of Henry B. Parkes, *The American Experience*, and Leo Gurko, *The Angry Decade*.)

"Etiology of the Image." *Poetry*, 72/3, June 1948, 156–61. (Review of Rosemond Tuve, *Elizabethan and Metaphysical Imagery*.)

"Review of Hermann Broch, *The Sleepwalkers.*" *The Commonweal*, 47/25–26, April 9, 1948, 620–22.

"Review of Beatrice Webb, *Our Partnership.*" *The Commonweal*, 48/7, May 28, 1948, 166–67.

"Review of Charles A. Lindbergh, *Of Flight and Life.*" *The Commonweal*, 48/24, September 24, 1948, 573.

"Review of *The Diary of Pierre Laval.*" *The Commonweal*, 49/5, November 12, 1948, 122.

"Editor's Mail." *The New York Times Book Review*, March 21, 1948, 29. (Reply to Howard Mumford Jones's review of *Ideas Have Consequences*.)

1949

"Culture and Reconstruction." *The Sewanee Review*, 57/4, Autumn 1949, 714–18. (Review of T. S. Eliot, *Notes Toward the Definition of Culture*.)

"Review of Samuel H. Beer, *The City of Reason.*" *The Commonweal*, 50/3, April 29, 1949, 73.

"Review of Bertrand de Jouvenel, *On Power: Its Nature and the History of Its Growth.*" *The Commonweal*, 50/19, August 19, 1949, 466–68.

1950

"The Rhetoric of Social Science." *Journal of General Education,* 4/3, April 1950, 189–201. (Reprinted in revised form as a chapter in *The Ethics of Rhetoric.*)

"Agrarianism in Exile." *The Sewanee Review,* 58/4, Autumn 1950, 586–606.

"Review of Henry Steele Commager, *The American Mind.*" *The Commonweal,* 52/4, May 5, 1950, 101–3.

"Review of Herbert Feis, *The Road to Pearl Harbor.*" *The Commonweal,* 53/1, October 13, 1950, 20–22.

"Review of George Orwell, *Shooting an Elephant and Other Essays.*" *The Commonweal,* 53/11, December 22, 1950, 283–84.

1951

George J. Metcalf, W. H. L. Meyer, Jr., John P. Netherton, James Sledd, and Richard M. Weaver. *Elements of English Grammar.* Chicago: University of Chicago Press, September 1951, pamphlet.

"Review of Ferdinand A. Hermens, *Europe Between Democracy and Anarchy.*" *The Commonweal,* 54/11, June 22, 1951, 266.

"Nehru: Philosopher, Prophet, Politician." *The Commonweal,* 54/18, August 10, 1951, 432–33. (Review of Jawaharlal Nehru and Norman Cousins, *Talks with Nehru.*)

"Review of Edward Crankshaw, *Cracks in the Kremlin Wall.*" *The Commonweal,* 54/24, September 21, 1951, 582.

1952

"Aspects of the Southern Philosophy." *The Hopkins Review,* 5/4, Summer 1952, 5–21.

"The Tennessee Agrarians." *Shenandoah,* 3/2, Summer 1952, 3–10.

1953

The Ethics of Rhetoric. Chicago: Henry Regnery Company, 1953.

Manuel Bilsky, McCrea Hazlett, Robert E. Streeter, and Richard M. Weaver. "Looking for an Argument." *College English,* 14/4, 1952–53 (January 1953), 210–16.

"Impact of Society on Mr. Russell." *The Commonweal,* 57/20, February 20, 1953, 504. (Review of Bertrand Russell, *The Impact of Science on Society.*)

"And for Yale." *The Commonweal,* 58/1, April 10, 1953, 31–32. (Review of Editors of the *Yale Daily News, Seventy-Five: A Study of a Generation in Transition.*)

1954

"Education: Reflections On." In William T. Couch (ed.), *Collier's 1954 Year Book.*
New York: Collier & Son, 1954, 182–84.

"The Pattern of a Life." *Asheville Citizen-Times,* August 22, 1954, B4.

"Liberalism with a Ballast." *The Sewanee Review,* 62/2, Spring 1954, 334–41. (Review of Lord Acton, *Essays on Church and State,* G. E. Fasnacht, *Acton's Political
Philosophy,* and Gertrude Himmelfarb, *Lord Acton.*)

"Battle for the Mind." *Chicago Sunday Tribune Magazine of Books,* October 24, 1954,
section IV, page 3. (Review of Russell Kirk, *A Program for Conservatives.*)

1955

"Introduction." In William James, *Pragmatism (selections)* [*sic*]. Chicago: Gateway
Editions, 1955, v–xi.

"Colleges and Universities." In William T. Couch (ed.), *Collier's 1955 Year Book.*
New York: Collier & Son, 1955, 145–47.

"Propaganda." In William T. Couch (ed.), *Collier's 1955 Year Book.* New York:
Collier & Son, 1955, 517–21.

Stuart Gerry Brown, Aaron Director, and Richard M. Weaver. "Who Are Today's
Conservatives?" *The University of Chicago Round Table,* #881, February 27, 1955,
1–11. (University of Chicago Round Table of the Air, Broadcast #1092, in coop-
eration with the National Broadcasting Company.)

"History in a Dry Light." *The Sewanee Review,* 63/2, Spring 1955, 280–86. (Review
of Clement Eaton, *A History of the Southern Confederacy,* and Thomas J. Pressly,
Americans Interpret Their Civil War.)

"Easy Conclusion." *National Review,* 1/2, November 26, 1955, 29. (Review of
Theodore L. Lentz, *Towards a Science of Peace.*)

"A Program for Conservatives." *Faith and Thought,* January 1955, 4–5. (Review of
Russell Kirk, *A Program for Conservatives.*)

1956

"Introduction." In James L. Weil, *Logarhythms.* New York: Poetry Library, 1956,
9–13.

"The Best of Everything." *National Review,* 1/11, February 1, 1956, 21–22.

"The Middle of the Road: Where It Leads." *Human Events,* 13/12, March 24, 1956,
5–8.

"The Land and the Literature." *The Sewanee Review,* 64/3, Summer 1956, 485–98.
(Review of Clifford Dowdey, *The Land They Fought For,* and Willard Thorp
[ed.], *A Southern Reader.*)

"Review of Arthur A. Ekirch, Jr., *The Decline of American Liberalism.*" *Mississippi Valley Historical Review*, 43/3, December 1956, 469–70.

"Misunderstood Man." *National Review*, 1/7, January 4, 1956, 30. (Review of Hudson Strode, *Jefferson Davis: American President, 1808–1861.*)

"From Poetry to Bitter Fruit." *National Review*, 1/10, January 25, 1956, 26–27. (Review of Joan Dunn, *Retreat from Learning.*)

"Mr. Hutchins as Prophet." *National Review*, 1/12, February 8, 1956, 26–27. (Review of Robert M. Hutchins [ed.], *Great Books: The Foundation of a Liberal Education.*)

"Language and the Crisis of Our Time." *National Review*, 1/13, February 15, 1956, 27. (Review of I. A. Richards, *Speculative Instruments.*)

"Cold Comfort." *National Review*, 1/16, March 7, 1956, 29. (Review of R. M. MacIver, *The Pursuit of Happiness.*)

"Flesh for a Skeleton." *National Review*, 1/19, March 28, 1956, 26–27. (Review of Tobias Dantzig, *Number: The Language of Science.*)

"Anybody's Guess." *National Review*, 1/22, April 18, 1956, 20. (Review of Paul M. Angle and Earl S. Miers [eds.], *The Living Lincoln.*)

"On Social Science." *National Review*, 1/25, May 9, 1956, 20. (Review of Stuart Chase, *The Proper Study of Mankind.*)

"Safe for a While." *National Review*, 2/5, June 20, 1956, 21. (Review of Lester Asheim [ed.], *The Future of the Book.*)

"Informed and Urbane." *National Review*, 2/6, June 27, 1956, 19. (Review of John P. Dyer, *Ivory Towers in the Market Place.*)

"Which Ancestors?" *National Review*, 2/10, July 25, 1956, 20–21. (Review of Russell Kirk, *Beyond the Dreams of Avarice.*)

"Inglorious Exit." *National Review*, 2/13, August 18, 1956, 20–21. (Review of Charles P. Smith, *James Wilson: Founding Father.*)

"Social Science in Excelsis." *National Review*, 2/19, September 29, 1956, 18–19. (Review of Leonard White [ed.], *The State of the Social Sciences.*)

"Education for What?" *National Review*, 2/27, November 24, 1956, 20–21. (Review of John D. Redden and Francis A. Ryan, *A Catholic Philosophy of Education.*)

"Person and Journalist." *National Review*, 2/29, December 8, 1956, 19. (Review of Joseph F. Wall, *Henry Watterson: Reconstructed Rebel.*)

"Review of Samuel F. Bemis, *John Quincy Adams and the Union.*" *Freeman*, 6, June 1956, 62–64.

"Review of Daniel Bell (ed.), *The New American Right.*" Submitted to the *Chicago Tribune* in February 1956 but no evidence of its publication.

1957

Composition: A Course in Writing and Rhetoric. New York: Henry Holt and Company, 1957.

"The South and the American Union." In Louis D. Rubin, Jr., and James J. Kilpatrick (eds.), *The Lasting South: Fourteen Southerners Look at Their Home.* Chicago: Regnery, 1957, 46–68.

"Life Without Prejudice." *Modern Age,* 1/1, Summer 1957, 4–9.

"The Middle Way: A Political Meditation." *National Review,* 3/3, January 19, 1957, 63–64.

"Roots of the Liberal Complacency." *National Review,* 3/23, June 8, 1957, 541–43.

"On Setting the Clock Right." *National Review,* 4/14, October 12, 1957, 321–23.

"Integration Is Communization." *National Review,* 4/3, July 13, 1957, 67–68. (Review of Hugh D. Price, *The Negro and Southern Politics,* Carl T. Rowan, *Go South to Sorrow,* and Leo Kuper, *Passive Resistance in South Africa.*)

"Cotton Culture." *National Review,* 3/11, March 16, 1957, 264–65. (Review of David L. Cohn, *The Life and Times of King Cotton.*)

"The Western Star." *National Review,* 3/15, April 13, 1957, 358–59. (Review of Clement Eaton, *Henry Clay and the Art of American Politics.*)

"Proud 'City of God.'" *National Review,* 3/24, June 15, 1957, 578. (Review of Rene Guerdan, *Byzantium: Its Triumphs and Tragedy.*)

"Trumpet-Tongued Foe of Coercion." *National Review,* 4/13, October 5, 1957, 307–8. (Review of R. D. Meade, *Patrick Henry: Patriot in the Making.*)

"Science and Sentimentalism." *National Review,* 4/22, December 7, 1957, 524–25. (Review of Andre Missenard, *In Search of Man.*)

"Review of Amaury de Riencourt, *The Coming Caesars.*" *Freeman,* 7, October 1957, 61–63.

"VU Prof. Explores Basic Human Issues." *The Nashville Tennessean,* April 14, 1957, 7G. (Review of Donald Davidson, *Still Rebels, Still Yankees.*)

1958

"Individuality and Modernity." In Felix Morley (ed.), *Essays on Individuality.* Philadelphia: University of Pennsylvania Press, 1958, 63–81.

"Up from Liberalism." *Modern Age,* 3/1, Winter 1958–59, 21–32.

"First in Peace." *National Review,* 5/14, April 5, 1958, 329–30. (Review of John A. Carroll and Mary W. Ashworth, *George Washington: First in Peace.*)

"The Lincoln-Douglas Debates." *National Review,* 6/1, June 21, 1958, 18–19. (Review of Paul M. Angle [ed.], *Created Equal? The Complete Lincoln–Douglas Debates of 1858.*)

"Open All the Way." *National Review,* 6/13, November 22, 1958, 339–40. (Review of Daniel J. Boorstin, *The Americans: The Colonial Experience.*)

"VU Prof. Describes Fugitive Agrarians." *The Nashville Tennessean,* July 6, 1958, 8-C. (Review of Donald Davidson, *Southern Writers in the Modern World.*)

1959

Education and the Individual. Philadelphia: Intercollegiate Society of Individualists, July 1959, pamphlet. Abridged versions reprinted as "The Purpose of Education," *The Wall Street Journal,* October 9, 1959, and as "Schools Increase, Minds Decay," *Milwaukee Journal,* October 29, 1959.

"Foreword." *Ideas Have Consequences.* Chicago: Phoenix, 1959, v–vi.

"Concealed Rhetoric in Scientistic Sociology." *The Georgia Review,* 13/1, Spring 1959, 19–32. Reprinted in a revised version (footnotes added) in Helmut Schoeck and James W. Wiggins (eds.), *Scientism and Values.* Princeton: Van Nostrand, 1960, 83–99.

"Contemporary Southern Literature." *Texas Quarterly,* 2/2, Summer 1959, 126–44.

"The Regime of the South." *National Review,* 6/21, March 14, 1959, 587–89.

"Christian Letters." *Modern Age,* 3/4, Fall 1959, 417–20. (Review of Randall Stewart, *American Literature and Christian Doctrine.*)

"Reconstruction: Unhealed Wound." *National Review,* 6/20, February 28, 1959, 559–60. (Review of Hodding Carter, *The Angry Scar.*)

"Review of Forrest McDonald, *We the People.*" *Freeman,* 9, May 1959, 58–62.

1960

"Lord Acton: The Historian as Thinker." *Modern Age,* 5/1, Winter 1960–61, 13–21.

"Conservatism and Libertarianism: The Common Ground." *The Individualist,* 4/4 (old series), May 1960, 5–8.

"Mass Plutocracy." *National Review,* 9/18, November 5, 1960, 273–75, 290.

"Illusions of Illusion." *Modern Age,* 4/3, Summer 1960, 316–20. (Review of M. Morton Auerbach, *The Conservative Illusion.*)

"Dilemma of the Intellectual." *National Review,* 9/10, September 10, 1960, 153–54. (Review of G. B. de Huszar [ed.], *The Intellectual: A Controversial Portrait.*)

1961

Relativism and the Crisis of Our Time. Philadelphia: Intercollegiate Society of Individualists, n.d. (1961), pamphlet.

Reflections of Modernity. Provo: Brigham Young University, 1961, *Speeches of the Year* pamphlet.

"Relativism and the Use of Language." In Helmut Schoeck and James W. Wiggins (eds.), *Relativism and the Study of Man.* Princeton: Van Nostrand, 1961, 236–54.

"The Importance of Cultural Freedom." *Modern Age,* 6/1, Winter 1961–62, 21–33.

"A Moral in a Word." *Modern Age,* 5/3, Summer 1961, 330–31. (Review of C. S. Lewis, *Studies in Words.*)

"Modern Letters Con and Pro." *Modern Age,* 5/4, Fall 1961, 426–27. (Review of Edward Dahlberg and Sir Herbert Read, *Truth Is More Sacred.*)

"History or Special Pleading?" *National Review,* 10/1, January 14, 1961, 21–22. (Review of Harvey Wish, *The American Historian.*)

"An Altered Stand." *National Review,* 10/23, June 17, 1961, 389–90. (Review of Robert Penn Warren, *The Legacy of the Civil War.*)

"More on Machiavelli." *National Review,* 10/19, May 20, 1961, 328. (Letter to the editor.)

1962

"Address of Dr. Richard M. Weaver, Chicago University." In Pearl M. Weaver, *The Tribe of Jacob.* Asheville: Miller Printing Company, 1962, 113–16.

"A Great Individualist." *Modern Age,* 6/2, Spring 1962, 214–17. (Review of Guy J. Forgue [ed.], *Letters of H. L. Mencken.*)

"A Hobble for Pegasus." National Review, 12/2, January 16, 1962, 30–31. (Review of Robert E. Lane, *The Liberties of Wit.*)

"Anatomy of Freedom." *National Review,* 13/22, December 4, 1962, 443–44. (Review of Frank S. Meyer, *In Defense of Freedom.*)

"Weaver Discusses English Course." *Chicago Maroon,* February 21, 1962, 4.

1963

Academic Freedom: The Principle and the Problems. Philadelphia: Intercollegiate Society of Individualists, February 1963, pamphlet.

"Language Is Sermonic." In Roger E. Nebergall (ed.), *Dimensions of Rhetorical Scholarship.* Norman: University of Oklahoma Department of Speech, 1963, 49–63.

"Two Types of American Individualism." *Modern Age,* 7/2, Spring 1963, 119–34.

"The Southern Phoenix." *The Georgia Review,* 17/1, Spring 1963, 6–17. (Review of the paperback reissue of Twelve Southerners, *I'll Take My Stand.*)

"A Further Testament." *Modern Age,* 7/2, Spring 1963, 219–22. (Review of Joseph Wood Krutch, *More Lives Than One.*)

1964

Visions of Order: The Cultural Crisis of Our Time. Baton Rouge: Louisiana State University Press, 1964.

"The Southern Tradition." *New Individualist Review*, 3/3, Autumn 1964, 7–17.
"The Humanities in a Century of the Common Man." *New Individualist Review*, 3/3, Autumn 1964, 17–24.

1965
Life Without Prejudice and Other Essays (ed. Harvey Plotnick). Chicago: Regnery, 1965.

1967
Rhetoric and Composition: A Course in Writing and Reading, 2nd ed. (revised with the assistance of Richard S. Beal). New York: Holt, Rinehart and Winston, 1967.
A Rhetoric and Handbook (revised with the assistance of Richard S. Beal). New York: Holt, Rinehart and Winston, 1967, paper. Reprinted as *A Rhetoric and Composition Handbook* (revised with the assistance of Richard S. Beal), New York: Morrow, 1974, and New York: Quill, 1981.

1968
The Southern Tradition at Bay: A History of Postbellum Thought (ed. George Core and M. E. Bradford). New Rochelle: Arlington House, 1968.
A Concise Handbook (revised with the assistance of Richard S. Beal). New York: Holt, Rinehart and Winston, 1968.
"The American as a Regenerate Being" (ed. George Core and M. E. Bradford). *The Southern Review*, 4/3 (n.s.), Summer 1968, 633–46.
"Realism and the Local Color Interlude" (ed. George Core). *The Georgia Review*, 22/3, Fall 1968, 301–5.

1970
Language Is Sermonic: Richard M. Weaver on the Nature of Rhetoric (ed. Richard L. Johannesen, Rennard Strickland, and Ralph T. Eubanks). Baton Rouge: Louisiana State University Press, 1970.
"Two Orators" (ed. George Core and M. E. Bradford). *Modern Age*, 14/3–4, Summer–Fall 1970, 226–42.
"Humanism in an Age of Science" (ed. Robert Hamlin). *The Intercollegiate Review*, 7/1–2, Fall 1970, 11–18.

ca. 1971
The Role of Education in Shaping Our Society. Philadelphia: Intercollegiate Studies Institute, n.d. (after 1970) pamphlet.

1976

"A Responsible Rhetoric" (ed. Thomas D. Clark and Richard L. Johannesen). *The Intercollegiate Review*, 12 / 2, Winter 1976 –77, 81– 87. See also 2000.

1987

The Southern Essays of Richard M. Weaver (ed. George M. Curtis, III, and James J. Thompson, Jr.). Indianapolis: Liberty Fund, 1987.

2000

"The Anatomy of Southern Failure" (ed. Ted J. Smith III).

"Conservatism and Liberalism" (ed. Ted J. Smith III).

"The Cultural Role of Rhetoric" (ed. Ted J. Smith III).

"How to Argue the Conservative Cause" (ed. Ted J. Smith III).

"On Liberty" (ed. Ted J. Smith III).

"'Parson' Weems: A Study in Early American Rhetoric" (ed. Ted J. Smith III).

"The Prospects of Conservatism" (ed. Ted J. Smith III).

"Puritanism and Determinism" (ed. Ted J. Smith III).

"Responsible Rhetoric" (ed. Ted J. Smith III).

"Two Diarists" (ed. Ted J. Smith III).

"The Weaver Family of North Carolina: The Prospectus of a History" (ed. Ted J. Smith III).

"William Maury Mitchell" (ed. Ted J. Smith III).

Index

Note: Page numbers followed by *(n)* indicate material in footnotes.

This book is set in 10.5 on 14 Caslon.
Caslon, designed by William Caslon in the early
eighteenth century, was modeled after late
seventeenth-century Dutch faces.

Printed on paper that is acid-free and
meets the requirements of the American National Standard
for Permanence of Paper for Printed Library Materials,
z39.48-1992. ∞

Book design by Erin Kirk New, Athens, Georgia
Typography by G&S Typesetters, Austin, Texas
Printed and bound by Edwards Brothers, Inc., Ann Arbor, Michigan